Mastering
Revit® Architecture 2009

Mastering

Revit® Architecture 2009

Eddy Krygiel

Greg Demchak

Tatjana Dzambazova

Wiley Publishing, Inc.

Acquisitions Editor: Willem Knibbe

Development Editor: Dick Margulis

Technical Editor: Phil Read

Production Editor: Dassi Zeidel

Copy Editor: Liz Welch

Production Manager: Tim Tate

Vice President and Executive Group Publisher: Richard Swadley

Vice President and Executive Publisher: Joseph B. Wikert

Vice President and Publisher: Neil Edde

Book Designer: Maureen Forys, Happenstance Type-O-Rama; Judy Fung

Compositor: Craig Johnson, Happenstance Type-O-Rama

Proofreader: Nancy Bell

Indexer: Ted Laux

Cover Designer: Ryan Sneed

Cover Image: © Pete Gardner/Digital Vision/Getty Images

Project Coordinator/Cover: Lynsey Stanford

Copyright © 2008 by Wiley Publishing, Inc., Indianapolis, Indiana

Published simultaneously in Canada

ISBN: 978-0-470-29528-1

For general information on our other products and services or to obtain technical support, please contact our Customer Care Department within the U.S. at (800) 762-2974, outside the U.S. at (317) 572-3993 or fax (317) 572-4002.

Wiley also publishes its books in a variety of electronic formats. Some content that appears in print may not be available in electronic books.

Library of Congress Cataloging-in-Publication Data

Krygiel, Eddy.
 Mastering Revit architecture 2009 / Eddy Krygiel, Greg Demchak, Tatjana Dzambazova.
   p. cm.
 Includes index.
 ISBN 978-0-470-29528-1 (paper/website)
1. Architectural drawing—Computer-aided design.   2. Architectural design—Data processing.   I. Krygiel, Eddy, 1972–   II. Demchak, Greg.   III. Title.
 NA2728.D98 2008
 720.28′40285536—dc22
               2008022836

10 9 8 7 6 5 4 3 2 1

Dear Reader,

Thank you for choosing *Mastering Revit Architecture 2009*. This book is part of a family of premium-quality Sybex books, all written by outstanding authors who combine practical experience with a gift for teaching.

Sybex was founded in 1976. More than 30 years later, we're still committed to producing consistently exceptional books. With each of our titles we're working hard to set a new standard for the industry. From the authors we work with to the paper we print on, our goal is to bring you the best books available.

I hope you see all that reflected in these pages. I'd be very interested to hear your comments and get your feedback on how we're doing. Feel free to let me know what you think about this or any other Sybex book by sending me an e-mail at nedde@wiley.com, or if you think you've found a technical error in this book, please visit http://sybex.custhelp.com. Customer feedback is critical to our efforts at Sybex.

Best regards,

Neil Edde
Vice President and Publisher
Sybex, an Imprint of Wiley

Acknowledgments

Hats off to the innovators who conceptualized, designed, and made Revit happen. You have changed the world!

Huge thanks to all the faithful followers! Without you, Revit wouldn't be what it is today.

Personal thanks to the Grand Master Philippe Drouant, without whose expertise, generous help, and amazing illustrations we wouldn't have been able to make this book. Many thanks to Guillermo Melantoni and Erik Egbertson, whose participation was crucial in getting the 2008 version of this book out of the door; to the inspirational leaders Mario Guttman and Ken Sanders for their contributions; to BNIM Architects, who continue to let us use their Revit models in our books and thus help raise the knowledge base in the community; to Tsvetan Tsvetanov, who put his life aside to make this release of Revit so much more powerful with the great new rendering features.

Sincere thanks to all the hardworking developers, product designers, and quality assurance testers from the development team of Revit, for their dedication, passion and love of Revit.

And finally, thanks are due to our friend and technical editor Phil Read and our excellent support team at Sybex, who helped us develop and focus the content. Thanks to Dick Margulis, for helping us form complete sentences; to Liz Welch for dotting the i's and crossing the t's; to Dassi Zeidel for keeping us honest; and a special thanks to Willem Knibbe, whose constant support and willingness to put up with our "issues" made us the high-maintenance authors we are today.

We would like to express our sincerest gratitude to our friends, the architects who generously shared their work, allowing us to inspire you with it: Suhail Arfath; Waseem Quadri; The Creations; ADD Inc, Richard Taylor, Kucarovik, Nemeth, Vlkovic, Polakova, and Senteska; Gensler; HOK; Jim Balding and WATG; Martin Taurer; Krisztian Hegedues; Max Bögl Bauservice GmbH & Co. KG; and Boston Architectural College.

About the Authors

Eddy Krygiel is a registered architect, a LEED Accredited Professional, and an Autodesk Authorized Author at BNIM Architects headquartered in Kansas City, Missouri. He has been using Revit since version 5.1 to complete projects ranging from single-family residences and historic remodels to 1.12-million-square-foot office buildings. Eddy is responsible for implementing BIM at his firm and also consults for other architecture and contracting firms around the country looking to implement BIM. For the last four years, he has been teaching Revit to practicing architects and architectural students in the Kansas City area and has lectured around the nation on the use of BIM in the construction industry. Eddy also coauthored *Green BIM*, a book on sustainability and BIM, with Bradley Nies.

Greg Demchak is a designer, a technology advocate, urban explorer, and post-apocalyptic film producer. He holds architectural degrees from the University of Oregon and Massachusetts Institute of Technology. He is a product designer for Autodesk, and has been working with Revit since 2000. He has been teaching at the Boston Architectural College since 2003, and is currently the principal investigator for the 2009 Solar Decathlon competition. He resides in Massachusetts.

Tatjana Dzambazova was the product manager for Revit Architecture between 2005 and 2007, after which she moved into global industry development for the AEC industry in Autodesk, Inc. Before joining Autodesk in 2000, she practiced architecture for twelve years in Vienna and London. At Autodesk, she focused on evangelizing technology and established herself as internationally renowned inspiring speaker who fosters relationships with architects and industry leaders from all around the globe. Powered with seemingly unlimited sources of energy and passion, Tanja manages to make three days out of one, always on the hunt for what's new and exciting in the world of architecture and technology. When she is not working or coauthoring technology books, she is advocating wildlife conservation, reading books like a maniac, cooking, riding her Ducati Monster, or playing Scrabble and Texas Hold 'Em.

Contents at a Glance

Contents

Foreword

BIM—or Building Information Management (not Modeling)—is not the *future*. It is the *present*. CAD is the *past*.

Back in the spring of 2000—with my pen in one hand, my checkbook in the other, and the phone cradled in my neck, I was waiting for the software vendor to tell me the total amount for the BIM-ish solution he was selling. And then there was a pause.

"We've kind of become friends," he said. "And I'd feel bad if I didn't tell you about something I've just come across. A small company in Boston—Revit Technology—has integrated documentation. You should at least take a look at it before you spend a lot of money."

Thanks, Mark. You didn't make the sale. But you kept your integrity.

It's been nearly nine years since the first public release of Revit. At the time, BIM was certainly a differentiator. Very few people understood the implications of a concurrent, bidirectional building design environment. There was a lot of resistance. So, after one of the three owners of the architectural firm I worked at in Charlotte, North Carolina, made it clear that Revit was perceived as "just another CAD package" (and we already had enough of a challenge juggling AutoCAD *and* MicroStation), I realized it was time to move on.

Thanks, Don. Being told "no" provided both clarity and opportunity.

Nine years later, BIM/Revit is no longer a differentiator. It is a commodity. As a matter of fact, it was already becoming a commodity in the spring of 2001, when in Singapore, I observed how you could buy a CD with AutoCAD *and* ADT in an illegal software shop for *five* Singapore dollars. But the CD with Revit (including a software crack) cost *ten* Singapore dollars. I expressed some frustration to my associate: Why would anyone buy Revit when AutoCAD was less expensive? To this, my coworker wisely replied, "This is good. In India we have a saying, 'Nobody steals a dead dog.' A good thief knows the value of what he has stolen."

Thanks Sunil. Shouldn't we have that bottle of vodka by now?

Working for Autodesk Consulting has been a wonderful experience and I have been exceedingly fortunate. I've watched the most extraordinary people design and create and support Autodesk Revit. As a result this wonderful tool is now being used by so many other extraordinary people on some of the most remarkable projects you can imagine. Yes—I've done a lot of training and mentoring and fire extinguishing. But overall, I've been a very lucky bystander.

Thanks James. Thanks Matt. I'll bring the scotch if you'll bring the glasses.

And here's another secret: For the most part, I'm a straight "B" student. There are so many other far more brilliant people. But the thing about brilliant people is that many times they already "know" what isn't possible. On the other hand, I'm fortunately not that smart. Enough monkeys, enough beer, and enough keyboards, right? So basically, I'm just really stubborn. And

I deeply hate to lose. And I really despise disappointing the people that I respect. So basically, I don't know when to give up. Which brings up a good life lesson:

A stubborn "B" student can outwit a shiny "A" student who has too much knowledge but not enough experience. Every. Damn. Time.

Architecture is a business. If you're young and impressionable and still in school you really need to learn this now. I'm absolutely *not* suggesting that you compromise your integrity and embrace mediocrity for the sake of financial gain. What I'm suggesting is that you fully embrace BIM in order to realize the best and the highest you can offer within the realities of time and budgetary constraints. More to the point: If you're not using BIM, you're doing a severe disservice to your client, your community, your profession, and your future.

The reason *Mastering Revit Architecture* is such a great book is because of its holistic approach to BIM. Eddy, Greg, and Tatjana have taken great care to help you understand the context of what you're trying to accomplish within the application of important design principles. Many books mistakenly view BIM as mere "technology"—or even one particular technology. It's not. BIM is a philosophical approach to architecture that emphasizes the integration of the design, development, and delivery process. It's about understanding the implications, complications, and context of design decisions as early as possible.

It's about being accountable for your own design decisions.

As a result, one can't fully implement BIM without rejecting one particularly insidious and conceited notion (espoused by so many signature architects) that great designers don't need to understand the tools that are used to implement their designs; they just need enough pencils, paper, and staff. As if tools the rest of us choose to embrace somehow stifle *their* creative genius. How does this make better buildings?

So I'm hopeful these notions of *technical apartheid* are a dying breed and the sooner, the better. BIM isn't just about the integration of technology; but the integration of people and processes. And if Michelangelo could mix his own pigments and plaster and paint while lying on his back, then I suppose it's not too much to remind some present (or future) signature designer he may do well to learn to move his own mouse.

Because most importantly, architecture isn't about buildings. It's about what we are able to accomplish with what little time we have. *This is the elegant essence of BIM.* BIM is about the time it affords to do *other* things; other far, far more important things than architecture.

Because if all you are able to accomplish in this life is the production of buildings at the expense of the other more important things, such as helping other people, creating meaningful relationships, enjoying good drink and food with friends, and even the occasional opportunity to roll around naked with someone you love—then you've missed out on a full life. And that's what the joy and wonder of architecture is *really* about.

And if an employer doesn't understand this balance between life and work, I hereby submit my closing advice:

Tell him to get stuffed and quit. Life is too short. Then send me an e-mail and I'll help you find a better gig.

But first make sure that you know how to use Revit. This book will help you accomplish that and more.

All the best,

Phil Read
June 2008

Introduction

Welcome to the second edition of *Mastering Revit Architecture*, based on the Revit Architecture 2009 release.

This book follows on the heels of our updated *Introducing Revit Architecture 2009* (Wiley, 2008). In preparing the 2009 edition of the *Mastering* book, we took the opportunity to introduce some of the features new to the 2009 release of the software, to rewrite large portions of the text, and to polish up the rest, taking into consideration comments and suggestions from many readers and friends. Working as a team of three authors, we kept one another in constant check, each of us writing, reviewing, editing, and updating as chapters rolled out. One additional change we made to the previous edition of the book was to break some of the longer chapters into more bite-sized morsels, which hopefully results in chapters that flow better and gives you some breathing room as you move through the book.

Writing books might seem easier than it truly is, but what drives and inspires us is the feeling that we're doing something important: sharing our best knowledge and practices about Revit and building information modeling (BIM) with those who have already been acquainted with its incredible power and feel the need to go deeper and further to fully leverage its abilities and values. We want to help you make better designs, be more efficient in creating correct documentation, learn some new techniques, and put some fun back into using software.

We wanted to write a book that is as much about architectural design and practice as it is about software. We think we've succeeded, because the book follows real-life workflows and scenarios; it's full of real-world examples that show how to use Revit practically and creatively.

Who Should Read This Book

This book is written for architects who have already gotten their feet wet with Revit and are eager to learn more so they can optimize workflow and leverage the full power of this tool. It's for architects of any generation—you don't need to be a high-tech wizard to dive into this book. However, a basic understanding of Revit will make it easier to work through the book. Revit is very rich, and the topics we've selected include those that are most widely used and those least understood. Many more books need to be written to cover the entire world of Revit.

This book is also for the seasoned user who has already received training or has started working on projects with Revit and is looking to discover useful best practices and tips that will make the work on a project smoother and the implementation easier. We've added many time-saving and inspiring concepts to the book, supported with examples from architect friends and colleagues from all around the world, to motivate you and help you on your journey into the new era of building information modeling. The book also offers insights for BIM managers into the best practices for creating good project or office templates; these managers should also take a sneak peek into the powerful world of building content and Revit families.

What You Will Learn

This book will help you take the basics of Revit and BIM that you already know and grow those skills by using real-world examples. It is intended to go beyond an introduction to Revit. Thus, we won't be starting a project from scratch and teaching you how to build a simplified BIM model from the ground up (if you are interested in that approach, please see *Introducing Revit Architecture 2009* [Wiley, 2008], which is meant to be complementary to this book). Instead, we show you how to take a preliminary model and add layers of intelligence to help analyze and augment your designs.

Our book begins with a brief overview of the BIM approach. As you are already aware, BIM is more than just a change in software; it's a change in architectural workflow and culture. To leverage the full advantages of both BIM and Revit in your office structure, you will need to make some changes to your practice, and the book is designed around an ideal, integrated workflow to help you make this transition.

Starting with the workflows for conceptual design and feasibility studies, it continues through best practices for design iteration and refinement. You'll learn about powerful modeling techniques, design documentation best practices, how to make compelling presentation graphics, parametric design with the family editor, and some strategies for sustainable design. The book concludes with a chapter on troubleshooting and best practices so you can avoid common pitfalls. But throughout the book we've tried to share our practical experience with you, particularly in the form of Real World Scenario sidebars.

Whether you're studying Revit on your own or in a class or training program, you can use the Master It questions in the Bottom Line section at the end of each chapter to test your mastery of the skills you've learned.

Also featured is a color project gallery containing inspirational Revit projects from friends and colleagues who were generous enough to share their good work with the rest of the world.

All the tutorial files necessary to complete the book's exercises plus sample families are hosted online at www.sybex.com/go/masteringrevit2009. To download the trial version of Revit Architecture, go to www.autodesk.com/revitarchitecture, where you'll also find complete system requirements for running Revit.

Enjoy! Revit has changed our lives. Maybe it will change yours as well.

We welcome your feedback! Please feel free to email us at GoRevit@gmail.com.

Go Revit!

Eddy, Greg, and Tanja

Mastering
Revit® Architecture 2009

Chapter 1

Understanding BIM: From the Basics to Advanced Realities

In this chapter we'll cover the principles of a building information modeling (BIM) approach and summarize how BIM differs from a traditional 2D computer-aided design (CAD) process. We'll explain fundamental characteristics of Revit, how Revit delivers the benefits of a true BIM tool, and why Revit is the tool best suited for a process motivated by an integrated and collaborative practice.

In this chapter, you learn how to do the following:

◆ Identify the advantages of building information modeling

◆ Know what to expect from BIM

Identifying the Advantages of Building Information Modeling

The production of design documents has traditionally been an exercise in drawing lines to represent a building. These documents become instruction sets: an annotated booklet that describes what the building should look like when complete. The plan, section, elevation, and detail are all skillfully drafted—line by line, drawing by drawing, sheet by sheet. Whether physical or digital, these traditional drawing sets are composed of annotated graphics—where each line and text is part of a larger abstraction meant to convey design intent so that a building can eventually be constructed. By and large, this is still the reality we face today, but the process of creating these drawings is being fundamentally changed as a result of BIM.

Let's put this into a historical context for a moment and briefly walk through the evolution of architectural design and documentation.

A Brief History of Design and Documentation

Andrea Palladio's *Four Books on Architecture* (trans. Robert Tavernor and Richard Schofield, MIT Press, 1997) presents an amazing array of drawing techniques that show buildings cut in plan and section and even hybrid drawings that show elevations and sections in one drawing. You can even see hints about construction techniques and structural gestures in the form of trusses, arches, and columns.

These representations were meant as simplified expressions of a project, and often they were idealized versions of the building—not necessarily how the building was built. The drawings were communication and documentation tools, themselves works of detailed craftsmanship. In those days (14th–17th centuries), the architect was brought up in the tradition of building and had integral knowledge of how buildings were constructed. Palladio, like many other architects of his day, grew up as a stonemason. Building techniques were deeply embedded in the construction trades, which in turn spawned the great architects of the time. Other master masons and sculptors who were also architects include the likes of Filippo Brunelleschi, Giovanni Bernini, and Francesco Borromini. These architects are often referred to as the master builders—they were integrated into all facets of the design and construction of architecture.

Over time, however, architecture became more and more academic as building typologies solidified, and classical reconstructions on paper and in model form became part of the formative education of the architect. The design profession began its gradual separation from the building trades. The notion of design process and iterative problem solving became critical attributes of a design professional—in many cases superseding knowledge of construction means and methods.

With modern architecture, solving abstract spatial problems, accommodating programmatic elements, and experimenting with new materials became driving forces. The machine age and the promise of mass production were idealized and fully embraced. Le Corbusier's (1887–1965) romantic vision of steamships and automobiles inspired a new generation of architecture, and buildings became increasingly machine-like. Consider all the office towers and commercial office parks that have emerged, with their internal mechanical systems used to keep buildings operational.

As buildings continued to grow in complexity, both technically and programmatically, the architect grew more removed from the act of physical construction. Modern materials such as steel and reinforced concrete became prevalent, and complex building systems were introduced. In turn, the production of more detailed drawings became a legal and practical requirement. Structural engineers and mechanical engineers were added to the process, as need for specialized knowledge of building systems grew. No longer could the architect expect to produce a few simple drawings and have a building erected. Complexity in building systems demanded greater amounts of information, and this information was delivered in the form of larger and more complex construction document sets. Architects today find themselves drafting, producing details, working with a wide range of consultants, and still having to create sketches for contractors in the field in order to resolve the complexity of construction assemblies.

The traditional production of plans, sections, and elevations continues to this day, but with far more drawings than in the days of Palladio. At the same time, we ask: Will all these drawings be necessary in the near future? Will the adoption of BIM lead to new ways of communicating the design, new delivery methods, new forms of construction, and new roles for the architect? Can a shift in technology lead to a shift in thinking about the building process?

Building Information Modeling

Fast-forward to the present context and the advent of building information modeling: the production of drawings is now streamlined by building a digital 3D model composed of virtual building elements. These elements are loaded with data that describe not only geometry, but also material, fire rating, cost, manufacturer, count, and just about any other metadata you can imagine. The focus moves from 2D abstractions to integrated model delivery. It's now possible to detect spatial clashes between the multitudes of complex systems in the building. You can know with confidence whether ductwork will interfere with the structural steel long before construction starts.

The goal of reducing errors and smoothing out the construction process is driving firms to be more efficient, effective, and productive. With BIM, all the plans, sections, and elevations are derivative representations on the model: producing these drawings is no longer a set of isolated, repetitive, and discontinuous tasks. A data-rich model also means that more analysis and iterative searching for optimal solutions can occur early in the design process. As detail is added, the model becomes an increasingly accurate representation of what will actually be built. The model itself can be used to generate parts lists, shop drawings, and instructions for industrially produced elements for the fabrication process. If you can send a digital file that can instruct machines to produce components, the need for traditional annotated drawings might disappear entirely. The ultimate benefits of BIM are still emerging in a market primed to radically change the way buildings are designed and built. A shift in process and expectation is happening in the architecture, engineering, and construction (AEC) world, with private and public sector owners beginning to demand BIM models as part of the delivery package.

The shift from traditional 2D abstractions to on-demand simulations of building performance, usage, and cost is no longer a futuristic fantasy but a reality. In the age of information-rich digital models, all disciplines involved with a project can share a single database. Architecture, structure, mechanical, infrastructure, and construction can be coordinated in ways never before possible.

Models can now be sent directly to fabrication machines, bypassing the need for traditional shop drawings. Energy analysis can be done at the outset of design, and construction costs are becoming increasingly predictable. These are just a few of the exciting opportunities that a BIM approach offers. Designers and contractors can begin to look at the entire building process—from preliminary design through construction documentation into construction—and rethink how buildings come together. The whole notion of paper-based delivery may become obsolete as more players adopt up-to-date, accurate, digital models.

With the Revit building information model, a parametric 3D model is created that produces traditional building abstractions such as plans, sections, elevations, details, and schedules. The drawings produced aren't discrete collections of manually coordinated lines, but interactive representations or, more accurately, different views of a model. Working in a model-based framework such as Revit guarantees that a change in one view will propagate to all other views of the model. As you shift elements in plan, they change in elevation and section. If you move a level height, all the walls and floors associated with that level update automatically and adjust their height/length to the new condition. If you remove a door from your model, it's simultaneously removed from all other views, and your door schedule is updated automatically. This unprecedented level of coordination allows designers and builders to better control and display information, ensuring higher quality and a leaner process.

The immediate access to 3D visualization of the building and its spaces makes it much easier to understand and communicate the building design. One model can contain many options, any of which can be explored at any stage in the design process. Integrated design and documentation keeps the data centralized and coordinated. This in turn leads to live and up-to-date schedules and quantity take-offs. That information can then be used to make decisions early in the design process, reducing risk and cost overruns. Not only that, but with the coordinated BIM model, you can start running energy analysis, solar studies, daylighting simulations, and egress analysis much earlier in the process, allowing you to iterate through design decisions earlier, not later.

Coordination with BIM is now required for many buildings to come into existence. Consider a complex project such as Daniel Libeskind's recently completed Denver Art Museum and its extreme geometric configuration (Figure 1.1). Integrating the mechanical and structural systems into a 3D model is essential to completing a building of this complexity. Exact spatial organization of structural members could be modeled, which in turn led to fewer field errors and fewer requests for information. In addition, parts could be sent directly to fabrication from the model, eliminating the need for 2D drawings entirely.

FIGURE 1.1
BIM makes it possible to build more complex buildings with fewer errors.

Denver Art Museum, Daniel Libeskind

Let's not leave out some of the more pleasurable aspects of BIM that go beyond all the technical, economic, and ecological benefits. With a 3D model, you can expect to see changes in how you interact with your team and your clients and in the way you produce presentations. No longer are you stuck with using 2D drawings or outsourcing to create perspective images. You'll find yourself working with your team in close quarters, sharing a model, and exploring it together. With your clients, you can now take them through the building, in full 3D, from the beginning. The experience of working with and visualizing 3D space can't be overemphasized, and people enjoy it immensely. In the BIM era, 3D experience is the norm, not the exception.

BIM and Process Change

When moving to a BIM work environment, you'll experience a change in process and workflow. Perhaps the most immediate and obvious difference is that a traditional CAD system uses many separate files to document a building, whereas a BIM project typically has only one file. With CAD, all the separate files are created individually and have no intelligent connection between them. Each drawing represents a separate piece of work to be managed and updated throughout the design process. With such an unwieldy process, the possibility of uncoordinated data, and thus errors, is very high. The manual change management enforced by CAD is a tedious and error-prone process that requires diligent project management and lots of red lines. BIM provides a different approach to the problem: rather than many files, you work with one file. With BIM, all information is consolidated and networked together for you, and the resulting drawings all relate back to a single underlying database, guaranteeing an internally consistent model.

If you understand the basic premise of an integrated building model, then you'll by now have realized that BIM removes the concept of drawing lines to represent objects. Instead, you build walls, roofs, stairs, and furniture. You model the building and its systems. Figure 1.2 shows a 3D sectional view of a Revit model. You can see that the model incorporates façade elements, floors, roofs, parapets, curtain walls, and materials. All this information is modeled and must be designed as it is to be built. You then add information to the drawings to explain the model in the form of parametric tags and keynotes. Although the end result is still a set of printed lines, you rarely draw these lines. This concept of modeling is so simple, and matches more closely the process of building design that you as an architect are familiar with, that you'll get used to the idea in no time.

FIGURE 1.2
The BIM model keeps you honest and focused on solving problems of a model, not lines.

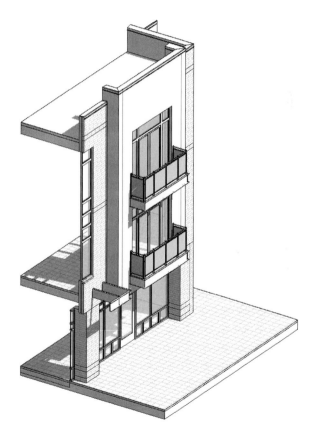

Revit is excellent at managing changes and keeping your model interconnected. Unlike CAD, the intent of BIM is to let the computer take responsibility for redundant interactions and calculations, leaving you, the designer, with more time to design and evaluate your decisions. With a BIM tool such as Revit, be prepared to change your expectations of how to use design software. Remember: you are modeling a building now—not drafting lines. You're doing what you do best: solving complex spatial problems.

Revit Encourages Creativity

Revit's tools are clustered in easy-to-access groups such as modeling, drafting, rendering, site, and so on. Most of these tools will get you where you need to go with minimal effort. For more complicated conditions, be prepared to put your creativity to use. Remember, Revit is a 3D modeling application that will let you build almost anything you want. For example, if you can't create the wall or roof you want with the explicit Wall or Roof tool, you can create your own custom-shaped walls or roofs using 3D solid geometry that, however, can be assigned to the wall category and will behave and schedule as walls. Figure 1.3 shows an example of custom-designed railings, curtain walls, and structural elements—all possible for a creative and engaged designer. These custom elements participate in the underlying data structure of Revit, making them schedulable and quantifiable.

FIGURE 1.3
Be creative, and work out your design solutions in 3D.

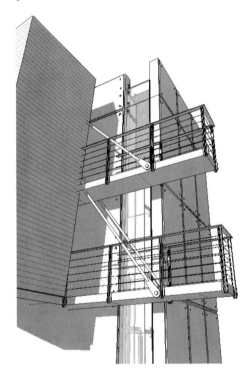

Every Element in Revit Has Properties

Throughout the design process of a project, you'll often need to adjust elements and change the model. Get used to the idea of clicking the Element Properties button to make interactive changes to the model. A member of the Basic Wall family, for example, has properties like width, height, bearing or nonbearing, demolished or new, interior or exterior, fire rating, and material. You can even define how layers wrap when inserts are placed in the wall, add integrated wall sweeps, and build stacked walls. Figure 1.4 shows the assembly options embedded in the type properties of a Revit wall.

FIGURE 1.4
The Element Properties dialog box of a wall contains many powerful features allowing detailed editing of the wall assembly.

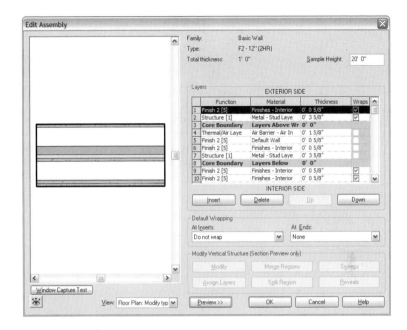

Elements Interact with Other Elements—All the Time

Remember: there is one model and many ways to look at it, called views; no matter in which view you change the model, the change will immediately be updated in all views. And in each view, you have total control over what information you want to display. Think of a view as a pair of glasses that can filter what you see—but the underlying model is still there, all the time.

A wall in Revit interacts with other walls to produce clean connections and appropriate levels of material abstraction. It connects to floors, levels, and roofs; forms rooms; and defines areas. Windows and doors placed in a wall move with the wall that hosts them when that wall is repositioned. Deleting a wall will delete all windows and doors in that wall and all dimensions associated with the wall. If you move a level, expect floors, roofs, walls, plumbing, and electrical features to also move as their parameters change. Keep the interaction of elements in mind, especially in multiuser scenarios where your changes to the model will affect many views at once.

Duplicating Views Takes Two Clicks

With Revit, you can duplicate floor plans quickly, allowing you to generate plans as in-progress working drawings, others for presentation purposes, and still others for final construction documents (CDs). Note that this is very different from making a copy of a drawing: duplicating does not create any copy of elements in a model—what happens is that you are simply duplicating a view of the model and you can have as many different views of the same model as you wish.

Revit Fosters Problem Solving

An advantage of a BIM methodology is that you can't cheat the documentation of your design. Because the elements have properties based on real-life constraints, you'll find it difficult to fake elements within the design. When you get stuck trying to resolve a roof condition, it's most likely that you have a complex roof to solve. You can't just fake the elevations and call it a day. Of course, in CAD-based systems, faking annotatons has always been possible and has no doubt led to some messy construction administration work. As you move into the BIM world, be prepared to take on some early design challenges.

Figure 1.5 shows what appears to be a simple house model, but it's more complex than it looks. With Revit, you model the dormers, the trusses, and the fascia and soffits. You need to determine how the walls and roofs connect to one another—and Revit is well suited to figuring these things out.

FIGURE 1.5
To build a BIM model, you need to solve problems in 3D space, from dormers to trusses.

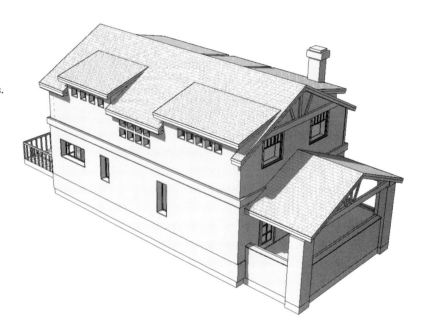

Revit Lets You Leverage Other Tools to Support Your Workflow

Other software packages, such as SketchUp, Rhinoceros, Maya, and 3ds Max, are excellent modeling applications. However, these modeling applications don't have the ability to document fully your design for construction, nor can they be leveraged downstream. While these tools are not BIM, they can still play a role in a BIM workflow; many architects use them to generate concept models that can then be brought into a BIM application and progress through design, analysis, and documentation. If you prefer to work with other tools for concept modeling, doing so isn't a problem. When the design starts to gel, import the geometry into Revit, convert the imported conceptual models into real building elements, and start taking advantage of BIM.

Not everything in a Revit model is modeled in 3D. You can create pure 2D drawings, drafting views, and details in Revit; import existing CAD details; and reuse details from other Revit projects.

Revit Allows You to Draft

The tools may be a bit different than those in AutoCAD or any drafting application, but there is nothing you can draw in CAD that can't be drawn in Revit. By using the intelligence of Revit families, you can build your details into individual components, thereby embedding drafting into the object. Figure 1.6 shows an example of a detail drawn entirely in Revit.

FIGURE 1.6

2D details can be drawn directly over the 3D model, allowing you to add much more information to the model.

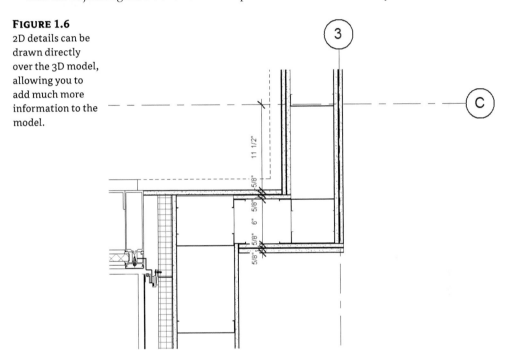

The Family Editor Is a Powerful Tool

Most elements (families) in Revit are made with the Family Editor and can be built with incredible behaviors. Don't be afraid to dig in to the editor and explore your creative side. We've seen many beautiful families and clever tricks put to use that make Revit fun to use. Figure 1.7 shows a curtain-wall system with nested panels and attachment clamps. As we'll discuss in Chapter 5 and reinforce in Chapter 10, creating such families isn't too difficult, and requires no programming or scripting knowledge. Using 3D modeling tools and parametric dimensions, you can create reusable and dimensionally flexible components for any architectural element. By taking your time, being patient, and problem solving, you'll be producing custom content in no time.

FIGURE 1.7
Using the Family
Editor, you can
model intelligent
part assemblies.

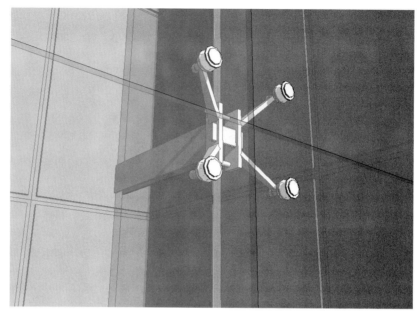

Revit Does Away with Layers and X-References

If you've already made the jump into Revit, then this will already be obvious: rather than user-defined layers, you use an intelligent architectural classification system to manage visibility, graphics, and selection. This may seem stringent at first, but once you get the hang of it, you'll see the benefits. Because a building model is an assembly of meaningful, to-be-built objects, you control the visibility and graphics of those objects using a rational list of well-understood categories. This also makes it easy to select similar elements and edit them. Figure 1.8 shows the list of classifications that manage visibility. You can't add to or alter this list, which means every project enjoys the same level of visual predictability. And of course, with an integrated model, you don't need to worry about referencing other drawings to keep the drawings up to date and in sync.

BIM Is More Than a Technology Approach: It's a Change in Process

One of the powers of Revit is the ability to work in a single-file environment where the design and documentation of the building happens on a holistic model. This can be a disadvantage if it isn't taken seriously. Users who are quick to make changes without thinking about how such changes will ripple through the model can cause unintended problems. Revit is a parametric modeler that maintains relationships between building elements to streamline the design process. For example, deleting a roof underlay in a view doesn't just delete the roof in that view—it deletes it *everywhere* in the model. You need to think before you delete that wall or ignore that warning message!

FIGURE 1.8

The Visibility/ Graphic Overrides dialog box contains the entire range of elements used in Revit.

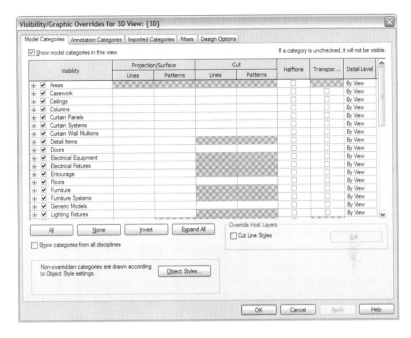

Be prepared to work in much tighter, more collaborative teams. As soon as you enter the BIM multiuser world, you absolutely need to be communicating with your team all the time. The changes that you make in the model will affect the whole model and other people's work. We think this is a great—perhaps unintended—consequence of moving into a model-based design paradigm.

Anticipate that tasks will take different amounts of time when compared to a CAD production environment. You'll perform tasks in Revit that you never had in CAD; and conversely, some CAD tasks that took weeks (such as chamfering and trimming thousands of lines to draw walls properly or making a door schedule) take almost no time using Revit. On the other hand, some tasks may seem to take longer in Revit. This may initially seem true, but remember that as you're modifying or adding something in plan, you're also adding it in section, elevation, and detail. Be prepared to discover and embrace new tasks with BIM that were never part of a 2D workflow.

In Revit you'll often feel as if you are working in traditional types of 2D views—just keep in mind that it's still a 3D model. Moving walls, windows, and doors in plan feels like a 2D operation, but of course it's not. If you've never worked in a model-based environment, it can be jarring at first to see the drawing you've been working on change as a result of an edit in a different view. As we mentioned, this becomes even more dramatic when you start working in a team and sharing a model. You'll learn that preventing movement of elements becomes just as critical as being able to edit elements in the model. Pinning down grids, levels, and exterior walls will become part of your workflow, especially in larger projects with many users working in a single file.

Revit Is Relatively New Technology

Revit is the latest and most technologically advanced BIM application, and it's under highly dynamic development. What began as a single tool for architects has expanded into a platform that is the base for the structural and mechanical disciplines as well. The evolution of the Revit software platform will continue. As with any new technology, you'll run into problems, get flustered, and no doubt pull out some hair. That said, no other application on the market delivers the advantages of BIM as well as Revit does. Consider this for a moment: most other architectural products in today's market are based on technology that is 20-plus years old, whereas Revit is a new technology that was designed from the ground up as a BIM tool to specifically address the AEC industry. From its inception, Revit has had the goal of improving design communication, coordination, and change management. It has a patented parametric change engine that is unmatched in sophistication. It's also the leading software package in the international market. Revit is not the only BIM package out there, but we feel it offers the most holistic approach.

As you complete more projects with Revit, you'll begin to understand some of its advanced functionality. In this book, we'll delve into advanced concepts and guide you through some really cool features. We'll touch on the fact that Revit is now a technological platform that supports architectural, structural, and mechanical disciplines. The fact that you can share a model with your structural and mechanical, engineering, and plumbing (MEP) engineers without any intermediate translation methods or change to the base environment is an exciting prospect, and one that will continue to drive changes in process.

Where Can You Go from Here?

Building information modeling is a revolutionary approach to the design, analysis, and documentation of buildings that takes full advantage of modern-day computational technology. At its core, BIM manages the flow of information throughout the lifecycle of a building-design process, allowing you to experience the building before it is built. Using BIM from early conceptual design through construction documentation and into construction administration and beyond, it's possible to better predict, plan, and execute the complex task of creating architecture to meet today's demanding requirements.

The flow of information in this new world consists of virtually all imagined inputs that go into a building design: the gross area of the building; its impact on the environment; the number of windows, doors, and plumbing fixtures; the cost of materials; the size of heating and cooling equipment—you name it. All this information is stored in a digital model—a virtual 3D database chockfull of information primed for extraction, analysis, and representation. The input turns into output in the form of coordinated document sets that can be shared across multiple disciplines and that serve as a centralized design-management tool for an entire project.

The AEC industry is at the cusp of a major shift in technology and the resulting impact on building—and by extension the greater environment—will be revolutionary. We can no longer build without considering the impact of the building, without considering the building as part of a larger network of interconnected flows. The promise of BIM lies in the ability to visualize and understand how a building participates in these complex networks: how it performs, how it will age, and how it will accommodate and adapt to dynamic economic and spatial requirements.

Revit, along with a change in process, can change the way you do business, structure your office, present ideas to clients, win new jobs, and ultimately build a new architecture.

Armed with the skills you'll develop in this book, you'll be able to take Revit to the edges of creative expression and maybe create something as ambitious as the skyscraper in Figure 1.9.

FIGURE 1.9
Taking Revit to the edges of creative expression

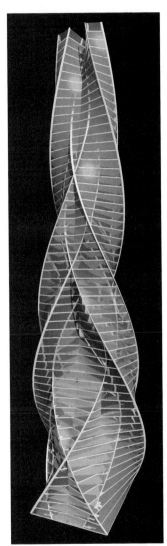

Image Courtesy of Phil Read

The Bottom Line

Building information modeling is a departure from the conventional approach of representing buildings with lines on paper; instead, BIM stores a description of the building as data that can be used to generate all of your drawings.

Identify the advantages of building information modeling   The traditional architectural design tools you've mastered are probably serving you well. New software and a new conceptual model of the building process will inevitably involve some adjustments, so they need to provide significant benefits.

Master It   What are some of the advantages of using BIM over traditional CAD tools?

Know what to expect from BIM   A BIM project is based on a single, centralized database of information. You need to anticipate how that change can affect workflows based on more independent functions.

Master It   How can your work process be affected by the adoption of BIM?

Chapter 2

Revit Fundamentals

The power of a database is that information can be easily accessed, managed, queried, and updated. A Revit project is essentially a database that makes it easy to quickly identify elements, control their visibility and graphics, and generate reports based on this information. The data is highly structured, but you have tremendous liberty when it comes to the representation of that data. This flexibility lets you have as many views as you want or need to convey your design intent. Every view is a filtered, graphical representation of an underlying database, and you're free to make as many views of this data as you deem necessary.

The sooner you embrace this concept and start exploring the opportunities it presents, the better. If you can't get your drawings to look just right, chances are you just haven't dug deep enough. Throughout this book we'll give you suggestions and techniques that we hope will inspire you to think creatively about how to exploit the data to get the output you want.

In this chapter, you learn how to do the following:

◆ Understand Revit parametric elements

◆ Work with the Revit user interface

◆ Use the Project Browser

◆ Navigate views and view properties

Understanding Revit Parametric Elements

Every element in Revit is considered a *family*, and each family belongs to a *category*. Figure 2.1 shows the basic Revit object model. In this section, we'll discuss how Revit organizes all these families into categories and why this makes sense from a workflow and consistency point of view. We'll next look at the different types of families, the principles of their behavior, and how to create them.

Revit uses a classification system to organize all the families in the model. This system of organization is based specifically on the AEC industry and is set up to help manage relationships between classes of elements as well as the graphical representation for each class. To see all the categories available in a Revit project, choose Settings ➢ Object Styles to open the dialog box shown in Figure 2.2.

FIGURE 2.1

The essential categorization of Revit elements

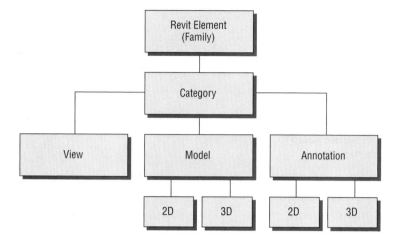

FIGURE 2.2

The Object Styles dialog box

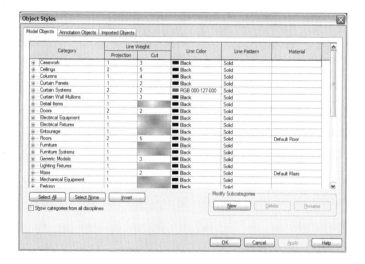

At the core of this organization is a fixed list of *categories* to which all elements ultimately belong. Although this may seem stringent, it works well and will help you maintain a consistent graphical representation across your projects. As you can see, every element belongs to a category, and that category is either a model or an annotation object. In addition, each element is either 2D or 3D in nature. Whenever the mouse hovers over an element, a tooltip appears and tells you what kind of element it is and what category it belongs to (see Figure 2.3).

TOOLTIPS INFORMATION

If you aren't working in a worksharing (multiuser) project, then the first bit of text in the tooltip tells you what category the element belongs to. If you're in a worksharing project, the category is preceded by the name of the workset containing the element. (See Chapter 24 for more detail on worksharing.) The next part of a tooltip tells you the family name, and then comes the family type. So, the tooltip follows this logic.

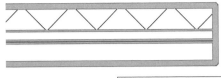

Model Categories

Model Object categories—the first tab in the Object Styles dialog box—include all the real-world
types of objects typically found in buildings. These object categories include elements such as
walls, floors, roofs, and furniture, along with other categories that make sense in an architectural project. The category *Detail Element* is used for elements that represent real-world objects
used for 2D detailing such as insulation and detail components. In Revit, these objects are not
modeled as 3D elements, but added as 2D representations, as shown in Figure 2.4.

FIGURE 2.4
Details such as
this steel connec-
tion at the roof are
composed of 2D
elements.

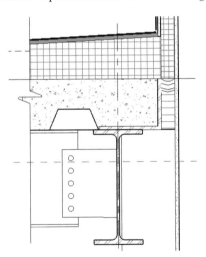

For elements that don't fit into any obvious category, there is the *Generic Models* category. This
can be used for objects or parts of an overall assemblage that do not need to be scheduled. An
example might be a canopy or reception desk. Model elements appear by default in all views. In
other words, if you draw a wall in plan, it will show up in any other applicable plans, elevations,
sections, and 3D views. Remember, you're working on a single building model—all views in
Revit are just different ways to look at the same model. Detail components, on the other hand,
appear only in the view in which they were placed. If you want them to appear in other views as
well, you will need to manually copy them to those other views.

As we'll discuss in more detail shortly, you can turn the visibility on and off for any category
or element in any view. For example, imagine you've placed furniture in your model. The furniture is 3D geometry that will be visible by default in many views. Revit lets you turn off the

visibility of the furniture in one floor plan while leaving it visible in another floor plan, or turn it off in plan view while having it visible in section view. The furniture isn't deleted; it's made visible or not depending on the information you need to convey in particular drawings.

Because model elements appear in all other views, two types of graphic representation are defined for each category: projection and cut, as shown in the Object Styles dialog box in Figure 2.2. The *projection* graphics define the graphics for the element in elevation, 3D views, or any other view where the element isn't being cut by the view. The *cut* graphics define how the element will look when cut by sections and plan views. Typically, the section cut graphic is bolder than the projection lines, to emphasize that the element is being cut by the view plane.

Surface and cut patterns are always drawn with line weight 1 and can't be made thicker.

Figure 2.5 shows how the wall line weight differs between cut and projection. Also notice that patterns are applied to the walls and floors. Patterns can be added to give additional graphic representation to a material and are always drawn with a thin line weight.

Categories also make it easy to interchange elements. You can swap out elements of the same category with another type of element with only few clicks of the mouse. This deliberate limiting of choices to only those that make sense is what streamlines the process of swapping out types of elements. For example, you can swap a lighting fixture with another lighting fixture by selecting the element and then seeing what other lighting fixtures are available in the Type Selector. Choosing another type swaps out the type instantly.

Revit is smart about this interchange—it offers only different types of the same category of elements. For example, when you select a door, you don't get a list of plumbing fixtures or windows to swap it with; you get a list of other door families.

Annotation Categories

Annotation Object categories include all the annotations, symbols, and descriptive data added to a view to describe the building. These are listed in the second tab of the Object Styles dialog box. Most annotations are view-specific 2D elements and appear only in the view in which they were created. Examples include dimensions, tags, callouts, and text notes. Annotations such as sections, levels, and grids are 2D graphics, but they have 3D characteristics and appear in other views. These elements (levels, grids, sections) appear in many views thanks to BIM application functionality. Levels, grids, and section marks extend throughout the model and can be edited from multiple views. You don't need to draw these elements in each view as separate, disconnected graphics. With Revit, they're truly 3D annotations. (Levels , grids, and section marks never appear in 3D views.)

DEPENDENT VIEWS

There is an exception to the rule that annotations appear only in the view in which they were placed. With *dependent views*, annotations are shared between views, so that if you change the annotation in one view, it affects other views as well.

FIGURE 2.5
Cut and projection graphics are defined for each element.

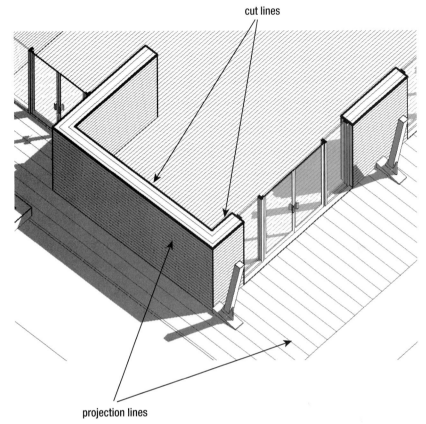

Subcategories

Within each category are many subcategories that let you control the graphics of an element with finer precision. This is what makes the concept of categories so much more powerful and natural to work with than layers. Select Settings ➢ Object Styles and look in the Modeling tab at the Door category: you can see that the category Doors (Figure 2.6) has a set of subcategories that relate to subelements in the door assembly, such as Elevation Swing, Frame/Mullion, Glass, Opening, Panel Swing, and any other user-defined elements that can be made when creating a door family. For each subcategory, independent line weight, color, and pattern can be assigned.

FIGURE 2.6
Subcategories allow finer graphic control over categories.

Doors	2	2	■ Black	Solid
Elevation Swing	1	1	■ Black	Dash 1/16"
Frame/Mullion	1	3	■ Black	Solid
Glass	1	4	■ Black	Solid
Hidden Lines	2	2	■ Blue	Dash
Opening	1	3	■ Black	Solid
Panel	1	3	■ Black	Solid
Plan Swing	1	1	■ Black	Solid

Imported Categories/Subcategories

When a CAD file is imported into Revit, all of its layers are represented as subcategories in the Imported Objects tab of the Object Styles dialog box. Layers have a projection line weight, a color, and a pattern.

IMPORTED FILE LIMITATIONS

There is no Cut line style for DWG, DXF, and DGN files. These files are just sets of lines, and lines can have only one line weight.

These can be overridden at any time to suit your requirements. Each import appears as a category in this dialog box, as shown in Figure 2.7. There is no need to remap CAD layers into Revit taxonomy. If you're used to the layer conventions set up in CAD, these will be mapped directly into the Object Styles dialog box with same names, line weights, and colors.

FIGURE 2.7
Imported CAD layers represented as subcategories

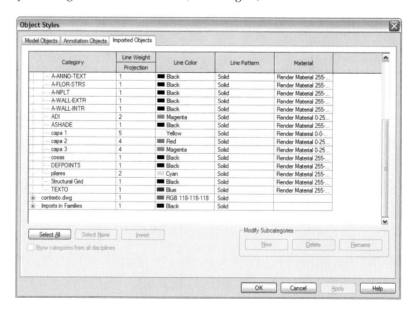

Views

Views are also considered parametric elements in Revit, and they have many properties to help you define how they should display information. A view doesn't change the model in any way—it only acts as a filter through which you view the model. This also applies to schedules and material take-offs. Although schedules are more abstract ways to think of a view, they're still parametric views into the model. Throughout the book, you'll be asked to make views, and we'll guide you through various methods for making views convey specific information about your design.

Type and Instance Parameters

A *parametric element* is something that can change size, material, and graphic look but is still the same fundamental element. Most elements in Revit are designed with parameters that allow for the creation of variations of a base type. Take a typical Revit door family as an example. Each family can have many types built into it, where each type typically represents a variation in size, material, color, or other defining characteristic. Although each type can vary in shape and size, the base geometry for each type is derived from the same family.

THE DIFFERENCE BETWEEN CAD BLOCKS AND FAMILIES

In a typical CAD environment, for each size of the same door you might create a separate block; each of those blocks would be a separate element unrelated to any of the others. So, 20 door sizes would mean 20 floor-plan blocks, 20 (or 40) section blocks, 20 elevation blocks, and 20 3D blocks if you were going to use them as liberally as we use them in Revit. All of those in Revit are represented with *one* family that can display itself in 2D and 3D and whose size, material, and visibility can be changed at any time.

Depending on how the family is built, parameters can affect either the *type* or the *instance*. A change of *type parameters* affect all families used in the model, whereas *instance parameters* affect only the family (the element, the instance) you've selected. This is an important distinction: you can change instance properties only when you have an element selected, but you can change type properties without selecting anything.

Consider a round table. You might define its shape using a type parameter for the radius. If you placed 20 types of tables with a 2′ (60cm) radius and then changed that radius to 3′ (90cm), all 20 tables would update automatically. Now, if the radius parameter was an instance parameter, changing the radius would affect only the table you currently had selected. The same logic can be applied to other dimensional constraints and materiality. Revit forces you to consider what an element is and what it means to change the element's defining characteristics. For example, most content in Revit doesn't let you arbitrarily change dimensions of every instance, on the fly, whenever you want—this would make tracking the notion of object type difficult and would make mass-updating more tedious. Think of a type as something you'll eventually have to schedule, spec, and install as a real-world commodity.

Bidirectional Relationships

Objects with parameters that can be edited are nothing new in the world of software. But what makes Revit unique is its ability to go beyond 3D objects with parameters and create relationships *between* objects. This ability has been referred to as the *parametric relationships and the resulting parametric change engine,* and it's a core technological advantage built into Revit.

For example, walls can be attached to roofs, and if the roof changes to a new shape or size, all walls attached to the roof automatically adapt to the roof shape. Figure 2.8 shows that changing a roof pitch automatically adjusts other roofs and walls to keep them joined.

FIGURE 2.8
Changing the roof pitch updates walls automatically.

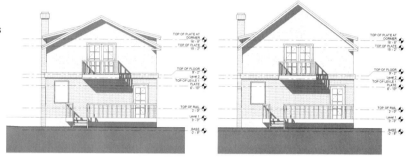

Another powerful manifestation of interrelationships occurs between walls, floors, roofs, components, and levels. They all have explicit relationships to levels, so that if a level changes elevation, all elements associated with that level update automatically. Not only do the bases of the walls attached to a level change, but the tops of the walls attached to this level also change. This is fundamentally different from other BIM software applications, where elements understand the relationship with the level on which they are placed but not the level to which they extend. Thus, if you change the height of a story (level), there will be a gap to the walls, columns, and other elements that, due to the lack of relationship to the level above, will not understand that they need to become taller. Similarly, when you change the size of a room by moving walls to new positions, you're changing not only the wall position but also everything that wall affects in the model: the size of the room (area and volume), color-fill schemes applied to the rooms, the shape and size of ceilings and floors. Doors, windows, and any other wall-hosted elements, such as light fixtures or sockets, will move with the wall when the wall changes position, and any dimensions to that wall will automatically update.

Revit tries to keep things joined and connected in order to eliminate huge amounts of tedious editing. You'll begin to take it for granted after a few days with Revit, but remember: when you drag a wall that has other walls attached to it, those other walls will automatically stretch with your move. Not only that, but rooms, dimensions, floors, components, and tags will also move. Of course, if you don't want all this intelligent behavior, Revit provides escape hatches. For example, if you right-click a wall's end control, you can disallow it from joining other walls (see Figure 2.9). Or you can select Disjoin from the Options bar once you've selected a wall, and then select the Move command—doing so will detach the smart relationships between the wall and the rest of the model and treat the wall as an independent entity.

FIGURE 2.9

By right-clicking the end of a wall join, you can stop the wall from autojoining to other walls.

This parametric behavior extends to annotations and sheet management as well. Tags aren't simple graphics and text; they're interactive graphical parameters of the element being tagged. To edit a tag is to edit the element or tag family, and vice versa. This is also known as a *bidirectional association*. You can edit the elements and the tag and maintain consistent data. A great example is easily demonstrated with a view and a sheet. When you place a section view onto a sheet, the section key automatically references the sheet number and detail number on the sheet. Change the sheet number, and the section tag updates instantly. *This* is what a real parametric engine is and what ensures total coordination of documentation. You've probably heard this phrase before, but it's worth repeating: the parametric engine guarantees that a "change anywhere is a change everywhere."

🌐 Real World Scenario

ADJUSTING A LEVEL AND ROOF SLOPE TO MEET DESIGN REQUIREMENTS

In a real-world project, the height of a level is bound to change in the design process, which in turn will change floor-to-ceiling heights and roof locations and will influence the building's overall height. Consider a scenario in which keeping the top of the roof below a maximum height was a design requirement. Not to worry—with Revit, changing the height of levels (floor-to-floor heights) at any point in the process updates all dimensions and elements associated with that level.

If changing the Roof level pushes the roof peak too high, this is easy to fix. By editing the roof and changing its slope parameter, you can lower the roof height and all the walls attached to the roof update to reflect the change. There is no need to edit the walls independently in order to get the correct results.

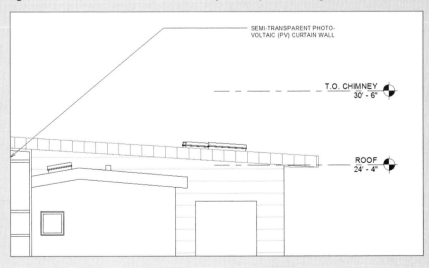

With one edit, you change the roof height. The walls and roof update immediately.

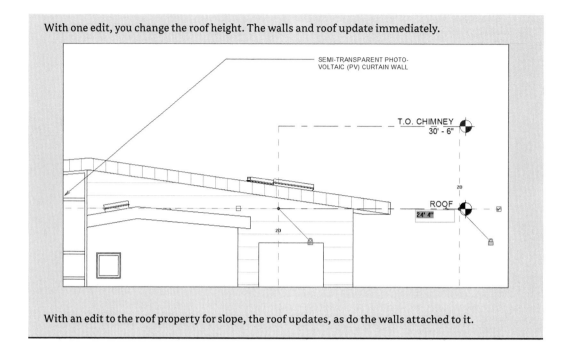

With an edit to the roof property for slope, the roof updates, as do the walls attached to it.

Constraints

During the design phase, you may want to apply some dimensional rules to the design and make sure they aren't altered. These rules might be a minimum hallway width for code compliance, or a maximum office square footage for a particular user. Whatever the restriction, Revit dimensions make it possible to lock it down and create a constraint. This constraint is independent, but it's related to the dimension. If you delete the dimension, you can keep the constrained condition and know that the model will maintain those relationships. The point is that a dimension can be much more than a 2D annotation.

These design rules are used all the time, but not many software applications let you capture this design intent in the model. If you run a dimension string from level to level and lock the dimensions (as in Figure 2.10), you're locking the relationship between these elements in the whole model. By locking down elements, you make it harder for other elements in the model to break this important design intent, and thus keep the model more intact and predictable.

Here are some practical examples of situations in which this is particularly useful: you may want your door jamb always positioned 4″ (10cm) from the wall corner; or you may want three windows in a room to be always positioned at equal distances throughout the length of the exterior wall in a room. By defining and locking these relationships, you embed design intent into the model. And these relationships will react to any later change of the model; if the side wall moves, the door will move as well, to keep the locked 4″ rule; or the windows will reposition to maintain the rule of being equally spaced.

FIGURE 2.10
Design intent can
be locked down by
adding constraints.

Revit Families

Revit families are used to create your model. There are three overarching methods for creating families in Revit:

◆ System families

◆ Standard families

◆ In-place families

The difference between them lies in their creation method, in what context they're created, and the types of parameters available. Let's review each of these types of families.

SYSTEM FAMILIES

Model system families are made up of a limited set of types: walls, roofs, floors, ceilings, stairs, railings, ramps, mullions, curtain panels, mechanical equipment, and toposurfaces (topography). See Figure 2.11 for examples of system families. These families are created in the context of each project, using some predefined types. These families also have various creation methods that are specific to the type of the family. For example, to make walls you can just start drawing (placing a wall), whereas to make a floor or roof, you enter a *Sketch mode* in which you define the outer shape with lines that then generate a 3D model of the floor. For stairs and railings, you enter a more detailed Sketch mode that has additional features not available for floors or roofs. When making toposurfaces, you use a Sketch mode that lets you edit 3D points specific to toposurfaces. As you can see, system families all have slightly different creation methods.

You can create new types of system families by duplicating existing types and editing their parameters. If you've been using Revit for any length of time, then this method of duplicating a type to create new types should be familiar territory for you.

You can't create new categories in Revit. These categories are predefined within Revit and limited to the list available. This is primarily to maintain control over the graphics from project to project.

FIGURE 2.11
System families

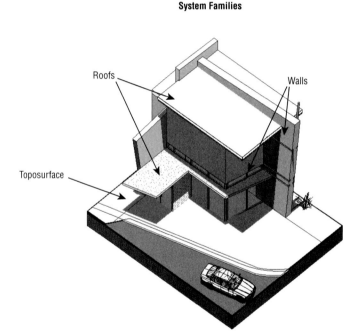

If you aren't sure whether an element is a system family, open the Element Properties dialog box and check the family name. Embedded in the family name, you can see whether the element is a system family. Figure 2.12 shows that a Basic Wall and a Section are both system families.

FIGURE 2.12
System families
include model
and annotation
elements.

System families are also used for many annotation categories, such as sections, elevations, levels, grids, text, and dimensions—they aren't limited to model elements.

Another characteristic of a system family is that you can't save them outside of your project to a shared library as a standalone component. Even so, it's still possible to reuse system families in other projects. To transfer system families between projects, choose File ➤ Transfer Project Standards to display the Select Items to Copy dialog box (Figure 2.13). This dialog box gives you a feel for the number of different types of system families used in a Revit project.

FIGURE 2.13

The Select Items to Copy dialog box

STANDARD FAMILIES

Standard families (see Figure 2.14) are created outside of the project environment using the Family Editor. They're stored in an external library (folders on your hard drive) and can be loaded into a project for use at any point. Every standard family belongs to a specific Revit category so that when it's loaded into a project, it adopts the graphic rules defined for its category in the Object Styles dialog box. This guarantees graphic consistency throughout your project without your having to constantly manage changes to new families. This also guarantees that when you schedule a category, you get all elements that belong to that category.

For example, if you find a lighting fixture family on the Web and load it into your project, it will use the Lighting Fixtures object style in your project to represent the family. It will be scheduled with other lighting fixtures. You aren't forced to open the family and adjust line weights or colors, or add metadata to the element, because this is all controlled at the project level. This illustrates the value of having a fixed number of categories to manage—you can rest assured that the project won't inflate with endless, oddly named layers that are difficult, if not impossible, to decode.

Standard families have their own file format extension (.rfa) and can be stored outside the project environment for later use in other projects. Revit ships with a predefined folder structure to help manage the vast numbers of families available. Choose File ➤ Load from Library ➤ Load Family to see how Revit organizes information (see Figure 2.15).

FIGURE 2.14
Standard families

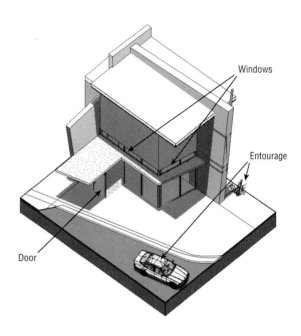

Windows

Entourage

Door

FIGURE 2.15
The Load Family
dialog box

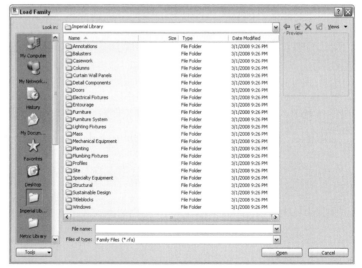

ORGANIZING YOUR OFFICE LIBRARY

In your office you're free to organize your families in whatever way makes the most sense. You can use a read-only, shared office library, or per-project mini-libraries. Whatever route you go, be sure to add your library locations to your Revit file load dialog box.

To do this from the Load Family dialog box, browse to your office library and choose Tools ➢ Add Current Folder to Places located at bottom of the dialog box. The folder will appear in the list of default folder locations.

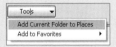

Another option is to use the Options dialog box. To open it, choose Options ➢ Settings, then click the File Locations tab. Add a new path to the Libraries table.

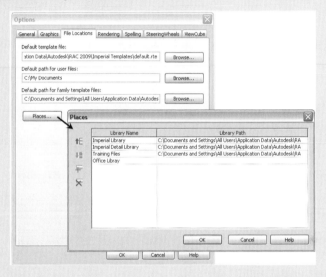

Once you do this, a new link appears in the Open dialog box with the name of your library. Clicking the icon takes you directly to your office library.

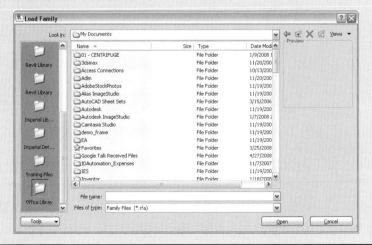

To create variations of a standard family, duplicate an existing one in the project and modify its properties. To make more radical geometrical changes to the family, you need to open it in the Family Editor and change the form there. The process of editing a family supports an iterative design workflow: by selecting any family, you have the option either to edit its properties or to open it in the Family Editor and make changes to it and then load it right back into your project. Families can be complex, but at least you won't need to learn any specialized scripting languages to create smart, parametric content. This goes for all forms of standard families, from totally parametric windows and doors to one-off pieces of furniture or lighting fixtures.

Revit provides a set of starting family templates you can use to make content from scratch. When you want to start creating a new library element (family), you first need to select the correct template. To open a template, choose File ➢ New ➢ Family. Choose the type of element you want to make, and the template will open. Embedded in each template are smart behavior characteristics of the family you're creating. Figure 2.16 illustrates a door family template, where geometry, parameters, and dimensions are already in place to help you get started.

FIGURE 2.16
The template for this door family includes geometry, parameters, and dimensions to help get you started.

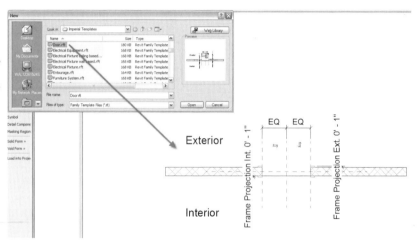

Doors, windows, balusters, casework, columns, curtain wall panels, entourage, furniture, massing elements, generic objects, and plantings are all examples of standard Revit family categories.

To move families between projects, you can use copy and paste or save your families to disk and then load them into another project.

IN-PLACE FAMILIES

In-place families are custom elements that are specific to a project and the conditions of the project. An in-place family accesses functionality available in the Family Editor in the context of a project environment. The model grays out and becomes unselectable when you make such families. A nonvertical, sweeping wall shape is a good example for when you would use an in-place family.

You can copy and paste in-place families from project to project, but you can't save them as RFA (Revit projects have the extension .rvt, Revit Families .rfa) as you can with standard families.

Figure 2.17 shows an in-place family added to a façade in order to create some nonorthogonal mullions.

FIGURE 2.17
Example of an in-place family used to add skewed mullions to the façade

FIGURE 2.17
Example of an in-place family used to add skewed mullions to the façade

---

USING IN-PLACE FAMILIES

There are some more advanced features of building information modeling that you will inevitably want to pursue, such as energy modeling or daylighting or direct-to-fabrication. Some of these features do not respond well with in-place families. Try to limit your use of in-place families if possible.

Overriding the Representation of Elements

Keep in mind that there are no layers in Revit. Revit uses object categories and subcategories (not layers) to define the graphics for each element class as well as to control visibility (which is the purpose of layers in other software). The Object Styles dialog box (accessed from the Settings menu) establishes the default graphics for every category; however, in any view, you can override these graphics using the View ➤ Visibility/Graphic Overrides dialog box shown in Figure 2.18. The two dialog boxes look very similar—the difference is that Object Styles shows the defaults preset for a project, whereas Visibility/Graphic Overrides is the place to review and make changes to those default settings on a per-view basis. The same familiar categories and subcategories displayed in the Object Styles dialog box are displayed in this dialog box as well.

FIGURE 2.18
The Visibility/
Graphic Overrides
dialog box

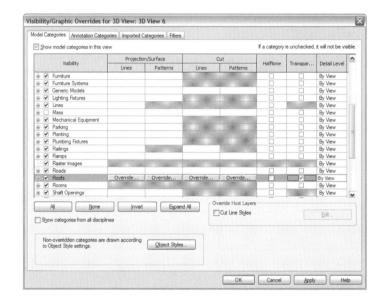

The same level of visual control for line weight, color, and pattern is provided here, but in a slightly different interface. In addition to line overrides, you can override cut and surface patterns and choose to show a category as halftone, transparent, or at a different level of detail. Figure 2.19 shows the Roof category overridden to be transparent in the 3D view, allowing you to see through the roof and look into the rooms beneath while keeping the shape of the roof visible. Changes made using this dialog box are applied only to your current view.

FIGURE 2.19
The Roof category
has been over-
ridden to be
transparent in
the 3D view.

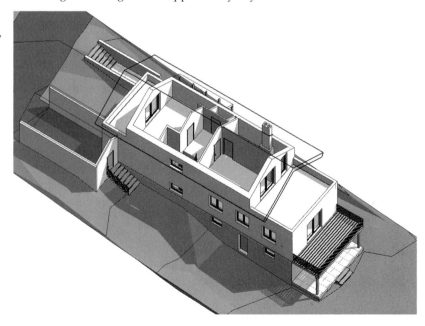

The same categories are used to control the visibility of elements in a view. You can turn off entire categories, subcategories, or individual elements in any view.

Working with the Revit User Interface

As you'll notice, the Revit interface isn't overburdened by a lot of toolbars. It may seem as if there are too few buttons to build an entire building. Don't worry, all the tools are there—they're just not visible all the time. The user interface (UI) is divided into five major components, shown in Figure 2.20:

◆ The *View window*, where all the views and drawing take place

◆ The *Design bar*, where you access all the creation tools

◆ The *Project Browser*, where all the views and families are stored and which is used to navigate the projects

◆ The *Options bar*, where you choose types, access properties, and edit context-sensitive options

◆ The *toolbars*, where you invoke various editing tools

FIGURE 2.20
The Revit user interface

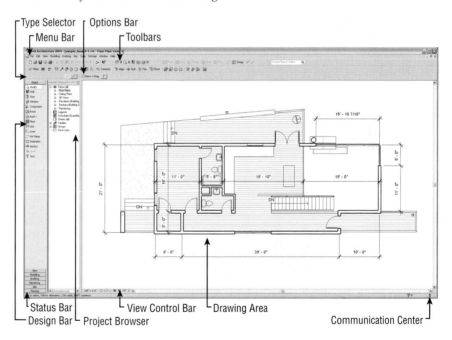

Next, we'll take a quick look at each of these components.

In addition to these major UI components, the *status bar* is located along the bottom of the application frame. It contains information about active commands and what is selected, progress meters, and the Communications Center.

The View Window

The View window is where all the action takes place. Here, you add elements, modify them, and construct and document your model. The view area can tile multiple views, allowing you to visualize the model from multiple vantage points concurrently. We don't recommend tiling the views if you have more than six or so open views because the views get too small and it becomes difficult to work effectively.

To arrange views, go to the Window menu and try the Cascade or Tile option. You'll also see the option Close Hidden Windows.

The Close Hidden Windows feature is a great way to clear your workspace when you have an unmanageable number of views open. Selecting Close Hidden Windows closes all but one view for each project or family you have open. This is advisable to improve performance when you're working on a complex project.

Views in Revit are showing the same model from different vantage points. Thus, when selecting an element in one view you'll see that the element becomes selected in all views. You can try this by opening two views (click on the view names in the Project Browser) and tile the views (Window ➢ Tile). This simple interaction shows that when you make a change to an element in one view the change is instantly reflected in other views. This is a great way to conceptually understand the reality of a true BIM modeler.

View Controls

Each view has properties, and some of these properties are exposed at the bottom of the View window in what is called the View Control bar.

These controls allow you to quickly change the display of the view without having to dig into a properties dialog box. The available controls include View Scale, Detail Level, Display Type, Shadows, Rendering, Crop View, Show Crop, Temporary Hide/Isolate, and Reveal Hidden Elements.

The Design Bar

The Design bar is a group of tabs located on the left side of the application window that contains creation tools organized based on common tasks, as shown in Figure 2.21.

The tools are grouped into tabs that suggest a certain task: Drafting, Modeling, Site, Massing, and so on. Some tools are repeated on multiple tabs because they're used for various tasks. The Dimension tool is an example: dimensions are used when modeling, drafting, and laying out structures. Which tabs are visible is entirely up to you. In fact, we've even seen some users turn off all design bars and only use menus and keyboard shortcuts.

FIGURE 2.21
The Design bar

Clicking a tab opens it and makes the tools available for use. You can hide/reveal design tabs using the context menu when the mouse is hovering over the Design bar. On some smaller monitor resolutions (less than 1280 × 1024), you may not see all the tools available in a design tab. To access these tools, click the More Tools flyout at the bottom of the tab, as shown here.

TURNING TABS ON AND OFF

The Massing tab can be turned off if you don't use massing. The same is true for any other tab—you can choose to turn any of them on or off. To see the full selection of tabs, right-click anywhere on the Design bar, and select only those you wish to view.

All the tools located in the Design bar are also available from the menu at the top of the application. You may notice that at times some tools are grayed out, depending on the type of view you're currently working in. If you open a perspective view, almost all the tools in the Design bars appear grayed out. This is because Revit doesn't let you create new elements in perspective views (don't be discouraged; you can place objects in any orthographic 3D view).

The Options Bar

The Options bar contains several parts: the Type Selector, Properties button, and dynamic option controls. The Type Selector becomes active when you're making new elements or when an element is selected. The tool is used to swap types of family elements—and works on all types of Revit objects—whether model or annotation. The Options bar looks like this when a wall is selected:

The Properties button takes you to the element properties of whatever you've selected. Everything to the right of the Properties button is dynamic and changes depending on what you're creating, what tool you're using, or what element is selected. For example, when the Move tool is activated, you'll notice some new options appear:

ALWAYS CHECK THE OPTIONS BAR FOR TOOL SPECIFIC OPTIONS

Look to the Options bar whenever you're using a tool, placing elements, or selecting elements, because it will show you options specific to the current task. It's easy to forget the Options bar exists, so train yourself to scan it, and get familiar with what it offers.

Toolbars

At the top of the application are the toolbars. These are used to save files, undo or redo commands, dynamically pan and zoom, modify elements in the model, and enable additional features such as worksets and design options. We won't go into each tool here, but throughout the book we will refer and direct you to various tools in these toolbars.

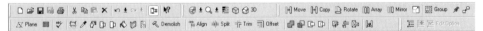

The Project Browser

The Project Browser allows you to navigate to all your views, create new views, access element properties, and place elements. All the views of your project are stored here, making it possible to organize and navigate a project from one location.

Figure 2.22 shows a collapsed view of a typical Project Browser. As you can see, the browser contains all your views, families, schedules, sheets, and linked files.

The Project Browser is the backbone of your project; we'll devote the rest of this chapter to exploring its use.

Using the Project Browser

You can navigate through a Revit project in a number of ways. As you start working in real projects, the number of views and drawings that accumulate will become quite large. Being able to find your views and move between them is critical to an effective workflow. We'll look at the various methods of moving between views, explore best practices, and show you how to customize the display of these views using the Project Browser.

Views

A *view* is a graphical way to look at the database of information you're creating. Plan, section, schedule table, 3D view—all of these are just different ways to look at and query the same underlying database of information that describes your building. Revit organizes all the views of your project in the Project Browser. Your plans, sections, elevations, 3D views, and schedules are all stored there. Double-clicking a view name from the Project Browser opens the view in the View window. When you close a window using the controls at the top right on each window, you don't need to save the view first—it's always accessible from the Project Browser.

The default organization of the Project browser is based on the view type and presented as nodes in a tree structure. The default organization when all the nodes are collapsed looks like this:

The Project Browser allows you to define an organization of views per your needs. We will go into how to do this in more detail later in this chapter.

With a node expanded, right-click a view name to access additional options for any view (see Figure 2.23). From the context menu, you can open views, rename them, duplicate them, and apply view templates.

FIGURE 2.23
Context menu
options for a view

Note that you can multiselect views in the Project Browser. When more than one view is selected, you can right-click to bring up the context menu:

For example, from the context menu you can create and apply view templates. This is a way
to give views a consistent scale and graphical appearance, among other things. Let's look at how
to use the Project Browser as a way to drive properties from one view to another:

1. Open Foundation.rvt from the Chapter 2 folder on this book's companion website
   (www.sybex.com/go/masteringrevit2009).

2. Open Plan: Level 1.

3. Right-click the view and duplicate it.

4. Rename the view **Level 1 - Presentation**.

5. Type **VG** to open the Visibility/Graphic Overrides dialog box.

6. Select the Annotations tab, and turn off visibility of all annotations by clearing the Show
   Annotation Categories in This View check box at the top of the table.

7. Go back to the view in the Project Browser, and right-click the view. Select Create View
   Template from View (see Figure 2.24).

FIGURE 2.24

Creating a new
view template

8. Name the template **Presentation Graphics**.

9. Duplicate Level 2, and rename it **Level 2 - Presentation**.

10. Right-click the view name, and choose Apply View Template.

11. Choose Presentation Graphics from the list in the dialog box in Figure 2.25.

FIGURE 2.25

Choosing the Pre-
sentation Graphics
template

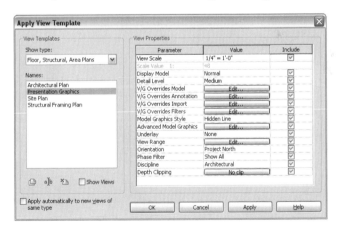

12. The plan now has the same properties as the Level 1 - Presentation view.

Working in a data-driven model, you can use view properties to customize how the browser sorts and organizes all your views. This is a great way to manage the large number of views that will fill your project. Clicking the top of the Project Browser window (not a view) makes it the active selection. You'll notice the Type Selector in the Options bar activates and some predefined options will be available (see Figure 2.26). Selecting any of these will re-sort the views in your project based on those criteria.

FIGURE 2.26
Browser organiza-
tion options

Customizing the Browser Organization

Use these steps to customize the browser organization:

1. With the `Foundation.rvt` file still open, select the Views icon in the Project Browser.

2. The Type Selector lists `Browser - Views : all`.

   Click the Properties button.

3. Change the type to Not on Sheets. You'll see the browser reorganize the list and remove views that are on sheets.

Now, let's make a custom sort based on your name (or initials) by applying a new Drawn By parameter to all views and then using that parameter to sort the views in the browser:

1. From the menu, choose Settings ➢ Project Parameters.

2. In the resulting dialog box, click the Add a New Parameter button.

3. Choose the Views category on the right side of the dialog box, and give the parameter the name **Drawn by**. In the Group Parameter Under drop-down list, select Identity Data (see Figure 2.27). Click OK.

FIGURE 2.27
Create a new
project parameter
for views.

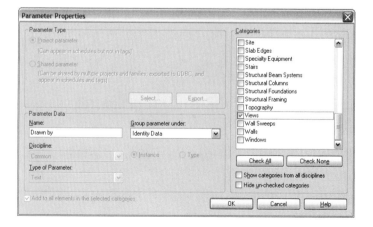

4. Go back to the Project Browser.

5. Go to Properties, and choose Duplicate ➢ Not on Sheets. Name the duplicate **My Drawings**.

6. Click the Folders button.

7. Change the Group By setting to Drawn By (Figure 2.28), and click OK.

FIGURE 2.28
Group views by
the new parameter,
Drawn By.

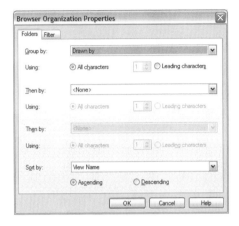

8. Go to any view, and open its view properties.

9. The project parameter you added appears in the Identity Data group as Drawn By. Type your initials or name in the value field, and click OK (Figure 2.29).

FIGURE 2.29
Change the Drawn
By parameter for
any view.

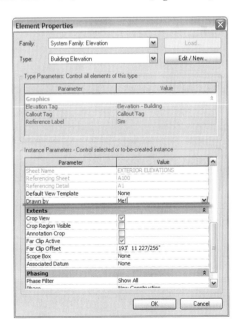

Sheets

Sheets are special views that are your final documents—the actual sheets you'll be sharing with your contractor, client, or team members. This is where the collections of drawings that eventually get printed are stored. Under each sheet node you see all the views placed on that sheet. As with any other view in Revit, if you double-click the node, the sheet view opens in the View window.

To make a new sheet, use the View tab or the View menu, and choose Sheet. This lets you select a title block family to use.

ACTIVATING A VIEW ON A SHEET

Double-clicking a view placed on a sheet is the same as opening the view from the view's node. Double-clicking the sheet name opens the sheet. From the sheet, you can directly edit views on the sheet by right-clicking a view and choosing the Activate View option. This opens the view and grays out the sheet context, allowing you to edit elements in the view from the context of your sheet. To get back to the sheet, use the context menu again, and choose Deactivate View.

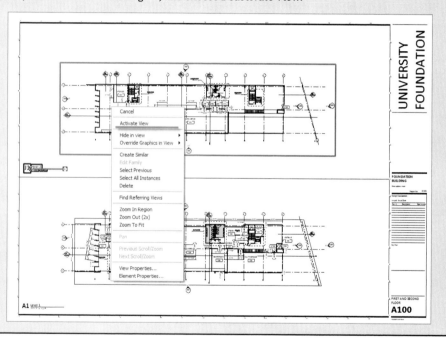

Families

In the Project Browser you can see all the loaded families in your project. *Loaded* means available from within the project and usually loaded along with the template. You can load additional families while working on the project, and each one you load will be available in this location in the Project Browser. From here, you can drag and drop families into the drawing area, query

NAVIGATING VIEWS AND VIEW PROPERTIES | **43**

their properties, create new types of elements, and even select all instances of a given element in the model in order to locate them or perform wholesale changes. The context menu for families (Figure 2.30) is different from that for views. Note that if you choose the option to edit a family, you'll open the family in the Family Editor, where you can make changes to the component and then reload it. If you expand the family node to expose all the family types, you can right-click a type and choose Select All Instances from the context menu. All instances in the model become selected, even if you can't see them in your current view. This lets you make edits to the family type in one interaction. For example, you can select all instances of a door family and swap it with a different door type.

FIGURE 2.30
Options for families in the Project Browser

Links

Revit *links* (other Revit files that are linked into your project) are also listed in the Project Browser. Using the context menu, you can reload, unload, open, copy, and visually identify the links in your project.

Groups

Groups are associated collections of elements that can be repeatedly placed throughout the model. Groups are used for repeating entities (furniture composed of a table and six chairs, a typical bathroom layout with fixtures and partitions, or a typical hotel room, for example). When one group changes, all other instances of that group also change. Whenever a group is created, it appears in the Project Browser. You can place a group from the Project Browser by dragging it into the View window.

Navigating Views and View Properties

As we've mentioned, all views have properties that determine characteristics such as scale, graphics display, and view depth. Each view type has special characteristics and options that are important to understand when you're using Revit. We'll look at the different view types and explain their defining features and how to use them. To access view properties, use any of these access methods:

♦ Right-click anywhere in the view window, and select View Properties from the context menu.

♦ Right-click a view in the Project Browser, and select Properties from the context menu.

♦ Select View ➢ View Properties.

♦ Use the keyboard shortcut VP to access the View Properties dialog box directly.

Floor Plans

Plan views are used to show horizontal slices through your building. Each plan view in Revit is associated with a level. A *level* is a horizontal datum that establishes major floor-to-floor heights and other critical horizontal working planes. Figure 2.31 shows that each level generates a plan view. By default, the plan is cut 4″ (1–1.2 m) above the actual level height, but this value can be customized to suit your requirements.

FIGURE 2.31
Levels generate plan views.

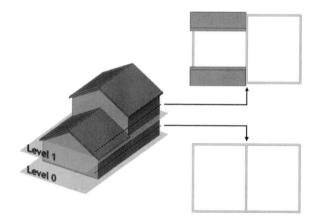

CAUTION WHEN DELETING LEVELS!

If you delete a level in your project, you will delete all views and elements associated with that level, including any walls, roofs, and furniture—so be careful when deleting levels!

Each plan view can show a range of the model based on levels. This aspect of Revit is often misunderstood, so let's take a moment to demystify it.

VIEW RANGE

When creating your documents, you care about correct representation of your elements. Using the Object Styles dialog box and graphic overrides, you can get your drawings to look exactly the way you want them to look. However, you'll often wish to add some abstraction to the drawing that involves elements that aren't typically visible in the view. You may want to see roof lines overhead, or see down into an atrium a few levels below. This is where the View Range options come in handy.

The options available in the View Range dialog box allow you to define how elements in a view are represented based on their location in space. View-range values are stored as a property of the view and are included when you save a view as a view template.

Figure 2.32 shows three ways to represent the same space and elements by using different view range settings. Think of the mess you might end up with if you had to do this using a layering system!

FIGURE 2.32
Three different representations of the same model in plan view

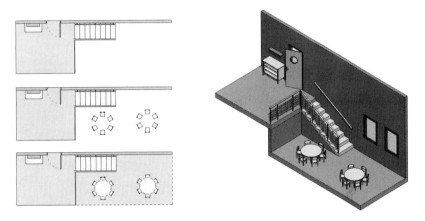

To access the View Range dialog box, go to View Properties of a plan or ceiling plan view, and choose to edit the View Range parameter. Doing so opens the dialog box shown in Figure 2.33.

FIGURE 2.33
The View Range dialog box

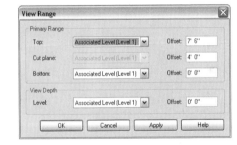

The View Range dialog box is divided into two parameter groups: Primary Range and View Depth. The view range is defined by horizontal planes—three of them define the primary range (Top, Cut Plane, and Bottom), and a fourth plane defines the depth of a view (View Depth):

Top   Defines the top limit of the view range

Cut plane   Defines the height of the Cut plane

Bottom   Defines the bottom limit of the view range

Note that the positioning of these is *always* relative to a level. The Cut plane *always* references the level of the view in which you're working, and the other two can reference *any* level of the project.

There is no graphical presentation of the view range settings, but it shouldn't be difficult to imagine their position in space. Look at Figure 2.34, a representation of different positions of the horizontal planes of a view range.

FIGURE 2.34
Various positions of the view range (top) and the associated plan view (bottom)

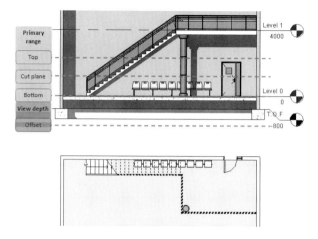

Floor plan   In a floor plan view, the direction of the view is from top to bottom—so you're looking from above.

Ceiling plan   In a ceiling plan, the view direction is exactly the opposite—you're looking from below, upward (see Figure 2.35).

FIGURE 2.35
Position of the view range for ceiling plans (top) and the associated plan view (bottom)

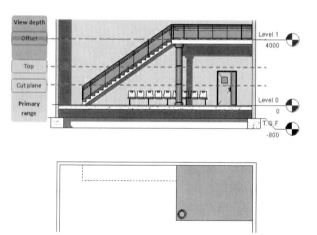

Depending on the positioning of the elements with respect to the view range and its parameters, the graphical display of those elements can vary. The Cut Plane parameter can radically change the appearance of your view, because every element in Revit has a physical location in space. Elements look different depending on whether they're *cut* by the Cut plane, *above the Cut plane*, or *below the Cut plane*.

DOES A CATEGORY ALLOW CUTTING?

How do you determine whether a category allows its elements to be cut? A fast way is to look it up in the Revit Help file under Creating Your Own Components (Families) ➤ Visibility and Detail Level ➤ Cuttable and non Cuttable Family categories.

There is another method as well, which may be more practical: in the Visibility Graphic Overrides dialog box or the Object Styles dialog box is a Cut column. For certain categories, this column is grayed out; this is the indicator that the category doesn't allow cutting.

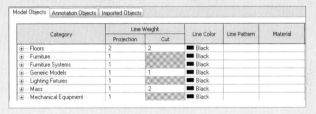

CUT PLANE

Not all Revit elements behave the same with respect to the Cut plane. Some Revit categories don't support the notion of being cut (furniture families, for example); even if a Cut plane intersects them, they're always represented as if viewed from above (not cut). Figure 2.36 shows that a stool looks the same, no matter where the Cut plane happens to intersect it.

FIGURE 2.36
Some categories, such as furniture, are not affected by the cut plane.

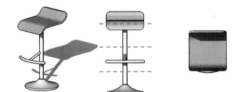

THE PRIMARY RANGE

Now that you have a general understanding of how the Cut plane affects elements in a view, let's dig deeper into the primary range concept. As we mentioned, this range consists of two other planes, Top and Bottom, which are placed respectively above and below the Cut plane. The exact positioning of these two planes is defined by an offset value relative to a level:

The Top plane can reference any level above the current one. The Bottom plane can reference any level below the current one. Let's look at some examples:

♦ If an element is cut by a Cut plane, it's visible in the view as shown in Figure 2.37.

FIGURE 2.37
The cabinet is cut
by the Cut plane
and is visible.

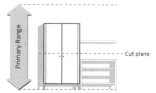

♦ If an element is *below* the Cut plane but within the primary range (partially or completely), it's visible in the plan view as if it were looked at from above, as shown in Figure 2.38.

FIGURE 2.38
The lower book-
case isn't cut but
is visible.

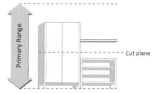

♦ If an element is *above* the Cut plane and completely within the view range, it doesn't appear unless it's the category Windows, Casework, or Generic Model. It appears as if seen from above, as shown in Figure 2.39. Because the wall shelf is the category Casework, and it's within the primary range, it appears in plan view.

FIGURE 2.39
The wall shelf
appears.

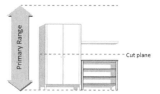

VIEW DEPTH

The View Depth is defined by a horizontal plane that is below the view range. The positioning of this plane uses the same principle as the planes in the view range—it's defined by an offset referencing a level:

This plane is often confused with the Bottom plane of the view range: the View Depth *cannot* be above the Bottom plane. View Depth allows you to see elements below. The default is set to show nothing, because it's associated with the active level and has no offset.

The View Depth is easy to misunderstand; it sounds confusing to have a Bottom plane in the view range and also have this additional View Depth parameter. The idea here is that you need the ability to control the display of elements that are below the primary range but within the View Depth. Consider a wall with a footing. The wall is placed on Level 0 and goes up to Level 1. In the plan view of Level 0, using the default settings, you don't see the footing (see Figure 2.40).

FIGURE 2.40

With the default View Depth, the footings aren't visible in plan view.

Figure 2.41 shows the effect of the default view range when it's set to be coincident with the view's associated level, in this case Level 0. To make the footing visible in the Level 0 plan view, you need to do one of the following:

◆ Lower the height of the Bottom plane in the primary range, and define the View Depth to be coincident with it.

◆ Define the View Depth so that it's below the base of the footing.

FIGURE 2.41

Modifying the view range for different visibility. Lowering the depth of the view makes the footings visible in plan view. They're represented with the Beyond line style, which in this example uses a dashed line.

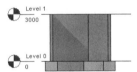

In the second case, you don't need to change anything about the Bottom plane. In addition, you can obtain a different graphic presentation for the footings (without modifying the Visibility/Graphic Overrides settings). The View Depth allows elements that are below the current level to appear in a unique line style named *Beyond*. To control that line style, choose Settings ➢ Line Styles.

To display the elements in view in a specific way, you'll need to play with various parameter settings in the view range (see Figure 2.42).

FIGURE 2.42
The view-range settings work in the vertical dimension (view shown in elevation) and affect plan views (corresponding plan view shown below).

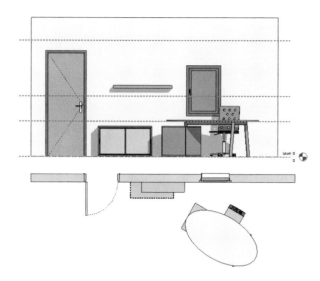

To fully understand this example, it's essential to understand the categories of the elements participating in this view (from left to right in Figure 2.42):

The door   The door belongs to the Door category. It's cut by the Cut plane. Its graphic presentation is controlled by the Cut style in the Object Styles or Visibility/Graphic Overrides dialog box. The arc representing the door swing is a 2D symbolic element and thus can't be cut by the Cut plane.

The low cabinet   The low cabinet belongs to the Furniture category. Because it's placed below the Cut plane but still within the View Depth, it's visible in plan view. It uses the Beyond line style.

The wall-mounted shelf   The wall shelf belongs to the Furniture System category. The shelf is above the Cut plane but within the view range. Its category allows it to be represented in plan view. Its graphics are controlled by the Projection column in the Visibility/Graphic Overrides or Object Styles dialog box.

The desk–chair–drawer family   The desk with a chair and a drawer (all one family) belongs to the Furniture category. This family is cut by the Cut plane. Its category doesn't allow for it to be cut, and its graphics are thus controlled by the Projection style in the Visibility/Graphic Overrides or Object Styles dialog box.

The window   The window belongs to the Window category. It's cut by the Cut plane. Its graphics are controlled by the Cut style in the Visibility/Graphic Overrides or Object Styles dialog box.

Creating a Plan View Using View Range and a Plan Region

Figure 2.43 is a model of a simple space that we'll use to understand view range. We have chosen a split-level example to show you the power of various settings and resulting displays of the view-range parameters. The goal is to create a plan view of Level 0 that displays information from a lower level. We want to display elements placed on Level 00B with a dashed line style. Follow these steps:

1. Open the file Foundation.rvt from the Chapter 2 folder on the book's companion web page.

   In the elevation view (South Elevation) you can see the various planes (Figure 2.44). The View Depth is defined to be the same as the Bottom plane.

FIGURE 2.43
Working with the view range

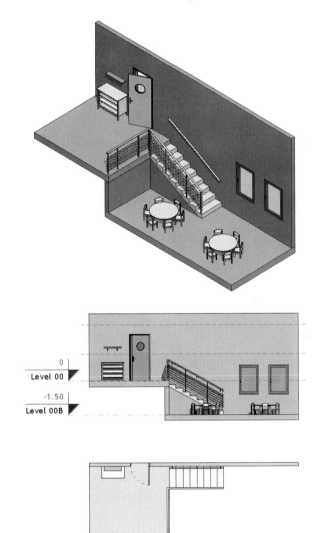

FIGURE 2.44
View range
settings

2. From the Level 00 plan view, go to View Properties, and open the View Range dialog box.

   The default Revit settings are currently being used. Notice in Figure 2.45 that Level 00B and all elements placed on it are *not* visible in this view. The low cabinet is visible in the view, because it's placed on Level 00 and is within the primary range. The wall shelf above the low cabinet belongs to the category Furniture Systems and is also visible, even though it's above the Cut plane.

FIGURE 2.45
You can see the
effect of moving
the Bottom and
View Depth to
Level 00B.

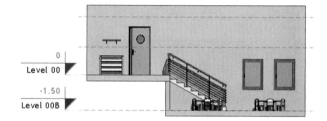

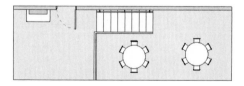

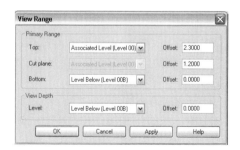

3. Change the Bottom and View Depth to Level Below (Level 00B), and click Apply.

   Having defined the Bottom plane as well as the View Depth to be coincident to Level 00B, you've managed to show the elements of Level 00B in the Level 00 plan view. The problem is that it will be difficult to assign a dashed-line style to the elements placed on Level 00B, as you initially desired. You could manually override all the elements, but you'd have to do so in each view manually—let's look at a smarter way to do this.

4. The furniture in this level is below the Cut plane. To change the graphic display of it, you could use the Projection column in the Visibility/Graphic Overrides or Object Styles dialog box; but in that case, the presentation of the furniture on Level 00 would be affected—and that isn't what you want to happen.

5. Set the Bottom plane to Level 00, and give the View Depth a –4′ (–1.2m) offset below Level 00. Click Apply. In the elevation in Figure 2.46, you can see the various planes in dashed-line style. As you'll notice, the chairs are now visible but not the table—this is because the chairs are partially within the view but the tables aren't (they're below the View Depth). The chairs belong to the Furniture category, which doesn't support a cut representation; they're shown as if they were seen from above, even though they're intersected by the View Depth.

FIGURE 2.46
Modifying the View Depth settings

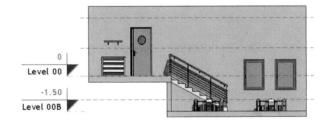

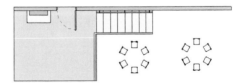

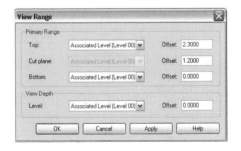

6. Set the View Depth to Level Below (Level 00B) and give it a –4′ (–1m) offset. In the elevation in Figure 2.47, you can see the various planes in dashed-line style.

By changing the View Depth, you have achieved your goal of seeing the furniture from below in a dashed-line style; however, the windows don't look quite right. To fix that, Revit provides a tool that allows you to selectively alter the view range for certain parts of the view using a *plan region*. This tool lets you draw a rectangle and then define the view range for that rectangle as a way to override the view range settings of the view.

FIGURE 2.47
Lowering the
View Depth

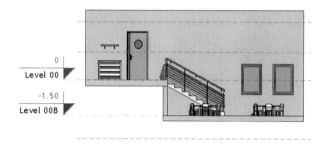

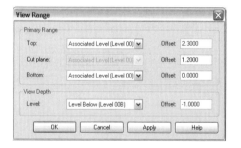

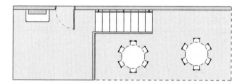

7. In the View Design tab of the Design bar, select the Plan Region tool, and sketch a rectangle around the windows as shown in Figure 2.48. This region will make it possible to show the windows as if they were cut.

FIGURE 2.48
Making a plan
region, annotated
here by the rect-
angle in the upper
right

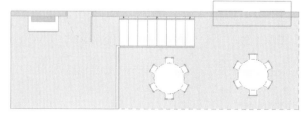

8. Click the View Range Properties button on the Design bar, and change the view range of the plan region. In this example, to show the window, set the level the Cut plane is referencing to Level 00B (see Figure 2.49).

FIGURE 2.49

View-range properties of the plan region

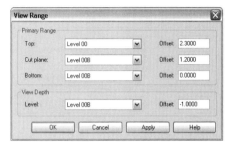

If you need to adjust the properties of the plan region later, select it and use the View Range button on the Options bar as a quick way to get back to the settings.

Sections

Section views are traditionally live cuts through the building model. They can be generated using the Section view tool from the View or Basics Design bar. You can place section lines in plans, elevations, and other section views, and they will appear in other views that cross the section perpendicular to the Cut plane. A section has two graphic symbols associated with it that appear at either end of the section line. Check the Options bar when placing a new section—you'll notice that you can choose a section type (Building, Wall, Detail) and also preset the scale. These are the options available when placing a section:

You define the section line by making two clicks in the view. Once a section has been created, you can move it by dragging it. The amazing thing is that when you move the section line, the view it references is automatically regenerated. A section line always shows what it's cutting when the view is displayed. It's impossible to have a section that is out of sync with the model.

Some special properties are available for sections that help you create the drawings you want. We'll focus on those next.

BROKEN SECTION LINES

The default section graphic is shown as a solid line with a section head and section tail at the ends. You can break a section cut line by clicking the little squiggle icon in the center of the line. Doing this lets you create a graphic as shown in Figure 2.50.

FIGURE 2.50
Clicking the
squiggle icon
breaks the
section line.

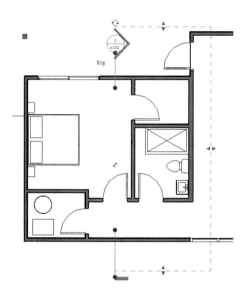

JOGGED SECTIONS

As you draw a section line, you'll notice that you can only draw a straight segment. Often, however, you'll want the section line to pass through important parts of the building that don't lie on the same line—you'll need to break the section line and make it jog. You can jog the section line around elements in plan to change what is shown in the view. To do this, click the Split Segment button on the Options bar when a section is selected. The cursor changes to a knife. Click to split the section, and begin dragging the segment. Figure 2.51 shows an example of a section split that jogs around an elevator core but cuts through classrooms.

FIGURE 2.51
Jogging a
section line

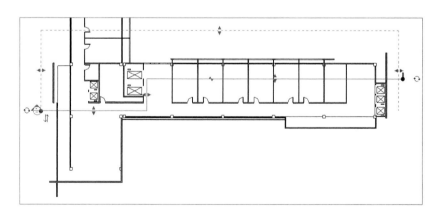

DEPTH OF A SECTION

When a section is selected, you can control the extents of the view interactively using the crop boundaries. The right and left sides directly affect the section view size on a sheet. The far clip limits how much geometry is visible in depth. To improve performance and get the right representation, be aware of how deep your sections are. Show only what is needed. By default, a new section extends the entire depth of the model. To change that, pull the far clip closer to the Cut plane (see Figure 2.52). The same logic applies to elevation depth as well.

FIGURE 2.52
Controlling the section depth

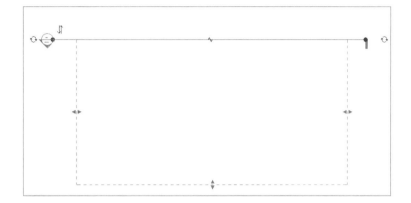

AUTOHIDING SECTIONS AND ELEVATIONS

It's possible for sections to disappear from time to time as you change the scale of a view. If you check the visibility settings or try Reveal Hidden Elements mode, it won't be clear why the sections aren't visible. This behavior is a result of a little-known feature: Hide at Scales Coarser Than. This parameter lets you set a scale beyond which the section will no longer be visible. In most circumstances, the benefit of this feature will be nearly invisible—Revit will do the right thing, and you'll go about your business as usual.

Elevations

Elevations are made by placing elevation tags in floor plan views. Depending on where you place the elevation in the model, you'll get different resulting views. Revit assumes that if you place an elevation in the model (in a room, for example), you're creating interior elevations. The view shows only the walls visible in that room. If you place an elevation outside your model, a building elevation is created that shows the entire façade.

Elevations are a lot like sections in terms of how they behave in Revit: they have a clip plane, a crop boundary, and a symbol; and they can be opened directly by double-clicking the symbol. Elevation tags can have as many as four views related to one tag for the purpose of creating interior elevations of rooms. This is great for interior elevations but limits your ability to customize the graphics of these tags.

Real World Scenario

HIDING SECTIONS AT COARSER VIEW SCALES

In a ¼″ (1:50) floor plan view, you may have many wall sections, building sections, and interior elevation tags visible. However, with a ⅛″ plan (1:100), you only want to see the building sections and exterior elevation tags. Using the Hide at Scales Coarser Than option, you can do this. Select your interior elevation tags, and set their type property to hide at scales coarser than ¼″ (1:50). (Make sure you select the view direction arrow, not the view reference part.) Next time you open the ⅛″ (1:100) plan, they won't be visible. Do the same for your wall sections. Because this is an instance property, you must first select the elements to which you want to apply this rule.

In many scenarios, the symbol used for an exterior building elevation is identical to the symbol used for section heads. Currently, in Revit, this can't be done with a standard elevation symbol. For this use case, we suggest a common workaround:

1. Create a building section, and open its properties. Click the Edit/New button, and then duplicate the section. Name the new type **Exterior Elevation**, as shown in Figure 2.53.

2. When you go to place an exterior elevation, choose the Section tool instead. Draw the section so that it creates an exterior view of the model.

3. Drag the section head to the middle of the model. Notice that the section extents stay where they are, so the view isn't affected by this graphical change.

4. Turn off the visibility of the section tail by clicking the cycle icon.

5. Drag the section line so it disappears into the section head.

FIGURE 2.53
Making a new
section type for a
building section

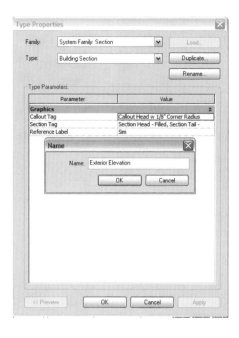

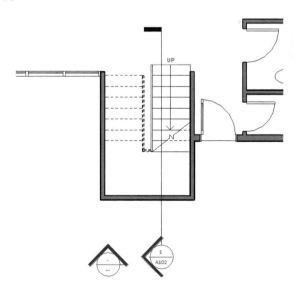

Sections (Exterior Elevation)
Section 3

6. Check your Project Browser. A new node appears for your Exterior Elevations.

7. In Figure 2.54, the elevation still appears in the sections node, but it's appended with the Exterior Elevation type. You can rename the section if needed.

FIGURE 2.54
The elevation tag
looks like the sec-
tion tag.

If you go this route, be aware that to adjust the cropping, you must select the section line you just worked so hard to hide. You'll need to zoom in close and use the Tab key to select that line again. Once it's selected, you'll have full access to the other controls associated with the section.

3D Views

One of the most obvious benefits of working with BIM is the 3D nature of the model. When using Revit, you'll find yourself constantly generating different 3D views, examining the space from various vantage points, and making presentations you would not be able to do using a 2D application. You can create two types of 3D views in Revit—axonometric and perspective—and each has special characteristics that you need to be aware of.

AXONOMETRIC 3D VIEWS

An *axon view* is a scaled drawing showing the model in three dimensions. These views allow you to dimension lengths in all three dimensions with no perspective distortion. The easiest way to make an axon view is to duplicate the default {3D} view using the Project Browser. Right-click the {3D} view name, and duplicate it. Once you do this, the next time you press the 3D icon, a new default {3D} view will be created automatically. Once you have a 3D view, use the mouse to spin around. Hold down Shift and the middle mouse button to orbit around the model. If you first select something and then orbit, you'll orbit around your selection. To pan the view, hold down the middle mouse button and pan. To zoom, scroll the mouse wheel back and forth.

ORIENTING TO OTHER VIEWS

Perhaps the most compelling feature of the axon view is its ability to orient to other views. When you do this, a 3D section box is enabled in the view that cuts the model with all six faces of the box. You can go from a very dense, hard-to-read model to a focused representation. Figure 2.55 shows a 3D view that was oriented to a section view. You're free to create new elements and edit the model from these types of views.

FIGURE 2.55
3D view oriented
to a section view
and then orbited

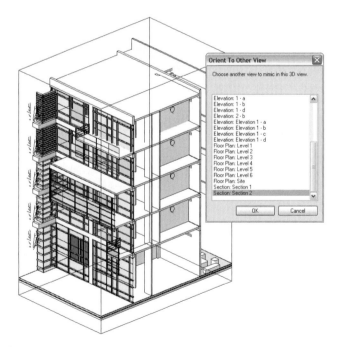

To create these types of views, open a 3D view and choose View ➢ Orient to Other View. Then choose which view to orient to. The section box is turned on and matches the extents of the view being oriented to. You can then spin the model to get a 3D representation. With Revit, these types of views are easily generated; they suggest a new type of drawing to be included in standard construction and presentation document sets.

Perspective Views (Cameras)

Perspectives in Revit (bird's-eye and worm's-eye views) follow the metaphor of placing a camera in space. To make a new camera, start from a floor plan, and use the Camera tool from the View Design tab. The first click establishes where the camera is placed in the model. Look at the Options bar: you can set the camera height prior to placement if you want. The default puts the camera 5′-6″ (1.8m) above the active level you're on. You then give the camera a direction and set the center of rotation by clicking a second time. The view automatically opens for you to reveal what your camera sees. The camera placement is shown in Figure 2.56.

FIGURE 2.56
Camera placement

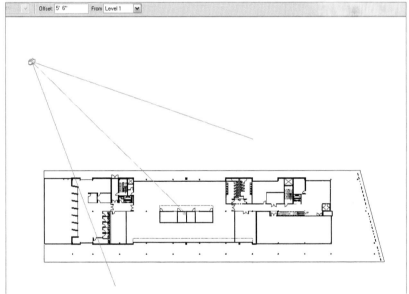

Once in the camera view, you can navigate around by using the mouse buttons to orbit and pan. For even more options, enable the SteeringWheels from the main toolbar, shown in Figure 2.57.

FIGURE 2.57
The Steering-Wheels: (A) full navigation; (B) tour building; and (C) view object

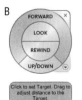

Use the small arrow icon in the lower-right corner of the SteeringWheel to access additional options and change which wheel is active.

Once a camera has been placed, you won't see it in other views. Its default state is to be invisible. To make a camera visible, select the view in the Project Browser, and choose Show Camera from the context menu. You'll see a graphic of the camera and its available controls such as the camera, target, and far clip plane (if it's enabled). Select any controls, and drag them around to alter the location of the camera. Clicking empty space or another element deselects the camera; it will disappear.

Unlike axon views, perspective cameras don't have a view scale that determines how big the view is. A perspective has no scale, so you use the crop region to define the size of the image. Select the crop region of a perspective view, and click the Size button on the Options bar.

The width and height are controlled here—this is the size of the image if it was printed out on paper. If you start editing the values, you'll see the crop boundary resize. The default option (Field of View) adjusts the width and height independently, and the model becomes more or less cropped. Figure 2.58 shows the effect of changing Width from 16″ to 12″.

If you choose the Scale (Locked Proportions) option and change either Width or Height, the image looks exactly the same but is scaled up or down. If you like the proportions of your shot but you want a bigger version of it, choose this option.

FIGURE 2.58

Changing the crop boundary

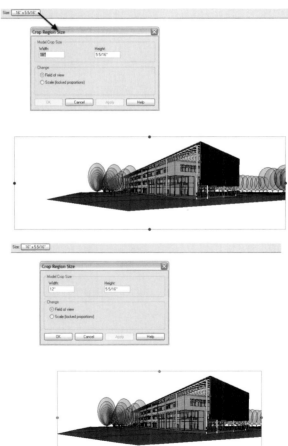

The Bottom Line

The Revit user interface is fairly straightforward. Once you know how to access settings, add elements to a view, and navigate views, you'll be off and running. Get used to the idea of editing properties of elements to change their appearance and behavior. This applies to model elements, annotations, and views.

Understand Revit parametric elements   Although you can find references to objects, families, instances, and components, in the end everything is an element.

Master It   What are Revit elements, and how are they managed graphically?

Work with the Revit user interface   As in any software application, you need to know where all the major components are and what tasks they support.

Master It   How do you change the graphics of a category for all views? What if you need to change the graphics for only one view?

Use the Project Browser   This UI component provides access to all elements in your model. Become accustomed to using it to locate views, families, groups, and links.

Master it   Knowing how to navigate views in Revit is essential to completing work. What are some of the ways to open views in Revit?

Navigate views and view properties   Views are also elements. Just like the walls, floors, and roofs you add to the model, you'll also add views. They have properties you should become familiar with.

Master it   You need to change the scale of a plan view from ⅛″ to ¼″. How do you do this with Revit?

Chapter 3

Know Your Editing Tools

Get to know Revit's basic commands, tools, and techniques. The faster you learn to work with the interface, the more productive you'll become. As you progress using Revit, you'll find that certain commands are better suited for certain tasks. For example, you'll develop a sense of when to copy and paste an element versus when to move and copy it; and when to use the spacebar instead of the Rotate tool.

There are also some tools whose function might not be obvious at the beginning but that we believe you should get acquainted with as soon as possible, such as the Join Geometry tools and the Split Face and Paint tools. These tools will help you produce the drawings you need with the added value of being intelligent and parametric.

In this chapter, you learn how to do the following:

◆ Select, change, and replace elements

◆ Edit elements interactively

◆ Use other handy editing tools

Selecting, Changing, and Replacing Elements

Knowing how to select, change, and replace elements of a Revit building model is fundamental to working with the software. These basic interface operations are the building blocks that you'll use throughout the process of making edits to your model.

Selection

Selection is straightforward in Revit: hover your cursor over an element and it highlights (turns gray)—click the highlighted element, and it turns red, meaning you have it selected. Once the item is selected, the Options bar adjusts to show you options relevant to the selected item (Figure 3.1).

FIGURE 3.1
The tool set offered by the Options bar depends on the type of element you've selected.

You can select multiple elements in several ways:

Additive selection   Hold down the Ctrl key while clicking new elements to add them to your selection. To remove elements from the selection, hold down the Shift key and click selected elements.

Window selection   You can select many elements by dragging a selection window across the view. Do this by holding down the left mouse button and dragging. A left-to-right drag selects only elements completely within the selection window; a right-to-left drag selects anything within or intersecting the selection window.

Chain selection   You can select connected lines and walls by holding down the Tab key and selecting a wall or line. All walls/lines that are end-joined to that wall become selected.

Selection Count tool   New in Revit 2009 is the selection count tool. This is displayed on the far right in the same zone as the status bar; it has the symbol of a filter as it actually is an addition to the selection filter functionality and gives information about the number of Revit elements currently selected.

After making a selection of elements, you will see the number of elements you selected; you can double-click on the count icon. This invokes the Filter dialog box, where you can narrow down a selection if needed. If you have nothing selected in the model, double-clicking on the count icon will not invoke the Filter dialog box.

You can also access the selection count tool by directly invoking the Filter dialog box from the Options bar that is also only active after a selection of elements in the model.

FILTERING YOUR SELECTION

You can filter what you've selected based on categories using the Filter button located on the Options bar. This allows you to make large, nonspecific box selections and then focus your selection by removing categories from it. For example, if you box-select an entire floor plan, you'll end up selecting many categories of elements. Using the Filter dialog box, you can limit the selection to just the Windows category (or the doors, or whatever element you need).

You can try this on a model you have open. Using a box selection, draw a big box around a portion of your model, and then click the Filter button in the Options bar. You'll get a dialog box like the one shown in Figure 3.2. Here, you can deselect categories to limit what you've selected. Think of this as a shortcut. Let's say you need to change the properties of 20 doors in a plan view. It's much faster to box-select an area of your model and then filter out all the elements except the doors than it is to Ctrl-select all 20 doors one at a time.

FIGURE 3.2
Use the Filter
dialog box to limit
what you've
selected.

SELECTING ALL INSTANCES

This option is available in the context (right-click) menu of an element and allows you to select all instances of a particular family in the entire model. This is great when you need to perform a wholesale swap of a certain family. For example, if you placed some generic wood doors in your project and you now want to swap all those with metal doors, this command is perfect. To use it, you select one door in the model, right-click, and choose Select All Instances from the context menu to select all the wood doors. Then, use the Type Selector in the Options bar to change the door type. With this command, elements become selected that may not be visible in your view (the elements might be hidden), because this type of selection isn't limited to what you see or manually clicked. Remember: you're selecting all instances of that family type used in the *entire* model.

Whenever you make a selection of elements, you can look at the count tool on the bottom right of your screen. Figure 3.3 shows that four elements were selected.

FIGURE 3.3
Count showing the number of items selected

USING THE TYPE SELECTOR

The best practices to model a building in BIM are to start to model using generic walls, floors, doors, and windows initially, and then over time, as you make more specific decisions and refine the details of the design intent, you can swap those for specific types of elements. Using Revit, you don't have to redraw the elements when you decide to get more specific with your design. You make new types or load new content, and then swap out the elements using the Type Selector on the Options bar. The elements on the Options bar are all in the same category, making it easy to locate relevant content.

You can take advantage of this feature the moment you start placing any Revit families. During creation, you can use the Type Selector to choose the type of element being placed. Once you select an element, the same list is available, making it simple to change the types.

MATCHING PROPERTIES

The Match Properties button allows you to select one type of element and then apply its properties (type and instance) to another element of the same category. Once you select an element, the eyedropper appears filled. Each subsequent click on elements of the same category will replace the selected element with the type currently in the eyedropper.

Be careful when you use this tool with walls, because it changes top and bottom constraints of the elements being matched. For walls, if you need to change the type but don't want any of the level constraints to change, use the Type Selector, not the Match Properties tool.

Copying and Pasting

Copying and pasting is a familiar technique used in almost all software applications, and Revit provides the basic features you'd expect with a copy and paste interaction (Ctrl+C and Ctrl+V).

It also has some additional time-saving options that are specific to working on a 3D building model.

To copy any element to the clipboard, select it and press Ctrl+C. Elements are copied and now ready to be pasted. To paste, press Ctrl+V. In the majority of cases, Revit pastes the elements with a dashed bounding box drawn around them. You then determine where to place the elements by clicking. In the Options bar, you can also choose Quit to abandon the operation, Finish to complete the paste, or Edit Pasted Elements to move the element prior to finishing the paste.

Paste Aligned

Once you've copied elements to the clipboard, you can paste them into other views with a variety of options. This allows you to quickly duplicate elements from one view to another (an entire furniture set from one floor to another floor, for example) while maintaining a consistent location in the X–Y coordinate plane. After selecting elements and copying them to the clipboard using Ctrl+C, choose Edit ➢ Paste Aligned from the main menu, as shown in Figure 3.4.

Figure 3.4

Paste Aligned options

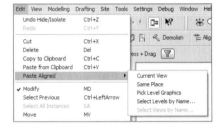

Five options are available. Depending on the view from which you copy and what elements you copy, the availability of these options will change. For example, if you select a model element in a plan view, you'll have all the options shown in the figure. The options are as follows:

Current View   This pastes the elements from the clipboard into the currently active view, in the same relative spatial location. For example, if you copy a series of walls in one view, switch to another view, and choose Current View, Revit pastes the walls into exactly the same X–Y locations in that view.

Same Place   This option places an element from the clipboard in the exact same place from which it copied or cut. One use for this tool is copying elements into a design option; see Chapter 10 for an explanation of design options.

Pick Level Graphics   This is a mode you can use to copy and paste elements between different floors. Once you select the elements and choose this option, you're placed into a pick mode where you can select a level in section or elevation. You must be in an elevation or section view to have this option available. The level you select determines the Z location of the paste and preserves the X–Y location. You might use this type of paste to copy balconies on a façade from one floor to another.

Select Levels by Name   This method is similar to the previous one, but the selection of levels doesn't happen graphically. Instead, you choose levels from a list in a dialog box, and you can paste to multiple levels at once. This is useful when you have a multistory tower; in such a case, manually selecting levels in a view can be tedious. Similar to other options, the X–Y position is maintained, and the pasted elements are translated in the vertical dimension.

Select Views by Name   This option allows you to copy elements to other views by selecting views in a dialog box. In the list available for selection, you don't see levels listed but rather a list of parallel views. For example, if elements are copied from a plan view, all other plan views are listed. Likewise, if you copy from an elevation view, only elevation views appear as possible views to paste into.

Create Similar

Rather than hunting through a list of families or making copies using copy and paste, try using the Create Similar tool to add new instances of an element to your model.

The tool is on the main toolbar, all the way to the right on the top of the screen. To use this tool, think about the type of element you need to make, and select an instance of it. Then, click the Create Similar tool, and you'll immediately be put into a placement–creation mode. If you use this tool to create a similar floor or roof (or any other sketch-based element), you're taken directly into sketch mode, where you can start sketching your new element.

Editing Elements Interactively

Revit provides a range of options to interactively edit elements in the model. The most obvious is to select elements to drag around the screen or use the blue control grips to extend walls and lines. At the same time, you often need more precise methods for moving and positioning things. Let's look at some ways to do this.

Moving Elements

Revit provides several ways to move elements, ranging from traditional tools to using intelligent dimensions that appear on the fly when you select elements. Become familiar with each method, and find what works best for your workflow.

USING TEMPORARY DIMENSIONS

You should have noticed by now that when elements are selected, dimensions appear. These dimensions are called *temporary dimensions* and are there to both inform you of the location of the elements relative to other elements in the model and to help you reposition the elements. Clicking the blue dimension value makes it an active, editable value. Type in a new value, and *the element you selected* moves to that point. Keep this in mind: when editing a position of an element via the dimensions, it will always be the selected element that moves. By the same token, you can't edit a dimension if nothing is selected.

If a temporary dimension isn't referencing a meaningful element, you can choose a different reference by dragging the small blue square attached to the dimension witness line to a new parallel reference (Figure 3.5). Parallel references highlight when the mouse moves over them.

FIGURE 3.5
Drag or click the small blue grip to change the reference of the temporary dimension.

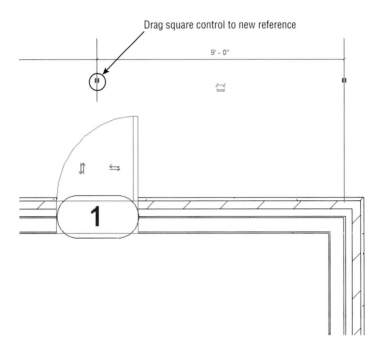

If you click a blue grip, it cycles to the next possible reference in the element. For example, clicking the blue grip of a dimension to a door or window cycles between the left and right openings and the center of the element. The same is true for walls: try clicking the blue grip control, and see how the temporary dimension cycles through the various references in the wall (interior face, centerline, exterior face).

To change which references temporary dimensions go to first, use the Temporary Dimension Properties dialog box shown in Figure 3.6 (Settings ➢ Temporary Dimensions). Here, you can specify how dimensions default to walls, doors, and windows independently.

FIGURE 3.6
The Temporary Dimension Properties dialog box lets you define default behaviors.

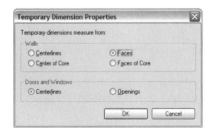

If you have many elements selected at the same time, temporary dimensions sometimes don't appear. Check the Options bar for the Activate Dimensions button; clicking it will make the temporary dimensions appear in the view.

USING THE MOVE TOOL

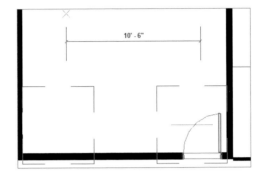

Use the Move tool to move elements precise distances by typing in values or using the temporary dimensions as helpers. When you have an element selected, the Move tool is enabled.

Moving elements is a two-click process: first you define a start point, and then you click to define an endpoint. If you know you need to move something to the left 10′6″, it doesn't matter where your two picks take place; all that matters is that the distance between the two clicks is 10′-6″. (Figure 3.7 shows the graphics provided during a move operation.)

FIGURE 3.7
Use the Move tool to move elements precisely.

When the Move command is active, there are a few options to be aware of on the Options bar:

Constrain When this option is selected, it constrains movements to horizontal and vertical directions. Deselecting it gives you free movement if the element is freestanding. Hosted elements such as windows and doors always move in a constrained manner parallel to their host axis.

Disjoin Hosted elements such as windows and doors can't change host and move to another host without explicitly being disjoined from their host. This option lets you disconnect inserts from their host and move them to new hosts. For example, if you need to move a door from one wall to another, you select the door, select the Move tool, select Disjoin on the Options bar, and move the door to another host.

Copy This option lets you make a copy of the element without moving the original element. In the strictest sense, this isn't really a *move* operation but a shortcut to making a *copy*.

NUDGING ELEMENTS (REPOSITIONING IN SMALL INCREMENTS)

Nudging is a great way to push things around quickly. When an element is selected, you can use the arrow keys on the keyboard to move the element horizontally and vertically in small increments. Each press of an arrow key nudges the element a specific distance based on your current zoom factor. The closer you zoom, the finer the nudge is. Likewise, as you zoom out, the nudge moves elements by larger increments. This is a good tool when you're working with views placed on sheets.

MOVING WITH NEARBY ELEMENTS

Another way to move freestanding elements, but in a more automatic way, is to use the Moves with Nearby Elements feature. This tool is designed to capture logical relationships between elements. When furnishing a space, you probably want to align the bed or dresser with a wall. If you change your design, you want the furniture to follow the wall to the new location. For this purpose, select the furniture and then select Moves with Nearby Elements on the Options bar. By doing so, you create an invisible relationship between the bed and the wall so that each time you move the wall, the bed moves with it (Figure 3.8).

FIGURE 3.8
When the bed is selected, the option to have it move with nearby elements is available on the Options bar.

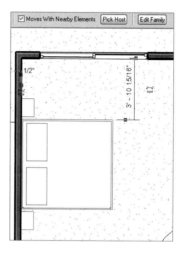

Copy

This is an interactive tool that is nearly identical to the Move tool but makes a copy of the selected element at the location of the second pick. This tool doesn't copy anything to the clipboard; it copies an instance of an element or selection of elements in the same view. If you change views while using this tool, your selection is dropped.

To activate this tool, first choose the element or elements you want to copy, and then select the tool. Using the Options bar, you can choose to make multiple copies in one interaction by selecting the Multiple option.

Rotating and Mirroring Elements

It's common to need to rotate an element. Just as with Move, Revit provides a few methods for rotating elements. The time-saving spacebar is a quick way to rotate elements in 90-degree increments: just press the spacebar when an element is selected; each press of the spacebar rotates the element another 90 degrees. If a diagonal reference (wall, grid, reference plane) is nearby, then the spacebar will locate this as a rotation candidate. For more precision, the Rotate tool is provided, which you can use to rotate elements to any specific angle you require.

USING THE SPACEBAR

Revit uses the spacebar to rotate elements both at the time of placement and once an element has been placed. This is a great time-saving command to become familiar with, because you can forgo using more traditional tools such as Rotate and Mirror by taking advantage of the spacebar. Here are a few examples:

Doors and windows   If you have a door with its swing in wrong direction, select it and press the spacebar. You can cycle through all four possible orientations of the door with a few clicks. The same holds true for windows; however, many window families are built to only let you flip the window from inside to outside, because many windows are symmetrical in elevation. If you are creating an asymmetrical window on your own, be sure to add flip controls to the window family during its creation—these allow the spacebar to work on hosted elements. Figure 3.9 shows the window opened in the Family Editor and where to access the flip controls for placement from the Design bar and the Options bar.

FIGURE 3.9
Flip arrows are used to flip elements. These can be added to families from the Family Editor.

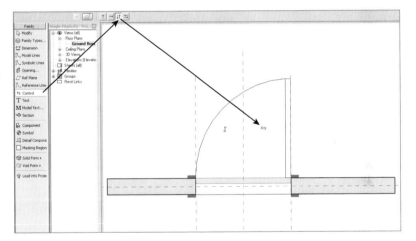

Walls   If you select a wall, pressing the spacebar flips the element as if it were being mirrored about its length. Walls flip based on the Wall Location Line, which often isn't the wall centerline. If you aren't sure which direction your wall is facing, select it and look for the flip-control arrows. These are always drawn on the exterior side of walls (Figure 3.10).

Freestanding elements   If you select a freestanding element like the loveseat shown in Figure 3.11, the spacebar rotates the element about the center reference planes defined in the family. Depending on how the family was built, the rotation origin may not make the most sense, but you can quickly orient your furniture and casework. If you decide to edit a family to change the location of the geometry relative to the center reference planes, be careful: when loaded back into a project, all your elements will jump to a new X–Y location based on the changes you made!

FIGURE 3.10
The flip arrow is another way to reorient an element. For walls, the flip arrow is always on the exterior side.

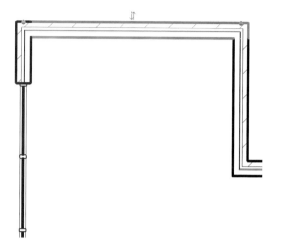

FIGURE 3.11
Center reference planes defined in the family determine the rotation origin.

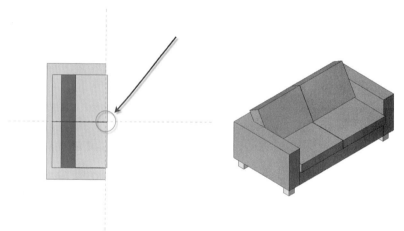

USING THE ROTATE TOOL

To rotate an element, select it and click the Rotate tool. This is a two-pick operation similar to the Move and Copy tools. Alternatively, you can enter numeric values. Revit locates the geometric center of the selected element or elements and uses that as the default center of rotation. This is fine if you don't need to be precise and just want to rotate something by a known angle. However, in most cases you first must designate a meaningful center of rotation.

To do so, select and drag the center of the rotation—the rotation cursor—to a new location before clicking to set start and end picks. Once the origin is established, begin rotating the element using the temporary dimensions as a reference or by typing in the angle of rotation explicitly.

You'll notice that while moving the origin, you lose the ability to pan and zoom the view. To overcome this, drag the origin into the Project Browser and release the mouse button; then, move the mouse back into the view. The cursor changes to a rotation icon, and you can freely pan and zoom all you want. The next click you make places the origin, and you can then designate the rotation.

USING THE MIRROR TOOL

The Mirror tool allows you to mirror elements across an axis in order to create a mirror image of an element, like the sinks in Figure 3.12. You can either pick an existing reference in the model (the arrow icon) or draw the axis interactively (the pencil icon). In the example shown, a mirror axis was drawn through the center of the top wall.

FIGURE 3.12
The sinks, toilet fixtures, and door are mirrored about the middle of the wall at the top of the view.

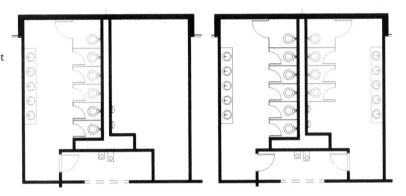

Use the pick method when you have an existing element with a meaningful center axis. If nothing in the model exists as a mirror axis, use the Draw mode and draw your own axis.

Arraying Elements

An *array* allows you to copy instances of an element with equal spacing between instances. Revit provides intelligent arrays that can be parametrically grouped and associated, as well as one-off, unassociated arrays. Like all the other tools we've reviewed, the creation options are presented on the Options bar.

You can create two types of array: *linear* and *radial*. Linear arrays are set as the default because they're the most common. As you would expect, a linear array creates a series of elements in a line. Each element in the line can be given a set distance from the previous element or be spaced equally based on a maximum line length. Figure 3.13 shows a linear array where the Move to 2nd option was selected in order to set the initial spacing correctly. Think of this type of array as additive and subtractive: if you change the number, the length expands or contracts.

FIGURE 3.13
This array uses the Move to 2nd option to set a fixed distance between groups.

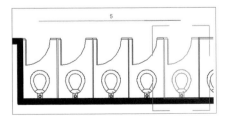

If you want to space elements in a fixed space, and the exact spacing between elements is a less important factor, use the Last option. Figure 3.14 shows an array where the location of the last element in the array was picked, and the elements (in this example, windows) were placed equally between the first and last elements in the array. With this option, the length is fixed, and the array squeezes elements within that constraint as the number changes. These two examples show that depending on your design criteria, you can use different arrays.

FIGURE 3.14
This array uses the Last option and backfills instances between the first and last group.

A radial array works in a similar fashion, but it revolves around a center point. With a radial array, elements autorotate so that each element faces the center of the array, as shown in Figure 3.15.

FIGURE 3.15
When you're making a radial array, you can specify the number of instances interactively.

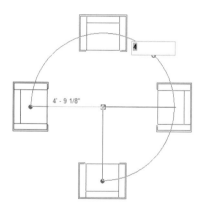

The Group and Associate option allows you to treat the array as a group that can be modified later to adjust the number and spacing of the array. If this option is unchecked, then the array is a one-off operation, and you have no means of adjusting the array after you create it.

When an element in a *grouped array* is selected, a control appears, indicating the number of elements in the array. Editing that number changes the number of elements in the array. This tool comes in handy when you're creating certain families, because the array number can be parameterized. See the Chapter 11 section "Parametric Arrays in the Family Editor" for a detailed exercise.

Resizing Elements

The Resize tool lets you scale certain objects that make sense to scale, such as imported raster images and 2D line shapes. In Figure 3.16, the Resize tool was used to make the lines surrounding a door tag a bit larger. The first pick was the center of the family, the second pick was the center of one of the lines, and the final pick finished the resize.

FIGURE 3.16
The Resize command sequence is a three-click process.

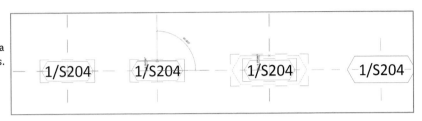

This tool is also well suited for working with imported images that need to be scaled to match real-world dimensions. For example, it's common to import an aerial photograph of a site to use as a contextual underlay; the Resize tool works great to get the image to the right scale.

This tool is active once you select an image. After you select the Resize tool, click a point to enter an origin (say, the lower-left corner of the image); the second point you click is the width of the image that you want to fit within a certain size; finally, the third click is the new length you want.

Keep in mind that you're working with a building information modeling (BIM) application full of real-world objects, not abstract primitive forms. Don't expect to resize most elements in Revit—it's not practical or meaningful. For example, you can't scale the size of a door, wall, or sink.

Aligning Elements

If you've been using Revit for any amount of time, you should have discovered the incredible power of the Align tool. If not, take time to get acquainted with this tool, because it's a real time-saver and supplants the need to use many of the tools we've already discussed. The Align tool lets you line things up in an easy, quick, and intuitive manner.

With this tool, you explicitly align references from one element to another. For example, you can align windows in a façade so their centers are all in alignment. To use the Align tool, first select a target reference and then select what you want to align to that reference. The second element picked always moves into alignment. This selection sequence is the opposite of the other editing tools we've looked at so far, so remember: first you select the aligning reference, and then you select the element to move into alignment with the reference.

As soon as you make your second pick, a lock icon appears so you can constrain the alignment. Once you click the lock icon, if either element moves, it brings the constrained element along with it.

Figure 3.17 shows the use of the Align tool to align windows on a façade. The left opening of the topmost window was used to align multiple windows using the Multiple Alignment option on the Options bar.

FIGURE 3.17
The Align tool is great for lining up edges of windows in a façade.

The Align tool also works for aligning geometry with surface patterns like brick or stone. Select a line in the surface pattern, and then select the geometry you want aligned. Figure 3.18 shows how you can align the edge of a window to a brick pattern. Use the Tab key if you cannot get surface patterns selected with first mouse click.

FIGURE 3.18
You can also align model elements to surface patterns.

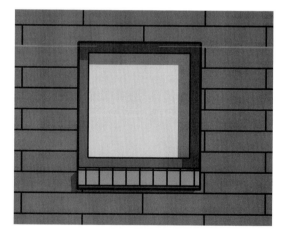

Trimming and Extending Lines and Walls

You can trim and extend lines and walls to one another using the Trim tool. With the Trim tool, you first select the tool and then operate on elements in the model. Again, like all the other tools we've covered, the Options bar gives you a number of ways to use this tool.

The first option is the default, Trim/Extend to Corner. It trims elements to one another, creating a cleaned-up end join between walls and lines. For example, Figure 3.19 shows two walls before and after using the Trim/Extend to Corner tool.

FIGURE 3.19
The result of trimming two walls to one another is a clean corner join.

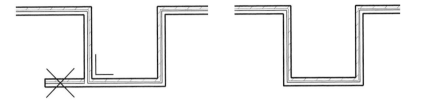

The second and third options are for extending lines and walls. First select a target wall; then select walls you want to extend to that target (Figure 3.20). The second option, Trim/Extend Single Element, is for extending a single wall, and the third option lets you extend many walls in one interaction.

FIGURE 3.20
Trim can be used to extend walls as well.

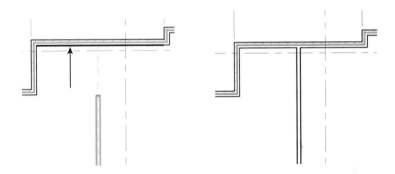

The Trim tool is used a lot for editing sketches of floors and roofs, because it's easy to end up with overlapping lines that need to be neatly trimmed. Keep in mind that with the Trim tool, you're selecting pairs of elements to *remain*, not be removed. Use the temporary preview graphics to help you. If you do trim the wrong thing, you'll see it immediately—just undo, and pick again.

Splitting Lines and Walls

The Split tool operates on walls and lines. This tool lets you slice a line or wall into pieces. To cut a wall, move the mouse over the edge of the wall—you'll see a preview of the split line before clicking.

The Options bar has a nice feature that removes the need to use the Trim tool: Delete Inner Segment. In Figure 3.21, you need to remove the middle section of the wall and end up with a clean set of wall joins. Using the Split tool with the Delete Inner Segment option selected, you can accomplish this with two clicks.

FIGURE 3.21
Use Split with the
Delete Inner Seg-
ment option to get
a clean condition
without having to
come back and use
the Trim command.

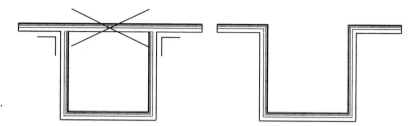

Offsetting Lines and Walls

Offset is similar to the Move and Copy tools in that it moves or moves and makes a copy of an element by offsetting it parallel to an edge you select. You can find the Offset tool either on the Edit toolbar or on the Options bar when you're sketching lines or walls.

This tool is especially useful in the Family Editor when you're making shapes that have a consistent thickness in profile, such as extruded steel shapes. Offset is also handy when you're making roof forms or soffits with known offsets from a wall. You can either offset a line and maintain the original (for that, make sure that the Copy option in the Options bar is checked) or offset the line, removing the original. Figure 3.22 shows the offset of sketch lines in the Roof Editor where the offset has been defined as 1´-0˝. Each pick of the wall offsets the line by 1´-0˝.

FIGURE 3.22
Offset lets you pick
existing elements
and create new
elements with a
specific offset
distance.

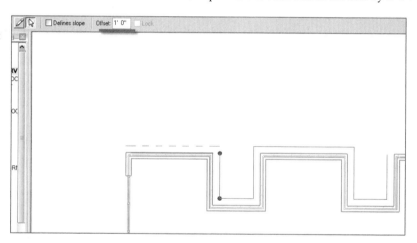

Keeping Elements from Moving

In many cases, you'll want to make sure some elements don't move, because the consequences could be bad. Imported drawings, grids, levels, and exterior walls are some of the most obvious cases. Revit provides a couple ways to deal with this.

PINNING ELEMENTS

You can restrict an element's ability to move by pinning it down with the Pin tool. This tool is located in the upper-right corner of the toolbar. Select the element you want to pin down, and click the Pin tool. If you try to move the element, nothing happens—you don't even get a ghost preview of a potential move.

Use this tool to lock down critical elements that need to remain fixed for long periods of time. This is a great feature for imported CAD files, because it's *very* easy to accidentally select an import and drag it or move it. This kind of accident can lead to coordination problems, even in a BIM environment. Use pins to lock down gridlines as well, because you certainly don't want those to move accidentally.

To unpin an element, select it and look for the pin icon. Clicking the pin removes it and frees the element.

CONSTRAINTS

Constraints aren't as rigid as the Pin tool, but they do allow you to create dimensional rules in the model so that elements remain fixed relative to one another. You can create a constraint using dimensions and alignments and then click the lock icon.

A simple example of using constraints is keeping a door a fixed distance from a side wall, so that if the wall moves, the door also moves. At the same time, if you try to move the door, Revit will not let you do it. Look at Figure 3.23: the door has been locked to be 5⅜″ from the wall face. If the wall moves, the door moves as well; but if you try to drag the door to a new location, you can't.

FIGURE 3.23
A constrained door can't be moved independently.

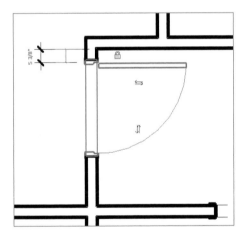

Another example is to lock the head height of a series of windows relative to a level. This prevents users from accidentally dragging windows into undesired locations while guaranteeing that if the level moves, the windows also move.

Exploring Other Handy EditingTools

A range of other tools are available in Revit, and these will be covered in subsequent chapters when they're used in specific operations. There are a few tools you should know about now, however, because they're generic tools that you can put to use on any project immediately.

Join Geometry

Revit does a good job of cleaning up joins between elements such as walls, floors, and roofs; however, in many cases elements don't look right unless they're explicitly joined. This is where the Join Geometry tool is useful. This tool creates joins between floor, walls, ceilings, roofs, and slabs. A common place to use this tool is in your building sections, where floors and walls appear overlapped and not joined. Figure 3.24 shows a floor intersecting some walls that aren't joined. Using the Join Geometry tool, these conditions can be cleaned up nicely.

To fix this condition, select the Join Geometry tool, and then select the floor and wall in sequence.

FIGURE 3.24
Joining floors to walls and walls to floors creates cleaner-looking drawings.

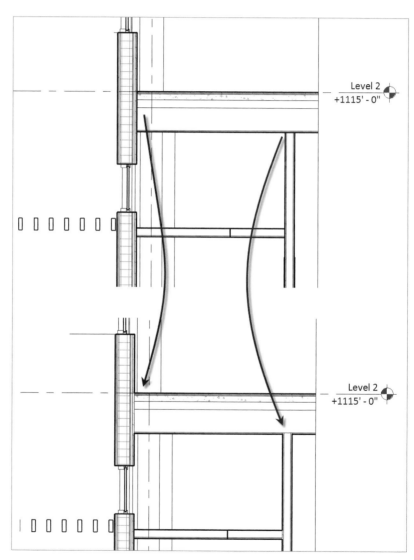

Split Face and Paint

To support painting of surfaces without having to make new types of elements, Revit provides the Split Face and Paint tools. You can paint the exterior faces of walls, floors, roofs, and ceilings with a material. This material has no thickness, but you can schedule (with a materials take-off schedule) and tag it. A typical use case for this feature is the application of a carpet material or tile to a floor.

Figure 3.25 shows the floor being split with the Split Face tool. Once the face has been split, activate the Paint tool. The Type Selector lists all the materials in your project (Figure 3.26). Choosing a tile material and then clicking the split face applies the material. The result is that the floor is unchanged structurally, and the bathroom appears with a tile finish (Figure 3.27).

FIGURE 3.25

Use Split Face to sketch an area of the floor to be painted with a new material.

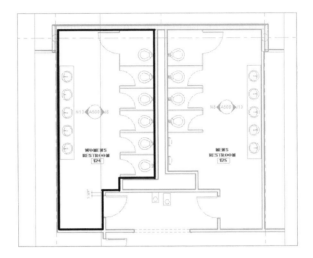

FIGURE 3.26

The Paint tool lists all materials in your project in the Type Selector.

FIGURE 3.27
You can paint the split face with a tile material to get the desired effect.

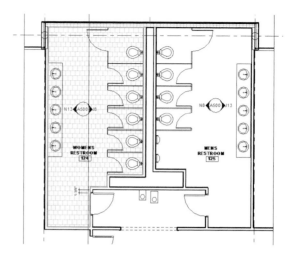

Keyboard Shortcuts (Accelerators)

Many users like using keyboard shortcuts to speed up common commands and minimize the need to interrupt workflow. When you open any of the menus in the menu bar, the keyboard shortcut is indicated to the right of the tool name:

Revit contains preset keyboard shortcuts when installed, but you can modify the default shortcuts by editing the Keyboard.txt file located in the C:\Program Files\Revit Architecture 2009\Program folder. Revit's shortcuts are two-key shortcuts and are available only for commands that already exist. When you change the shortcuts in the Keyboard.txt file, Revit shows these abbreviations in the menu.

The Bottom Line

Get to know the basic commands with Revit. The faster you become, the more productive you'll be. The more you use Revit, the more you'll find that certain commands are better suited for certain tasks.

Select, change, and replace elements Learning the basic mechanics of the interface is crucial to just about everything you'll do in Revit.

Master It Selecting elements in the model happens all the time. What are some of the capabilities that the Revit user interface provides when you select elements?

Edit elements interactively   The architectural process inevitably involves revision, so be sure you know how to make changes on the fly.

> **Master It**   You need to make some major changes to a floor plan, moving the bathroom 20′ down a corridor. How might you do this with Revit?

Use other handy editing tools   Revit provides a wide range of tools for making changes in a project.

> **Master It**   In a section view, you notice that the walls and floors aren't cleaning up neatly—you're seeing lines overlap. What tool could you use to try to clean that up?

Chapter 4

Setting Up Your Templates and Office Standards

In this chapter we discuss how to set up your office standards and how to prepare a project template that is rich with information, going beyond the out-of-the-box content. We show how templates assure graphic consistency in your projects and how the reuse of work will increase productivity in the future, making the process of creating documents more seamless. We tackle the Family Editor and the creation of custom annotation symbols, titleblocks, object styles, and view templates.

In this chapter, you learn how to do the following:

◆ Start a project with a custom template

◆ Create custom annotation tags

◆ Create custom titleblocks

Starting a Project with a Custom Template

The type of building you're planning, the geographical area in which your building will be built, and even the style of the building you're designing will require settings and content that differ from the out-of-the-box Revit template. Software vendors make a great effort to provide locale-specific content libraries that respect local traditions as well as incorporate local regulations in their documentation, but as we all know, that is only a good starting point and can't cover all the types of elements you'll need in the course of a project. Like many other software packages, Revit allows you to start with a basic template and then spawn your own custom templates to suit your specific requirements.

As your knowledge of the software progresses, you'll begin to create new wall types, roof types, ceilings, stairs, and other families in order to meet your design and documentation needs. This is also the case with regard to the graphical language that you or your firm has established over the years *and* probably wants to continue using in Revit. How you graphically present elements like text, dimensions, annotations, keynotes, and hatch patterns defines your style of design documentation. The reality of the architectural profession is that we tend to develop stylized graphics, and Revit respects this need by letting you customize your starting templates. One possible example of graphic style in a CD phase of a project done by BNIM Architects is shown in Figure 4.1.

FIGURE 4.1

Example of stylized annotations used in a custom template

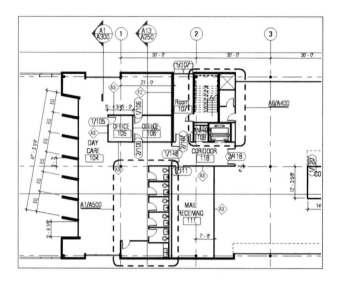

With Revit, you can expect to set up your templates by doing one or more of the following:

◆ Defining all the project settings to meet your graphic requirements

◆ Preloading model and annotation families

◆ Defining system families before you start a project

Once everything is in place, you can then save the file as a new template (.rte) and use that template whenever you start a new project. Once you've saved a new template, you can have Revit open that template when you're starting new projects. To do so, follow these steps:

1. Choose Settings ➢ Options, and click the File Locations tab.

   The first option in the dialog shows the default template location.

2. Click the Browse button to choose a new path to your default template (Figure 4.2).

Creating and reusing templates can increase your productivity and keep your documentation looking consistent. Specifically, using templates allows you to do the following:

◆ Easily reuse work that you've already created

◆ Maintain consistency in a project (very important when many team members work on one centralized file)

◆ Assure a graphic consistency across all your projects

In this chapter we focus on personalizing (customizing) the Revit template file (.rte). The following list lays out items we suggest you go through one by one when setting up templates. This doesn't represent *all* possible settings you can predefine in a template, but it includes those that we think are most pertinent.

Settings for graphics:

◆ Object styles

◆ Materials

◆ Line styles

◆ Line patterns

◆ Fill patterns (hatches)

◆ View templates

Setting up annotations:

◆ Dimension styles

◆ Text styles

◆ View tags

◆ Annotation tags

Setting up titleblocks

Global project settings:

◆ Keynoting external file locations

◆ Project units

FIGURE 4.2
Change the path
to your default
template.

Strategies for Making Templates

Architectural firms tend to address template files in one of two ways: a generic, one-size-fits-all office template, or a project type–specific template. Some firms focus on one type of building (healthcare, office, retail, and so on) where a single template is sufficient, and others do a wide range of projects and may even work across cultures with very different requirements between project types. If you work all over the globe or have many types of projects, then a generic office template probably isn't the best strategy. Instead, create new templates for each type of project. On the other hand, if you're focused on predictable, similar projects, you can start all projects from the same template.

Templates not only contain all graphic and visibility settings but also contain loaded families that you are likely to use in each project. Don't overburden your template with too many families—especially if you don't intend to use them all. To systematically remove families from your template, use the Purge Unused option in the File menu and select what you want to remove. You'll experience better performance when launching Revit and reduce the file size footprint of your model by starting out with a lean template.

When creating your own personalized template, be sure to avoid starting from an empty file (do not select the No Template option); rather always use an existing RTE file. You'll save yourself a lot of time by doing this.

Settings for Graphic Consistency

One of the goals of using a template is to assure graphic consistency across a project or even across an office. To achieve that, you need to set up the object styles that control the graphic appearance of everything in your Revit project, from 3D elements to 2D lines and hatch patterns.

Object Styles

As we mentioned in Chapter 2, object styles control the graphics for all the categories in your project. To access these settings, choose Settings ➢ Object Styles. This dialog box has three tabs: Model Objects, Annotation Objects, and Imported Objects. In this section we'll discuss the first two types of objects. The third tab, for imported objects, is where all DWG, DXF, or DGN files that you import in your Revit file appear. Even though these file types are based on a layering system, Revit still gives you full control over the graphics of each individual layer by translating each layer into a subcategory. When you define your template, focus on the first two tabs: Model Objects and Annotation Objects. They both organize categories and subcategories into a collapsible tree structure. From here, you can define graphics for the main category as well as any subcategories. If we take a door family as an example, you can define different graphic settings (line weight, color, and pattern) for the panel, the frame, and the door swing. The settings on these tabs are as follows:

Model Objects As shown in Figure 4.3, six columns are used to control graphic properties of model elements. The first holds the list of all available categories and their subcategories of model elements in Revit.

The next two columns define the line weight that will be used when these elements are drawn in projection (elevation and 3D) or section (plan or section) view. In some of the categories, you'll notice that the Cut column is grayed out; this indicates that the category of element will never be cut by Revit. The furniture category, for example, will not be represented as cut in plan or section views. The next two columns define the color and pattern of the lines used to draw the geometry of these elements. The last column on the right lets you define a default material that will be associated with the category or subcategory in the event that elements in that category don't have materials explicitly defined. If a family has materials set to *By Category*, it looks to the material set in the Object Styles dialog box.

FIGURE 4.3

The Object Styles dialog box gives you independent graphic control of all Revit categories and their subcategories.

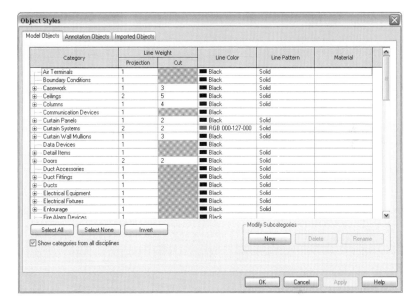

Annotation Objects   This tab is similar to the Model Objects tab. The difference lies in the material definition (lines don't have materials!) and the line weight (there is no distinguishing between projection and cut line weight), because annotation objects are 2D only.

All these settings may look like overkill at first, but you usually only need to customize these values at the beginning of a process when building your office templates. Once you've assigned all the desired line weights, colors, and materials, you shouldn't mess around with them as these settings will affect the appearance of the entire project. While object styles are global, you do have the ability to change the graphic style of any element for a specific view using overrides (View ➤ Visibility/Graphic Overrides, or you can use the keyboard shortcut, VG).

Object styles allow you to establish the graphical standard for the drawings that leave your office, contributing to an appearance of professionalism, so be sure to take your time and invest in getting them right. These powerful settings shouldn't scare you—they will ensure that your drawings have a consistent look and feel.

Line Styles

Much like object styles, a *line style* is composed of a line weight, line color, and line pattern and controls how all 2D and 3D lines will appear. Keep in mind that these settings are for the more traditional use of nonintelligent lines. To put this in context, when you draw lines or detail lines, they use a line style. To access the line styles, choose Settings ➢ Line Styles. The dialog box that opens (Figure 4.4) has four columns to control the appearance of each line type.

FIGURE 4.4
Line styles define weight, color, and pattern for all lines used in a project.

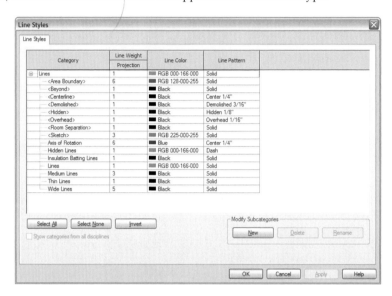

The Category column is organized in a tree structure, with all line styles listed as subcategories of lines. As you can see, each style is defined by Line Weight, Line Color, and Line Pattern. Line Weight can have a value between 1 and 16, corresponding to a physical pen thickness that varies slightly based on view scale. This is the actual thickness of the line when printed on paper at 100 percent. You'll notice that lines have different thickness as you zoom in and out of a view; this is because the lines have a real thickness.

Line weights are managed from the dialog box shown in Figure 4.5, which you access by choosing Settings ➢ Line Weights. As the scale gets coarser, line weights adjust so the drawing is still readable. Examining the Line Weights dialog box, you'll notice that line thickness varies for heavy pens between scales.

CAUTION WHEN DELETING LINE STYLES

If you delete a line style that is used by elements in a project, those elements cannot reference that line style anymore and will automatically reference the first line style that was above the one deleted. This could create undesirable results, so use caution when deleting line styles from your projects or templates.

FIGURE 4.5

FIGURE 4.5

Model line weights vary depending on the view scale.

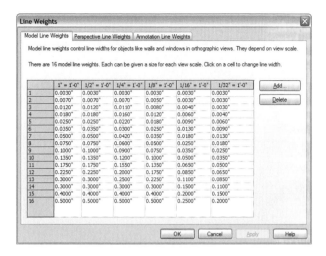

Back in the Line Styles dialog box, notice that some of the line style names are bracketed but others aren't. The bracketed line styles are internal, system types of lines, which can't be renamed or deleted. Any unbracketed line style can be renamed or deleted at any time.

To create a new line style, click the New button in the Modify Subcategories button group. Enter a new name in the dialog box that opens, and confirm it by clicking OK. The new style appears in the tree structure on the left, and you can now set the rest of the parameters (Line Weight, Line Color, and Line Pattern) to suit your needs.

Line Patterns

A *line pattern* is a repetitive series of line segments, spaces, and points. To create a new line pattern, choose Settings ➤ Line Patterns. The resulting dialog box displays a list of existing line patterns in the project. On the right side are four buttons: New, Edit, Delete, and Rename (see Figure 4.6).

FIGURE 4.6

Line patterns are made of dashes, spaces, and dots.

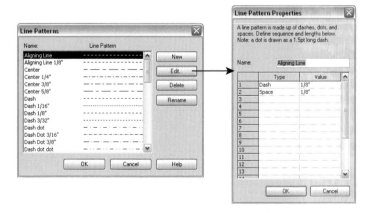

To edit an existing line, click the Edit button. To create a new line pattern, click New. You can then create a line pattern by specifying line and space lengths that form a repeating sequence. To rename a pattern, click Rename. Be careful when naming line patterns: if you give a line pattern a name that already exists in the list, Revit overrides the existing pattern with the new one and overrides all elements that use that line pattern.

A pattern sequence can contain dashes, dots, and spaces. For dashes and spaces, you need to define their length; for points, a value isn't necessary. The construction of a sequence is simple: in the Type column, you select Dash or Dot from the drop-down list, and in the Value column, you provide a length (if it's a dash or space). For each row you add, only the available choices are shown in the drop-down list. Notice that in the first row, the drop-down only offers Dash and Dot as options—this is because Revit does not allow a sequence to begin with a space. Following the same logic, you can't have a dot after a dash or the opposite, because they will merge and the result will look like a longer dash.

Before deleting any line pattern, you must verify that it hasn't been used anywhere in your project. If you fail to do so, you'll lose information, as the lines using the deleted style will be assigned to the Line category. This can only be done manually by checking line patterns used in the Object Styles, Line Styles, and Visibility/Graphic Overrides dialog boxes.

Creating a New Line Pattern

Follow these steps to create a new line pattern:

1. Choose Settings ➢ Line Patterns.

2. In the Line Pattern dialog box, click New.

3. Give the new line pattern a name.

4. Define the sequence, as shown in Figure 4.7.

5. Confirm by clicking OK.

6. The resulting line pattern looks like this:

FIGURE 4.7
Make a new pattern using this sample as a guide.

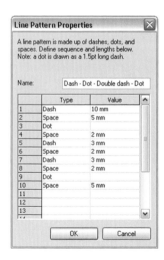

Materials

Defining materials in your project template is something you should not neglect. Materials fundamentally drive the graphic representation of elements. They don't just affect the display of an element in rendered views—a big misconception—they are responsible for representing the chosen material in symbolic patterns for documentation purposes. Materials are also responsible for cleanups, and they merge with one another when elements of the same materials are joined. For example, concrete walls join and appear contiguous with concrete floors when the elements' geometry is joined together. A material also defines how an element's surface looks in shaded views, when cut in plan or section, and when seen in 3D and elevation views. In Figure 4.8, the surface patterns are all derived from the material used in the element.

FIGURE 4.8

Materials define the surface and cut patterns, color, and render material of the elements.

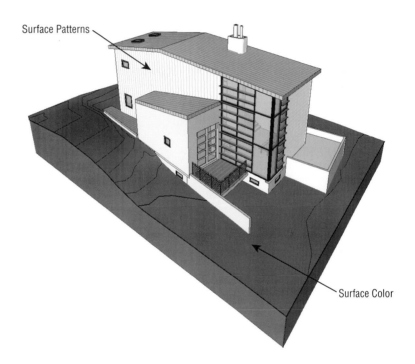

Surface Patterns

Surface Color

To access the Materials Editor, choose Settings ➤ Materials. You'll see the dialog box shown in Figure 4.9.

The Materials Editor has two components: a list and a tabbed properties interface. On the left is a list of all available Revit materials in the project. Below the list are options to duplicate, rename, and delete materials:

Duplicate   Use this button each time you need to create a new material. As with most elements you want to customize in Revit, always duplicate a material before you change any of its properties—if you fail to do so, you may change a material definition already used in the project and risk inadvertently changing and thus losing a lot of work. To create a new material, find an existing material that closely matches what you want to make. Once you click the Duplicate button, you'll be prompted to provide a name for the newly created material.

FIGURE 4.9
Use the Materials
Editor to define the
hatch patterns on
elements.

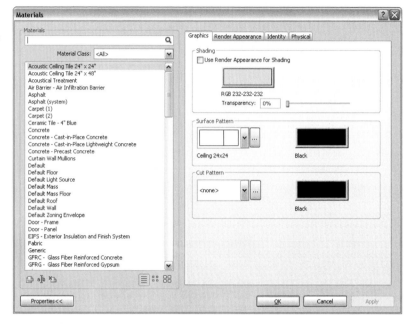

Rename   This works like all other Rename buttons in Revit. Clicking the button lets you
rename the material. If you use a name that's not unique, Revit will warn you and prompt for
a unique name.

Delete   You'll rarely need to delete an existing material. If for some reason you decide to do
so, select the material that you wish to delete, and click the Delete button. You'll need to click OK
to finalize the deletion. Be sure you don't delete a material that is already being used by elements.

On the right side of the editor are four tabs that contain material properties:

◆   *Graphics*—Defines shading color, surface patterns, and cut patterns

◆   *Render Appearance*—Defines rendering attributes

◆   *Physical*—Defines structural properties of a material (used for structural analysis)

◆   *Identity*—Defines schedule values and keynotes

We'll concentrate on the Graphics and Render Appearance tabs, because those include the
graphical properties of materials. The other tabs are used for scheduling and structural analysis
and aren't critical to this chapter.

GRAPHICS

Here are the Graphics tab's options:

Shading   This allows you to define the color and transparency used for the selected material when a view is set to Shaded or Shaded with Edges display mode (Figure 4.10). Note

that the color can be dependent on the associated render appearance. In that case, when the option Use Render Appearance for Shading is checked, the color and transparency are taken from the render appearance.

FIGURE 4.10
Shading properties

Surface Pattern This allows you select a model pattern that will be displayed on the faces of the elements in elevation, plan, and 3D views. Click the button next to the preview to see a graphical list of available patterns (Figure 4.11). You can control the color of patterns here as well.

FIGURE 4.11
Use the visual preview to help choose the appropriate surface pattern.

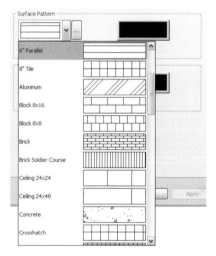

Cut Pattern The fill pattern that you select here is a drafting pattern, and it will be the pattern displayed when an element is cut through. Some Revit elements can't be cut, as we discussed in Chapter 2; in these cases, this parameter has no effect on the graphic display and the pattern will not show.

RENDER APPEARANCE

Click the Render Appearance tab to view render properties. These properties will only become visible when you render a view, and will not affect construction documentation graphics.

It may seem impossible to imagine all the materials you'll need in a project, making building a template seem daunting. Think of the basic materials you're likely to use—woods, brick, concrete, glass, and so on—and build from those. Remember, a template is just a starting point, and you can always expand it. If you end up making a lot of nice materials over the course of a project, use the Transfer Project Standards function to move materials back into your templates.

Fill Patterns (Hatches)

Materials are often represented with simple hatch patterns. For any material used in Revit, you can define a *surface pattern* and a *cut pattern*. For simple parallel hatches and crosshatches, you can use the patterns already supplied in Revit or you can make your own custom hatches.

For more complex patterns, you need to import an external pattern file (.pat). To create, modify, or view an available fill pattern, choose Settings ➤ Fill Patterns (see Figure 4.12). On the left side of the Fill Patterns dialog box, you can view the names and small graphic previews of the patterns to help you visualize as you select and edit the patterns. Below those are the Pattern Type options, where you choose what type of patterns to create and specify what type of pattern you wish to edit (drafting or model). As with the Line Styles dialog box, the New, Edit, and Delete buttons appear on the right.

FIGURE 4.12
Fill patterns are defined separately for drafting and model representations.

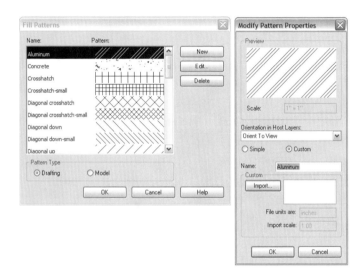

There are two types of fill patterns: *model patterns* and *drafting patterns*. Use the model patterns when you want to convey real-world dimensional patterns to represent a material. Use drafting patterns for symbolic representations. For example, a model pattern is used to show a brick pattern in 3D and elevation views, whereas a drafting brick pattern is used to represent the cut pattern in plan and section. Figure 4.13 shows how concrete masonry units (CMUs) are represented with a running bond pattern (model) as well as a crosshatch (drafting).

Model and drafting patterns have specific behaviors. In our example, we have a CMU wall with blocks that measure 16″ × 8″ (40mm × 20mm), regardless of the view scale. With a drafting pattern, the opposite is true: the pattern adjusts with the view scale so the pattern looks identical in all scales.

To create a new pattern, first choose either Model or Drafting, and then click the New button. A generic pattern appears in the New Pattern dialog box. You can then design your pattern and assign some behaviors.

FIGURE 4.13
The CMU wall has both a drafting pattern (cut) and a model pattern (surface) defined.

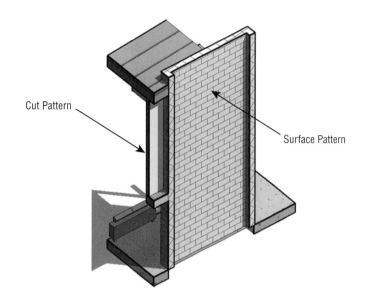

Cut Pattern

Surface Pattern

The option Orient in Host Layers is particularly useful when you're making drafting patterns. This allows you to specify how a pattern orients itself relative to host elements such as walls, floors, roofs, and ceilings when they're represented as cut. (Note that the option isn't available for model pattern types.)

The three options shown in Figure 4.14 are described here:

FIGURE 4.14
From left to right: pattern orientation Orient to View, Keep Readable, and Align with Element

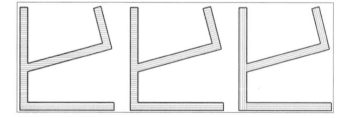

Orient to View   When this orientation is applied, the patterns used in the project all have the same orientation and the same origin. They're always perfectly aligned with the origin of the view.

Keep Readable   This orientation is best understood when compared with the Keep Readable attribute of text—it stays readable (will not appear upside down) regardless of its orientation.

Align with Element   This orientation ensures that the pattern orientation depends on the orientation of the host element. Patterns essentially run parallel with the element.

You can choose to make either simple or custom patterns with this dialog box, using the radio button options. Figure 4.15 shows the result of each option:

FIGURE 4.15
From left to right: simple fill pattern, simple fill pattern with the crosshatch option selected, and a custom fill pattern

Simple   These patterns are generated with parallel or crosshatch lines that can have different angles and spacing. With both the crosshatch and parallel options, you can specify only one angle for the entire pattern. Using crosshatch, you can set two spacing values. The exercise in the sidebar "Creating a Simple Fill Pattern" demonstrates creating a fill pattern.

Custom   To create a more complex custom pattern, you have to import a pattern (.pat) file from an external source. This is often necessary due to Revit's current limitation in creating natively complex patterns. Your office may have a set of established patterns they've been using for years, and the Custom option allows you to import and reuse them without having to make them again from scratch. Custom patterns let you import a PAT file from anywhere on your hard drive or on a network and use it as a base pattern for a new fill pattern in Revit. The next section shows some best practices for importing a PAT file.

CREATING A CUSTOM PATTERN USING A PATTERN FILE

Custom patterns require an external file that contains the definition of the pattern. The file extension of that pattern should be .pat, which is what you'll make in this section by editing an existing AutoCAD PAT file. An advantage of specifying patterns in the template file is that the PAT file won't need to be installed on each computer where Revit is installed; Revit stores each pattern internally in each template or project.

Before modifying PAT files, always make a copy of the original PAT file you intend to use as a base; you don't want to risk messing up other files that might already be using that original PAT file. PAT files can be edited with Notepad, but any text-editing application will also do. For this exercise, you'll choose the AutoCAD pattern called Grass, which you can find in acadiso.PAT (in metric units) or acad.pat (Imperial units) located in the Chapter 4 folder on the book's companion web page (www.sybex.com/go/masteringrevit2009).

IMPORTING A CUSTOM PATTERN

Follow these steps to make a custom fill pattern by importing an existing pattern definition:

1. Using Notepad, open the file acadiso.PAT or acad.PAT.

2. Highlight the lines that define the pattern, and select them:

```
45, 6.35, 0, 4.49013, 4.49013, 1.5875, -5.80526, 1.5875, -8.98026
*GRASS, turfed surface
90, 0, 0, 17.9605, 17.9605, 4.7625, -31.1585
45, 0, 0, 0, 25.4, 4.7625, -20.6375
135, 0, 0, 0, 25.4, 4.7625, -20.6375
*GRATE, grid

0, 0, 0, 0, 0.79375
```

 Real World Scenario

CREATING A SIMPLE FILL PATTERN

Often, the default templates don't have all the patterns you need. Following these steps, you can make a new simple fill pattern:

1. Choose Settings ➢ Fill Patterns.

2. In the Fill Patterns dialog box, choose to make either a Model or a Drafting pattern, and click New.

3. In the New Pattern dialog box, enter a new name for the fill pattern.

4. If Drafting is selected, also choose an option from the Orientation in Host Layers drop-down.

5. In the Simple group, enter a line angle. Choosing to create a crosshatched pattern lets you define the line spacing in both directions of the crosshatch. Note that a crosshatch always makes the second set of parallel lines perpendicular to the first.

6. The preview window shows the pattern. Click OK to commit the pattern to the model.

3. Choose Edit ➢ Copy.

4. Open a new text file, and paste the selection. (Note that you can also open the PAT file located in C:\Program Files\Revit Architecture 2009\Data, in which all Revit patterns are already saved. In that case, you can paste the selected text in that file.)

5. This is the important part: in the new text file where you pasted the selected text, add the two lines shown highlighted here:
   ```
   ;%UNITS=MM

   *GRASS, turfed surface
   ;%TYPE=DRAFTING
   90, 0, 0, 17.9605, 17.9605, 4.7625, -31.1585
   45, 0, 0, 0, 25.4, 4.7625, -20.6375

   135, 0, 0, 0, 25.4, 4.7625, -20.6375
   ```

   The first line that you write before the pattern text, ;%UNITS=MM, can appear only once in the text file. It defines the value for the units used in the pattern. In the example, the units are millimeters (MM); if you wanted to work in imperial units, it would be ;%UNITS=INCH. (If you followed our second option to not create a new note for each file but collect them in one file, then this line already exists and you don't need to add it.)

   The second statement, ;%TYPE=DRAFTING, helps define whether you're creating a drafting or model pattern. In this example, the pattern is the Drafting type.

IMPORTING PAT FILES

It's important to know that when you import a new pattern, the type of pattern needs to be the same as the new type of pattern you're making. In other words, if you're making a new model pattern, you can't import a drafting pattern. If you try to do so, you'll see a warning message like the one shown in Figure 4.16.

FIGURE 4.16
If you try to assign a drafting .pat pattern to a Revit model pattern, you'll see a warning.

6. Save your text file with a .pat file extension.

7. In Revit, choose Settings ➢ Fill Patterns.

8. In the Fill Patterns dialog box, verify that the Drafting option is selected, and click New.

9. In the New Pattern dialog box, select the Custom option. The lower part of the dialog box offers new options.

10. Click Import.

11. Navigate to the place on your hard drive or network where you saved the PAT file, and click Open.

12. In the list that appears to the right of this button, you can see the name of the pattern you created: Grass. (If you have a PAT file with many patterns defined, you see all the other drafting patterns available in that list.) The name of the pattern automatically becomes the name of your fill pattern, but you can change that if you like. See Figure 4.17.

FIGURE 4.17
The New Pattern dialog box displays the imported PAT file in the Custom group.

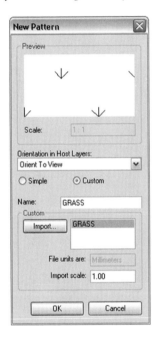

13. If necessary, you can adjust the scales of the imported pattern. The Preview window displays the graphic of the pattern, always in 1:1 scale. This informs you if you need to scale the pattern up or down. You'll know that you need to scale the pattern if the preview appears as a solid black box—that means the pattern is too dense.

14. If you're happy with the result, confirm by clicking OK.

Dimension Styles

Dimensions are system families used to dimension the model. Dimensions can be linear, angular, or radial, each of which has a set of type parameters that control their graphic characteristics.

In Revit you have dimension styles in which predefined type parameters are set. When placing dimensions in the project, you can choose between aligned, linear, angular, radial, and arc length dimensions. Depending on the choice you make, a corresponding dimension style will be chosen for you:

◆ Aligned, linear, and arc length dimensions are associated with the system family Linear Dimension Style.

◆ The angular dimensions are associated with the system family Angular Dimension Style.

◆ The Radial dimensions are associated with the system family Radial Dimension Style.

PROPERTIES OF DIMENSION STYLES

Dimension styles can vary from a rigid technical appearance to more creative and sketchy types. Figure 4.18 shows three variations of a liner dimension style, each using a different type of tick mark. A wide range of graphic controls is at your disposal. Most conventions can be achieved using the options located in the type properties of your dimension types. Options include tick marks, length of dimension lines, extension, text type, spacing of text, spacing between the text and the dim line, and so on. Figure 4.19 shows the type properties of a linear dimension.

FIGURE 4.18
Dimension string types from top down: Continuous, Baseline, and Ordinate

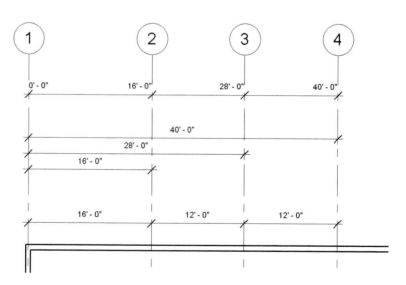

Let's look at the various ways you can customize the appearance of dimensions:

Dimension String Type   This is a new parameter, introduced in the 2009 version of Revit. It allows for control of how a string of multiple dimensions will appear. It has three options: Continuous, Baseline, and Ordinate. The continuous type is typical of architectural drawings; the others are seen in structural drawings. Figure 4.18 shows the difference between the appearances of the three string types.

Tick Mark   This option allows you to select the type of graphic called a *tick mark* that marks the crossing between the dimension line and the extension lines. You can select the type of the tick mark but not its size. Adjusting the size isn't possible directly from the dimension type dialog box. To edit a tick mark or make a new one, choose Settings ➤ Annotations ➤ Arrow Heads. You'll see the Type Properties dialog box shown in Figure 4.20.

FIGURE 4.19
Type properties are used to define different graphic styles for dimensions.

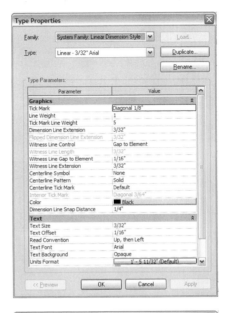

FIGURE 4.20
Type properties of a tick mark

Line Weight This sets the thickness of the line that represents the dimension line and can be any value from 1 to 16. These numbers correspond to the weights defined in the Line Weights dialog box (Settings ➤ Line Weights ➤ Annotation Line Weights).

Tick Mark Line Weight You can set the thickness of the tick mark to any value from 1 to 16.

Dimension Line Extension This setting allows you to define the length of the extension of the dimension line beyond the tick mark. In this example, the line extension has been highlighted in bold:

Flipped Dimension Line Extension This setting is grayed out unless Tick Mark is set to Arrow Head. It inverts the direction of the arrows when the space between them is too small to accommodate both arrows in the dimension space. This parameter controls the length of the extension of the dimension line after the arrow symbol.

Witness Line Control This setting controls the position of the witness lines with respect to the element that is dimensioned. You can choose one of the following options: Gap to Element or Fixed to Dimension Line.

Witness Line Length This parameter defines the length of the witness line. It's active only when Witness Line Control is set to Fixed to Dimension Line.

Witness Line Gap to Element This parameter sets the distance between the element that is dimensioned and the witness line. It's active only when Witness Line Control is set to Gap to Element.

Witness Line Extension This parameter controls the length of the witness line above the dimension line.

Centerline Symbol Some local standards require a specific graphic representation of the dimensions that reference to center axis of an element. By loading custom annotation symbol families into your project, you'll be able to choose which one is best suited to your needs.

Centerline Pattern   Using this parameter, you can define a line style when you're dimensioning to the center axis of an element. Again, this is to accommodate various local standards that require the center of elements to be graphically different from other dimensions.

Centerline Tick Mark   This is the third graphical way to make the axes or centers of elements easily recognizable. This parameter allows for a different graphic to be used as a tick mark when dimensioning centerlines of elements.

Interior Tick Mark   If more than one set of arrows doesn't fit in the space in a dimension chain, you can define smaller or simpler tick marks for the interior portions of the dimension segment.

Color   This parameter allows you to define any color for a dimension style (text and lines are both affected).

Dimension Line Snap Distance   Before you click the second line in a dimension chain, a dimension help line in a dashed green style appears, to help with positioning. The snap distance defines the automatic offset between two dimension lines. When you place a second dimension chain, the second one snaps to this designated offset.

Text   Text height, offset from the dimension line, reading convention, text font, background (opaque or transparent), and unit format can all be set, allowing for a high level of customization when you create your own style.

Show Opening Height When selected, this parameter displays the opening height of the element that is dimensioned, as shown here:

You can customize and rename the existing types and also create your own. To create your own type, you need to select an existing type, duplicate it, give it a name, and then edit the parameters:

Create a new type In the Type Properties dialog box, click Duplicate, give the new type a name, and click OK.

Rename a type In the Type Properties dialog box, select a type from the Type list, click Rename, give the type a new name, and click OK.

Delete a type To delete a type, choose File ➢ Purge Unused. In the Purge Unused Elements dialog box, select the dimension types you wish to delete, and click OK.

Text

Text is used to add notes to your drawings and can be customized to suit your needs. By default, Revit provides a couple of styles for you—feel free to edit these and add more as you see fit. Standard graphical control over size, font, color, and style are provided as well as the ability to add leaders to text.

Text is another form of system family and offers a range of graphic options for customization. Realistically, Revit isn't a full-blown text-editing application and it would benefit from many improvements when it comes to text editing; so you won't see the same level of font and paragraph style control that you might find in regular text editors. However, a number of common parameters let you change the appearance of text.

PROPERTIES OF TEXT

Some text parameters are exposed directly in the Options bar when text is selected for editing, such as justification and the bold, italic, and underline options:

However, most properties are managed through the Element Properties dialog box. The following text properties can be accessed by selecting text and going to the Element Properties dialog box:

Color Text can be assigned any color using a standard color picker.

Line Weight Any text note can be accompanied by leader lines—this parameter controls the weight of the leader lines.

Background   The background on which text is written can be opaque or transparent. An opaque background is solid white and obscures other elements beneath it; a transparent background lets elements show through the text area. The usage of this parameter depends on the style of graphics you want to show. In busy drawings, setting the background opaque can help keep text readable. Figure 4.21 shows the effects of this parameter.

FIGURE 4.21
Text with
(left) opaque and
(right) transparent
backgrounds

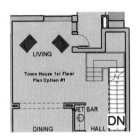

Leader Arrowhead   This parameter defines the leader arrowhead used in the leader line. You can't define the size of the leader arrowhead here. If you wish to create another size of leader arrowhead, choose Settings ➤ Annotations ➤ Arrowheads.

Read Convention   This parameter accommodates different reading conventions for the text with respect to the screen and sheet.

Text Height   This parameter controls the height of the text in dimensional values. Revit doesn't support the use of standard point sizes; you type in values in inches (mm).

Tab Size   This parameter controls the length of text when a tabulator is included in the text string.

Bold   This parameter forces the text to be bold.

Italic   This parameter forces the text to be in italic style.

Underline   This parameter forces underlining of text.

Width factor   This parameter lets you control the length of text without affecting its height. The default value is 1. If you want the text to be narrower, change this value to less than 1. If you need the text to be wider, the value must be greater than 1. In the example shown here, on the left the width factor is 0.5, in the center it's 1.0, and on the right side it's 2.0:

You can customize and rename the existing types and also create your own. To create your own type, you need to select an existing type, duplicate it, give it a name, and then edit the parameters to suit your requirements:

Create a new type   In the Type Properties dialog box, click Duplicate, give the new type a name, and click OK.

Rename a type   In the Type Properties dialog box, select a type from the Type list, click Rename, give the type a new name, and click OK.

Delete a type   To delete a type, choose File ➢ Purge Unused. In the Purge Unused Elements dialog box, select the dimension types that you wish to delete, and click OK.

Creating Custom Annotation Tags

Many kinds of annotations are used in design and construction documents. These range from door and window tags, to wall and room tags, to view tags for sections and elevations. You can see the full list of annotation categories in the Object Styles dialog box, under the Annotations Objects tab (Figure 4.22). Using the Family Editor, you can customize all of these tags (with exception of elevation tags) to meet your graphic conventions. In this section, we'll walk through the creation of some common tags and show you how to make your own.

ARCHIVING AND MANAGING YOUR CUSTOM FAMILIES

Many new users of Revit are unsure where to store custom created families. It isn't advisable to save them in the system folders created during the installation of Revit, because you may lose track of them or inadvertently delete them when you reinstall the software. Reinstalling Revit erases just about any folder and the entire contents of it. It is thus advisable to keep your personally created content somewhere else, under a separate independent folder; if you are not a single user, store that folder on a shared network drive.

You should also keep your templates up to date as you add more content; that way, you only need to maintain a few template files rather than dozens of separate family files. It's even better if you can establish this as a role within the office so everyone isn't making graphical changes to your templates.

FIGURE 4.22
The Annotation Objects tab of the Object Styles dialog box

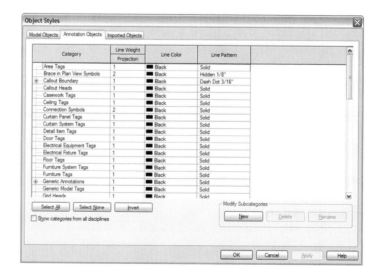

View Tags

Section, callout, and elevation tags are graphic indicators that reference (link to) other views in your project. The graphics for these elements can be customized to meet most scenarios. To create a custom section tag, for example, you have to first create a custom section tag family. To access the view tags, choose Settings ➤ View Tags. From here, you can customize a view tag through its Type Properties. By default, there is a predefined view tag for each view type. The graphics can vary depending on the language version of Revit you have installed on your machine. The tags shown here are displayed and available by default in the USA English version:

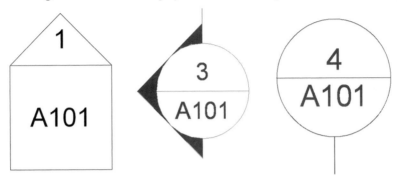

You can use the existing one, rename it or duplicate it, and amend its properties to create your own custom tag.

The creation of custom view tags slightly differs depending on which view tag you're working with. Some require you to load a family file (.rfa) that can be fully customized with the Family Editor; others don't have corresponding family files and allow only limited customization directly within the project.

SECTION VIEW TAGS

Before selecting a section tag, make sure you can load multiple section tags from the family library to have a good selection. This can be useful when you decide to use different section tags for building sections and wall sections as one example, and maybe even different tags for presentation plans than for construction documents. To implement these options in your project, you need to create each set of tags and load them into the project environment so they're available to select from the tag's Type Properties. All the section tags are defined in Settings ➤ View Tags ➤ Section Tags. In the Type Properties, you will find the following parameters:

Section Head   With this parameter, you can select different symbols for the section head. The drop-down list contains all loaded section view tag families (RFA files). Note that you can create your own fully customized section head using the Family Editor. Once selected from the list, the section head family appears at the beginning of the section line.

Section Tail   In some countries, a section line is described with the same symbol at the beginning and the end; in others, a section head appears on only one end of a section line, and at the other end is a section tail (a simplified graphic). This parameter lets you select the tail graphic. Like the section head, this symbol can be fully customized in the Family Editor and loaded as a family (RFA file). Once selected from the list, the section head family appears at the beginning of the section line.

Broken Section Display Style It's usual practice when documenting a building to make *nonlinear sections*—sections that change direction and cut through the more important aspects of the design. With the section line selected, use the Split Segment tool from the Options bar to split a section in many segments. To split a section line with gaps, click on the break icon located on the section line (see Figure 4.23).

FIGURE 4.23
Click the "gaps in segments" icon in the middle of the section line to split the line.

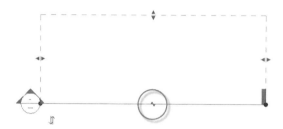

Creating a Custom Section Tag

To create your own section tag, you first need to select the tag family to which your new tag will belong. You have two options:

♦ The family already exists in your library, in which case all you need to do is load it into the template.

♦ The RFAs from the library don't correspond to your needs, and you wish to create a custom section tag. In this case, you first have to create a section tag in the Family Editor and then load it in the template.

This section's examples show how to create a custom tag family that you'll then use for your custom section tag.

Static Text and Parametric Labels

Creating annotation families in the Family Editor is by no means difficult, but you must understand the principle of using parametric labels and text:

Text In the Family Editor, placing text in an annotation or titleblock means you're defining text that will always be the same and is unchangeable when that annotation is placed in the project environment. Figure 4.24 shows the words *AREA* and *VOLUME* as text. Regardless of where this room tag is placed, the text will always say *AREA* and *VOLUME*. Section tags work the same way: if you add static text, that text appears exactly the same for all section marks. This isn't typically used for sections, because each section is a reference to a unique view, and you want that information to be dynamic and parametric. That's where label functionality comes into play.

FIGURE 4.24

A custom room tag showing room name, number, area, and volume

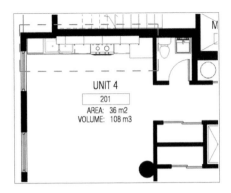

Labels   A label offers textual information, but unlike static text, it's a live reference to a parameter value of an element in the project. It pulls information about a parameter directly from the BIM model. So, if you add an Area label, it will pull the value of the area of the room; if you add a Sheet Number label in a Section Head family in the Family Editor environment and then use that section head in a project, the label will automatically display the actual sheet number on which this section is placed in the project. If you move the section from one sheet to another, the label will automatically report the new sheet number.

In Figure 4.24, Unit 4 is a label of the room name; the number 201 is a label of the room number. The label behaves as dynamic text and is always fully coordinated with the value of the parameter it represents.

Like text, labels have graphical properties such as height, color, and font.

Creating a Custom Section Tag Family

An exercise will clarify what we just discussed. Imagine you would like to create a section tag that looks like the one shown in Figure 4.25. You need to first create a section tag family using the Family Editor and then load it into your template before you can create the tag in the project. Follow these steps:

FIGURE 4.25

Custom section tag

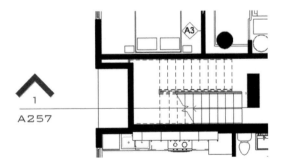

1. Choose File ➤ New ➤ Annotation Symbol.

2. In the Open dialog box, select the family called Section Head.rft or M_Section Head .rft, and click Open.

3. The Family Editor environment automatically opens, and the drawing area shows a view in which three green reference planes (two vertical and one horizontal) have already been drawn. Do *not* change the position of either the horizontal reference plane or the vertical reference on the right. In some templates, this is indicated with help text in red (which you can later remove).

The intersection of horizontal and right reference planes defines the connection location with the section line. This means your annotation will be located in between the two intersections points.

A proposed geometric shape is drawn for the annotation: a circle (two arcs) and a horizontal line. You're free to delete this default geometry and create your own tag shape. The default shape is there to help you visually understand where to begin drawing your new tag geometry.

4. Select the arcs that create the circle (use the Ctrl key for faster selection), and delete them.

 5. Click the Label button in the Design bar. Position your cursor between the two vertical reference planes and below the horizontal plane, and click to position the start of the label. The cursor changes as shown here:

6. In the Edit Label dialog box, select Sheet Number. Click the Add parameter(s) to Label button. In the Value column, you can enter a value; the default is A101.

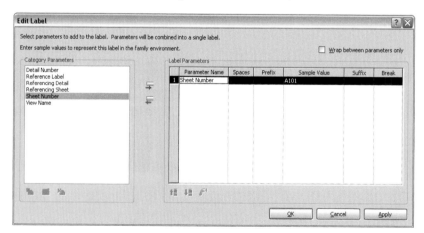

This isn't an actual value that will be displayed—it's a sample value that is visible only in the Family Editor. The text is a placeholder for an eventual real parameter value and is only here to help as a reference with layout. Once you load the family into a project template or project, this value will be replaced with the actual parameter value pulled from the database of your model. The default value is logical, so confirm by clicking OK. The label is placed and displays blue grips when selected. These let you change the length of the label text field. The length is important, because any value that is added (in a project) that is longer than the length of this box will begin to wrap and could mess up your graphics.

7. Following the same principle, place the label **Detail Number** above the horizontal reference but still between the vertical references.

8. You can reposition a label by selecting it and using the Move button to move it around. For more precise positioning, use the arrow keys on your keyboard to nudge elements in small increments. You can also help yourself by zooming in for a better view. (Note that zooming in makes the increment for the nudge tools finer.)

🔲 Filled Region 9. On the Design bar, click the Filled Region button. You'll be put into Sketch mode. Using the Line tool, draw the shape shown here. In the Region Properties, check that Color is set to Black and Cut Fill Pattern to Solid Fill. Make sure the lines form a closed loop (no gaps or overlapping lines).

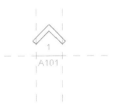

10. On the Design bar, click Finish Sketch. If you did everything correctly, you should have a custom designed family, as shown here:

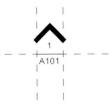

⬆ Load into Projects   Save the tag you just created somewhere on your hard drive or network, and you're ready to use it in the template or a project. To load it into your project, click the Load into Projects button on the Design bar. Choose the project you want to use the symbol in, and click OK.

In the next exercise, you'll assign this tag to a section mark in the context of a project.

Creating a Section Tag with a Custom Head/Tail Graphic

To create a section type that utilizes the section head family you created previously, you need to load the created section head in the template file:

1. Choose File ➢ Load from Library ➢ Load Family.

2. In the Load Family dialog box, find the section head you created previously, select it, and click Open.

3. In the Settings menu, click View Tags ➢ Section Tags.

4. In the Properties dialog box, click Duplicate.

5. In the Name dialog box (Figure 4.26), name the new tag **Filled Arrow** and click OK.

FIGURE 4.26
Naming the new
section view tag

6. In the section head's Type Properties dialog box, click the drop-down menu and select your custom head family. For Section Tail, click <none>. This means the other end of the section line will not use a symbol (Figure 4.27). Click OK.

FIGURE 4.27
You just created
a new section tag
that you now wish
to associate with a
section type.

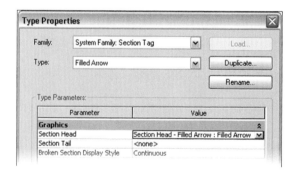

7. In the View menu of the Design bar, select Section.

8. From the Options bar, select Properties.

9. In the Element Properties dialog box, click Edit/New and then Duplicate.

10. Name the new type **Filled Arrow - No Section Tail**, and click OK (Figure 4.28).

FIGURE 4.28
Create a new section type with a unique name.

11. Under Section Tag, click the drop-down menu, select the tag you created, and click OK.

You can now place a section in your drawing area and see the results shown in Figure 4.29.

FIGURE 4.29
Draw one of your new sections—it should look like this.

Note that each time you create a new section type, Revit creates a new folder for it in the Project Browser. Our example uses two types of sections: building sections and detail sections. When you place one of each in a project environment, they're each placed in a new folder named by section type.

As you'll see next, the same principles apply when you make callout views.

CALLOUTS

In order to have a variety of different callout tags in the project environment, you must load some customized callout tags into the project. To do that, select Load from Library ➢ Load Family and under Annotations find the available callout tags. The properties of callout tags offer a few options:

Callout Heads   This parameter defines the family and the callout type that will be used. The drop-down list contains all loaded callout head families (RFA files); you can also use no family (None). Using the Family Editor, you can create callout head families just as you can for section heads and tails.

Corner Radius   A callout in Revit usually has a rectangular shape with filletted edges. This parameter lets you define the radius of those arcs on the corners of the callout tag.

Creating a Custom Callout Head

Figure 4.30 shows on the left the callout tag family you'll create in this exercise. Follow these steps:

1. Choose File ➢ New ➢ Annotation Symbol.

2. In the Select Template dialog box, select the family template called `Callout head.rft` or `M_Callout Head.rft`, and click Open.

FIGURE 4.30
(left) Custom call-
out annotation;
(right) custom
callout annotation
associated with
callout boundary

3. The Family Editor opens, and a view with two crossing reference planes appears. Again, if you want to avoid problems later, don't move either of these two planes. In red, you'll see important guideline text: always read it before deleting it. This text informs you that the tag will be positioned in the center of the crossing of the two reference planes and that the callout leader will be trimmed (adjusted) to match the width of the drawn elements. Select the help text and delete it.

4. On the Design bar, click the Label button. Click the vertical reference plane and above the horizontal one to position the label.

5. In the Edit Label dialog box that opens, select Detail Number; in the Value zone, you can place a value as explained in step 6 of the exercise in the section "Creating a Custom Section Tag Family."

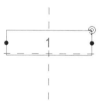

6. Following the same principle, add another label—this time using Sheet Number—and position it below the horizontal reference plane.

Filled Region   **7.** From the Design bar, select Filled Region. Revit goes into Sketch mode. Using the Line tool, draw the shape that represents the graphic of the callout tag you wish to create. Make sure the filled region uses a solid fill black pattern by editing its type properties.

8. Click Finish Sketch on the Design bar.

9. You can also adjust the text to be a different font or font size if desired. The annotation in the Family Editor should look like this:

10. Save your callout tag, and load it into your project.

11. In the project, choose Settings ➤ View Tags ➤ Callouts. Make a new type, or edit an existing type by choosing the family you just loaded in. You should do this in order to take advantage of your custom tag. Simply loading it into your project won't automatically assign it to a callout.

CHANGING THE GRAPHIC APPEARANCE OF THE FILLED REGION IN A CALLOUT TAG

You may want to use colors other than black for the filled region, and you may want to make it transparent or opaque. This will result in a different graphic presentation when you place the tag in the project and a different graphical presentation when it's printed, because most reprographics companies don't print full-sized sheets in color.

Callout Views—Type Properties

The following are the type properties of a callout view:

◆ *Callout Tag*—Lists all available callout tags

◆ *Reference Label*—The default label for referenced callouts

Creating Callout Tags

You've already created your Callout Head family. Now you'll load it in the template file and associate it with a callout tag:

1. Choose File ➢ Load from Library ➢ Load Family.

2. In the Load Family dialog box, find the callout head you created previously, select it, and click Open.

3. From Settings menu, choose View Tags ➢ Callout Tags.

4. In the Properties dialog box, click Duplicate.

5. In the Name dialog box, name the new tag **Filled Rectangle**, and click OK (Figure 4.31).

FIGURE 4.31

Give the callout tag type a unique name.

6. Under Callout Head, click the drop-down list and select your callout family. Under Corner Radius, set the angle that will be applied to the corners of the callout boundary line (Figure 4.32).

FIGURE 4.32

Choose the callout head, and set the radius for the callout corners.

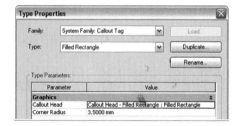

7. Click OK. You just created a new callout tag that you can now associate with a callout type.

8. In the View menu of the Design bar, click Callout.

9. On the Options bar, click the Properties button.

10. In the Element Properties dialog box, click Edit/New and then click Duplicate.

11. Give the new type a name (**Filled Rectangle - Corner Radius 3.5mm**), and click OK (Figure 4.33).

12. Under the Section Tag parameter, click the drop-down list and select the callout tag you created.

13. Click OK.

FIGURE 4.33
Create a new call-
out view type.

You can now place a callout in your drawing area and see the results shown in Figure 4.34.

FIGURE 4.34
The final appear-
ance of the new
callout type

ELEVATION TAGS

Unlike all other tags in Revit, elevation tags don't reference a family file and are customizable only to a limited extent. You can't create custom elevation tags—the only thing Revit lets you do is choose between a round or square shaped elevation tag and make a few small modifications to those shapes. However, you can create different elevation tags for exterior and interior elevations. Figure 4.35 shows the properties for elevation tags.

FIGURE 4.35
Type Properties
dialog box of an
elevation tag

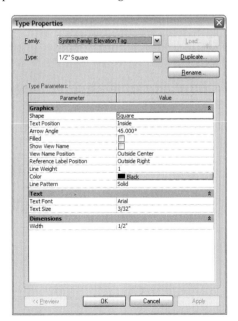

Elevation Tag Properties

The following parameters are available in the Type Properties dialog box for elevation tags:

Shape   This provides the two possible shapes for elevation tags: Circle and Square.

Text Position   Each elevation tag allows text to show the number of the view when placed on a sheet. This value is empty until that elevation view is placed on a sheet. You can also decide to add the name of the view to the elevation tag. This can make the tag busy and illegible, so consider your options carefully. Figure 4.36 shows the options from left to right: Outside Left, Outside Center, Outside Right, and at the end, Inside. In the last case, it's preferable for better legibility to select an empty arrowhead.

FIGURE 4.36

Elevation variations, left to right: Outside Left, Outside Center, Outside Right, Inside

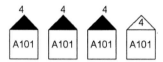

Arrow Angle   The arrow indicates the direction of the view, and this parameter controls the angle of the arrow.

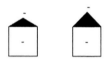

Filled   This option controls whether or not the arrow associated with the tag is filled. Set this option depending on your graphical requirements.

Show View Name   This parameter allows you to add the information about the name of the view in the elevation tag.

View Name Position   If you've decided to add the view name in the elevation tag, this parameter allows you to control the position of the name.

Reference Label Position   This parameter controls the position of the reference label with respect to the tag. Figure 4.37 shows the different positions, from left to right: Outside Left, Outside Center, Outside Right.

FIGURE 4.37

The name of the elevation can appear on each arrow.

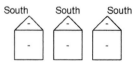

Line Weight   This parameter defines the weight of the lines used for the entire tag. The Line Weight value can be any number from 1 to 16.

Color   This parameter defines the color of the lines.

Line Pattern   This parameter defines the line pattern for lines used in the tag.

Text Font   This parameter defines the font used in the tag.

Text Size   This parameter defines the height of the text used in the tag.

Width   This parameter defines the size of the shape. If you choose Circle, this value is the diameter; if the tag is square, this is the size of the square.

As we mentioned previously, elevation tags are the only tags in Revit for which you can't create your own graphics using the Family Editor. For example, many firms use the same symbol for sections as they do for exterior building elevations. A common workaround to this problem is to use sections in lieu of elevations to get the right graphic appearance.

This workaround works well and is simple. The only downside is that your building elevations will appear under the Section tree in the Project Browser.

Elevation View Type Properties

The following parameters are available as elevation type properties:

Elevation Tag   This parameter lists all available elevation tags in the project. You create elevation tags in the Settings ➢ View Tags ➢ Elevation Tags dialog box.

Callout Tag   This parameter lists all available callout tags in the project. You create callout tags in the Settings ➢ View Tags ➢ Callout Tags dialog box.

Reference Label   This parameter defines the default label for referenced elevations.

Creating an Elevation Tag

Unlike section and callout tags, to create a new elevation tag you don't need to load an elevation family, because there are none. You can create your custom elevation tag only by duplicating an existing one and changing its properties. You will be able to change the appearance of the elevation tag to a degree and then associate it with a new elevation view type. Follow these steps:

1. In the View tab of the Design bar, select Elevation.

2. On the Options bar, click the Properties button.

3. In the Element Properties dialog box, click Edit/New and then click Duplicate.

4. Give the new type a name (**Elevation Tag Presentation**), and click OK.

5. Under the Elevation Tag parameter, click the drop-down list and select the elevation tag you created.

6. Click OK.

You can now place an elevation in your drawing area and see the results as shown here:

Assigning a Family to a View Tag

We discussed how to create custom annotation families that are used to create custom tags. To put these annotations to use, you need to assign them to a view tag type. For sections and callouts, you use a section head family and a callout family. To assign an annotation to a section or callout view tag, choose Settings ➤ View Tags ➤ Section Tags. In the resulting dialog box, you can choose what symbols to use for the section head and tail. The same procedure is used for callouts.

LEVELS

Levels in Revit usually indicate stories or represent levels used for referencing heights of certain elements. Graphically they are represented with a line and a level symbol that can be placed at one or both ends of the level line. Creating level types allows you to define the graphical characteristics of the level line, the level family symbol, and Z-coordinate system used by the level tags. All these parameters are stored in the level type properties; you can create as many as you please.

Level Properties

The following properties are available for levels:

Elevation Base   You'll find two options for Elevation Base: Project and Shared. When you select Project, the project's coordinate system is used. When you select Shared, the coordinates correspond to the shared coordinates.

Line Weight   This parameter allows you to set the line weight of the level line. Line Weight can be any number from 1 to 16. These numbers correspond to virtual pens with various thicknesses, which can depend on different scales applied to a view. To review the current settings, choose Settings ➤ Line Weights ➤ Annotation Line Weights.

Color   This parameter defines the color of the level line.

Line Pattern   This parameter defines the pattern of the line used for the level line.

Symbol   This parameter provides a list of all available level symbols that can be placed at the ends of the level lines. This list shows all level head family files currently loaded into your project. Just as with other tag families, you can create custom level tags and load them in your template. To create a custom level tag family, you need to use the correct family template: Level Head.rft or M_Level Head.rft.

For the level tags shown in Figure 4.38, we created a custom level tag family and selected it in the custom level tag.

FIGURE 4.38
Level tags can be
fully customized.

Symbol at End 1 Default and Symbol at End 2 Default   These options allow you to define whether to place the level head symbol at both sides of the level line (in which case this and the next option should be selected) or just one of them. End 1 is the start point when you draw the level line; End 2 is the end point.

GRIDS

The principle of customizing and creating grid types is similar to that of levels. The one parameter that grids don't have is Elevation Base. You can fully customize the appearance of a grid line, design your own symbol family, and define these in the type properties of grids. For custom symbols, there is a Grid Head.rft or M_Grid head.rft family template to use when you need to create your own.

Customizing Element Tags

During the construction documentation phase of a project, architects need to annotate various building components with symbolized descriptions (tags) in order to give additional information about the elements to be built. In the majority of cases, Revit allows automatic placement of the tags during the placement of components. If you don't want to fill your drawings with annotations early in the process (and to be honest, that might not even be possible, as in early design stages you might not be sure which exact types you will be using), you can choose to not tag elements during placement. You can add the tags later, in a manual or automated way (see "Tag All Not Tagged" in Chapter 19). The tags are annotation families, meaning that they are created in the Family Editor, loaded into a project, and then used wherever you need them. You can customize the graphics for all tags to meet your specific requirements.

It's advisable to load all tag families that you intend to use in your project or office template. That way, you can guarantee coherence and consistency in the way you document your project across the project team or office.

You can load the various tags in the template using several tactics:

♦ Choose File ➤ Load Library ➤ Load Family.

♦ Using Microsoft Explorer, select `.rfa` tag families and drag and drop them to place them in the Revit project environment. (You'll need to have the template file open.) When you try to load more than one family at the same time, Revit prompts you either to open each of those files in an independent window (so you can modify them) or to load them all in the current project. Choose the second option.

♦ Use the tool available in Settings ➤ Annotations ➤ Loaded Tags (Figure 4.39). The advantage of this method is that you have a preview of all loaded and preset tags that will be used throughout the project.

FIGURE 4.39
Tags dialog box

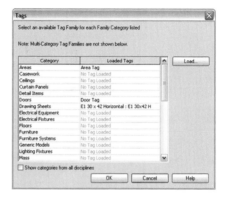

Certain tags are indispensable in a project template. These include door tags, window tags, room tags, revision tags, material tags, keynotes, and area tags. Out of the box, Revit offers at least one of each of these tags, but you'll probably want to create your own in the Family Editor and load them into your template.

CREATING A CUSTOM DOOR TAG

As an example of creating custom tags for a basic element, the following steps show you how to create the custom door tag shown in Figure 4.40:

FIGURE 4.40
The custom door tag you'll create in this exercise

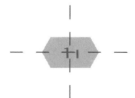

1. Choose File ➤ New ➤ Annotation Symbol.

2. In the Select Template File dialog box, select the family template called `Door Tag.rft` or `M_Door Tag.rft`, and click Open.

   The Family Editor opens in a view with two crossing reference planes. To avoid problems later, don't move the two reference planes. The intersection point is the center point of the tag.

3. On the Design bar, select Label. Click the intersection of the two planes to position the label.

4. In the Edit Label dialog box that opens, select Mark and click the Add Parameter(s) to Label button. In the Value column, you can enter a value that will be a symbolic value visible only in the Family Editor and that will be replaced by the number of the door to which this tag is associated. In this case, accept the proposed value and click OK.

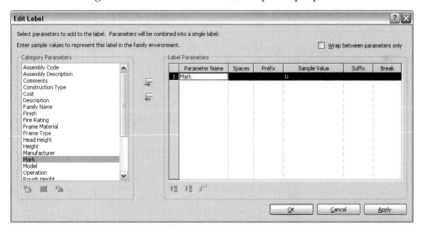

   Everything you learned about repositioning and changing the length of the section tag label in the exercise in the section "Creating a Custom Section Tag Family" applies here as well.

5. Click to select the label you just placed. On the Options bar, click the Properties button.

6. In the Element Properties dialog box, click Edit/New.

7. In the Type Properties tab, select the text color, set the background to Transparent, and select a font style and size consistent with your office standards.

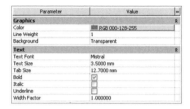

8. Click OK. Your graphic should look like this if you've followed the steps so far:

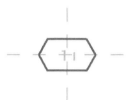

9. In the Design bar, click the Filled Region button, and sketch the shape of the tag.

10. Click Element Properties on the Design bar, and click Edit/New. In the Type Properties dialog box, change the color of the fill pattern (select a color that allows you to see the color of the text—gray or yellow). Set Cut Fill Pattern to Solid Fill.

11. Click OK in all open dialog boxes.

12. While holding down the Ctrl key, click one of the lines in the sketch (and thus select all connected lines); from the Type Selector, select <Invisible Lines>. Doing so defines the shape of the tag, which has colored fill but no drawn boundary, as shown previously in Figure 4.40.

    Invisible lines are for reference only in the Family Editor and in Sketch mode. They're selectable but not visible in the project environment, and they never appear on printed documents.

13. On the Design bar, click Finish Sketch. The result should look like this:

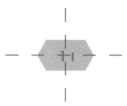

14. Save your tag. It's ready to be reused in a project or a template.

CREATING TAGS FOR OTHER CATEGORIES THAT DON'T HAVE FAMILY TEMPLATES

While creating custom tags, you'll notice that family templates aren't available for all Revit categories that exist. For example, if you need to create a furniture tag, you won't find a corresponding template for the furniture tag. What do you do? For such tags, you use the template called Generic Tag.rft or M_Generic Tag.rft. As a first step when starting the template, you assign it to the category you wish it to be associated with. Here are the steps to do that:

1. Choose Settings ➤ Family Category and Parameters. (This exists *only* in the Family Editor.)

2. In the resulting dialog box, select the desired category (Furniture, in this case), and click OK.

3. Select the red information text, and delete it.

You can now proceed, using the techniques shown in our previous examples.

Keynotes and Textnotes

Notes are a critical part of communicating design and construction intent to contractors, subcontractors, and owners. No drawing set would be complete without textual definitions and instructions on how to assemble the building. *Keynotes* are element specific and can be scheduled and standardized in the Revit database.

Keynotes are textual annotations that relate text strings to specific elements in the model, which are in turn linked to an external text file. You can format font style, size, and justification in the same manner as for standard text, but keynotes behave like a Revit family. This means you can insert different text family types in Revit, just as you would door or window families.

KEYNOTE TYPES

The Keynote command is located on the Drafting tab in the Design bar. Adding keynotes in Revit gives you three options similar to those mentioned in our discussion of adding tags:

Element This option allows you to note an element in the model, such as a wall or a floor. This type of note is typically used if you want to note an entire assembly, such as a wall assembly. You can find this value in the family properties of that element.

Material   This option lets you note a specific material in Revit. You can add a note to concrete, gypsum board, or acoustical tile, for example.

This value can also be found in the Settings ➢ Materials dialog box. The Identity tab lets you add keynote values directly to each material.

User   This option allows you to select any model-based component in Revit and define a custom keynote for it. Notes defined this way differ from those defined under Element or Material because they're unique to the particular object selected. They can be used in conjunction with element and material notes.

CREATING A CUSTOM KEYNOTE

To create a custom keynote, follow these steps:

1. Choose File ➢ Open, select the Imperial library (or Metric, depending on your installation), and then choose Annotations ➢ Keynote Tag.rfa. You'll use an existing note block to edit in lieu of making one from scratch; this note is great to use as a template because it has each type of note already created.

   The Family Types include Keynote Number, Keynote Number Boxed, and Keynote Text note types; checkboxes under each allow you to customize the notes further. As an example, here is Keynote Number Boxed:

2. For your keynote, select the Keynote Text option from the drop-down list, and click OK. As we discussed with the other tag families, you can add labels, text, lines, filled regions, and other graphic tools to customize your keynote.

3. Because you're using the text and not the numbers for this note, delete the box surrounding the note.

4. Select the label for the note (the 1), and go to the label properties. Here, you can adjust the font size and style. Also change the justification from Center to Left. Click OK to exit the dialog boxes when you're finished editing.

5. A critical part of a keynote is the note length. The overall length of the note before the texts begins to wrap to a new line is controlled by the size of the box for the note label. In this case, you want your notes to be 25 characters long (roughly 2¼″ at ³⁄₃₂″ scale). The best way to do this is to number the characters. Remember, the value you enter in this box now is only an aid to create the family.

1234567890121456789012345

When you insert notes into the model and annotate a wall, you can see how the text responds, on one line or on two (Figure 4.41).

Figure 4.41
Examples of material keynotes

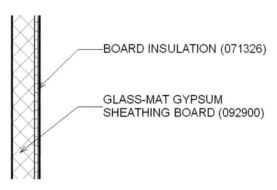

Creating Custom Titleblocks

While you're building a rich BIM model and adding more detail and intelligence in each phase of the project, you also have to document each phase and share it—deliver drawings (sheets) for others. No matter whether you share this information digitally (DWF, PDF) or via printed documents, you need to place information that is company specific (logo and contact information), project specific, and sheet specific on those sheets. Consistency between the sheets is essential.

Sheets in Revit can be created in the project environment. Their creation starts with the selection of a titleblock that can have any shape, graphic layout, and size. Figure 4.42 shows a couple of examples; you'll create the second in this section's exercise. Titleblocks are external families—you can create any kind of a titleblock in the Family Editor and add project number, sheet number, or company-specific information on it, both textual and images. (You can include your logo, an image of your project, and any other graphic.) Companies have different titleblock styles for document sharing with different parties.

Figure 4.42
Different titleblocks: left for presentations, right for construction documents

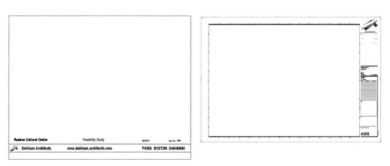

To use the titleblock families you've created in the Family Editor on a sheet, you must load them in the project. If you've created office standards, the project templates are the best place to store titleblock families you created on your own. There is no need to create final sheets in the template file—loading the titleblock families is sufficient. However, different offices have different strategies.

Creating a Custom Titleblock with the Family Editor

Revit lets you easily create sheets to any standard you require. Sheets usually have standard dimensions based on standard paper sizes. These vary from country to country but are more or less standardized within each country.

The first thing to think about when creating a titleblock is the paper size on which it will be printed. You then think about the layout graphics as well as the information you want included on the sheet. Various world standards (DIN 680, BS 4264, SFS 2488, ISO 11180, ANSI/ASME Y14. 1, and U.S. National CAD Standards) define precise layout requirements for sheets and the content displayed in them.

Revit accommodates all these requirements—many of them in an automated manner. You can add any shapes, graphics, and textual information as well as use parametric labels capable of extracting information from the project. As you'll see, labels are part of the coordinated BIM concept and will help streamline your process.

The following steps demonstrate how to create the custom titleblock illustrated in Figure 4.43:

1. Open the Family Editor by choosing File ➤ New ➤ Titleblock.

2. From the list, either select one of the prepared sheet sizes or select New Size. This opens a titleblock template where you can start laying out your titleblock. Let's assume that the size you need to duplicate doesn't exist in the list; select New Size.

3. A blank template file opens with nothing but a rectangle. Click the lines of the rectangle to activate temporary dimensions. You can then edit the dimension text value to drive the size of the rectangle. Make the sheet 42″ × 32″.

4. Draw lines with the Line tool, creating a layout as shown in Figure 4.43. For each variation in line thickness or color, you'll need to make a new line style using the Line Styles dialog box. Add new subcategories to the Titleblock category.

FIGURE 4.43
The vertical title-
block you'll make

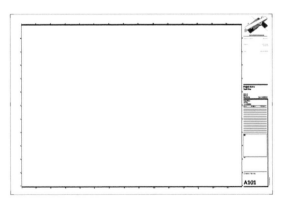

Once you're finished with the lines, you'll continue by adding images, fill patterns, text, labels, and symbols.

1. Add an image by choosing File ➤ Import ➤ Image and selecting the example on the book's companion web page or any image on your computer. Place it anywhere, resize it using its grips when selected, and position on the titleblock. This is how you can place your company logo into your titleblocks.

2. Add fill patterns with the Filled Region tool to add a color banner or hatched area to your sheets. You can't add a fill pattern on a sheet in the project environment, so you need to add them in the Family Editor.

   Fill patterns added in the titleblock are always displayed *in front* of any views placed on the sheet. In other words, you can't use a filled region to create a colored backdrop view. There are other ways to achieve that.

3. Add text with the Text tool. Text is always the same and is unchangeable from the project environment. *Drawn by*, *Scale*, and *Date* are all examples of text. For each variation in font or size, you need to create a new type of text.

4. Add labels with the Label tool. These are textual fields that report information stored in individual projects. As with text notes, you need to create new types for every variation in font or size. By adding the label *Project Name* to the titleblock, you can reuse the titleblock in many projects; the label will update in each project with the appropriate name. The same principle works for the other labels, shown in the Edit Parameter dialog box (Figure 4.44). Using this dialog box, you can add prefixes to the label. Be sure to add some blank spaces after the prefix if you go this route.

FIGURE 4.44

In this example, Project No. is prefix text and remains unchanged in the project environment. The number 00.0000 is a label and will reflect the number of the project set in the project information.

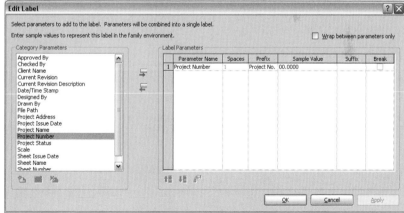

Figure 4.45 illustrates the difference between text and label elements, which behave as described in "Static Text and Parametric Labels" earlier in the chapter.

FIGURE 4.45
Place labels
with standard
parameters.

5. Place text and labels on the sheet to reflect the example shown in Figure 4.46.

FIGURE 4.46
Continue to build
the titleblock.

6. Add a revision schedule to the titleblock so you can track changes in your document set. Changes are stored as revisions and can be displayed parametrically in your titleblocks. We'll review the revisions in more detail in Chapter 23, but you'll add the revision schedule now.

Choose View ➤ New ➤ Revision Schedule (Figure 4.47). The Revision Schedule dialog box opens, and you can choose which parameters to schedule. Choose Revision Number, Description, and Date. To adjust the font and size, use the Appearance tab. New in Revit 2009, you can now specify if the schedule adds new revision rows from bottom up or from top down. Additionally, you can set the height to User Defined, which allows you to dynamically set the height in the titleblock family to a fixed number of rows. Choosing Variable for the height will allow the revision table to get taller as new revisions are added. See Figure 4.48. When you're finished, click OK. An empty schedule appears; close that view.

FIGURE 4.47
Place a revision
schedule.

FIGURE 4.48
New parameters
added to revision
schedules in Revit
2009: Bottom-up,
and User Defined
height

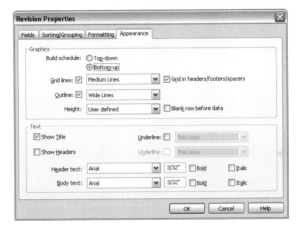

7. In the Project Browser, click the Views node, and then open the Schedules node. Drag and drop the revision schedule into the titleblock to place it. The revision schedule appears empty, but not to worry—it will be filled automatically when used in a project. If you have set the height to be user defined, go ahead and adjust the height using the blue grip control (Figure 4.49).

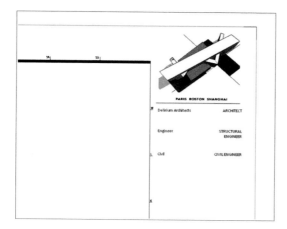

FIGURE 4.49
User-defined height control for revision schedule

Once you've placed all these elements, the titleblock is good to go. Save it to your hard drive with a unique name, and click the Load Into Projects button. Choose a project file, and the title-block will be loaded.

Best Practices and Workarounds: Positioning Views on a Sheet

Revit has no automated way to place similarly scaled floor plans in the exact same location across many sheets; you'll have to eyeball the placement. However, a useful aid is available to help, which takes advantage of the invisible line type. Choose an origin in your titleblock by drawing two intersecting invisible lines. These lines aren't visible in the project but provide a snappable intersection you can move views relative to. Another aid is to add tick marks to the titleblock to create a basic cell division.

The Bottom Line

If you set up your templates from the beginning, you'll save yourself headaches downstream. Experiment with object styles, annotations, and tags to get the right look and feel for your practice.

Start a project with a custom template   Creating a template that incorporates your firm's styles and preferences is an essential first step in putting Revit to work.

> **Master It**   Your firm has some deeply established graphic conventions that were defined in AutoCAD. How would you go about matching these graphics and setting up a Revit template?

Create custom annotation tags   Styles for annotations, dimensions, and text are all governed by office standards, and the Family Editor is your tool for setting up those standards in Revit.

> **Master It**   You need to create dimensions, text, and annotations that match your office standards. How do you do this with Revit?

Create custom titleblocks   Titleblocks are another important element of office standards that you can configure in the Family Editor.

> **Master It**   Most offices have several titleblocks with lots of information embedded in them. How would you add multiple titleblocks to your project template file?

Chapter 5

Customizing System Families and Project Settings in Your Template

In this chapter, we'll dig into customizing the Revit system families (see Chapter 2 for a definition of system families) so that you can make your office templates exactly as you need them. Knowing how to adapt the system families—by using view templates, type catalogs, and other global project settings—and include them in templates can save you headaches early in the design process. In addition, the documentation process will be a lot easier because the assemblies are created correctly from their inception.

In this chapter, you learn how to do the following:

◆ Create new types of system families

◆ Use type catalogs

◆ Customize project settings in your template

Creating New Types of System Families

System families in Revit are a bit different from the other family types. They represent a limited list of building elements (walls, curtain walls, floors, ceilings, roofs, stairs, mullions) that cannot be saved out as a file external to your project (.rfa files). There are only three ways to create or add new system families to your model:

1. Create them in your project by duplicating one that already exists and modifying its properties.

2. Copy and paste them in as objects from one project to another.

3. Use the File ➤ Transfer Project Standards method (again, from one project to another).

The first way is the most commonly used one in Revit. In the following sections, we will review how to modify the system families in Revit, allowing you to create your own, unique types.

Wall Types

Walls are made from layers that represent the construction materials used to build real walls. In Revit, these layers can be assigned functional values, allowing them to join and react to other layers in the model when walls, floors, and roofs meet. Each wall has at minimum a core, with the option to add layers of material to the core in order to create multilayered assembly wall types. These layers can be added inside the core or placed outside the core. As you'll see, this special wall *core layer* is a powerful element; understanding it is essential to mastering Revit.

A wall core is much more than a layer of material. The core identifies the structural part of the wall; it influences the behavior of the wall and how the wall interacts with other elements in the model such as floors and roofs. Every wall type in Revit has a core material with a boundary on either side of it. These core boundaries can be snapped and dimensioned to when laying out your model.

For example, when you draw a floor above your exterior walls and use the "pick walls" method, the option to extend to the core of the wall is available in the Options bar. You can choose to offset your floor from the core layer as well. This floor creation method results in an explicit relationship between the floor and the underlying wall core layer. If any wall changes position, the floor follows and stays related to the wall core layer—even if the wall type is changed (see Figure 5.1). If you created your floor using the pick walls method, the relationship between the floor and the wall will happen automatically.

If you decided to use the draw method instead of the pick walls method and you still want your floors to be dependent on the position of the walls and have a relationship with them, you need to manually lock the relationship so that the dependency is established. To get the locks (that create constraints between aligned elements) to appear, drag sketch lines of the floor over the walls (or use the align tool) so that they are coincident with the boundary or core lines of the walls, and then click the blue lock icon. If your floor sketch lines were already coincident with the wall lines, just select one, drag it away from the coincident wall line, and drag it back. The lock icon will appear and you will be able to lock it.

To access and edit wall-core boundaries and material layers, select a wall, open the Element Properties dialog box, click the Edit/New button to open the Type Properties dialog box, and then select the Structure parameter to edit. Doing so opens a new Edit Assembly dialog box. Here you can define materials, move layers in and out of the core boundary, and assign functions to each layer (see Figure 5.2).

CREATING YOUR OWN WALL TYPES

If you have a series of wall types that are standard in your office, you'll want to create them and add them to your project template right from the beginning so that they are available to all team members at all times. The creation of new wall types consists of duplicating an existing type, then modifying wall structure and type properties. A wall can be a simple structure (single-layered wall) or a complex structure (multilayered wall). If you need to make new types that are not part of your template, you can create new wall types on the fly, at any stage in a project by duplicating existing types, adding or removing wall layers, and adjusting parameters to meet your requirements. The Edit Assembly dialog box, shown in Figure 5.3, is where you define the layers of the wall type. This dialog box is divided into four zones: the Preview window, the Layers table, the Default Wrapping , and the Modify Vertical Structure (Section Preview Only) options.

FIGURE 5.1

Section through wall and floor: the sketch of a floor representing its boundary can be constrained to a certain layer or offset from the core boundary of the wall.

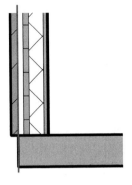

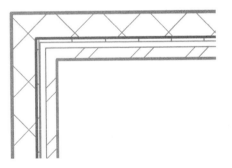

FIGURE 5.2

Each wall type is composed of layers of material, defined in the Layers portion of the Edit Assembly dialog box.

FIGURE 5.3
The Wall Edit
Assembly
dialog box

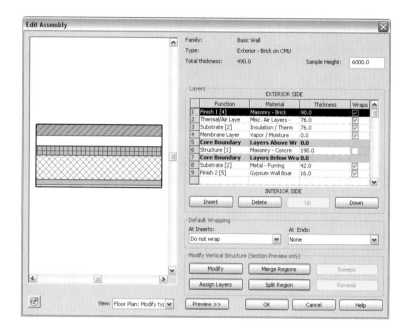

The Preview Window

On the left side of the dialog box, you will see a graphical preview of the wall structure in plan (the default) or section view. (If you don't see the preview, click the Preview button at the bottom left of the dialog box.) To switch from the default plan view preview to section view preview, and vice versa, click the drop-down list under View to choose another viewing option. In the preview, the core boundaries of wall are drawn with green lines. Note that in the section preview, when you select a row in the Layers table the layer is highlighted in red.

The Layers Table

The Layers table is where you add, delete, move, and define layers of the wall structure. Each wall layer is represented as a separate row of information. Note that two of the rows are gray: they represent the boundaries of the core of the wall (the structural part of the wall). They don't represent any physical component but are just a visual representation of the separation between the structural and nonstructural components of the wall. In between those two gray zones is the wall's structural core layer.

The table is divided into four columns: Function, Material, Thickness, and Wraps:

Function This column provides six choices for wall functions that relate to the purpose of the material in the wall assembly. Each of those functions defines a priority that determines how it joins with other walls, floors, and roofs:

Structure [1]: Defines the structural components of the wall that should support the rest of the wall layers This function gives the highest priority to a wall layer and allows it to join with other structural layers by cutting through lower-priority layers.

Substrate [2]: Forms a foundation for other layers (materials such as plywood or gypsum board).

Thermal/Air [3]: Defines the wall's thermal insulation layer.

Membrane Layer: A zero-thickness material that usually represents vapor prevention.

Finish 1 [4]: A finish layer to use if you have only one layer of finish (gypsum wall board).

Finish 2 [5]: A secondary, weaker finish layer (plaster, tiles, or brick).

With the exception of the membrane layer, which has no priority assigned, all the other layers have a priority value from 1 to 5, with 1 being the highest priority. Revit uses the priorities of the layers in a wall to understand how to clean up the intersections between various layers when two or more walls meet at an intersection. The principle is simple: priority 1 is the highest in order; a layer that has a value of 1 will cut through any other layer with a lower priority value (2, 3, 4, 5). A layer with priority 2 will cut layers with priority 3, 4, or 5, and so on. Logically, the layer with priority 1 should be placed between the core limits and represents the core of the wall (the bearing component); the other layers should be outside the core. Revit starts sorting out wall joins by beginning with the highest-priority components and then working down the priorities (Figure 5.4).

FIGURE 5.4
Layers with the same priority clean up when joined. Layers with priority 1 join and clean up first, and then the layers with priority 4 clean up.

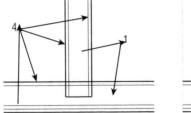

Material Associating a material to a wall layer provides graphical as well as physical characteristics for the wall. With a material, you can calculate the quantity of that material used in your project and schedule this information. The material also knows how to graphically clean up when it joins with other walls, floors, and roofs that are made of the same material. Finally, a material will define the color and graphical pattern of a layer.

How does a material definition affect the cleanup? The material usage informs Revit how to treat wall layers at intersections. If the priority of the layers is the same and the material is the same, Revit cleans up the join between these two layers, creating a graphically consistent material representation. If the materials are different, even though their priority is the same, Revit separates the two layers graphically with a thin line (Figure 5.5).

Thickness This value represents the actual thickness of the material. Note that the membrane layer is the only layer that can have a zero-thickness value.

FIGURE 5.5

Two layers with the same priority (1) but different materials: the cleanup between the layers isn't taking place because of the different materials used. The separation between the two layers is indicated with a thin line.

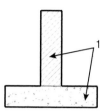

Wraps Wall layers rarely end with a straight-cut finish at wall ends or wall penetrations (windows and doors). This option allows a layer to wrap around other layers (Figure 5.6). You can define different settings for wrapping the end of walls or openings.

To create a wrapping solution for openings that reflects a real-life condition, this setting probably won't be sufficient. All you can define in the Wall Editor is *if* a material layer will wrap and whether it's an exterior or interior wrap. The Wall Editor alone can only solve wrapping conditions in a generic way. To achieve more complex wraps like the one shown in Figure 5.6, you must define another set of rules in the Family Editor, while creating the window or door family itself. These additional settings, combined with the wrap function of the wall layer, will produce more complex wraps at opening conditions such as the one shown.

FIGURE 5.6

Layer wrapping. Left: Wrapping is applied only to the first exterior component of the wall, and only that layer wraps around the window opening. Right: The first and second exterior components have wrapping active, so they both wrap around the opening of the window.

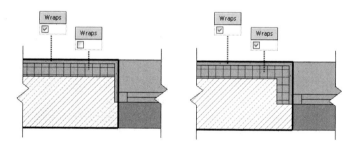

To summarize, editing the wall structure means adding or deleting wall layers. Each of those layers needs to be associated with a priority, material, thickness, and wrap information. To move layers up and down in the table, or to add and remove layers, use the buttons at the bottom of the dialog box.

Once layers have been defined and positioned, you need to consider a few more properties.

The Default Wrapping

Each wall layer can either wrap or not wrap at the ends of the wall or at inserts (windows, doors, openings). To make this happen in the project, you must decide whether the wrapping should occur at openings or wall ends or at both. For inserts, you can choose Do Not Wrap, Exterior, Interior, or Both. Similarly, for wall ends, the options are None, Exterior, and Interior. The default wrapping parameters appear in both the Edit Assembly dialog box (Figure 5.3) and the wall's Type Properties dialog box, as shown here:

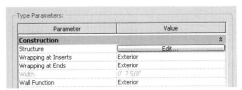

Modify Vertical Structure (Section Preview only)

Walls are often complex and articulated in their composition. Cornices, reveals, corrugated metal finish, and other elements are used all the time. Revit can accommodate any of these types of design articulation, and this is the place where all that is handled. See "Adding wall Articulation" in Chapter 12 for a detailed explanation of these functions.

Level of Detail

Walls have only two different styles of graphic display for the three levels of detail: one for Coarse views and another for Medium and Fine views. You will notice that changing from Medium to Fine view, and vice versa, has no effect on the graphic display of the wall, because they use the same representation.

Coarse Display   This is defined as a type property for each wall family, and is typically used for 1:200 scaled drawings. You can set both Coarse Scale Fill Pattern as well as Coarse Scale Fill Color. If no Coarse Scale fill is set, then the wall category material (set in Object Styles) will be used.

Medium/Fine Display   This is defined in the Type Properties dialog box in the wall assembly. The materials used for each layer establish the cut and surface patterns of the wall. These types of display will be rich in detail and show each layer of the wall.

In Figure 5.7, Coarse Scale Fill Pattern is set to a solid fill and Color to black. You can see the difference in how these walls present in the same plan at different scales, and thus different levels of detail.

FIGURE 5.7
On the left is the
Coarse view:
Individual layers
are not displayed; a
black Coarse
Fill pattern is
assigned. On the
right: Medium/
Fine view displays
all wall layers.

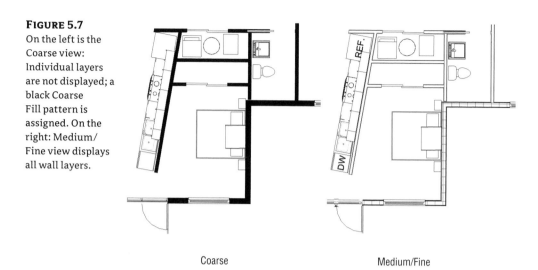

Coarse   Medium/Fine

MANAGING LAYER POSITION

When you insert new wall layers, you will notice in the Layers table that the newly created wall layer is always positioned below the active wall layer (the selected layer). To position your new wall layer where you want it, either you can click the Insert button and use the Up and Down buttons to position the new wall layer, or you can select the layer you want to reposition with the mouse (place the mouse at the beginning of the line and select the entire line as shown in Figure 5.3) and, again, use the Up and Down buttons to reposition it where you need it. By default, each time you insert a new wall layer, it has a Priority value of Structure [1], a Material setting of By Category, and a Thickness value of 0. Also, Wrap is selected.

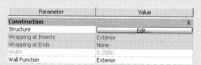

Note that you cannot delete the wall layer between the two gray lines (the structural portion of the wall) if it is the only layer or the last one. A structural layer must exist and have at least one layer that has a value greater than zero. If you create a wall that has only one material (like a concrete foundation wall), you must place that one concrete layer between the gray core-boundary lines.

Wall Function

Each wall assembly) has a function whose value is Interior, Exterior, Foundation, Retaining, Soffit, or Core-Shaft, as selected in the Wall Type properties. Changing this parameter doesn't affect the geometry of the wall, but setting it correctly allows you to control the visibility of walls and is useful for scheduling purposes. Another important use of this categorization is during export to DWG: you will be able to assign each functional wall type to a different CAD layer for export.

Floor and Roof Types

The process of creating floor and roof types is similar to that for walls. Editing the floor structure follows the same principles as editing the wall structure. One notable difference is that floors and roofs do not involve Wraps—in the Floor Editor, this parameter is always grayed out. On the other hand, multilayered floors have an additional parameter that wall layers don't have that allows the layer to vary in thickness if the floor is sloped. This appears in the Layers table as a new column named Variable (Figure 5.8).

FIGURE 5.8
The Variable parameter is available only for Floor and Roof structures.

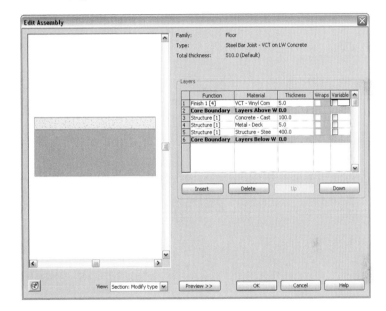

Revit allows you to slope floors and roofs by adding points and ridges that can then be manipulated to create creases and sloping forms. You do so using Shape Editor tools, which are available in the Options bar when a floor or roof is selected. The Shape Editor tools are explained in more detail in Chapter 13.

Floors or roofs that have been dynamically edited with these tools will have the Variable parameter enabled. If you select the Variable property, that layer can have a non-uniform thickness, as shown in Figure 5.9.

FIGURE 5.9
The property Variable is selected, so the floor layer has a non-uniform thickness.

If the Variable property isn't selected, as in Figure 5.10, the layer in question has a uniform thickness, and the entire floor structure is going to be sloped.

FIGURE 5.10
The Variable property isn't selected, so the floor layer has uniform thickness and the entire structure slopes.

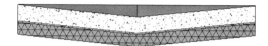

Ceiling Types

Ceilings are also system families. Revit includes two different ceilings families: a simple ceiling that has no thickness or internal layers, and a multilayered ceiling that is identical to floors and roof in terms of functionality (Figure 5.11). Ceilings don't support the variable-layer thickness functionality we just mentioned, and they don't have a wrap function. What they can do (that floors and roofs cannot) is host ceiling-mounted lighting fixtures. This is very important to know: if you need to place light fixtures, you're going to have to add a ceiling.

FIGURE 5.11
Ceilings can be generic (represented as one simple line) or compound (represented with layers).

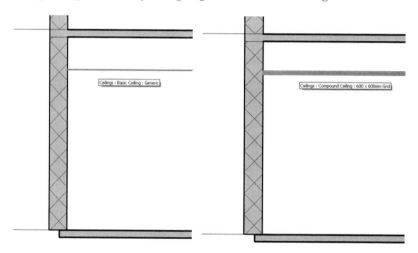

Use the simple ceiling to model drop ceilings that are hung from the structure. These are typically only as thick as the acoustical tiles and don't need to be modeled as fully 3D forms. The multilayered ceiling is good for gypsum ceilings placed on joists.

Stair Types

Stairs are complex building elements and require a deep understanding of local standards, rules, and requirements. Check the local building code requirements (minimum width, maximum height) to confirm that you're using the correct stairwell dimensions and proper headroom.

Formulas for calculating stairs are based on common codes and ergonomics. These may have slight variations in different regions, based on local conditions.

A number of parameters define the representation of stairs, including rules for risers, treads, and stringers; selection of construction techniques; and material used. All of these can be adjusted and made into types for use in your templates so that you always have the types of stairs that conform to the local building rules where you operate. Figure 5.12 illustrates different types of possible stairs created in Revit.

FIGURE 5.12
Stair types representing different construction approaches and material selections

Courtesy of Phil Read

PROPERTIES OF STAIRS

In the Element Properties dialog box for stairs, you can control the following properties:

Calculation rules In the stair's Type Parameters dialog box, in the Construction/Calculation rules, click the Edit button to open the calculation rules. To use the calculation functionality, select the option at the top of the Stair Calculator dialog box (see Figure 5.13). The calculation rule is based on the universal calculation formula that sets the value that should result depending on the size of the runs and risers. If this value can't be achieved, it should at least be within the minimum and maximum range you've defined.

FIGURE 5.13
Stair calculation options

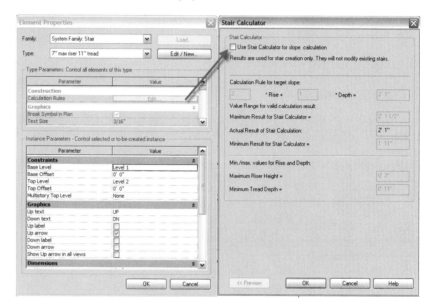

Extend Below Base This field defines an offset between the base of the stair and the level where it starts. A positive value means the stair starts higher than its base level, and a negative value starts the stair below the base level. The top of the stair isn't affected by this parameter. This option is needed for conditions where the floor material demands that the stair start a bit higher or lower than the level.

Monolithic Stair When this option is checked, it changes the stair into a monolithic form where the stringers, risers, and treads are treated as the same material. This is great for making concrete stairs.

Landing Overlap This option is active only when the Underside of Winder option is selected (see following explanation).

Underside of Winder This option is available only with monolithic stairs and has two values: Smooth and Stepped. They represent the treatment of the underside of the stairs, as shown in Figure 5.14.

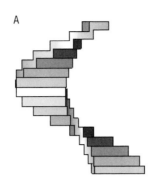
A

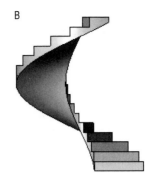
B

FIGURE 5.14
Monolithic stairs with Underside of Winder set to (A) Stepped and (B) Smooth

Break Symbol in Plan   This parameter shows a break line in plan. If it's selected, the break symbol appears at the cut height of the stair. The part of the stair that is beyond the break symbol (above the cut plane of the view) is shown with special subcategories of stairs: Stairs Beyond Cut Line and Stringers Beyond Cut Line. Each can be assigned a different color and line type. This setting is unique to the rest of the graphics used for the stair.

Figure 5.15 shows on the left a stair with a visible break symbol and on the right the same stair with no break symbol.

FIGURE 5.15
The same stair with and without the break-line graphic enabled

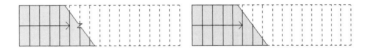

Text Size and Font   When creating stairs, you can set automatic appearance of Up and Down text that indicates the direction of the stairs. The text size and font define the properties of that text.

Material   You can set different materials for various components of the stairs. When the Monolithic Stair option is selected, some of the options under Material will become grayed out as only one material will be considered for the entire stair.

Minimum Tread Depth   This parameter controls the depth of a tread. Once you place a stair in a project, you can set the Actual Tread Depth in the stair's instance parameters. If this value is less than the type property Minimum Tread Depth, Revit gives you an error message alerting you to the problem.

Tread Thickness   This parameter controls the thickness of each tread.

Nosing Length   As the name suggests, this parameter controls the length of a nosing in a stair. When this parameter has a value of 0, no nosing is applied to the stair. A positive value for this parameter results in a nosing being exposed on all treads.

Nosing Profile   This is where you can set the nosing profile that is used when Nosing Length has a positive value. You can create any custom Profile family for the nosing—the

Family Editor includes a Profile–Stair Nosing family template you need to use. Once you have the custom nosing family, you load it in the template (project) and associate it with a certain stair type.

Apply Nosing Profile   This determines where the nosing profile is placed relative to the tread. The available values are Front Only; Front and Left; Front and Right; and Front, Left, and Right. No Back option is available.

Maximum Riser Height   This field defines the maximum allowed value for a riser. Usually, this setting depends on regulations set in the local building code as well as the type of building.

Begin with a Riser, End with a Riser   These settings control the start and end of the stair and the connection with the landing.

Riser Type   There are three possible types: None, Straight, and Slanted. As shown in Figure 5.16, this is fairly self-explanatory for the riser. For the slanted type, you can't define the angle of the slope; that value is a result of the length of the tread and the profile of the nosing.

FIGURE 5.16
Riser types: left to right, (A) no riser, (B) straight riser, (C) slanted rise with value 1″ (2 cm) for nosing, (D) slanted riser with value 1.5″ (3cm) for nosing

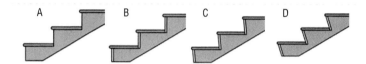

Riser Thickness   This value defines the thickness of the riser material.

Riser to Tread Connection   There are two options: Extend Riser behind Tread, as shown on the left; and Extend Tread under Riser, as shown on the right:

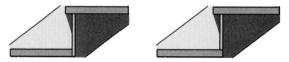

Trim Stringers at Top   This option controls how the stringer finishes its geometry at the top of the flight (see Figure 5.17).

Stringer Left/Right   This setting provides three options for stringer geometry:

None: No stringers applied to the stair.

Closed: The stringers are placed on the sides of the stair.

Open: The stringers are placed below the stair and are cut away by risers and treads.

Note that if you have a stair with stringers and decide to change the type to Monolithic Stair, the stringer will disappear.

FIGURE 5.17
Trim stringer
options

- Do Not Trim: The stringer continues above the level.

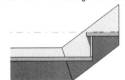

- Match Level: The height of the stringer is coincident with the level.

- Match Landing Stringer: The top of the stringer is cut at a height that matches the landing stringer.

Middle Stringers   This option allows you to add one or more stringers below the stair. When more than one is added, they're evenly spaced.

Thickness/Height of Stringers   This option gives you dimensional control over the stringers.

Open Stringer Offset   This option is active only if the stringers are defined as open. This parameter controls the position of the stringer relative to the stair.

Stringer Carriage Height   This is the value between the stringer height and the treads. The larger the value, the deeper the stringer goes below the treads (the tread position stays the same).

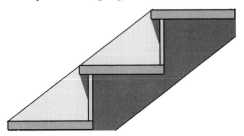

Landing Carriage Height   This value controls the distance between the bottom of the landing and the bottom edge of the stringer.

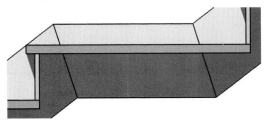

Door and Window Types

Doors and windows are external families (RFA files) and are loaded into a project as needed. You should include door and window families that you use most frequently in your templates and, by extension, remove content that you do not use.

You can create initial types using the Family Editor or loading from the existing library, and there is no limit to the number of additional types you can create in the context of a project. The same principle applies to other standard families such as furniture, plumbing fixtures, lighting fixtures, and so on. As you develop doors and window families that you think will be used downstream in many projects, be sure to load them into your default templates.

Using Types and Type Catalogs

To see why type catalogs are useful, you need to understand the various ways types of families can be created.

Library elements (referred to as standard families) often come in different sizes and colors while maintaining the essential shape. Revit allows you to embed many variations of an element in terms of size and material in a single family by creating different types of that family. Each type corresponds to a combination of user-defined values that control the size and material. In Figure 5.18, you can see three types of the same table that come in three different sizes and three different chair configurations. They're all the same family, but each variation in table size is captured as a separate type. The geometry and number of chairs are all controlled parametrically, allowing for many types to be generated.

FIGURE 5.18
One family with
three types:
4-chairs type,
6-chairs type, and
8-chairs type

You can create types of Revit elements in different ways and places, depending on the elements as well as the intended purpose of the types or their number:

◆ You can create types of families in the project environment using the duplication method.

◆ You can set them in the family environment.

◆ You can also use a type-catalog approach. This is used in cases where you need more than five or six types, such as 50-plus different sizes of manufactured steel columns.

Creating Family Types in the Project Environment

When you create new types in a project environment, they exist only in that project. The process for creating a new type of element involves duplicating an existing type and giving it new parameter values. For example, select a wall, open its Element Properties dialog box, click Edit/New and then click Duplicate, give it a new name, and change its properties to reflect the new type you need. If you want to reuse that new type in another project, you can use the File ➤ Transfer Project Standards function. This copies those types in another project, and they will be available for use from then on. You can create types of both standard and system families using this method.

Creating Family Types in the Family Editor

Creating family types in the Family Editor applies only to standard families. You create new types using the Family Types dialog box on the Design bar in the Family Editor. (To open the Family Editor you'll need to open any existing RFA family, or from the File menu, select File ➤ New ➤ Family to make a new family.) By creating the types in the Family Editor, you save time downstream by providing a collection of common sizes that will be available when loaded into any project. Creating types in the Family Editor also ensures consistent library components across projects, as they are likely shared by the whole office. If you make unintended changes in a project, you can always reload the original family file from the library and override the values you changed. The strategy of defining types in the Family Editor isn't always applicable depending on the number of types you need per element. If you think you'll have more than five or six different types, consider using the type-catalog strategy instead of making the types in the family. Type catalogs are the best way to define many types by entering textual information that a family then uses to construct a list of possible types.

Creating Family Types with Type Catalogs

Each family type uses a certain amount of memory for its definition. When you load a family into a project, every type in that family is automatically loaded. There is no way to selectively load types of a given family created in the Family Editor. If you have lots of families with lots of types, this can consume unnecessary memory and bloat your file size, especially if you need just one type of each and many remain unused. Additionally, when you have several types defined in a family and you load them in a project, the list of available types can become long and the Type Selector becomes difficult to search through.

This is where type catalogs can help. They allow you to define many different types (size combinations) of an element, which can then be selectively loaded into your project. A *type catalog* is a text-formatted list that contains all the dimensions of the family for each type variation and can include an infinite number of types. The catalog is a separate .txt file related to the family. To create a type catalog file, all you need is a simple text editor (Notepad, for example). When you load a family associated with a type catalog, you get the option to choose which types to load in.

When you're creating a type catalog, the .txt file has to have the same name as the RFA family and be located in the same folder as the family. Figure 5.19 shows a steel column that comes in many different sizes (for example, in cases when you need more than 20 types) and what the corresponding type catalog looks like.

FIGURE 5.19
The type catalog
lets you create
many types using a
text editor.

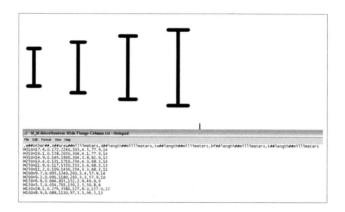

Let's take a look at how to create a type catalog.

TYPE-CATALOG SYNTAX

To create and edit a type catalog, keep in mind these syntax rules:

◆ The type catalog must have the exact same name as the family it's associated with. The
only difference should be the file extension (.txt). In the example in Figure 5.19, the family
is called MMiscellaneous Wide Flange-Column.rfa and the matching type catalog is
MMiscellaneous Wide Flange-Column.txt.

◆ The type catalog has to be stored in the same directory as the family. The example mentioned
can be found in the following standard installation locations:

Imperial sizes: C:\Documents and Settings\All Users\Application Data\Autodesk\
RAC 2009\Imperial Library\Structural\Columns\Steel

Metric sizes: C:\Documents and Settings\All Users\Application Data\Autodesk\
RAC 2009\Metric Library\Structural\Columns\Steel

◆ Each value must be delimited with a comma or semicolon, depending on the regional
settings of your PC. Note that the first line must also begin with a delimiter.

The first line in the type-catalog file declares the parameters that will be taken into account
in the type catalog:

```
,W##other##,A##area##inches,d##length##inches,tw##length##inches,bf##
length##inches,tf##length##inches,k##length##inches
```

or

```
;Width##Length##millimeters ;Height##Length##millimeters;Frame##other##
```

Let's look at the second example in more detail. The syntax is as follows:

```
Name of Parameter##Type of Parameter##Units
```

Name of Parameter corresponds to the name of a parameter in the family. You have to be
careful when typing, because this value is case-sensitive. For example, if you have a Width

parameter in the family, it should be shown as Width in the catalog as well. This parameter must be followed by two # symbols. *Type of Parameter* also must correspond to a type parameter in the family. The supported types are Length, Area, Volume, Angle, Force, and Linear Force. If the parameter in the family doesn't correspond to any of these, type **Other**.

Next, enter the units. These are the valid units that will work in a type catalog:

For *length*: inches, feet, meters, centimeters, and millimeters

For *area*: square_feet, square_inches, square_meters, square_centimeters, square_milli-meters, acres, and hectares

For *angle*: decimal_degrees, minutes, and seconds

For *force*: newtons, decanewtons, kilonewtons, meganewtons, kips, kilograms_force, tonnes_force, and pounds

For *linear force*: newtons_per_meter, decanewtons_per_meter, kilonewtons_per_meter, meganewtons_per_meter, kips_per_foot, kilograms_force_per_meter, tonnes_force_per_meter, and pounds_per_foot

For *other*, you don't specify a value; it can be anything. In our case, it's Yes/No.

In the example, Width is a *length* parameter defined in millimeters, Height is also a *length* parameter defined in millimeters, and Frame is a parameter that has *other* as its value and no defined units.

After editing the first line in the catalog, type in values to define types. Here is an example showing four types. Notice that each definition consists of name, length, height, and frame:

```
900mm x 400mm - D;900 ;400 ;1
900mm x 400mm;900 ;400 ;0
1200mm x 600mm - D;1200 ;600 ;1
1200mm x 600mm;1200 ;600 ;0
```

By having set this in the type catalog, you create four types for one family. The first type is named 900mm x 400mm – D. The width of the element is 900mm, the height is 400mm, and there is a frame (Frame is defined in a family as a Yes/No parameter; in the type catalog, this value uses 1 for Yes and 0 for No). To better understand the principle of the type catalog, it's best to see it in table form:

Type Name	Width	Height	Frame
900mm x 400mm - D	900	400	1
900mm x 400mm	900	400	0
1200mm x 600mm - D	1200	600	1
1200mm x 600mm	1200	600	0

Loading from a Type Catalog

When you have a type catalog associated with a family and you load the family into a project, you are given the option to selectively load types from a table. This table lists type properties, to help you sort and choose which types you want. Select one or many of these types (use Shift or

Ctrl for multiple selections), and then click OK to load the family and selected types. Figure 5.20 shows a Shift-selection, and Figure 5.21 shows a selection using the Ctrl key.

FIGURE 5.20

When you load a family with a type catalog, the Specify Types dialog box allows you to choose which types to load.

FIGURE 5.21

Using the Ctrl key, you can select several types that aren't sequential.

Customizing Project Settings in Your Template

Having a well-thought-out project template not only can save you time but can also guarantee a higher level of graphical consistency between projects. This way, you don't have to become familiar with the settings in Revit and modify them each time you start a new project; you simply have to do it once and save it to a location that is accessible by everyone.

Graphic Overrides of Host Objects

When dealing with multilayered walls, Revit uses object styles and represents the wall layers with a single cut-line style for all walls. As shown on the left in Figure 5.22, this cut line applies to the wall's outermost layer. This isn't flexible enough for some representations, where you may want to show only the core as a thick line and reduce the line weight of finish layers, as shown on the right in Figure 5.22. To add richer and more descriptive graphics to complex host structures, you need the ability to assign line thickness, type, and color to individual layers in a host structure (walls, floors, and roofs). You can do so on a per-view basis using graphical overrides; however, the settings can be stored in a view template and applied to other views.

FIGURE 5.22

(Left) The default representation of a cut line. (Right) The core layer can be made bolder and the finish layers thinner.

To do this, open the Visibility/Graphic Overrides dialog box from a plan view. Then, choose the Overrides Host Layers option for Cut Line Styles (Figure 5.23).

FIGURE 5.23
You can change the line weight, color, and pattern of host layers.

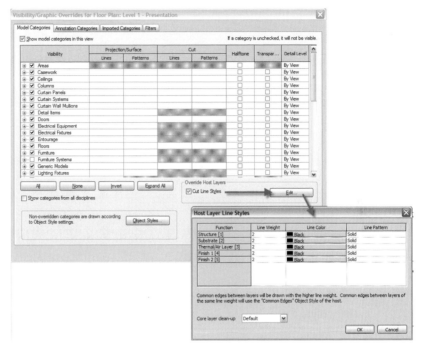

When the Host Layer Line Styles dialog box opens, you see that the wall functions are listed with options to adjust the line weight, color, and pattern. Changing these values lets you generate wall graphics, as shown in Figure 5.24.

FIGURE 5.24
The effect of changing line weight, color, and pattern for walls

You can also control the line styles for *common edges*. A common edge is a line that is common between two layers of different functions. The common edge is drawn with the line weight of the higher priority of the two layers that touch. If both layers are drawn in line styles with the same pen weight, the properties assigned to Common Edges are used. Common Edges is a property of every host, and you can set its style in the Object Styles dialog box (Figure 5.25).

FIGURE 5.25

Override Host Layers in the Host Layers Line Styles Dialog box

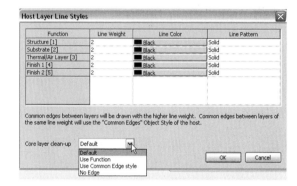

The Host Layer Line Styles dialog box also lets you define how the core layers should clean up:

Default   All line weights, colors, and patterns use standard behavior.

Use Function   This setting ignores the material settings (the line is never invisible) and sets the style of the separating line based on the layers' functional priorities. The style of a separating line is determined by the layer with the higher functional priority.

Use Common Edge Style   This setting ignores the functional priorities and material settings and always uses the common edge style.

No Edge   This option sets the separating line to invisible whenever the layers have the same fill pattern.

 Real World Scenario

USE VIEW TEMPLATES

As your use of Revit on projects progresses, you'll find that you will have view settings you will use over and over again that will help quickly define many of the parameters in a new view. These can easily be for plans, details, sections, or any other view within the project. Once you've defined these view templates, add them to your project template so that you can quickly access them when you begin new projects.

Additional Global Project Settings to Consider When Making Your Templates

In addition to setting up the object styles for your templates, you should set up some other global settings in advance. In the Settings menu (Figure 5.26), you'll find global project settings that can be stored on a per-template basis.

FIGURE 5.26

The Settings menu

AREA AND VOLUME COMPUTATIONS SETTINGS

Area and volume computations settings include several predefinitions for you to consider. In this dialog box (Figure 5.27), you can set the rules for room surface calculation (the cut height at which room areas are calculated) and enable automatic calculation of room volumes. We don't suggest enabling the volume calculation option at all times because it can slow down overall performance when you're working on your model. Do it only when you need the information or have to print out the documents that contain that information.

Finally, you can apply different rules for room calculations that relate to boundary options in walls. These include wall finish, center, core layer, and core center.

These settings affect area plans that are used to convey building usage that extends beyond the shape and size of individual rooms, such as rentable area or office space. You access area plans from the View list of the Project Browser.

FIGURE 5.27
Area and Volume calculations are based on the height of the cut plane and the layer in a wall to which the calculation is measured.

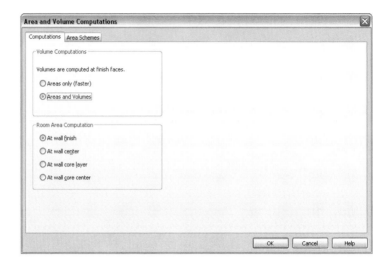

UNITS

Depending on where the project is located or what country you work in, you'll use either metric or imperial units. In the Project Units dialog box (Figure 5.28), you can set the units for length, area, volume, angles, slope, and currency. Under each of these options, you can define a rounding value, rounding increment, and units suffix and decide whether you wish to show the plus symbol (+) for positive values.

FIGURE 5.28
Set up your units and rounding in advance in your templates.

Note that Revit allows for a combination of imperial and metric units within the context of the same project. For each unit type in the Project Units dialog box, you can specify any formatting that is most suitable. Also note that while the project settings establish a consistent baseline, you can override project unit settings for elements such as dimensions and schedules.

IMPERIAL FEET OR INCHES?

When you're using Revit for the first time and working in imperial units, you'll notice that numeric values resolve in feet instead of inches, which is different from the way AutoCAD works. A majority of Revit users have extensive experience (and thus established habits) with AutoCAD, so this can be frustrating at first. If you want to make sure your workflow isn't inhibited by this issue, you can modify the setting here to work in inches instead of feet.

KEYNOTE SETTINGS

Keynotes are a great way to standardize on a numeric system for calling out materials and assemblies. When setting up keynotes, define the following keynoting settings at the outset. First, set the keynote table path, as shown in Figure 5.29. The path defaults to the Revit library locations, but you may want to change this if you're using customized keynote files located on the office network. In this dialog box, you establish whether the numbering method for keynotes is By Keynote or By Sheet. We'll go into more detail about how to use keynoting in Revit in Chapter 19.

FIGURE 5.29
The Keynoting
Settings dialog box

MATERIALS

When you upgrade your templates to Revit 2009, you will most likely need to remap rendering settings to your materials, especially if you set up custom Accurender materials. The Materials dialog box has been reworked to accommodate this (Figure 5.30). A brand-new render appearance library also ships with Revit 2009, and you can use it to map rendering appearances to your existing Revit materials. To do so, select materials from the list on the left, and then click the Replace button to go to the Render Appearance Library (Figure 5.31).

If you were using custom texture maps previously, then use the Generic Render appearance and remap the image files. Be sure to set appropriate scale using the Sample Size control. Keep in mind that for this to work in your templates, the images need to be accessible over the network by anyone who uses the template.

FIGURE 5.30
Concrete material
needs to be
remapped.

FIGURE 5.30
Concrete material
needs to be
remapped.

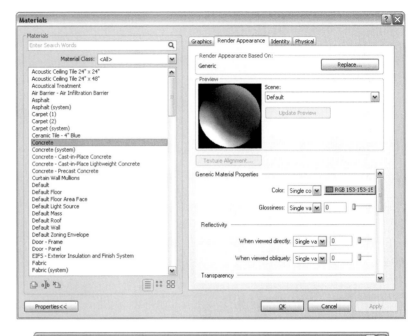

FIGURE 5.31
Use the new
Render Appear-
ance Library to
select a render
material.

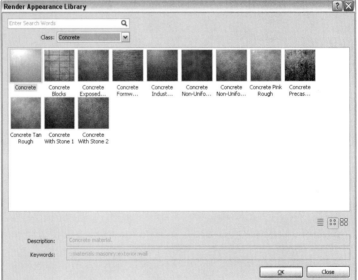

SETTING UP GOOD DEFAULTS

Whatever type of element you selected last with the Type Selector will be set in the project
template as the default type during creation. Revit remembers the most recently used settings
across sessions. It's therefore important that you set the types of your selected Revit elements as
desirable defaults.

Default Wall

To set a default wall type, activate the Wall tool. Then, under the Type Selector select the wall type that you wish to be the default choice. In the Element Properties or from the Options bar, select the wall height or set a top level, and select the wall location line. You never know which wall type you'll need in the next project, so we suggest setting this to a Generic type. The selection of exact wall types can come later.

Default Doors and Windows

Your project template is loaded with windows and doors that are typically used in projects. Activate the window or door tools, then using the Type Selector, choose a default door and window family, and save your template. The last selected door and window will be default elements in the Type Selector when you place new elements. This applies to all other family elements in your template.

Default Dimension Types

To streamline your workflow, set the dimension style used most commonly in your template. You can consider presetting many settings in the Options bar:

- The type of dimension (we suggest selecting Linear).

- The reference selection that will be used when dimensioning a wall (to or from). Here the choices are the usual wall references: wall center, face, core face, and core center.

- The selection method, or what we call *manual* versus *automated* dimensioning. In Revit, the Pick method can be Individual, where you're asked to click each instance you wish to dimension, or Entire Walls, where you click an element and it's dimensioned automatically. With the Entire Walls option, another dialog box prompts you to further define what elements are used as auto-dimension references when you click walls (Figure 5.32).

FIGURE 5.32
Dimensions can be preset in your template to be automatic if need be.

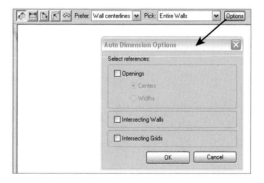

Align Tool

Many users find this to be one of the most helpful tools in Revit, as it aligns elements to any reference target in the model. Setting its options correctly will aid in smoothing your workflow. Preset which wall layer to which you want the Align tool to default. The options available for a wall are shown in Figure 5.33.

FIGURE 5.33

Set up a default alignment preference with respect to wall references.

Levels and Plan Views

Set up levels and corresponding plan views in advance in your template to save time downstream. You can predefine the number of levels, their typical height, and naming convention (Figure 5.34).

FIGURE 5.34

Levels in the Project Browser and in section view

Elevations

If you've started building your template from an existing Revit template, you'll already have four default exterior elevations defined. If you started from scratch with no template, you'll need to create all four base elevations (south, east, north, and west) by placing elevation markers. (Note that we don't recommend that you ever start Revit using the None option under Template file as you'll have to define a great many things to make Revit work that are already defined in the default template.) It's very important that you also set the width and depth of the elevations. To do so, select the arrow of the elevation mark that activates the current width and depth; then you can adjust them accordingly (Figure 5.35).

Views

For each view that you preset in the Revit template, you can define a scale, a level of detail, the state of the crop region (visible or not), and display settings (hidden lines, shaded view, and so on). But mostly, think of view templates when you preset your views, because they're the biggest time-savers—setting them in the templates will increase productivity significantly and help you maintain graphical consistency.

View Templates

View templates let you define a desired set of view properties for any of your view typical types (plans, section, elevations, schedules, etc.). This is a great way to enforce graphic consistency across views. For example, if you want your architectural plan views to always show furniture as half-toned, you can define this in your plan view template. If someone changes the appearance of furniture to no longer be half-toned, you can reapply the view template to get the drawing back to its original configuration. To do this, right-click the view name in the Project Browser, and choose the Apply View Template option. Choose the desired template, and click OK.

Look at the view templates that ship with the default template, and adjust these to suit your requirements. For example, the architectural plan scale (1:100) is set to ⅛″=1′-0″. If this is too coarse for your needs, change the value to ¼″=1′-0″ (1:50).

Every view can have a default view template assigned to it (Figure 5.36). This doesn't automatically keep the view in sync with the view template, but it lets you select many views in the Project Browser and push their default view template back into the view. To do this, select multiple views in the Project Browser, and choose to apply the view template. Choose the option Default View Template (Figure 5.37).

FIGURE 5.35

Two different settings for elevation tag depth and width

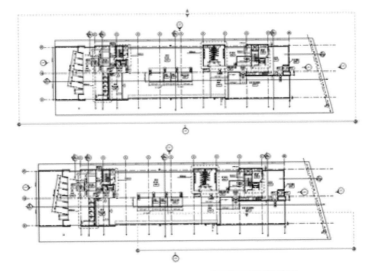

FIGURE 5.36

Views can have a default view template assigned to them to help streamline updating the view later in the process.

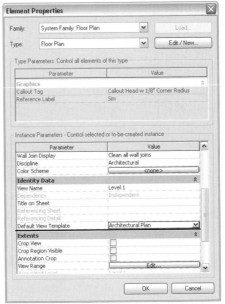

FIGURE 5.37
To apply the view's default template, use the Default View Template option.

Color Fill Schemes

Color fill schemes let you apply color to room and area parameter values to help graphically illustrate spatial organization. Applying a color fill scheme to a plan or section view color-codes room properties such as department, name, and usage. It's good practice to predefine different color schemes that you're likely to use. Once a color scheme is defined, it can be applied to any number of plan views. Keep in mind that color is applied only to spaces that have been populated with room or area elements. If you want to make department-usage plans, think about prepopulating your color schemes with commonly used department and usage names. This will make the value available for rooms later so you don't have to manually type them in each time. For example, if you add "Accounting" as a value to a color scheme in your template that colors by department, then when you later go to a room's element properties to assign it a department, you'll see "Accounting" as a predefined choice in the drop-down list.

The Bottom Line

Project templates save you time by capturing settings and modeling standards in a preset file that will help your office maintain a consistent look and feel across different projects. Templates allow you to load a set of commonly used families in advance, so that you won't have to search and load those elements with each new project you start. Having complete and well designed templates will help create a more efficient and productive working environment.

Create new types of system families   Incorporating common building components in your project template is fundamental to using Revit effectively.

Master It   How do you add/remove wall, floor, and roof types to your template?

Use type catalogs   Revit's type catalogs are an important tool for keeping the types you create accessible in a project.

Master It   What are type catalogs used for?

Customize project settings in your template   View templates allow you to tailor views according to the requirements of a project.

Master It   How would you set up a new view template for plan views where the surface pattern of floors is turned off?

Chapter 6

Modeling Principles in Revit I

Creating a BIM model requires modeling in 3D. This is very different from working with abstract 2D lines in order to represent your design. To work with Revit and be able to build a BIM model, you need to have an understanding of how objects are constructed at various scales, ranging from the building mass down to furniture assemblies. You need to know how various building elements interact with each other and depend on each other, what materials they are made of, and how they are constructed and assembled. To this end, Revit provides a set of tools that enable you to build your model and all the elements that go into the model. Understanding the principles of modeling in the context of Revit will be essential to your success as you move deeper into building information modeling.

This chapter is the first half of a description of the basic modeling principles that support the design process in Revit.

In this chapter, you learn to do the following:

♦ Understand the basics of modeling with Revit

♦ Understand sketch-based design

♦ Understand work planes, levels, grids, reference planes, and reference lines

Understanding the Basics of Modeling with Revit

Designers have a long tradition of modeling before building. This activity involves the use of pliable and tactile materials such as clay and wood to model designs fluidly. With these materials, form can be explored with ease, as designs iterate directly in our own hands. The use of software to model form has become a popular extension of this activity, and you only need to look so far as the latest animated film to see how far the technology has come.

Many software modeling tools are available that allow direct editing and intuitive shaping of form. Tools such as Maya, Rhinoceros, 3ds Max, and SketchUp allow you to create free-form shapes with relative ease. These tools are great for modeling, but they are not geared for a BIM approach to design and documentation. The elements created with these modelers are meshes, nurbs, ACIS solids, and other generic geometrical shapes that are used to represent walls, slabs, roofs, and windows; but they do not have embedded intelligence or relationships among themselves or with other elements in the model. Further, they barely contain any metadata that can be quantified and analyzed. So—as it stands today—you will find great modelers that are not BIM and BIM applications that are not powerful modelers. One way that Revit approaches this problem is to allow importing of free-form geometry into the project and family environment, where it can then be used to derive walls, floors, and roofs. And while not as free-form, Revit natively supports the creation of parametric 3D forms.

The entire modeling concept in Revit is based on some base class modeling forms—extrusions, revolves, sweeps, blends, and swept blends—and the combinations these can produce.

Each of the five base modeling techniques can produce either a positive or negative shape (solids and voids) that can be combined to create more complex forms. Each form is derived from 2D sketches that are drawn on work planes and then given a third dimension. We'll explore sketch-based forms in more detail in the next section.

While there is clearly room for improvements when it comes to the generic modeling capabilities of Revit, you will be pleasantly surprised with the variety of 3D geometry you can generate in a short time. Those who have already used Revit will also notice the addition of the new Swept Blend tool, long desired by seasoned Revit users, in Revit 2009.

Figure 6.1 shows an example of what's possible using the five basic modeling tools.

FIGURE 6.1
Example of expressive architecture using Revit

Courtesy of architect Kamal Malik

Understanding Sketch-Based Design

All internal modeling techniques in Revit rely on an approach called *sketch-based design,* where you draw a shape in a special Sketch mode by creating 2D lines that then generate 3D forms. When you model most Revit elements, you enter a mode in which the entire model is grayed out and not selectable, so focus is given to the sketch, which is represented in strong magenta lines. Once you've defined your shapes by creating closed loops of lines, you click Finish Sketch, and the geometry is generated. This Sketch mode is used throughout Revit, so you should get acquainted with its behavior early on.

For example, the Floor, Roof, Ceiling, Stair, and Railing tools require you to first sketch 2D shapes and then generate the form by "finishing the sketch." Revit then applies a thickness, or other element-specific property, based on the element type, to the sketch. Even walls have an underlying sketch, but in the case of walls, this is a sketch that can be edited in elevation, not plan view, as is the case with the rest of the elements, as shown in Figure 6.2. To edit the elevation of a wall, select the wall in an elevation or 3D view and click the Edit Elevation Profile button in the Options bar. Note that this only applies to linear walls.

Courtesy of E. Di Giacomo

FIGURE 6.2
Moorish architectural example:
(A) Standard straight rectangle shaped wall;
(B) elevation profile of that wall changed to the desired shape using simple lines;
(C) wall shape result achieved by simple editing of the sketch in elevation; (D) the wall used in a building.

A
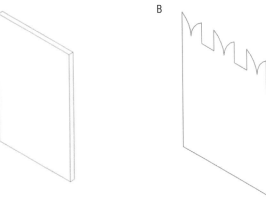

B
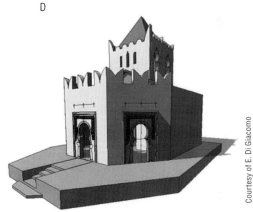

C
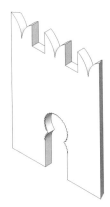

D

Floors and Roofs

One of the first places you'll encounter sketch-based modeling is with the Floor and Roof tools. When you initiate either of these tools, you are instantly placed in Sketch mode. The Design bar changes, indicating the new mode (Figure 6.3), and you'll get a set of tools specific to the task of creating 2D sketch lines and creating lines with relationships to other model elements.

FIGURE 6.3
The Design bar in Sketch mode

Sketch
⟲ Modify
⊟ Dimension
Ⅰ⌐ Lines
◿ Ref Plane
⫯ Pick Supports
⊩ Pick Walls
◈ Slope Arrow
◪ Set Work Plane
🗒 Floor Properties
⟳ Finish Sketch
❌ Quit Sketch

For example, you can either draw lines freely using the Lines tool in Draw mode, or use the Pick Walls tool from the Options bar to generate the floor or roof sketch lines for you by picking on walls. When using the pick walls method, you create an explicit relationship between the floor or roof sketch and the walls. The result is that when walls move, the sketch (and thus the floor or the roof made of it) adapts and updates with the walls.

The rules for creating a valid closed-loop sketch are straightforward:

♦ The sketch has to form a closed loop of lines, and the lines have to be perfectly trimmed at the ends. You cannot have gaps or overlapping lines in the sketch. Whenever a sketch is not complete or has overlaps, you will not be able to finish the sketch, and Revit will indicate that something is wrong with an error message.

♦ When creating certain types of elements, you are allowed to sketch more than one closed loop within or outside of the same sketch—this is fine as long as the two loops do not intersect. If one loop of lines is within the boundaries of the other, it creates an opening in the outer shape (Figure 6.4).

FIGURE 6.4
Creating a closed loop within another closed loop of lines results in an opening.

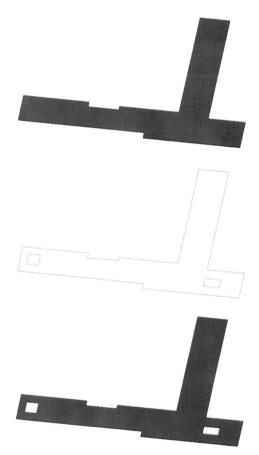

If you were to draw another loop within those openings, it would be positive and create another solid piece of floor of the same type. The logic of the loops is: one is positive, the next one within it is negative, the next one within it is positive. Remember that (Figure 6.5).

FIGURE 6.5
An additional loop of lines results in a positive shape.

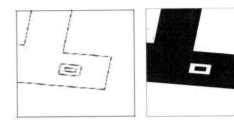

Sketching Rules of Thumb

Here are some rules of thumb you will need to know and follow when sketching:

◆ To edit a sketch, you need to be in a view that is parallel to the sketch or a 3D view. For example, it is not logical to edit the sketch of a wall profile in a plan view as you would not be able to see the sketch in a way that is relevant. If you attempt to do this in plan view, Revit alerts you and proposes other views in which you *can* execute the task. The same goes for a floor—only in plan or 3D will you be able to edit the sketch.

◆ Sketch mode cannot be activated in perspective (camera) views. If you select a wall or any other element and want to edit its shape but cannot find the Edit button in the Options bar, you are in camera view. Switch to an axonometric, 3D, or any other view in which the sketch makes sense to edit.

Understanding Work Planes, Levels, Grids, Reference Planes, and Reference Lines

Reference planes, reference lines, levels, work planes … what are they? To master modeling techniques in Revit, you need to understand the concept of a work plane.

Work Planes

The work plane is a 3D plane that you sketch on. For example, when you are in a plan view and start sketching a floor, the work plane is set to the level associated with the plan view you are working in. The majority of views in Revit (plans, 3D views, or views set in the family templates) have predefined work planes set automatically when they are created. Views such as sections and elevations require you to manually pick a work plane in order to add 3D elements to those views. In some cases, as with placing windows or doors in an elevation view, this is done implicitly—the cursor locates planes (walls) automatically.

A work plane can be understood as a surface on which you draw or place something. Imagine you are holding a marker in your hand and have a space in front of you. Can you draw with the marker in the space? No. You need a piece of paper, glass, wall—some kind of a surface to draw on. So, a work plane defines a surface on which you can build geometry. You can define a work plane by drawing a reference plane, picking a face from an existing element, or use an existing level (datum) as a reference.

Figure 6.6 graphically explains the work plane. There are a few simple rules when using or understanding a work plane:

FIGURE 6.6
Concept of
work planes

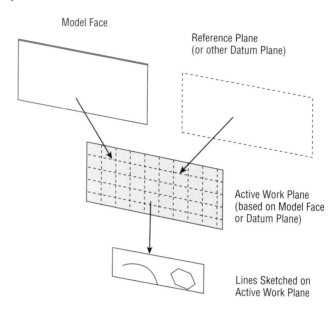

Model Face

Reference Plane
(or other Datum Plane)

Active Work Plane
(based on Model Face
or Datum Plane)

Lines Sketched on
Active Work Plane

♦   The work plane is set by selecting a reference plane/reference line; a datum plane (like a level or grid) or a planar face of a model element. Often it is preset and you do not need to explicitly set it.

♦   Many elements in Revit use the active work plane to know where to sketch or place objects (some objects are limited to only horizontal or vertical work planes).

♦   The work plane is also used when you are modifying objects. When you drag or move an object, it is typically constrained to that plane.

♦   When you set the work plane to be based on other selectable elements, it creates a *dependency*, or relationship to the underlying reference you selected. If the underlying object is moved, the work plane is moved to stay aligned to it. Any objects created on the work plane will also update.

Let's look a bit more closely at the types of work planes available in Revit.

Levels

Levels are horizontal work planes that define the levels in a building and can also be used to denote important horizontal references in a building (such as attic height). Levels are only created and visible in section or elevation views. Each level typically has a corresponding floor plan view associated with it, although it is possible to make levels with no associated floor plan. For example, a level may define the Top of Steel in a building section, but there is no need to have a floor plan view of that level. For that case, you can create levels without plans by clearing the option Make Plan View in the Options bar when the Level tool is activated. This creates a level that appears black and white, rather than blue—indicating that there is no hyperlinked view.

Note that when you create new levels using the Copy tool, the newly created levels are black and white, as copying levels does not autogenerate new floor plans. If you need to convert a black and white level so that it has a floor plan associated with it, use the Floor Plan tool in the View tab in the Design bar. You will then be able to add a view to any existing level in the project.

When you place families, they automatically become associated with the level they are placed on. Walls, roofs, and stairs all have top and bottom constraints to levels. This guarantees that when the level changes height, so too will all the elements on that level. All sketch-based families such as floors, roofs, ceilings, and stairs are also associated with at least one level. Note that if you delete a level , all the elements associated with that level will also be deleted—so use caution when deleting levels!

Grids

Grids are vertical planes used as standard references in the construction industry for creating location grids on the site as well as a communication reference between the building participants. These construction datums are used to accurately define locations for elements such as columns and beams or positions of main structural walls or the exterior shell. You can associate elements with the grids so that when the grid system changes, it controls the position of the associated elements. A good example for that would be columns associated with grid intersections. As with a level, when a grid is moved, associated elements move with the grid (Figure 6.7).

FIGURE 6.7
Grids are reference planes that can be used to control other elements such as beams and columns.

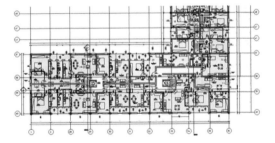

EXTENDING LEVELS AND GRIDS

If you wish to expand grids or levels to encompass a larger portion of your model, you can use the context menu of the grids and select Maximize Extents. This extends the datum planes you have selected to the maximum extents of the model geometry.

Reference Planes

Reference planes are used to drive other geometry. They are planes that exist in 3D space that other elements can be attached to. While not visible in 3D views, they can be seen when perpendicular to plan, section, and elevations and are represented as green dashed lines. Similar to levels and grids, these lines are not view specific and will appear in all perpendicular plans, sections, and elevations. Even though reference planes look and feel like ordinary lines, they are very different. Think of them as symbolic representations of infinite planes. The ends of reference planes are selectable and you can drag them to make them longer, but you will not be able to rotate the end of a reference plane freely, as you can with lines.

USING REFERENCE PLANES IN THE FAMILY EDITOR

Reference planes are the essence of parametric content creation in the Family Editor, as they are used to create the parametric skeleton to which geometry is then attached and allowed to vary. The reference planes in a family are what you dimension to when they are loaded into a project—not the geometry.

Giving the reference planes various states also affects how other elements relate to the family. A reference plane can be set as *not a reference*, *weak*, or *strong*; and it can be defined as a reference for the left, right, front, bottom, back, or center position. The selection of these options is important in the Family Editor environment, as they define references for snapping. When you have two crossing references set as Strong, they define the insertion point of an element when you place it in the project environment. In Figure 6.8, the two centrally positioned strong references define the insertion point of the element. The weak references serve only as secondary snaps.

FIGURE 6.8
A work desk

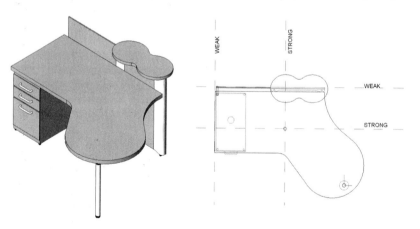

In a project, reference planes can be used to drive geometry (see Figure 6.9).

FIGURE 6.9

Reference planes are used extensively in the Family Editor to create parametric constraints that can drive forms and define snapping references.

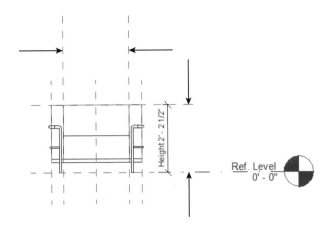

Reference Lines

Reference lines were designed mostly for use in the Family Editor to overcome the limitation of the reference planes and their inability to define constraints that reference a point, direction, and angle. Unlike with reference planes, the start and end points of a reference line can be referenced and used for dimensioning. A popular use of a reference line is to define door swing opening angles by creating an angular relationship between the door leaf position and the closed state of the door leaf. This will let the user set any angle of door opening later in the project. Other differences between reference lines and reference planes are that you cannot name the reference lines and you can only select them graphically.

Reference lines define two work planes—one is the plane on which the reference line was drawn, and the other is perpendicular to it (see Figure 6.10).

FIGURE 6.10

Reference lines are used to control door swings and opening angle in families.

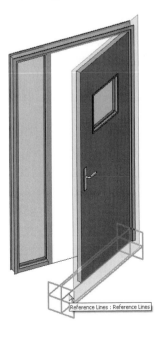

SCOPE BOXES

As previously mentioned, reference planes extend in all views. The Scope Box tool limits the range in which reference planes (grid lines, levels, and reference lines) appear. Scope boxes are used when you have multiple floor plans where the gridlines aren't the same for all levels. In our example of a building with a base and tower, two separate scope boxes are created, one for each major volume of the building. The grids in each part of the building are then assigned to the appropriate scope box. Figure 6.11 shows how scope boxes work in a 3D view.

FIGURE 6.11
(A) This building consists of two main volumes, a low volume with shopping function and a tower with hotel use. These two volumes use separate grid systems, and thus two different scope boxes are created to control the visibility of the separate grids.
(B) Grid element properties indicate the scope box to which the grid belongs.

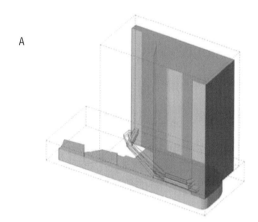

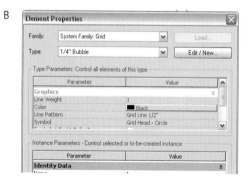

Scope boxes are visible in 3D views—although not in camera (perspective) views—and you can easily manipulate their extent directly using the grip controls. Assigning gridlines or other datums to a scope box is easy: select the gridlines, and in the Element Properties dialog box choose the Scope Box parameter and select the scope box where the datums should belong. Figure 6.11 shows the Element Properties dialog box for the gridlines and the associated scope box.

If you are working on a project in a system of grids, you need to draw the grid system only once in a floor plan view, and the grids will be visible in every other plan or ceiling view. But let's say your project has a base of five floors of shopping with a 30-story hotel above (like the model shown in Figure 6.10). It's likely you'll have separate structural bays for each part of the building. You don't need to see all grid lines of the shopping base in the tower, and vice versa. To deal with these scenarios, you use a scope box. This will allow you to control in which views a grid will appear.

VISIBILITY OF GRID LINES IN SECTIONS AND ELEVATIONS

Grid lines will show in section or elevation view *only* if the view is cut perpendicular to the grid line. In no other case will the grid line appear. This is done to avoid confusion on the construction site due to misleading graphic description.

Work Planes in a Nutshell

Before moving on to look at using work planes in practice, let's take a moment to summarize the basic theory.

WORKING WITH WORK PLANES

When creating elements that do not necessarily fall on a standard reference plane (such as a level), you will need to select the Work Plane tool from the toolbar to establish your work plane. This brings up the Work Plane dialog box shown in Figure 6.12. Let's review the options in the dialog box:

FIGURE 6.12
The Work Plane dialog box lets you specify the active work plane for a view.

Name   This option displays available levels, grids, and named reference planes. Note that only reference planes that you have explicitly given names appear in this list. To name a reference plane, use the element properties of the reference plane.

Pick a Plane This option allows you to select a plane interactively in the model. The selection is visual and you need to click on a reference plane, wall face, or faces of an element. Figure 6.13 shows the effect of selecting different planes on which to sketch and create a void extrusion.

FIGURE 6.13
The same mass and the same 2D shape extruded as a hole: (A) the extrusion shape is drawn on the front face of the mass; (B) the extrusion is drawn on the back face of the mass.

A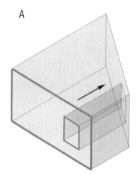

B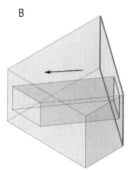

Pick a Line and Use the Work Plane It Was Sketched In With this option, Revit converts the work plane on which the line was created into the active work plane. When you select a work plane that is perpendicular to your current view, Revit opens a new Go to View dialog box that gives you options to select a view in which the chosen work plane can be worked on (Figure 6.14).

FIGURE 6.14
The Go to View dialog box lists views where you can work on the active work plane.

WORK PLANE VISIBILITY

You can visually show the active work plane in your view using the Work Plane Visibility toggle located in the main toolbar. When visible in 3D, the work plane is shown as a semitransparent grid face (Figure 6.15). By activating work plane visibility, you'll see where you will be adding new elements. You can see the work plane change location by using the Pick Plane option in the Work Plane dialog box. Select model faces and you'll see the active work plane change.

If you are not sure where your active work plane is, click the Work Plane Visibility tool in the toolbar.

FIGURE 6.15
Making the work
plane visible helps
you understand
the active work
plane in a 3D view.

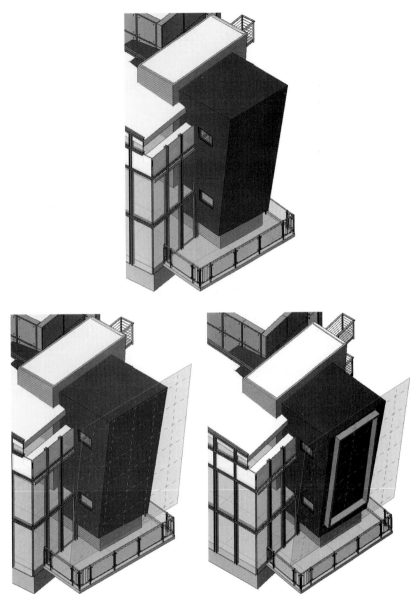

OTHER WORK PLANE OPERATIONS

Revit will let you rotate a work plane grid by clicking on it and selecting Rotate from the toolbar. This in turn affects how new elements will be placed on that work plane. You can also align elements to the work plane grid, and lines will snap to the grid (Figure 6.16).

FIGURE 6.16
When the work plane grid is rotated, new elements placed on the work plane will also be rotated.

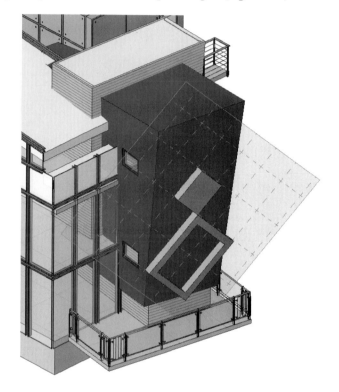

To change the work plane an element is associated with, select the element, and then click the Edit Work Plane button in the Options bar and select another work plane using one of the methods in the dialog box.

To dissociate an element from a work plane, first select the element. Then click the Edit Work Plane button in the Options bar to display the dialog box shown in Figure 6.17, and click the Dissociate button. The element will then be free to move anywhere in the model. Note that this option is only available for work plane–based families.

Once you have dissociated an element from its work plane, you will notice that the value for the work plane instance parameter (located in Element Properties) will be set to <not associated>. Most importantly, you will notice that the element is free from constraints and is free to be moved in any 3D direction.

FIGURE 6.17
The Work Plane dialog box allows you to set the work plane of an element or dissociate it from its work plane.

To rehost elements from one host (wall, floor, or roof, for example) to another, you can use the Rehost button in the Options bar when an element is selected. This allows you to select a new host to place the element. With this tool, you can choose any new host—it does not have to be in the same plane as the original. For example, you can select a window in one wall, click the Rehost button, and then choose a new wall for the window.

Figure 6.18 shows an extruded shape originally created on a horizontal work plane. Using the Rehost tool, you can place the form on any surface in the model.

FIGURE 6.18
(A) original condition; (B) desired repositioning of the curved element; (C) the element is rehosted and a relationship between the two elements has been created; (D) the host changed its geometry and the hosted elements follows the change.

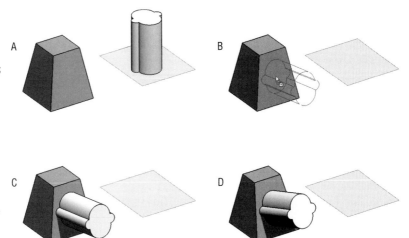

 **Real World Scenario**

USING WORK PLANES WITH REVIT ROOFS

Here are two versions of the same building, with roofs that use the same sketch profile but are drawn on two different work planes. Image A shows a roof by extrusion sketched on a work plane parallel to the exterior wall; B shows the same roof sketched on a work plane rotated 45 degrees with respect to the exterior wall. Notice the difference!

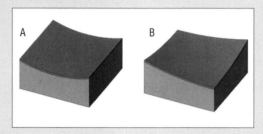

CREATING A ROOF BY EXTRUSION (DEFAULT WORK PLANE)

Take the following steps to see for yourself how version A was created:

1. Draw four walls in plan view in the shape of a square.

2. From the Basic tab in the Design bar, select the Reference Plane tool and draw a reference plane parallel to the south wall:

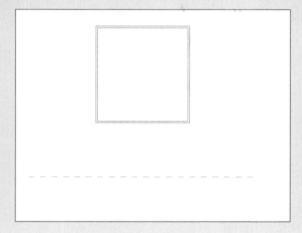

3. Pick the reference plane and go to Element Properties. Give it a name, **Front Roof Plane**.

4. From the Modeling design tab, select the Roof tool and select Roof by Extrusion.

5. You will be prompted to select a work plane:

6. From the Name list, select the named reference plane you just drew. You'll be asked to open a view to begin sketching. Choose the south elevation.

7. Sketch a roof in arc shape as shown here and finish the sketch:

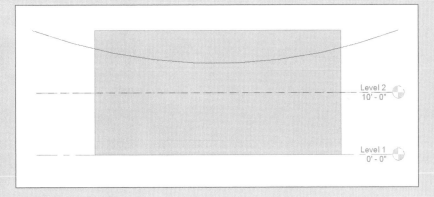

8. Go to the default 3D view and using the blue arrows; adjust the length of the roof to make sure it extends beyond the exterior walls, as shown here:

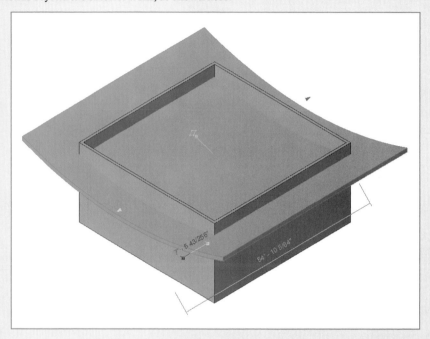

9. While still in the 3D view, select all the walls. Click the Attach button in the Options bar and then select the roof to attach the walls to the roof. The resulting roof should look something like this:

10. To make the roof end at the edge of the exterior walls, select the roof in plan view and select the option Cut Plan Profile in the Options bar. This allows you to cut off the extruded roof exactly at the edge of the building, regardless of its shape. In this example, draw two rectangles that cut the roof up to the face of the walls.

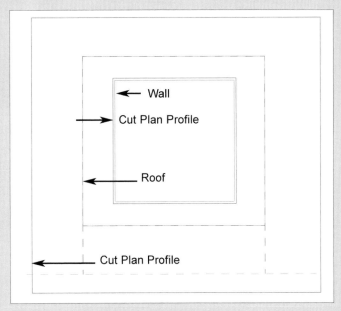

After using Cut Plan Profile, the final result for the first roof looks like this:

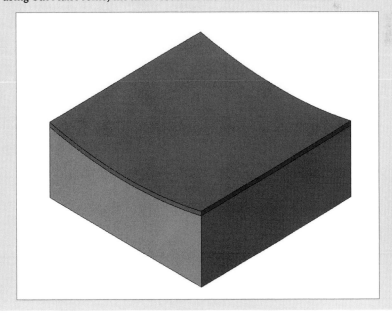

CREATING VERSION B: A ROOF USING A 45-DEGREE WORK PLANE AS A REFERENCE

To obtain the second roof (B), repeat all the previous steps, but draw the reference plane at a 45-degree angle to the building, as shown here. Remember to give the reference plane a different name in the Element Properties dialog box. If drawing at this angle is awkward, you can also use the Orient command in the View pull-down.

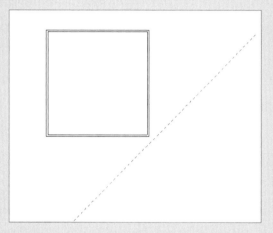

The finished roof looks like this:

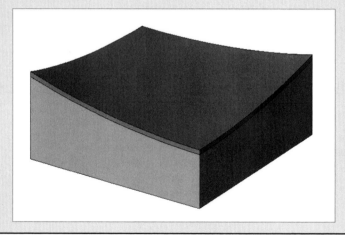

The Bottom Line

Creating elements in Revit requires modeling in 3D, which can be quite a change from traditional 2D workflows. Learning how to model your building project in Revit is the first step to leveraging the functionalities of BIM.

Understand the basics of modeling with Revit   Modeling with software is an extension of the traditional art of modeling with the hands. Free-form 3D modeling tools are not designed with BIM workflows in mind, however, it is still possible to import shapes into Revit for downstream use. At the same time, Revit provides some basic tools for 3D design, and you should familiarize yourself with these.

Master it   Tools such as Rhinoceros, 3ds Max, Maya, and SketchUp allow you to create free-form shapes with relative ease. How does Revit let you take advantage of such shapes?

Understand sketch-based design   Sketch-based design allows you to define some basic parameters and shapes in Sketch mode within Revit.

Master it   Revit uses a 2D sketch-based approach to modeling. What modeling elements in Revit use this 2D sketch principle to generate their form?

Understand work planes, levels, grids, reference planes, and reference lines   Using these tools gives you the ability to better control your model and your design by applying and controlling parameters.

Master it   In order to sketch a form, the form must reside on a work plane. How do you define and visualize the work plane in Revit?

Chapter 7

Modeling Principles in Revit II

Creating a BIM model requires modeling in 3D. This is very different from working with abstract 2D lines in order to represent your design. To work with Revit and be able to build a BIM model, you must understand how objects are constructed at various scales ranging from the building mass down to furniture assemblies. You need to know how various building elements interact with each other and depend on each other, what materials they are made of, and how they are constructed and assembled. To this end, Revit provides a set of tools that enable you to build your model and all the elements that go into the model. Understanding the principles of modeling in the context of Revit is essential to your success as you move deeper into building information modeling.

This chapter is the second half of a description of the basic modeling principles that support the design process in Revit.

In this chapter, you learn how to do the following:

◆ Understand the principles of modeling in Revit

◆ Model with five basic forms

◆ Combine solids and voids to create complex and intriguing forms

Understanding the Principles of Modeling in Revit

Revit is much more than a 3D modeler. It was designed specifically for architects and has behavioral rules built into many of the architectural elements that make up the building. For example, walls are usually vertically oriented rectangular shapes; floors and ceilings are horizontal shapes with constant thickness. These major building elements use a restricted sketch-based approach because those restrictions make sense for these types of elements. This is one of Revit's major differences when compared to a generic modeler where you can model anything, any way you like. In essence, with Revit, the type of element you are modeling will present a tailored set of creation tools.

You draw a wall by defining its start and endpoint, which will determine its position and length. The width of the wall and its height are determined by the wall properties. The wall becomes 3D immediately with each click of the mouse. Roofs and floors, on the other hand, require definition with a sketch that determines their outer shape, while their thickness is what is defined in the element properties of the roof or the floor.

Once the envelope of the building has been established with walls, floors, and roofs (the system families), you progressively add windows, doors, furniture, plumbing fixtures, and so on (standard families) to the model. These elements rarely depend on the context of the building and are usually built offsite and manufactured in some factory in real life. In Revit, a good selection of these elements is predefined and saved in a library for use across multiple projects. These loadable elements are all created in the Family Editor using a combination of simple geometric forms that can be associated with parametrically driven dimensions and materiality. For example, a chair can be created with a combination of sweeps, blends, extrusions, and revolves. The same applies to a lighting fixture, a sitting bench, a plumbing fixture—you name it. Figure 7.1 shows samples of standard "loadable" family types.

FIGURE 7.1
These windows and doors belong to the standard loadable family types.

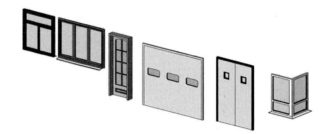

In some cases, you need the full flexibility of the Family Editor in the context of your project. When you want to create a custom design feature tightly related to the context of the building or the landscape around it (such as an entrance canopy or a reception desk in welcome area), you'll need a robust set of tools that are not available using the basic walls, floors, and roofs. These types of elements are created using the Create tool from the Modeling tab in the Design bar (see Figure 7.2). They use the same features available in the Family Editor, and are referred to as "in-place families." Figure 7.3 shows a fireplace built as an in-place family.

FIGURE 7.2
The Modeling tab on the Design bar

FIGURE 7.3
Example of an
in-place family

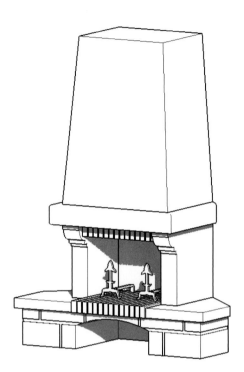

Another workflow where free-form modeling comes into play is at the early stages of conceptual design, where massing studies are explored. These mass forms are done with the Massing tools, as combinations of various geometric shapes made using extrusions, blends, sweeps, and revolves. Again, with massing, the tools need to be flexible and not constrained to a specific use case. In Revit, the same set of primitive form-making tools is available when making massing geometry. Figure 7.4 shows a massing study using Revit form making tools.

FIGURE 7.4
Early massing
concept studies

Courtesy of RJMJ Hiller

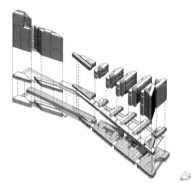

Images courtesy of Gensler

Courtesy of RJMJ Hiller

Modeling with Five Basic Forms

As we've mentioned, there are five basic form-making options in Revit. With these forms you can create almost any shape you need for various scales of design, from large-scale massing studies down to sink faucets. By combining forms and using forms as subtractive elements, you can model nearly anything in Revit. The five primary forms are:

◆ Extrusion

◆ Revolve

◆ Sweep

◆ Blend

◆ Swept Blend

All of these are accessible from a few places:

◆ The Family Editor when selecting Solid Form or Void Form (Figure 7.5A)

◆ Under the Modeling tab, when you select the Create tool, Solid Form, or Void Form (Figure 7.5B)

◆ Under the Massing tab, when you select Create Mass, Solid Form, or Void Form (Figure 7.5C)

FIGURE 7.5

The (A) Family Editor, (B) Modeling tab, and (C) Massing tab all enable you to create solid or void forms, which you can then model by any of the five basic techniques.

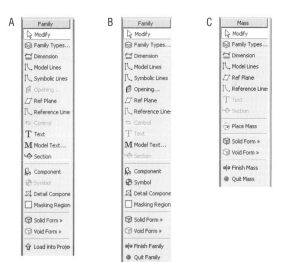

Selecting Solid Form or Void Form from any of these toolbars displays the options shown in Figure 7.6.

FIGURE 7.6

Solid and Void
Extrusion, Blend,
Revolve, Sweep,
and Swept Blend
options

Solid Extrusion	Void Extrusion
Solid Blend	Void Blend
Solid Revolve	Void Revolve
Solid Sweep	Void Sweep
Solid Swept Blend	Void Swept Blend

Extrusion

Extrusion, the simplest of all modeling transformations, is based on a closed 2D sketch (shape) that is given a thickness value. The thickness is always perpendicular to the work plane of the sketch (see Figure 7.7).

FIGURE 7.7

An extrusion is a
2D sketch shape
with depth added.

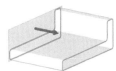

The element properties of an extrusion allow you to set the thickness of the extrusion as well as an offset from its work plane.

Extrusion Start   This defines where the extrusion starts and has a default of 0, but it can have any positive or negative value. The effects of this parameter are shown in Figure 7.8.

FIGURE 7.8

(A) Extrusion start
is set to 0; (B) has
a positive value
and the extrusion
starts above the
work plane; (C) has
a negative value
and starts below
the work plane.

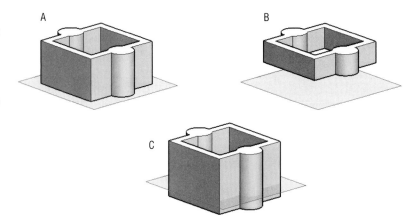

Extrusion End   This feature defines the end of the extrusion relative to the work plane. This value can be positive or negative. The default is set to 1′-0″ (250mm). The total thickness of an extrusion is the difference between the extrusion end and extrusion start.

When an extruded element is selected, check the Options bar for relevant options:

Edit   This feature takes you back to Sketch mode so that you can make changes to the underlying shape. Once you have changed the shape, don't forget to click Finish Sketch in the Design bar.

Depth   Depth defines the value of the extrusion depth—this value can be positive or negative. With vertical extrusions, the depth actually is the height of the extrusion.

Visibility   Visibility defines in which view types or levels of detail you want the extrusion to be visible. Figure 7.9 shows that the selected extrusion will be visible only in plan and reflected ceiling plan views, and only in medium and fine level of detail.

FIGURE 7.9
Forms can be made visible or invisible in different views and at different levels of detail.

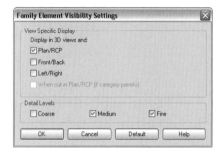

Edit Work Plane   This feature allows you to change the work plane of the extrusion. Note that a new work plane is only valid if it is parallel to the one that you wish to change.

Figure 7.10 demonstrates how a furniture element can be constructed from two extrusions that create the entire shape.

DIRECTIONS IN A REFERENCE PLANE

The direction in which you draw a reference plane determines which way is positive and which way is negative.

These images demonstrate in plan view how the different direction in which the reference plane was drawn affects the direction of the extrusion:

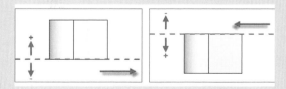

Because it is not easy to remember which way you drew each reference, we suggest that you name each reference plane you create. If you do that, when the reference plane is selected you will see the name of the reference plane, and it is always placed at the *end* of the direction in which it was drawn.

FIGURE 7.10
A cozy lounge chair
made of two simple
extrusions

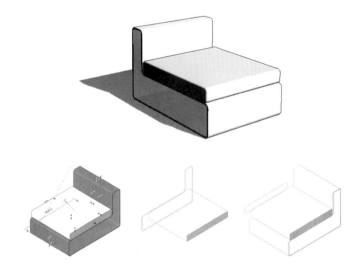

When you use the *face* of an element as a work plane (rather than a reference plane), as shown in Figure 7.11, the direction of the extrusion will depend on whether you are making it a solid or a void shape.

FIGURE 7.11
A void extrudes
into the solid face.

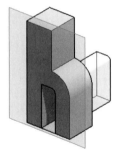

When you sketch a shape that is going to be a *void*, the void extrudes positively *toward the interior* of the object that you used to define the work plane.

When you add a *solid* shape, the shape extrudes positively *away from the exterior* of the object face, as shown in Figure 7.12.

FIGURE 7.12
A solid extrudes
away from the
solid face.

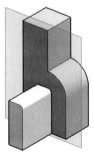

Revolve

A *revolve* takes a 2D profile and rotates it around an axis. A revolve is composed of two elements: a 2D profile (think of this as a cross section) that will define the surface once it is revolved, and an axis that the profile revolves around. As with extrusions, the profile sketch must be a closed loop of lines for the revolve to be valid. The bollard shown in Figure 7.13 is an example of a revolve form.

FIGURE 7.13

A revolve consists of a closed loop sketch and an axis of rotation.

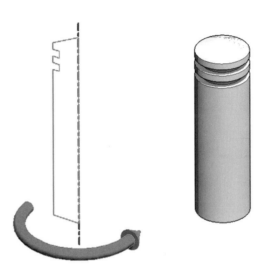

A revolve follows a full 360-degree path by default. In the element properties of a revolve, you can adjust this angle so that the profile can appear open, as shown in Figure 7.14.

FIGURE 7.14

The end angle is set to 270 degrees.

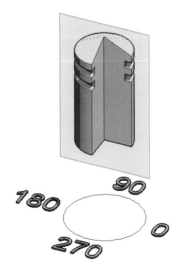

End Angle   This positions the sketch relative to the work plane of the end of the revolution. Figure 7.14 shows a revolve with an end angle set to 270 degrees.

Start Angle   This positions the sketch relative to the work plane at the beginning of the revolution. By setting the start angle to a value other than 0, you can get shapes like that shown in Figure 7.15.

FIGURE 7.15
The start angle is set to 90 degrees and the end angle is set to 270 degrees.

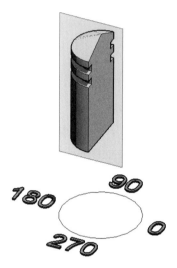

When an element that is revolved is selected, you will find the following tools in the Options bar:

These are similar to the options available when selecting other modeling forms. You can change the sketch that you used to execute the revolution with, set the visibility, edit the work plane, or re-host the form to another plane.

To understand how sketches create revolve shapes, we will look at three different results based on three different types of sketches. Figure 7.16 shows a standard revolve made out of one closed loop of lines; Figure 7.17 shows a revolve made out of two closed loops, where one loop is a subtractive element; and Figure 7.18 shows another revolve with two closed loops, where each loops is an additive element.

FIGURE 7.16
One closed loop of lines revolved around an axis

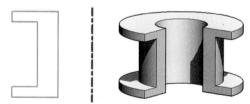

FIGURE 7.17
In this example, the two closed loops of lines are placed one inside the other. Following the principle of sketch-based design, the inner loop creates a hole in the first loop.

FIGURE 7.18
The two loops are independent of one another and thus the resulting revolution creates two solid shapes.

A revolve can be composed of multiple closed loops to define the profile sketch. Keep in mind that a sketch must not intersect another sketch; if it does, it will fail, and Revit will warn you when you try to finish the sketch. Depending on the positioning of the different loops, you can achieve different results, as shown in Figures 7.17 and 7.18.

A common example of a revolve form appears in Figure 7.19. The profile defines the cross section of a dome (cupola) roof. By rotating this profile around the center axis, we can generate a dome form.

FIGURE 7.19
The profile is revolved around the center axis, resulting in a dome form.

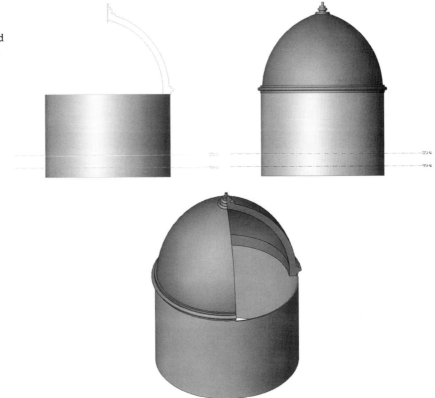

Another example of a revolve is this doorknob (Figure 7.20), where the cross section is drawn and then revolved around an axis.

FIGURE 7.20
A revolve can be used to create elements such as doorknobs as well.

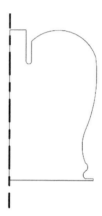

Sweep

A Sweep is conceptually similar to an extrusion, but you define a path for the extrusion profile to follow. The resulting form is generated by sweeping the profile along path segments. The profile is always swept perpendicular to the path segment it follows.

A sweep is defined by two sketches: the *path* and the *profile* that you sweep along the path. The path can be drawn on any work plane, and the profile will always be drawn perpendicular to the path. The first segment of the path you draw determines the default work plane for the profile sketch. To change the default location of the profile sketch plane, delete the line segment of the path that hosts it: the profile plane will jump to next available line segment in the path. Figure 7.21 shows a swept form, along with the path and profile used to create it.

FIGURE 7.21
Example of a sweep. In the sketch, the dashed rectangle is the profile plane—always perpendicular to the path.

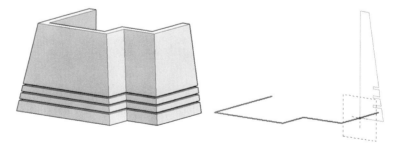

DEFINING THE SWEEP PATH

You can make a path either by selecting existing geometric edges to create new lines or by drawing lines. These options are available either from the Design bar:

or the Options bar:

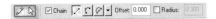

Sketch 2D Path allows you to draw the path using the various draw tools to make lines. You can use the Pick command to select edges and lines from the other elements to speed up creation.

Pick Path allows you to select existing lines or edges of geometry as the path for your sweep. With this method, you create a dependency between the swept element and the object that you selected for edges to define the path. Thus, when the geometry of the referenced object changes, so too will the swept element. We strongly recommend working in a 3D view when using this method, to make it easier to understand the relationships and effects of changing geometry (Figure 7.22).

FIGURE 7.22
Example of a sweeping path that is created by selecting existing edges of a solid geometry (in this case a wall opening). If the opening changes its size, the sweep will also change because of the dependency established with the Pick method.

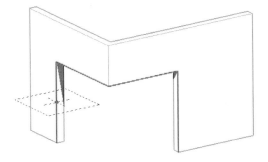

DEFINING THE PROFILE

A profile can be created using one of two methods: by drawing the profile on the spot, or by using a loaded, predefined profile. These options are shown in the Options bar when the Sweep command is activated. The default, By Sketch, lets you draw the profile using standard draw tools. You can also select a profile from the pull-down list of profiles that can be loaded into the project or family. This method is applicable in cases where you need to sweep the same profile on many paths. For example, you would first create a 2D profile family using the Profile (imperial) or M_Profile (metric) template. The profile has to be a closed loop of lines. Save the profile on your hard drive and then load it in your project.

Once you've made a sweep profile, the profile will be available in the drop-down list in the Options bar.

Figure 7.23 shows the Options bar with both options.

FIGURE 7.23

The default method for creating profiles is by sketching (top). You can also load premade profiles and use those (bottom).

If you use a loaded profile, you are given controls to position the profile relative to the X and Y axes (see Figure 7.24). These values are distances from the point of insertion of the profile (the intersection of the two reference planes in the Family Editor) and the point of reference of the profile and the path (the green cross). You can also rotate the loaded profile by adding a value under the Angle option (see Figure 7.25). The Flip button mirrors the profile, if you need it.

FIGURE 7.24

Offsetting the profile from the point of reference of the path. In this profile, the crossing of the references in the Family Editor was set to the lower-left corner of the profile. Thus, the offset values start from that point.

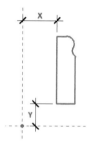

FIGURE 7.25

The angle of rotation is applied to the profile that is to be swept.

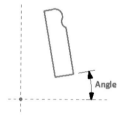

Once a sweep is created, you can always change the values that are available in the Element Properties dialog box of the sweep:

Parameter	Value	=
Constraints		≫
Work Plane	Level : Niveau 0	
Horizontal Profile Offset	0.1000	
Vertical Profile Offset	0.0500	
Angle	0.000°	
Construction		≫
Profile	Plinth : #01	

The advantage to using premade profiles is enormous. Figure 7.26 illustrates a concrete example of a sunshading family that needs to be edited.

FIGURE 7.26
Sweeps can be
used to create a
sunshade.

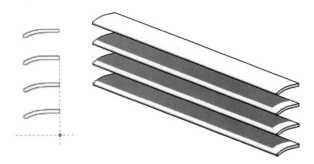

If you drew your profile manually and then used the Copy Multiple command to repeat the shade, you would need to change each shade separately to apply a new profile. If you had drawn the shape as a loadable profile family and loaded it into the family, you would only need to change the profile family once and reload it. All instances of the profile will update automatically when reloaded.

 Real World Scenario

PUTTING THE SWEEP TOOL TO WORK

Here are some real-life scenarios in which the Sweep tool is very handy. We'll let the pictures do most of the talking.

First consider the modern shower fixture in the bathroom shown here:

This design was created as a simple sweep on a circular path.

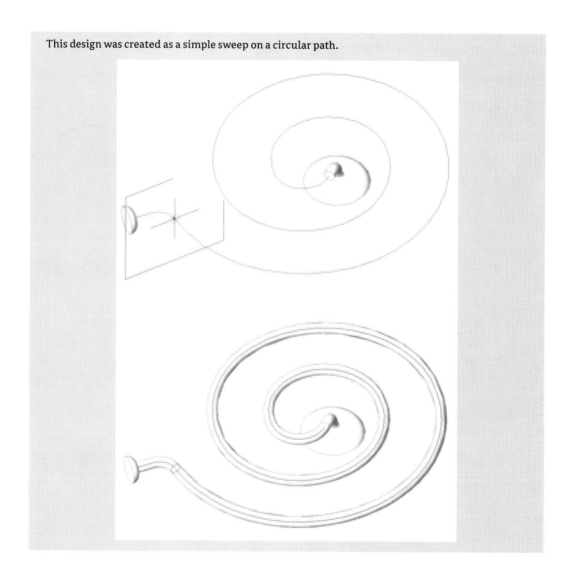

The architectural example shown here demonstrates another use of sweeps, to create a highly specific wall shape. The retaining wall was created as an in-place wall using the Create function and the Sweep method.

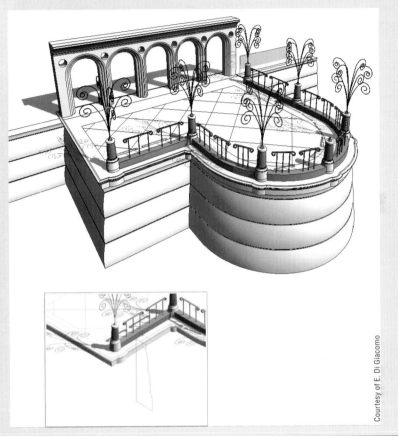

TRAJECTORY SEGMENTATION

The Trajectory Segmentation parameter (see Figure 7.27) provides a way to segment smooth arcs into linear segments. This can be useful when rationalizing a form into planar, constructible elements. When the option is checked, it makes the parameter Maximum Segment Angle active. The value you set defines the maximum value of the angle between two segments of the arc. The smaller that value, the higher the number of linear segments that will replace the arc. Figure 7.28 shows the effects of this parameter.

FIGURE 7.27
Sweeps can be segmented using the Trajectory Segmentation parameter.

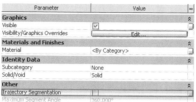

FIGURE 7.28
An arc path can be segmented using the Maximum Segment Angle parameter.

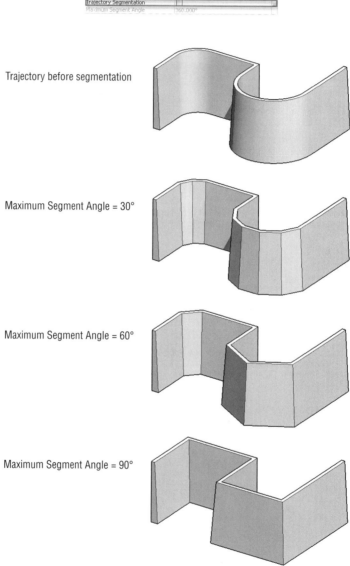

Trajectory before segmentation

Maximum Segment Angle = 30°

Maximum Segment Angle = 60°

Maximum Segment Angle = 90°

Blend

A blend creates a form by connecting two different 2D shapes on two different planes along a linear path (see Figure 7.29). The distance between the two shapes—the base and top—is what defines the depth of the blend. The two shapes for the top and base of the blend do not need to be the same shape or have the same number of segments. Revit can even blend arcs into linear segments.

FIGURE 7.29

A blend is created from two sketches that blend together along a linear path.

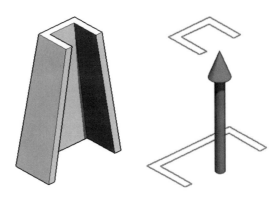

When the top and base shapes are the same, the resulting form will look exactly like an extrusion or sweep along a single, linear segment. You can think of a blend as an extrusion with two sketches—one for the base, and one for the top.

The properties of a blend resemble those of an extrusion. You can set the blend depth as well as the offset from the work planes on which the shapes will be drawn:

First End   This defines the offset of the base shape relative to its work plane. This value can be negative or positive. The default value is set to 0.

Second End   This defines the offset of the top shape relative to the work plane on which the blend is drawn. This value can be positive or negative. The default is set to 1′0″ (250mm).

The total depth of the blend is the resulting value between the first end and the second end. When a blended element is selected, you will find new tools in the Options bar:

These are the same as the options for extrusions, with the addition of two other features that take you to the sketch of the base or top of the blend:

Edit Top   This allows you to enter Sketch mode, where you can modify the top sketch.

Edit Base   This allows you to enter Sketch mode, where you can modify the base sketch.

Whenever you select one of those two options, the Options bar will change as well as the Design bar, as shown in Figure 7.30. Click Finish Sketch to exit either option.

FIGURE 7.30
Options in the
Design bar depend
on whether you are
editing the base (A)
or the top (B) of the
blend.

As you can see, when creating blends there is not one single work plane; this means that the two sketched shapes are always on parallel work planes.

The Vertex Connect tool is specific to blends, and it shows up in the Design bar when you're editing the blend sketch. This tool allows you to set the connection between the vertices that the two shapes have. Manipulating the vertices alters results in the final blend.

When you click the Vertex Connect tool, you see graphic controls indicating existing connections between the vertices of the blend shapes.

There are two different things you can do here:

Twisting After selecting Vertex Connect, two tools, Twist Left and Twist Right, appear in the Options bar.

These control the number of twists between the two shapes. Figure 7.31A shows a basic blend between two 45-degree oriented square shapes. Figure 7.31B shows one additional twist, and Figure 7.31C yet another twist.

Editing Vertices This is another way to affect the blend in order to arrive at alternative shapes. By clicking one of the open blue circle controls that appear when you first select the Vertex Connect tool, you can change the direction of the vertices by clicking on the control. Once you change the connection point, the circle will be filled in solid blue, and a line will be drawn showing a preview of the connection from one vertex to another. Revit connects the vertices from the base shape to the top shape in an automated way with each click. But each of the vertices has an option to be connected to the top vertex that lies to the right of it, or to the left, or both. The example shown in Figure 7.32 demonstrates how the same blend with the same base, top, and depth all look different depending on the vertex connections.

FIGURE 7.31
Various looks for
the same element
depending on the
number of vertex
connections or
twists: the forms
shown can be a
tower shape or a
table leg.

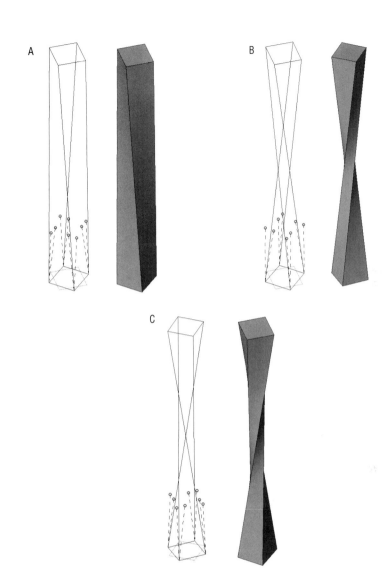

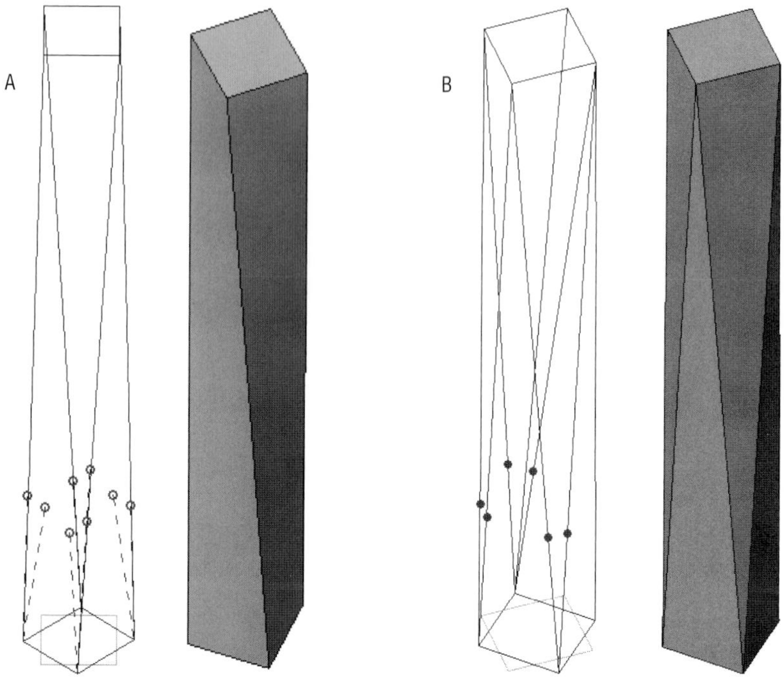

FIGURE 7.32
Changing vertex connections results in different blend forms.

TROUBLESHOOTING BLENDS

When the base shape of a blend has the same number of vertices as the top shape, the results are pretty much predictable. But often the number is not the same and you may not get the results you expect or desire. A tip to consider when working with more complex blends:

If one of the shapes is a circle, you might want to break it up into segments to get additional vertex points so that you arrive at a shape you need, as shown in Figures 7.33 and 7.34.

FIGURE 7.33
A standard blend you will often see, with the base shape a square and the top shape a circle

FIGURE 7.34
The same shapes with the circle split into four segments to add three more vertices. In example A, the vertex points are orthogonal; in B, they are rotated 45 degrees. Note the difference in the results.

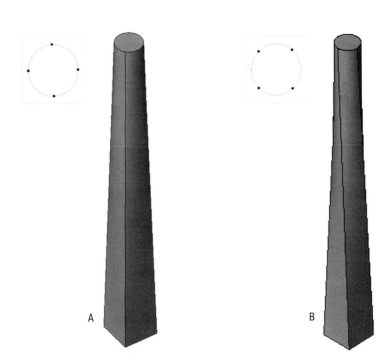

A

B

CREATING A LAMP WITH BLENDS AND SWEEPS

A real-world application of blends and sweeps can be seen in the Revit lamp family illustrated here.

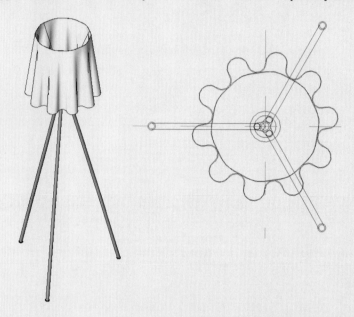

The shade is constructed using a blend between a segmented circle for the top (A) and a more complex series of arcs for the base (B).

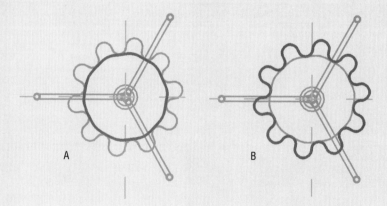

The top sketch has been divided into many segments to match the number of vertices of the base. This file can be found in the Chapter 6 folder on the book's companion web page if you want to explore it some more on your own (PS Lamp.rfa).

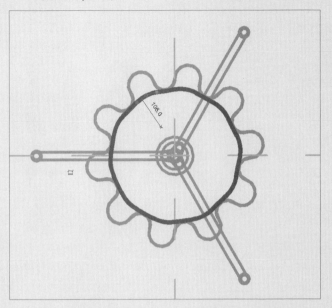

The legs of this lamp can be made using sweeps. A void extrusion was used to cut the bottom of the legs horizontally so that it sits flat on the floor.

EXAMPLES OF BLENDS IN PRACTICE

The shapes in Figure 7.35 are inspired by the sculptor and designer Isamu Noguchi's lamps, but as you can imagine, they could just as easily represent a lamp, a column, or an entire shape of a building. They are constructed as simple combinations of connected blends.

FIGURE 7.35
A series of blends used to form a more complex form

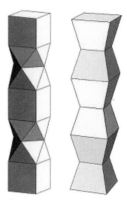

The blend sketches cannot contain more than one loop of closed lines. If your intention is to create something like the lampshade shown in Figure 7.36, you need to add a void. If you try to make such a shape, Revit will give you a warning message telling you that "more than one loop is not allowed."

FIGURE 7.36
This blend sketch with multiple loops is not allowed and would generate a warning message.

To obtain the result needed, you need to first create a solid blend and then a second one, done with a void that has a smaller radius, as shown in Figure 7.37.

FIGURE 7.37
A lampshade can be made by creating a void blend that is smaller than the solid blend.

Swept Blend

The Swept Blend feature was added to Revit 2009 and is a combination of a single segment sweep with a blend. The principles for creating a swept blend follow from the sweep and blend workflow. With a blend, you have no control over the path: it is always perpendicular to the sketch plane. With the swept blend, you can now create arc paths for the profiles to blend along. Examples of this include a roof or roof segment with a shape that changes over a nonstraight path, an elbow pipe that changes diameter between the two ends, funky furniture shapes or parts, and walls beneath curved stairs.

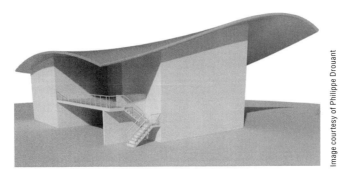

Image courtesy of Philippe Drouant

Combining Solids and Voids

Many complex shapes you wish to design go beyond the basic form-making techniques we just explored. Designs often require a combination of forms that are both additive and subtractive. To accommodate richer modeling, Revit approaches this problem by allowing any form to be solid or void. Solids are positive, physical elements, and voids are invisible, cutting elements that remove form from solids.

All the forms we covered (extrusion, revolve, sweep, blend, swept blend) can be made as either a solid or a void. This is represented in the Design bar, where you have the two options: Solid Form and Void Form.

NOTES ON SOLIDS AND VOIDS

◆ Voids that don't cut a solid and solids that are not joined may be switched from one to the other (from solid to void and vice versa) within their properties. Once they are joined or cut, they cannot be toggled in this way.

◆ Once a void is cut, it is no longer visible unless selected.

◆ Not all joined solids can be cut by the same void.

Examples Showing Use of Voids

Voids can be used in many ways to arrive at some surprising geometric forms. Think of a void as a way to carve away from a solid chunk of clay; you can truly sculpt with this tool!

VAULTS

In Figure 7.38, complex vaults have been created out of solid pentagonal extrusion and half-circle void extrusions cutting through it.

FIGURE 7.38
Vaulted space created out of a combination of solid and void extrusions

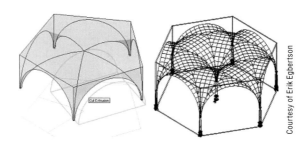

Courtesy of Erik Egbertson

JOIN GEOMETRY TOOL SOLVES GEOMETRY CONNECTIONS

You will need to use the Join Geometry tool to have the void cut the solid.

TOWER SHAPES

The basic shape of the tower shown in Figure 7.39 is a simple blend. A plow shape is used at the base, and a triangular shape is defined for the top. Then a simple curved shaped void extrusion is used to carve out the blend. The result is an interesting shape that is far more complex than what you'd expect to be able to do with the four basic modeling forms.

FIGURE 7.39

A blend with a void extrusion results in some very interesting forms!

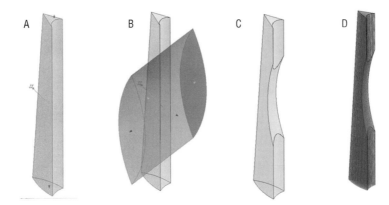

COMPLEX ROOFS

A shape like the one shown in Figure 7.40 could be created using two revolved shapes and then cut off using a void square around the edges.

FIGURE 7.40

Use of a simple void to cut out geometry from a revolved shape

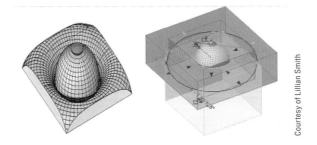

WHERE CAN YOU GO FROM HERE?

Mastering the modeling techniques in Revit and understanding the power of parametric relationships will open the doors to some powerful modeling skills. Even if it seems like science fiction that you can make highly complex forms using Revit, with time, creativity, and practice, you will get there. Here are some examples of highly creative uses of solid and void forms, made with Revit's native form-making tools.

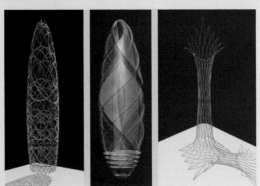

The Bottom Line

Revit provides a set of modeling tools and techniques that enable you to build your model and all the elements that go into the model. Mastering them is what will make the transition to working in 3D BIM easy.

Understand the principles of modeling in Revit   Understanding how to use Revit's modeling tools is an important part of project documentation. Knowing which modeling tools to use when will aid not only in project visualization but also in documentation, scheduling, and rendering.

Master it   There are many unique design elements in any project. Know when to use the appropriate modeling tools at the right times. What tool in Revit might you use to model the following elements?

◆ Reception counter

◆ Entry canopy

◆ Massing study

◆ Custom furnishings

Model with five basic forms   These tools are at the root of practically all form modeling.

Master it   Having learned the basics of Revit's form-making tools, imagine how you would build this faucet designed by Philippe Starck.

Master it   In some cases, a form uses multiple sketch lines to generate its form. What form-making tools in Revit use more than one set of 2D sketches to generate the form?

Combine solids and voids to create complex and intriguing forms   Revit's five basic forms can be expressed as either positive space (solids) or negative space (voids).

Master it   To make more complex forms, both solids and voids can be used. Think of a case where the using voids as a subtractive element makes sense.

Chapter 8

Concept Massing Studies

In this chapter you'll explore the early stages of design and the how to generate the first massing studies used to explore conceptual ideas. We introduce you to the tools in Revit that support workflows related to massing studies and the early conceptual design process, where form is not only explored, but also analyzed. Revit allows you to maintain continuity in design as you move from the massing study into real building elements, making it possible to easily transform massing studies into buildings that can be documented and eventually built. We discuss various approaches for creating massing studies and the underlying principles of creating parametric mass elements using the Family Editor.

In this chapter, you learn how to do the following:

◆ Understand massing workflows

◆ Start a conceptual massing study

◆ Understand how massing can be used downstream as the design progresses

Understanding Massing Workflows

There are many ways to start a new design. It often starts as a napkin sketch that you make while having a conversation with your client in a coffee shop. These first ideas often encapsulate the essence of the design and, unless some unforeseen changes are demanded in the design, are usually easily recognizable in the final building. Many architects are known for the re-markable similarity between the first napkin sketches of their ideas and the final outcomes of the built buildings, as can be seen in drawings by architects such as Frank Gehry, Jorn Utzon, Daniel Libeskind, Frank Lloyd Wright, and countless others. Figure 8.1 shows a hand sketch using very gestural lines, tones, and hatches. The ability to sketch freely and with gestural expression is a fundamental aspect of design iteration and has been part of the architectural profession for centuries.

FIGURE 8.1
An inspiring early
sketch

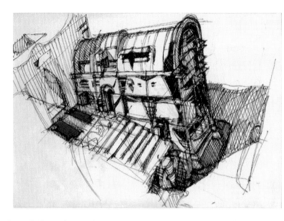

Courtesy of E. Di Giacomo

Architects have long realized that the only way to make an investor buy in to their early ideas and designs is to make those early designs understandable to them. Many investors have difficulty reading technical drawings, so architects use creative methods to communicate the design, the space, and the experience of that space from the early stages of the design on. Perspective drawings, photo collages, and 3D physical models made of wood, Styrofoam, cardboard, balsa, Plexiglas, and metals are all used to help the client, and sometimes the public, understand the implications of a given design.

In more sophisticated building studios, physical models are constructed so that the design can be evaluated by deconstructing the model into parts representing different levels or functional parts of the building. This lets people examine individual stages of construction and integrated systems. Models can range in fidelity from very rough massing studies to highly photorealistic models, as Figure 8.2 demonstrates.

Three-dimensional physical models offer some obvious advantages for conveying design intent:

◆ You get an immediate feel for proportion, scale, and composition.

◆ You can get a sense for the spatial volume.

◆ Light and shadow can be easily simulated (hold a real lamp in your hands and simulate the shadows).

◆ If you model the surrounding site, you can easily understand how your design relates to its context.

Three-dimensional physical models also have some potential disadvantages:

◆ They take a lot of time and patience to create.

◆ They require space for creation as well as storage.

◆ They are created in one scale only.

◆ They can't handle design options easily, and thereby require building multiple models to convey each design option.

◆ They require manual work—both in the physical modeling and in performing calculations of area and space.

◆ They can be costly in terms of skilled personnel, materials, and equipment.

As clients become more demanding, they aren't satisfied with just understanding how the future building will look but also want to know how the building will perform in terms of lifecycle costs. With sustainability now an integral part of any conversation, they also need to understand how sustainable the future building will be. Making a final decision is not always easy, and they ask for the ability to compare and contrast multiple proposed solutions in order to arrive with you at an optimized design solution that meets their taste, fulfills all the program requirements, and is sustainable economically.

To accommodate all that, architects and owners need to analyze the building and experience it in the early stages of design before it's built. Traditional hand-built models don't provide this kind of analytical flexibility. This is where using digital models backed up by real data comes into play. See Figure 8.3.

FIGURE 8.2
Models can range from very rough (A and B) to highly refined representations (C and D).

A

B

C

D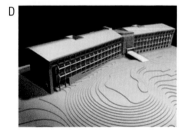

FIGURE 8.3
Early massing
studies

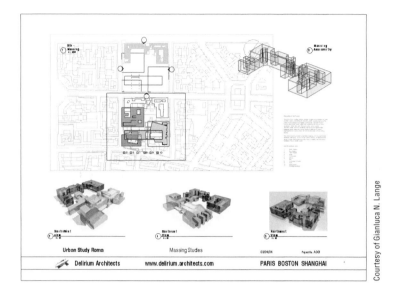

Courtesy of Gianluca N. Lange

Massing Study Workflows

Regardless of how a massing study is done (digitally or in a physical medium), there has always been a break in the workflow between this conceptual design stage and the next phase of more detailed analysis of how the building will behave or will be constructed. In the case of built physical massing models, once they are done, to move to the next stage and start working on criteria design and detail design development you would need to create a digital project from scratch, usually in AutoCAD, without having a way to reuse the information you previously created.

Even when you make a study using digital tools such as Rhinoceros, SketchUp, Form Z, Maya, or 3ds Max, in order to document those studies you still need to start from scratch because these tools are mainly modelers—not architectural documentation tools—and the data created in them is not reusable in any intelligent manner. In these cases, the documentation phase traditionally occurs in the form of 2D drawings produced with tools such as AutoCAD. With the advent of building information modeling, this is all changing; you can now carry a conceptual model through to construction documentation in one environment.

An important aspect of using BIM is the ability to move and reuse previously created data throughout the design process, from start to finish—without having to start over from zero. Revit provides specific tools for keeping the design process integrated. For early conceptual studies, Revit lets you either import geometric massing studies created in other applications or you can create them natively within Revit, using the massing tools. Regardless of how you create the concept massing studies, (either within or outside of Revit), both can later be transformed into Revit building elements such as walls, floors, and roofs. In essence, Revit provides a set of tools for converting an abstract mass form into a full-fledged building model.

With the massing tools, you can create flexible preliminary designs and create massing models out of building blocks long before you make decisions about walls, roofs, and floors. You can create the blocks quickly, run through and visualize alternate configurations, and then, when you're ready, generate a building shell.

 Real World Scenario

COMMON USES FOR THE MASSING TOOLS

Here are some common scenarios where using Revit massing tools makes sense.

SITE STUDIES: USING MASSING TO QUICKLY BUILD THE CONTEXT ENVIRONMENT AROUND THE BUILDING

You can use Revit's massing tools to quickly model the surrounding context of your building to get a feel for how it fits the site. This is a standard practice used to demonstrate how your design relates to its environment. Once you have modeled the environment around your building, you can make walkthroughs around your building and experience it from different points of view. You can also make initial solar studies to better understand how your building affects the environment and how the environment affects your design.

Courtesy of Kubik+Nemeth+Vlkovic

MASSING STUDIES FOR TESTING DIFFERENT DESIGN OPTIONS

You can do a quick conceptual massing study to work out a functional design arrangement, make more options, and look for an optimal solution. For each design, separate masses can be made and given color to indicate their function. This allows you to see spatial relationships in simplified geometric forms but also get precise area and volume values for each mass option you explore.

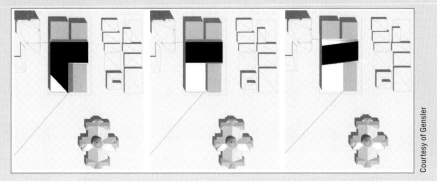

Courtesy of Gensler

FEASIBILITY STUDIES AND PROGRAM VERIFICATION

You can take the massing study a step further and make feasibility studies to explore how to fit the client's program on the site, calculate the floor area ratio (FAR), mass floor area, and volume. With mode information added to the model, you can get better estimates about building cost, energy analysis, and aesthetics.

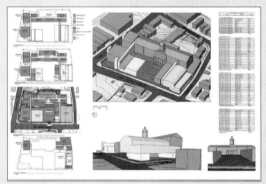

Courtesy of RMJM Hiller

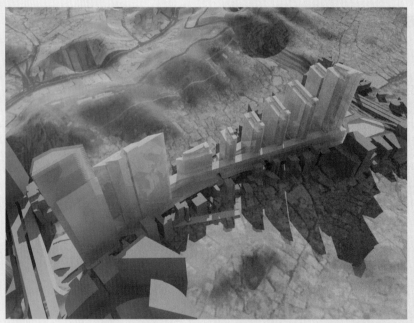

Courtesy of Gensler

Massing Tools

The massing tools are located on the Massing tab of the Design bar (Figure 8.4). If you don't see it, you can activate it by right-clicking anywhere on the Design bar and selecting Massing from the menu. To create, study, analyze, and later convert a massing form into a building, you need to understand the available tools first; then, we'll walk through a real exercise in which you can experience the entire workflow.

FIGURE 8.4
The Massing tab provides tools needed to create a massing study.

The tools for creating masses in Revit are directly connected to the modeling tools and techniques we discussed in Chapters 6 and 7. You'll use the same modeling tools (Solid Extrusion, Solid Blend, Solid Revolve, Solid Sweep, and Solid Swept Blend) as well as the logic of modeling on work planes. The Massing tab is divided into three groups of tools that we refer to as mass-creation tools, Building Maker tools, and view tools.

The first group allows you to make masses from scratch or place massing families.

The second group contains tools to support the concept of *Building Maker*—a term that doesn't exist in the Revit user interface but is commonly adopted among Revit users to describe the process of converting a conceptual mass into a real building. Using the faces of a conceptual mass element, you can attach walls, curtain systems, floors, and roofs to the mass form with a click of the mouse. Throughout this chapter we'll refer to this grouping as Building Maker tools.

The third group contains the standard Section and Level tools; these are the most important additional tools to have at hand during creation of mass studies. They are the same Section and Level tools that you find on the Basic menu or in the views.

Creating a Mass Element

There are two ways to create a mass element in the project environment:

Create Mass tool   This method allows you to create a new mass element.

Place Mass tool   This method allows you to place a massing family or load a mass family from your library.

Before we look in detail at these two methods, you need to understand how massing visibility is handled in Revit, because you'll encounter this issue the moment you start creating masses.

Visibility of Mass Elements

When you try to place mass or create mass for the first time, you may get the following message, which conveys information about the visibility of the mass elements:

This message can be disconcerting at first, so let's understand what is going on. Visibility of mass elements can be controlled either via the toolbar or as a category in the Visibility/Graphic Overrides dialog box. The toolbar control is a global on–off switch for massing that affects all views temporarily. It's located at the top of the screen, near the 3D button:

When you click this button, all masses in all views become visible. This is great for early massing studies, allowing you to move from view to view and see your mass without having to turn the category on or off for each view separately. When this mode is enabled, it *does not* affect the Visibility/Graphics Overrides state of your views—this Massing toggle is a temporary view control and doesn't affect printed output.

To see the mass elements in specific views only, you should use the Visibility/Graphics Overrides settings for view control. Even when the Show Mass button is turned off, if you activate the Mass setting in the Visibility/Graphic Overrides dialog box, it will be visible in that view.

To print and export massing, turn the mass category on using the Visibility/Graphic Overrides dialog box.

As you develop your design further by moving from the conceptual phase into the early design development phase, you will start creating the real building components (walls, floors, and roofs) by adding elements to the mass model. This will slowly but surely obscure the visibility of the massing form. A great way to maintain a view where only massing is visible is to create a 3D view where *all categories are turned off except the Massing category*. To do this, use the Visibility/Graphics Overrides dialog box. Be sure to duplicate a view when doing this, and name the view **Massing** or something appropriate. Figure 8.5 shows two views: one with only the massing category visible and the other with all categories visible. This is handy when you want to make adjustments to the basic shapes that define the geometry (masses) without being distracted by the presence of the building elements. When you change the underlying mass, the architectural elements created from it follow the change automatically. You'll learn more about this workflow in Chapter 9.

FIGURE 8.5
The same view
with different
visibility states for
massing and model
elements

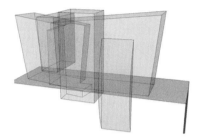 

View with only the massing category visible   View with all categories visible

Starting a Conceptual Massing Study

You can create massing forms using Revit's 3D modeling tools. Use these tools to quickly generate site plans and initial building shapes in the early phase of design development.

Creating a Mass

When you select Create Mass from the Massing tab in the Design bar, you're first prompted to name the mass you're about to create. Once you provide a name, the interface transforms and you will find yourself in a mass-creation mode, with a new set of tools on the Design bar (Figure 8.6). Using these tools, you proceed to create the massing form using combinations of solid and void forms.

FIGURE 8.6
The Design bar for
massing creation

This creation mode is similar to that of the Family Editor, where a select set of tools are presented that are relevant to the creation of parametric forms. You'll also notice some overlap with the Create tool in the Modeling tab of the Design bar. The underlying principles in all these environments (Family Editor, in-place Family Editor, and Massing Editor) are the same.

Most tools on this Design bar should be familiar. The only unique feature is the Place Mass tool. When selected, this tool does the same thing as the Place Mass tool on the main Massing tab of the Design bar: it lets you place a mass family. This is a component-placement tool that only places premade components (families) of the mass category.

When you're in mass-edit mode, you can create and edit mass elements that are represented by a single shape or by a combination of solids and voids. Everything you add during the same mass editing session creates one single mass element. You can place as many different solids or voids in this mode as you require. Your decision to make each shape a separate mass element will depend on what you need it to represent and how you intend to interact with it. For example, one mass element could have five extrusions representing five buildings. Or, you could make five separate mass elements for each building. Do you want to move each building independently? Or will you likely want to move all the buildings together, as one element? Let these kind of questions guide your decision-making process.

When you've finished modeling the mass sketch, click Finish Sketch, and when you've finished modeling the entire mass, click Finish Mass. Don't forget to always look at the Design Bar and finish the elements. Otherwise you will be wondering why the interface is all washed out and what you should do. After clicking Finish Mass, everything you modeled becomes one mass element. To edit a mass, select it and click the Edit button on the Options bar.

A mass element must have solid geometry in it—it can't be made of voids alone. If you try to make a void massing, you'll get a warning message like the one shown in Figure 8.7.

FIGURE 8.7
Error message for a mass without solids

It's possible to get the same message even if you do have a solid but the void isn't cutting through the solid.

For example, if you draw a solid first and then a void, the message won't appear. If you do the opposite and add the void before the solid, you'll get this error message. To solve this problem, you need to use the Cut Geometry tool to make the solids and voids intersect. Only by using the Cut Geometry tool will this message be cleared so you can finish the mass. Figures 8.8 and 8.9 show this.

FIGURE 8.8
If you draw a void before you add a solid, they won't intersect or have any relationship— the mass can't be completed in this case.

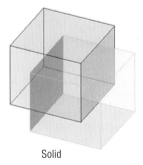

Solid   Void

FIGURE 8.9
Adding a void after placing a solid cuts it from the solid. The mass can then be completed.

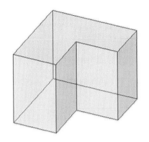

The Cut and Join Geometry tools are both available on the toolbar when massing forms are selected. These tools are important when you're dealing with massing, so let's look more closely at them:

Cut Geometry   This tool cuts voids out of solids. You select the tool, select a void, and then select what you want the void to cut. Voids can cut multiple solids.

Join Geometry   This tool joins solids (voids can't be joined together) to form one connected element. It merges the shapes (masses) into one, both graphically and as data (Figure 8.10). To use this tool, select the tool, and then select solids you want to join. Multiple solids can be joined together.

FIGURE 8.10
Joining two masses together creates a single, seamless element.

If you change the position of one of the joined masses, the intersection (called the *joining*) instantly updates. However, if you move one of the joined masses outside the boundaries of the other joined masses so they don't intersect any more, you'll get a warning message. To resolve the problem, you can use the Unjoin Geometry command. Note that even if the mass elements are joined, selecting the mass results in the selection of just one of them (Figure 8.11).

FIGURE 8.11
Joined masses can
still be selected
and edited
independently.

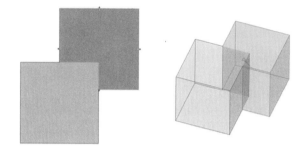

Placing a Mass Family

The other way to create a mass is to load it from the library. You do so with the Place Mass tool, which gives you access to the predefined massing families that represent basic geometric 3D shapes. You can load these from the library into your project while working on the project or you can preload them in your office template if this is something that you do often. You then use those primitive shapes and start stacking them together to build the shape that you need (Figure 8.12). In practice, these predefined parametric mass families are great for building the context around your building in order to quickly create a sense of the environment in which your project will be situated.

FIGURE 8.12
Mass families that
ship with Revit

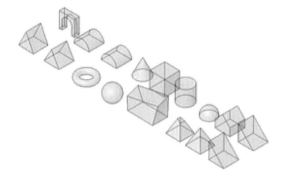

The difference between predefined loaded mass elements (Place Mass) and those created in place (Create Mass) is that you get different levels of interactivity with the produced masses. For example, a mass created in-place lets you edit its base sketch directly, whereas a family-based mass requires you to edit the family and then reload it if you want to change its sketch. You also get different grip controls when you select each type of massing form. If you select an in-place mass in a 3D view, you get drag controls that allow for dynamic manipulation. However, with a loaded mass family you don't get the same grip controls.

Figure 8.13 shows two boxes of the same size: one created in the project using the Create Mass tool and the other placed in the projects using the Place Mass option.

FIGURE 8.13

Loaded massing
family on the left,
and mass built in
the project on the
right

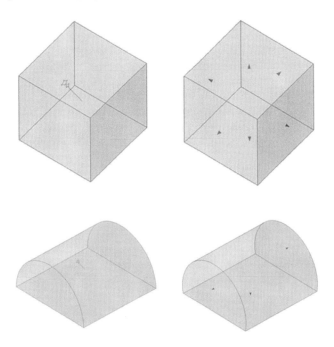

By default, when you're loading a mass element for the first time, you may get the following message:

The message tells you that there is no host on which to place the massing based on the current placement mode. Host-based placement doesn't let you place an element floating freely in space.

To better understand this, look at the Options bar. You'll see two placement modes for massing: Place on Face and Place on Work Plane.

By default, this is set to Place on Face; if you try to drag and drop an element from the type list onto the workspace, your cursor looks like a crossed circle if it doesn't find any geometric face to be a placed on, and you will not be able to place the mass. To be able to place the mass, switch out of this mode, and change from Place on Face to Place on Work Plane to place masses freely. From then on, your mass elements will be placed on the current level or whatever the current work plane of the view is set. Once you select the Place on Work Plane option, you will see the Place selection list in the Options bar (see Figure 8.14).

FIGURE 8.14

Work plane choices
in the Options bar

Here you can select a level that represents the plane where you will place the mass, or you can use the Pick option to select a face of an element, a level, or a workplane to set a new plane for placing the mass.

The Place by Face option is usually used when you need to continue placement or creation of a mass on the face of another element. We covered this when discussing modeling techniques in Chapters 6 and 7.

One more option you should be aware of on the Option bar is Rotate After Placement. When this option is deselected, you need just one click to place a mass element. The click is the center of the mass element, which is placed at 0 degrees. When the option is selected, you need two clicks to place the mass element: the first click positions the center; the second defines the rotation angle.

In a new Revit session, try the Place Mass function. In the Revit templates, no mass element is preloaded, so you're prompted to load one. If you confirm by clicking Yes, the Family Library opens so you can load masses from the Mass folder. The choices include arch, gable, box, sphere, pyramid, and other predefined shapes. You can load more than one at the same time with Shift-click or Ctrl-click. When you load a mass, don't expect it to immediately be dropped in the drawing area: loading it just adds it to the project. To place it, you must select it from the Type Selector or the Mass folder in the Family Tree of the Project Browser, select the Place on Work Plane option and place it in the view.

Creating a New Mass Family

You can create your own mass families in the Family Editor and load them later in any project. To create a mass family, you use a special family template called `Mass.rft`. If the shapes shown in Figure 8.12 don't represent what you need, and you wish to create your own custom shapes that you'll use in more than one project, you can start a new family using `Mass.rft` and create your own parametric mass. Later in this chapter, we'll guide you through the creation of a parametric mass family in the Family Editor.

If you haven't been modeling much yet in Revit, you can learn a lot by editing one of these families. Load it in a project, select it, and click Edit Family in the Options bar. The family will open in the Family Editor. Look at how the mass element was created.

When you're modeling a mass, it is nothing more than a static 3D object. To make that mass parametric, you need to add labeled dimensions to it. That way, the mass will not just represent one shape and size but will have the ability to be several predefined sizes. Of course, once an element has parametric dimensions, you're free to make as many variations of that shape as necessary.

For example, if you open the Cylinder mass family from the library, you'll find that it has two parameters related to its size: Radius and Height. Defining parameters lets you predefine types (size combinations) that can be changed in the project environment. In the Family Editor, we made the Radius and Height dimensions into labeled dimensions, and thus they became parametric constraints (see Figure 8.15).

The mass elements shown in Figure 8.12 are all simple, created from simple solids or combinations of solids and voids. You can create more complex mass elements by *nesting* one mass within another mass family. Nesting means you're loading one mass family into another mass family to create a more complex assembly.

CREATING A PYRAMID MASS FORM

The Pyramid mass family (in the mass family folder) is an example that shows how to create a special mass element shape by combining solids and voids. When you edit this family, you'll notice that it was created with the following elements: a solid box was created as a simple extrusion, and two void extrusions were added to remove geometry from the box and create the pyramid shape.

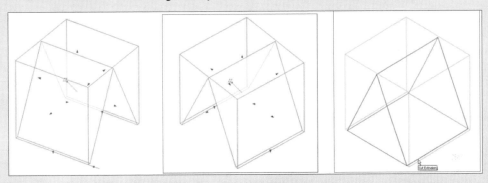

Reverse engineering is a good method to learn how more complex shapes have been done. If you are intrigued by models created by other users and shared on public forums, download them and look at how they were created.

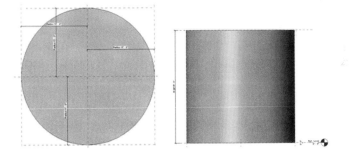

FIGURE 8.15
A cylinder mass element with two main parameters: Radius and Height

Putting Theory into Practice: Making a Parametric Mass Family

In the following exercise we'll guide you through the creation of a simple parametric mass family so that you understand some of the principles of creating a mass in the Family Editor. (In the next chapter, we'll explore creation of a mass model within the project.)

The result will be the mass shape shown in Figure 8.16, which is parametrically adjustable in several dimensions.

FIGURE 8.16

The parametric
mass family you'll
create in this
exercise

First, when you're creating a new family, it's essential to select the correct family template. In this case, you wish to create a new mass family, so you need to select Mass.rft or Metric Mass.rft. Follow these steps:

1. Choose File ➤ New ➤ Family. In the New dialog box, select the template Mass.rft or Metric Mass.rft and click the Open button.

   The Family Editor opens, and the drawing area shows the plan view. There are two pre-defined reference planes: the vertical one is called Center (Left/Right), and the horizontal one is called Center (Front/Back). The intersection of these two planes defines the insertion point of the family when you later place it in the project. You want to create a parametric family, not just a static mass, and thus you need to create reference planes to which you can constrain dimensional parameters that will allow you to change the size of the family by changing properties.

2. Using the Reference Plane tool from the Design bar, add four more reference planes in the plan view:

   These will be used to control the size of the mass in plan.

3. Open the front elevation and add two additional horizontal reference planes. These will be used to control the height of the mass:

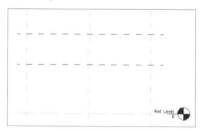

4. Place dimensions between the reference planes in plan and elevation. You'll eventually convert these dimensions to labels that represent the future parameters to be tweaked;

you'll do that by selecting the dimensions and clicking the Label button on the Options bar. For now, let's keep adding dimensions.

5. Select the reference plane you created in elevation and that is coincident with the level. It isn't easy to see it (it can be completely covered by the level geometry), so use the Tab key and verify in the tooltip or in the command line that you have selected the reference plane and not the level (using the level can create potential problems). Click Properties on the Options bar, and change the value of the Is Reference parameter from Not Reference to Weak Reference. This makes the bottom of the massing form display blue grip controls when selected.

6. Look at the reference planes that define the center axis, because they need to remain centered relative to the other reference planes. You'll set an equality (EQ) dimension constraint between these three reference planes to keep the design symmetrically balanced.

   Select the two Reference Planes that define the axis, and set their Is Reference parameter to Not Reference.

7. Open the plan view Ref. Level. On the Design bar, click Dimension.

   Click each reference plane to create the dimensions between them, and then click the EQ symbol:

   Repeat the same action in the other direction:

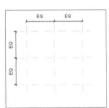

Dimension

With these steps, you've ensured that the axes in both the X and Y directions will always be in the middle of the element. You now need to create the parameters that will control the size of the mass element: D for depth and W for width.

8. Still in plan view, select the Dimension tool, and place a dimension between the two outer reference planes. Don't worry about the value of the dimension:

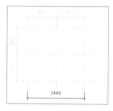

9. On the Design bar, click Modify, and select the dimension you just created. On the Options bar, click the drop-down list next to the label, and select Add Parameter.

10. In the Parameter Properties dialog box (Figure 8.17), enter **W** for Name. In the list for Group Parameter Under, select Dimensions, and select the Instance radio button. Click OK to confirm your selections.

FIGURE 8.17
Defining the width
parameter

Following the same principle, create a dimension in the other direction and name it **D** for depth:

Note that from now on the value in the dimension text has the prefix D or W.

11. Open the front elevation view, and add a dimension between the reference plane that is coincident with the level (again, make sure that you select the bottom reference plane and *not* the level line) and the first horizontal reference plane above:

Add another dimension between the other two horizontal reference planes:

Following the principle previously described for labeling these, name them **H1** and **H2**:

12. You've created the framework that will drive the geometry, so all that is left to do is to make the geometry. But before that, you need to test the parameters you just created—what is called *flexing* the model:

On the Design bar, click the Family Types button. In the Family Types dialog box (Figure 8.18), select the parameters you just created and modify the values. Click the Apply button to see the effects in the view (the reference planes move as you change values).

FIGURE 8.18

The Family Types dialog box

Make sure you change the parameters one by one; if you get an error message, and you've changed many values at the same time, you won't know which one is the problem. If you try changing all the values and don't get any error messages, you have done well and are ready to create the geometry.

13. Open the plan Ref. Plane and, on the Design bar, select Solid and then Solid Extrusion.

You're placed into Sketch mode, and the Design bar changes to show only tools relevant to the extrusion sketch mode. On the Options bar, select the Rectangle shape:

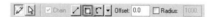

Click the intersection of the left and bottom reference planes to define the start point of the rectangle:

Click the intersection of the top and right reference planes to define the diagonal finish point of the rectangle:

Click the four padlocks that appear automatically; by doing so, you create constraints between the lines of the sketch and the reference planes on which they're drawn. This means that later—when you move the position of the reference planes by changing the values in the Family Types—the sketch lines of the geometry will follow the change parametrically.

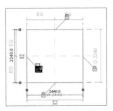

In the Design bar, click Finish Sketch.

14. Open the front elevation, and select the solid you just created. Click the blue arrow on the top of the solid, and move it up to the upper reference plane. It should snap to it.

When the geometry coincides with the reference plane, a padlock icon appears, allowing you to constrain the relationship. Click the padlock. You've now defined the relationship between the top of the solid and the reference plane, so that if you change the reference plane position (the value of the parameter) again, the top of the solid will move with it.

15. Using the Family Type option from the Design bar, start changing the H1 and H2 parameters, and see what happens. While working with the family parameters, you can also change (flex) the values for W and D to verify how they affect the geometry. Note that to review the correct functioning of the parameters while flexing them, it's best to be in 3D view.

16. Now add a void to the solid. For that purpose, you'll use the Sweep tool. Start by adding a new reference plane that will control the position of the new shape in plan view.

Open the plan view Ref. Level, and add a reference plane:

17. Add a dimension between this new reference plane and the one that defines the axis front-to-back, and transform this new dimension into a label as previously described. Name the new label **O** (for offset).

18. Open a 3D view. On the Design bar, click Void Form ➤ Void Sweep.

19. Click the Pick Path tool. This time, instead of sketching the path, use existing geometry for the path you want to define.

Click the solid's four top edges. For this exercise, make sure you first select the edge that is in the front. On that first edge, a cross appears, with a red spot in its center. This represents the work plane of the profile sketch. You can sketch the shape of your profile directly in 3D, but it's easier to draw the shape in the same plane as the profile work plane—especially when dimensions are important. Switch to a view that is parallel to the sketch's work plane—in this case, the left or right elevation.

On the Design bar, click Finish Path.

20. On the Options bar, select Sketch Profile. Open the right elevation. On the Design bar, click the Line tool, and then trace three sketch lines:

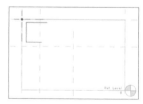

21. Click the Align tool, select the vertical reference plane, and then select the vertical line of the newly created sketch. By doing so, you align the sketch line to the reference plane. To establish the relationship, click the padlock icon.

LOCKING A LINE ALREADY PLACED

If you ever forget to click the lock, and the next time you want to do so the lock doesn't appear, click the sketch line, move it to the left or right, and reposition over the reference plane—the lock will appear again, and you can lock it.

---

22. Still using the Align tool, click the top horizontal reference plane and then the top horizontal line of the sketch, and again lock the padlock.

23. Click the horizontal reference plane just below the lower horizontal sketch line and then click that horizontal sketch line to align. Again, lock the padlock:

24. You have one more task, and it's more delicate. Zoom in closer in the lower-right corner of the sketch and the vertical reference plane.

Still using the Align tool, click the vertical reference plane (the second from the left, if you're in the right elevation), and then place your cursor next to the free end of the horizontal sketch line. A little square appears at the end of the sketch line, which fades slightly. (If this doesn't happen, try moving the cursor. Help yourself with the Tab key.) Once you see the small square at the end of the sketch line, click it to define the alignment to the vertical reference plane:

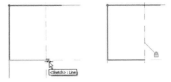

25. On the Design bar, click the Line tool, and draw the last line segment to close the sketch:

26. Click Dimension on the Design bar, and select Angular from the Options bar:

27. Add an angular dimension between the diagonal sketch line and the vertical reference. Create a label out of that dimension, and name it **A** (for angle):

28. On the Design bar, click Finish Sketch and then Finish Extrusion. Don't forget to finish both of these; otherwise, your drawing will look grayed out, indicating that you are still in Sketch mode. Go to 3D view to see the result:

Congratulations! You just created your first fully parametric mass family! Save it as **My First Mass** somewhere where you can find it again. You can open a new project and load this newly created mass. In the project environment, start to flex the parameters and see how they affect the shape of the mass. If you already have a project file open and want to quickly load the family into it, press the Load into Projects button. This will load the family into your active project, and you won't have to go hunting around your network for the file.

Also note that when you import the mass element in the project and select it, small blue controls appear on the edges of the solid. Using them, you can change the size of the mass element on the fly:

To change the angle of the shape you carved out with the void, change the angle in the parameters and see how it affects the look of your mass. The value of the angle can be positive or negative, allowing you to create variations in shape like those shown in Figure 8.15 at the beginning of this exercise.

Tagging and Scheduling Mass

The value of doing early massing studies in Revit is that they all contain information about the spaces you're designing. You can quickly tag the masses, visually categorize them, or schedule them to get feedback about the area and volume the building will occupy.

THE MASS TAG

The mass tag is Revit's tag for mass elements. By default this type of tag is not loaded in Revit. When you decide to tag the mass families and select Tag ➤ By Category from the Drafting tab on the Design bar, you get a message that a mass tag has not yet been loaded and that you can load such a tag from the library. If you confirm with Yes, the library folders open and you will find the Mass tag family under the Annotations folder. The default mass tag extracts the gross floor area of each mass, but you can add any other instance property to be extracted by the tag or any shared parameters you may need in the process of a feasibility study for stacking and blocking diagrams (see Chapter 19 for more on tagging). Note that the default mass tag only displays the floor area value if you have applied the Mass Floors option (available in the Options bar when you select a mass) to a mass. If you haven't, the tag displays a question mark. We'll explore this workflow in more detail in the next chapter. There is no special `Mass tag.rft` template file. To create a new mass tag to match your graphic needs, you can either duplicate the existing one or start with a generic tag template.

PROJECT PARAMETERS AND SCHEDULING MASSING

To create schedules that can give you information about various functional groups to which mass elements belong, the departments they represent, or the space IDs, you can use project parameters. You can create project parameters for program group, department, or space ID; assign these to your masses; and then schedule them to analyze and track how your model fits the program.

To add a project parameter, choose Settings ➤ Project Parameters. Choose to add a new parameter, and then select Mass as the parameter's category. Once you do this, the parameter shows up in all mass instances, and you can assign values for this parameter in each of the mass instances. Should you also want to tag the properties in question (Program Group, Department, and so on), you'll need to create shared parameters instead. You'll learn more about shared parameters in Chapter 19.

Importing 3D Conceptual Models Created in Other Applications

You can import geometry from conceptual modeling applications (3D models, created in AutoCAD, SketchUp, Rhinoceros, Maya and 3ds Max, among others) into a mass instance or mass family in the same way you import geometry into other families. You may want to do this in several scenarios:

- You have users who are comfortable with 3D modeling tools like those listed. They prefer to do the massing there and then use Revit's conceptual analysis capabilities as well as Building Maker to turn the mass into a building.

- There are shapes and NURBS forms that Revit doesn't do easily (or at all), so you need to create the shape in another application. You need not import a whole building shape, as shown in Figure 8.19—it may be just a face of a shape that you'll need later to design a specific portion of a complex-shaped building, such as its roof.

FIGURE 8.19
NURBS shape created in Rhinoceros is converted to a real wall using the Wall by Face functionality of the Building Maker.

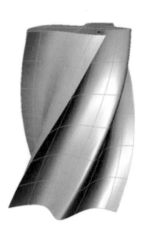
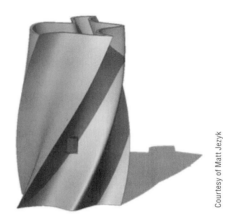

You can import individual masses (a complex shape, for example) or a fully developed massing study model. Regardless of what the import represents, the strategy is to never import it directly into the project file but to go through a family import:

◆ If the geometry is an individual element that you're likely to reuse, open the Family Editor by opening a mass template, and create a new mass by importing the geometry.

◆ If you have a full study model, it's advisable to import it as an in-place mass family in the project (use the Create Mass tool and then File ➢ Import CAD Formats to import the 3D geometry created elsewhere).

We'll talk more in Chapter 9 about how the behavior of the imported items depends on how they're imported, whether directly into the project, in a massing family in the Family Editor, or in an in-place mass family.

Rapid Prototyping and 3D Printing

Three-dimensional digital massing studies allow architects to use advanced technologies and make physical prototypes for demonstration or testing purposes using the 3D printing services that are becoming more affordable. For many architects as well as investors, a physical model is still something they like to have in order to study the design.

Rapid prototyping is the automatic construction of physical objects using solid freeform fabrication. The first techniques for rapid prototyping became available in the 1980s and were used to produce models and prototype parts. Thanks to advances in technology, and the increasing affordability of 3D printing, professionals in many fields now rely on rapid prototyping—architects to create models, industrial designers to make first-draft prototypes, and even artists to sculpt complex shapes for fine arts. The process of rapid prototyping takes virtual designs from a digital model, transforms them into virtual cross sections, and creates each cross section in physical space one after the next until the model is finished. This is often done by layering liquid and powdered material for each section and using glue or a laser; the material is fused together as shown in Figure 8.20.

FIGURE 8.20
3D physical models can be printed directly from a digital model.

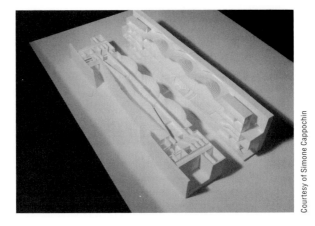

Courtesy of Simone Cappochin

The most common file format for sending this data is .stl. The .stl export is not natively built in Revit—you can find a prototype for an .stl exporter for Revit on the Autodesk Labs site, http://labs.autodesk.com/utilities/revit_stl/.

Figure 8.21 shows a rapid prototype model of an un-built Louis Kahn building.

FIGURE 8.21
Hidden-line view, shaded view, sectional 3D view, and a rapid prototype physical model from the same Revit model

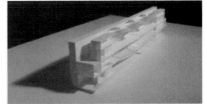

Courtesy of Simone Cappochin

The Bottom Line

Projects begin with broad, gestural strokes that are eventually refined with more detail. The ability to quickly generate conceptual 3D massing form aids in the development of a project.

With Revit, you can make parametric abstract mass forms and use those forms downstream in your process as the design progresses.

Understand massing workflows   Using generic forms, you can create early conceptual models and then use the mass to create the walls, floors, and roofs.

Master It   You need to explore a design idea early on, in 3D, using abstract forms. How would you do this with Revit?

Start a conceptual massing study   In the project environment, you can make massing forms at any time. For generic forms that might appear in multiple projects, consider using the Family Editor and create mass families.

Master It   You've imported a 2D site plan, and now you need to start building a massing study model in the project. How would you approach this with Revit?

Understand how massing can be used downstream as the design progresses   Creating a mass is one thing, but leveraging that mass for conceptual analysis and quantity take-offs can further aid and inform the design process.

Master It   Once you've settled on a basic massing study, what information can you derive from it? How can this be represented?

Chapter 9

From Conceptual Mass to a Real Building

In this chapter, we describe the use of an early conceptual mass model to help you understand program fit and the creation of early feasibility studies. You'll see how easy it is to convert a massing study—whether done within Revit or imported from another application—into building elements such as walls, floors, and roofs. The premise of a BIM approach to design is that a fluid workflow can be maintained as you move from early concept models into design development and eventual construction documentation, all the while maintaining the same underlying geometry and design intent. Revit provides specific tools that accommodate early massing model studies for program validation and feasibility studies, which can then be quickly converted to real building elements.

In this chapter, you learn how to do the following:

◆ Make conceptual designs and early studies in Revit

◆ Build a real building out of a 3D concept mass

◆ Use imported geometry from other applications for massing

◆ Use smart relationships between building mass and the underlying mass

Understanding Conceptual Design and Early Studies

A project usually starts with a rough conceptualization of first ideas in which the architect's mind wanders between the creativity of fantasy and the reality of customer needs, merged with the influence of the context, the genius loci.

Conceptual designs are the first graphical words an architect exchanges with a client to get approval for the architect's first thoughts and sense the client's taste. When the initial idea is approved, the architect continues in the next stage of development of her design and makes more detailed studies supported by concrete measurements and numbers that prove the applicability of the design and its feasibility.

We'll review how this process of initial conceptualization and form finding can be done using Revit. Figure 9.1 shows an example of an early massing study made in Revit. Let's walk through how this workflow is supported.

FIGURE 9.1
Massing
study model

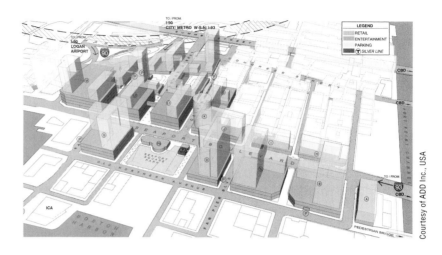

Courtesy of ADD Inc., USA

Getting Site Data and Building the Context

A project usually starts with a client's wish, vision, and expectations that are described in initial conversations with the architect. A list of program requirements is compiled, listing the types of spaces the building will have and its rough area. The architect then starts gathering information and data about the site—aerial photos, photos of the site and context, site-survey files with land information, and building footprints and blocks. Using site analysis, program requirements, and creativity, the architect proceeds to study what shape and size building fits best. Variations of the design are studied, analyzed, critiqued, and presented to the client.

Getting site data into the digital model is the first step in moving from loose napkin sketches to a real project. By importing DWG or DGN site information into Revit or using a CSV points files, you'll have a real-world underlay from which to work. (For small projects, this can also be a scanned image of a hand-drawn site situation.)

CAD drawings with site information usually come with a rich amount of information that needs to be culled. Using the Visibility/Graphic Overrides dialog box, after having imported the DWG or DGN file you can hide unnecessary layers to make the drawings more legible. Setting the correct scale and orientation of the site relative to the building will be the most critical initial steps, and they should be carefully considered during the import.

SCALE

In the Import dialog box, setting the Import units to Automatic usually works well if the CAD file was drawn correctly, that is, at 1:1 scale. If the drawing was scaled, you may find that the scale of the imported file is incorrect. If this is the case, you can rescale the image using the Element Properties dialog box.

ORIENTATION

The next step is to deal with the orientation of the imported site plan. Maps are usually created so that north is always at the top, and that is how site information should be displayed in final documents. However, when you're working on developing a site plan, you'll probably prefer to work in a way that is most comfortable for you, in a way that the site is oriented parallel to your computer screen (meaning you don't have work under some strange angles)—not to true north.

 Real World Scenario

ORIENTING A SITE PLAN TO FIT YOUR SCREEN

Suppose you're starting your design study and you open a site plan view to import the CAD file with the site. An imported CAD drawing usually comes in its original coordinates' orientation, with north and south in the vertical axis:

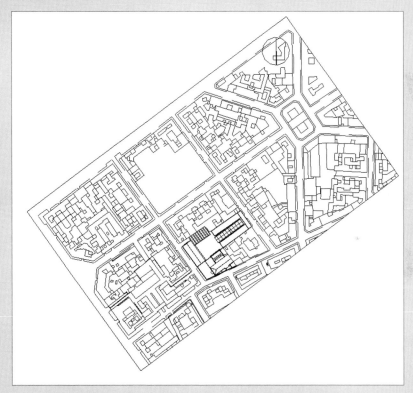

If you open the view's properties, you'll notice that the Orientation parameter indicates Project North:

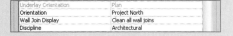

Underlay Orientation	Plan
Orientation	Project North
Wall Join Display	Clean all wall joins
Discipline	Architectural

By default, the orientation of a view is set to Project North. By changing the Orientation parameter to True North and rotating the True North setting, you can work in a comfortably oriented plan relative to your screen.

In the View Properties dialog box, change Orientation to True North, and rotate true north using Tools ➢ Project Position/Orientation ➢ Rotate True North. A rotation control appears in the view. Rotate to an angle best suited to work on. Note that this does not mean you've rotated the project but rather the world.

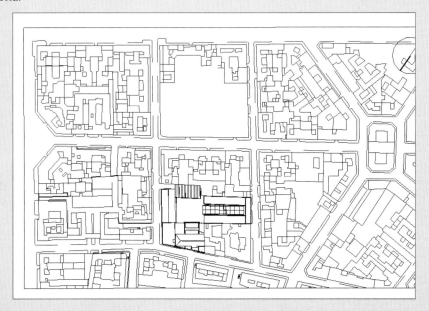

This procedure is more than enough if you don't intend to send information back to the person you received the file from. However, if you're collaborating with a civil engineer and need to send back the building footprint or an early mass study, you need to establish a connection between the two files so they have the same coordinates. This can be achieved using Linking (an option during the Import) as well as the Acquire Coordinates functionality.

Positioning Imported Files Relative to the Revit Project

You can choose an automated or manual placement of the imported file in your Revit project. With Automatically Place (under the Positioning drop-down in the Import dialog box) you have the following options:

Auto - Center to center aligns the 3D center points of both models.

Auto - Origin to origin places the world origin of the linked file at the Revit model's origin point. If the linked model was created far from the origin point, linking with this option may put the linked file far away from the main model.

Auto - By shared coordinates places a linked Revit file according to the shared coordinate system created between the two files (this is available only if you're linking files). If no shared coordinate exist between the two files, Revit alerts you and uses the Auto-Center to Center positioning. The Shared Coordinates settings can be found in the Tools drop-down menu; you have the following options:

Acquire Coordinates allows you to take the coordinates of the linked file into the host model. There is no change to the host model's internal coordinates; however, the host model acquires the true north of the linked model and its Origin setting.

Publish Coordinates allows you to publish the Origin and True North settings to your linked model. Revit understands that there may be other things in your linked file and you may not want this to be a global change to the linked file. An additional dialog box appears that gives you the option to name separate locations for each set of coordinates.

Specify Coordinates at a Point allows you to manually key in X, Y, and Z coordinates relative to the origin or define where you want your (0,0,0) point to be.

Report Shared Coordinates shows the E/W (east–west) (x), N/S (north–south) (y), and elevation (z) coordinates of any point in the model.

Manual - Origin The imported document's origin is centered on the cursor.

Manual -Base point The imported document's base point is centered on the cursor. Use this option only for AutoCAD 2009 files that have a defined base point.

Manual - Center Sets the cursor at the center of the imported geometry. You can drag the imported geometry to its location.

You can import a CAD file so that it appears in all views of your project, or you can import it so that it is visible only in the current view in which you are importing it. You will find these options at the left side of the dialog box.

Remember that for topography files, as an exception to the rule, you should *not* select the Current View Only option because you will not be able to convert the imported file into topography. This might be slightly counterintuitive because this is exactly a case where you would logically import it only in site view as you don't need the topography in any other view (and thus the Current View Only option would have rather been the logical way to proceed). However, because of some settings concerning the site in Revit, you will need to remember this exception. In any other case, if you need to see an imported file just in one view, select the Current View Only option.

If you forget this rule during the import and import the site plan using the Current View Only option, we advise that you delete the import and re-import the file, making sure that the Current View option is *not* checked. As you will probably not want the site file to be visible in all other views, you can turn its visibility off in the other views later.

Building the 3D Context

After positioning the imported CAD file in your site plan and reorienting it to true north, you can start building a 3D environment using the massing tools. The base shapes of buildings in the CAD file can be used to quickly generate a massing model of the surrounding site. Use photos or actual data to establish building heights.

To make a 3D study of the surrounding site, use the Create Mass features and begin developing solids out of the existing geometry:

1. From the Massing tab in the Design bar, select Create Mass. Give the mass a name, such as **context buildings**.

2. Select the Solid Form – Solid Extrusion, and switch from the default Draw mode (the pencil symbol) to the Pick Lines mode using the Options bar. Select lines from the imported file and use them as a base sketch for the 3D masses you wish to create to generate the surrounding in 3D.

3. In the Depth field in the Options bar, change the height of each mass to match the real-world conditions.

4. Still in editing mode, open the Extrusion properties and give each mass that you created a material that suits your graphic needs. A neutral gray or white is common. Figures 9.2 to 9.5 show the use of massing to create abstract forms that represent the context.

FIGURE 9.2
Massing used to add surrounding context buildings

Courtesy of Kubik+Nemeth+Vlkovic

FIGURE 9.3
Massing used for abstract contextual representation

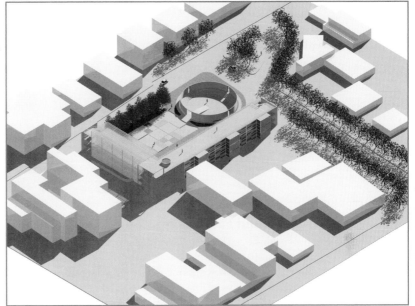

FIGURE 9.4
Massing used to model existing buildings on site

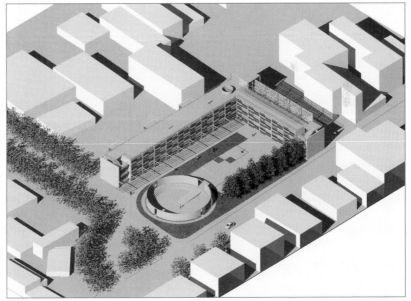

FIGURE 9.5
Massing used
to create an initial
conceptual form

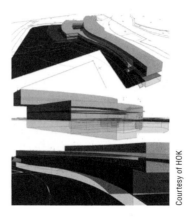

Courtesy of HOK

Program Check and Feasibility

Many of the activities in early design revolve around exploring the commercial viability of the site and figuring out the right mix of uses (for example, residential versus office versus retail). All these uses have different economic returns. Zoning regulations can be complicated in how they allow different amounts of total development based on the mix ratio. In essence, two numbers govern almost all urban properties: floor area ratio (FAR) and lot coverage ratio (LCR). FAR is a number that says how many multiples of the site area the building area can be. LCR specifies the percentage area of the site that can be covered by the building footprint. Usually the architect is required to maximize the FAR by determining the right mix of uses placed at the right location on the site.

At this stage, the problem is not only about forms or shapes but about the program, construction costs, and rents and the functional distribution on the site horizontally and vertically. The architect usually attempts to determine what physical forms, in what location, and with what use will provide the best economic return to the owner. This study then needs to be consolidated and documented. While studying this problem, the architect may generate tens if not hundreds of slightly different alternatives for numerical comparative purposes. A few of the most promising are then developed further for client and authority presentation purposes.

At early stages in design, you need to check the program and how well your proposed design fits into it. Programs can be less or more precise, depending on the client and the task in question. It can be as bold as 15,000 sq. ft. (4,570 sq. meters) offices, 40,000 sq. ft. (12,200 sq. meters) hotel space, and 20,000 sq. ft. (6,100 sq. meters) retail space for a bigger complex, or it can be an exact number of rooms and spaces when working on one building. Figure 9.6 shows an early massing study annotated to show usage and areas.

Architects are constantly thinking about architectural expression, fitting in the site, and accommodating the program. They're also evaluating whether the client's requirements can fit the allowed buildable area and height of the site, zoning regulations, land uses, traffic requirements (they usually always want more), and information about the number of parking spaces and other support functionalities. This phase of the project can also involve shadow studies and energy modeling, as discussed in Chapter 18.

The next step is to propose multiple solutions to the client, so proposals with different mixes of functions and spatial solutions can be reviewed and analyzed. This is where the Design Options tools you'll learn about in Chapter 10 come in handy.

FIGURE 9.6
Early study
documenting
maximum allowed
heights and total
square footage of a
proposed solution

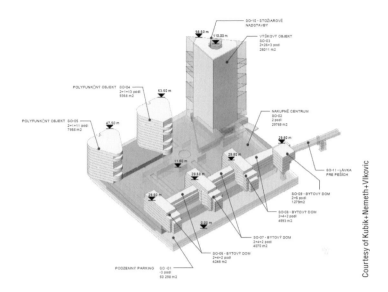

CREATING MULTIPLE MASSING STUDY DESIGN OPTIONS

Here is a suggested workflow based on a real-world use case.

The architectural firm Gensler created an option set with three options, each with a distinct name. They duplicated the 3D views, made three different variations of the design and schedules to document project information of the three design options early on. In each view, the Visibility/Graphic Overrides were set to display only one option at the time (one set to Option 1, another to Option 2, and the third to Option 3). Doing so not only visually described the new option but also presented the data behind each design.

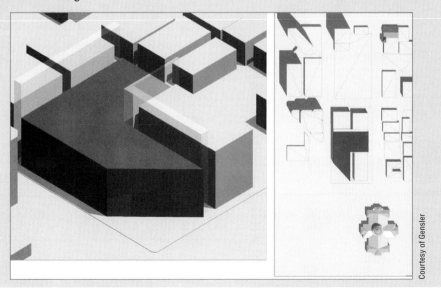

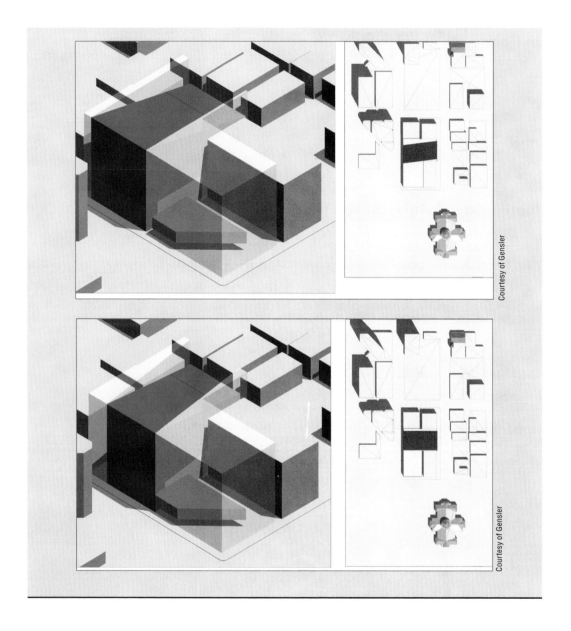

Courtesy of Gensler

Courtesy of Gensler

Building Maker

After several iterations and tweaking, the client makes up their mind. One of the solutions is selected, and you're ready to convert that early massing study into a real building project. Here is where the Building Maker tools come into play. With these tools, you can convert the mass into a building and move to the next stage of design attaching walls, floors, and roofs to the massing shapes.

This approach has two major advantages over traditional 3D systems:

◆ The need to re-create the digital data from scratch is eliminated. Instead of building a new project with walls, floors etc. you simply use the created mass as a reference.

◆ A connection between the building elements made by referencing the mass and the mass itself is established, so that the massing design can change later and this will automatically update the building elements made out of its faces or floor slices.

The nice thing about the Building Maker workflow is that it also supports the import of massing elements or studies from other tools, such as Maya, Rhino, 3ds Max, Inventor or Sketch-Up, and converts them into Revit mass elements, to which you can then attach walls, floors, and roofs and thus convert the mass into a real building.

Chapters 6 and 7 discussed the principles of modeling, and Chapter 8 analyzed the basic principles of the massing tools for creation of massing studies. Thus, by now you should have a good understanding of how to create a mass element or an entire mass study and the proper use of the first set of tools in the Massing tab of the Design bar.

In this chapter we'll focus on the second group of tools located in the Massing tab: the Building Maker tools.

Let's get an overview of the available tools and then examine their real-life application.

Mass Floors

The first tool you should know about isn't visible in the Massing tab. And agreed—this is confusing! It's the Mass Floors tool, which is designed for getting early square footage take-offs from the massing model. This tool only appears in the Options bar when you select a mass element.

Assuming you've created a mass study in which you defined the basic volumes and shapes that will form your building or complex of buildings, you're ready to start setting up levels. Depending on the type of building you're making, code regulations, and functional usage, you can begin to lay out levels for the building. Let's say the maximum allowed regulated height for your building is 70′ (22m), and your building is a hotel, which will usually have a 10′ (3m) floor-to-floor height. In that case, you can get approximately seven levels.

Switch to any elevation view, and using the Level tool, start adding as many levels as your building needs to have. It's obviously much easier to copy a level graphically using the Multiple Copy or Array command than to manually draw a level seven, eight, or however many times you need it; however, if you use the Copy or Array method for level creation, you won't create actual floor plan views associated with each of the levels, something that would have automatically be done when you manually draw levels. (The difference between drawing and copying a level was covered in Chapter 3.) If that's OK with you, and you don't need floor plan views for each of the levels, then all is well and you can go ahead. If not, and you do wish to have a relevant floor plan generated for each level you are creating, you can either use the Level tool and draw each level or use the copy method to create levels but then additionally create floor plans from those levels by using the View/Floor Plan tool and selecting which levels should have a floor plan view associated with them.

Once you have established the number of levels your building will have, select the mass and click the Mass Floor button from the Options bar. (It is good to do this in a 3D view as you will instantly understand what that tool does.) Upon selection of the Mass Floor button, you get a list of all available levels in the project and are prompted to choose the levels for which you want to generate floor area faces. If you check all levels, a mass floor will be created for each level and can thus be later calculated. If you want to skip a level because of double room height, for example, don't check that level. You can do this for all masses at the same time or separately for each volume. And you can also add or remove levels later: anything in Revit can be changed at any time.

Select the Levels of choice and click OK in the Mass Floor dialog box. You will notice that your mass is sliced by all selected Levels, and Mass floors are indicated on the Mass.

Figure 9.7 shows Mass Floors being applied to the main building only. In Figure 9.8, all other masses representing other buildings have also been sliced by the Mass Floors tool.

FIGURE 9.7
Mass Floors tool applied to one of the masses

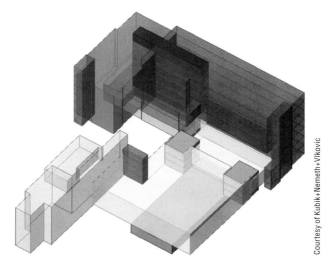

Courtesy of Kubik+Nemeth+Vlkovic

ASSIGNING LEVELS FOR MASS FLOORS

In cases where you have multiple individual mass bodies representing different buildings, you can have them all use the same levels for the floor slicing, or you can select them individually and have each one use different levels. Imagine you have set up levels at a distance of 3m and have seven levels. You have a hotel building and a conference center building. The conference building might have a floor-to-floor height of 6m and thus you'd select only Level 1 and Level 3 as floor area slicers—as opposed to the hotel rooms that will need a floor sliced each 3m.

Courtesy of Kubik+Nemeth+Vlkovic

FIGURE 9.8
The different masses can be sliced using different level selection.

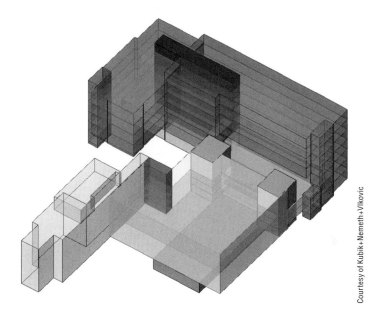

You now understand why the Level tool is handy on the Massing Design bar. Revit is fantastic because you can add, delete, and reshuffle levels at any moment in your project development without needing to redo work or lose any invested work.

The *slicing* of masses done by the Mass Floors tool doesn't just visually help you understand the number of floors and divisions—it also gives a lot of numerical information essential for early conceptual analysis. With the help of this tool, you can find out the following:

◆ Floor area (RO)

◆ Exterior surface area

◆ Floor perimeter

◆ Floor volume

◆ Usage

There is quite an improvement of this tool in the Revit 2009 release. In the previous release, you could only get information about the Gross Floor area, Gross Surface area, and Gross Volume, all of which were a collective value for all floor faces of the mass, which was useful and is still available. You couldn't, however, get information about any of those properties on a per-level basis. This was quite limiting when it came to further assessment and analysis of usage of the floors as well as calculating the cost factors. That has now been improved with a new Mass Floor Area parameter that has been added in the schedules, so that you can call out and schedule all those and some additional values per level (Figure 9.9).

FIGURE 9.9

Mass floor areas in schedules

An additional improvement allows you to get information about the floor perimeter and the exterior surface area (Figure 9.10).

FIGURE 9.10

Floor perimeter and exterior surface in Revit schedules

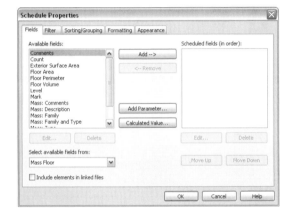

◆ You can calculate gross floor area, surface area, and volume, and for that you make a schedule of the Mass category.

◆ You can also calculate and schedule floor area, exterior surface area, floor perimeter, floor volume, usage, and some additional parameters inherited from the mass, all per individual level—and to do that you schedule the Mass Floor category.

The improvements in Revit 2009 also allow for individual tagging of the floor area faces. You can schedule them, and they each have individual properties that relate directly to the slice of the mass above the floor area face.

All this provides a powerful set of data that can help you make easy conceptual analysis and validate the program fit or make variations. By scheduling, sorting, and filtering the data from these, you can find out the exterior skin material for each usage on each floor and calculate its percentage of the entire exterior surface of the building. You can do similar calculations for the floor area to determine the total usage of various functions and their percentage of the total usable area of the building.

Even though the floor area faces represent volumetric slices of the mass, they do not show this volume geometrically in 3D. Only the floor area face geometry that was previously part of the mass becomes a new element in the model.

Verifying Your Design and Its Fit within the Defined Program

You can schedule the parameters and values of the masses like you can any other Revit element. In the earliest phase of the project, you'll probably want to schedule the functional zones. To create an understandable schedule, it's a good idea to give the mass elements you created names according to their function—Hotel, Conference hall, Parking, Restaurants, and so on—and assign them different colors (materials) so it's easy to visually represent the data. If you need to rename the mass element once it is created, you can do that from the Project Browser—find the mass element in question and rename. As mentioned in Chapter 8, you can also add project parameters to the mass elements, such as Public or Private Space, Department, and so on. If you wish to tag those new parameters so that they are shown in the mass tag, you must make them shared parameters and add them in the Massing Tag family. See Chapter 19 to understand shared parameters and their applicability.

Out of the box, the Mass category in Revit can report the following numeric properties:

◆ Gross floor area

◆ Gross surface

◆ Gross volume

If you create an initial mass study and schedule the mass elements, the schedule reports gross surface and gross volume of the entire shape, as shown in Figure 9.11. Note that the Gross Floor area is blank: the reason for that is that you can't schedule the gross floor area without first adding levels and creating Mass floors as explained at the beginning of the chapter.

Figure 9.11
Example of a mass element without mass floors applied (no floor area faces generated as of yet)

Mass Schedule			
Family	Gross Floor	Gross Surfac	Gross Volum
Building 1		58080 SF	517251.44

By defining levels and creating floor area faces using the Mass Floor tool, the floor area slices will show in the mass and the missing information about the gross floor area will be automatically filled in the schedule (Figure 9.12).

Mass Schedule			
Family	Gross Floor	Gross Surfac	Gross Volum
Building 1	52113 SF	58080 SF	517251.44

The Gross Floor area of the mass is the sum of all the Mass floor slices belonging to that one mass element. Periodically, you need to get separate data about the floor area per floor, sorted and grouped by use or function. This is now possible by creating a schedule for the Mass Floor category (Figure 9.13).

FIGURE 9.13
Scheduling new
parameters can
help you make a
more accurate
conceptual
analysis about
the usage of space
and materials.

Mass Floor Schedule					
Usage	Level	Floor Area	Floor Perimet	Exterior Surfa	Floor Volume
hotel lobby	Level 1	1979 SF	211' - 7 13/32	1101 SF	19788.02 CF
restaurants	Level 2	1979 SF	211' - 7 13/32	1101 SF	19788.02 CF
conference rooms	Level 3	1979 SF	211' - 7 13/32	1101 SF	19788.02 CF
hotel rooms	Level 4	1979 SF	211' - 7 13/32	1359 SF	22377.33 CF
hotel rooms	Level 5	2468 SF	249' - 8 9/32"		
hotel rooms	Level 6			5836 SF	54346.62 CF
hotel lobby	Level 7	2944 SF	265' - 8 25/32	2102 SF	30392.79 CF
hotel rooms	Level 8	3128 SF	271' - 7 11/16	2148 SF	32031.56 CF
hotel rooms	Level 9	3272 SF	276' - 2 1/32"	2183 SF	33261.66 CF
hotel rooms	Level 10	3374 SF	279' - 4 1/32"	2205 SF	34067.64 CF
restaurants	Level 11	3433 SF	281' - 1 25/32	6131 SF	30055.76 CF

The reported values are useful for further conceptual analysis: you can apply different cost factors for different exterior skins. For example, you can get a good idea about how much more expensive it would be to make the last five floors of your building glass skin versus having them all be solid walls.

The massing tools in Revit have been extensively used by many architects. Figure 9.14 shows a project of the firm HOK in which they used the massing tools to produce colored diagrams that are great for explaining to the client the spatial organization of the project. This book is black and white, so you will need to apply your imagination as to how such a colorful diagram looks. Know that investors love this simple but informative way of understanding functional distribution.

FIGURE 9.14
Transparency and color in massing studies used as a language to explain programming

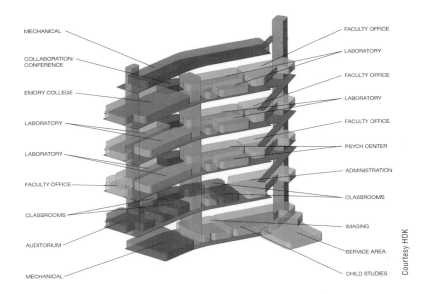

MECHANICAL

COLLABORATION/ CONFERENCE

EMORY COLLEGE

LABORATORY

LABORATORY

FACULTY OFFICE

CLASSROOMS

AUDITORIUM

MECHANICAL

FACULTY OFFICE

LABORATORY

FACULTY OFFICE

LABORATORY

FACULTY OFFICE

PSYCH CENTER

ADMINISTRATION

CLASSROOMS

IMAGING

SERVICE AREA

CHILD STUDIES

Because you can now quickly generate metrics and graphics showing the functional distribution of program elements, you should be able to get feedback on the fitness of the design early on. This will in turn allow you to fine-tune the design and make sure you're keeping pace with the client's requirements. Once you've built a parametric massing model, the elements are all adjustable in size and shape, and any change you make will instantly be reflected in the visual and schedule data (Figure 9.15).

FIGURE 9.15
Conceptual mass analysis

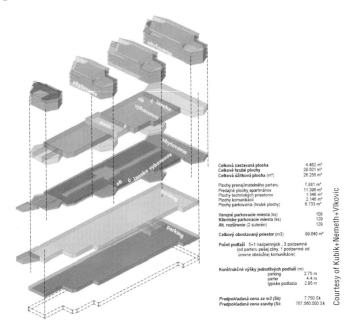

Celková zastavaná plocha	4.462 m²
Celkové hrubé plochy	29.501 m²
Celková úžitková plocha (m²)	26.255 m²
Plochy prenajímateľného parteru	7.881 m²
Predajné plochy apartmánov	11.396 m²
Plochy technických priestorov	1.346 m²
Plochy komunikácií	2.146 m²
Plochy parkovania (hrubé plochy)	6.733 m²
Verejné parkovacie miesta (ks)	108
Klientske parkovacie miesta (ks)	129
Alt. rozšírenie (2.suterén)	129
Celkový obostavaný priestor (m3)	99.040 m²

Počet podlaží 5+1 nadzemných , 3 podzemné
(od parteru pešej zóny, 1 podzemné od
úrovne obslužnej komunikácie)

Konštrukčné výšky jednotlivých podlaží (m)
parking   2.75 m
parter   4.4 m
typické podlazia 2.95 m

Predpokladaná cena za m3 (Sk)	7.750 Sk
Predpokladaná cena stavby (Sk	787.560.000 Sk

After you've reviewed a couple of design options with the client, a decision is made and you need to move forward. To the real project! Moving to the next stage is simple: you can convert the mass into building components using specially designed tools. Let's look at these tools now.

WALL BY FACE

You can start converting the mass into real building elements and can start by generating walls from the mass faces. For that you will use the Wall by Face tool on the Massing tab in the Design bar, and start applying it to faces of the masses. Note that you can only create walls by face on vertical and inclined faces or arc faces of a mass. Wall by face cannot be applied to horizontal faces. You can begin applying generic walls that you later swap with exact wall types that you'll be using; or, if you want to make early renderings that convey color and texture, apply the types of walls that you believe represent your idea the best and contain the texture, material, and color information. Cost estimates are generated early in the process, so you'll soon need to move from abstract forms to the real wall types.

Many of the rules and principles behind standard wall creation should be followed here as well. It's important to correctly set your wall location prior to applying it on the face to save post-editing—but of course if you make a mistake, you can always fix that later. Depending on how you built the mass—to represent the outer-most envelope or to represent the interior envelope—will determine how you want to set the location line for your walls. Use Exterior face if you modeled the massing to the exterior envelope of construction. For example, imagine that you've created a conceptual mass study in Rhinoceros, Maya, or SketchUp and imported it into Revit as a mass element. Using the Wall by Face tool, you can start applying generic walls to the mass immediately.

Keep these limitations in mind:

- Any wall in Revit can be converted into a curtain wall. Unfortunately, this isn't the case with walls created with the Wall by Face option. To make curtain walls, you need to use the Curtain System by Face tool.

- You can't apply the Edit Profile tool that allows for the shape of the wall to be changed on walls created with the Wall by Face tool. To do that, you must change the shape of the underlying mass first.

FLOOR BY FACE

Only after you've applied the Mass Floor tool and generated Mass floor area faces in the masses can you apply real floor elements to them. Select the Floor by Face tool, and start selecting the Mass floor area faces to which you want to assign a floor. To create the floors, you will have to click the Create Floors button on the Options bar, or nothing will happen.

To accommodate floor creation in a tower with many floors, for example, you can check the Select Multiple option on the Options bar. You can then begin selecting all the floor area faces to which you wish to apply floors and finish with the Create Floors tool.

The Mass Floor tool slices the mass horizontally, creating horizontal floor plates by default. If you need floors to be sloped (such as ramps), you can always slope them later using the Floor Edit tools available from the Options bar when a floor is selected, or edit the sketch of the floor and add a slope arrow when in Sketch mode of the floor (Figure 9.16).

FIGURE 9.16
Click a grip control
to change the floor
slope.

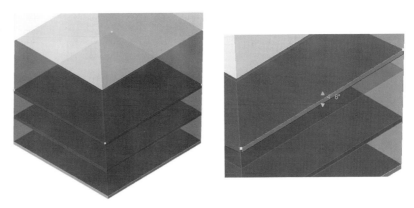

It's worth mentioning that when you create a floor by face, the Options bar includes an Offset parameter:

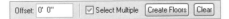

This isn't the vertical offset of the floor from the level you can find in the floor properties; it's an offset of the floor sketch from the current floor area boundary. If you add a positive value to the offset, the floor plate becomes smaller than the actual floor area (Figure 9.17).

FIGURE 9.17
Use offset to make
slab smaller or
larger than the
floor area face.

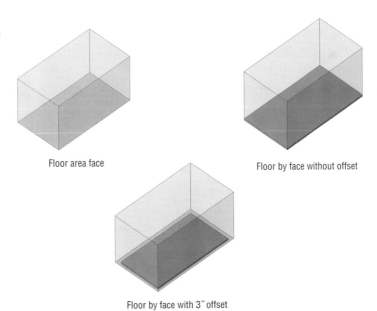

Floor area face

Floor by face without offset

Floor by face with 3″ offset

Roof by Face

You've learned how easy it is to apply walls and floors by face. Roofs follow the same basic principles but are more flexible. You can create roofs by face on planar faces, arcs, or other shapes created by extrusions, revolves, sweeps, and blends.

Note these limitations:

♦ You can't select a vertical face to create a roof by face.

♦ Once a roof is created using the Roof by Face method, you can't edit its sketch to change the shape of it in plan. If you created a roof by face and need to change its sketch, you must change the shape of the underlying mass from which the roof has been derived; only in that way can you affect the shape of the created roof.

Curtain System by Face

Curtain systems are a handy tool. With one click, you can convert a face of a building into a curtain system that you can predefine with parameters to match your needs. Curtain systems can be applied to any nonplanar face and are composed of grids, panels, and mullions. Make sure the curtain system type you choose has a predefined Curtain Grid layout.

Keep these limitations in mind:

♦ You can't edit curtain system sketches. A curtain system made by face requires editing the shape of the underlying mass.

♦ You can't always predict the X–Y coordinate system applied to the face. You may have to make new types in order to meet your requirements.

♦ Only masses that are planar or curved in one direction can host custom curtain panels. Compound curved systems have to use the default system panel.

Technical Details You Should Be Aware of When Scheduling Mass Elements

It's important that your mass model be modeled properly from a geometrical point of view to support correct reporting and downstream applications of walls, floor, and roofs. Look at the towers shown in Figure 9.18. If you simply draw the two towers and schedule them, the schedule reports the values for the individual towers.

If you move the position of the towers so that they intersect, the schedule reports the same calculated values: Revit doesn't join the geometries and eliminate the overlapping areas automatically (Figure 9.19). If you place different masses that aren't joined but overlap, when you use the Floor by Face tool the intersecting portions of floor slabs overlap and cause duplicate area calculations. To resolve this issue, you need to join geometry.

To get the correct schedule that represents the actual volume, surface, and floor area values, use the Join Geometry tool in the main toolbar to join the two masses. Whichever mass you used first is the one that penetrates into the other mass. The schedule now reflects the values of the joined, merged geometries (Figure 9.20).

FIGURE 9.18
Unconnected
mass forms and
their schedule

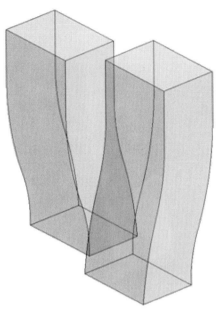

Tower B

Tower A

Tower A   Tower B

Tower A   Tower B

Mass Schedule			
Family	Gross Floor	Gross Surfac	Gross Volume
Tower A		172052 m²	3915914.77 m³
Tower B		172052 m²	3915913.75 m³

FIGURE 9.19
Mass forms inter-
sect but are still
not joined; the
schedule still
reports the sum
of the area and vol-
ume (incorrect).

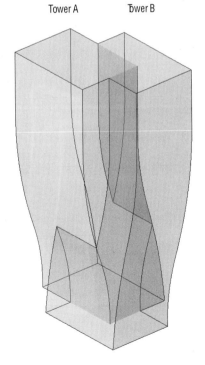

Tower B

Tower A

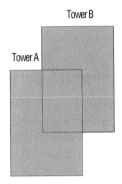

Mass Schedule			
Family	Gross Floor	Gross Surfac	Gross Volume
Tower A		172052 m²	3915914.77 m³
Tower B		172052 m²	3915913.75 m³

FIGURE 9.20
Mass forms joined. The schedule reports the correct surface and volume.

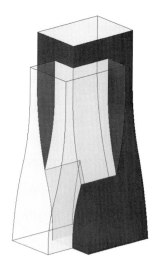

Tower A Tower B Tower B

Tower A

Mass Schedule			
Family	Gross Floor	Gross Surfac	Gross Volume
Tower A		164685 m²	2415856.24 m³
Tower B		172052 m²	3915914.32 m³

Joining the masses creates a relationship between the two masses. This means that if you move the location or edit the shape of one, the joined geometry automatically updates in a Boolean manner. Only in cases where you move one mass completely away from the other mass will you get an error message that the two masses don't intersect anymore and you need to use the Unjoin Geometry option to fix the error.

Once the masses have been joined, you can begin to apply elements by face (Figure 9.21).

FIGURE 9.21
Mass with applied walls by face

Using Imported Geometry from Other Applications for Massing

You can use various applications to create geometry to be imported into Revit for massing. This section looks at using SketchUp, Maya, Rhinoceros, 3ds Max, Inventor, and many more.

SketchUp

SketchUp is a fantastic piece of software. It's considered by many to be a useful concept modeling and visualization tool that is easy to use, produces great results, and really feels architectural. Many architects adore SketchUp for conceptual studies or early images of design ideas. Revit users use SketchUp to make initial massing and conceptual studies to produce nice graphic outputs for their clients. They can then move the model into Revit for the documentation phase.

SketchUp files can be imported in either of two file formats, which are tied to different workflows and expectations:

SKP   Use this format if you've created a complex geometric element in SketchUp that is pretty much final and you just need to import it into Revit using the direct import of the SKP file. An example is a building with a complex shape or roof that you couldn't easily do in Revit.

DWG   If you expect a dynamic workflow where the models need to move back and forth and maintain some intelligence, use file linking and link in the DWG files. This way, if the DWG changes, the model will update to show the latest version of the DWG.

IMPORT THE SKETCHUP MODEL IN PROJECT ENVIRONMENT TO LEVERAGE LINKING

You can only leverage the linking functionality if you import the SketchUp model within the project environment. If you import it as a mass, the reload link functionality will not work.

Here is how we suggest working with a SketchUp file:

1. In SketchUp, make a quick and easy initial concept design like the one shown in Figure 9.22, and save it.

FIGURE 9.22
Massing created
in SketchUp

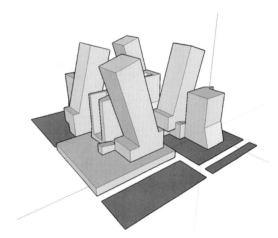

2. Start a new massing by using the Create Mass tool in the Massing tab of the Design bar, and then import the file (Figure 9.23).

FIGURE 9.23
The Import/Link
CAD formats
dialog box

3. Finish the family.

4. Switch to 3D view, and switch the model graphics of the view to Shaded with Edges. The SketchUp model appears in Revit. You can also activate shadows to see the model better (Figure 9.24).

FIGURE 9.24
Imported SketchUp
file with shadows
turned on

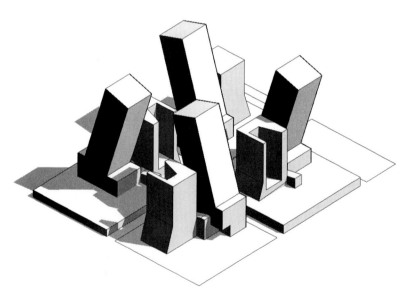

Often, when you finish the mass family after importing the SKP file, you'll get a warning message:

It's important to read this message in order to understand the future expectations for the import. If a mass family imports only nonvolumetric geometry, you can't create floor area faces in Revit. This is the case with any imports that come from surface or polymesh modeling applications. When imported in Revit, NURBS and solids can to be fully understood by Revit and generate the Mass floor area faces and all future reporting needed for conceptual studies. Maya and Rhinoceros deliver good NURBS for this workflow.

Rhinoceros

Rhinoceros (known popularly as Rhino) is a neat application that many architects love for the powerful shapes it can create and its relative ease of use. Rhinoceros produces NURBS surfaces, and while Revit doesn't natively create NURBS, they can be easily imported and used as a reference to create a building out of the Rhino massing concept.

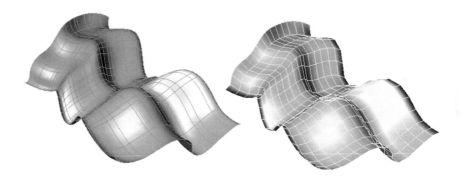

You can use Rhino to create concept studies or a complex-shaped building element. As an example, a draped form was created using Rhino and then imported into a Revit massing element (see Figure 9.25), just as you'd do with a SketchUp import. The form was then used as a reference and a curtain system by face was applied to it to generate the roof in Revit.

FIGURE 9.25
NURBS turned
into curtain
systems using the
Curtain System
by Face tool

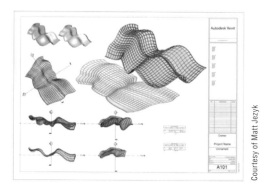

Courtesy of Matt Jezyk

Rhino models are imported in Revit as SAT files. To import a SAT file from Rhino into Revit, the best approach is to make a mass family in the project environment and import the SAT file while in mass editing mode. This allows Revit to use the imported geometry for Mass floor area faces and to perform other calculations and cuts in section and plan. When you're importing a mesh into the family, you get a message about calculation limitations:

This warning can safely be ignored. Finish the family; then, from the Massing tab, select the Curtain System tool. You can select a different type from the Type Selector. Click the imported file geometry, and click the Create Roof tool on the Options bar.

The new object—a curtain system—is generated out of the underlying geometry (Figure 9.26). It's important to understand that glass panels don't conform to the surface—the panels remain planar and attempt to fit the surface as best they can. So, as the panel cell size gets smaller, deviance decreases. You can always change the type later, just as you can for any element in Revit. Once you're happy with the type and the size of the panels, you can apply mullions. Depending on the complexity of the imported file, this can take up to a few minutes—but don't worry, it's a one-time action! Note that tighter grids give better results but also increase the processing time.

FIGURE 9.26
You can apply a
curtain system to
a NURBS imported
geometry.

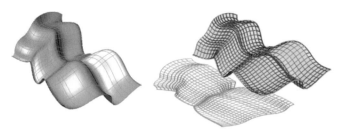

Autodesk Maya

As technologies become more powerful, they have the ability to influence trends in many industries, including architecture. Organic, free-form, generative buildings are all over the architectural magazines: this in a way is provoked by the fact that building technologies have become more sophisticated but also because modeling tools to create such forms have become better and easier to use. And while no software can make something beautiful unless it is in the hands of a creative person, these inspiring tools certainly capture the creative mind of talented architects.

In the myriad of available modeling tools today, the question is not only if you can make a shape or inspiring design but *how*. Maya is considered one of the best tools with a most artistic approach to form-finding. No wonder that it started to capture the mindshare of many famous architects and is being implemented in the curricula of the most advanced architectural schools that teach generative techniques and methodologies of computational modeling.

Maya helps artists not just explore forms that are approximations or alternatives to creative visions, but in itself sparks ideas and forms not previously explored or considered in a creative process.

Maya can create the most amazing shapes (Figure 9.27) and supports three major types of geometry: polymeshes, NURBS, and subdivision surfaces. You can import any of those into Revit, but if you want to leverage the full power of Building Maker and get area, volume, and skin calculations from the Maya model, you'll get best results by using NURBS while working with Maya.

FIGURE 9.27
There is no limit
to your fantasy
when modeling
with Maya.

Courtesy of Marcel de Jong

FIGURE 9.28
Conceptual mass created in Inventor, imported as Revit Mass, turned into building, and rendered.

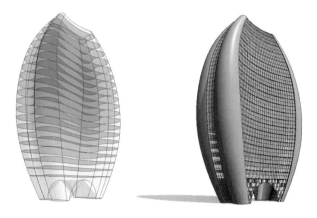

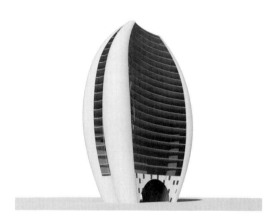

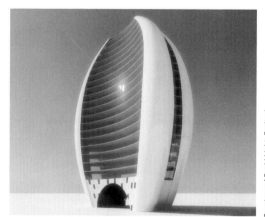

The workflow from Maya to Revit is either via DWG directly to Revit, or via AutoCAD where the DWG is converted into a SAT file and then imported in Revit. As a general rule, use the latter only in cases where you have trouble importing the DWG created with the plug-in.

The DWG export from Maya is not native in Maya but is a separate plug-in and can be found at the Autodesk Labs website: http://labs.autodesk.com/utilities/maya_export_dwg/.

Autodesk Inventor

Autodesk® Inventor™ is a software solution for the manufacturing industry, but it starts to provoke a growing interest among architects for its parametric rules-based form generation as well as for its fabrication capabilities. Using rule-based techniques, you can create a complex conceptual mass in Inventor and then use them in Revit to make initial conceptual analysis, Mass floor area, volumes, etc., and then move the concept to a real building by creating elements by faces, just as you can do that from the other modelers. You should export the conceptual mass done in Inventor in SAT file format to be able to import it in Revit (see Figure 9.28).

Inventor can serve later in the stage of creation of implementation documentation and fabrication details. You can design, for example, your curtain wall layout in Revit but can make fabrication exact drawings of each of the elements using Inventor.

FIGURE 9.29
Detailed design and fabrication documentation can be easily done with Autodesk Inventor

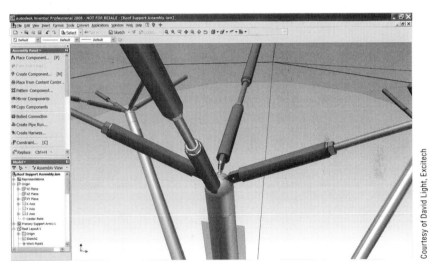

Courtesy of David Light, Excitech

Using Smart Relationships between Building Mass and the Underlying Mass

The idea behind attaching building elements to massing faces is that you can come back to the massing and make large gestural edits to the underlying form and have the walls, floors, and roofs update. When you're working in the conceptual design phase, you experiment a lot during the form-finding and creative thinking stage. In Revit, the change of the underlying mass form is designed not to update automatically and change the Revit building elements created by its faces, as this would present regeneration slowdowns and impede a fluid workflow. That said, it's easy to keep your model in sync. You might first play with the shape, and then when you're happy with it, use the Remake button located on the Options bar to update your building elements. So, how does that work? When elements that are tied to a massing are selected, a Remake button appears on the Options bar (Figure 9.29). Clicking that button updates the element to match the newly edited shape of the underlying mass form, as shown in Figure 9.30.

Figure 9.29 shows a series of elements updated.

FIGURE 9.30
A: The starting form. B: The mass is made larger. C: The wall is re-made to match the mass. D: The roof and other walls are remade to match the mass.

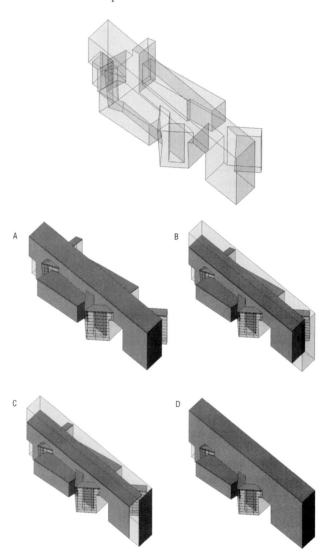

The Bottom Line

One typical way to start a design process is a creation of conceptual masses. Revit can create or read concept masses created in other tools and apply conceptual analysis and convert those masses in real building elements using a set of smart tools called the Building Maker.

Make conceptual designs and early studies in Revit   You can use massing studies to validate a design against the program requirements.

> **Master It**   Conceptual modeling is used early in the design process to explore building shape and program. How do you approach schematic design using Revit and perform feasibility studies?

Build a real building out of a 3D concept mass   Moving from massing to actual building components is easily done with Revit.

> **Master It**   You've got the basic massing nailed down, and now you need to study more details such as wall and window fenestrations. How do you approach this with Revit?

Use imported geometry from other applications for massing   You can make your own conceptual massing forms using standard Revit form-making tools or by importing geometry from other applications.

> **Master It**   How can you reuse conceptual models created in other modeling applications and turn them into a measurable and documentable building in Revit?

Use smart relationships between building mass and the underlying mass   It's not always possible to start a project directly within Revit. Knowing how to import model geometry from other applications is critical to a good workflow. You can also avoid replicating model geometry just because you're moving from one software package to another.

> **Master It**   Import model geometry from other applications (such as Rhino or SketchUp) into Revit in a way that allows you to cut them in plan and section.

Chapter 10

Working with Design Options

Revit supports workflows where multiple design options need to be explored, evaluated, and presented. This type of workflow is an integral part of developing and iterating on a design solution. With Revit's design options, you can create a range of variations of a design that can vary in scale—from entire façade studies down to kitchen layouts—and, most important, all in the same integrated model.

In this chapter you learn to do the following:

◆ Use Revit design options

◆ Decide on a design solution

◆ Use design options with parametric design

Using Revit Design Options

Revit provides a set of tools for developing multiple design iterations in the context of one project. These tools allow you to explore alternative designs without having to constantly save multiple independent versions of your model as you move in different directions. With Revit's design options, you create, evaluate, and mock up a wide range of options in the context of your project file. You're free to investigate multiple roof configurations or different entry canopies, explore various furniture and office layouts and stairs—quite literally anything that can be modeled. Figure 10.1 shows an example of the same model with two different entry canopies. Each canopy belongs to a separate design option that can be displayed or hidden in any view. This lets you create views that show each option so the two designs can be evaluated against each other.

FIGURE 10.1
Revit design options used to explore alternative design solutions

Design options work in the following manner: you have a *main model*, which includes all the elements you've modeled that are fixed and not affected by the options you want to explore. The main model can be thought of as a backdrop or stage on which different options play. Elements in the main model are always visible, whereas design options come and go—appearing and disappearing depending on what you're editing. The options could include different furnishing for the interior or different canopies over an entrance, and the main model includes everything else that's *not* in the option.

You can make as many options as you need—there is no limit. You can create views for each option that only shows that option displayed against the main model, and thus be able to place these views on a sheet in order to compare and contrast your designs.. You can then present them to a client, to the project architect, or to other stakeholders in the design process. Once a design option has been settled on, you *accept* it as the primary design solution going forward by adding it back to the main model. Doing so deletes all elements in the design option that aren't going forward. That is, some elements become embedded in the architecture, while others disappear forever.

Enabling the Design Options Tool Set in the Toolbar

To enable design options, first make sure the Design Option group of tools is visible in the toolbar by right-clicking the toolbar and checking Design Options in the context menu. You can also access design options from the menu: Tools ➢ Design Options ➢ Design Options. A new set of tools appears at the upper right on the toolbar:

By default, only one button (Design Options) is enabled in a new file that has no design options. That button launches the Design Options dialog box, where you create and manage all the design options in a project. We'll cover the other buttons in the next few sections.

Enabling design options doesn't create anything at first—it simply sets up the work environment so you can begin making various designs using the feature.

Design Option Sets

In Revit, every design option belongs to a *design option set*, where a *set* is a way of structuring the design options into clusters to aid your workflow. For example, in a project you may have three design options for an exterior façade, two options for a bathroom configuration, and three options for room and furniture layout. Revit allows you to have several sets for each major type of option you're exploring. You may have a design option set called Exterior Façades, one called Bathrooms, and another called Room Layout. In each set, you can have as many options as you need for the design in question. This hierarchy is structured as a tree interface in the Design Options dialog box, as shown in Figure 10.2. Each option set is shown in a top-level node of the tree, and each design option is shown as a child of a set.

As you can see in the dialog box in Figure 10.2, there is always a *primary* option in each set, designated by the "(primary)" suffix. This option is always visible by default in any view. You can change the primary option by selecting an option in the dialog box and clicking the Make Primary button. In your views, the new primary option will then be visible by default, hiding the previously defined primary option.

When you reach a point in your design where you'd like to explore multiple design solutions, you're ready to start creating option sets. Think about how you'd describe the option—Façade Studies, for example—and name your option set accordingly. Add at least two options to the set—more, if you think you'll be exploring more than two options. You don't have to define all the options in the beginning; you can always come back and add or remove options if needed.

Creating new design option sets is straightforward. Click the New button, and a new set is created. To give the set a unique name, select it in the tree and click the Rename button. Adding new options follows the same pattern: make a new one, and then give it a unique name.

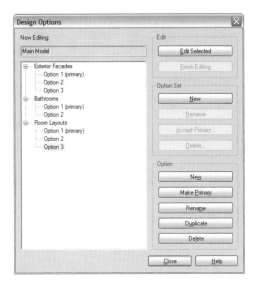

You can delete sets and options at any time; doing so effectively deletes any elements added to a design variation you've made using that design option, so be wary of deleting before you're ready to do so. It will also delete any views that you have set up specific to those design options. In both cases, you will be warned by Revit before the views and option sets are removed. The same effect is achieved when you click the Accept Primary button—all other options in that set are deleted.

Adding Elements to a Design Option

Once you've formally established design option sets and design options, you can do a number of things depending on the scope of your options. You can add elements from the main model into each option to experiment with variations of the element; this is applicable if you want to explore different expressions of the same object without adding new elements. For example, if you want to show two roofs with the same footprint but different slopes, this method of adding the roof into each design option will work nicely. Once the roof is added to each option, you edit the option and then edit the roof slope. The roof is essentially a copy and can be edited independently in each option (Figure 10.3).

FIGURE 10.3
Design options in
the same model

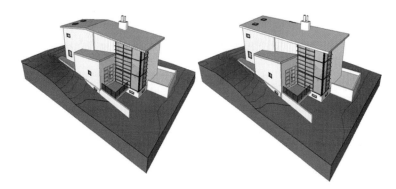

Another way to work with options is to start editing the option directly, without first adding elements to the option. This approach works well if you have a design idea but don't want to add it to the main model just yet. When you begin editing an option, the main model grays out, and any new element you add is added to the active design option. For example, let's say you haven't yet designed the entry canopy for your model, and you want to experiment with some different ideas. Start editing the option and you can then model whatever you want. The main model is still visible for reference, but it won't be editable.

You can use both methods in combination as well. For example, you might add a wall from the main model to two options and in each option add new, but different, window types to the wall. You'd use the Add to Design Option Set button to put the wall into both options, and then you'd edit each option to add the new windows.

To add elements to an option, first select them, and then add them to the appropriate design options by clicking the Add to Design Option Set button on the toolbar. Select only the elements you wish to make variations of—you don't need to add elements that you won't be editing. Once you click the Add to Design Option Set button, you're taken to a dialog box that allows you to copy the elements into the desired design option or options. Again, this method is best if you know the elements will be essentially the same in each option and may vary only in type, material, or arrangement. Figure 10.4 shows the same walls in two options with different windows inserted, and using a different wall type to change material.

FIGURE 10.4
Add walls to multiple options in order to experiment with different window placements.

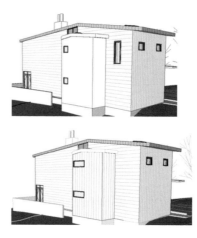

To edit a design option, click the Edit Option button in the toolbar, and choose an option to edit. You're taken to a special edit mode, where anything you create is added to the active design option automatically. Use this method if you're starting from a blank slate and laying out several options for furniture layout or exterior shading devices, like those shown in Figure 10.5.

When you're adding elements to design options, keep the following basic rules in mind:

◆ Host-based elements that cut the host (such as windows or doors) need to be included with the host when you make design options, meaning both the host and the insert have to be a part of the same option. You cannot have the host be a main model but the inserts an option.

◆ Inserts are automatically copied with the host when you add hosts to design options. Using our example of a wall with a window in it, if you add the wall into a design option, the window is automatically added as well.

◆ By the same token, if you're editing an option and try to place a window or door into a wall that's not included in the option, you'll get a warning:

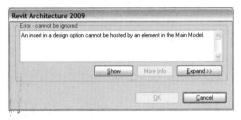

You need to add that wall to your design option if you want to place inserts in the wall. Host-based elements that *do not* cut their hosts *can* reside in different design options without the host. For example, a wall-hosted sink can reside in a different design option than the wall on which it's mounted (which resides in the main model), but a window that cuts a wall can't.

◆ When you're adding curtain walls from the main model to a design option, the grids, mullions, and panels are automatically added for you.

◆ When you're adding a roof to a design option, you should include all walls that attach to that roof. Otherwise, you won't be able to attach walls to the roofs in your design options.

◆ When you create groups or arrays within a design option, selected elements must be in the active option.

FIGURE 10.5
Use this dialog box to choose the design options into which you want to add elements.

Once an element has been added to a design option, by default it's no longer selectable when you work on the main model. You can override this behavior by deselecting the Exclude Design Options check box on the Options bar.

Because the elements in a design option can't be selected from the main model, to edit elements you'll need to use this feature or activate a design option. For example, if you add all your exterior walls to design options in the Exterior Façades option set, the walls won't highlight or be selectable unless you're editing the design option. If you add elements to a secondary option, they won't be visible by default in the main model.

Editing a Design Option

To start experimenting with design variations, you edit your design options after having created them. To do so, use the drop-down menu associated with the Edit Option button on the toolbar, and choose the option you want to edit (Figure 10.6).

FIGURE 10.6
Use the Edit Option button to access a drop-down list of available design options.

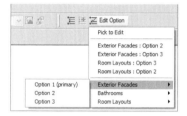

The main model grays out and becomes unselectable. This allows you to modify the elements in the design option without worrying that you'll mess up other parts of the model. Any element created while in the design option's Edit mode is automatically added to the option. For example, if you're editing Option 2 of an Exterior Façade set, and you insert new windows in a wall in that option, the windows are added to the design option—they aren't added to the main model. Remember that the wall must be in the design option in order for you to place the window.

EDITING AN OPTION BY SELECTING AN ELEMENT

If you want to start editing an element in a design option directly, click the Edit Option button and choose the Pick to Edit option. Hover the mouse over the model, and elements in design options will highlight; you can then begin editing an element as soon as you select it. This shortcut lets you edit elements in a more direct manner and opens the desired option automatically.

Take the example of two views showing different roof options. In each view, to start editing the option, choose Pick to Edit, select the roof, and start editing the roof—you don't have to think about the name of the option.

Real World Scenario

MAKING DIFFERENT EXTERIOR SKINS

Using design options, we added the exterior skin of a building to two options in an option set. By creating a new wall type with different materials, we easily exchanged one wall type for another in each option. Once the wall types were swapped in each option, we duplicated the perspective view showing the exterior skin and changed it to show both options (spandrel glass on the left, wood on the right) using the Visibility/Graphic Overrides dialog box. To make the northeast perspectives easy to find in any list, we assigned the views meaningful names: Glass NE and Wood NE.

Displaying Design Options

To visualize different design options and have them represented in separate views that you can drop on a sheet, you need to create a new view that displays the desired option. To do this, right-click any view in the Project Browser, choose Duplicate, and give the view a name that indicates which design option it represents. You'll then adjust the Visibility/Graphic Overrides settings of that view to show the desired design option.

As you can see in Figure 10.7, once you've created option sets and design options, a new Design Options tab appears in the Visibility/Graphic Overrides dialog box. The default visibility setting is Automatic, which shows the primary option and the main model. Using the drop-down menu under Design Option, you can override this setting and show any of your other options.

FIGURE 10.7
By default, views are set to show the primary design options and the main model.

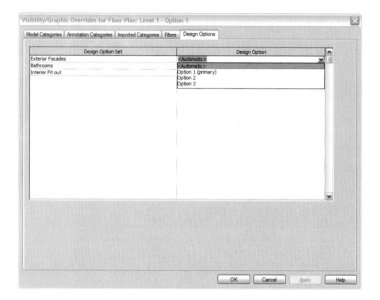

In Figure 10.8, three options are shown for a building façade: Option 1 has no canopy over the third-floor deck, Option 2 has a solid canopy, and Option 3 has a louvered canopy. All three options exist in the same model and can be visualized next to one another by duplicating the view and changing the visibility of the design option.

FIGURE 10.8
By duplicating views and changing the default design option visibility, it's easy to compare options and even place the views on sheets for printing.

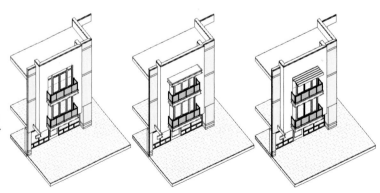

Deciding on a Design Solution

When you've decided which option to build, with one click you can make the chosen option become a part of the main model and get rid of the rest. First, decide which option you intend to keep, and designate it as the primary option by clicking the Make Primary button in the Design Options dialog box. Then, select the option set, and click the Accept Primary button. Doing so brings up a confirmation dialog box asking if you're sure you want to do this (Figure 10.9). As the message suggests, if you proceed *all* secondary options will be deleted, and whatever is in the primary option will be pushed into the main model. (Make sure you're ready to implement the decision!) The elements will again become selectable without your having to edit a design option. This approach is recommended if you've made a definite design decision and intend to move forward with that decision. Keeping unused and out-of-date options in the project needlessly inflates the file size and adds unwanted complexity.

FIGURE 10.9
To add an option back to the main model, click the Accept Primary button in the Design Options dialog box.

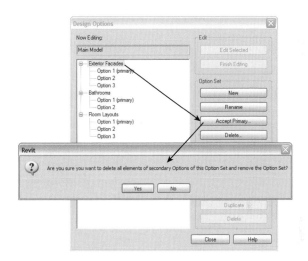

You're also asked to delete any views that were set up to display options that you're deleting (Figure 10.10).

FIGURE 10.10
You're prompted to delete views associated with options you're deleting.

Click Delete to continue, and the views will be removed from your project. You can't keep any views that were set to show secondary options that no longer exist.

Putting Design Options into Practice

In the following exercise, you'll make three different office layouts, shown in Figure 10.11, using design options. Option 1 is a hybrid design of open space and closed offices, Option 2 is an open office with cubicles, and Option 3 has only enclosed offices. Once created, all the options will exist in one file and can be separately displayed in different views and dropped on one sheet for comparison. Follow these steps:

1. Open the Foundation model in the chapter 10 folder of the book's companion web page (www.sybex.com/go/masteringrevit2009).

2. Open the Level 1 Presentation plan view.

3. Enable Design Options.

4. Create a new option set called **Interior Fitout**.

5. Create three options, and set Option 1 to be primary by clicking the Make Primary button, as shown in Figure 10.12 (this should be set by default).

FIGURE 10.11
The three office layouts you'll create as design options

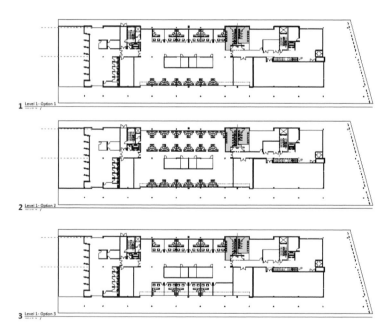

FIGURE 10.12

Add a design option set and three design options.

6. Close the dialog box.

7. Choose to edit Option 1, using the Edit Option drop-down menu in the toolbar.

8. While editing Option 1, place a series of workstation families (`workstation.rfa`), interior partitions, and offices, as shown in Figure 10.13.

FIGURE 10.13

Add a series of workstations to design Option 1.

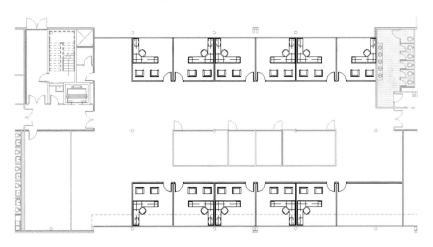

9. Finish editing the options by clicking the Edit Option button.

10. Choose Option 2 from the Edit Option drop-down menu.

11. Create the open floor plan shown in Figure 10.14. To speed up the process, you can choose Edit Option 1, copy the row of cubicle desks to the clipboard, choose Edit Option 2, and paste them in using Edit ➤ Paste Aligned ➤ Same Place. Don't be thrown off by Same Place; this pastes the workstations only into the active design option.

FIGURE 10.14
Add cubicles to
Option 2.

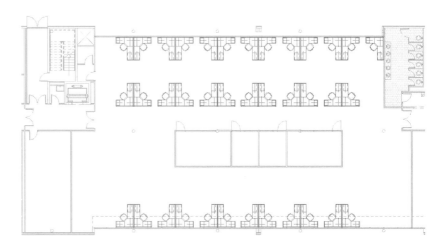

12. When you're finished, click Edit Option in the toolbar to return to the main model.

The elements in Option 2 will disappear from the view. The primary option (Option 1) is set to be visible by default, and as mentioned earlier, you can't view more than one option per view.

13. To make a third option that has enclosed offices and no cubicles, choose to edit Option 1, select all the offices in the top half of the space, and copy them to the clipboard using Ctrl+C.

14. Choose Option 3 from the Edit Option drop-down menu in the toolbar.

15. From the main menu, choose Edit ➤ Paste Aligned ➤ Same Place (Figure 10.15).

The workstations are copied into Option 3.

16. Continue to fill the space with offices, as shown in Figure 10.16. You can use the Mirror command to speed up the process.

Next, you need to place each option on a sheet so you can show the options to your client and get feedback about the different layout options. Follow these steps:

1. Duplicate the plan view from the Project Browser, and rename it **Level 1 - Option 1**.

2. Duplicate the view two more times, and give each view a unique name: **Level 1 - Option 2** and **Level 1 - Option 3**.

3. In Level 1 - Option 3, open the Visibility/Graphic Overrides dialog box, and go to the Design Options tab. Change the Design Option value from Automatic to Option 3.

4. Open Level 1 - Option 2, and repeat step 3, but make sure Design Option is set to Option 2.

FIGURE 10.15
Use the Paste Aligned feature to copy elements from one design option to another.

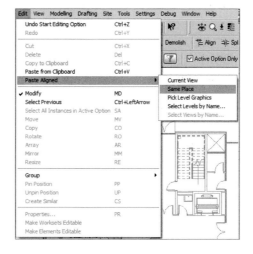

FIGURE 10.16
Design Option 3 contains offices.

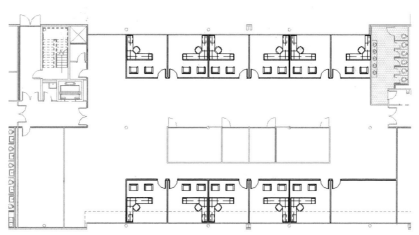

5. Create a new sheet view, and drag each of the plans onto the sheet, as shown in Figure 10.17.

6. You're now ready to present your alternatives.

FIGURE 10.17
All three options can be placed on a sheet by duplicating the plan views and adjusting the settings in the Visibility/Graphic Overrides dialog box.

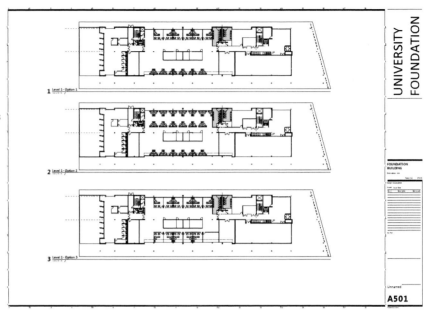

Using Design Options with Parametric Design

Now that we have discussed the ability to have different design options within Revit and how to show these various solutions, let's dig into a little more detail and talk about other ways to consider the various solutions. As any designer knows, multiple factors come into play with any design solution—beauty, functionality, cost, and sustainability, to name a few.

Showing Quantities and Cost Schedules for Multiple Options

You can compare design options and discuss with your client cost versus features desired, contrasting the cost of options using schedules. A schedule, like any view, can be tailored to show specific design options. To create a schedule of elements in a design option, first click the Schedule/Quantities tool from the View tab in the Design bar to make a new schedule. Choose the category you'd like to schedule, and the appropriate parameters. The properties of the schedule include a parameter for Visibility/Graphics Overrides (Figure 10.18). Clicking the Edit button brings you to the Design Options tab (in this case, the only tab in the dialog box), where you can choose a design option to schedule. Here is the real power: only elements belonging to the selected category in the selected design option are included in the schedule.

FIGURE 10.18
From the schedule's properties, you can access the Visibility/Graphic Overrides dialog box and change the design option.

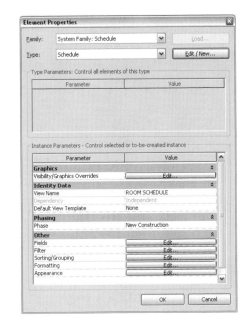

Working with Rooms and Design Options

You can create rooms in design options to compare areas and create color schemes for various options. For example, you can create two office layouts with different sizes and number of offices in each option and then add rooms to the offices. You can then create views of each option that are color-coded to provide a nice visual comparison. To get a feel for how this works, consider this simple example.

Start with a corridor and rooms on either side. You need to create two design options that show different room configurations. Follow these steps:

1. Draw a simple layout of walls, as shown here in plan view:

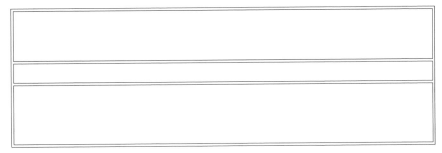

2. Open the Design Options dialog box from the toolbar, and create an option set named **Office Configurations**. Add two design options to the set, as shown in Figure 10.19.

FIGURE 10.19
Adding the design options

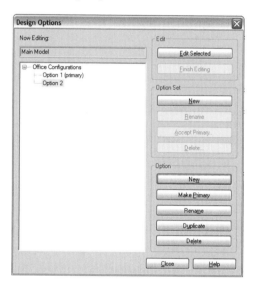

3. Back in the plan view, duplicate the view from the Project Browser. Name the view **Level 1 Plan View - Option 2**. In the Visibility/Graphic Overrides dialog box for that new view, go to the Options tab and set Option to Option 2.

4. Go back to your original view and change the Options Visibility/Graphic Overrides setting to Option 1.

5. In the Option 1 plan view, choose to edit the option. Draw walls to create 12 offices:

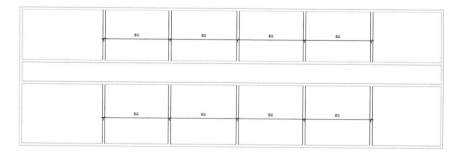

6. Add rooms to each office using the Room tool on the Basics tab of the Design bar:

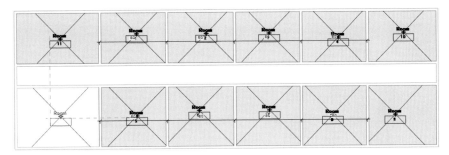

These rooms are added to the primary option.

7. Open Plan View - Option 2, and click to edit Option 2 from the toolbar. Place walls so that you make 10 offices rather than 12, and place rooms in each office space:

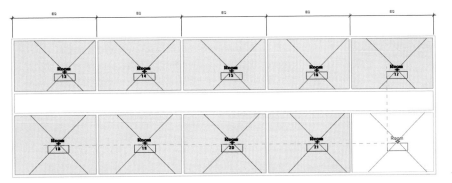

As you can see, Revit allows you to create two independent room layouts in the same model.

8. To create a schedule of the rooms in each option, select the Visibility/Graphics Overrides parameter in the Element Properties of the room schedule, and set the design option to the desired option (Figure 10.20).

FIGURE 10.20
Displaying the
rooms in the
schedule's design
options

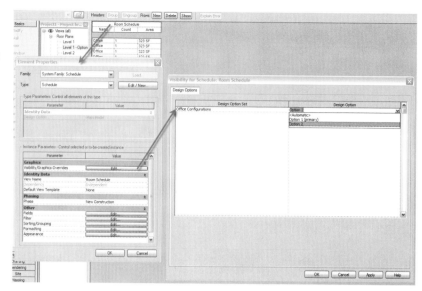

9. Make a schedule for each design option showing rooms, areas, and count. Be sure to
name each schedule so that it corresponds to your design options. You can then place
each schedule and plan view on a sheet for comparison (Figure 10.21).

FIGURE 10.21
The design options
in schedule form

Room Schedule - Option 1		
Name	Count	Area
Office	1	254 SF
Office	1	254 SF
Office	1	254 SF
Office	1	254 SF
Office	1	299 SF
Office	1	299 SF
Office	1	299 SF
Office	1	299 SF
Office	1	316 SF
Office	1	267 SF
Office	1	323 SF
Office	1	381 SF
Grand total: 12		

Room Schedule - Option 2		
Name	Count	Area
Office	1	323 SF
Office	1	323 SF
Office	1	323 SF
Office	1	323 SF
Office	1	323 SF
Office	1	381 SF
Office	1	381 SF
Office	1	381 SF
Office	1	381 SF
Office	1	381 SF
Grand total: 10		

The Bottom Line

If you need to explore alternate design ideas in your model, try using design options. Doing so will
save you from having to try to merge information downstream if you tend to make separate files

for each design. Rather than going through a laborious copy–paste workflow and maintaining two or three models in separate files, you can use design options in one model of your building and thus streamline your workflow. Just keep in mind that you're working with a 3D parametric model that creates lots of relationships between elements. Often, editing a floor or roof also involves editing walls that are attached to that roof, even if you aren't burdened with having to make the edits manually.

Use Revit design options   Design options provide a means to maintain two or more alternative designs for the same project or component.

Master It   What are design options in Revit?

Decide on a design solution   The end result of exploring multiple options is to choose one alternative and implement that choice.

Master It   You've explored a number of design options for an entry scheme. Your client has selected one, and you need to incorporate it into the rest of the model and remove the unwanted alternates.

Use design options with parametric design   Making quantitative differences visible is an essential part of presenting multiple alternatives.

Master It   You need to look at some seating layout options for an auditorium space based on different-sized seating and show the seating counts.

Chapter 11

Creating Custom 3D Content

In this chapter we explore how to build your own designed library elements (families) for use in a project. We'll look at how parametric constraints and parameters can be used to build flexible, time-saving, beautiful, and smart content. By learning a few simple rules supported with the knowledge of form making that we covered in Chapters 6 and 7, you can build just about any element and assign it a behavior that you wish it to have—and all of this, without writing one single line of code or knowing a programming language. Building intelligent content is a key feature of Revit and deserves an entire book in its own right, but we will introduce you to some useful concepts and get you going. This chapter will take you through fundamental principles and some compelling use cases using the Family Editor.

In this chapter, you learn how to do the following:

◆ Model parametric 3D families

◆ Nest one family into another

◆ Build relationships between parameters with formulas

Modeling Parametric 3D Families

As a design progresses from the generic to the more refined, you'll need to add more detail and realism to your model. This process involves more faithfully representing what will be built and requires you to start building your own families. Although many types of families are provided out of the box or can be downloaded from websites such as www.bimworld.com, www.revitcity.com, or www.arcat.com, or using the new integrated search tool that connects to Autodesk Seek, you'll inevitably reach a point where your design intent isn't matched by any of those, and you'll need to create new elements yourself. This is when you'll need to dig into the Family Editor and create new building components (Figure 11.1).

Up to now we've covered many of the basic principles of families, including understanding the different family categories, the principles of modeling, form making, and constraints—but we haven't put all this into practice beyond some simple shapes. In the following sections, we'll look at more advanced techniques used to create parametric families with embedded intelligent behaviors.

FIGURE 11.1
Custom design
for a sunshading
element

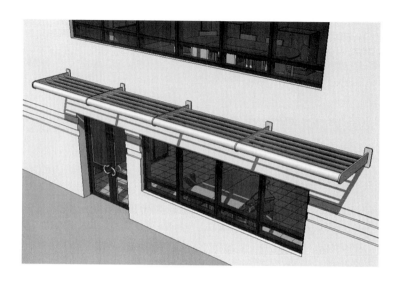

Choosing the Right Family Template

Every family belongs to a category, making it essential to categorize new families correctly so they can be controlled and scheduled logically when loaded and used in a project. Choosing the correct family template when making new families will set the appropriate category. Revit provides templates (see Figure 11.2) for most families. These are hard-coded, provided by Revit, and you cannot create a new template from scratch. That shouldn't be understood as a limitation, since there is a template for all major necessary architectural elements, and those few rare elements for which you might not find a corresponding template can be created using the generic template.

FIGURE 11.2
Family templates

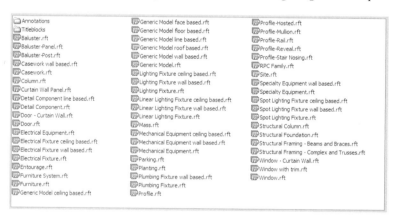

When you decide to create an element on your own, you need to select the correct template. These templates are time-savers, because they already have the right category assigned, provide the most important reference planes that drive the behavior and geometry, and in some cases include text notes to help explain how the family will work in the context of a project. Figure 11.3 shows a window template file, which includes text indicating the exterior and interior of the wall; parametric dimensions for width, sill height, and opening height; and a sample host wall. This is the template to start with when you're creating a new custom-shaped window that you designed.

FIGURE 11.3
Plan, elevation, and 3D views of a template for windows. Text notes, reference planes, and dimensions have been preset.

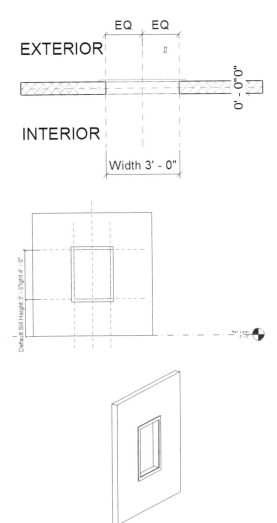

The reference planes that appear in the family environment are the essential "bones" of any family. They establish the critical dimensional rules for the family, define the origin, and provide references that can be dimensioned to when loaded into a project. All templates provide at least two reference planes to start with—without reference planes, you can't make parametric content or dimension it in the project.

Types of Families

Families can be grouped, at the highest level in two categories: those that will appear in one view only (drafting, annotation, 2D families) and those that when placed in a model will appear in any view (model-based).

For model-based families, there are two high-level types: 2D and 3D model-based families. 2D families are used for making 2D details of the model, and 3D families are for making 3D geometric representations.

For 2D families, you can make standard detail components and line-based (2-pick) detail components. Three-dimensional family types include various host-based types (floor, wall, roof, and ceiling), profiles, line-based, work plane–based, and generic model. Note that 3D families can contain nested 2D elements as a way to embed more detailed information about that element directly into the families.

Choosing the correct template is essential to getting the desired categorization and behavior of the element you are creating. To better understand what that means, let's drill deeper.

Host-Based Families

Windows, doors, skylights, and lighting fixtures are all discretely manufactured objects, but they have something in common: they're installed into something else. Without the wall, ceiling, or any other mounting surface, the object has no place to ground itself in a typical building project and it will not be able to be placed. In other words, these types of elements require a host in which they can be placed or by which they can be supported. Thus, for these types of elements, Revit provides host-based families and templates.

When you need content to have an explicit relationship with a wall, floor, or roof, then a host-based family is absolutely the way to go. These are the most common types of families used in Revit and include components such as doors, windows, skylights, solar panels, light fixtures, and balusters. Assuming you've placed some windows and doors in a Revit project, the benefits and behaviors of host-based families need not be covered here in detail. The basic principles are quite simple: once a host-based element is placed in or on a host, there is a dependency established between the element that requires a host and the host in which it is placed. In an example of a wall (host) and window (host-based family), if you move the host, the hosted element will move as well; if you delete the host, the hosted element will be deleted as well. Bear this in mind going forward in developing your model. Figure 11.4 shows several examples of such host-based families.

The golden rule when making a new family is to first think from a category point of view. What am I making? How does it need to behave (in a view or schedule, parametric, limited parameters, etc.)? And once it's made, how is it likely to need to change? Then, use an appropriate template as a starting point. For example, if you need to make a new window, start with the `Window.rft` template; if you are making a table, the `Furniture.rft` template is the way to go.

Windows and doors don't exist in the model in isolated, abstract form, but are always hosted by a wall. This is why when you start creating or editing a window family, you will see a sample host element (a small wall, roof, or floor). The sample host in the family is there just so that it can help you construct the family so it behaves properly in the model—to give you a context in order to build the family so it correctly relates to wall thickness.

FIGURE 11.4
Examples of host-based families

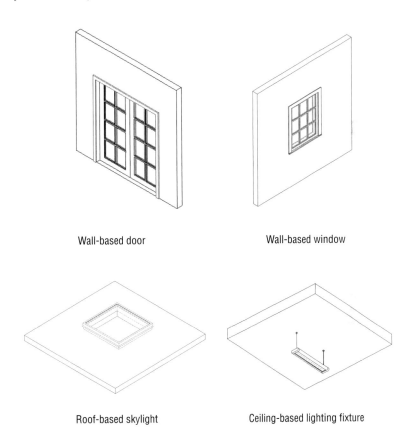

Wall-based door   Wall-based window

Roof-based skylight   Ceiling-based lighting fixture

Note that the host that exists in the family template (such as the wall in the window template) isn't loaded in the project when you load the window—it's present in the Family Editor only as a reference to help you understand how the window will work when loaded into a project. Only the geometry, symbolic lines, and reference planes that you create will end up in your project. This is very important to understand.

PROFILE FAMILIES

Many architectural details have distinct cross sections that run in a linear fashion. Geometrically, these details are constructed by extruding that profile along a path, which maps to how many of the elements are physically manufactured. Baseboards, cornices, handrails, and mullions are all good examples of profile-based elements:

Revit provides special templates designed for elements like these. To create one of these elements, you choose to create a profile family. You will notice that there are a few different profile family templates: Hosted, Mullion, Rail, Reveal, and Stair Nosing. Make sure you pick the correct one when creating a profile family. Once you do that, you start sketching with 2D lines, defining the shape of the profile cross section. Like many sketches in Revit, the profile must be made of *a single closed loop* of lines—multiple loops will lead to errors downstream. For example, if you created a mullion profile like that shown in Figure 11.5 and then tried to load it and use it in a mullion family, you'd get a warning message. Delete the inner loop of lines to get the mullion to work properly.

FIGURE 11.5
Invalid profile: profiles with more than one loop won't work in a project.

If this is true, you must be asking yourself how you can make something like the shape shown in Figure 11.5. Although you can't have multiple loops in the profile family, you can import a detail component into the profile family that will mimic the representation you need; this is possible because there is no penalty for having multiple loops of lines in the detail component. The detail family showing the rest of the content within the outer profile adds much more detailed information about that element. It can be visible in a section of that element in the model (think plan and section views), and you can decide in which levels of detail you want that detail component to be visible.

To control when this level of detail is visible in the model, set the visibility of the detail component so it appears only at fine levels of detail. Continuing with the mullion example (Figure 11.6), take these steps:

1. Start a new family using the `Profile Mullion.rft` family template.

2. Load a complex detail component done by a manufacturer into the mullion profile family. You will find a myriad of them on the Web, usually offered in DWG format, although with every passing day more manufacturers offer their content in `.rfa` format as well.

3. Trace the loaded component with a single loop of lines to get the outer shape of the profile (see Figure 11.6).

4. As you probably don't need to see that level of detail in coarse or medium level of detail (they will probably just make black marks in your drawings in small scales), set the options in the Family Element Visibility Settings dialog box to show the detail only in fine views.

FIGURE 11.6
On the left is the profile sketch, and on the right is a detail component.

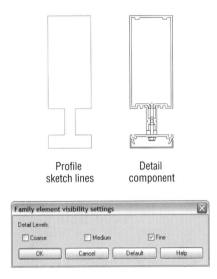

Profile
sketch lines

Detail
component

5. Load the Profile Mullion family into the project by using the Load into Project button.

6. From the Project Browser, under the Curtain Wall Mullions node, locate the Rectangular Mullion family. Right-click to duplicate it and give it a specific name. Open the Type Properties dialog box of that new mullion, and under Construction, then Profile, assign the new profile that you just loaded in the project to the mullion family (see Figure 11.7).

FIGURE 11.7
Choose the profile from the mullion's type properties.

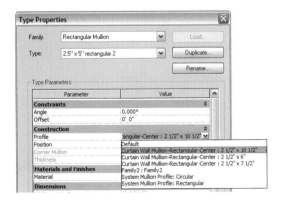

Once a profile is loaded into Revit, it doesn't take 3D form until it's assigned to system families such as mullions, rails, wall sweeps, and gutters. To do this, open the Type Properties dialog box of any of these families and assign the profile to the family. You can use a 2D profile in the definition of a wall as a precast parapet cap, as shown in Figure 11.8.

FIGURE 11.8

Assigning a profile to a system family

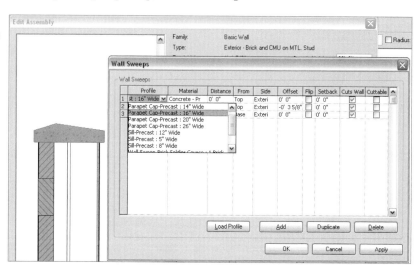

Many companies that sell finish molding provide 2D CAD drawings that you can import directly into a Revit profile family. This is a great time-saver and will keep you from having to draw complex profiles from scratch.

Profiles can be used for many different purposes. To accommodate more specific behavior as well as categorization, six different profile family templates are available: Profile.rft, Profile-Hosted.rft, Profile-Mullion.rft, Profile-Rail.rft, Profile-Reveal.rft, and Profile-Stair Nosing. Be careful to select the correct one, because Revit looks only for specific profiles depending on what you're making. For example, a mullion family won't let you choose a wall-sweep profile; only mullion profiles will show up in the list.

2D Line-Based Families

Working on a 3D model does not mean that all elements need to be modeled in 3D; some are represented using 2D detail drawings. Most details can be drawn using lines and filled regions, but these are inherently difficult to maintain and reuse. For details that are likely to be used in other drawings or projects, you should create detail families. With Revit, you can make stand-alone detail components or line-based families. The line-based family type is great for making elements where length is the primary variable and for making 2D repeating components.

The 2D line-based template (Detail Component line based.rft) allows you to draw a detail element as if you're drawing lines with two picks, but the component can contain as many lines and filled regions as you want. For example, you can draw a detail component that represents plywood (lines plus wood hatch) with two clicks of the mouse.

Making a Plywood Line-Based Family

When we had to make a plywood detail element, we went to the line-based detail family. With this detail template, we created a filled region between the left and right reference planes and assigned a plywood fill pattern to the region. As long as the left and right lines of the filled region are coincident with the reference planes, they will follow the planes when the family is placed in a project and drawn. The cross-sectional dimension of the filled region can be driven by a Thickness parameter, which is set to ¾″ and can later be modified if you need new types:

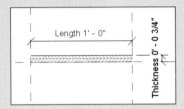

When the plywood family is loaded into the project, we were able to make a symbolic 2D plywood representation with two clicks that defines the length. Once the plywood was placed, we could reselect it and drag either end using the blue grips to stretch the detail. Compared to using a filled region in the project, this method provided parametric constraints, reusability, and incredible ease of use.

3D Line-Based Families

Just like the 2D drafting line-based families, you can make 3D line-based families. For these families, use the template `Generic Model line based.rft`. Examples where you need such 3D line-based families are molding details, sunshades, grating, and any other elements that have length as their primary variable and repeating 3D components. Figure 11.9 shows a 3D chair family that adds chairs as the family is made longer.

Figure 11.9
3D line-based chair family

 With two clicks of the mouse, you can quickly add rich 3D content to your model. Figure 11.10 shows a sunshade example. (Figure 11.1 showed this same sunshade in 3D.) The brackets at the left and right side were modeled in the family using solid extrusions and constrained to the left and right reference planes. The blades were modeled as sweeps between the two horizontal reference planes, using a profile. When placed in the model, the sunshade can be stretched dynamically.

FIGURE 11.10

3D line-based
Sun Shade family

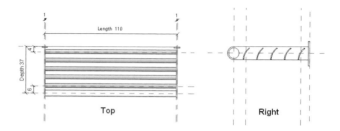

FACE-BASED AND WORK PLANE–BASED FAMILIES

For elements that need the flexibility to be placed on any model face, such as electrical outlets, signage, or coffee pots, there are work plane and face-based families. Not only do these families attach to any surface of the model during placement, but you can also re-host them at any point later to any other surface if need be. Any time you have a component that needs to be installed on multiple types of hosts, think of making the family face-based.

Face-Based Families

You create face-based families with the template `Generic Model face based.rft`. When you open the template, you'll see an abstract host surface on which you can model your family. When you load your family into your project, the host surface in the family maps to whatever face you choose in the project, and your family reorients to be placed on that face automatically. The face you choose can be anything from another family to geometry of a linked file. An example of a face-based family is an HVAC supply register, which you need to be able to place on walls, ceilings, or even floors. Figure 11.11 shows another application of a face-based component, where the curved surface doesn't have a work plane.

FIGURE 11.11

A sign created as a
face-based family
can be placed on a
curved wall.

Work Plane–Based Families

Work plane–based families are placed on the active work plane of the current view. Every view has an active work plane that you can manipulate using the Work Plane tool (see Chapter 6).

Be sure to give the family an appropriate category before loading it so you can control its visibility and graphics.

RICH PHOTOREALISTIC CONTENT (RPC) FAMILIES

When you're rendering a view, it's possible to substitute real model geometry (the family) with highly photorealistic images (such as ArchVision content, available at `http://www.archvision .com/`). For example, a simplified stick figure can turn into a real-looking person when the view is rendered (see Figure 11.12).

FIGURE 11.12
Left: Entourage
family, non-
rendered. Right:
same family when
rendered.

This can be a cool feature when you're rendering, and it makes rendering faster because there is no complex geometry to render. You can create plants, cars, and people using these families.

ASSIGNING A RENDERING APPEARANCE

RPC families are specialized and have specific behavior when rendered. In addition to the 3D and 2D representation that you normally add to a family, you can assign a rendering appearance to the family. This appearance shows up only when you render a 3D view.

You create RPC families using the template `RPC Family.rft`. RPC appearances can only be added to the Entourage and Planting families. When the family is set to either of these categories, a Rendering Type parameter is enabled in the dialog box that opens when you select Settings ➢ Family Category and Parameters. RPC families in these categories have additional type parameters (located in the Family Types dialog box; see Figure 11.13) to control the associated RPC file used when the family is rendered in a project, along with specific properties. Figure 11.14 shows the Render Appearance library and some of the people that come with Revit.

FIGURE 11.13
RPC parameters in
the Family Types
dialog box

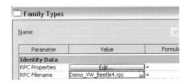

FIGURE 11.14
Render Appearance library for RPC content

Once you've selected an RPC object, you can further refine the properties of the object by clicking on the first Render Appearance parameter. Figure 11.15 shows the properties of a Steelcase Think chair, with options to change the back and seat fabric. You'll also notice that RPC content supplies you with 3D model geometry.

FIGURE 11.15
Editing the render appearance properties for a chair

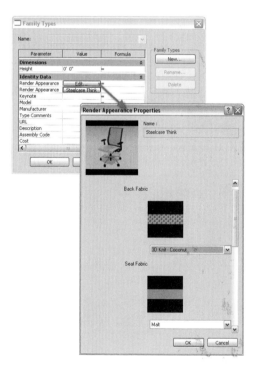

DETAIL COMPONENT FAMILIES

As you'll see in Chapters 20 and 21, a typical workflow to complete a construction document set involves enriching the model with 2D details in detail views. These detail elements typically depict cross sections or elevation views of elements that don't need to be modeled in full 3D (to do so would only bog down the model and not add much value). For this use case, you can use detail component families to add detail to model or drafting views; these details are visible only in the view in which they're placed. Examples include blocking, studs, steel sections, bolts, flashing, and so on:

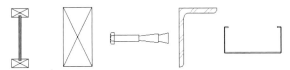

Detail components can contain lines, filled regions, masking regions, symbols, and other detail components. Detail components are meant to represent real building components and assemblies, so they scale with the model when the view scale is changed. To create a new detail component family, use `Detail Component line based.rft` or `Detail Component.rft`.

3D FAMILIES

To accommodate fast and easy creation of architectural content, many templates have been made for you with the appropriate category selected. Examples include `Furniture.rft`, `Furniture Systems.rft`, `Mechanical Equipment.rft`, and `Plumbing fixture.rft`, to name a few. Use these templates to make content when starting from scratch.

CURTAIN PANEL FAMILIES

Curtain walls and aluminum storefront systems are composed of mullions, panels, operable windows, and doorways. In Revit, the Curtain Wall tool organizes all these components into an integrated system of parts. For panels, the default solid and glazed options are usually sufficient. Adding doors and windows to a curtain wall requires you to make custom windows and doors made with a special template in the Family Editor. Figure 11.16 shows a curtain wall door family in the Family Editor—you'll notice that these templates don't contain host walls as other door family templates do.

Keep this in mind: to add doors to a curtain wall, you must use one of the special *curtain wall doors*—you can't place a standard door into a curtain wall. Use the `Door - Curtain Wall.rft` template to create these families. Essentially, they're like regular door families, but the width and height are dynamically tied to the size of the curtain wall cell in which the door is placed. As the curtain grid spacing changes, so does the size of doors placed in the wall. As you can see in Figure 11.17, the door family adapts to the size of the curtain grid spacing.

FIGURE 11.16
Double-panel
curtain wall door

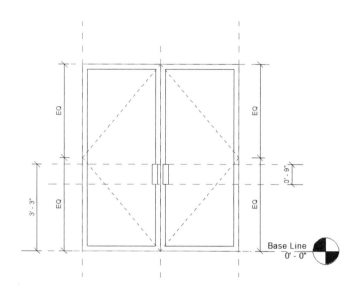

FIGURE 11.17
The curtain wall
door adjusts its
width and height
to the size of the
cell in which it is
placed.

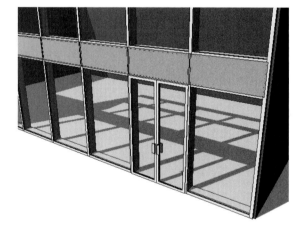

Family Categories and Parameters

In every Revit family, settings control specific behavior of the family and set the category. Depending on what category you assign the family, you can get a different set of type parameters and category-based parameters. For example, in a window family template, preset parameters for sill height, width, and height are hard-coded into the family (see Figure 11.18). In a furniture family template, you don't see these parameters.

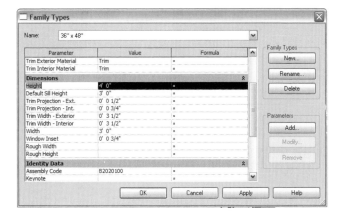

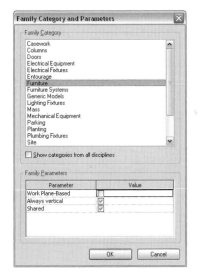

FIGURE 11.18
Family parameters
for windows

Another set of parameters affects the entire family based on the category it belongs to. You can access these settings by choosing Settings ➤ Family Category and Parameters. In the resulting dialog box (Figure 11.19), you can set or change the category and also adjust other parameters that affect how the family will behave when placed in a model.

FIGURE 11.19
The Family
Category and
Parameters
dialog box

In the figure, the Entourage category has four family parameters listed: Work Plane–Based, Always Vertical, Rendering Appearance Source, and Shared. Remember that changing the active category at the top of the dialog box may enable or remove family parameters displayed in the bottom of this dialog box. Let's briefly review what these parameters do:

Work Plane–Based Enabling this option allows the family to be hosted by the active work plane when placed in the project or nested into another family. Any nonhosted family can be set to be work plane–based. Any family using the generic template (furniture, site, casework, and so on) can be set to work plane–based, as such families aren't required to be hosted by another component (like doors or windows).

Always Vertical   This parameter keeps a family oriented in the positive Z direction when placed in a project. In most cases this is desired, because levels are always horizontal. But when you have sloped floors or sloped site conditions, you may want the component to be oriented perpendicular to the surface it's placed on. Parking stripes and cars placed on a sloped slab of a parking structure are examples where making the family *not* always vertical makes sense (see Figure 11.20).

FIGURE 11.20
Family set to not
be always vertical

As another example, the Always Vertical parameter comes into play with trees placed on a toposurface. As the site changes slope, you want to keep the trees vertical and not have them look like they're falling over.

Rendering Appearance Source   This only applies to the categories Planting and Entourage. There are two options here: Third-Party or Family Geometry. Choosing Third-Party automatically imports 3D geometry from RPC content. Choosing Family Geometry does not use RPC geometry but rather the geometry you construct yourself in the Family Editor.

Shared   This parameter controls the visibility in a project of a family that is nested in another family component. You may choose to nest families to create assemblies or save time modeling components that repeat. Nesting has implications when you need to tag or schedule the family. For example, consider a window assembly with a main light and two side lights—one on each side. If the design intent is that the window is to be tagged and scheduled as a unit, then the families will be nested into a host family and the Shared parameter will remain unchecked. In this situation, only the host family (the family containing all nested windows) will schedule. If the intent is that the assembly be constructed from separately purchased units and assembled on site, then the nested families should have the Shared parameter checked. This allows each nested window to appear on the schedule as if placed separately.

Additional Family Parameters for Structural Content   When you choose various structural categories, you'll see additional options show up that are specific to structural framing, foundations, and columns. We will not go into detail here on each of these, but structural engineers should be aware that special functionality has been built into family templates depending on the type of family you are creating.

Nesting One Family into Another

When you open a family in the Family Editor, you can load another family and place instances of it into your host family much as you would in a project. This powerful feature allows you to manage your content and reuse existing work. For example, consider the workstation family illustrated in Figure 11.21.

FIGURE 11.21
Nested families used to create a workstation

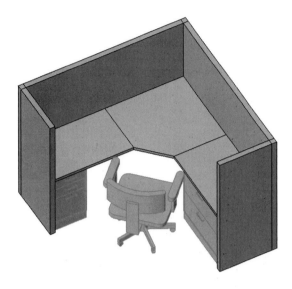

This family is composed of loaded filing cabinets, a desktop, partitions, and a chair. This makes building the family much more manageable and also makes it much easier to place and manipulate the family as a unit when placed in a project.

One common example of family nesting is the combination window. Rather than model the entire unit from scratch, you can load and insert existing window components into a base window family. You place the windows just as you would in a project. For example, you can place a fixed-window family in the center and two double-hung windows on either side (see Figure 11.22). You can then save the family and load it into a project. The entire assembly acts as one element when placed in the model.

FIGURE 11.22
Combination window: One family, created from two nested families

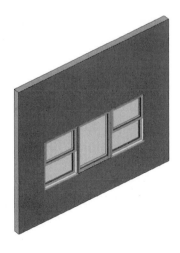

Choosing to use nested families not only saves modeling time but can also simplify your work in the Family Editor. It's often easier to manipulate and constrain an assembly of extrusions as a nested family than to model the same geometry in the host family. In another example, a bracket for a sunshade is modeled separately and nested into the host sunshade family (Figure 11.23). Two instances of the bracket can now be placed and constrained in the family much more easily than modeling the same elements as separate extrusions. Later in the chapter, we review some powerful features that you can use via family nesting.

FIGURE 11.23
Nesting a bracket
into a Sun Shade
family (host)

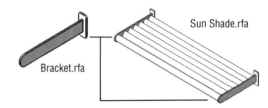

Sun Shade.rfa

Bracket.rfa

Finally, nesting of one family in others allows for centralized change management: if you create a handle, you can nest it in doors, windows, or curtain wall doors and windows; and if any change is made to the handle, it will propagate to all other families where it has been nested.

Scheduling Nested Families

When a family is nested in another family, by default it doesn't appear in project schedules and isn't taggable. For the most part, this is the desired behavior because it avoids overburdening your schedules with unneeded subassembly elements. A nested family's geometry displays, but is treated as part of the host family.

In some cases, you may want to schedule nested families—for example, if you've nested chairs within a table family. To expose nested families to tagging and scheduling, you need to enable a parameter called Shared, as we detailed earlier. To do so, follow these steps:

1. Open the nested family.

2. Choose Settings ➤ Family Categories.

3. Select the Shared option in the Family Parameters group.

4. Reload the family into all its host families, and then reload those host families into your project.

Once all your nested families have sharing enabled, they will be schedulable and can also be tagged in your project.

Linking Parameters

When families are nested, the parameters of the nested family *aren't visible in your project* by default. Only the parameters of the host family are visible, and they can be modified in the project environment. If the element you're nesting is unlikely to change parametrically, this may be desirable. However, if you want to control the nested element's parameters as well, you must explicitly link them to parameters in the host family.

In our example, the support bracket of the sunshade is a nested family, and you need to be able to drive its dimension from the context of the project. Let's look at how you'd accomplish this:

1. Open a new project and draw a wall.

2. While in plan view, load the `sunshade.rfa` family found in the chapter folder and place it somewhere along the wall.

3. In the host family, select an instance of a nested family, and open its Type Properties dialog box.

4. To the far right of the Value field, click the button to open the Associate Family Parameter dialog box.

5. The parameters *in the host family* are listed. Select one that you want the nested family to be constrained to.

   Doing so ties the nested family to a parameter of the host family. Only parameters of the same type can be associated with one another. (Types include Text, Integer, Number, Length, Area, Volume, Angle, URL, Material, Yes/No, and <Family Type>.) For example, two lengths can be associated with each other, or two material parameters can be associated, but a length and a material parameter can't.

6. Click OK. Once the link is made, the small button in the Type Properties dialog box displays an equal sign.

In Figure 11.24, the depth of the nested bracket family is associated with the depth of the host Sun Shade family. Changing the Depth parameter of the sunshade causes the depth of all support brackets to also change to the same value.

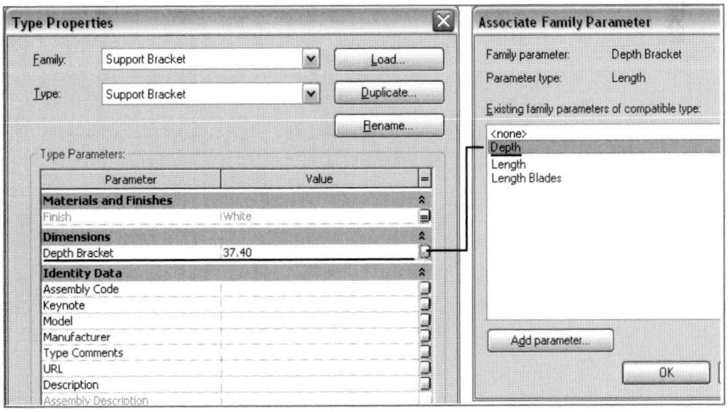

FIGURE 11.24

Linking a parameter in a nested family to the host

You can link any kind of parameter, from dimensions to materials to text. For example, the Sun Shade family has two material parameters: Material Supports and Material Blades. By selecting one of the nested brackets and opening its type properties, you can assign its Finish Material parameter to the sunshade (host) material parameter Material Supports. When this is done, you can control the bracket material from the project by assigning a material to the sunshade's Material Supports property.

Parameters in many nested families can be linked to a single parameter in a host family to provide powerful control over size, quantity, and even display of family subassemblies from within a project. This is a great way to limit exposing a family's internal complexity when the family is loaded into a project.

Linking Parameters (Conditional Visibility)

Every nested family or piece of solid geometry has a Visible parameter. This parameter allows you to control the visibility of nested families by creating a Yes/No parameter in the host family and then linking the nested family to that parameter. Checking or clearing this check box controls the element's visibility in the host family when viewed in a project.

For example, let's look at a window family that has a shutter family nested in it and two instances placed on either side of the window. You can create a Yes/No parameter called "DisplayShutters" in the window family and link the Visible parameter of the shutter family to this parameter (Figure 11.25).

Two types are then created: Window w Shutters and Window w/o Shutters. The former has DisplayShutters selected and the latter has it deselected. When loaded into the project, you can use the two types to control whether or not the shutters are visible (Figure 11.26).

FIGURE 11.25

Linking a Yes/No parameter to the Visible parameter allows the same window to be shown with and without shutters.

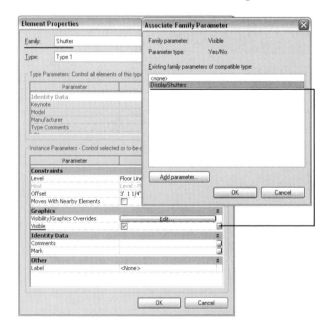

FIGURE 11.26
Two types of a single family—conditional geometry display

Building Relationships between Parameters with Formulas

There are many examples of building components that have repetitive subcomponents built into them: evenly spaced shelves, brackets, structural members, nested chairs, or other components—the list goes on. Figure 11.27 shows a perfect example where using an array to place vertical and horizontal shelves makes sense.

FIGURE 11.27
Arrays can help maintain element spacing in a family and allow you to control the number of grouped element instances.

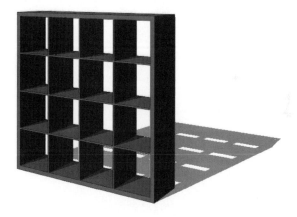

In the Family Editor, you can use arrays on any geometry you've created or on any nested families you're using. The Array tool in the Family Editor works the same as it does in the project, but in the Family Editor, it can also be driven parametrically.

Making a Parametric Array

To make a parametric array in the Family Editor, you need to use the Group and Associate option in the Options bar. This allows you to parametrize the number of instances of the element in the array. When you select the array, a number appears that corresponds to the total number of groups in the array. If you change this number, the number of groups in the array updates. If the array was created with the option Move to: Last, elements are added or removed between the start and end of the array as defined when it was created. If the array was created with the option Move to: 2nd, elements are added or removed after the end of the array.

You can turn the array number into a parameter by selecting the array and labeling it as a parameter (see Figure 11.28). Once the number is selected, the Options bar displays a Label drop-down menu. Select <Add parameter…> to create a new number parameter.

FIGURE 11.28
Assigning an
array number to a
parameter

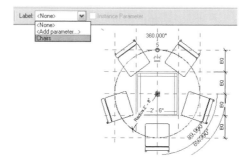

Once you make the assignment of the array number to a type parameter, the number of elements in the array can be controlled from the Family Types dialog box. In Figure 11.29, the number parameter Chairs controls the number of chairs in the radial array. Changing the number automatically changes the number of elements in the array.

FIGURE 11.29
Array of chairs
in Table-Dining
Round w
Chairs.rfa

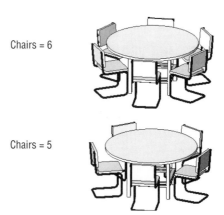

Chairs = 6

Chairs = 5

Encoding Design Rules

Proportion has been an important consideration in the design of objects for centuries. Relating width, height, and depth to a design rule informed the design of architecture dating back to early Greek and Egyptian times. The dimensional size of one element often drives the size of other related elements. Think, for example, of a window with muntins; the number of muntins often grows in proportion to the size of the window (see Figure 11.30). To this end, Revit provides ways to relate parameters to one another using formulas. By changing one dimension of a component, you can effectively change many other dimensions and thereby maintain design intent. Often, your family will have parameters that determine its dimensions, and it's the relationship between these dimensions that you want to maintain.

FIGURE 11.30
Window with
muntins added as
function of height

EXAMPLE: USING A FORMULA TO CONTROL DIMENSIONS

In a simple case, you can imagine using a formula to set the width of a shutter in a window family. The window family may already have types that control its width and height. Knowing that the shutters should always be equal to the window height and half the width, you can use a formula and let Revit do the calculation for you. Follow these steps:

1. Load the shutter family into your window family, and place an instance on either side of the window.

2. In the window Family Types dialog box, create a new parameter by clicking the Add button:

3. In the Parameter Properties dialog box (see Figure 11.31), give the parameter the name **Half Width**, and set Type of Parameter to Length. You can group the parameter under Dimensions to make it easier to find.

FIGURE 11.31
Use the Parameter
Properties window
to give the new
parameter a name
and type.

4. Back in the Family Types dialog box, in the parameter's formula field, enter **=Width / 2** (see Figure 11.32). This ensures that the parameter is always half the window's width. The Value field displays the calculated value; when the family is loaded into your project, the parameter will display but won't be editable.

5. Select the nested shutter in your family, and link its dimensions to the window so they change together. To do so, in the Associate Parameter dialog box (accessed from the small button at the far right of the parameter row), click the button in the correct row of the Shutter element properties. Associating the shutter's Width parameter with the window's Half Width parameter and its Height to the window's Height connects the two objects.

The shutter will now adapt its dimensions to the window whenever its shape is adjusted.

FIGURE 11.32
A simple formula for half width

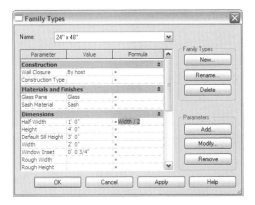

USING A FORMULA TO CONTROL AN ARRAY

In the next example, you'll see how you can use a formula to control the number of elements in an array used to construct a sun-shading family (Figure 11.33). (You'll find this file on the book's companion web page, www.sybex.com/go/masteringrevit2009, as Sunshade.rfa.)

FIGURE 11.33
A sunshade family can be parametrically defined with a formula.

This family is constructed of a support bracket and blades that make up the shade. The design calls for supports to be added dynamically as a function of length. In this example, both the brackets and the shades are arrayed so that their quantity is determined by the size of the family when placed in the project. The number of brackets is controlled by the Support Quantity parameter, and the number of blades in the shade is controlled by Blade Quantity. Both of these can be driven by formulas. The calculated value of a formula is always displayed in the Value column. Let's look deeper at this design problem and see how it can be solved.

Support Quantity uses a conditional statement to guarantee that there are always at least two support brackets in the family. A conditional statement takes this general form:

If (*condition*, do this, else do this)

In the support case, if Support Minimum is true, then the number of supports is set to **Length / 60**. If it's false, then the value is **2**.

Support Minimum is a Yes/No parameter that's also set to a formula. In this case, if Length (the length of the family) is greater than 135″, Support Minimum is Yes (true); otherwise, it's No (false).

In Figure 11.34, you see the default Length value is 110″. So Support Minimum is false, and Support Quantity is set to 2. When the length exceeds 180″, Support Quantity equals 3, and an additional support bracket is introduced via the array.

FIGURE 11.34
Formulas used to control arrays

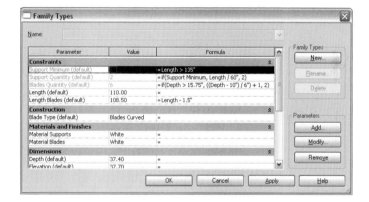

Blade Quantity is simpler. The conditional statement determines whether the depth is greater than 15.75″. When it's larger (shown as 37″). The number of blades is one more than **Depth – 10″ / 6**. When the depth is less than 15.75″, there are only two blades.

Figure 11.35 shows how changing the length to 180″ causes a new bracket to be added based on the formula.

FIGURE 11.35
Different shade sizes evaluated via the formula. On the left, two supports are added. On the right, three supports are added.

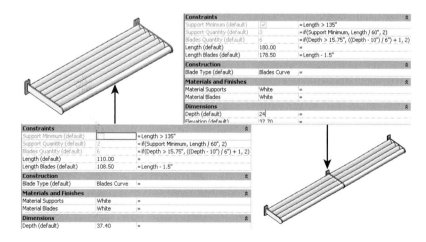

Real World Scenario

MAKING A PARAMETRIC SUNSHADE

We constructed an advanced line-based family to model an exterior shading element. The family uses arrays with a formula to capture the design intent regarding the number of blades, proper support spacing, and blade angle. The resulting family can be quickly placed with two clicks, and the correct number of supports are placed. Note that the way this family is constructed, it must be placed in a plan view of the model. Once you place the family, you can experiment with different blade angles and numbers of blades in the system by changing a few properties:

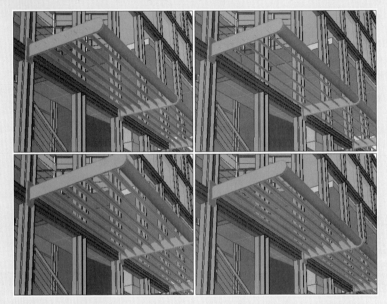

Building a Parametric 3D Family

In this exercise, you'll assemble a furniture ensemble consisting of a round table surrounded by chairs (see Figure 11.36). To accomplish this, you'll do the following:

◆ Nest families

◆ Create an array

◆ Use a formula to lock in design intent

◆ Use parameter linking to control element visibility

FIGURE 11.36
Table family with
nested chairs

FIGURE 11.36
Table family with
nested chairs

NESTING THE CHAIR

To nest a chair into the table family so the whole family works as a unit, follow these steps:

1. Open Table Round.rfa from the Chapter 11 folder of the book's companion web page (www.sybex.com/go/masteringrevit2009).

2. Open the Ref. Level plan view using the Project Browser, and fit the view to the screen.

3. Choose File ➤ Load from Library ➤ Load Family to load Chair-Breuer.rfa from the Chapter 11 folder.

4. Activate the Component tool on the Family Design bar.

5. The active component in the Type Selector should be Chair-Breuer.

6. Place a single instance of the chair, as shown in Figure 11.37. Use the spacebar to rotate the chair to face the table, and type **SI** to use the intersection snap override to snap the chair origin to the reference-plane intersection.

FIGURE 11.37
Place an instance
of chair in the table
family

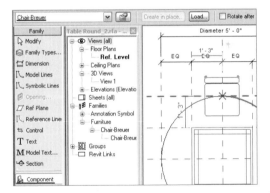

CREATING A PARAMETRIC ARRAY

Next, you'll make the chair array become parametrically driven. Follow these steps:

1. Click the Family Types command on the Design bar to launch the Family Types dialog box.

2. In the Parameters group, click Add.

3. In the Parameter Properties dialog box, enter the information shown in Figure 11.38 for the parameter, and click OK.

FIGURE 11.38
Adding a new
Chairs parameter

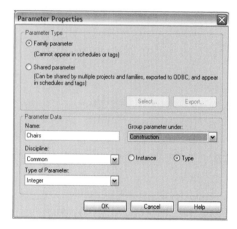

4. Add a Radius parameter (Figure 11.39), and click OK.

FIGURE 11.39
New Radius
parameter added

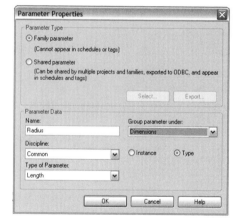

5. For the Radius parameter, enter the following in the Formula column: **Diameter / 2**. This ensures that the radius is half the diameter.

6. For the Chairs parameter, enter the following in the Formula column:

(Diameter *3.14)/2'6"

This formula sets the desired number of chairs relative to the circumference of the table.

7. Select the chair instance you placed earlier, and select the Array tool. Change the array type in the Options bar to from linear to radial. A red box appears around the chair, with a blue rotate control in the center. Drag the blue control to the intersection of the two reference planes at the center of the table to set the center of the array.

8. Define the start of the array by clicking at the origin of the chair, and then move your mouse into the Options bar area. Set the Move To radio button to Last, and enter **360** in the Angle field.

9. Press the Enter key twice. Revit creates three chairs.

10. To constrain the array to the radius of the table, activate the Dimension tool, and choose the Radial placement method from the Options bar:

11. Hold the tool over the table edge, and press Tab until the status bar reads *Array : Array : Reference*. Click in any whitespace to finish the dimension.

12. Select the dimension. In the Options bar, set the Label drop-down menu to the Radius parameter. This sets the radius of the array to match the radius of the table.

13. Select a chair group, and then the array reference (the line that connects the chair groups and displays the array number). You may need to press Tab until you see the status bar read *Array : Array : Reference*.

14. Once you make this selection, the number of chairs should change to match the value of the formula-driven Chairs parameter (Figure 11.40).

FIGURE 11.40

Assign the array reference to the Chairs parameter.

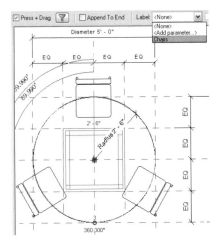

CONTROLLING VISIBILITY

To modify the family so that chairs can be made visible (or not visible) as part of the family definition, follow these steps:

1. Click Family Types on the Design bar to open the Family Types dialog box.

2. In the Parameters group, click Add.

3. In the Parameter Properties dialog box, enter the data shown in Figure 11.41.

FIGURE 11.41
Fill out the Parameter Properties dialog box as shown here.

4. Click OK.

5. Select one of the chair groups, and choose Edit Group from the Options bar.

6. Select the chair, and edit its element properties, either by right-clicking and using the context menu or by clicking the Element Properties icon in the Options bar.

7. Under the Graphics group, find the Visible parameter. At the far right end of the row, click the small button to launch the Associate Family Parameter dialog box.

8. In the dialog box, choose the displaysChairs parameter you created earlier.

9. Click OK twice to dismiss the Associate Family Parameter and Element Properties dialog boxes; then, click Finish Group.

10. Click the Family Types Design bar command to launch the Family Types dialog box.

11. Choose the type 36″ Diameter in the Type drop-down list at the top of the dialog box.

12. At the right, in the Family Types group, choose New.

13. Type in the name **36″ Diameter no Chairs**, and then click OK.

14. In the Graphics group, select the displaysChairs parameter, and then Click OK to close the Family Types dialog box.

15. Save the family. Choose Load into Project from the Design bar to view the completed family.

16. You should have four types of families available. Place an instance of each to see the results (see Figure 11.42).

FIGURE 11.42
Finished family types placed in a project. All four types are displayed, illustrating the use of the array with the formula and the conditional display of the chairs.

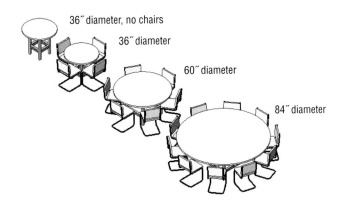

36″ diameter, no chairs

36″ diameter

60″ diameter

84″ diameter

The Bottom Line

Models are full of content, and while the majority of the time you can find the needed content in the Revit library or on the Web, at some point you'll need to make your own designed content. Don't be afraid to dive into the Family Editor and start creating your own custom content. Begin with simple families, and elaborate as you go. When approaching an element you wish to model, think first of how it's constructed and what aspects of it you need to control parametrically—not all components need to be full-blown parametric objects. Also think about how you might break a component into subcomponents. Consider the eventual application of the family—will it be hosted in walls, ceiling, or roofs? Or is it a stand-alone object? As you become more familiar with how parameters work, start considering formulas and parameter linking to save time and embed intelligent behavior.

Model parametric 3D families   When you're making a new family, consider how it will be used in the model, and choose an appropriate template.

> **Master It**   You found a ceiling-mounted lighting fixture that you want to use in your existing project, but you can't find a Revit family for it in any libraries or online communities. How would you start?

Nest one family into another   The ability to nest families in other families lets you create content that's easier to manage and improves your workflow.

> **Master It**   Building components are often composed of a series of subcomponents that form an overall assembly. Think of some common examples and what strategies you could use to build such content in Revit.

Build relationships between parameters with formulas   Create smart connections between geometry and dimensions to create efficient and parametric content.

> **Master It**   You can use dimensional relationships to tie the size of one object to the size of another. How do you do this in the context of a family?

Chapter 12

Extended Modeling Techniques—Walls

In the previous chapters we covered basic modeling techniques for constructing a simple building. We skipped over many additional features to give you a handle on essential workflow, the user interface, and making modifications to the model. In this and the following two chapters, we'll cover more advanced features that are available any time you're modeling in Revit. As you'll see, with a little refinement and creativity, you can create a wide range of building components with the standard tools.

In this chapter, you learn how to do the following:

◆ Use advanced modeling techniques for standard walls

◆ Use advanced techniques to create stacked walls

◆ Use advanced modeling techniques for curtain walls

Using Advanced Modeling Techniques for Standard Walls

Walls are made from layers of materials that represent the construction assemblies used to build real walls. In Revit, these layers can be assigned functions, allowing them to join and react to other, similar layers in the model when walls, floors, and roofs meet. The wall *core* is one of these special layers, and understanding it will help you when designing your walls.

Wall Core

Revit has a unique ability to identify a *wall core* that is much more than a layer of material. Every wall type in Revit has a core material with a boundary on either side of it. The core defines the structural part of the wall and influences the behavior of the wall and how the wall interacts with other elements in the model. The core of a wall creates a reference to which you can dimension, designating the location of structural wall components rather than finish materials. The core boundary can also be used as the location definition when drawing host elements (walls, floors, ceilings, roofs). For example, you can constrain a floor sketch to the structural stud layer of walls by using the wall-core boundary to create the sketch. If walls change size or are swapped, the floor sketch maintains its relationship to the core boundary and will automatically adjust to the new wall.

To access and edit wall-core boundaries and material layers, select a wall and choose Element Properties ➤ Edit/New. In the Type Properties dialog box, select Structure as the parameter to edit. This will open a new Edit Assembly dialog box. From here you can add or delete wall layers, define their materials, move layers in and out of the core boundary, and assign functions to each layer (see Figure 12.1).

FIGURE 12.1
The Edit Assembly dialog box of a wall type lets you define the construction layers of a wall.

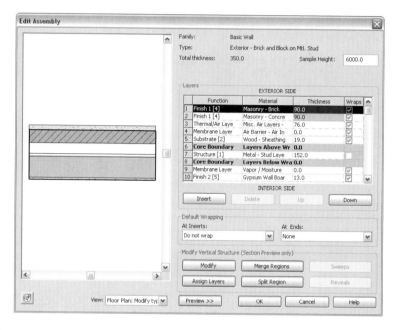

To get a feel for how core layers are used in relation to a floor, start a new session of Revit and follow these steps:

1. Open a new project, select the Wall tool from the Basic tab in the Design bar, and draw a simple rectangular floor plan. Prior to drawing it, from the type selector, select a multilayered wall type in order to understand the value of the exercise—the Brick on CMU wall type works well. Draw at least four connected walls that represent a simple floor plan.

2. Use the View Control bar to switch to fine or medium detail view so you can see the wall layers. (In coarse views, wall layers are never displayed.)

3. From the Modeling tab of the Design bar, select the Floor tool, keep the default Pick Walls option, and in the Options bar, check the Extend into Wall (to Core) option.

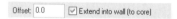

4. Position your cursor over an edge of the wall (do not click yet), press Tab to highlight all connected walls, and then click to select and zoom in. A sketch line indicating the shape

of the floor will be created. This sketch line indicates the position of the floor boundary relative to the wall—it's drawn at the exterior edge of the wall core. Make sure you've selected all walls as a reference to create the floor and click Finish Sketch.

5. Create a section through the wall and open the section view. Again, make sure your view is set to medium or fine. You'll see the edge of the floor and how it aligns with the wall construction. Figure 12.2 shows the sketch in plan and how the floor looks when finished in section.

FIGURE 12.2
Floor sketch indicated in plan view and section through the floor and the wall in section view

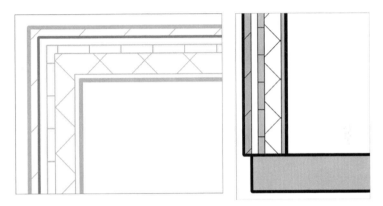

If you change the wall type later on or move its position, the floor will update to match its relative position to the wall's new core position.

Layer Join Cleanup

Having clean and legible drawings is important when representing construction design intent. To this end, Revit provides a wall layer priority system that intelligently manages the cleanup of wall layers between touching or intersecting multilayered walls. Revit provides six functions (levels of priority), with *Structure* having the highest priority (Figure 12.3).

FIGURE 12.3
Each wall layer has a function.

When you create a new wall type and begin defining and adding layers to the wall, you need to assign a material, thickness, and priority to those layers. When you're assigning a priority, think about the function of the layer in the wall—is it finish? Substrate? Structure? This decision will help Revit understand your intent and help clean up your walls down the road.

Editing Wall Joins

If you encounter situations in which the automated wall cleanup doesn't correspond to your expectations, Revit lets you cycle through a range of possible layer configurations using the Edit Wall Joins tool, located in the Options bar.

With the Edit Wall Joins tool, you can edit wall join configurations. The default wall join is set to butt join (See Figure 12.4). Activate the Edit Wall Joins tool, and place your cursor over a wall join. (This can be a corner where two walls meet.) The Options bar shows some alternative configuration options: Miter and Square. A miter join is also shown in Figure 12.4.

FIGURE 12.4
A butt wall join
and a miter
wall join

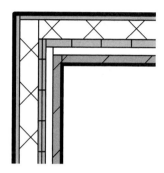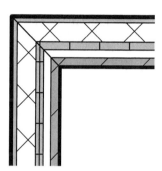

Disjoining Walls

In some cases, you will want to override the intelligent wall cleanup that Revit provides. For example, a nonrated partition should not interrupt the gypsum board in a fire-rated wall. The Disallow Join option lets you create this condition. To access this command, right-click the blue control dot at the end of any wall and select Disallow Join from the context menu. Doing so breaks the auto-join cleanup. Figure 12.5 shows the default cleanup (left) and the same join after disallowing the join and adjusting the wall end (right).

FIGURE 12.5
The Disallow Join
option provides
extra flexibility.

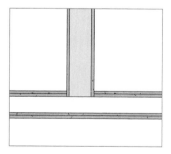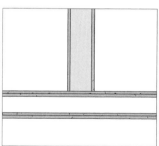

A wall on which Disallow Join has been applied displays a new Allow Join symbol upon selection (Figure 12.6). This is an improvement in Revit 2009, and its purpose is to give you a visual aid so you know when a wall has been consciously set to not join. Note that the symbol only appears when a single wall has been selected.

FIGURE 12.6
The Allow Join option indicates a wall that has Disallow Join applied to it.

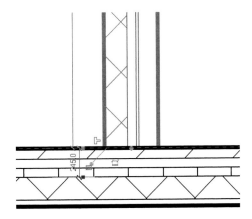

Stacked Walls

Walls in a building, especially exterior walls, are often composed of different wall types, made out of different material combinations and with different widths, that stack one on top of another over the height of the façade. At the very least, most walls sit on top of a foundation wall. You can create such walls by creating individual walls of different types at different heights, but if you want an intelligent relationship of all different wall types that make up one wall and that act together as one wall (for example, the foundation wall moves and you expect walls on top of the foundation to also move), a *stacked wall* might be a good way to go.

Stacked walls allow you to create a single wall entity composed of different wall types stacked vertically on top of each other. The wall types used in a stacked wall need to be types already defined in your project. To understand how stacked walls work and how to modify one, follow these steps:

1. Open a new session of Revit, and make sure three levels are defined (if you don't have three levels defined, switch to an elevation view, add a few new levels, and then go back to your floor plan view).

2. Pick the Wall tool and select Stacked Wall: Exterior - Brick Over CMU w Metal Stud (located at the bottom of the list in the Type Selector). In the Element Properties dialog box, click the Edit/New button and then duplicate the wall type to create a new stacked wall.

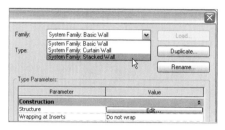

3. Edit the structure parameter and click the Preview button to see the wall in section (Figure 12.7). When you're editing the Stacked wall type, you'll notice that the user interface is slightly different from when you're working with a basic wall. Rather than editing individual wall layers, in this dialog box you are editing stacked wall types.

FIGURE 12.7
Section preview of stacked wall type

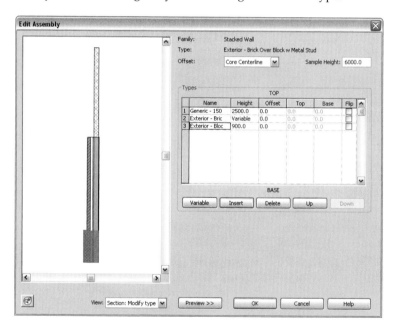

4. Click the Insert button to add a new wall. A new row appears in the list and allows you to define a new wall. Select the Generic wall type from the Name list, and set the Height value. With a new row selected, click the Variable button. This will allow the wall to vary in height to adjust with level heights.

5. Go back to your plan view and draw the new wall, setting its top constraint to Level 3.

6. Cut a section through the model and change the heights of Level 1 and Level 3 to see the effect this has on the wall. (Make sure the level of detail is set to medium or fine so you can see the wall layers.) You'll see that changing Level 2 does not change the bottom walls because they are fixed in height. However, changing the height of Level 3 changes the height of the variable wall (Figure 12.8).

FIGURE 12.8
The middle section of this stacked wall varies on a per-instance basis.

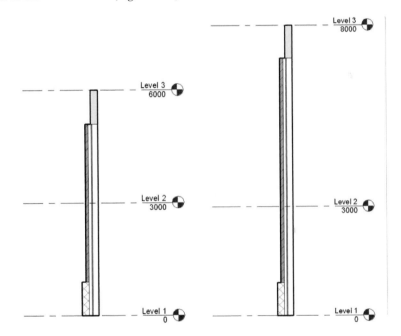

Adding Wall Articulation

Walls are often complex and articulated in their composition. Cornices, reveals, corrugated metal finish, and other projections are used all the time. Some wall finishes have more than one material on them, and they can be flush or of different thickness. Revit can accommodate any of these types of design articulation in smart wall assemblies. Some examples of such walls, called compound walls by Revit users, are shown in Figure 12.9.

FIGURE 12.9
Compound vertical walls: (A) brick wall with horizontal sweeps, reveals, and a top finish; (B) compound wall with aluminum corrugated finish, trapeze-shaped; (C) compound wall with aluminum corrugated finish curved; (D) compound wall with slanting wall finish.

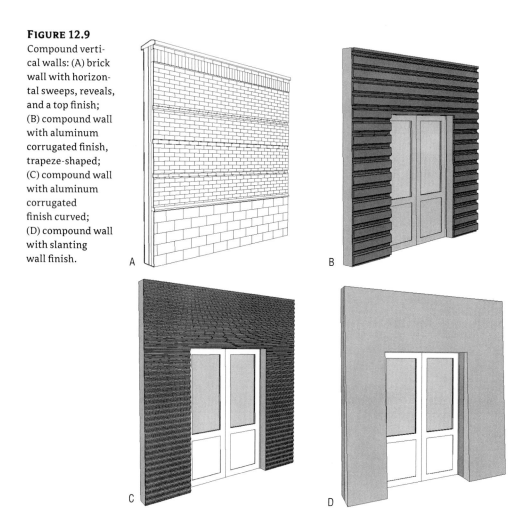

From the Edit Assembly dialog box of any basic wall type, you can enable a preview of the wall. This preview allows you to view the wall in either plan or section. When the section preview is active, additional tools also become active and allow you to place geometric sweep and reveal components on the wall (Figure 12.10).

FIGURE 12.10
With section view
active, tools for
modifying the
vertical structure
become active.

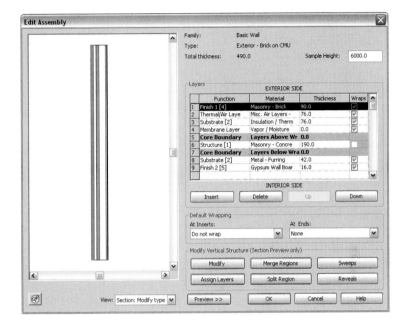

EXAMPLE: ASSIGNING TWO DIFFERENT MATERIALS ON THE FINAL FINISH OF A WALL

Let's start with a case where you need to create a wall that has two different material finishes
that are flush aligned (Figure 12.11).

FIGURE 12.11
Exterior wall layer
built of two differ-
ent materials
arranged vertically

1. Select a multilayered wall as a base and duplicate it to create a new wall type.

2. In the wall's Edit Assembly dialog box, switch the view to show a section view of
   the wall.

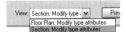

In this exercise, the exterior wall layer is plaster, but what we need is the lower 4′ (120cm) to be brick and to keep the walls flush with one another.

3. Place your cursor at the beginning of the exterior finish layer. This highlights the wall component in the section preview. Select the Split Region tool and split the layer at the 4′ (120cm) height (Figure 12.12).

FIGURE 12.12
The Split Region tool applied to the exterior component

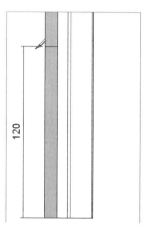

4. The moment you split the layer, you will notice that the Finish layer reports a thickness of 0.00, meaning that it is variable.

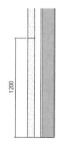

5. Add one more layer. Use the Insert button and add that layer right after the first exterior finish layer. Change its function to Finish 1, its material to Brick, and its thickness to **0**.

6. Place the cursor at the front of the row of the new material and select it. This highlights the material and shows a thin red line in the section view (Figure 12.13).

FIGURE 12.13

Highlight the lower portion of the split wall layer to assign a new material to it.

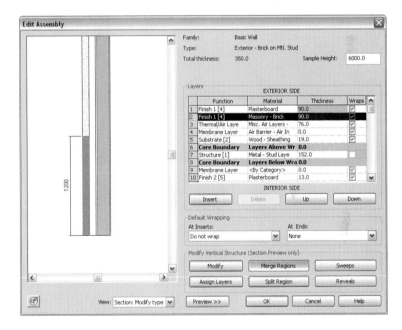

7. After adding that layer, click the Assign Layer button and select the portion of the wall that you wish to assign the zero thickness layer to (in this example, the lower portion).

The result is that the selected portion of the wall has the new layer assigned and your wall exterior face shows two different materials.

While working on a complex compound wall, you might have a situation where you need to merge horizontal or vertical wall layers that already exist in the wall. For that, use the Merge button and select the line between two layers. Once the cursor is over a line between two layers, an arrow indicating which layer will override the other one during the merge shows up, as shown in Figure 12.14.

FIGURE 12.14
(A) Merge layers
vertically;
(B) merge layers
horizontally

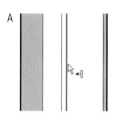
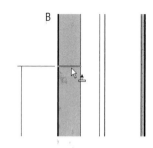

FIGURE 12.14
(A) Merge layers
vertically;
(B) merge layers
horizontally

Wall Wrapping

The way materials are detailed at insert conditions (doors, windows, and openings) varies depending on the construction type, building conventions, and aesthetics. Layer wrapping options are available in the wall Edit Assembly dialog box; however, they aren't sufficient to accommodate a complex wrapping situation specific to a particular door or window. To achieve more control over these construction conditions, you need to set parameters in the window or door family itself.

In the Family Editor, you can assign a *Wall Closure* property to reference planes; it defines a plane to which wall layers that have wrapping assigned to them will wrap.

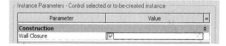

In a door or window family, in the Element Properties dialog box for the reference plane check the option Wall Closure. This means that the exterior wall layers that have wraps assigned terminate at this reference plane. The effect can be seen in Figure 12.15.

FIGURE 12.15
(A) The reference
plane in the Family
Editor and (B) its
effect when set
to Close

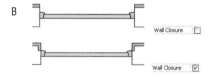

Sweeps and Reveals

Many walls have linear embellishments that are attached or embedded in the construction. Cornices, brick soldier courses, and reveals are all examples. Using basic walls, you can add these elements directly into wall types.

Clicking the Sweeps or Reveals button in the Edit Assembly dialog box opens a new dialog box where you can define profile families to use as sweeps or reveals.

These profiles (more on profiles in Chapter 11) are 2D shapes made out of simple lines and then swept along the length of the wall at a specified height. Many profiles representing cornices, skirting, and chair rails ship with Revit, but if you need to create a custom profile, you can use the Profile Family template. Choose File ➤ New Family ➤ Profile to access the Revit Family Editor. From here, you draw a single closed loop of lines at the desired real-world scale and load the profile back into your project. Follow these steps to get a feel for the workflow:

1. Click the Wall tool and select Generic Wall and duplicate it.

2. Open the Wall Assembly dialog box.

3. In the preview view, switch to section view. The six Modify Vertical Structure options become active at the bottom of the dialog box.

4. Click the Sweeps button to bring up the Wall Sweeps dialog box, shown in Figure 12.16.

FIGURE 12.16
The Wall Sweeps dialog box before inserting any profiles

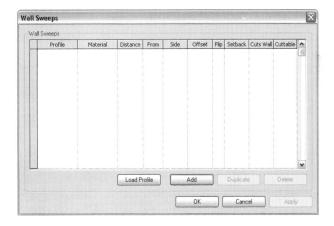

5. Click the Load Profile button, browse to the Profiles folder, and load these two profiles:

   ◆ Cornice profile: Traditional (1)

   ◆ Skirting profile: (Base 2, Ogee or similar)

6. Click the Add button. This adds a row in the dialog box that lets you select one of the loaded profiles and set its position relative to the wall geometry.

7. Add both profiles. Set the Traditional profile's From value to Top and the Ogee profile's From value to Base. Doing so attaches the profiles to the top and bottom of your wall. Figure 12.17 shows the profiles attached to the top and bottom of the wall.

FIGURE 12.17
Profiles attached to
wall top and base

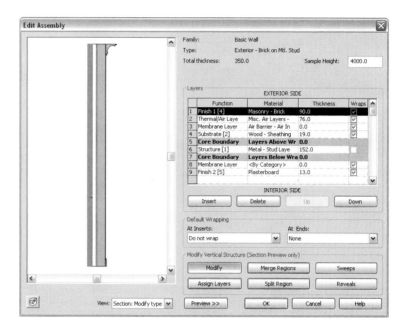

8. Click OK. Draw a segment of this wall in the drawing area. Check out the wall in section and 3D views to see the result (see Figure 12.17).

Using the same principles outlined for adding traditional elements, you can get creative and add any type of profile you want. Figure 12.18 shows a wall with corrugated siding added as an integrated wall sweep.

FIGURE 12.18
Wall with corru-
gated siding created
with integrated
wall sweep

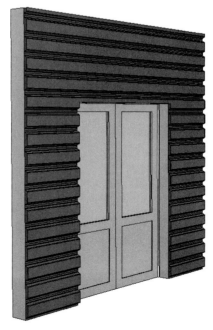

REVEALS

Reveals can be added to a wall using the same workflow you use with sweeps; the only difference is that the profile is *subtractive* rather than additive.

WALL SWEEP RETURNS

When you're working on traditional architectural projects, the wall sweeps usually wrap around door openings in thick walls. Revit can accommodate that using the Change Sweep Return command. To understand this feature, follow this simple exercise:

1. Open a new session of Revit and place a generic wall. Switch to a 3D view.

2. Rather than placing a sweep in the wall type (as we just did), we can use another method for placing sweeps: the Host Sweep tool in the Modeling tab of the Design bar. From the Host Sweep menu, choose Wall Sweep.

These sweeps can be placed either vertically or horizontally using the Options bar.

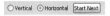

3. Add a horizontal sweep to the middle of the wall. Use the temporary dimensions to place the sweep at the desired height.

4. Choose the Opening tool, also located in the Modeling tab.

Select Wall Opening, and using this tool, draw an opening that intersects the sweep (Figure 12.19).

5. Select the sweep—it will display a blue grip at the end (the edge of the opening). Click the Change Sweep Return button in the Options bar. While in the options bar, you can also set the angle of the return or decide to make a straight cut. The cursor turns into a knife symbol, and when you click somewhere on the profile it creates a new segment that can be wrapped around the edge of the opening. Press Esc or use the Modify tool to exit the command. You will need to zoom in close to the end of the sweep to really see the effect. (If you zoom very closely, the lines might become thick and ugly—in that case, click the Thin Line Mode button in the toolbar.)

FIGURE 12.19
A manually placed wall sweep intersected by a wall opening shown in (A) perspective, and (B) elevation

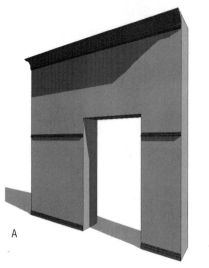
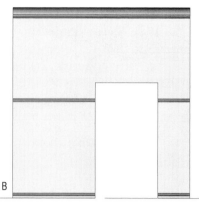

A

B

6. Select the sweep again, and drag the control to adjust the length of the sweep. Figure 12.20 shows how the return can be modified.

FIGURE 12.20
Wall sweep returns

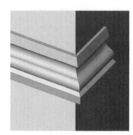

EXTENDING WALL LAYERS PAST THEIR BASE

In many construction scenarios, you need layers of materials to extend beyond the base of the wall. A typical example is the extension of sheathing and siding on an exterior wall (Figure 12.21). Letting layers extend requires you to unlock the bottom edges of the wall from the sectional preview in the Edit Assembly dialog box. Once the layers have been unlocked, an instance parameter of the wall becomes enabled, either Base Extension Distance or Top Extension Distance (depending on which edges you unlocked). This value can be entered directly in the Element Properties dialog box or adjusted graphically when you select the wall by dragging the small blue triangle control at the bottom of the unlocked layer.

FIGURE 12.21
Example of wall layers extending past the base of the wall

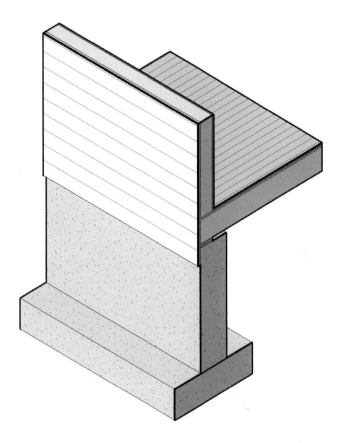

Follow these steps to enable the Base Extension parameter of a wall:

1. Select a generic wall type and draw one in a new project. Select it and duplicate it. Name it **Exterior wood siding**.

2. Select the structure parameter to open the Edit Assembly dialog box.

3. Add a new layer to the exterior of wall, set its function to Finish (4), use the material *siding - clapboard*, and give it ¾″ thickness.

4. Open the preview and look at the section view. Zoom into the bottom of the wall.

5. Select the Modify button, and then click on the bottom edge of the exterior siding layer. Click the padlock icon to unlock the layer (Figure 12.22). Note that if you wanted to unlock additional layers, they all need to be adjacent—you cannot, for example, extend layers on either side of the core.

FIGURE 12.22
Use the padlock icon to unlock layers.

6. The layer is now unlocked. Click OK twice to get back to the Element Properties dialog box. You'll see that the Base Extension Distance parameter is now enabled. Type in **-10"** for this parameter, and check the wall in 3D. You'll see that the wood siding layer is now extending 10˝ below the level shown in Figure 12.23.

FIGURE 12.23
Modifying the wall layers

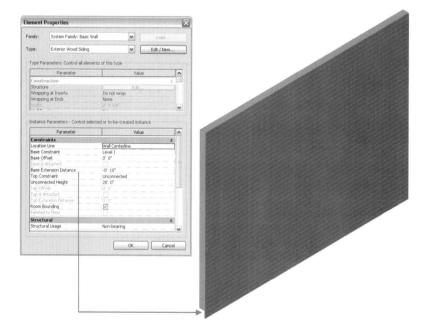

Creating Custom In-Place Walls

When you're working on traditional architecture or restoration of historic buildings, you often need to create walls that are irregular in shape. The Create tool, found under the Modeling tab of the Design bar, lets you address such wall styles. Figure 12.24 shows an example. This tool allows you to draw solid geometry using one of four modeling methods. Each created form is assigned a specific category that is later used to control visibility and behavior in the model. For example, assigning a sweep to the category Wall allows the wall to host inserts such as windows and doors.

FIGURE 12.24
Manually constructed wall used to create nonvertical wall surfaces

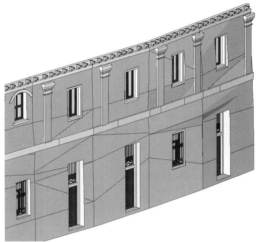

The finished wall

The two wall blends combined to make the wall

Courtesy of Simone Cappochin

🌐 Real World Scenario

USING BLENDS TO MAKE NON-STANDARD WALL SURFACES

The wall in Figure 12.24 was created using a series of blends assigned to the category Wall using the manual Create method under the Modeling tab of the Design bar (also referred to as creation of *in-place* families). It still behaves like a wall: you can insert doors and windows into it; they will cut through the geometry and create openings. If you are making a wall schedule, you will also be able to schedule these walls and get correct documentation—very slick!

Various wall types can be created using this method. Consider the modeling tools we've covered previously and how you can use them to generate unique wall profiles.

Using Advanced Modeling Design Techniques for Curtain Walls

Curtain walls in Revit are unique wall types that don't behave like the rest of the wall families. While they share some similar traits, there are additional elements unique to curtain wall assemblies.

The curtain wall A curtain wall is drawn like a basic wall and is available in the Type Selector when the Wall tool is active. It has top and bottom constraints, can be attached to roofs, can have its elevation profile sketch-edited, and is scheduled as a wall type.

Curtain grids These are used to lay out a grid that defines the physical divisions of the curtain wall. The layout grid can be designed freely as a combination of horizontal and vertical segments or can be a type with embedded rules that specify regular divisions. Figure 12.25 shows a typical grid division and expressive curtain panels in between.

FIGURE 12.25
Curtain wall with regular orthogonal grids and expressive curtain panels

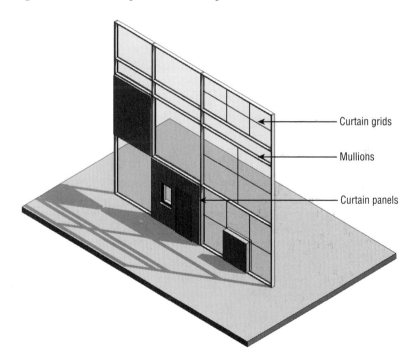

Curtain grids

Mullions

Curtain panels

Mullions These represent the metal profiles on a glass façade, and in Revit they follow the geometry of the grid. They can have any shape that is based on a mullion profile family. Mullions can be vertical or horizontal. If you have a playful spirit, however, you can make curved mullions as shown on Figure 12.26.

FIGURE 12.26
With a little bit of
inventive spirit,
you can have
curved mullions
as well!

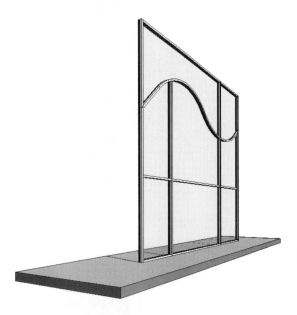

Curtain panels These fill in the space between gridlines and are always one of the following:

Empty panels No panel is placed between the grids.

Glazed panels These can be made out of different types of glass that can have any color or transparency.

Solid panels and panels with wall types These can take on any geometry you wish and thus create the most interesting structures, like the one shown in Figure 12.26.

Wall types as infill You can also choose from the Type Selector a wall type to fill the space between the gridlines (mullions). All wall types in the project will be available for your selection. Adding a wall type is usually a typical case in office partitions where the lower portion is a parapet wall and glass fills the upper portion of the metal stud wall.

Designing a Curtain Wall

In this exercise, we'll walk through the creation of a simple curtain wall. To draw a curtain wall, you can either draw a standard wall and then change its type to Curtain Wall or select a Curtain Wall type from the Wall Type Selector first. Follow these steps:

1. Select the Wall tool.

2. From the Type Selector, select Curtain Wall.

3. In the Level 1 plan view, draw a simple curtain wall (Figure 12.27). Use the wall type Curtain Wall 1.

FIGURE 12.27
A generic curtain
wall before adding
any grids or mul-
lions looks like a
simple glass wall.

4. Toggle the view to see the result in 3D.

5. Divide the wall into panels using the Curtain Grid tool on the Modeling tab in the Design
   bar. Mouse over the edges of the wall to get a preview of where the grid will be placed.
   Revit has some intelligent snapping built into grid placement that looks for midpoints
   and points that will divide the panel into thirds. Place the grid so that you get something
   like Figure 12.28.

FIGURE 12.28
Curtain wall with a
few added grids

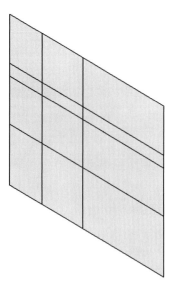

6. Place mullions on the wall. You can place one mullion at a time by selecting separate grid segments. If you want to apply the same mullion on all segments, hold the Ctrl key and click a gridline to select all segments and apply the mullions. With mullions placed, your wall should look like Figure 12.29.

FIGURE 12.29
Mullions applied to the grids on a curtain wall

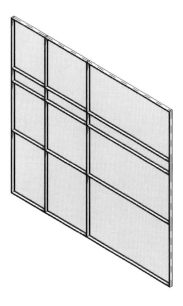

7. Let's say you want to add more mullions, but this time you don't want them to extend the entire height of the curtain wall. Select the Curtain Grid Line tool, and place new grids (Figure 12.30).

FIGURE 12.30
To add more mullions, you will need to add another grid.

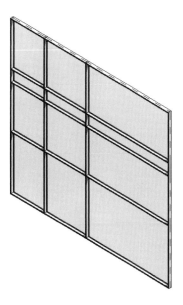

8. Before applying a mullion to the new gridline, delete the segments of the gridline where you don't wish the mullion to occur. Close the Curtain Grid tool, and select the newly created gridline. Click the Add or Remove Segments button in the Options bar, and click the segment you want removed.

Add or Remove Segments

Remove the top and bottom segments, and then add mullions (Figure 12.31).

FIGURE 12.31
Removing portions of the grid and applying a mullion on the remaining segment of the grid

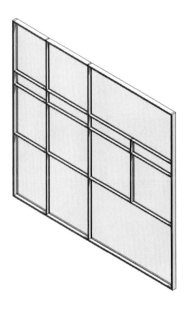

Curtain Panels

Curtain panels fill the space between the curtain grids and mullions. These elements are created in the Family Editor using the Curtain Panels family template. They can be found under File ➢ New Family ➢ Curtain Wall Panel.rft. The Revit default template has a couple of curtain panels preloaded: System Panel Glazed and System Panel Solid. You can duplicate different types of these families and change the material, thickness, and offset to customize the appearance.

Figure 12.26 earlier in the chapter shows some very creative curtain panels.

SELECTING THE ELEMENTS WITHIN THE CURTAIN WALL

Revit provides specially tailored selection options in the context menu to aid with workflow and interaction when you're working with curtain walls.

When you hover the mouse over or select an element in a curtain wall, take note of the status bar in the lower-left corner of the screen: it tells you exactly the type of element you're about to select or have already selected. Depending on what the mouse is hovering over, various selection options are available. The elements you can select include the following:

- The entire curtain wall entity (indicated by a green dashed line surrounding the curtain wall)
- A gridline
- A mullion
- A curtain panel

To select the element you want, use the Tab key until that element is highlighted.

Curtain Wall Doors and Windows

Curtain walls can host specially designed doors and windows. Keep in mind that standard doors and windows cannot be hosted by a curtain wall. These specially designed elements are recognizable by a name that indicates they are curtain wall doors or windows. Revit schedules them as doors and windows, but their behavior is dependent on the curtain wall. Curtain wall doors and windows adapt their width and height to fill in grid cells. Essentially, they behave exactly like panels—they've just been made to appear and schedule as doors or windows. To insert a door within a curtain wall, choose File ➢ Load Library ➢ Load Family. Navigate to the Doors folder, and select a curtain wall door (single or double). Figure 12.32 shows a curtain door panel that has been swapped with a glazing panel. To make your own doors, choose File ➢ New Family ➢ Door - Curtain Wall.rft.

FIGURE 12.32
A special curtain wall door family is used to represent a door within a curtain wall.

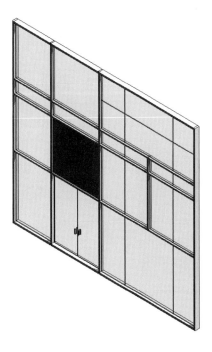

Complex Curtain Wall Panels

Look at the complex-shaped curtain panels in Figure 12.33. You may think, "Oh, I can *never* do that!" Well, Revit can help you do it—and do it easily. The creation principle behind any of these types of curtain walls is the same as you learned in Chapter 10. By being smart about nesting and linking parameters, it is possible to build sophisticated curtain panel families.

FIGURE 12.33
Complex curtain wall panel example using a series of nested components

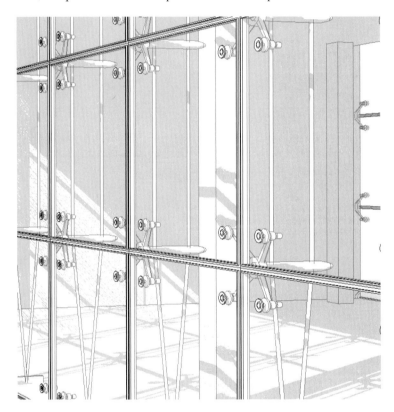

The Bottom Line

Revit provides you with the tools to create everything from standard walls to more complex assemblies. In all cases, the walls will behave intelligently and relate to other elements in the model. Digging deeper into the wall properties, you'll discover some great ways to improve workflow, and get more detailed designs out of the model.

Use advanced modeling techniques for standard walls Many design situations require more than just the basic wall features; learn to use the more advanced Revit tools.

Master It A design calls for a horizontal soldier course in a brick wall every 12′ on the façade. Using Revit, how would you build this into a wall element?

Use advanced modeling techniques to create stacked walls   Walls along a building façade usually have different construction layers from foundations to the top of the building. Stacked walls allow for a single wall to be constructed with varying wall types along its height.

> **Master It**   You have a building project where you are still experimenting with a number of floors but have already defined the wall types for the foundation, typical floor, and the attic and have combined them in a stacked wall type. How do you define the stacked wall so that it will accommodate middle floors with varying heights?

Use advanced modeling techniques for curtain walls   Curtain walls find their way into many architectural projects and designs. Knowing how to manipulate curtain walls in Revit is a key piece of the software for many design solutions.

> **Master It**   You've got to add a doorway to a storefront façade you've made. How would you go about doing this?

Chapter 13

Extended Modeling Techniques— Roofs and Slabs

In the previous chapters we covered basic modeling techniques for constructing a simple building. We skipped over many additional features to give you a handle on essential workflow, the user interface, and making modifications to the model. In this chapter we cover more advanced features that are available any time you're modeling in Revit. As you'll see, with a little refinement and creativity, you can create a wide range of building components with the standard tools.

In this chapter, you learn how to do the following:

◆ Understand the various roof creation methods

◆ Create all kinds of roofs

◆ Work with advanced roof and slab shape editing

Understanding the Various Roof Creation Methods

Roofs can come in many shapes, sizes, and degrees of complexity. They can be as simple as a single-pitch shed roof, or they can involve complex sine curves or intersecting vaults. Once you understand Revit's primary concepts, logic, and tools, you will be able to design just about any roof shape.

In general, roofs in Revit can be constructed in four different ways:

Roof by footprint   Use this method to create any standard roof that more or less follows the shape of the building footprint and is a simple combination of roof pitches.

Roof by extrusion   This method is best applied for roof shapes that are geometrically generated by extrusion of a profile, such as sawtooth roofs, barrel vaults, and waveform roofs.

In-place roof   This technique is used to accommodate roof shapes that cannot be achieved with either the footprint or extrusion methods. They are either done by using the general modeling techniques and applying a roof category to that geometry, or by using an underlying mass form.

Roof by face   You select faces of massing forms to create standard thickness roofs. You can create those underlying massing forms within Revit, or import geometry created in other modeling applications into a mass family and use it as an underlay to create the roof by face.

The following sections provide a close look at these approaches and review their application to real-world scenarios.

Footprint Roofs

Use the roof by footprint method to create any standard roof that more or less follows the shape of the footprint of the building and is a simple combination of roof pitches (Figure 13.1).

FIGURE 13.1
Simple roof created using the roof by footprint method

These roofs are based on a sketched shape that you define in plan view at the soffit level and that can be edited at any time during the development of a project from plan and axon 3D views. The shape can be drawn as a simple loop of lines, using the Line tool, or can be created using the Pick Walls method. The latter means that the exterior walls are used to define the shape of the roof.

The best way to conceptualize the roof by footprint method is to understand that the sketched shape defining the main shape of the roof is just a simple, closed loop of lines—nothing more than that, regardless of whether it's drawn or picked.

The Pick Walls method provides an intelligent selection method, so if you select walls as references to generate the sketch lines, with or without an offset to the walls, the lines will maintain a smart relationship with the walls. The Pick Walls method is the suggested approach for creating roofs by footprint. By selecting the walls to generate the sketch for the roof, you are creating an exclusive relationship between the walls and the roof so that if the design of your building later changes (wall position, level height, wall height, etc.), the roof will follow that change and adjust to the new wall position without any intervention from you (Figure 13.2). Like any change in Revit, this happens everywhere in all views, and thus not only the model but also its entire documentation and related quantities will be updated.

To guide you through the creation of roof by footprint and explain some of the main principles and tools, here is a brief exercise demonstrating the steps:

1. Open a Level 2 plan view and create a building footprint similar to Figure 13.3.

2. From the Basics or Modeling tab of the Design bar, click the Roof tool and choose Roof by Footprint.

3. From the Sketch tab of the Design bar, select the Pick Walls tools (this should be the default).

FIGURE 13.2
Using the
Pick method:
(A) original roof;
(B) the entrance
wall position has
changed, and the
roof updates
automatically;
(C) the angle of the
wall to the right of
the entrance has
changed, and the
roof changes to a
new shape.

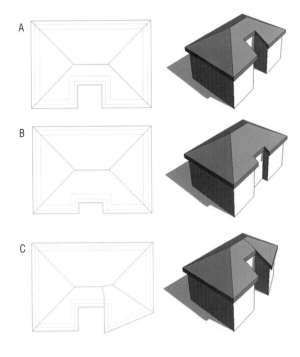

FIGURE 13.3
Draw a simple set
of walls.

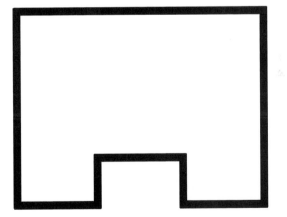

4. To define whether you want a sloped or flat roof, use the Defines Slope check box in the Options bar. The Overhang parameter allows you to define the value of the roof overhang beyond the wall. When the Extend into Wall (to Core) option is checked, the overhang is measured from the wall core. If the option is deselected, the overhang is measured from the exterior face of the wall. When you've chosen to create a roof by footprint, the Options bar makes these tools available:

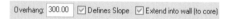

5. After defining these settings, place your cursor over one of the walls (don't click), and using the Tab key, select all connected walls. Your display should look like Figure 13.4.

FIGURE 13.4
Roof sketch lines are automatically drawn after Tab-selecting the bounding walls and entering the command, and they are offset from the walls by the value of the overhang as defined in the Options bar.

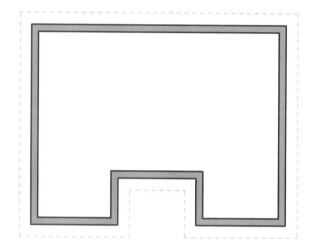

6. Click the Finish Roof button.

If the shape of the roof doesn't respond to your expectations, at any time you can select the roof and select Edit from the Options bar to return to sketch mode, where you can edit lines or sketch lines or the slope.

To change the slope definition or angle of individual portions of the roof, select the roof, and then click Edit on the Options bar. This brings you back to Sketch mode; select the sketch line of the roof portion for which you wish to change the slope and either toggle the Defines Slope button in the Options bar to remove or add a slope, or click the slope value that is displayed when you select the sketch line. If you mistakenly made all roof sides with slope but wanted to make a flat roof, you can Tab-select all sketch lines that form the roof shape and clear the Defines Slope box in the Options bar.

Roof slope can be measured in different ways: it can be set as an angle or percentage rise. All slope measuring options can be found by choosing Settings ➢ Project Units ➢ Slope ➢ Units (see Figure 13.5). If the current slope value is not in units you wish to have (suppose it displays percentage but you want it to display an angle), change the slope units in the Format dialog box—you will not be able to do that while editing the roof slope. Setting it here means specifying the way you measure slopes for the entire project.

FIGURE 13.5
Format dialog box
for slopes

Here are some of the important instance properties you should be aware of and need to set properly; all are found in the dialog box shown in Figure 13.6.

FIGURE 13.6
Roof Properties
dialog box

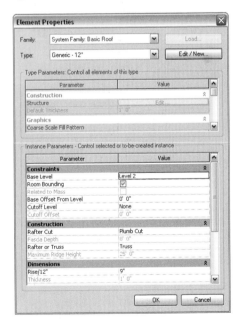

Base Level   As in other Revit elements, this is the level at which the roof is placed. The roof moves with this level if it changes height.

Room Bounding   When this is checked, the roof geometry has an effect on calculating room area and volume.

Related to Mass   This property is active only if a roof has been created with the roof by face method (Massing tools).

Base Offset from Level   This option lowers or elevates the base of the roof relative to the base level.

Cutoff Level   Many roof shapes require a combination of several roofs on top of each other—for this you need to cut off the top of a lower roof to accommodate the creation of the next roof in the sequence. Figure 13.7 shows an excellent example of this technique.

FIGURE 13.7
The cutoff level applied to the main roof, and a secondary roof built on top of the main roof using the cutoff level as a base

Cutoff Offset   When the Cutoff tool is applied, the Cutoff Offset value also becomes active and allows you to set the cutoff distance from the level indicated in the Cutoff Level parameter.

Rafter Cut   This defines the eave shape. You can select from Plumb Cut, Two Plumb Cut, or Two Plumb Square. When Two Plumb Square is selected, the Fascia Depth parameter is activated and you can set the value for the depth.

Rafter or Truss   With Rafter, the offset of the base is measured from the inside of the wall. If you choose Truss, the plate offset from the base is measured from the outside of the wall. Figure 13.8 is a typical example of a roof by rafter cut.

FIGURE 13.8
Construction
drawing of a
rafter detail

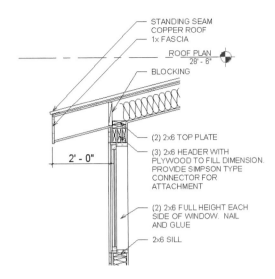

STANDING SEAM
COPPER ROOF

1x FASCIA

ROOF PLAN
28' - 6"

BLOCKING

(2) 2x6 TOP PLATE

(3) 2x6 HEADER WITH
PLYWOOD TO FILL DIMENSION.
PROVIDE SIMPSON TYPE
CONNECTOR FOR
ATTACHMENT

2' - 0"

(2) 2x6 FULL HEIGHT EACH
SIDE OF WINDOW. NAIL
AND GLUE

2x6 SILL

Roof by Extrusion

The roof by extrusion method is best applied for roof shapes that are generated by extrusion of a profile, such as sawtooth roofs, barrel vaults, and waveform roofs. Like the roof by footprint method, it is based on a sketch; however, the sketch that defines the shape of the roof is drawn in elevation or section view (not in plan view) and is then extruded along the plan of the building (see Figure 13.9).

FIGURE 13.9
A barrel-shaped
roof extended
with sunshades.
The main roof is
an extruded arch
sketch.

The Roof by Extrusion tool offers additional settings in the Options bar when selected:

Roofs by extrusion do not have an option to follow the building footprint, but that is often needed to complete the design. To accommodate this, a special tool called Cut Plan Profile is provided. This tool is available from the Options bar when a roof by extrusion is selected.

To briefly explain the concept: you create your roof by extrusion by defining a profile in elevation that is then extruded above the building. The extrusion follows a straight path, which is not necessarily the same as the building footprint. If the shape of the building is nonrectangular in footprint or the shape of the roof you want to create is not to be rectangular, this tool will let you carve geometry from the roof to match the footprint of the building using a plan sketch.

You will recall that with sketch-based design, any closed loop of lines creates a positive shape, every next loop inside it is negative, the next one inside that negative one will be positive, and so on. In Figure 13.10, a roof by extrusion was drawn at an angle to the walls. To clip the roof to meet the walls, the Cut Plan Profile tool was used to draw a negative shape.

FIGURE 13.10
The Cut Plan Profile tool applied in plan view to an extruded roof to follow the exterior shape of the building

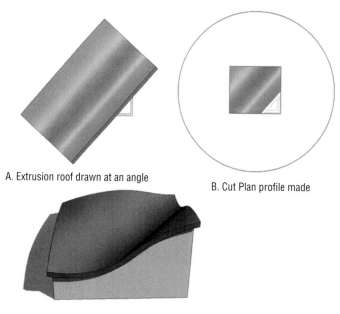

A. Extrusion roof drawn at an angle

B. Cut Plan profile made

C. Resulting roof

In-Place Roofs

The in-place roof technique accommodates roof shapes that cannot be achieved with either of the previously mentioned methods. It is the usual way to model historic roof shapes or challenging roof geometries such as domes and onion-domed roofs (see Figure 13.11).

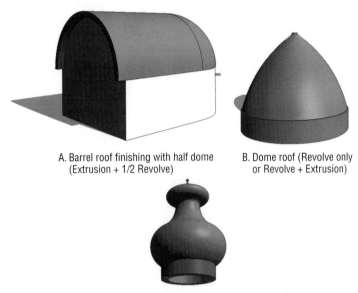

A. Barrel roof finishing with half dome
(Extrusion + 1/2 Revolve)

B. Dome roof (Revolve only
or Revolve + Extrusion)

C. Traditional Russian onion dome (Revolve)

Here's the concept: you create a geometry using the Create tool from the Modeling tab of the Design bar, assign a roof category to it, and go wild with your creativity.

To start an in-place roof family, click the Create button on the Modeling tab. Select Roofs from the Family Category list (Figure 13.12), and click OK. This list allows Revit to schedule the new element as a roof.

FIGURE 13.12
Set the category for
an in-place roof.

Family Category and Parameters	
Family Category	
Generic Models	
Lighting Fixtures	
Mass	
Mechanical Equipment	
Parking	
Planting	
Plumbing Fixtures	
Roofs	
Site	
Specialty Equipment	
Structural Columns	
Structural Foundations	
Structural Framing	
Topography	
Walls	
Windows	

☐ Show categories from all disciplines

Family Parameters

Parameter	Value

OK   Cancel

You can create any roof shape using the modeling techniques of extrusion, sweep, revolve, blend, or any combination of them (see Figure 3.13). You can, using the Edit Shape tools, edit any roof shape manually, adding points and slopes. There is more about advanced shape editing later in this chapter, in the section "Working with Advanced Roofs and Slab Shape Editing."

FIGURE 13.13
Organic-shaped roof created using the new Swept Blend modeling technique

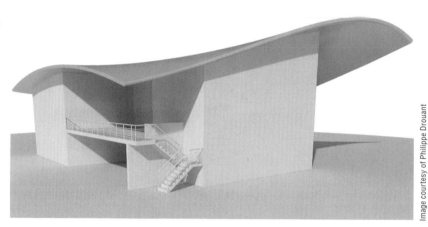

Image courtesy of Philippe Drouant

Sloped Glazing

You saw earlier that a curtain wall is just another wall type made out of panels and mullions organized in a grid system. Similarly, sloped glazing is just another type of a roof that has glass as material and mullions for divisions. Using sloped glazing, you can make roof lights and shed lights, and use them to design simple framing structures.

To create sloped glazing, make a simple pitched roof, select it, and using the Type Selector switch to the Sloped glazing type. Once you have done that, switch to a 3D view and use the Curtain Grid tool to start applying horizontal or vertical grids that define the panel sizes; then you can apply mullions. Figure 13.14 demonstrates the process of converting a standard roof into sloped glazing.

FIGURE 13.14
(A) Standard roof.
(B) Convert a
standard roof into
sloped glazing.
(C) Divide with
curtain grid.
(D) Add mullions to
the grid. (E) Finish
applying all mul-
lions to the grid.
(F) Change curtain
panel from glass to
empty. (G) Finished
rafters.

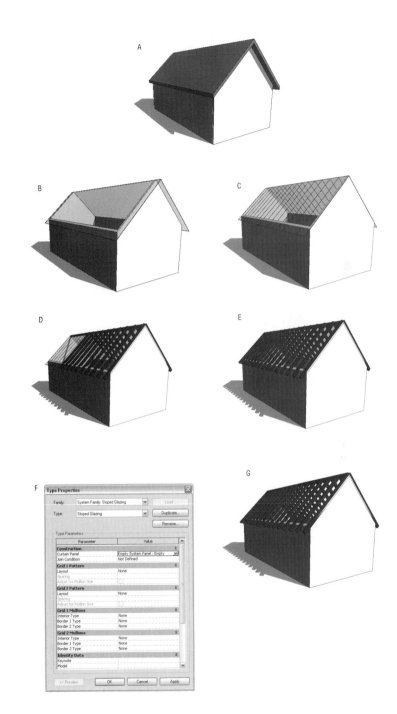

Real World Scenario

CREATING A RIDGE SKYLIGHT ROOF

Suppose we are planning a factory whose roof needs to be a ridge skylight on a pitch:

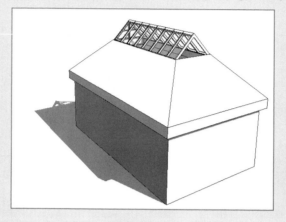

Here's how we make this roof:

1. In Level 1, draw the floor plan of the building. For the sake of simplicity, we will assume that the floor plan is a rectangle.

2. Define two new levels in the drawing: Level 2 at 12´ (4m), and Level 3 at 18´ (6m).

3. Switch to Level 2 and select the Roof tool.

4. Select Roof by Footprint.

5. Click the Pick Walls option in the Design bar.

6. In the Options bar, define an Overhang setting of 1´6˝ (50cm), and check the Defines Slope option.

7. Click Finish Roof in the Design bar.

Once you complete these steps, this is the resulting roof:

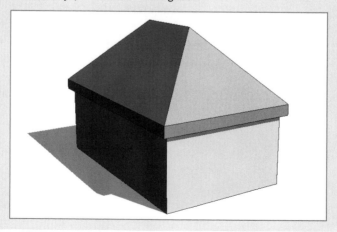

We now need to cut the top of this roof at Level 3.

1. Select the roof and, in its instance properties, select Level 3 under Cutoff Level and −1′8″ (−57cm) for Cutoff Offset (the roof thickness value); then click Finish Roof. The result looks like this:

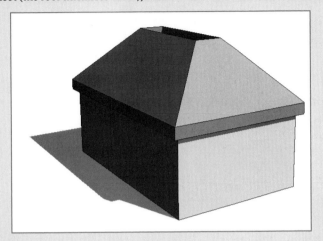

Next, create the second roof and use the opening in the first roof as a reference for the sketch lines defining the new roof.

1. Switch to Level 3 and select the Roof by Footprint tool. Instead of selecting the Pick Walls option, select the Lines tool, and in the Options bar, change from the Draw option to Pick. Select the four edges of the opening of the first roof and lock all padlocks that appear when the four pink sketch lines are selected.

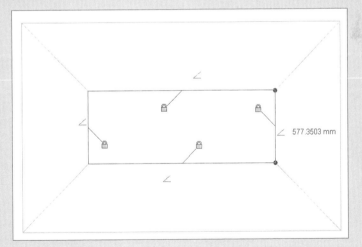

By doing this, you are creating a relationship between the two roofs so that if you later change the cutoff level or the geometry, the second roof will change to match.

Select the second roof, and from the Type Selector, pick Sloped Glazing to get the following configuration:

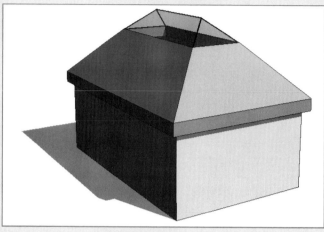

If the slope of the second roof isn't what you desire, you can change it at any time. Select the roof, click Edit on the Options bar, click each of the sketch lines, and type in a new value over the slope value displayed. In this example, we have set 40 degrees for the second roof (the skylight).

The last thing to do is to divide the sloped glazing into segments and apply mullions. For that, use the Curtain Grid tool and start dividing the glazing.

At the end, add mullions by selecting the Mullion tool from the Modeling tab of the Design bar and picking the gridlines on the glazing. The final outcome should be similar to this:

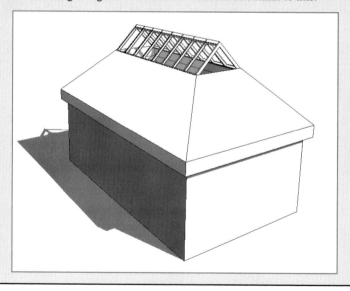

Sloped Arrows

Another way to slope a roof is by manually adding slope arrows to flat roof slabs. This can be useful for unusual shapes, especially if the roof edges are not straight.

Slope Arrow

First create the sketch lines to define the shape of a roof, and do not check Defines Slope on the Options bar. Instead, choose the Slope Arrow tool from the Design bar. Draw the slope arrow in the direction you want your roof to pitch and at the intended height between the base of the roof and sloped end (see Figure 13.15).

FIGURE 13.15

A slope-defining arrow added to the sketch in roof by footprint

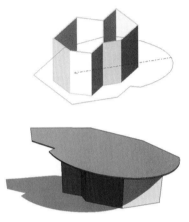

Once you've drawn the slope arrow, you can select it; in the Element Properties dialog box, you can set any of the parameters shown in Figure 13.16. The most critical parameter to check is Height Offset at Head. This defines the height of the roof slab from the base to the top of its slope.

FIGURE 13.16

Slope arrow properties

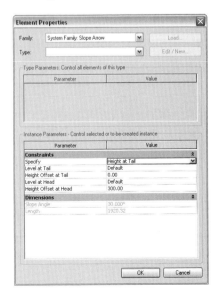

To create a shed roof, you can draw a roof without any slope-defining sides and then apply a slope arrow that defines the exact sloping (see Figures 13.17 and 13.18).

FIGURE 13.17
A shed roof defined using the Slope Arrow tool

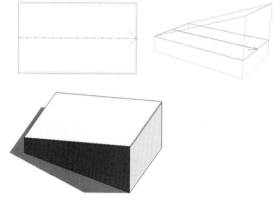

FIGURE 13.18
The same roof, with the slope arrow shortened. Note that the roof became much steeper.

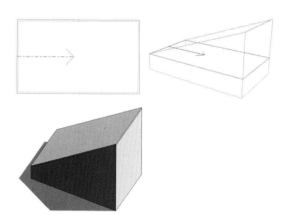

Creating All Kinds of Roofs

The following section demonstrates a series of typical roof conditions and the appropriate strategy to use in Revit to create these roofs. For any roof, there can be many ways to solve it geometrically; use this as a guide and to shore up your skills with the roof tools, using the methods described previously in this chapter.

Each roof in the typology is represented with roof plan view, sketch plan, and 3D view of the roof.

FLAT ROOF

This flat roof was created using roof by footprint and the Pick Walls method, checking Defines Slope.

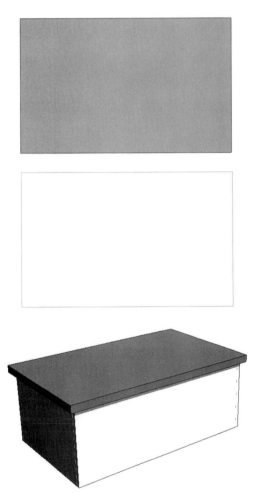

GABLE ROOF WITH ASYMMETRIC SLOPES

This roof is also created using roof by footprint and the Pick Walls method, but in this case Defines Slope is checked only for the shorter sides of the roof, with slope angles that are not identical.

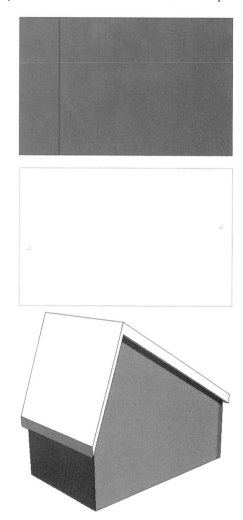

SHED ROOF

This roof by footprint was created using the Pick Walls method with Defines Slope checked only for one of the short sides of the roof.

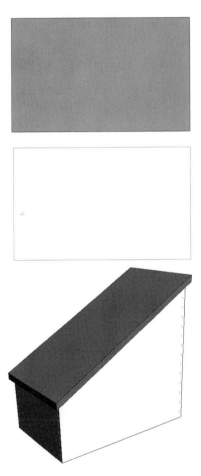

Note that you could also make this same roof by adding a slope-defining line to a flat roof:

HIPPED ROOF

This roof by footprint was created using the Pick Walls method, and Defines Slope was checked for all sides of the roof.

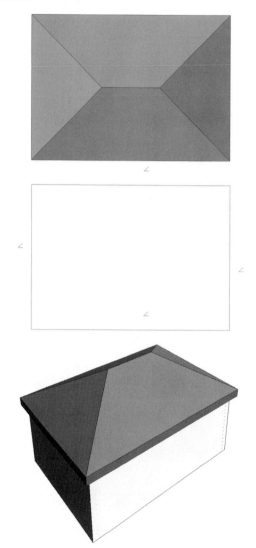

Hip Roof Following Recessed Walls

This roof by footprint was created using the Pick Walls method. Defines Slope was checked for all sides of the roof except the three walls that recess toward the inside.

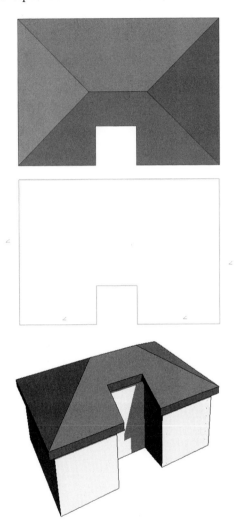

GABLE ROOF

This roof by footprint was created using the Pick Walls method with Defines Slope checked for all sides of the roof but the one that recesses toward the interior of the building.

GABLE ROOF WITH EXTENDING PERGOLA

This roof by footprint was created over a rectangular floor plan using the Pick Walls method. Its sketch was then edited and additional sketch lines added to shape the extension. Slope is defined only for the sides indicated in the sketch.

HIP AND GABLE HYBRID ROOF

This roof by footprint was created with the Pick Walls method with Defines Slope defined for all sides.

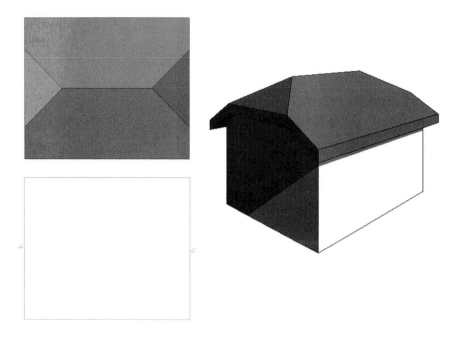

Notice that the sketch lines of the shorter sides have been split in thirds and Defines Slope is checked *only* for the middle portion of the line, as shown here.

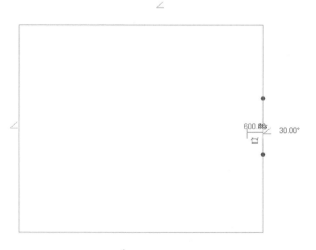

GAMBREL ROOF

This roof by footprint was created using the Pick Walls method. Defines Slope was checked for the two long sides of the roof only. The roof is cut off at a certain height (cutoff level), and a second roof has been created using as a sketch the cutoff shape of the first roof. The second roof also has Defines Slope Option checked for its two longer sides.

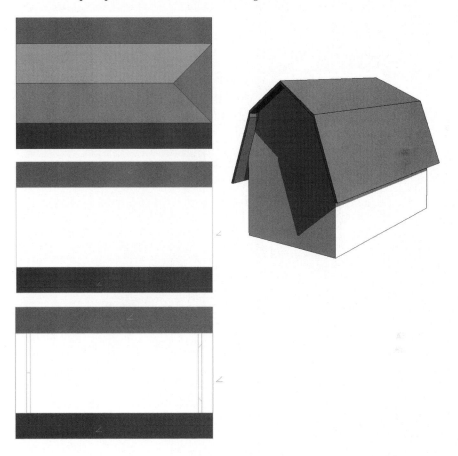

DUTCH GABLE WITH GLAZED ROOF

This roof by footprint was created with the Pick Walls method with Defines Slope checked for all sides of the roof. The roof is cut off at a certain height (Cutoff level), and a second roof has been created using as a sketch the cutoff shape of the first roof. The Type value of the second roof is set to Sloped Glazing. The second roof also has Defines Slope checked for all sides of the roof, but the slope of the second roof is slightly steeper than that of the first roof. Curtain grid and mullions are applied to the sloped glazing. (See "Real World Scenario: Creating a Ridge Skylight Roof" for a full step-by-step procedure for this example.)

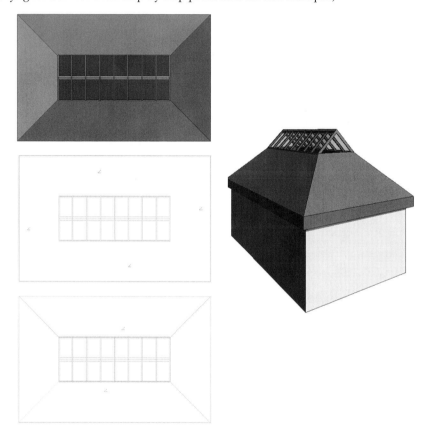

DUTCH GABLE

This roof by footprint was created with the Pick Walls method with Defines Slope checked for all sides of the roof. The roof is cut off at a certain height (Cutoff level), and a second roof has been created using as a sketch the cutoff shape of the first roof. Defines Slope is also checked for all sides of the second roof; the slope of the second roof is slightly steeper than the slope of the first roof.

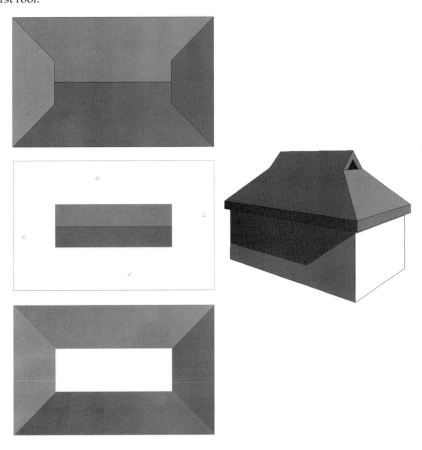

Hipped Roof with Sloped Arrow Dormer

This roof by footprint was created by using the Pick Walls method with Defines Slope checked for all sides of the roof. The sketch line on the south of the building is split into four segments to allow for the dormer creation. Sloped arrows facing each other and meeting in one point have been added to the middle two segments of the split sketch line.

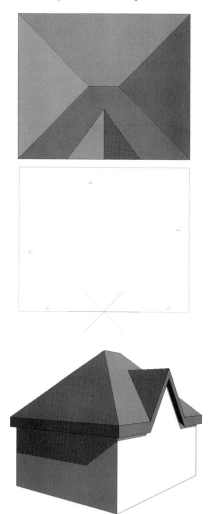

HIPPED ROOF WITH TWO DORMERS

This roof by footprint was created using Pick Walls method with Defines Slope checked for all sides of the roof. The two dormers are also separate roofs created by the footprint of the walls defining the sides of the dormer. The roofs are then joined. The opening in the roof slab is made up of two simple closed loops of lines (this can be done directly in the sketch or with the Opening tool later).

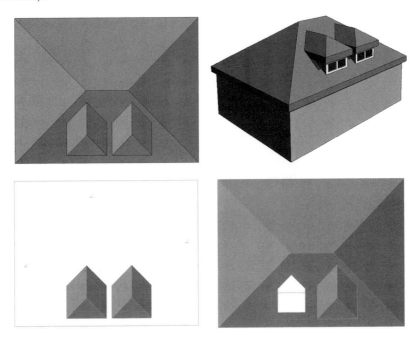

FOUR-SIDED GABLE

This roof by footprint was created using the Line Draw method in the shape indicated in the sketch. Defines Slope is checked for all four corners (see the blowups of the corner and middle roof edge).

Mastering Revit Architecture Project Gallery

This gallery comes from architects from all around the globe who have embraced the move to a smarter way of working on projects. They all have different skill levels with Revit, but what ties them together is that they have produced beautiful architectural examples using BIM.

BIM is not a myth. These are real architects, real projects, and real sources of inspiration. And don't forget, it's technology, it's digital—but still, what really matters is that it's good architecture. Enjoy!

COURTESY OF KUCAROVIC, NEMETH, VLKOVIC

Competition project for Jasna Centre

ADD Inc

USA

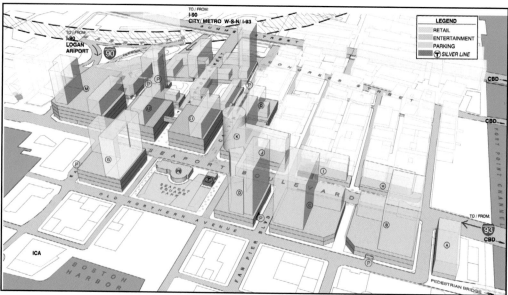

Retail Projects

Nemeth, Polakova, Senteska
Slovakia

Hviezdoslav Apartments

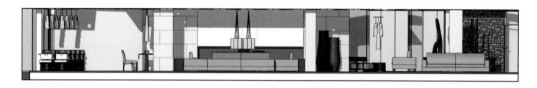

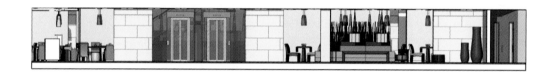

Hotel Helios

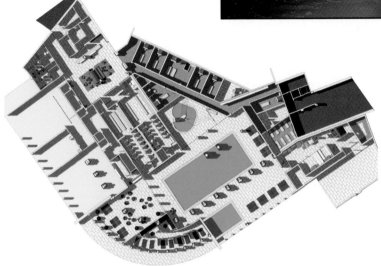

Hotel Helios

Gensler
USA

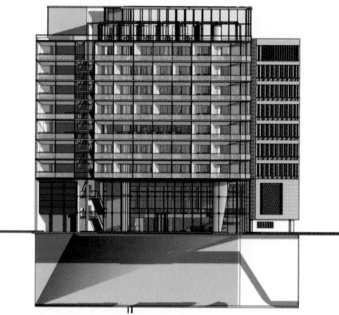

Corporate headquarters building

Corporate headquarters building

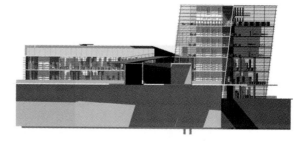

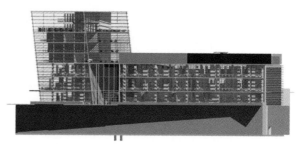

American University of Beruit, School of Engineering

HOK
UK

Florence Airport

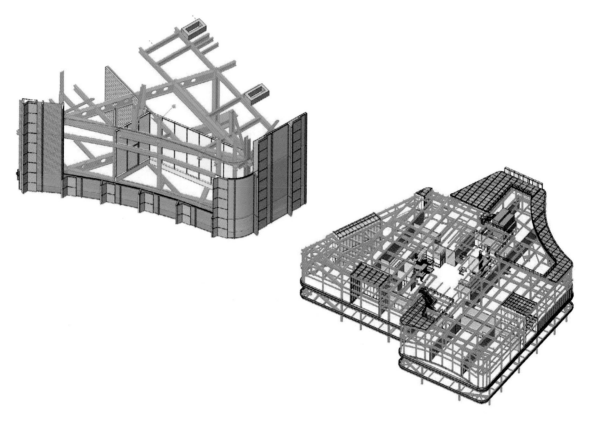

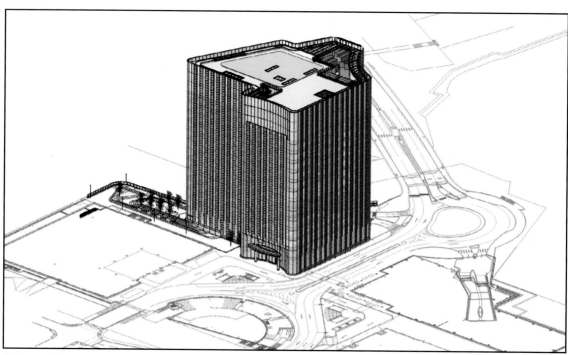

Office Building, Canary Wharf

Pavilion in London Square

WATG
USA

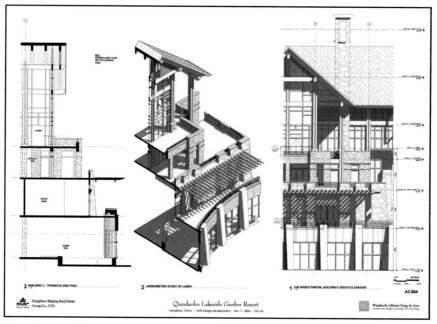

Four Seasons Cove 4 Restaurant and Sofitel Qiandaohu Lakeside Resort

The Creations
India

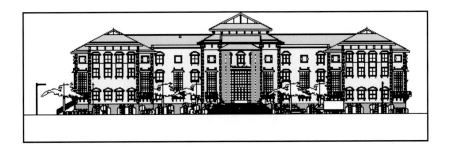

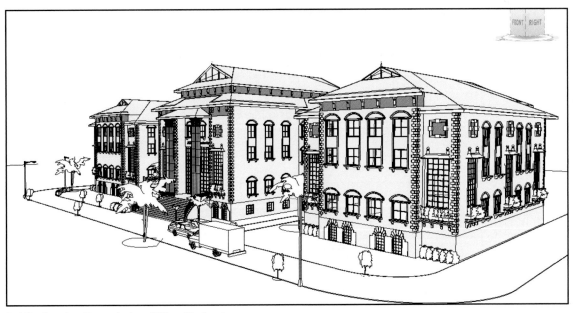

Public Service Commission Office, Kashmir

Martin Taurer
Netherlands, Japan

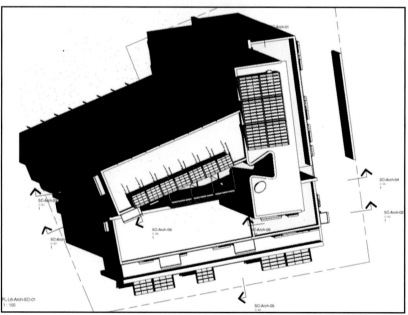

Condominium and office building, Japan

Max Bögl
Germany

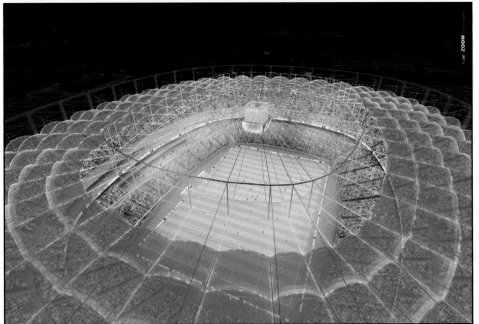

Max Bögl Bauservice GmbH & Co., KG, Germany, and Zoom Visual Project GmbH, Austria

Stadium Bucharest, Romania

Boston Architectural College
USA

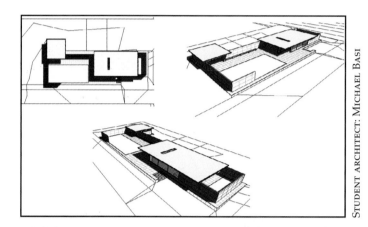

STUDENT ARCHITECT: MICHAEL BASI

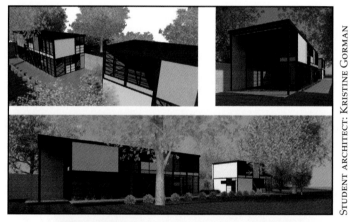

STUDENT ARCHITECT: KRISTINE GORMAN

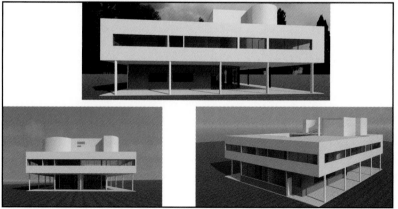

STUDENT ARCHITECT: ANGELA PETITTO

Barcelona Pavilion (Mies van der Rohe); Eames house (Charles and Ray Eames) and Villa Savoye (Le Corbusier)

HIPPED ROOF WITH EXTRUDED ROOF DORMER

This roof by footprint was created using the Pick Walls method with Defines Slope checked for all sides of the roof. The dormer roof is created as a roof by extrusion using the wall face as a work plane and then joined with the other roof in the sketch or with the opening tool later.

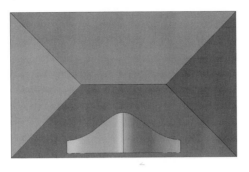

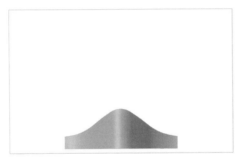

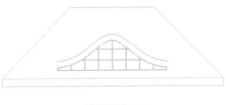

CONE ROOF

This is an in-place roof, created using the Create tool from the modeling Design bar with Roof as the category assigned to it. A simple closed line loop sketch is revolving around an axis.

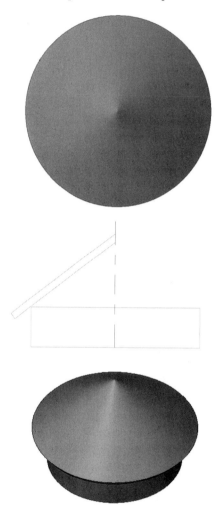

DOME

The dome was created using the revolve modeling technique. You will first need to draw a reference line in plan view that crosses the center of the circle describing the exterior walls, and then in section view, you will draw the revolving shape as well as the axis of rotation.

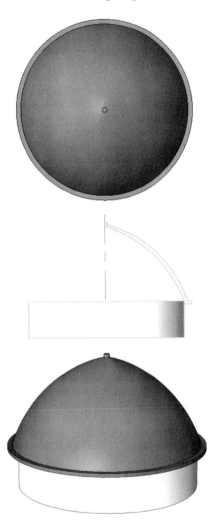

BARREL ROOF

This example was created using the roof by extrusion method. A simple line in arc shape defines the main shape of the roof extruded over the building footprint. In this particular example an additional roof by extrusion is added, converted into sloped glazing. The sloped glazing curtain panel type is set to Empty glazing, which allows the mullion structure to create a sunshade.

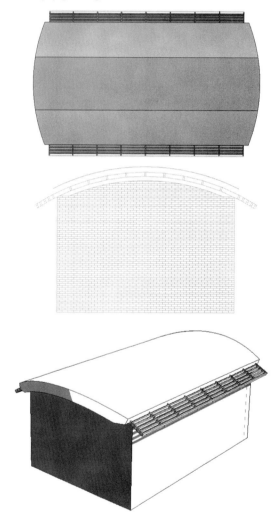

MULTIPITCH ROOF

This roof by footprint was created using the Pick Walls method with Defines Slope checked for all sides of the roof. Regardless of how complicated the underlying footprint, Revit correctly calculates the ridges as long as the eaves are aligned.

🌐 Real World Scenario

CREATING A DORMER

Roofs with dormers generally cause grief for architects, so we'll guide you through the creation of one.

1. Create the base of a building, set up three levels, and create a roof by footprint with Defines Slope checked for all sides.

2. Approximately in the position indicated below, on Level 2, create the four walls of a dormer. Set their height to a value that they extend above the roof.

3. Create a pitched roof on the dormer.

4. As you will notice, the dormer roof probably does not extend to meet the roof, so you will need to use the Join Roof tool, located in the main toolbar, to join the main roof and the dormer. Select the Join Roofs tool, select the main roof as the target, and then select the edge of the dormer roof to extend.

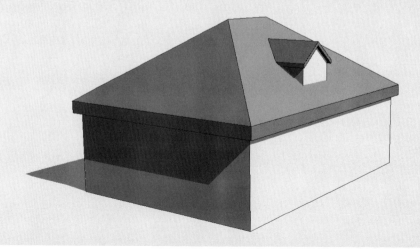

5. From the Modeling tab of the Design bar, select Opening/Dormer. Select the main roof, select the dormer roof, and then select the sides of the walls that define the dormer. Select the *inside* faces of the walls. Unlike most sketches, in this case you will not need to provide a closed loop of lines. Finish the dormer opening.

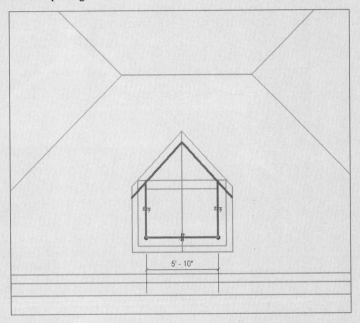

6. The last thing to do is to make a section through the dormer and edit the elevation profile of the walls. Note that you should *not* attach the top or the base of the dormer walls but edit its elevation to get the triangular elevation profile as shown.

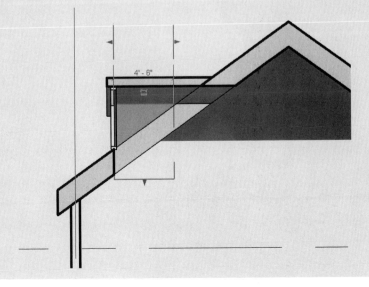

Your dormer opening is now correct and you will see that it has cut the roof in two directions, as a true dormer needs to.

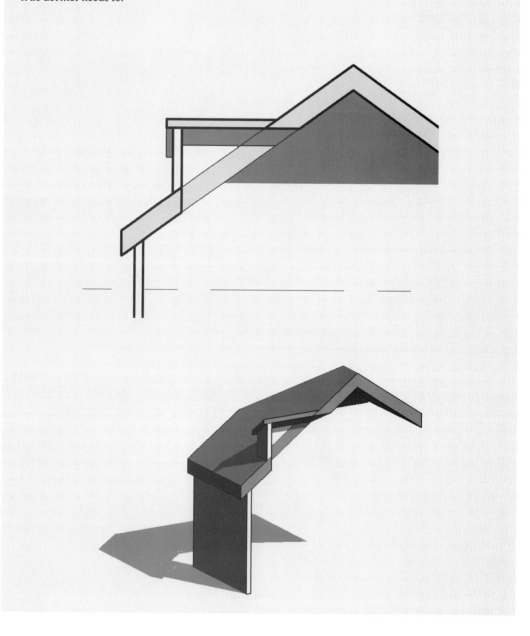

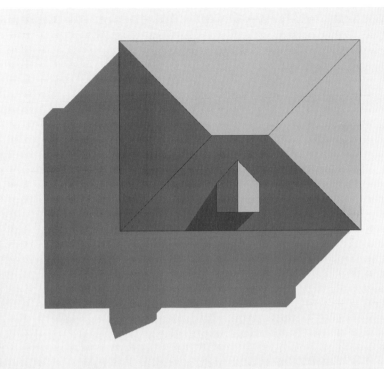

As a last thing, you can convert the front wall to a storefront or add a window.

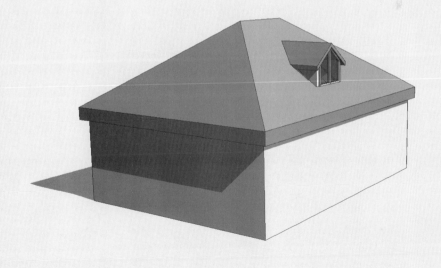

Working with Advanced Roof and Slab Shape Editing

No flat roof is ever really flat! And Revit is equipped with smart tools that allow for tapered insulation over a flat roof and similar conditions. A rich set of shape editing tools for roofs and slabs help create and modify such conditions in no time. These powerful tools are modifiers that are applicable to roofs and floors and will allow you to model concrete slabs with multiple slopes, often referred to as warped slabs (see Figure 13.19).

FIGURE 13.19
Sloped roof with
drainage

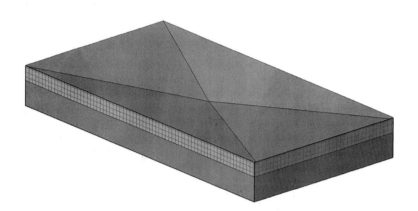

The modification tools appear in the Options bar when a flat roof or floor is selected.

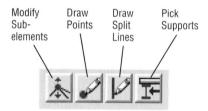

Modify Subelements   Draw Points   Draw Split Lines   Pick Supports

Here is what each tool is meant to do (left to right):

The Direct Editing tool (Modify Subelements) This tool allows you to edit element geometry using selection and modification of points (vertices) and edges.

The Draw Points tool This tool allows you to add points on the top face of a roof or floor. Points can be added on edges or surfaces.

The Draw Split Lines tool This tool allows you to sketch directly on the top face of the element, which adds split lines to the floor and roof so that hips and valleys can be created.

The Pick Supports tool This tool allows you to pick linear beams and walls to create new split edges at the correct elevation automatically.

As you can see, there is also a Reset Shape button. This button removes all modifiers applied to the floor or roof that is selected.

Sloped Roofs

Let's do a short exercise that shows how to make a sloped roof like the one in Figure 13.20 (shown in plan view).

FIGURE 13.20

A roof plan showing a roof divided in segments, with drainage points

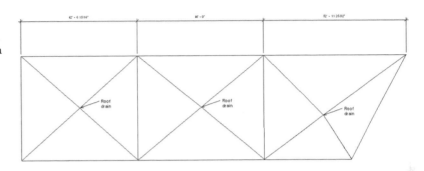

Follow these steps:

1. Open Modifying Roof Shape start.rvt from the book's companion web page (www.sybex.com/go/masteringrevit2009).

2. Select the roof that has already been prepared for you.

3. Activate the Draw Split Lines tool (note that the color of the rest of the model grays out).

4. Sketch ridge lines to divide the roof into areas that will be independently drained.

5. Using the same tool, draw diagonal lines within those areas to create the valleys.

    You have split the roof surfaces into many subslabs, but they are still all at the same height and inclination. You should have a roof that looks like Figure 13.21.

FIGURE 13.21

Using the Draw Split Lines tool, you can create ridges and valleys.

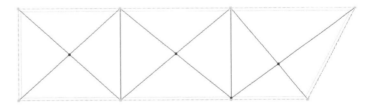

6. Switch to a 3D view.

7. To add a slope, you need to edit the height of the drainage points. Tab-select the crossing point of the diagonals. New controls that allow you to edit the text appear, and you can either move the arrows up and down or type in a value for the point height. As shown in Figure 13.22, type in -0′ 5″ (-13cm).

8. Repeat steps 1–7 for all three drainage points.

9. If you need to move the point to another position (perhaps to accommodate what's happening in the room below the roof), select the point and drag it.

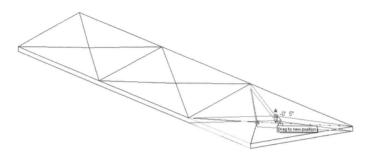

10. Make a section through the roof—if possible, somewhere through the drainage point. Open the section; change the detail level to Fine to see all layers. The entire roof structure is now sloped toward the drainage point.

What if you wanted the insulation to be tapered but not the structure? For that, the layers of the roofs can now have variable thickness. Let's see how to apply a variable thickness to a layer.

1. Select the roof, and navigate to its type properties to edit its structure.

2. Activate the preview. You will notice that in the roof-structure preview, you do not see any slopes. That is correct and will not change. This preview is just a schematic preview of the structure and does not show the exact sloping. Look for the Variable column under Layers (see Figure 13.23). This allows layers of the roof to vary in thickness when slopes are present. Check Variable for the insulation material.

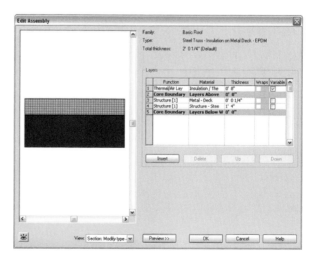

3. Go back to the section view and take a look at the difference that this change provoked. As you can see, only the insulation is tapered now, while the structure remains flat.

Warped Surfaces

Warped surfaces can also be created using this tool. Using the roof by footprint method, draw a flat roof (no slopes) and then select the roof. Using the Modify tool in the Options bar, you can start moving edge points up and down (Figure 13.24).

FIGURE 13.24
Warped roof

The Bottom Line

Revit provides extensive tools for modeling roofs, allowing for tremendous flexibility.

Understand the various roof creation methods There are multiple methods for creating roof forms in Revit, and you should become familiar with each.

Master it When would you use a Roof by Extrusion method?

Create all kinds of roofs   Roofs are an integral part of any building. Knowing how to create them in a variety of shapes and sizes is critical to the success of a project.

Master It   In the early design phases of a project, you are exploring a variety of roof forms for your building. Create the base building form and explore different roof options and shapes.

Work with advanced roof and slab shape editing   Roofs are another seemingly simple element that present architectural challenges, and Revit has tools for them.

Master It   You are working on a flat roof retail project, but the roof is not really flat and will need to drain. Using Revit roof tools, how would you go about modeling this?

Chapter 14

Extended Modeling Techniques— Railings and Fences

In the previous chapters we covered some advanced modeling techniques for making complex walls and curtain walls and for accommodating various specific conditions with roofs and floors. In this chapter we cover some advanced stair and railing features that enable you to make some quite creative and smart designs. As you'll see, with a little refinement and creativity, you can create a wide range of building components with a simple set of standard tools.

In this chapter, you learn how to do the following:

◆ Work with railings and fences

◆ Use balusters and rails to construct railings

◆ Adjust additional settings

Working with Railings and Fences

Railings and fences can range from very simple shapes to quite complex ones, as you can see by looking at the examples in the Revit help system (Figure 14.1). They can be represented as simple walls that follow the sides of a stair flight, balcony, or the boundaries of your garden; you can also create glass frameless railings or complex combinations of balusters and posts in different materials (wood, metal, glass panels). Revit allows most combinations of railings to be built, but this does require a thorough understanding of one of the more complicated systems in Revit.

FIGURE 14.01
From the Revit help system, a variety of possible railings and fences that can be created with Revit

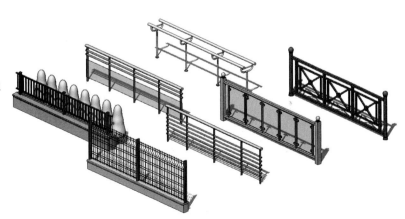

Here we cover some of the main principles used to create different types of railings in Revit.

Railings

When you need to create a railing in your model, Revit provides a customized tool to accomplish this. From the Modeling tab of the Design bar, choose Railing. You'll enter a Sketch mode where you have to first draw the path of your railing (Figure 14.2). The actual geometry of the railing is defined in the type properties, where you set up rail and baluster placement rules.

FIGURE 14.2
You define the position and length of a railing by drawing a base line in sketch mode. You can draw the base line of the railing wherever you please: in the center of the stair or on the side.

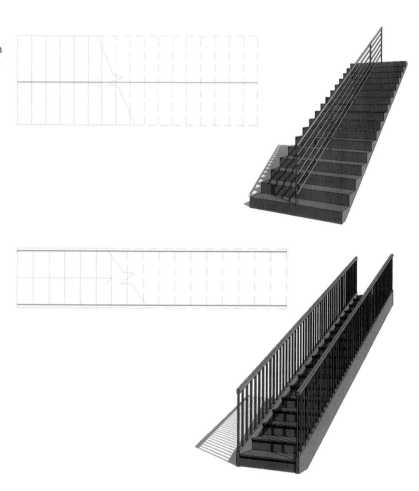

Set Host

Like many elements in Revit, railings must be placed on a host object. A valid host for a railing can be a slab, a floor, a stair, a ramp, or a level. If you draw a railing sketch line without first defining a host, it is drawn on the active level and you will create a horizontal railing. If you want to add a railing to a stair, select the Railing tool and, before or after drawing the railing path but definitely before selecting Finish Railing, use the Set Host option from the Design bar to select the stair as the host for the railing.

If you do not set a host prior to finishing drawing the railing, the railing is placed below the stair, on the active floor or level. If you forget to do that and need to re-host the railing to a stair after sketching the railing, this is not a problem; you can re-host it later. To re-host, select the created railing, edit its sketch from the Options bar, select Set Host, and pick the stair as a host. Finish the sketch, and the railing will jump from the level to the stair.

Since a railing is based on a sketch line that defines its path, you can have your railing follow just about any path by drawing any line shape (Figure 14.3).

FIGURE 14.3
A freestanding railing and a railing hosted by a stair, both following the sketch line shape

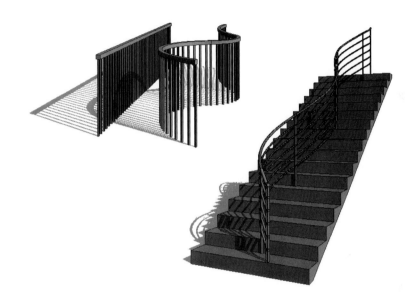

Subelements of the Railing Element and Principles of Railing Structure

A railing element consists of the subelements shown in Figure 14.4:

FIGURE 14.4
Railing components

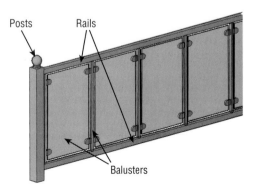

Balusters   These can be any shape or form. A baluster repeats itself in a railing based on spacing rules. To place balusters, you first need to load existing baluster families into your project. These could be baluster families provided by Revit or your own custom content. To create your own designed baluster families, use one of three available family templates: `Baluster.rft`, `Baluster-Panel.rft`, or `Baluster Post.rft`. Using the basic modeling tools explained in Chapter 6, you can make balusters such as those shown in Figure 14.5.

FIGURE 14.5
Balusters can have
any shape and size.

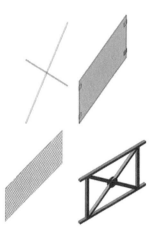

Posts   Posts can also have any shape, as shown in Figure 14.6. They are created using the `Baluster-Post.rft` template in the Family Editor.

FIGURE 14.6
Various post types
created using
`Baluster-`
`Post.rft`

Rails   Rails are horizontal elements that connect posts (should there be any) or can represent handrails attached to a wall. The geometry of the rails is defined by profile families that you create in the Family Editor using the `Profile-Rail.rft` family template. Here are some examples of typical rail profiles:

Rails can appear attached to a wall as a handrail, as shown in Figure 14.7. In this case, no posts are used and the wall mount brackets are custom-designed balusters. The rail is following the stair and is given an appropriate offset from the wall.

FIGURE 14.7
Handrail attached
to wall

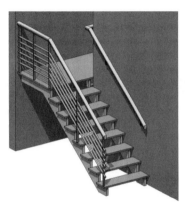

Railing Construction

The order and combination of subelements of the railing element can create unlimited variations of railings. In the type properties of the railing, under the Rail Structure and Baluster Placement parameters (Figure 14.8), you can define any combination of rails and balusters.

FIGURE 14.8
Type properties of
a railing element
with embedded
editors for rail and
baluster placement

Setting Up Rail Structure

From the type properties of a railing, selecting Rail Structure ➤ Edit Rails displays the dialog box shown in Figure 14.9, where you define the number, shape, and position of the rails in your railing. Figure 14.10 shows a railing with two rails: one set to 1′ (30cm) height and the upper one set at 3′-6″ (1m). Both of them use the profile Rectangular Handrail. The 1″ (2.5cm) offset pushes the rail away from the sketch line, as you can see in the front elevation.

FIGURE 14.9

The Edit Rails dialog box

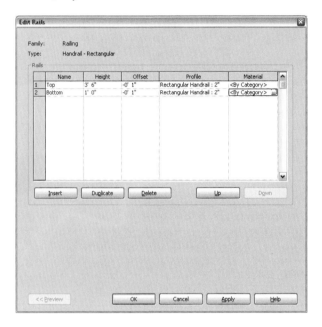

FIGURE 14.10

(Left) Elevation of a railing with two rails (lower and upper); (right) the rails are placed with an offset to the mid-axis of the rail sketch line (balusters have no offset).

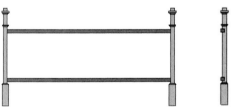

To define post and baluster patterns, click the Edit button for Baluster Placement in the type properties of the railing. You'll see the dialog box shown in Figure 14.11.

FIGURE 14.11
The Edit Baluster Placement dialog box

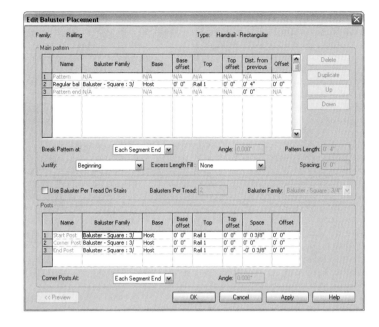

OPTIONS FOR POSTS

Depending on their position in the railing, posts can be placed at the Start, Corner, or End conditions of the railing. You can choose to have different families for the three positions and thus select a different baluster-post family for each, or you can keep it simple and use the same family. You also don't have to have them at all—you can set the post placement to None for any of them (for example, you can have start and end but no corner). Figure 14.12 shows various possibilities for the placement of posts.

FIGURE 14.12
(Left) Railing with start, corner, and end posts using the same post family. (Right) Railing with corner post set to None and different post families used for start and end posts.

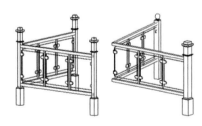

You can define corner posts to be dependent on the angle of the railing or to only appear under certain conditions, or you can choose to not place them at all.

The option Angles Greater Than allows for inclusion of the element dependent on the set angle. This means that if the individual segments of sketch lines of a railing turn into angles greater than 70 degrees (for example), a corner post will be placed (Figure 14.13). If smaller, none will be placed.

FIGURE 14.13
When the sketch lines of a railing meet at an angle greater than the angle defined for corner posts, a corner post will be placed.

As mentioned, railings can be hosted only on a slab, stair, ramp or level. So their placement is usually defined as an offset from the host. In the Edit Baluster Placement dialog box, you will find that you can also define the position of a rail as an offset from another rail that exists in the structure.

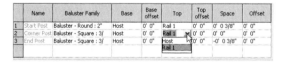

	Name	Baluster Family	Base	Base offset	Top	Top offset	Space	Offset
1	Start Post	Baluster - Round : 2"	Host	0' 0"	Rail 1	0' 0"	0' 0 3/8"	0' 0"
2	Corner Post	Baluster - Square : 3/	Host	0' 0"	Rail 1	0' 0"	0' 0"	0' 0"
3	End Post	Baluster - Square : 3/	Host	0' 0"	Host	0' 0"	-0' 0 3/8"	0' 0"
					Rail 1			

That is what the Top parameter means—here you can either select the host of the entire railing or choose from a list of existing rails in the railing as a top reference. The top offset can be a positive or negative value.

The Space parameter defines the distance of the post centerline to the railing viewed in a longitudinal direction, as shown in Figure 14.14. This value can be positive or negative.

FIGURE 14.14
Space parameters define the longitudinal position of the rail.

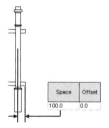

	Space	Offset
	100.0	0.0

DESIGNING THE MAIN PATTERN

The Main Pattern section of the Edit Baluster Placement dialog box is where you define the pattern of the railing between the posts to generate a complex railing, as in Figure 14.15. The options (Figure 14.16) are similar to those just discussed for the rails.

FIGURE 14.15
Baluster main pattern

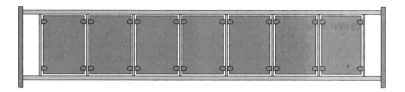

FIGURE 14.16
The Main Pattern options

Note that all parameters that define position (such as Dist. [distance] from Previous or Offset) are calculated from the center reference planes of the baluster families.

The Dist. from Previous setting allows placement of balusters at a specific set distance from one another. To keep balusters from running into one another, you should know the actual dimensions of your different balusters prior to defining this (Figure 14.17).

FIGURE 14.17
The baluster position is always measured to the mid-axis for all positioning parameters.

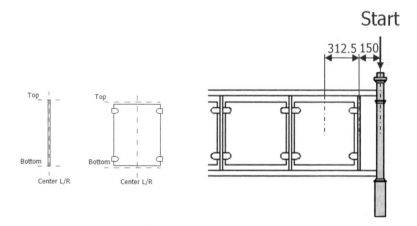

As you can imagine, the railing length will not always fit an even number of panels or balusters based on the pattern length. How do you deal with that?

Revit provides four different justifications for the pattern fit: Beginning, End, Center, and Spread Pattern to Fit.

Their names explain the usage, but Figure 14.18 shows the different justifications and their implications on a design.

The justification you select obviously depends on your design, but you may also be using prefab standard railing patterns that come only in certain dimensions.

FIGURE 14.18
Different pattern options for seven defined panels results in different distribution of the panel along the railing length.

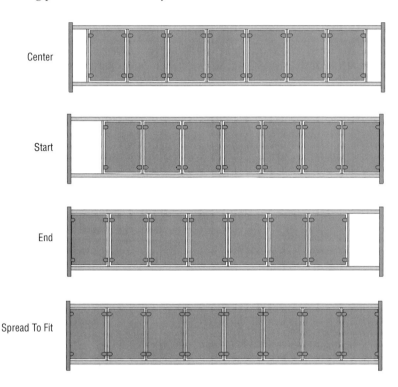

Center

Start

End

Spread To Fit

BALUSTERS PER TREAD

Revit allows you to set a specific number of balusters per tread on stairs.

If you want to control the number of balusters per tread, check the first option: Use Baluster per Tread on Stairs. This makes the next option active and you can then type in the number of balusters you want to have per tread. You can also change the baluster family by clicking the Baluster Family option to display a list of all loaded baluster families available in the project.

Figure 14.19 shows a railing with a two balusters per tread setting, a railing with a one baluster per tread setting, and a railing with a changed baluster family (when the Use Baluster per Tread on Stairs option is not activated, the effect is to change the baluster family).

FIGURE 14.19
Spiral stairs with different settings: (A) two balusters per tread; (B) one baluster per tread; (C) Use Baluster per Tread on Stairs is not activated, so the railing follows the main pattern.

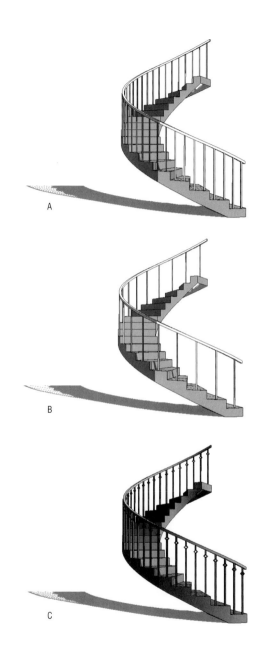

As you can see, the moment you use the Use Baluster per Tread on Stairs option, the Baluster Family selection overrides the one set in the Main Pattern section.

ADDITIONAL CONTROLS

Landings can be difficult to work with when designing railings. Revit has a set of additional tools and type parameters to control them (Figure 14.20).

FIGURE 14.20

Landing parameters: Use Landing Height Adjustment

By default, each railing in Revit follows the stair flight and the landing and creates the most logical solution. Often, however, the height of the railing on a landing is not calculated according to your design intent. With the Use Landing Height Adjustment parameter, you can change the railing at the landing to a specific height.

Landings can also generate unresolved situations where segments of the railing meet. By default, the joins at the angles are unresolved and the segments are not connected. You can fix that by adding vertical or horizontal segments and refine it further by setting the rail connections to Trim or Weld (see Figure 14.21). All these settings are also part of the type properties for the railing.

FIGURE 14.21

Angled joins: (A) no connector; (B) add vertical or horizontal segments; (C) with rail parameter set to Trim/Weld

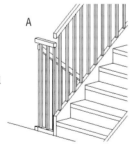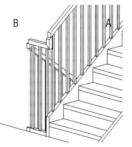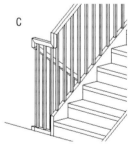

The Tangent Joins tool does a similar job but affects connections of different segments of the railing that are on a continuous tangent. The options are located in the type properties of a rail.

Tangent Joins	Extend Rails to Meet ▾
Rail Connections	Add Vertical/Horizontal Segments
Identity Data	No Connector
Keynote	Extend Rails to Meet

The effects can be seen in Figure 14.22.

FIGURE 14.22
Mid-landing railing segments cleanup: (A) No Connector; (B) Add Vertical Segments; (C) Extend Rails to Meet

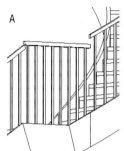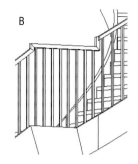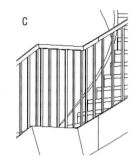

Finally, there are a few more adjustment tools needed to refine the railing and bring it closer to your design goals. These last tools are available in Sketch mode of the Railing tool only.

Edit Joins   Use this tool to clean up segment joints while in the railing sketch. Once you're in a Sketch mode, this option appears in the Design bar.

Click the Edit Joins button, hover the mouse pointer over the sketch line joins, and then click the join (Figure 14.23) to activate options in the Options bar. These provide the same controls you saw in the previous example.

FIGURE 14.23
Edit joins by clicking on the end join of sketch lines.

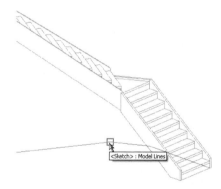

In Sketch mode, after you select one of the railing sketch lines, the following Options bar tools appear:

These tools let you manipulate the sketch lines in order to adjust the slope of the railing or correct the height connection.

The Slope tool offers you three possibilities:

By Host   This option follows the slope of the host, which is what you would most probably need in the majority of the cases.

Flat   This option keeps the railing flat, regardless the slope of the host.

Slope   This option defines a custom slope to your railing that ensures uninterrupted connection between adjacent segments.

Similar to what we have shown about the height adjustment on the landing, there is an additional adjustment of the height of a railing useful for controlling the extension of a railing. This is also available when in Sketch mode only and offers two options:

By Type   The railing height for the selected segment depends on the properties of the railing type.

Custom   The railing height for the selected segment can be forced to a different custom value. Figure 14.24 demonstrates both situations.

FIGURE 14.24
Railing height adjusted By Type or forced to a new height value (Custom)

🌐 Real World Scenario

ADDING A RAIL ONTO A WALL

Adding a rail to stairs is easy, but adding a rail on top of a wall is more difficult the way Revit elements are set up today. Shown here is a railing design consisting of a base wall and a railing element on top of it. This is a common type of railing in institutional buildings or outdoor stairs, so let's see how it is made.

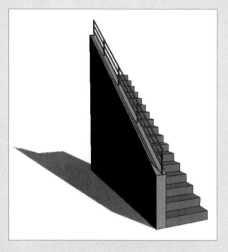

The challenge we face is that a wall is not considered a host for a railing element in Revit, so we have to find a workaround for how to place a railing that will follow the stair angle and is based on the wall.

Start by creating a stair without any railings (or delete the default railings later) and create a wall next to it with an edited elevation profile.

Then create a very thin floor on top of the wall that will play the role of a host for the railing (a floor is a valid host for railings):

1. Create a floor type that is very thin.

2. Switch to elevation view. Using the Dimension tool, measure the height of the top of the wall at the beginning and end of the stair. You will need these values when you slope the floor to match the stair.

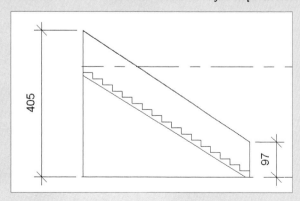

3. Define the floor shape by switching to plan view and drawing a floor. Use the Pick method and select the four lines representing the top of the wall.

4. While still in floor Sketch mode, click the Slope Arrow tool and set the properties as shown:

For Specify, choose Height at Tail.

For Height Offset at Tail, set the value of the lower height of the wall to 3′-0″ (97cm).

For Height Offset at Head, set the higher value of 12′-0″ (405cm).

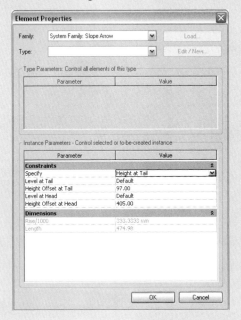

Draw the slope arrow in the middle of the floor starting at the beginning of the stair and finishing toward the end of the stair. By doing this, you have added a slope to the floor that matches the slope of the wall.

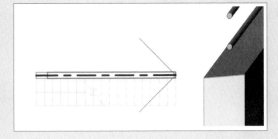

5. Select the Railing tool, click on Set Host, select the floor, and draw the railing in the middle of the floor.

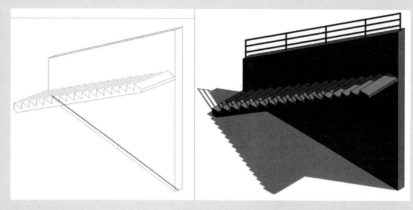

This workaround proves to be quite practical when dealing with railings in big auditoriums. Auditoriums are rarely done using huge stairs but rather stairs divided into many floors, and a railing can only have one host, so it won't be possible to host the railing on many floors at the same time. Using this workaround, you will be able to create a railing that runs through many auditorium levels and is still hosted.

The Bottom Line

Revit provides extensive tools for modeling basic elements such as walls, roofs, and railings, allowing for tremendous flexibility.

Work with railings and fences   Railings are a bread-and-butter architectural element whose design can be streamlined with Revit.

Master It   You've found some nice-looking railing panels and balusters while scouring the Web for interesting rail designs. How do you go about building the railing in Revit?

Use balusters and rails to construct railings   A Railing is a complex set of sub elements that Revit lets you organize and control with series of rules and settings.

Master It   You want to make a railing where the balusters are glass panels with fixed width. You wish to a railing that contains the maximum number of those panels and you wish them to be spread symmetrically. How do you do that?

Adjust additional settings   Stair railing details are particularly difficult to design and plan at landings. Revit helps you fine tune the details using additional settings.

Master It   After designing the stair railing, you notice that there is a gap between the Rails following the Stair flight and the horizontal Rail on the landing. What options do you have to resolve this situation?

Chapter 15

Presentation Techniques for Plans, Sections, and Elevations

As design professionals, we are deeply rooted in the art of representation and expression. Our drawings are not just collections of lines, but powerful communication devices that gain personal expression at our hands. The use of color, contrast, light, and shadow are manipulated to give a drawing life and dramatic poise. From the loose napkin sketch to the photorealistic rendering, we imbue our designs with a sense of purpose and intent. This intent is a driving force in architecture and critical to its progression. Without models and drawings that challenge the senses, that make us imagine the otherwise unimaginable, where would we be today? For a moment, consider the drawings of Piranesi, Boullée, Wright, Woods, and Hadid. Each is distinct, thoughtful, evocative—at times utopian. Consider your own practice and your techniques—your role in shaping the built environment.

Think about how your drawings are interpreted, received, and understood. How do they shape the evolution of a design? How have digital tools changed the way you present and evaluate a design? Keep these questions in the back of your mind as we move through the next two chapters. Consider how the techniques we look at can help you, and also think of how you might push some boundaries and extend your own creativity using the tools available in Revit.

You've seen with Revit that many traditional documentation drawing types are generated on the fly with little or no effort. With a few clicks of the mouse, you can generate entire building sections and elevations. Likewise, a perspective view now takes only a few seconds to generate. Revit does a fairly good job of producing these drawings, but it can't fully replace the skill and decision-making process of an artist. Design intent and the message still need to be considered by the designer, despite the affordances provided by technology. Knowing this, Revit provides some tools to help you make your drawings more legible and expressive. If need be, you can also export a drawing as vector lines (.dwg, .pdf, .dfx) or as pixels (.jpg, .png, and so on) and further refine it to meet your design requirements.

In this chapter, you learn how to do the following:

◆ Use shadows for presentation purposes

◆ Create presentation-quality plans and sections

◆ Create elevation drawings that convey depth

Using Shadows for Presentation Purposes

Shadows tend to be used for two purposes: analytical (Figure 15.1) and expressive (Figure 15.2). For analysis, shadows are used to see how a building will be affected by its environment and real-world sun angles based on the location of the site. This analytic use is explored in depth in Chapter 18 and is covered here primarily to introduce the shadowing tools for presentation purposes. The expressive use of shadow, our focus in this discussion of presentation issues, conveys depth in drawings and gives them more character; it may or may not be tied to real-world sun positions.

FIGURE 15.1
Analytical use of shadows in a site plan shows the effect of buildings on their environment.

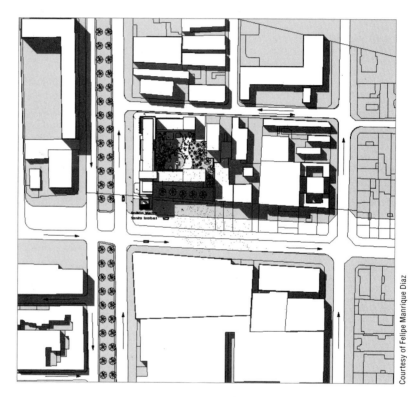

Courtesy of Felipe Manrique Diaz

FIGURE 15.2
A more expressive view using shadows in a shaded view without edges

Courtesy of Felipe Manrique Diaz

Revit provides a tool for each of these use cases, and you'll see how to use both. The nice thing about shadows in Revit is that it's easy to enable them, and voilà!—shadows are there.

Analytical Drawings: Sun and Shadow Studies

Using shadows analytically allows you to see (and demonstrate) the effect of a building on its environment and, likewise, the effect of the environment on your building. Using real-world sun and building positions, you can evaluate the design impact on its surroundings. You need to know whether the building will have a negative impact and make sure building codes are satisfied. You'll also want to see the effect of the sun on the building itself, to study light penetration and how other buildings will affect light and shadow. Figure 15.1 shows a site plan view with shadows turned on.

To get accurate sun shadows, you must establish where the building is on the planet, and the date and time that you wish to analyze. For example, it's common practice all over the world to represent the extreme sun angles at both the summer and winter solstices. Both of these are provided in the default templates. These angles vary based on latitude and longitude. In Revit, every project has a location that is defined in the Manage Place and Locations dialog box (Settings ➤ Manage Place and Locations); this location has a direct influence on sun position. In the Place tab (shown in Figure 15.3), choose from a list of cities; the latitude and longitude are set for you automatically. If you don't find your city in the list, choose a nearby city, and then edit the latitude and longitude to match your location.

FIGURE 15.3
Set your building location using the Manage Place and Locations dialog box.

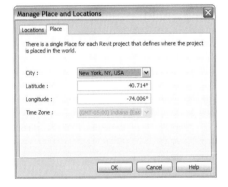

You need to set your location only once per project; this will affect all sun angle calculations based on the selected location.

To turn on shadows and see the effect of date, time, and location, choose the Shadows On option from the view controls at the bottom of any view:

ENABLING SHADOWS

Shadows are enabled on a view-by-view basis. This means that for each view in which you wish to display the shadows, you need to activate them independently. The downside of this is that if you have activated the shadows in many views, there is no one global button to turn them all off; you might well have to do that throughout the course of the project, as shadows can slow down the performance of the project significantly.

To understand how shadows are being cast, click the Advanced Model Graphics option to open the dialog box shown in Figure 15.4, where all the shadow settings are defined, including a direct link back to the Manage Place and Locations dialog box. From this dialog box, you can access the Sun and Shadows Settings dialog box, play with the brightness and darkness of the sun and shadows, and override silhouette edges.

FIGURE 15.4

The Advanced Model Graphics Settings dialog box

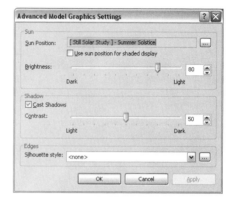

SUN AND SHADOW SETTINGS

Clicking the ellipsis button next to the Sun Position field opens a dialog box where you set the angle of the sun. For analytical views, choose meaningful times and dates. Revit ships with the presets shown in Figure 15.5.

FIGURE 15.5

The Sun and Shadows Settings dialog box for still images

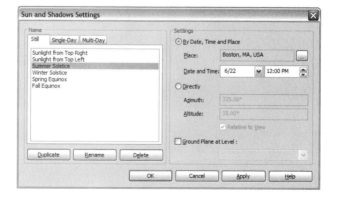

There are two methods for setting the sun angle: By Date, Time and Place; and Directly. Making any changes to them could cause serious problems later. For example, if you set Summer Solstice to a manually set azimuth and altitude that aren't accurate, you can create misleading settings. If you need to create a unique setting, the method to approach that is to *duplicate an existing setting* and only then go from there, rather than editing the preset options. Or, if you really intend to change the setting, go ahead and rename it with an appropriate and meaningful name.

INTENSITY

To get different graphic results using the same geographical settings, try experimenting with the Sun and Shadow intensities in the Advanced Model Graphics Settings dialog box:

If you give the sun 100 percent intensity, the model will appear brightly lit, and shadows appear more subdued. Figure 15.6 shows the different effects that can be achieved by adjusting the intensity values. Keep in mind that the sun and thus shadows only affect views set to Shading or Shading with Edges model graphic styles. In other words, for Hidden Line views, you can only change the darkness of the shadows but not the intensity of the sun.

To create several graphic versions of the same view, you must duplicate the view and apply different sun and shadow settings using the Advanced Model Graphics Settings dialog box.

FIGURE 15.6
Adjust intensity to get different graphic results.

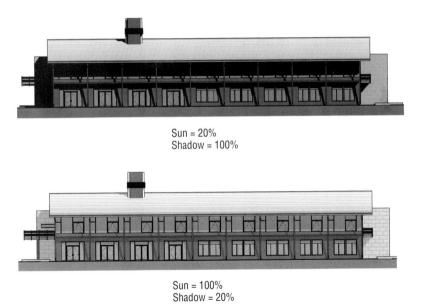

Sun = 20%
Shadow = 100%

Sun = 100%
Shadow = 20%

Create Expressive Drawings with Shadows

When you use shadows expressively, the need for accurate lighting conditions is not as important as the need to define consistent angles so that your drawings express depth. Without shadows, a façade appears flat and difficult to interpret. By adding shadows and setting them to be Relative to View, you can create an image that discloses information about the depth in that flat image, allowing it to be much better understood. To do that, you establish a shadow angle that suits your needs and reuse the settings for multiple views. The default template includes two presets for this in the Sun and Shadows Settings dialog box: Sunlight from Top Right and Sunlight from Top Left (see Figure 15.7).

FIGURE 15.7
Sun locations
in the default
template

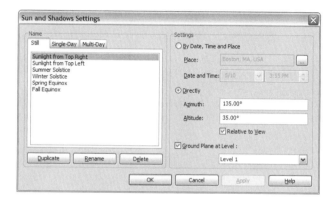

The combination of Azimuth and Altitude with these presets produces 45° shadows on an elevation.

HIGH-CONTRAST BLACK AND WHITE EFFECTS

Using hidden line display and increasing the shadows to 80–90 percent produces nice, high-contrast elevations. As you can see in Figure 15.8, this is a great way to create visuals that will read from far away.

FIGURE 15.8
High-contrast
black and white
elevation

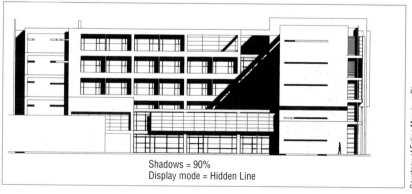

Shadows = 90%
Display mode = Hidden Line

Courtesy of Felipe Manrique Diaz

SOFT SHADOWS

If you prefer to give an image a softer appearance, try using a shading view (shading without edges) and setting shadows to 30 percent and sun to 70 percent. You'll get a very even-colored, washed-out feel, as shown in Figure 15.9. Because the book is printed in black and white, you might not be able to appreciate the finesses in these, so make sure you try them out yourself!

FIGURE 15.9
Soft edges and low-contrast shadows

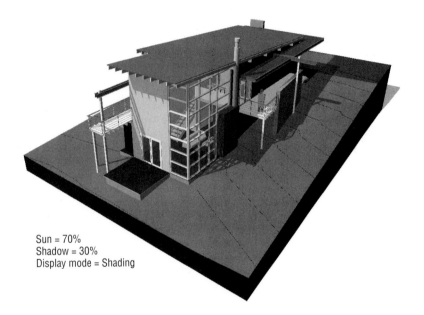

Sun = 70%
Shadow = 30%
Display mode = Shading

Performance Considerations

As you'll discover when working in views with shadows enabled, the speed of panning and zooming in the model degrades when shadows are on. So, as you start to use shadows, keep this in mind: *turning off shadows is always two clicks away.* If you want to start panning and zooming around the view, turn off the shadows for a while. When you're done zooming about, turn them back on. Remember that the settings are persistent, and turning off shadows is just a simple way to improve performance while working with your model. But don't worry—your work is saved and you will not need to remake them again the next time you turn them on.

Color-Coded Plans and Sections

Colors, when associated with a legend, are an effective way to signify meaning. In the context of architectural drawing, the colors are often applied to convey how space is used or intended to be used. With Revit, you can use color to differentiate one room from another or to communicate ideas about usage, size, importance, and cost. By assigning parameter values to colors and patterns, you can quickly make views that show how a building is spatially organized (Figure 15.10). For example, you can create a department floor plan by assigning department values (names) to all your rooms and then apply a color fill scheme to the view that changes the color of rooms based on what department they're assigned to.

FIGURE 15.10
Use color and parameters to generate color-fill plans.

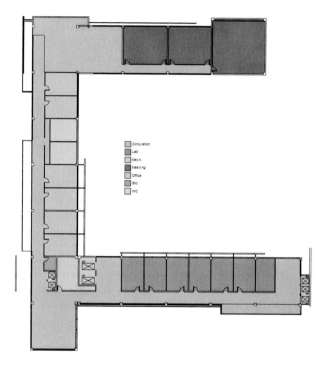

To make a color-coded plan, first duplicate an existing plan view and give it a unique name. Then add rooms if they have not been added already. The reason for adding rooms is that the color-coding is based on the properties of room elements and will have no effect unless room elements exist in the project. You can also create new area plans and use area separation lines to divide space at a more macro scale. You can then assign values to each area that can then be colored with a color fill scheme. Once rooms and areas have been placed, you can access their element properties. All of the properties grouped under the Identity Data parameter group can be color-coded. Using project parameters (Settings ➤ Project Parameters), you can also add custom parameters to the room and area categories.

From the View Properties of a plan, area plan, or section view, you can assign a color-fill scheme to the view. Clicking that parameter takes you to the Color Fill Schemes dialog box, where you set up and assign various schemes. Whatever is selected in that dialog box is applied to the view, and the rooms will become colored.

You can also create color scheme using the Color Scheme Legend tool in the Drafting tab of the Design bar. The moment you place the legend, you will be prompted to select the space type (Rooms or Areas) and a color scheme.

COLOR FILL SCHEMES

Color fill schemes are applied to views on a per-view basis (in other words, they appear only in the view where you created them), and are exposed as an instance property of floor plan, area plan, and section views. To access and create color fill schemes, choose Settings ➤ Color Fill Schemes to open the dialog box in Figure 15.11 (you can get to the same dialog box from the View Properties dialog box). In the Edit Color Scheme dialog box, you'll see a list of schemes on the left and all the rules and colors for those schemes on the right. Each scheme colors one parameter and all its values. For each unique value, a unique color or hatch pattern is assigned. For example, if you choose to color by name, the table fills with all the room names in the project and assigns a color to each unique name. Clicking the button in the Color column allows you to choose your own colors. While Revit will create new colors for you automatically with each new value, you are free to change those to your own colors, and can even save these into a template for use in other projects.

FIGURE 15.11
The Edit Color
Scheme dialog box

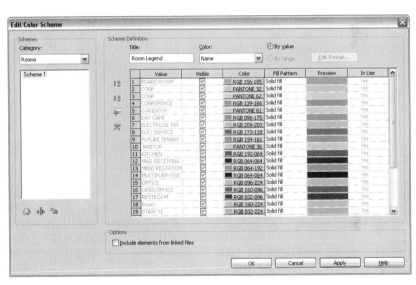

Information in this dialog box is also used to fill out color-fill legends, which are essentially graphical tags of the color scheme and are placed next to the plans to explain the color coding. The legend shows the title, values, and color swatches for the scheme applied to a view. To place a legend in a view, use the Color Scheme Legend tool in the Drafting tab of the Design bar.

The color-scheme legend allows you to edit its type properties to control the visibility of the title, swatch size, fonts, and color (Figure 15.12).

FIGURE 15.12
Color Scheme
Legend properties

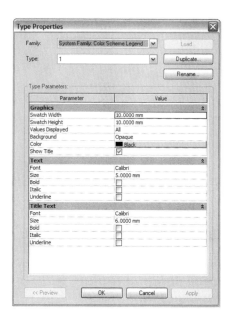

Note that the order of the values in the legend coincides with the order set up in the Edit Color Scheme dialog box. The default behavior lists each entry alphabetically, but you're free to change that by using the Move Up and Move Down buttons when a row is selected. Doing so simultaneously updates the color-scheme legend:

Another important graphical control of the legend is the Values Displayed parameter. This gives you the option to show only values in the legend that are also in the view (By View). In a project where the number of departments and room names can be large, and they aren't used in all floor plans, this is a great way to focus the legend on what is important to that view instead of listing all possible colors that might not be applied in that view and are thus irrelevant. Many designers do not want to display all the color swatches, but this is ultimately up to your own personal taste and what the drawings are intended to convey. Revit allows you to do both, so it's really up to you. Choosing the All option shows all values used in the project, whether used in the view or not.

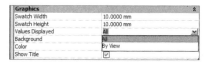

CREATING PREDEFINED COLOR SCHEMES

If you've created a list of room names, departments, and a carefully chosen color palette of colors that are likely to be reused in future projects, you can transfer the color scheme from one project to another or reuse it in your office template. This transfers all the values and colors, even if the project you're transferring to doesn't contain that value.

 **Real World Scenario**

TRANSFERRING COLOR FILL SCHEMES BETWEEN PROJECTS OR TEMPLATES

Imagine you have invested quite a bit of time setting up a color scheme in your current project, adding room names and departments and assigning them colors in the Color Fill Scheme dialog box. Should you want to reuse the same values and colors in other projects so that you maintain your graphical language, use the following strategy:

1. Open the source project, and then open the project into which you want to transfer. (You need to have two projects open to transfer from one to another. If you have only one project open, Revit will inform you that there are no open projects to transfer project standards from.) Remember, the project in which you invoke the Transfer project standard is the one you wish to import the standards to.

2. Choose File ➢ Transfer Project Standards. Select Color Fill Schemes in the Select Items to Copy dialog box:

3. Values are transferred into the project. You can then access the list of values from the room's Element Properties dialog box:

This saves you from having to manually retype all these commonly used values, and the colors will be consistent from project to project.

COLORED SECTIONS

In architectural practice, section views are often color-coded just as are floor plans, showing the stacking of various functional zones (Figure 15.13). New to Revit 2009, you can now get automated coloring of the rooms in section just as you can in plans:

1. Open a section view.

2. From the context menu, under View Properties, open the Visibility/Graphics Overrides dialog box (type **VG**) and make sure the Rooms category in the view is checked as visible.

3. Open the View Properties dialog box and assign a Color Scheme setting to the view. Use Name as the parameter to color if you have not assigned any departments (departments are the default setting, which comes from the fact that the selection is alphabetical). You're likely to get an image where the rooms do not fill the entire space being cut by the section, similar to Figure 15.13 (as the book is black and white, use your imagination: purple is used on the first two floors and gray on the third).

FIGURE 15.13
Use the grip controls when a room in section is selected—or the Limit Offset parameter in the room properties— to change the height of the room.

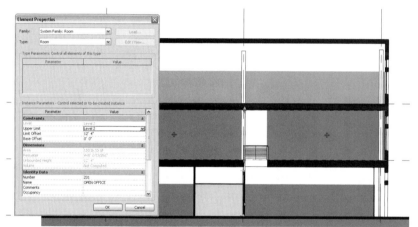

4. You can see that the rooms are not extending up to the next floor and roof. To fix this, select the room and drag the blue arrow controls at the top, or change the Limit Offset parameter from the element properties of the room.

5. To change how the color is drawn relative to the model geometry, you can set the color to be drawn in either the foreground or the background. This parameter is called Color Scheme Location and is a property of the view you are working in. Figure 15.14 shows the color in the background; the result is that you see walls and doors *not* colored by the color fill. Figure 15.15 shows the color in the foreground, and now doors and walls appear filled in.

FIGURE 15.14
Color fill drawn in
the background

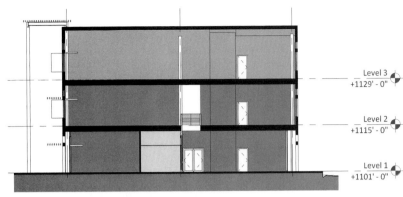

FIGURE 15.15
Color fill drawn in
the foreground

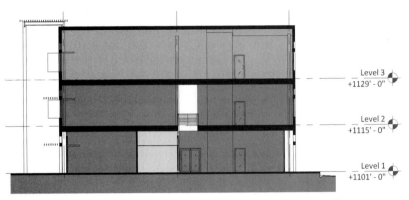

Creating Presentation-Quality Plans and Sections

Not all plans and sections end up as drawings full of dimensions, tags, notes, and layers of construction information. Easy-to-read, graphically clean drawings are used all the time in marketing collateral, on project websites, in print magazines, for competition boards, and for client presentations. A great way to create presentation-quality plans and sections is to clear out most of the textual information and fill in walls, floor, and roofs with a solid fill when they're cut. This creates views that are easier to read and that convey solid and void effectively (Figure 15.16). With Revit, this kind of representation is a few clicks away, and the fill hatch is tied directly to the element. You don't need a paint-bucket tool or special hatch tool to get results.

There are two strategies for dealing with solid fill for elements that are cut: as a property of the element or as a property of the view. Each strategy has its own merits. Let's review the options.

FIGURE 15.16
Plan view with
walls and columns
filled with solid
black

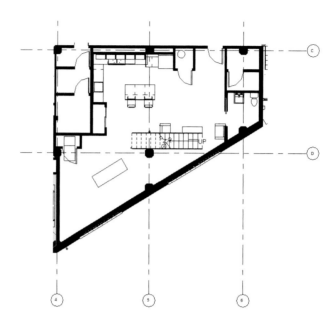

Coarse Scale Fill Patterns

Walls, floors, roofs, ceilings, and columns all have a Coarse Scale Fill type parameter. This allows
you to define how the element will appear when cut in the view if the view detail level is set to
Coarse.

The downside is that the property is stored with each type, so making all walls have the
same hatch requires you to edit every wall type. The same goes for floors and roofs. And if you
decide to change the color of the fill, you have to again edit every type.

Also, not all elements have this property. For example, in-place family walls, floors, and roofs
don't have this parameter, so you'd have to go a separate route to get correct graphics if you
chose to use this type of element.

Graphic Overrides and View Templates

The other way to think of this problem isn't as a property of the element but as a property of
the view that can be reused in other views. Think of a view as a multidimensional lens through
which you look at the model. Once you've set up the right lens, you can apply it to any number of
views and get the right results using view templates. We recommend this direction for graphic
overrides, as it makes for an easier way to deal with entire categories of elements. For example,

most Revit categories can have their cut pattern overridden with a hatch or solid fill. If you go to the Visibility/Graphic Overrides dialog box and select the Wall, Floor, Roof, and Column categories (by holding Ctrl with each row selection), you can then click the Fill Override button and apply a solid fill hatch (Figure 15.17). This applies to elements in your active view but isn't stored with the element. These overrides are stored on a per-view basis and are distinct from the project-wide object styles.

FIGURE 15.17
Use pattern overrides to apply a solid fill to categories.

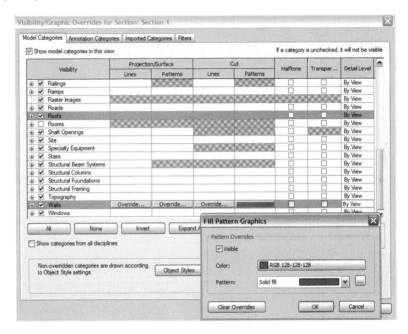

This view setting is great—but what if you want to apply the same graphics to other views? Follow these steps:

1. Once you have the overrides set up, choose View ➢ Create ➢ New View Template from View.

2. Name the view **Cut Overrides**.

3. New to the Revit 2009 release, if you only want to store the cut pattern values and not affect scale or any other graphic settings when applying this view template, clear all other view properties except for the V/G Overrides Model (Figure 15.18).

4. Right-click the view name you want to apply the overrides to in the Project Browser, and choose Apply View Template. Choose the view template you just created.

FIGURE 15.18
New to Revit 2009, you can now selectively choose which view properties are stored in a view template.

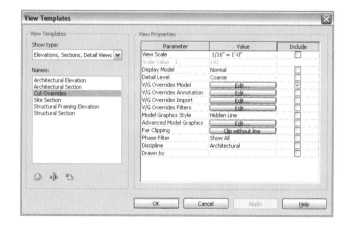

Creating Elevations That Convey Depth

Revit applies the same line style to all edges based on the cut or projection settings in the Object Styles dialog box. This can lead to elevations that appear flat and lack depth. Strategies for dealing with this issue range from highly parametric to using lines and drafting right on the view. In Figure 15.19, the Linework tool and some graphic overrides were used to punch out the building elements in the foreground and halftone elements in the background.

FIGURE 15.19
Edges can be made thicker with the Linework tool.

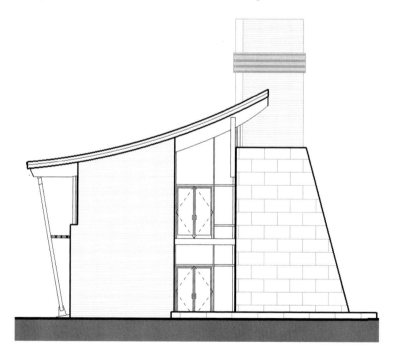

Linework

The Linework tool allows you to select a line style and then apply it to edges of the model as an override. Any edge can be overridden by this tool in order to change the line's graphic appearance. When activated, the Type Selector displays a list of available line styles in your project:

The cursor changes to a pencil and highlights edges of the model as you move the mouse around the view. With each click, the override is applied to the edge. This override is associated with the element; if you move the element, the linework moves with it. The line style applies to the entire edge of an element by default, but this can be adjusted. For example, if you need to make the diagonal line of this wall with a thicker line style, you select the Linework tool, choose the Wide line style, and then select the edge of the wall. The line goes the entire length of the wall (Figure 15.20A). While still in the Linework command, click and drag the blue control dot to adjust the length of the linework override (Figures 15.20B–C). Note that if you have your view set to thin line display, you will not see the effects of using linework.

FIGURE 15.20
(A) Initial condition; (B) linework applied; (C) cleaning up the line by dragging the control at the end of the line

A
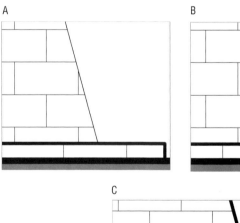

B
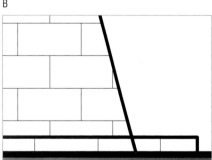

C
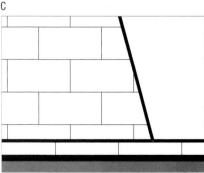

To reedit the length of linework, you need to activate the tool and then again select the edge you're concerned with. The same blue controls appear, allowing you to adjust the length of the line.

If you need to remove a linework override, the same principle applies: activate the Linework tool, choose By Category in the Type Selector, and then select edges in the model that you don't want overridden.

Drafting Lines

The other way to punch out the elevation is to use drafting lines and draw directly over the model in the view. This means you are not changing the appearance of a line in a view but adding new lines on top of the model. With this method, you also choose a line style, and you can even use the Pick tool to get the same behavior you would with the Linework tool. The only difference is that the lines aren't automatically associated with the element you draw on. Depending on your workflow and where you are in the process, this may be the best way to create a final elevation drawing. A nice benefit to this method is that you have access to all the familiar, time-saving tools such as Trim, Align, and Multi-select.

True-Color Elevations

Every material in Revit has a shading color and transparency—this is the color you see when the display mode is set to Shading or Shading with Edges. Be aware that the transparency is graphically visible only in 3D view. In elevations, a glass window will not appear as transparent so as to keep drawings clear of unwanted visual noise. After all, who wants to see interior furniture showing through the glass of a hotel façade in an elevation? The color you select in the Materials dialog box is an RGB or Pantone color (see Figure 15.21), but it often doesn't look like that color in shaded elevation views. That has confused many users, so here is the explanation: the reason behind this is that shaded views use a hidden fixed light source to light the scene, which causes the color to appear washed out or brighter in different views.

To overcome this limitation, you can control where the light comes from by using the Sun and Shadows Settings dialog box. You can also force the light to come from directly above the model so it doesn't affect any vertical surfaces. To do this, follow these steps:

1. Open the Sun and Shadows Settings dialog box, and duplicate the Sun from Top Right setting—give it a name like **True Color Shading**.

2. Change Azimuth to 0 and Altitude to 90 (see Figure 15.22).

3. Open an elevation view, and go to the Advanced Model Graphics dialog box from the view frame. Set the Sun Position to True Color Shading. Set Shadow Intensity to 0. Set Sun Intensity to 80.

   Be sure to enable shadows in the view. The effect should be immediately obvious.

FIGURE 15.21
Every material has a shading color, transparency, and options for cut and surface patterns.

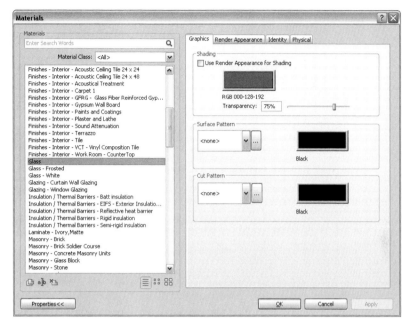

FIGURE 15.22
Use these settings to get accurate RGB colors in elevation.

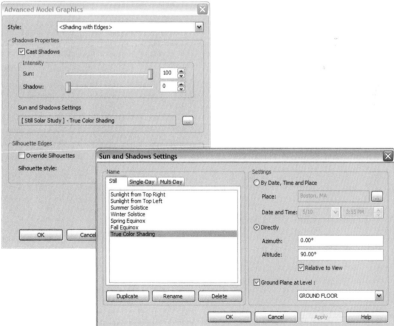

Elevations with Transparent Materials

Using the standard Revit elevation views, transparent surfaces are always rendered as opaque surfaces. This generally produces the right quality and meets most expectations, but it can also seem limiting. Luckily, creating an elevation view with enabled transparency is easy using the 3D views and orienting them to display elevation view. Here is how you can do that:

1. Open the default 3D view.

2. Choose View ➢ Orient ➢ South (or any other elevation view):

3. The camera swings around so it's lined up with the elevation view, and transparent surfaces appear transparent.

Using Images in Elevation Views

You can import image files (File ➢ Import/Link ➢ Image) into a Revit view to create effects such as gradient fills, add a backdrop to the view, or add a photo-style entourage to a nonrendered view. By taking advantage of the draw-order options for images when placed in a view, you can position the image either in front or behind the model. When you select an image, the Options bar gives you the ability to position the image in the foreground or background.

To add a gradient fill to the background of an elevation, follow these steps:

1. Import a gradient image file into an elevation view.

2. Select the image, and send it to the background using the Options bar.

3. Stretch the image to fit using the grip controls. You can unlock the proportional scaling using the Options bar (see Figure 15.23).

FIGURE 15.23
Elevation with
the gradient JPEG
import set to
Background

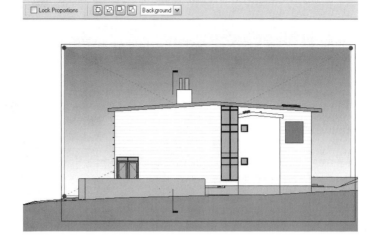

Another great technique is to use the transparency channel available in PNG-formatted images. By making a color transparent and pushing images to the foreground and background, you can add trees, people, and cars, and the image won't mask the model. In Figure 15.24, the tree image was imported into an elevation view and then copied and scaled. The copy on the right is set to Foreground, and the copy on the left is set to Background.

FIGURE 15.24
Imported PNG
file of one tree set
to Foreground
and another to
Background—note
that the transparency channel is
preserved.

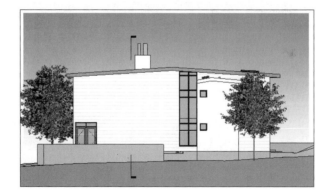

The Bottom Line

Revit is a complete solution that allows you to conceptualize a design and generate construction documentation while also providing powerful presentation tools. Using some automated routines to render shadows, depth, color, lighting, and materiality, you can create compelling plans, sections, and elevations directly in Revit and at any stage of your design. The value of doing this is that as the model changes, your presentation views automatically change as well. You won't have to redo your presentations as is usually the case when you exit modeling software and go to image-editing tools such as Photoshop. Your nice-looking views you've set up are maintained and updated automatically.

Use shadows for presentation purposes   Presenting your design to stakeholders is a critical part of your workflow and allows you to sell your ideas. Having tools that make this process easier without compromising your creativity is essential to being successful.

Master It   You've been asked to show the effect of your building's shadow on its surrounding site during the winter solstice. How would you do this with Revit?

Create presentation-quality plans and sections   Creating clean, easy-to-read plan and section views using Revit is a huge time-saver.

Master It   Your latest design is all the rage, and you've been asked to publish the plans and sections in a magazine. How do you make these?

Create elevation drawings that convey depth   Two-dimensional drawings can be hard for clients to read, which makes shadows a useful mechanism for illustrating recesses and projections.

Master It   You need to give your elevation view more variation in line weight to convey depth beyond the default line styles established in the Object Styles dialog box. How do you do this?

Chapter 16

Presenting Perspective Views

One of the many advantages when working with BIM models is the fact that you can produce perspective views of your model as often as you wish—and it takes only a few mouse clicks to do it. Think about how tedious the process of creating 3D axonometric or perspective was when creating perspective views manually or even digitally, when working with CAD drafting tools. Perspective views are greatly appreciated by owners as they visually communicate the intent of the design better than any other representation.

If you open a Revit project that has been in development for a while, you'll find dozens of perspective views. Although most of these views will never make it onto sheets, it's becoming standard practice to include one or two exterior perspectives on the cover sheet. Sheets aside, these views are critical for understanding your design from a human point of view and are used consistently for client meetings and internally when fleshing out a design. In many cases, a hidden line perspective view with shadows enabled provides an excellent graphical representation of your model. You can also take the visualization up a notch and produce photorealistic renderings without having to be a rendering guru.

In this chapter, you learn how to do the following:

- ◆ Create perspective views
- ◆ Create photorealistic renderings
- ◆ Create animated walkthroughs
- ◆ Export the 3D model for use in other applications

Creating Perspective Views

 Use the Camera tool to create perspective views in Revit. This tool can be found in the View tab of the Design bar. For perspective views, a good exterior shot typically shows a corner of the building from a human vantage point (Figure 16.1).

FIGURE 16.1
Street-level per-
spective view

For exterior views, start by placing the camera approximately 100′ (30m) from where you intend to aim the camera. Placing a camera too close to the model will often put you right up against a wall, and you'll have to readjust the camera to see more of the model.

When you activate the Camera tool, you first establish the eye position and then set the target. It's a simple two-click operation, and the next thing you know, you're taken directly to the camera view, looking at a perspective of your model. Revit puts the camera at eye level by default when you place a new camera in a plan view. This is usually fine, but you're free to adjust the camera dynamically or by manipulating the elevation of the eye and target levels through the properties of the camera.

To adjust your camera dynamically, enable the SteeringWheel from the main toolbar, and use the options to orbit, zoom, pan, and move through the view.

The walkthrough options allow you to walk, look, and move the camera up and down. To adjust the focal length of the camera (zooming camera in or out without moving the camera), click the small arrow at the bottom right of the SteeringWheel, and choose Increase/Decrease Focal Length (Figure 16.2). It acts as if you're zooming your lens in and out, while keeping the camera stationary—not to be confused with walking the camera closer to the building.

FIGURE 16.2

Focal length controls are accessed from the SteeringWheel.

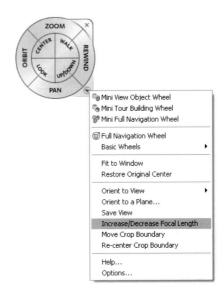

PERSPECTIVE VIEWS ARE FOR VISUALIZATION

Currently, perspective views are used only for visualization. You can select elements and change their properties (or delete them) from a perspective view, but you cannot edit any of the model using grips or edit commands within these views.

SHOWING THE CAMERA

To see a camera from the context of other views, right-click the 3D view name in the Project Browser and choose Show Camera. The camera appears in all views as a camera icon with the view extents shows as red lines (Figure 16.3); you can visualize where the camera is relative to your model. At this point, the camera is selected, so you can move it to a new location, and the view updates automatically to reflect the change. You can also adjust the target position in this mode. Just be careful where you click—clicking anything else (including nothing) deselects the camera, which causes it to disappear.

FIGURE 16.3
When a camera is
shown, the view
extents appear red
in all views.

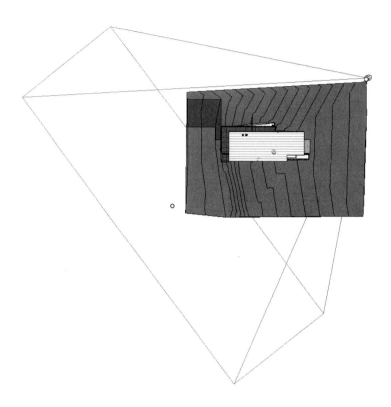

Silhouetted Edge Display

As you saw when we discussed elevations, overriding the edges of elements can help make a drawing more legible and graphically clear. In addition to using the Linework tool, you can use a more dynamic feature built into Revit that accounts for the fact that perspective views are more likely to be spun around and reoriented (and thus make the Linework tool irrelevant). From the shadow icon in the view frame control tools you can access the Advanced Model Graphics dialog box—at the bottom is a control for setting a line style called *Silhouette style*.

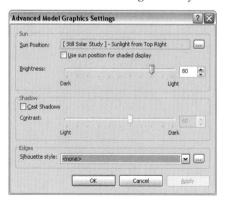

By choosing a line style with a thicker line weight, you'll see the effect of this feature. The line style isn't applied to specific edges of the model but is dynamically redrawn depending on your point of view. Revit applies the line style to the outer edges of elements visible in the view, giving the model a bold outline. The effect can be subtle but nice, as shown in Figure 16.4. If the effect is too subtle, try making the view larger (the default is a 6″ x 4.5″ view) and making a new line style with a heavier line weight.

FIGURE 16.4
Top: No silhouette edges applied; bottom: silhouette edges applied with a line style using a line weight of 6

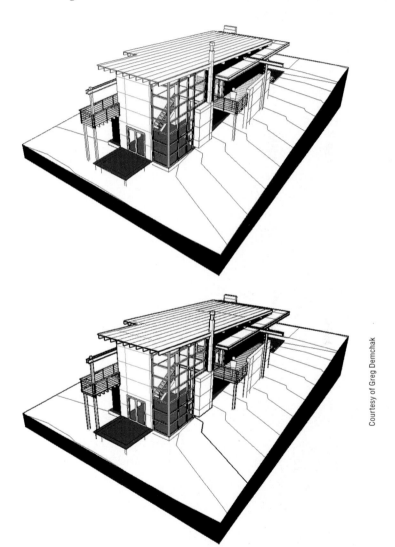

Courtesy of Greg Demchak

Creating Photorealistic Renderings

New to Revit 2009 is a completely reworked rendering workflow and integrated rendering engine. The former AccuRender engine has been replaced with a mental ray engine, which delivers stunning photorealistic renderings. Also added is a new library of rendering materials custom-designed for architectural visualizations. With the new features in Revit 2009, you can assign some materials, set up a camera, click Render, and expect to get some great results right out of the box (Figure 16.5).

FIGURE 16.5
Example of rendering from 2009

The Rendering Dialog Box

To render a perspective view, click the teapot icon in the view frame controls at bottom of the view. This launches the Rendering dialog box (Figure 16.6), where you set all the parameters for the rendering, such as quality, output, lighting, background, and exposure settings. You can also open the dialog box from the Rendering tab on the Design bar by right-clicking the Design bar and selecting Rendering. Once the tab is open, you'll see one button, and that button launches the dialog box shown in Figure 16.6.

Let's look at this dialog box in more detail, as each setting will affect how the rendering looks.

QUALITY

The first set of options when rendering an image consists of the quality settings (Figure 16.7). These affect the overall quality and, perhaps more important, the time it takes to render the view. The higher you go in quality, the longer the rendering time will be. We recommend rendering at draft and low quality initially and only going to higher quality after you have validated the material and scene selection assigned to the model.

The settings have been pretuned for optimal results, but if you want to experiment further down, under the hood, so to speak, you can select the Edit option. This opens the Render Quality Settings dialog box (shown in Figure 16.8), where you can see all the variables that affect the rendering quality. Any change you make to these settings is stored in the file as a Custom (view specific) setting. This prevents your changing any of the factory presets, but at the same time gives you total flexibility to go beyond what has been preset.

FIGURE 16.6

The new Rendering dialog box

FIGURE 16.7

Quality setting options range from Draft to Best

FIGURE 16.8

To see all the parameters that affect quality settings, open the Render Quality Settings dialog box.

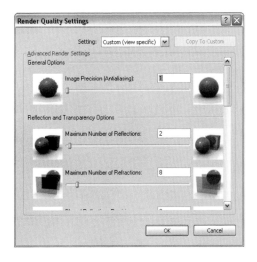

The image on the right and left side of each setting is a visual cue to help you understand the effect of the setting. To see what each factory preset uses, use the settings drop-down list at the top of the dialog box. To edit these settings, click the Copy to Custom button. This copies all the settings into the editable custom setting and allows you to refine the settings.

OUTPUT

The output settings allow you to set the resolution of the image being rendered. The default uses Screen, and you'll see the size of the image (width and height) in pixels, as shown in Figure 16.9A. Choosing Printer allows you to select from some standard DPI settings. The width and height values update automatically for you, giving you an idea of the final output size and the Uncompressed Image Size—this is the size of the file if saved as an uncompressed TIFF (see Figure 16.9B).

FIGURE 16.9
Use Screen or Printer to set the output size for the rendering.

Unless you are ready to send the rendering off for printing (150 dpi draft or 300 dpi finished print quality is recommended), keep the resolution at Screen (72 dpi); this will improve the speed of the renderings without compromising overall quality.

LIGHTING

The Lighting options (Figure 16.10) set exposure levels, let you select what kind of lighting to use, and establish the sun position. The options are self-explanatory: just match the setting with the kind of camera you've set up. Are you outside? Inside? Do you want to see the effect of sun, just artificial lights? Both?

FIGURE 16.10
Lighting options

Sunlight

The sun position is enabled for any scheme that includes the sun as a light source. The list includes sun settings. To access and edit these settings, click the Edit option at the bottom of the list. You can also access this same list by choosing Settings ➤ Sun and Shadow Settings. The resulting dialog box (Figure 16.11) lets you edit the sun position by adjusting time, date, and place. Be careful not to edit a setting without changing its name—you would be changing carefully prepared and geographically correct settings. Always duplicate an existing one, give it a new name, and only then set your desired values.

FIGURE 16.11
Sun and Shadow
Settings dialog box

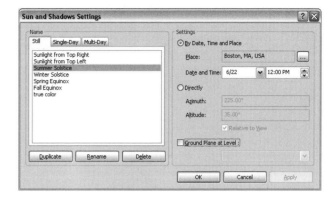

FIGURE 16.11
Sun and Shadow
Settings dialog box

Artificial Lights

When you choose a setting that includes artificial lights, Revit calculates and renders light that emits from lighting fixtures in the view. All the lighting fixtures that ship with Revit 2009 are designed to cast light when rendered. For lighting fixtures that were previously placed in earlier versions of the software, you'll need to manually upgrade the fixture. This is not as hard as it sounds; simply select the fixture, click the Edit Family button in the Options bar, and then load it back into the project once it opens in the Family Editor.

By default, Revit calculates all the lighting fixtures in your model, which can lead to extra long rendering times. To improve speed, click the Light Fixtures button in the Rendering dialog box. This opens the Artificial Light dialog box, where you can choose whether or not fixtures will cast light. You'll see a list of all lights in the project in this dialog box, and you can turn them on or off.

In a real project, say you want to make an interior rendering. To improve performance, you want to only render lights that are visible in the view. In the Rendering dialog box, click the Artificial Lights button (Figure 16.12). As you select lights in the resulting dialog box, they become selected in the model (they turn red), making it easy to know which lights are on or off.

FIGURE 16.12
Using the Artificial
Lights dialog box

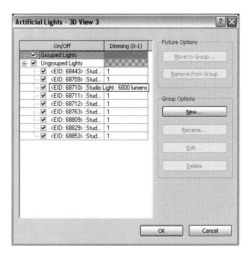

Real World Scenario

TURNING OFF LIGHTS YOU DON'T NEED IN A RENDERING

In Figure 16.13, we created a new group by clicking the New button and naming the group **First Floor Lights**. We moved lights to the group by clicking on each light to see if it highlighted in the view. When the light did highlight, we clicked the Move to Group button to move the light into the First Floor Lights group. Then, to improve rendering performance, all we had to do was clear the Ungrouped Lights option to turn off all the lights not in our view.

You can group lights together from any view in Revit when a lighting fixture is selected. To do so, select a fixture and check the Options bar. You'll have the option to assign the light to an existing group, ungroup it, or create a new group by choosing Edit/New, as shown in Figure 16.14.

FIGURE 16.13
Grouping lights that are visible in the view

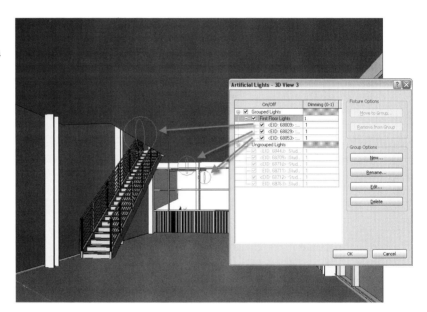

FIGURE 16.14
When a fixture is selected, the option to add it to a group is available in the Options bar.

You can also choose to interactively edit the group (if the light is in a group) by clicking the Edit button. This changes the model to halftone and shows all lights in the group as green. A floating toolbar appears that allows you to select light fixtures and either add or remove them from the group (see Figure 16.15).

FIGURE 16.15
When editing a light group, you can add or remove fixtures from the group using a floating toolbar.

BACKGROUND

The background settings (Figure 16.16) help give your model some context by using a sky, a sky with cloud cover, or color. The sky in Revit is tied directly to the sun and shadow settings, and will accurately color the sky based on time, date, and place. As you get toward dawn or dusk, the sky will change color to reflect this. You won't need to manually specify any color gradients. If you intend to use images in your background with a tool like Photoshop, you'll be glad to know that the background is saved as its own channel when images are exported as PNG. This means you can use whatever background image you want, and you'll get a clean, perfectly blended look. This also allows you to position and edit your background graphics in Photoshop, where you have total control.

FIGURE 16.16
Background options

To add some clouds to the background, choose from the options available in the drop-down menu. Clouds will appear wispy and subtle when using these options. If you want strong, high-contrast clouds, add them in the postprocessing by doctoring your images in image-editing programs—just be sure to export to PNG. You can also use a single color for a background.

RENDERING THE VIEW

Once you've chosen the quality, output, and lighting scheme, you're ready to render the view. Click the Render button and Revit will start the rendering process. Actually, a new process starts that is independent of Revit, so if the rendering were to get stuck or crash, you can stop the rendering process without having to stop Revit. You can see this in the Window Task Manager as fbxooprender.exe (see Figure 16.17).

FIGURE 16.17
Rendering is managed as a separate process by the CPU.

A progress dialog box will also appear:

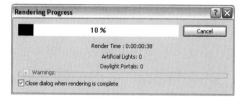

Here you will see how long the rendering is taking, how many artificial lights and daylight portals are being calculated, and if any warnings are encountered during the rendering process. An example of a warning would be if the path to images used for rendering were no longer intact. To cancel the rendering at any time, just click the Cancel button, and confirm you want to stop.

You can also decide to render just a portion of a view, to save time and get an idea of the results to be achieved. To render only a portion of the view, check the Region option next to the Render button. This enables a box in the view that you can adjust by selecting it and then dragging the grips to resize it. Use this option if you want to render only portions of the model to check materials, rather than rendering the entire view.

ADJUSTING EXPOSURE

When you choose a lighting scheme, Revit automatically determines some exposure settings for you. You can adjust these either before or after running a rendering. Click the Exposure Control button to open the Exposure Control dialog box, shown in Figure 16.18.

FIGURE 16.18
The Exposure Control dialog box gives you a series of settings for adjusting the exposure.

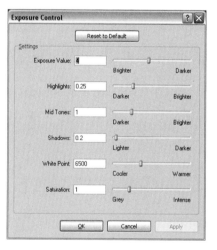

After the rendering is complete, you can change the values of these options. Click Apply to change the appearance of the image after the rendering is complete. For example, if the rendering seems too dark, try decreasing the Exposure value. To return settings to factory defaults, click the Reset to Default button at top of the dialog box.

SAVING RENDERINGS AS IMAGES

Once you've produced a rendering that you're happy with and want to keep, there are two options available to you in the Rendering dialog box. You can either save to the image to the project or export the image to disk. When saving to the project, the rendering is saved in the Rendering branch of the Project Browser and can be dragged onto sheets like any other view. When Exporting, the image will be exported and not stored in the project environment. A new feature in Revit 2009 is that the Save command no longer overwrites the previously created images. If you need to do some postprocessing with Photoshop, click the Export button. You can save the rendering in standard image formats (BMP, GIF, JPG, PNG, or TIF).

Materials

The new rendering materials added to Revit 2009 are designed to convey characteristics of texture, color, reflectivity, and transparency that you'd expect to see in reality. An entire library of new materials (branded as "ProMaterials") was designed specifically for architectural workflows. If you are just starting a project in Revit 2009, all the materials will be based on the new content. If you are upgrading from previous versions of Revit and have been using custom texture maps, you'll need to remap them from the Materials dialog box. Although this could be a tedious process, we think the end results will be well worth it, and you will need to do it only once.

EDITING A RENDERING APPEARANCE

All Revit materials now have a new tab associated with them that contains information about how the material will look when rendered. This information is located in the Render Appearance tab in the Materials dialog box, shown in Figure 16.19.

FIGURE 16.19
The new tab in the Materials dialog box: Render Appearance

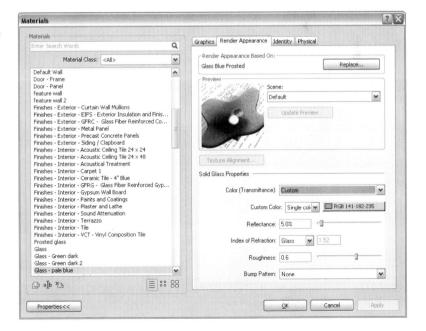

REPLACING MATERIALS

If you're not satisfied with the default render appearances or are upgrading and need to manually assign new materials, then the Replace button will be your first stop. Click that button to bring up the Render Appearance Library (Figure 16.20), where you can search for and assign render appearances.

FIGURE 16.20
The Render Appearance Library

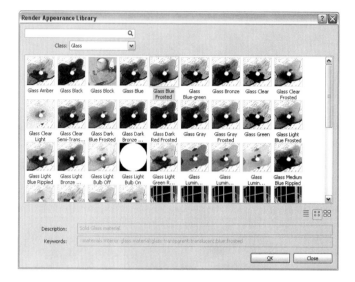

In this dialog box, you can search for materials by typing in the search field, or you can sort the materials using the Class drop-down list. Selecting a render appearance and clicking OK closes the dialog box and replaces your active material with a new render appearance. Consider using this library before making your own customized materials, as they have been carefully tuned to work well in Revit models.

CUSTOM RENDER IMAGES

Many good-looking materials use digital images that are scaled to match the building model. These images are often professionally produced and edited so as to not tile in an obvious manner when repeated over a surface in the model. You'll notice a bad image map if you can see where each image begins to repeat. We don't recommend making your own texture maps, because this tiling effect is difficult to manipulate on your own. Go to a website such as www.turbosquid.com or do image searches for materials.

If you have your own high-quality images that you'd like to use when rendering, this is not a problem. Locate your material in the Materials list. If your material was previously using a custom image, you won't see it listed anymore. Instead, you'll see a generic material assigned that renders as a solid gray color. To remap your image, choose the Color parameter and select Image File (Figure 16.21). This takes you to a dialog box where you can browse to your image file.

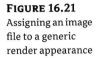

FIGURE 16.21
Assigning an image
file to a generic
render appearance

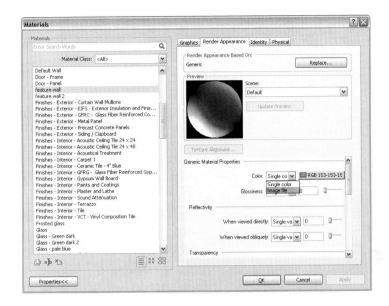

You'll then need to set the scale and change the preview to something more appropriate. Change the scale by typing in a value next to the image preview. This value sets up the repetition module for the image—relating a pixel-dimensioned image to a real-world scale. You can play with other parameters available in the generic render appearance, but for the most part, getting scale correct will be the most important task.

To change the preview, use the drop-down menu next to the preview swatch scene at the top (Figure 16.22). In this example, we are using a custom brick image and changing the preview to use the Flat Surface setting.

FIGURE 16.22
Changing the
Scene preview

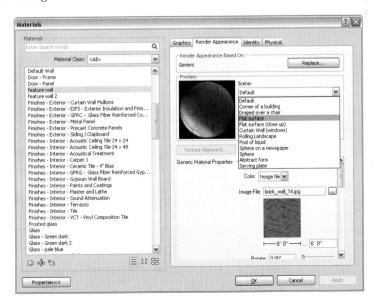

ADDING ENTOURAGE FOR RENDERING

Adding people, cars, and trees to a rendering will give it a sense of scale and context. This technique is usually applied to give a rendered image a more realistic and human effect. This can be achieved by placing entourage and planting families into your model. When rendering a view, this content takes advantage of Rich Photorealistic Content (RPC) technology to show photographic images in the context of the rendering.

For trees, any trees placed in previous versions of Revit will not render. You'll need to load new trees and replace the old ones manually. To do so, load from the planting folder and select an RPC tree. Doing so will load many types, and you can choose from a list of RPC trees (Figure 16.23).

FIGURE 16.23
Some new RPC tree types provided in Revit 2009 planting content

To replace trees quickly, use the Select All Instances option in the context menu when a tree is selected. This selects all instances and allows you to change the type to an RPC type. Be aware that the graphics will change, as the new RPC trees use a different mode of representation than previous versions of Revit. To see what RPC file is associated with a type, select the tree, open Properties, select Edit/New, and click the Render Appearance parameter. This opens a Render Appearance Library with all of the available RPC trees (Figure 16.24).

FIGURE 16.24
Render appearances for trees are accessed via type properties.

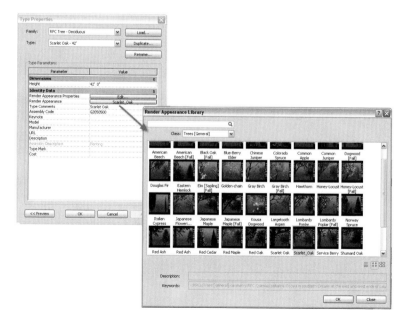

Once you have placed your trees, render the view, and you'll see the results (Figure 16.25).

FIGURE 16.25
Example new
RPC trees when
rendered in a
perspective view

Rendering Tips

Here are some guidelines for rendering efficiently:

- Don't set the quality settings to Best when iterating through material selections; doing so only slows down the time it takes to render. Keep quality at Low or Medium until you're ready for a final pass.

- Use screen resolution until you're ready to export a final image for printing.

- Turn off lights that aren't visible in your view using the Artificial Lights dialog box. Group lights by floor if you are doing interior renderings of various floors in your model. This will speed up your renderings.

- Only adjust quality settings if you absolutely have to. Changing one value could inadvertently slow down your renderings and return unnoticeable effects. All of the presets were carefully calibrated and should do the trick.

- Export rendered images to PNG in order to composite the image with background imagery.

Creating Animated Walkthroughs

Moving through a building in a virtual manner is a great way to experience a design before it gets built. Static images are nice, but it's becoming a common method to create animation sequences that showcase key aspects of the design. Revit provides tools for creating walkthrough sequences for the model, which you can then export as an AVI file.

To make a walkthrough in Revit, the process is as follows:

1. In a plan view, create a path through the model by starting the Walkthrough tool located in the View tab of the Design bar.

You're put into a Sketch mode where each click creates a keyframe that lets you change the direction of the camera. Think about how a camera would move through or around a building. When you've finished sketching, click the Finish button on the Options bar.

2. Edit the keyframes along the path, so the camera looks in the proper direction, by clicking the Edit Walkthrough button on the Options bar.

In this mode, you can edit the camera and path. The default setting allows you to step through each keyframe using the VCR-style controls and adjust the camera direction in the view. You can only edit the camera direction at keyframes. To see what the camera sees, click the Open button. Keep stepping through keyframes and adjusting the camera. In the camera view, you can enable the SteeringWheel and change the direction the camera is looking just as you can in a 3D perspective view.

3. With the walkthrough view open, export the walkthrough to `.avi` format by choosing File ➤ Export ➤ Walkthrough. Figure 16.26 shows the resulting Export Length/Format dialog box.

FIGURE 16.26
The Length/Format dialog box lets you set output values for the length and size of the animation.

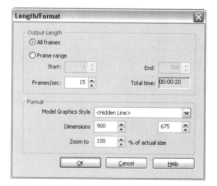

Exporting the 3D Model for Use in Other Applications

If you have established ways of working with vector or pixel based artwork, you can always export Revit views and use them as backdrops for your artistry. From the Export menu, you'll find CAD formats for DWG, DXF, DGN, and SAT formats. You can also export any view as an image file using the Export Image option. Supported formats include BMP, JPEG, PNG, TARGA, and TIF.

Once you've made edits to the exports in applications such as Photoshop, Illustrator, or Piranesi, you can always re-import the artwork into Revit and place it on sheets with your other views.

For rendering purposes, and new to this latest version of Revit 2009, you can export a Revit file to FBX format (Figure 16.27) and open it in the latest version of 3ds Max. In addition to the geometry, the FBX file contains information about the materials in the model (Figure 16.28) and to what elements the materials are applied. This information is available only if you *open the file with 3dS Max or 3dS Max Design 2009.*

FIGURE 16.27
On the Export menu you'll find a new option: 3ds Max (FBX).

FIGURE 16.28
Rendered model using 3ds Max

Courtesy of Andrea Sader and Ines Magri

Note that FBX export cannot be executed from a wire frame mode.

The Bottom Line

Revit is a complete solution that allows you to generate construction documentation while also providing powerful presentation tools. Using the new rendering functionality, you'll be able to generate photorealistic results with minimal effort. That said, setting up cameras and assigning good materials is still an integral part of creating a solid presentation, and they deserve attention.

Create perspective views Design visualization is a key benefit to using Revit as a documentation solution. Being able to snap quick perspectives of your spaces and building forms can be critical to making good design decisions.

Master It Create a new perspective view showcasing a critical design feature. Using the Rendering tab, apply lighting and materials and complete the rendering.

Create photorealistic renderings   You know those signs that are put up at the site before and during construction—the ones with the nice rendering showing the final product? Well, you can generate those directly in Revit!

> **Master It**   You've been asked to produce an exterior rendering of the building. Can you do this in Revit? Can you tweak the results in Photoshop?

Create animated walkthroughs   Creating animated walkthroughs is an excellent way to visualize the spaces within the project in a more dynamic fashion than still renderings.

> **Master It**   You want to create a compelling animation showing an entry approach to the building. How would you do that with Revit?

Export the 3D model for use in other applications   Revit is an excellent application, but there are a variety of other tools out there that you might want to use for rendering, modeling, or other BIM features such as 3D printing.

> **Master It**   You've modeled your project in Revit and assigned materials, and now want to make an animation sequence with 3Ds Max 2009. What should you do?

Chapter 17

Fine-Tuning Your Preliminary Design

The next step we'll explore is taking a preliminary building design and doing spatial analysis of the Revit model. You'll see how creating simple schedules of building and room areas can verify program information and start to generate preliminary cost analysis. We'll show you how to verify program data and evaluate a project's initial feasibility.

In this chapter, you learn how to do the following:

◆ Quantify your preliminary designs

◆ Create schedules

◆ Use schedules for preliminary cost estimates

Quantifying Your Preliminary Designs

Moving ahead, we're introducing a scenario that we'll build on for the next several chapters. As this is a Mastering book, we'll not go into significant detail about how to perform some of the more basic skills in Revit, such as how to make simple walls, floors, and roofs. Instead, you'll work from an existing, more developed design and build skills by adding and extracting information from this base model. You will move the design from a preliminary design level into a set of design documents based on common architectural requirements that occur in a typical project workflow. We will also explore some sustainable design strategies.

The Foundation Model

The model we'll be using for the next several chapters can be downloaded from the book's companion web page, www.sybex.com/go/masteringrevit2009. Called the Foundation, it was part of a design competition for a university alumni facility and was created by BNIM Architects. The building is approximately 46,000 sq. ft. and comprises office space, meeting areas, and multipurpose space spread out over three floors of the building. It is located at a major university in the Midwestern United States (see Figures 17.1 and 17.2).

FIGURE 17.1
Perspective view
of the Foundation
model

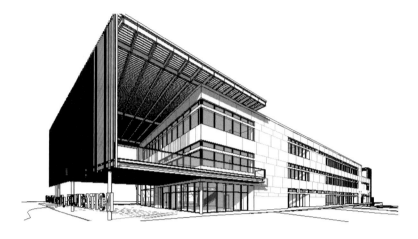

FIGURE 17.2
Another view of
the Foundation
model

We recommend doing a few things to familiarize yourself with this model:

◆ Open the project, and in the Project Browser, choose View ➤ All. This will give you a list of all the views in the model and provide you with an opportunity to browse through them and see what has been given focus and importance.

◆ Take a look at the generic 3D view. Using the ViewCube, spin it around a bit and kick the tires, so to speak. Take a look at the overall building form and geometry to help acclimate yourself to the overall design. That will give you a sense of direction within the building.

◆ Browse through any sheets that have been set up. Not only will this give you an idea of what the building looks like, but it will also tell you what stage the project is in and where the focus has been so far.

In the Foundation model you will find many preestablished 3D views, as well as some sections and generic plan views. Sheets have been started and views placed on those sheets. A structural grid, elevations, and the primary building materials have all been defined. Based on the plans, you can get a clear idea of what the building program is and how the spaces are organized. At this stage in a project workflow, you'll often need to take a short timeout from design work and do some program verification and evaluation, with the goal of creating an initial cost per square foot assessment. To do that, you will first create area plans for the Foundation's total and rentable areas and then create schedules of materials so you can check costs against some square foot assumptions. (Under a leaseback agreement, the building will be owned by its builder rather than the university—hence the need to calculate rentable area.) This is where we'll begin with this model.

Calculating Area Plans

For the purpose of program verification, you need to establish how area values are calculated and represented. The simplest method is to use room tags, which can report room area, but you'll quickly see the limitations of that approach. It is only the *carpet area* of the room and does not take into account walls. For the feasibility study in this chapter's example, you'll need to create area plans for both total area and rentable area. Then you'll see how to add areas and area tags manually.

Room Tags

The room tag shown in Figure 17.3 has been placed in the model and is tagging a room. This is used to label the room and its area. The surface value or the value expressed in square feet (SF) on the room tag is the usable area within the room, sometimes referred to as the carpet area.

FIGURE 17.3
Room area as a property reported in the room tag

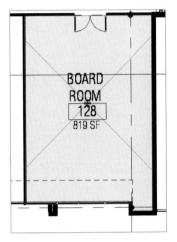

Revit calculates this area by finding all of the entities that touch the floor bounding a space. As you can see in Figure 17.4, it does not include things like the area below the column (at the upper left) or other objects that penetrate the space, giving you a truly usable floor area. Later in this chapter, we will discuss how to schedule those areas so you can report them in a way that they are all visible at the same time.

FIGURE 17.4
By default, room areas do not include the area below the columns.

While this is certainly a useful feature, it does not accommodate calculation of the precise areas you will need to verify your program or perform any cost take-offs.

Area Plans

Area plans are views of the model used to calculate the areas of your model according to various calculation standards. Some of the standards for area calculations are as follows:

Gross area   This is the overall area of a floor or footprint of the building.

Rentable area   Different developers and leasing companies have different standards for rentable area. For example, it may include all the spaces in a building except egress corridors, vertical transportation, and mechanical spaces. However, this includes the floor area taken up by columns and some walls.

Usable area   This area defines only the usable space in a plan. It doesn't count areas taken up by columns, walls, mechanical rooms, and shafts or other nonusable space.

BOMA area   BOMA is the Building Owners and Managers Association. Widely used in the United States by architects, developers, and facilities managers alike, it was created to help standardize office building development. BOMA has its own set of standards used to calculate areas. More information on BOMA standards can be found at www.boma.org.

Revit allows you to choose from two predefined area schemes, or it gives you the option to create your own scheme based on standard area calculation variables. To add or modify the area settings, choose Settings ➤ Area and Volume Computation to open the dialog box shown in Figure 17.5.

FIGURE 17.5
The Area and Volume Computations dialog box, with the Computations tab displayed

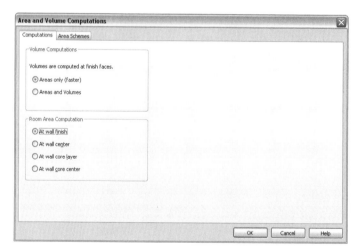

The Computations tab allows you to change how the areas and volumes are calculated in the model. You can set how areas are calculated relative to the wall geometry here (wall finish vs. wall core, for example).

The Area Schemes tab, shown in Figure 17.6, lets you add different schemes to calculate room areas, allowing you to calculate multiple area types.

FIGURE 17.6
The Area Schemes
tab of the Area
and Volume
Computations
dialog box

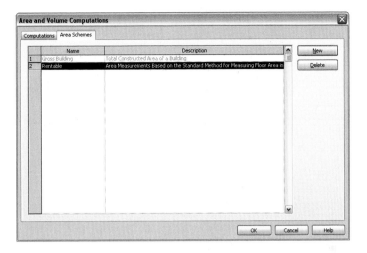

In the sample Foundation model, you first need to establish the *gross area per floor* of the building. To do this, start by adding an area plan to the model.

MAKING A GROSS AREA PLAN

Take the following steps to begin creating a gross area plan:

1. Open the Foundation model.

2. Select the Room and Area tab in the Design bar (if it is not visible, right-click anywhere in the Design bar and activate the Room and Area tab) and click the Area Plan button. This opens the New Area Plan dialog box (see Figure 17.7), where you select the area scheme, level, and scale. Select Gross Building from the drop-down menu at the top. Using Ctrl-click, select the floor plans for Level 1, Level 2, and Level 3. Leave the scale at 1/8″ = 1′-0″ (1:100), the default setting, and click OK.

FIGURE 17.7
Creating area
plan views

3. Revit automatically adds a new node called Area Plans (Gross Building) to the Project Browser and adds plans for each level you selected. Open the Level 2 area plan.

4. In the View window, you'll see a duplicate of the Level 2 plan view you selected. The difference between the original Level 2 and this one is that it has purple lines defining the area boundaries (see Figure 17.8). This might be a challenge to notice in this black and white image, but you will get the idea if you open the project. These purple lines are placed on the walls according to the type of area plan you selected, which in this case was Gross Building Area. You can make manual adjustments to these lines, move them, or delete them if they don't appear where you want them.

FIGURE 17.8
Area boundary
lines for gross area

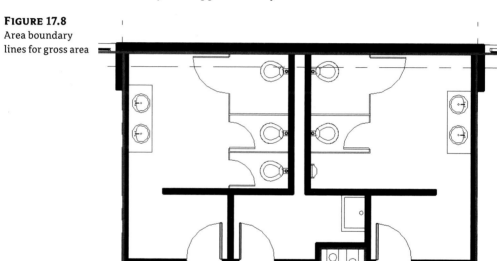

5. Revit has generated Gross Building Area plans for each floor and you can start adding area tags to get an idea of what your floorplate areas are for this project. As you can see, you have about 22,800 sq. ft. (~ 7,000 m²) of area for the first floor.

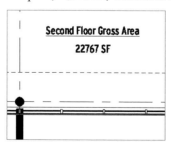

The boundaries that Revit applies automatically are not set in stone. Should you need to manually change them and add new boundaries, you can do that using the Area Boundary tool. When adding new boundaries, note that they must form closed loops of lines in order for Revit to calculate areas. Any breaks or gaps between the area lines, or lines that don't intersect, will result in Revit returning a "Not Enclosed" value for the area. If you get that message, inspect all your lines, and close gaps using the Trim tool or by extending the boundary lines. It is not possible to add Area Boundary lines to anything but an area plan. That option will be grayed out in all other views.

Making a Rentable Area Plan

Now that you have gross area defined and have a good idea of what floorplate sizes are, you can move on to getting a better understanding of the building program. For the program verification, you need to figure out the rentable area for each of the spaces so you can see how well you fared against the program supplied by the client for this project. Using the same process described earlier for the gross building areas, you can make rentable area plans for the building. Repeating the technique described earlier and selecting Rentable Area this time, you'll create a new view in the Project Browser—Area Plans (Rentable).

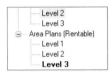

You'll notice that in displaying rentable areas, Revit draws the area boundary on the *inside* of the exterior walls (unlike with the gross area, where the lines were drawn on the *outside* of the exterior walls), but it also draws boundaries down the *centerline* of the interior walls. All of this happens automatically—all that is left for you to do is to verify the lines and make sure you have them where you need them.

For this exercise, you'll want to modify the results slightly from what Revit provides by default. For the program and client on this project, you're not going to calculate core areas (areas around the elevator and stair cores) as part of the rentable area, so you'll need to adjust the area boundary lines around the core walls to reflect this and turn the many spaces into one area.

AUTOMATING AREA CALCULATIONS DURING DESIGN

When Revit creates area boundary lines, those lines by default are locked to the walls on which they are created. This is to aid you so as your design changes and walls are relocated, the area boundaries automatically update as well, keeping your area plans always up-to-date.

In the case of the restroom core, start by deleting the lines that separate the restrooms from the janitorial closet (see Figure 17.9).

FIGURE 17.9
Modifying an
area plan

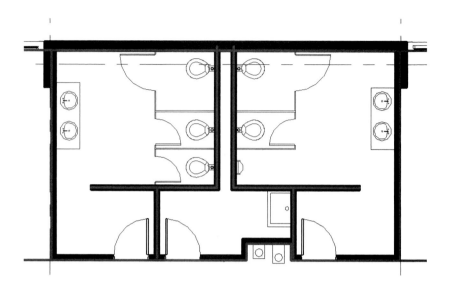

As you delete area lines, you'll more than likely get the warning message shown in Figure 17.10. This message tells us that we have removed the boundary between two areas, and Revit is asking what we would like to do with them. Before we answer this question, let's discuss what areas are in Revit.

FIGURE 17.10
Area warning
message

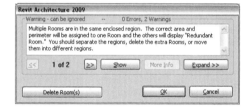

In the context of Revit, areas are elements, similar to walls, doors, or furniture. They are selectable, have properties, and can be scheduled. When selected, they will highlight in yellow and appear within the space as a box with an *X* through it, as seen in Figure 17.11.

Because areas are elements, you can tag them. An area tag reflects the properties of the element it is tagging. The tag itself is only an annotation.

At this point, you might be asking yourself, "Where did those areas come from? I didn't insert them." Revit generated them automatically when you created the area plans. This is the essential difference between *rooms* and *areas*. By default, when you create a new area plan, it creates an area element within all of the closed area boundaries, so provided there are no adjustments for you to make, it is only necessary for you to tag and label the areas.

FIGURE 17.11
Areas are select-
able elements with
properties.

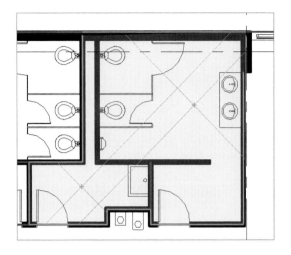

In this case you needed to make some changes to what Revit provided by default and now
have more areas than you have spaces. So let's jump back to the warning dialog box. You've
been given two choices: delete all but one of the areas or click OK and accept having multiple
areas in the space. Both of these options have viable workflows. If, as in our case, you do not
plan to subdivide the room again, you can click Delete Area(s) to delete the extra areas and
continue with our work. If you had deleted these lines with the intent of drawing new ones in
a different location within this boundary, you could click OK, knowing you would have redundant areas for a short time until we finish this part of the model.

Clicking Delete Area(s) deletes the redundant areas and gives you a single core area for the
restrooms shown in Figure 17.12.

FIGURE 17.12
One area is used for
the restroom core.

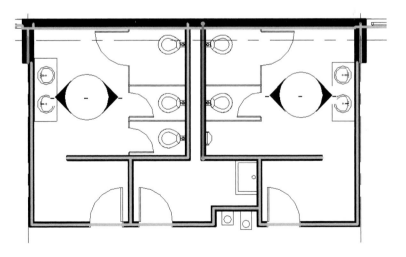

Since you don't want to count any of the core areas, you'll need to move the boundary lines from the centerlines of the walls to the inside face of those walls. Because the area boundaries surrounding the restrooms are locked to the walls themselves, you need to delete these lines and redraw them in desired locations. By now, you'll be used to the warning message about redundant areas, and in this case you know that you want to keep the areas and click OK instead of the Delete Area(s) button.

To draw the new area boundary lines, use the Area Boundary tool described earlier in this chapter to add the new area lines to surround the core. If you choose the Pick option, it will automatically choose the line location based on the rules established for that area plan type. Since we specifically want the area lines on the outside of the core, it is best to draw them manually. So, very quickly, our new core boundary will look like Figure 17.13.

FIGURE 17.13
Revised core boundary

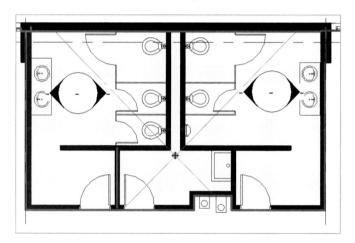

CREATING COMPLEX AREA PLANS

In some cases, such as General Services Administration (GSA) projects, there is a need to create and maintain a series, possibly many area plans. All these additional calculations, depending on the complexity of the building, can slow file performance. One way around this is to make a separate project file for the area plans. By linking the building model to a separate file with area plans, you cannot improve model performance, but you can create the area plans quickly without interfering with other workflows.

Adding Areas and Tags

⊞ Area

As we mentioned earlier, areas are actually elements within the model. When we made the area plans, Revit automatically populated the plan with areas for you. However, you might want to create your own areas that Revit cannot automatically generate. These might be units in a condominium building, for example. To add them manually use the Area button in the Room and Area tab on the Design bar. This adds an area and a tag (provided Tag on Placement is checked in the Options bar) at the same time to your area plan.

 To tag an existing area element, use the Area Tag button located directly below the Area tool.

DON'T DRAW MORE THAN NECESSARY

When designing office buildings, you will probably have your building cores as a repeating element on each floor of the building. In many cases, these cores will be identical. If that is the case, there is no need to redraw your area lines. You can simply copy those elements between floors.

To copy area boundaries between floors, select them and copy them to the clipboard.

1. To select area boundaries, you have several options:

   ♦ Ctrl-click each line individually.

   ♦ Highlight one line by mousing over it and press the Tab key. This will highlight the chain of all the connected lines, and you can then click to select them.

    ♦ Alternatively, you can drag a selection window around all of the lines, and using the Filter tool in the Options bar, filter out all but the <Area Boundary> lines, as shown in Figure 17.14.

FIGURE 17.14
Filtering your
selection

2. Once they are selected, you can use Ctrl+C or Edit ≻ Copy to copy them to the clipboard. Now, by choosing File ≻ Edit ≻ Paste Aligned ≻ Select Views by Name (see Figure 17.15), you can paste your copied area boundaries directly into the same location on other floors, ensuring consistency in your area calculations.

FIGURE 17.15
Pasting into
selected views

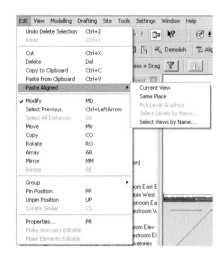

3. Now that you have all the areas defined, you can present them by printing the individual views to see graphically how the spaces are assembled (see Figure 17.16).

FIGURE 17.16
Area and tag
graphics

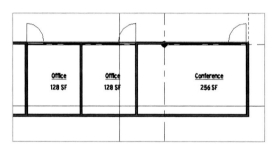

But what happens if you want to show this information in a tabular, spreadsheet format? Often you'll need to share information of this kind in a table format. Because Revit is based on a bidirectional information model, it can do all of these calculations and update tasks for you in real time. All you need to do is set up a view type in the model that allows you to look at the data in a list format instead of showing the information graphically. For this, use schedules.

Creating Schedules

Schedules are lists of elements within the model. They enumerate items, including building objects such as walls, doors, and windows; calculate material quantities or areas and volumes; and list the number of sheets, text notes, keynotes, and so on. The ability to dynamically create and update schedules is a core aspect of both BIM and Revit.

Creating schedules of objects, areas, or material quantities in a project is usually one of the most painful (if not boring) but necessary tasks for architects. Needless to say, performing a manual calculation takes a long time and can result in errors. Using CAD tools can partly automate this process, but when it comes to calculating numbers of objects, the calculation can only count the number of blocks that are predefined in a file. In Revit, all elements have information about their physical properties, and you can add information to individual elements. For example, doors can have properties such as size as well as material, color, fire rating, and whether they are exterior or interior.

Revit lets you schedule any element based on properties of the element. In effect, this means that almost anything placed in a Revit model can be scheduled and quantified. Additionally, because the schedule is linked to the objects in the model, you can use the schedule to locate objects within the model or to change their types and properties. This ensures that in any view, regardless of type, the count and properties of all elements are always synchronized. As we often state, the view in which you add or change something doesn't matter. The changes will be reflected in all the views.

If you're unfamiliar with database concepts, don't worry; we'll explain the options in the New Schedule dialog box. The following types of elements can be scheduled:

Areas	Gutters	Rooms
Casework	Lighting fixtures	Site
Ceilings	Mass	Slab edges
Curtain panels	Mass floors	Specialty equipment
Curtain systems	Mechanical equipment	Stairs
Curtain wall mullions	Parking	Structural columns
Doors	Planting	Structural foundations
Electrical equipment	Plumbing fixtures	Structural framing
Electrical fixtures	Property line segment	Structural trusses
Fascias	Property lines	Topography
Floors	Railings	Wall sweeps
Furniture	Ramps	Walls
Furniture systems	Roofs	Windows

There are also some other schedules you can create that are not limited to specific types of elements:

Multicategory   This type of schedule is for objects that span across Revit category organization. For example, you may want to create a list of windows and doors in the same schedule. You may also want a schedule showing all the casework and furniture in a project. A multi-category schedule allows you to combine a number of different categories into one schedule. It is also the only way to schedule generic model elements. The one limitation of a multicategory schedule is that you can't schedule host elements (walls, floors, roofs), only their materials and family components.

Area (gross building)   This schedule lists the gross building areas created with the area plans.

Areas (rentable)   This type can be created with a rentable plans schedule. Later in this chapter, we'll walk through an exercise demonstrating how to create a simple schedule showing the program areas we created in our area plans.

Although we've listed quite a few, we haven't included all the schedules available in Revit. There are still a few more worth mentioning. These schedules can be accessed only from View ➤ New.

Material take-off   This type of schedule can list all the materials and subcomponents of any Revit family and allow an enhanced level of detail for each assembly. You can use a material take-off to schedule any material that is placed in a component. For example, you might want to know the cubic yardage of concrete within the model. Regardless of whether the concrete is in a wall or floor or column, you can tell the schedule to report the total amount of that material in the project. As we will show later, you can use this schedule type to make some preliminary calculations regarding the use of recycled materials in the project to support sustainable design goals.

Revision schedule   This schedule shows a list of all the active revisions in the project. We discuss this schedule in detail in a later chapter.

View list   This schedule shows a list of all the views and their properties in the Project Browser.

Drawing list   This schedule shows a list of all the sheets in the project, sorted alphabetically.

Note block   This schedule lists the notes that are applied to elements and assemblies in your project. You can also use a note block to list the annotation symbols (centerlines, north arrows) used in a project.

Keynote legend   This schedule lists all the keynotes that have been applied to materials and objects in the model. You can either use this list as a complete index of all the notes in the drawing set or filter it by sheet. The legend can then be placed on multiple sheets.

These schedules are separated from the main list of schedules because they aren't commonly used in building documentation. They are primarily for data coordination that happens outside of the project documentation.

STANDARDIZE YOUR SCHEDULES

You will find yourself making the same schedules for each and every project. Take the ones you find the most universal and make them a part of your default template. As you add content to the model, these will start to autopopulate.

Making a Simple Schedule (Rentable Area)

Schedule/Quantities...   You can begin making a new schedule by selecting the View tab on the Design bar, choosing View ➤ New ➤ Schedule/Quantities or clicking the Schedule/Quantities button. When you begin a new schedule you're presented with a number of format and selection options. These will help you set the font style and text alignment as well as organize and filter the data shown in the schedule. Remember that Revit is a database at its core, so many of the same functionalities that are available in database queries are also available in Revit.

SORTING YOUR DRAWING LIST

The drawing list can also be used as a sheet index to the documents. By default, Revit sorts sheets alphabetically. It is traditionally desirable to prepare the sheet index with civil sheets first, then architectural, structural, and so on. One way to customize sheet sorting is to add a Discipline field to the schedule and number the sheets so civil is 1, architectural 2, and so on. You can then sort by that numbered column.

The process of creating a new area schedule is best demonstrated with an example. Take the following steps to create a new rentable area schedule for the Foundation model:

1. Open the Foundation.rvt file (www.sybex.com/go/masteringrevit2009).

2. Navigate to View ➤ Schedule/Quantities or click the Schedules/Quantities button on the View tab.

3. Choose Areas (Rentable) from the Category menu, name the schedule Rentable Area Schedule, and confirm by clicking OK.

   You will see a series of tabs that allow you to specify the schedule's graphic appearance and choose exactly what data you would like to show. Figure 17.17 shows you the dialog box for the rentable area schedule. As each grouping of elements within Revit is unique, the list of possible schedule values changes accordingly.

FIGURE 17.17
Rentable area scheduling options

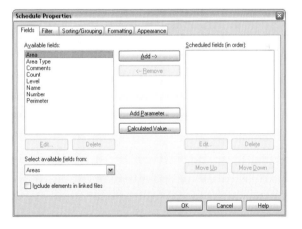

Each tab controls different ways to sort and view the data within a schedule. Here is a basic explanation of their functions.

Fields   The Fields tab lets you select the data that will appear in your schedule. For the wall schedule, it shows all the properties available in the wall family.

Filter   On the Filter tab, you can filter out the data you don't wish to show. You'll use this tab, for example, to restrict displayed data so that only information about the concrete walls in the project appears in the schedule.

Sorting/Grouping   This tab lets you control the order in which information is displayed. You can also decide whether you want to show every instance of an item or only the totals for a given family.

Formatting   The Formatting tab controls the display heading for each field and whether the field is visible on the schedule. It's possible to add fields that are necessary for calculations or sorting but don't show on the printed copy of the schedule. Additionally, this tab can tell Revit to calculate the totals for certain fields.

Appearance   The Appearance tab controls the graphical aspects of the schedule, including the font size and type of text for each of the columns and headers in the schedule. It also allows you to turn the grids on and off or modify the line thickness for the grid and boundary lines.

The following example walks through the different options in the New Schedule dialog box while you create a new wall schedule.

In this example, you'll create the schedule, filter out all but the concrete walls, and calculate the volume of recycled content in the walls based on the assumption that you're using 15 percent recycled content in all the concrete you pour on this project.

4. For your schedule, choose the following fields from the Fields tab and sort them in this order:

Level
Name
Area

5. Select the Sorting/Grouping tab to give the schedule some parameters to sort by. First, sort by level, so you can see which floors you have the areas on, and then sort by area name. You will also want to see a total of the areas by floor, so include a footer showing totals only for the levels. Also check the Header check box so you can tell which floor you're on in each grouping. Finally, you'll want to see a grand total of all the areas in the building. Your dialog box should look like Figure 17.18.

FIGURE 17.18
Set the Sorting/
Grouping tab to
match this.

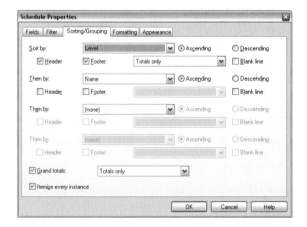

6. Select the Formatting tab as you'll also want to make a couple of changes here. Select the Level parameter and select the Hidden Field check box. You don't need to see a level heading for each item in the list, especially since you have one established already as a header for each floor. You'll also want to select the Area field and make two changes: first, right-justify the areas so they align properly, and then check the box to have the schedule calculate totals as shown in Figure 17.19.

FIGURE 17.19

Set up the Formatting tab to look like this.

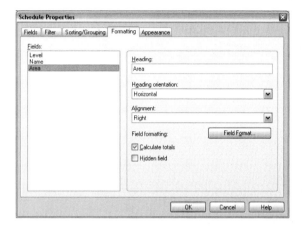

7. Clicking OK at this point will give you a schedule broken out by level and totaling each floor's areas. Your schedule should look something like Figure 17.20.

FIGURE 17.20

The area schedule

8. For areas, we are concerned only with the rentable spaces and don't need to see how much area the cores take up in the building. By right-clicking on the schedule, you can view its properties and make some modifications. Choose the Filter tab this time, filter out any name that does not contain the word *Core* (with a capital C), as shown in Figure 17.21, and click OK.

FIGURE 17.21
Filter the areas
to remove the
word *Core*.

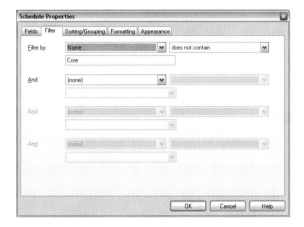

9. Pan down to the bottom of the list and you will notice that you still have the name *Restroom core* in the list (see Figure 17.22).

FIGURE 17.22
Check the schedule
to see the effect of
the filter.

10. The name *Restroom core* is still in the list because the filter and fields in the schedules and families within Revit are case-sensitive. *The fields need to match exactly.* However, there is an easy fix. By simply clicking within the cell itself, as you would do in Excel, you can modify the word *core* so it has a capital *C* and the name will then be filtered from the list. The finished schedule should look like Figure 17.23.

Placing the Schedule on a Sheet

Now that you've created the schedule for the program, you need to put it on a sheet. As you've figured out by now, schedules work like any other view: to place the schedule on a sheet, drag and drop it from the Project Browser onto the sheet you wish to place it on. One of the nice things about schedules is that you can actually place them on multiple sheets and they will always provide the most current information.

We want to create a set of sheets you could provide to the client that demonstrates the program for each floor in both graphic and list format. When finished, you should have an 11 × 17 presentation sheet that looks like Figure 17.24, with a floor plan and schedule for each floor.

1. Expand the sheets in the Project Browser and find the sheet 01 – First Floor Program.

FIGURE 17.23
The finished area
schedule

Rentable Area Schedule	
Name	Area
Conference	256 SF
Conference	256 SF
Daycare	2054 SF
Electrical	233 SF
Entry	214 SF
Mechanical	674 SF
Multi-purpose space	2695 SF
Office	104 SF
Office	163 SF
Office	128 SF
Office	128 SF
Open Office	8872 SF
Restroom	48 SF
Restroom	48 SF
Restroom	48 SF
Restroom	48 SF
Storage	252 SF
Telefund	838 SF
Vestibule 1	237 SF
Vestibule 2	70 SF
	18525 SF
Level 2	
Conference Rm	608 SF
Office	125 SF
Office	125 SF
Office	125 SF
Office	125 SF
Open Office	17989 SF
	19097 SF
Level 3	
Open Office	16215 SF
	16215 SF
	53837 SF

FIGURE 17.24
Finished
presentation sheet
with area plan and
schedule

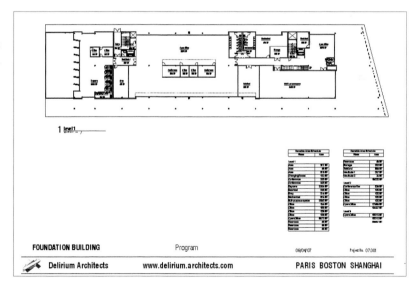

2. Expand the rentable area plans and drag and drop the Level 1 Plan onto the sheet.

3. You will notice that the plan is much larger than the sheet, since we made the area plan at ⅛″ scale originally. Right-click on the plan and choose Activate View from the context menu. In this view, you want to do two things: change the scale, and turn off some of the unnecessary annotations. So, first, adjust the scale of the drawing to be ¹⁄₁₆″ = 1′-0″ (1:200). Second, open the Visibility Graphics dialog box (by typing **VG** or choosing View ➢ Visibility/Graphics). On the Annotations tab, turn off visibility for the following categories:

   ◆ Elevation tags

   ◆ Grids

   ◆ Reference planes

   ◆ Section tags

   Once the view is resized and the display reconfigured, place the plan at the upper portion of the sheet.

4. Drag and drop the rentable area schedule onto the same sheet. When it first appears, it will look something like Figure 17.25. You'll need to do a bit of rearranging to get the schedule to fit the sheet properly.

FIGURE 17.25
Unformatted
schedule placed
on sheet

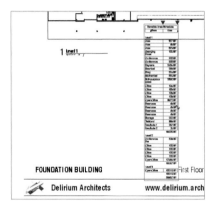

5. There are two different ways to modify the schedule directly from the sheet. On the upper portion of the schedule header, there is one blue triangle for each column. By dragging them left or right, you can resize the width of each column. You will notice some of our longer room names have wrapped to the next line. Grab the left triangle and drag it to the right to lengthen the Name field. Note that this also shortens the schedule by removing the wrapped lines.

6. The other tool you can use to modify how the schedule fits on the sheet is the squiggle, located in the center of the schedule. Clicking this tool splits the schedule into two columns. It is important to note that you cannot choose where this split occurs. However, you end up with two separate columns that you can now drag independently of each other. Now that the columns fit within the space you have remaining, you can locate them to the right-hand portion of the sheet. The sections of the schedules can be subdivided as many times as you need, and each section subdivides independently of the others. Your final sheet will look like Figure 17.24.

🌐 Real World Scenario

KEEPING BUILDING AREA SCHEDULES UPDATED

To most clients, building areas are a critical part of the development pro forma (the pro forma is typically a spreadsheet that outlines the financial goals of the project or development). In practice, you will create area plans that coincide with how the owner needs areas computed for their calculations. You keep these in a schedule, allowing owners to make regular updates to the building areas so they can compare them to the current pro forma. Since you can keep the schedules dynamically updated, you can set this up once and know that the areas will always be up-to-date.

Additional Schedule Capabilities

Now that you've generated a schedule of spaces, let's look at some of the other advantages of using schedules in the design process. Since Revit is a parametric modeler, all parameters are linked to elements within the model. You might notice that at the top of your schedule, the label is simply labeled Area. This is easy to change.

If we were not using BIM as a modeler, it would become tedious to locate these areas so they could be properly labeled. In Revit, we have two options to rename these spaces. First, if you know what the areas are supposed to be, you can either type the name in or select it from the list of already used names. However, what happens when you need to locate the room on the plan before making changes to it? This is easy to do within Revit. By selecting the area name in the schedule, you'll get useful tools in the Options bar.

Clicking the Show button repeatedly cycles through all of the existing views within Revit and zooms into the one that would best show the area in question. Clicking the button gives you a view similar to what you see in Figure 17.26. As you can see, the restroom does not have a descriptive name and is shown highlighted in the view.

FIGURE 17.26
Showing the
elements from
the context of a
schedule

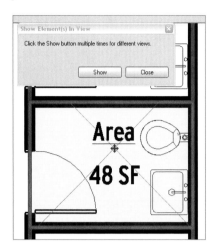

This is a powerful tool because it can be used to locate any of the elements within the Revit model directly from any schedule. Not only do Revit schedules report information about elements in the project, they can also be used to control elements. If you decide to exchange one wall type for another, you can do so by clicking in the schedule—under wall types, for example. A drop-down menu appears, listing all available types currently in the model, and you can choose the type you want. Again, this automatically changes the instance of the wall to another wall type in all views in which the wall is present.

Using Schedules for Preliminary Cost Estimates

At this stage, we're still in preliminary design for this project, and have not gone through the rigor of cost estimating the project yet. Nonetheless, you can use some of the scheduling tools to help calculate a rough cost of the building based on a cost per square foot assessment. The disclaimer here is that Revit is not a cost-estimating package. It is a database that can count, total, and tally the number of items, areas, or other properties within the model. Cost estimating itself is part counting and part experience; we can work on the counting part with the BIM model.

Since you already created gross area plans earlier, go ahead and create a new schedule to analyze the area plans to create a rudimentary cost estimate based on the building square footage. This time, only include the Level and Area fields in the Fields tab. Next, you'll need to add a parameter for cost. That parameter is *not* a standard property of the areas, so you'll need to add it to the list.

1. To add the Cost parameter, use the Add Parameter button on the Fields tab. This allows you to add a new custom parameter to the Areas field. You need to add one for Cost and you need the parameter type to be a number so we can get a cost per square foot. See Figure 17.27 for the dialog box properties.

FIGURE 17.27
FIGURE 17.27

Adding a new
parameter

2. Use the Calculated Value button to add a new field to the schedule. The button displays a new dialog box (Figure 17.28) where you can create new fields that are basically custom formulas defined by combining numerical values with other fields.

FIGURE 17.28

Calculated Value
dialog box

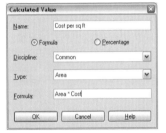

In our example, we want Revit to calculate a total cost for the project based on a cost per square foot we consider close to accurate based on previous experience.

1. For our Type setting we made the type an area. In Revit, you need to make sure the types of fields are compatible so you are not multiplying length times something like material. Also, as we mentioned before, the fields are case-sensitive. In the formula line, you will need to type in **Area * Cost** to get the total project cost. Click OK to exit the dialog box.

2. Finally, on the Sorting tab, check the box for Grand Totals, and on the Formatting tab, highlight the Cost per Sq Ft field you just created and check the box to calculate totals. Once you enter an estimated cost of $169.00 for each floor, the final schedule will look like Figure 17.29.

FIGURE 17.29

Building cost per
square foot

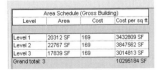

Now you have a constantly updated area of each floor of the building multiplied by our estimated cost per square foot for a continuously accurate total, based on those metrics. However, the costs are being reported as SF values and not dollar amounts. You can fix that problem using the Schedule Properties dialog box.

Editing the Graphic Appearance of a Schedule

When you create a new schedule, you're presented with a number of format and selection options on the Appearance tab of the Schedule Properties dialog box. These let you set the font style and text alignment and decide how to organize and filter the data for display in the schedule. Let's explore the options in the Schedule Properties dialog box.

Under the Appearance tab (see Figure 17.30), you'll see the options to change the font styles, gridline visibility, and other variables for header and body text of the schedule.

FIGURE 17.30
In the Appearance tab, you can control font, size, and header visibility.

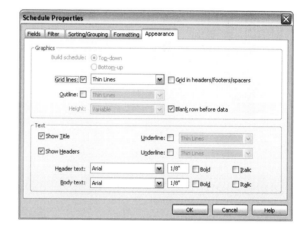

However, the change you need to make to the appearance of the data in the schedule is found in the Formatting tab of Schedule Properties. For our purposes in our cost per square foot schedule, select Cost per Sq Ft and make some adjustments:

1. Change the alignment to right justified, which is conventional for money totals.

2. Select the Field Format button and uncheck the option Use Project Settings. Here is where you can choose to change the Unit suffix and remove SF from the cost per square foot values (see Figure 17.31). Click OK to close all the dialog boxes and return to our schedule.

FIGURE 17.31
The Format dialog box

You also have the ability to add headers to our schedule. By selecting the Headers check box, you can group them under another title.

1. Select Level and Area by clicking in one of them and dragging the mouse to the other one (see Figure 17.32). They will show as highlighted. While Level does not look selected, it currently is.

FIGURE 17.32

Selecting headers

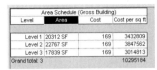

2. Doing this activates some of the different tools on the Options bar above. You'll now have the option to group (or ungroup) these headers. Choose the Group button.

3. You now have a header that spans the two headers selected, and we can add some more descriptive information to help clarify the schedule. In this example, we have added the text "Preliminary Design Plan" to the header (see Figure 17.33).

FIGURE 17.33

Grouped headers

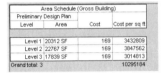

NOT ALL SCHEDULES NEED TO APPEAR ON SHEETS

You can use schedules to document objects used in your project (number of doors or windows, furniture pieces, material quantity, areas of rooms, etc.), but you can also use them to locate elements in the model or look for inconsistencies. For instance, you can keep a schedule of text notes only within a model and not use them on sheets. This schedule can then be used to look for odd items inserted into the model. In essence, you can schedule the text note name and the number of times it appears in the model. Perhaps the schedule indicates that a particular note is used only one or two times in the model. You can then decide if the note was inserted incorrectly into the project and determine whether it's inconsistent with the other notes in the model. The same thing can be done for wall types or anything else in the model.

The Bottom Line

Remember that area plans and schedules are nothing more than different ways to view your model and the parametric data inside it. Learning how to leverage these view types can be a huge time-saver for your project. In this chapter you created some area plans and schedules, but remember that this data will be constantly updating itself to reflect the most current status of your project. Set it up once and you have a tool you can regularly refer back to for project metrics.

Quantify your preliminary designs   Once your plans are established, create your own area plans to dynamically track changes in the project.

> **Master It**   Establish your preliminary design, and then create area plans so you can keep up to date with space sizes, allocations, and your project program.

Create schedules   One of the benefits of Revit is the ability to manage not only your drawings, but also other information about the project. Create schedules for your project templates to manage the materials within the project.

> **Master It**   Schedules have a multitude of uses and value at all levels of the project. Explore a variety of schedules to optimize your workflow and maximize what you can get from the model.

Use schedules for preliminary cost estimates   Create a schedule that tracks project costs based on an estimated cost per square foot.

> **Master It**   Many developers and facilities managers use BOMA calculations for figuring rentable area, gross area, and R/U (rentable/usable) ratios. Establishing area plans and schedules can help you find these numbers much quicker than a legacy CAD system would have allowed.

Chapter 18

Evaluating Your Preliminary Design: Sustainability

In this chapter, we will take our preliminary building model and investigate sustainable design strategies using the building information model geometry.

Revit does a number of things to support a sustainable design process and workflow, ranging from accurate material take-offs to energy analysis with third-party software. As you move to Revit from a more traditional drafting approach, you will begin to see more opportunities to engage in model-based simulation. This represents a shift in office workflow and culture. Revit changes how teams communicate, since everyone works with one centralized model that can aggregate linked structural and MEP models. This close integration allows team members to better understand the overall direction of the project from many vantage points. This ability to see the model from different points of view makes a BIM project perfect for exploring sustainable design strategies. We will explore how Revit can help support those strategies.

In this chapter, you learn how to do the following:

◆ Incorporate a sustainable approach from the very beginning of a project development

◆ Use Revit to create sun studies

◆ Track recycled materials and other sustainability strategies using schedules

Incorporating a Sustainable Approach from the Beginning

Sustainable design has been a long-standing practice in the construction industry, but it has recently received mainstream recognition and grown in popularity. Sustainable design can address many issues, such as energy use, access to natural light, human health and productivity, water conservation, use of recycled materials—the list goes on. One of the primary goals of sustainable design is to reduce a building's *carbon footprint* (the net amount of carbon dioxide emitted by a building through its energy use) to zero. This means the finished building uses no more energy than it can produce or offset. At the same time, sustainability means creating better conditions for the people who work, live, or play in the buildings.

An important factor in sustainable design is the huge effect that construction has on the environment. The United States, as an example, uses 25 percent of the world's energy, and the U.S. building industry uses 40 percent of global energy. Buildings, taken together, are the largest single resource consumer in the world. To solve the problem of global warming, we need to look at the low-hanging fruit of the architecture, engineering, and construction (AEC) industry and work toward a more efficient, more sustainable building practice.

Preliminary Design Tools

In the preceding chapter, we introduced the Foundation model by working with the preliminary design, and we discussed verifying program and area information by creating area plans and schedules. We will be building on the same model in this chapter to investigate sustainable strategies.

Since we have a digital building model, we can also rapidly iterate different variations of the design using sustainable strategies. When designing for sustainability, the important thing is to understand which questions to ask—and to ask them early enough in the process that you can make appropriate changes. There are five simple things you can do to help make any project more sustainable:

- ◆ Optimize the building mass.

- ◆ Create good site orientation by maximizing north–south exposure and minimizing east–west exposure.

- ◆ Optimize the use of daylight and sun shading.

- ◆ Optimize the building envelope assembly.

- ◆ Optimize the use of carbon-free resources such as sunlight, wind, and rain.

Although it's not designed primarily as a sustainable design tool, Revit does provide an integrated 3D model that can be used as input by other applications for the purpose of running analyses. This saves you the time of having to remodel geometry in these applications and thus reduces the amount of time and money spent on analytical modeling. With Revit, you are building a 3D model by default, so testing a number of simple but effective sustainability strategies early on makes sense and does not require you to remodel anything.

The LEED Rating System

One widely used tool for measurement and rating of sustainability in the building industry in the United States is the LEED rating system. Created by the U.S. Green Building Council (USGBC), the Leadership in Energy and Environmental Design (LEED) system is a nationally recognized benchmark for high-efficiency design and construction. The LEED rating system consists of five key areas:

- ◆ Sustainable site development

- ◆ Water savings

- ◆ Energy efficiency

- ◆ Material selection

- ◆ Indoor environmental quality

Each of these areas has point values assigned to a variety of methods and processes of sustainable design. The goal of the ranking system is the ability to determine and rank a building's sustainability. For more information on the USGBC and LEED, visit www.usgbc.org/leed.

TAKE ADVANTAGE OF THE DESIGN CYCLE

As any designer can attest, design is an iterative process. The process of design—especially sustainable design—can involve a series of intuitive and creative movements followed by periods of research, testing, and validating the design decisions. This is again followed by some manner of redesign to adapt to any changes that are needed due to the new information or direction.

Use the energy and sun tools in a similar fashion. If you wait until the end of the design process to begin using these tools, they will be of little value to help mold and inform your process. Begin your investigations and testing right away to see how the energy and sun tools can shape the form and design of your project.

Using Revit to Create Sun Studies

Chapter 15 introduced Revit's tools for applying physically accurate shadows for presentation purposes and showed how to enable and control them. Here we take a closer look at using these features analytically.

Good sustainable design optimizes the use of natural daylight within a building and thereby minimizes the need for heavy use of electrical (artificial) lighting. The design should take into account the direction the daylight is coming from because this dictates the amount of solar gain the building takes in during the course of the day. East and west daylight is much harder to control, while north elevations (in the Northern Hemisphere) provide a great amount of indirect lighting and the southern elevations get a great deal of direct exposure, which can be mediated with the proper use of sun shading devices (see Figure 18.1).

FIGURE 18.1
Sunshades and
natural ventilation

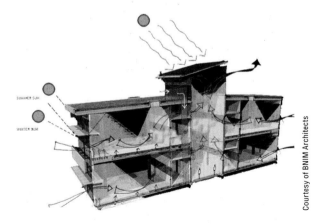

Courtesy of BNIM Architects

Sunshading devices are specific to the local climatic conditions; however, there are some fairly typical rules of thumb. North and south sunlight is the easiest to control since the angles of exposure are not nearly as dramatic as the east and west façades. Because of this, sunshading on the south side is typically horizontal, to allow more sun exposure to the interiors during winter months when the sun is lower in the sky and less exposure in the summer months when the sun is higher. Conversely, sunlight affecting the east and west façades is more difficult to control and sunshading is typically vertical.

Working directly, early on, with a mechanical engineer who is knowledgeable about sustainable principles and approaches can help direct and maximize the use of natural light and heat in your design. However, even without an expert, a simple daylighting view can help a design team make good decisions regarding daylighting.

Sun studies are views (they can be still or animated) that you can generate to reflect the solar conditions during specific times of the year to visually gauge light and shadow conditions. By creating camera views at key locations within the model, you can see the resulting shadows based on the location of the model on the planet and the date and time. In Figure 18.2, you can see the effect of sun on the Foundation model during four peak times of the year: the summer solstice (June 21), the spring and fall equinox (March 21 and September 21), and the winter solstice (December 21). We will be using these same dates as we study the model from other angles.

FIGURE 18.2
Sun studies at various times of the year. Since the spring and fall equinox replicate the same solar condition, only one image needs to be shown.

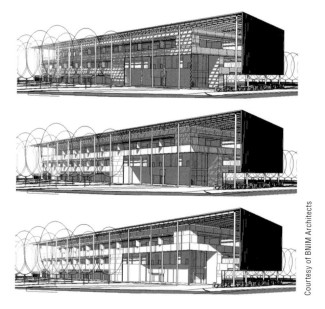

Courtesy of BNIM Architects

Remember, once we establish these views, they will be constantly updated as we make modifications or design changes to the model.

Making a Sun Study

Open the Foundation model in the Chapter 18 folder on the book's companion web page (www.sybex.com/go/masteringrevit2009), and let's establish a few views from different locations. We'd like a better understanding of the play of sun and shadow within the model from these locations. To do this, we are going to set up some sun studies in these spaces.

1. Set up the following camera views:

   A. From the second floor, place a camera from the View Design tab looking at the southern elevation of the building, eastern half (because of the building's length, we will not be able to see sufficient detail if we look at the entire façade at once). Name it **Sun Study-South E Facade** (Figure 18.3).

FIGURE 18.3
Exterior camera placement looking at south façade

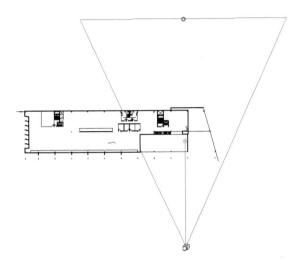

   B. From the second floor, place a camera looking at the western elevation of the building, east half. Name it **Sun Study-West Facade** (Figure 18.4).

FIGURE 18.4
Exterior camera placement looking at west façade

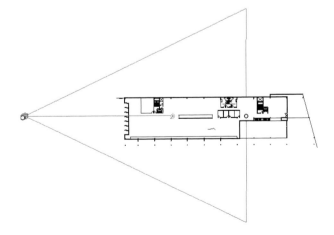

    c. From the interior third-floor office space, place a camera looking to the southwest. Name it **Sun Study-3rd Floor Interior** (Figure 18.5).

FIGURE 18.5
Exterior camera
placement looking
at the third-floor
interior

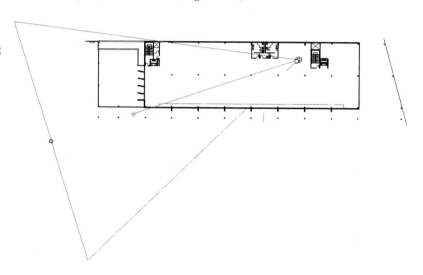

2. Now if you go back to the first view, the *Sun Study-South E Facade,* the view by default will look like a colorless perspective of the south façade (see Figure 18.6). You can either choose to accept the way this view looks or choose Shaded Lines or Shaded Lines with Edges from the View Control bar at the bottom of the view window.

You need to turn on the sun and cast some shadows.

3. In the View Control bar, the third button from the left is the Shadows button. Clicking this button toggles the shadows on and off. It also gives you the option to go to the Advanced Model Graphics dialog box, where you can then set the parameters for what time of day to show the shadows. Choose Advanced Model Graphics from the menu. Note that you can save these settings in a View Template to quickly be applied to other views.

FIGURE 18.6

Default appearance of perspective view

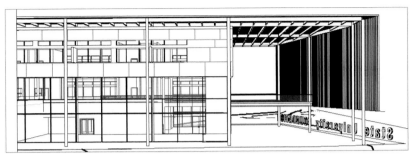

4. In the Advanced Model Graphics Settings dialog box, select the Cast Shadows check box (Figure 18.7).

This activates the browse button for the Sun and Shadows Settings dialog box. Click it to access that dialog box.

FIGURE 18.7

The Advanced Model Graphics Settings dialog box

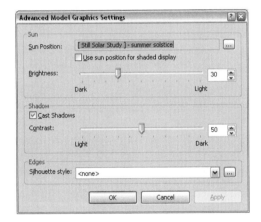

5. In the Sun and Shadows Settings dialog box, you have three options:

Still casts the sun at a specific time of day based on the parameters you choose.

Single-Day allows you to animate the sun and export the animation to an AVI file to show it over the course of a single day.

Multi-Day casts the sun in the same position (same time of day) over the course of multiple days.

For this exercise, choose Still (see Figure 18.8).

FIGURE 18.8
Sun and Shadows
Settings dialog box

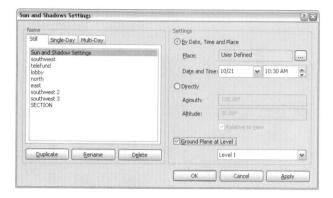

6. Here you need to start by setting the location of the building as well as the Date and Time of the year for which you wish to analyze the effect of the sun and thus shadows. Choosing the By Date, Time and Place option, we can give our building a geographical location.

7. Click the browse button to open the Manage Place and Location dialog box. Here you'll find a long list of choices available. Choose Kansas City, Missouri, and click OK. For the date, choose June 21, because we want to see the sun during the summer solstice. Set the time to 10:30 A.M. Finally, make sure Ground Plane at Level is selected and set to Level 1. This will allow Revit to cast shadows against the ground.

8. Before you click OK and let Revit calculate the effect of the sun for the location you have selected, you need to name your settings. Choose Rename from the buttons on the left of this dialog box and rename Sun and Shadows Settings to **6/21, 10:30 am**.

9. Click OK twice to exit the dialog boxes. It will take a moment for Revit to calculate all the shadows. The finished view should look like Figure 18.9. It looks like the sun canopy extends far enough to reach all the floors at this time of day in the summer, and it will give us an interesting play of light on the façade.

FIGURE 18.9
How the sun affects
the south façade on
a summer day

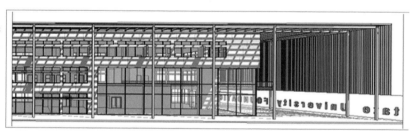

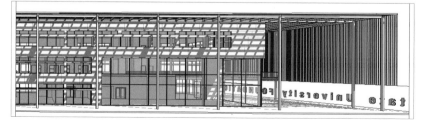

In Figure 18.9, you can see the results of the sunshades on the southern façade. Both solar studies were done at the same time of day, but there is an obvious impact of the shading devices on the second elevation over the first. Later in this chapter, we will discuss different energy modeling strategies that are designed to report the actual load differences the building will have with or without the shades.

SUN STUDIES THROUGHOUT THE YEAR

By going back to the Sun and Shadows Settings dialog box, you can duplicate the settings and modify only the date or time of day to include a sun study for the equinoxes and the winter solstice. You can then export each view using the Export Image option. Choose File ➢ Export Image and export each view to keep a record of the sun at different times of the year. Here are some examples of how shadows are cast on the building: the top is winter; the middle is spring and fall; the bottom is summer.

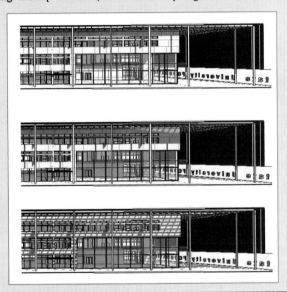

Animated Sun Studies

A great feature in Revit is the ability to create animated solar studies. You can see the effect of sun and shadow over time. For example, it is possible to animate the sun over the course of an entire year to see the extent of light penetration and shadow cast by your building and other buildings in its context. This is an excellent communication tool for explaining the impact of your building on the site and can be used very early on in massing studies to make adjustments to orientation, placement, and form.

Any view can be animated to show the effects of the sun. To access this feature, use the Advanced Model Graphics Settings dialog box and navigate to the Sun and Shadows Settings dialog box. There you will find three tabs: Still, Single-Day, and Multi-Day. The default tab is Still, and the settings on this tab affect static views. The other two tabs are specifically designed for creating multi-image representations of the model over time (Figure 18.10).

FIGURE 18.10
Use the Single-Day and Multi-Day tabs to define time and time intervals for the animation.

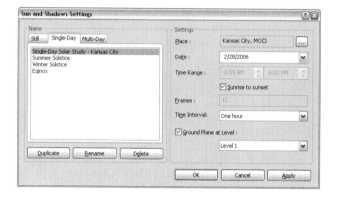

Single-day studies   Create single-day studies with the settings on the Single-Day tab. These settings will show the effect of sun on a specific day at various intervals (15, 30, 45, or 60 minutes). By setting the date and checking the Sunrise to Sunset box, you'll be able to animate the effect of sun on your model.

Multi-day studies   The settings on the Multi-Day tab (Figure 18.11) are just like the settings on the Single-Day tab, but the interval is days, weeks, or months, and you can see the effect of sun over the course of an entire year.

Once you select either a single-day or multi-day setting, a new control will become available in the View Shadow flyout menu to help facilitate visualizing and generating the animation.

FIGURE 18.11
Sun and shadows settings for a multi-day sun study

PREVIEWING A SOLAR STUDY

To preview the solar study, click the Animated Solar Study option; the following controls will appear in the Options bar:

You can use the controls to step through the frames of the animation and access the Sun and Shadows Settings dialog box. The animation will play slowly because the frames have to be redrawn one by one to recalculate the shadows. We do not recommend playing the animation using these controls as it is very time consuming for Revit to redraw all these views. To get a feel for the final output, you need to export the view and see it play back at real-time speed in a video viewer.

EXPORTING THE ANIMATION

Once you've set the correct values for the solar study, you can export it and play it in a media player. To do so, choose File ➤ Export ➤ Animated Solar Study. The Save As dialog box includes options to set file type, duration, size, and model graphics style (Figure 18.12). For better performance, drop the image size to something reasonable for a monitor (800 × 600, for example). As with the interactive preview, it will take Revit some time to process all the frames. The more frames, the longer the export will take, but the final result makes for compelling demonstration media. Revit also gives you the option to compress the video upon export.

FIGURE 18.12
Set the values for your animation.

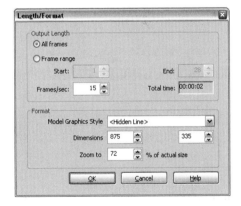

ANIMATED SOLAR STUDIES

Animated solar studies can track the course of the sun over the period of a day or at one time of day over a period of many days or months in an animated video format. These studies help us to better understand the impact of the sun on a building and of the building on the surrounding context. To set up an animated solar study, follow these steps:

1. Open the second perspective, Sun Study-West Facade.

2. Using the View Control bar at the bottom of the screen, or by navigating to View ➤ Advanced Model Graphics, open the Sun and Shadows Settings dialog box.

3. Choose the Multi-Day tab. You will notice that since you have set our location previously for the still study we did earlier, you don't need to set a new location for the project. Set the start date to **1/2/2007**, the end date to **12/28/2007**, the time interval to one day, and the time of day to 3:30 P.M. The dialog box should look like this:

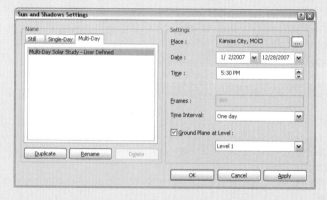

4. Clicking OK to exit the dialog box will give you a perspective with the sun located in a position to support the first date (1/2/2007) at the 3:30 time. If you go to the View Control bar and click the Shadow button again, you will notice a new option: Preview Solar Study.

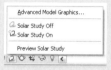

5. Choosing this tool highlights the view window and gives you a new set of tools in the Options bar, as shown here:

6. The controls work the same as they do on your DVD player. Clicking the time and date button will take you back to the Sun and Shadows Settings dialog box. The other controls are there to set the frame rate and initiate playback. Playback time will vary depending on the size and complexity of your model and your processor speed.

7. You also have the ability to export this animation to an AVI file. Choose File ➤ Export ➤ Animated Solar Study and you can set the dimensions of the image, the model graphic style, and the frame rate for your AVI. You can play around with the settings until you get the right proportion of size and time for each slide.

8. Once you have begun the export, you can view the progress of the AVI at the bottom of the View window.

Viewer Animator : PlayFoundation-13.rvt - 3D View: Sun Study- West façade [3 of 360] [Elapsed Time : 0:00:00:30]

These types of sun and shadows studies are not designed to provide you with quantifiable metrics for the amount of daylight in a given space. However, they are a good, quick tool during the earliest design decision phase to help check your design assumptions regarding where, when, and how the daylight enters the space.

Tracking Recycled Materials and Other Sustainability Strategies Using Schedules

In this section, we will be reviewing how to leverage schedules to track sustainable design strategies. Including recycled content in your building design is only part of the solution. To document credits for LEED points, it is important to know how much recycled content is in the building.

Recycled Materials

In Chapter 17, we discussed maximizing the power of schedules by adding custom variables to the calculations. We did this by doing a basic cost analysis on the Revit model and calculating a square foot cost against the gross square footage of the building. It is possible to use this same method to track the amount of recycled materials used in the project.

In our project, we have decided to substitute a percentage of Portland cement with fly ash in all of the cast-in-place concrete. As a by-product of burning coal, fly ash will help count toward the recycled materials points we need for LEED accreditation. Based on a number of concerns, we have chosen to use 21 percent fly ash in our concrete. We can calculate this very quickly using a simple schedule:

1. Navigate to View ➤ New ➤ Material Takeoff and choose Multi-Category from the list.

2. In the next dialog box, you will be asked to choose fields for the schedule. Choose the following fields and place them in this order:

Material: Name

Material: Volume

3. Clicking OK at this point would give you a list of all the materials in the project. Since we want only the concrete, select the Filter tab. Choose Material: Name and then Contains from the Filter By drop-down menu and type **Concrete** in the Filter field (see Figure 18.13).

Calculated Value...

4. Now, you'll need to add another calculated value to tabulate the percentage of fly ash in the project. Click the Calculated Value button. Name the field **Volume of Fly Ash**. Change Type to Volume and enter the following formula: **Material: Volume * 0.21**.

Remember, it is all case-sensitive, so make sure you type it properly. The finished dialog box should look like Figure 18.14. Click OK.

FIGURE 18.13
Use a formula to calculate a value for fly ash.

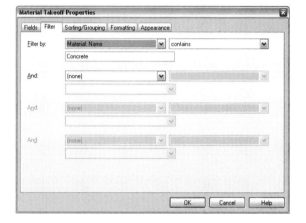

FIGURE 18.14
Set the schedule so that it filters for concrete materials.

5. On the Sorting/Grouping tab, check the Grand Totals check box.

6. Finally, on the Formatting tab, select Volume and change the alignment to Right. Select Volume of Fly Ash and change the alignment to Right. Also, check the Calculate Totals box. Click OK.

When the schedule is complete, you will get an up-to-date list containing all the instances of concrete in the building and a calculation showing how many cubic feet of fly ash each contains. This will all be totaled at the bottom of the schedule. As you can see, there are 6,898 cubic feet (CF) of fly ash so far in the project if we are using 21 percent recycled content (Figure 18.15).

Each of these schedules can be added to a template. Even if the percent of fly ash varies from project to project, you will have the basis for the schedule already created.

FIGURE 18.15
You can see the total amount of fly ash in the schedule.

Multi-Category Material Takeoff		
Material: Name	Material: Volume	Volume of Fly Ash
Concrete - Cast-in-Place Concrete	258.04 CF	54.19 CF
Concrete - Cast-in-Place Concrete	210.28 CF	44.16 CF
Concrete - Cast-in-Place Concrete	239.44 CF	50.28 CF
Concrete - Cast-in-Place Concrete	66.89 CF	14.05 CF
Concrete - Cast-in-Place Concrete	804.91 CF	169.03 CF
Concrete - Cast-in-Place Concrete	230.04 CF	48.31 CF
Concrete - Cast-in-Place Concrete	699.80 CF	146.96 CF
Concrete - Cast-in-Place Concrete	86.00 CF	18.06 CF
Concrete - Cast-in-Place Concrete	272.33 CF	57.19 CF
Concrete - Cast-in-Place Concrete	4286.33 CF	900.13 CF
Concrete - Cast-in-Place Concrete	476.81 CF	100.13 CF
Concrete - Cast-in-Place Concrete	230.70 CF	48.45 CF
Concrete - Cast-in-Place Concrete	191.17 CF	40.14 CF
Concrete - Cast-in-Place Concrete	258.04 CF	54.19 CF
Concrete - Cast-in-Place Concrete	5109.22 CF	1072.94 CF
Concrete - Cast-in-Place Concrete	0.00 CF	0.00 CF
Concrete - Cast-in-Place Concrete	537.35 CF	112.84 CF
Concrete - Cast-in-Place Concrete	13.70 CF	2.88 CF
Concrete - Cast-in-Place Concrete	13.88 CF	2.91 CF
Concrete - Cast-in-Place Concrete	13.88 CF	2.91 CF
Concrete - Cast-in-Place Concrete	12.33 CF	2.59 CF
Concrete - Cast-in-Place Concrete	211.37 CF	44.39 CF
Concrete - Cast-in-Place Concrete	19.87 CF	4.17 CF
Concrete - Cast-in-Place Concrete	12.89 CF	2.71 CF
Concrete - Cast-in-Place Concrete	10.96 CF	2.30 CF
Concrete - Cast-in-Place Concrete	10.96 CF	2.30 CF
Concrete - Cast-in-Place Concrete	10.96 CF	2.30 CF
Concrete - Cast-in-Place Concrete	10.96 CF	2.30 CF
Concrete - Cast-in-Place Concrete	10.96 CF	2.30 CF
Concrete - Cast-in-Place Concrete	10.96 CF	2.30 CF
Concrete - Cast-in-Place Concrete	18527.22 CF	3890.72 CF
Grand total: 31		6898.13 CF

FINDING "CONCRETE" IN THE MODEL

Remember, by scheduling things within Revit, you can easily use the schedule to locate them. Simply select the element within the schedule view. The Options bar will provide a button labeled Show. Clicking this button will cycle you through all of the relevant views showing the element selected. This is true for any schedule.

Window Surface Percentage vs. Room Area

We discussed concepts of sustainability earlier in this chapter and specifically the use of sun-shading devices to allow natural daylight into spaces but minimize the effects of solar gain at unwanted times of the day or year. Another way to keep out the sun is to simply minimize the amount of glazing on a given façade. There is a delicate balance between the amount of glazing on a façade and the amount of daylight that enters a space. In the ideal design, we want to maximize daylight but still be efficient with glazing. Again, north and south light is easier to control, the north particularly because it includes no direct sunlight. East and west light can be more challenging. One way to work toward the most efficient amount of glazing is to work directly with your mechanical engineer or energy modeler to calculate the ideal percentages of glazing for a given façade or cardinal direction. Once you have these goals, you will want to quickly calculate the percent of glazing versus wall area or room area. Revit can help you do this with the Room/Area Report (Figure 18.16).

FIGURE 18.16

Analytical views
of room area and
window area

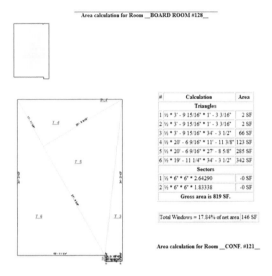

One of the export commands available within Revit is Room/Area Report (File ➤ Export ➤ Room/Area Report). If all the room objects are placed within a given floor in the model, this report creates an HTML file detailing how the areas for the rooms were calculated. The report lists in graphic and table format each room, its perimeter, and the triangulated areas within the room that generate the areas. If you choose the Settings option before you export the table, you can check a box to additionally report window area as a percentage of the room. This gives you the square footage of window area within the room as a percentage of the overall area of the room. This square footage percentage can also assist in the documentation you will need for LEED credit EQ 8.1 (for more information, see www.usgbc.org/leed).

Energy Analysis

Energy analysis is a useful tool in estimating building life cycle costs and is becoming more and more important to facility managers and owners early in the design process. The tool gives you the ability to predict building energy use. By making design changes to the model and running a series of energy analyses based on the various design iterations, you are able to estimate the building's loads based on the design schemes, thereby helping to minimize energy use and overall life-cycle costs.

In its current incarnation, Revit Architecture does not provide energy analysis. The software is primarily created for architects to model and document their designs; you'll need to use one of the third-party applications discussed in the following pages. At the same time, the design of a building involves not only its function but also its aesthetic and social implications and its environmental impact. Today, the focus on energy efficiency is becoming increasingly important to stakeholders involved with architecture. Owners and facilities managers alike are looking to get up-front data on predicted energy footprint and short-term and long-term costs and other information at the early stages of design.

Energy modeling can involve a complex set of analytical calculations, and entire careers are based on deriving accurate and predictable results. This type of analysis can encompass building energy use, daylighting, alternative power sources, computational fluid dynamics (CFDs), thermal gain, and carbon footprint, to name a few. Essentially, energy modeling allows you to understand the building from a more holistic, ecological point of view.

It is important to keep in mind that any value you get out of the Revit model with respect to energy analysis is only as useful as the information you put into the model. Good input will lead to good output.

There are a couple of applications that can be used in conjunction with the Revit architectural model for additional energy analysis data.

IES <VE>

IES <Virtual Environment> (www.iesve.com) is one application that provides a direct link to Revit Systems (Revit application for MEP) and Revit Architecture. IES <VE> is advanced simulation software that provides analytical tools for energy, daylighting, computational fluid dynamics (CFDs), and a variety of other analysis features. Opening a Revit Architecture model in Revit Systems, you can link to Integrated Environmental Solutions (IES) with a single click and get an estimation of the building's energy consumption based on rooms, location, and construction type (Figure 18.17). Revit allows you to export the whole model to IES so that a full-blown analysis can be performed.

FIGURE 18.17
A model as seen
in Revit MEP
heating and cooling
interface

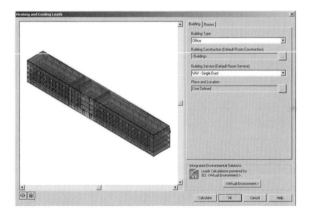

In Revit 2009, you can install an IES plug-in for Revit Architecture. This allows you to get peak energy loads in the form of reports.

GBXML

gbXML, or Green Building XML (www.gbxml.org), was designed as a neutral file format to transfer the data required for an energy model into various analysis applications from a Revit model. This file format, while not quite an industry standard, has been quickly adopted by a number of leading CAD vendors and is one way to transfer design intent into an energy modeler without having to re-create the building form in another application. IES <VE>, for example, will import a gbXML file, but it will not have all the geometric and spatial data that you will have if you imported directly from Revit.

Exporting to gbXML

Exporting to gbXML is a simple, fluid process; one of the primary benefits of using this file format as a basis for your energy analysis is that it is easy to create. To begin, you need to set a few variables before you start the export.

1. There is a location in the Revit file to set some energy data parameters of the project specifically for the energy analysis. Navigate to Settings ➤ Project Information. Click the Energy Data button. In this simple dialog box (Figure 18.18), define the following project variables:

FIGURE 18.18
Set basic variables to establish some assumptions about the energy requirements for your building.

Building Type—Such as office, residential, museum.

Postal Code—The five-digit postal code of the project. This variable defines the building's global location for sunlight.

Ground Plane—Where the ground level will be calculated.

Shading Surfaces—This is a simple check box. Shading allows you to take into account sunshades and other exterior features in the gbXML model.

Project Phase—Based on any phasing you have in your project.

Sliver Space Tolerance—By default, this value is set to 1′-0″. This specifies the tolerance for areas that Revit considers sliver spaces.

For our Foundation project, let's declare it an office building with a 64105 zip code (Kansas City). The ground plane is at Level 1, Shading Surfaces turned on, and we can leave the other variables at their defaults.

2. Now that you have set those variables, exporting is a simple process. Choose File ➢ Export ➢ gbXML. It will automatically begin calculating the export before you are given the option to save the file. The export will take a little time, depending on the speed of your computer. Once it's created, you'll have a small, compact file you can easily share with your mechanical consultant or upload directly into your energy analysis application.

Green Building Studio

Green Building Studio (www.greenbuildingstudio.com) is an online service that provides a simple energy analysis based on your gbXML file and some basic energy demand assumptions you provide. The results are reported in an easy-to-interpret web format with a lot of visual cues and graphics. The report takes into account TMY2 (Typical Meteorological Year 2) data (historical data of sunny vs. overcast days), regional utility demands and costs, and climatic data. It will return information such as the predicted annual utility costs, building life-cycle costs, and carbon footprint (see Figure 18.19).

FIGURE 18.19

Example from Green Building Studio showing the estimated energy cost of the building

General Information	Location Information
Project Title: Foundation	Building: KANSAS CITY, MO 64105
Run Title: Foundation-13.xml	Electric Cost: $0.057/kWh
Building Type: Office	Fuel Cost: $1.286/Therm
Floor Area: 52,697 ft²	Weather: TMY2 weather for Kansascity, MO

Estimated Energy & Cost Summary

Annual Energy Cost $35,642
Lifecycle* Cost $485,441
Annual CO₂ Emissions

Electric† 743,613 lbs
Onsite Fuel 167,846 lbs
H3 Hummer Equivalent   41.4 hummers

Electric Power Plant Sources‡

Fossil: 80%
Nuclear: 19%
Hydroelectric: 0%
Renewable: 1%
Other: 0%

‡ Based on US EPA EGRID 2006 Data (2004 Plant Level Data).

This is a free service for basic energy calculations, and there is a nominal charge for more developed results. You must download a small client application that will help coordinate the uploading and calculations of the gbXML files. You can download it from www.greenbuildingstudio.com/Tutorial.aspx.

Even if you do not understand the results from an energy analysis application such as this, it can always be used as a comparative tool. Take, for example the large sunshading device on this project. At some point during the design, it can likely become necessary to discuss with the client how much energy something like this can save your project. Within Revit, this element can be set to a design option and we can run an energy simulation using Green Building Studio (GBS) with and without the sunshade. Figure 18.20 shows the building model with and without the shades.

Images courtesy of BNIM Architects

FIGURE 18.20
The Foundation model with and without the sunshades

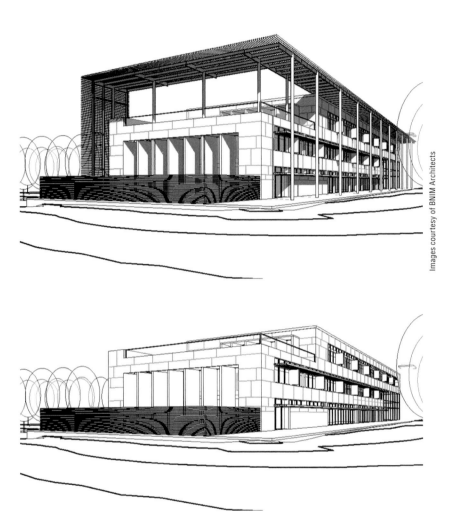

By comparing the annual energy costs from the GBS analysis, we can quickly see a 68 percent increase in energy savings over the course of a single year (Figure 18.21). Over the lifetime of this building, that can lead to a substantial energy savings for the client and more than offset the initial costs of the shading device.

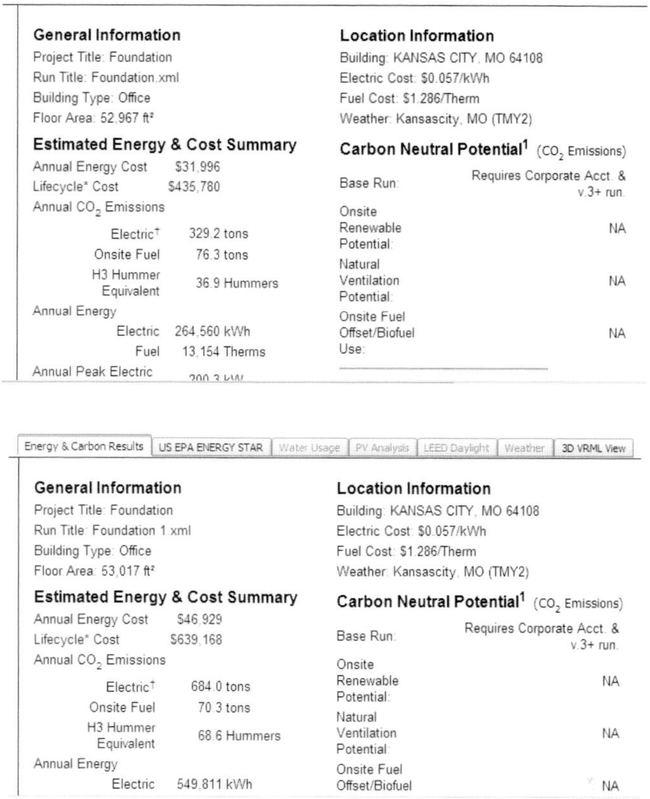

FIGURE 18.21

The energy analysis
for both designs
shown in
Figure 18.20

FIGURE 18.21

The energy analysis
for both designs
shown in
Figure 18.20

General Information

Project Title: Foundation
Run Title: Foundation.xml
Building Type: Office
Floor Area: 52,967 ft²

Location Information

Building: KANSAS CITY, MO 64108
Electric Cost: $0.057/kWh
Fuel Cost: $1.286/Therm
Weather: Kansascity, MO (TMY2)

Estimated Energy & Cost Summary

Annual Energy Cost	$31,996
Lifecycle* Cost	$435,780

Annual CO$_2$ Emissions

Electric†	329.2 tons
Onsite Fuel	76.3 tons
H3 Hummer Equivalent	36.9 Hummers

Annual Energy

Electric	264,560 kWh
Fuel	13,154 Therms

Annual Peak Electric   200.3 kW

Carbon Neutral Potential[1] (CO_2 Emissions)

Base Run:	Requires Corporate Acct. & v.3+ run.
Onsite Renewable Potential:	NA
Natural Ventilation Potential:	NA
Onsite Fuel Offset/Biofuel Use:	NA

Energy & Carbon Results | US EPA ENERGY STAR | Water Usage | PV Analysis | LEED Daylight | Weather | 3D VRML View

General Information

Project Title: Foundation
Run Title: Foundation 1.xml
Building Type: Office
Floor Area: 53,017 ft²

Location Information

Building: KANSAS CITY, MO 64108
Electric Cost: $0.057/kWh
Fuel Cost: $1.286/Therm
Weather: Kansascity, MO (TMY2)

Estimated Energy & Cost Summary

Annual Energy Cost	$46,929
Lifecycle* Cost	$639,168

Annual CO$_2$ Emissions

Electric†	684.0 tons
Onsite Fuel	70.3 tons
H3 Hummer Equivalent	68.6 Hummers

Annual Energy

Electric	549,811 kWh

Carbon Neutral Potential[1] (CO_2 Emissions)

Base Run:	Requires Corporate Acct. & v.3+ run.
Onsite Renewable Potential:	NA
Natural Ventilation Potential:	NA
Onsite Fuel Offset/Biofuel	NA

The Bottom Line

Sustainability is an increasingly important goal for your clients. Revit, thanks to its BIM database of project information, provides tools that greatly simplify sustainability analysis.

Incorporate a sustainable approach from the very beginning of the project development
Sustainability is quickly becoming a core approach to any design. Learn to leverage the Revit model for a more holistic approach to sustainability.

Master It BIM is also a computational database that can report information about the virtual building. The important thing about a sustainable approach is to know which questions to ask and to ask them at the right time. What is a strategy for doing this?

Use Revit to create sun studies Understanding the sun's effect on a building is paramount to sustainable design.

Master It How can you use the tools within Revit to produce still and animated solar studies from interior and exterior views in order to understand shading and the sun's effect on the building and space?

Track recycled materials and other sustainability strategies using schedules Keeping track of project goals is an important part of any project process. By using the schedules and other tools in Revit, you can also track key sustainability goals.

Master It Tracking recycled material usage is key to LEED credits and sustainability. Create a material schedule that tracks recycled content volume for concrete.

Chapter 19

Annotating Your Model

No set of documents is complete without annotations to describe the drawings. Even when working in BIM and having a digital parametric model, you will still need to provide annotated documents by adding dimensions, tags, text, and notes to the drawings, thus making communication of the design to the owner, contractor, and design team clearer and more informative.

In this chapter, you learn how to do the following:

◆ Annotate views

◆ Use schedule keys

◆ Leverage tags

◆ Understand shared parameters

◆ Add text and keynotes

Annotating Views

In any set of documents, showing geometry alone isn't sufficient to communicate all the information a builder or fabricator needs in order to construct the building. Annotations assist in clearly describing your model for others to read and understand. Tags, dimensions, text, and keynotes all need to be added to the drawing to cleanly and concisely guide construction or fabrication. Revit provides a rich set of tools for accomplishing these tasks.

Text, dimensions, and tags are placed in the views, in relation to real elements, not on the sheet. This allows you to annotate a view at any point in the process, before or after the final (sheet) document has been created. Figure 19.1 shows a floor plan annotated in a drawing set.

FIGURE 19.1

The annotated
floor plan

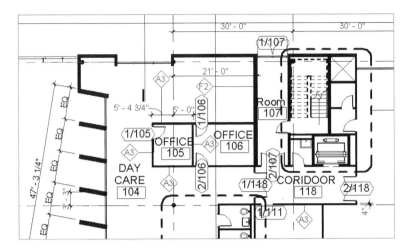

Creating and Annotating Rooms

Rooms help define areas and spaces within the Revit model. Even if a room represents the empty space between boundaries of physical elements, it is still considered an *element* in Revit, similar to a door, window, or wall. Rooms have properties and can be created, moved, deleted, modified, queried, and scheduled like every other element in Revit. Rooms can also be used for energy calculations and are critical to gbXML export. For more information on this feature, see Chapter 18.

You need bounding elements to define a space in which you can place the room element and thus generate a room that can calculate its area and volume. Bounding elements for rooms include roofs, walls, floors, columns, and room separation lines.

These elements all have an instance property called Room Bounding that determines whether that element participates in calculating room extents. By default, all these elements are set as room bounding. If you do not want an element to affect the calculation of room areas and volumes (for example, toilet partition walls are usually not deducted from the area and should be marked as non-room bounding), select it and clear the Room Bounding option in the element properties dialog box (shown checked in Figure 19.2).

FIGURE 19.2

A checked Room
Bounding param-
eter makes a wall
room bounding.

Every model element in Revit can be tagged, including rooms. The room tags report information stored in the room element properties. This means you can have the tags report anything about the room based on parameters of the room: name, number, area, finish, and so on. Rooms are separate elements from room tags, which, like all other tags used in Revit, are just annotations that can report any information stored in the building elements they are associated with.

Door and wall tags, for example, report values of the door or wall elements. Room tags do the same.

Even when rooms exist in a view, they are not visible in the view by default, but if they are tagged, the tag is visible so it can be easy to confuse the tag with the element. As with other elements in Revit, the tag can be placed automatically when adding a room using the Tag on Placement button in the Options bar. Clearing this box mean that when you create a room, no room tag will be added for that room.

In such cases, you can add room tags later in the project, individually for each room or for all rooms that are untagged at once. An improvement of the Revit 2009 release is that the Tag All Not Tagged tool in the Drafting tab of the Design bar now works with rooms. This means it tags any existing rooms in the active view and places the tags in the center of the X formed by the room element. You need to have created the room objects in the project first; then, wherever a room element is found, a room tag is placed in the room. This tool does not create rooms for you if they don't exist.

It's important to note that the tags only report the properties of the room. Deleting the tag does not delete the room element or the information shown in the tag.

Rooms can be inserted from either the Basics tab or the Room and Area tab of the Design bar. To insert a room, you must be in a plan view of the model, so choose one of the plan views and select the Room tool from the Design bar. When you select this tool, all of the rooms already placed within that view will highlight transparent blue and an X will be shown across the area that bounds that room (Figure 19.3).

FIGURE 19.3
Placing a room

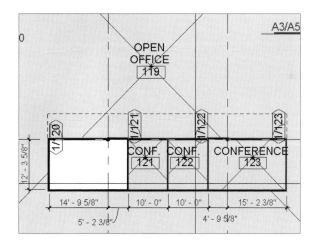

This is a visual aid to show you where room elements already exist within the model. As you can see in Figure 19.3, we are missing a room element in Room 120. To place a room in that space, with the Room tool selected, click in the white area in the middle of the space, to place a room element. A blue box appears and a room tag is automatically placed in the room. The Room tool remains active after the placement of each room and allows you to keep placing rooms in sequence. You'll notice that Revit autoincrements each room tag as you place the rooms. If you change a room number, the number of the room you place next is based on the number of the last room you placed.

Once a room is placed, it extends itself to the boundaries of the space in which it is placed and becomes an object in the model. As we mentioned, the room tag is a separate element and can be removed without removing the room element itself or any of the information you might have added to the room element. In fact, deleting the tag from a room will prompt a warning message alerting you that the room element still exists (see Figure 19.4). In a schedule, these rooms will continue to all show up with their proper room names and any other information you've added, regardless of whether they have been tagged.

FIGURE 19.4
Deleting a
room tag

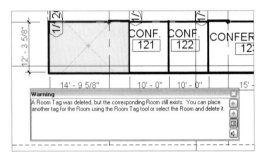

Once the tag has been removed, you can still select the room element. By default, the room element is not visible within Revit. This is intentionally done to avoid cluttering up precious space in a view. To select a room for further editing or to access its properties, drag the mouse over the space where the room is placed and click when the room element highlights (click close to one of the crossing diagonal lines to select the room).

There are a couple more features critical to rooms that you will want to be aware of as you begin placing them within your model:

◆ Room bounding elements need to create a closed loop. Placing a room in a nonenclosed area generates an error message like the one shown in Figure 19.5.

FIGURE 19.5
An unenclosed
room error

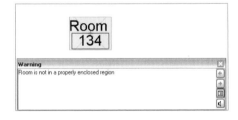

If a room that reports that it is unbounded is not resolved and is left unbounded in the model, it will not properly report in the schedules. There are a few ways to resolve an unbounded room:

◆ If you are still in the midst of design, simply finishing the design may give you the walls or other bounding elements you need to complete the enclosure. Once the room is properly enclosed, the room element will recognize this and dynamically stretch to fill the room.

◆ You can delete the room if it has been incorrectly placed. If you decide to remove a room, you must delete the room element itself, not just the room tag.

◆ You can use the Room Separation lines tool (you can find it on the Room and Area tab of the Design bar), which lets you draw a boundary and create room boundaries to define the edges of the space and close the areas where the room leaks.

SMALL GAPS WILL BE IGNORED BY ROOM BOUNDARY CALCULATION

Revit will tolerate a small gap in room boundaries. In that case, the error message does not appear.

◆ Room elements must not overlap (or Revit does not accept overlapping rooms and will report an error). You may come across this issue in any of three ways:

◆ First, you might mistakenly attempt to place a room in a space that already has a room element. If this occurs, Revit will alert you to the issue by showing you both room elements in the space and an error message asking what you'd like to do (see Figure 19.6). Clicking OK in this dialog box will leave both rooms in place. Clicking the Delete Room(s) button will remove the most recently placed room element.

FIGURE 19.6
Placing one room within another

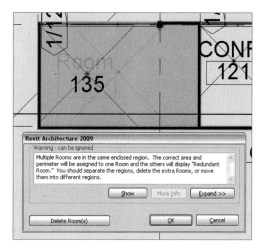

◆ The second way this can occur is if you remove a wall or other bounding element between two rooms. Revit will give you the same warning and ask how you would like to resolve the problem (see Figure 19.7).

FIGURE 19.7
Overlapping rooms

FIGURE 19.7
Overlapping rooms

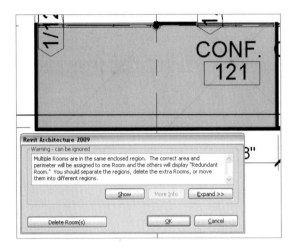

◆ A third way to get overlapping rooms is when the heights of rooms overlap. If a room extends vertically into a room on the next floor, a similar warning message will occur. To view the conflict, you will need to go to section view and check the room extents. It is important to understand that rooms can be volumes with 3D dimensions. Room volumes are covered in more detail in the section "Room Area and Volume" later in this chapter.

Room Separation Lines

So, what happens when you need one room to end and another to begin and you don't have a wall in between? For example, you might want a room to end at the end of a corridor that opens to an entry space, or you may have an open living room and dining room not separated by a wall.

For these conditions, use the Room Separation tool found on the Room and Area tab of the Design bar. This tool allows you to draw lines in plan that will act as bounding elements.

Room separation lines show in plan views as distinctive green lines (see Figure 19.8). These lines can be turned on or off in the Visibility/Graphic Overrides dialog box, or by right-clicking and hiding the category using the context menu.

FIGURE 19.8
Room separation
lines

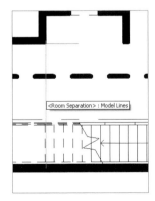

Room separation lines will print in the plans if left visible. If they are turned off, they will still maintain their room boundaries—but just remember they are there! "Out of sight, out of mind" can cause problems later when you move walls and the rooms seem to react in strange ways; so if you do decide to turn off the visibility of room separation lines, make a note for yourself about it and turn them back on after the printing.

 Real World Scenario

ADDING A ROOM SEPARATION LINE

In the Foundation project, there was a room named Corridor 127 that needed to be separated into a corridor and an entry area because they have slightly different finishes in the finish schedule.

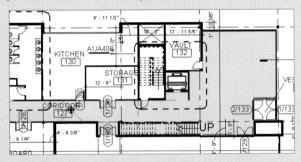

The Room Separation tool was used to divide the spaces.

Drawing a room separation line from the stairwell across to the wall created a boundary, allowing a new room to be added named "Entry 139." In the following view, you can see where the room element ends without requiring us to create a wall to divide the space:

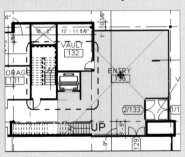

Selecting Rooms

You can select rooms in one of two ways: graphically and from a schedule table.

GRAPHICAL SELECTION

When hovering your cursor over a room object, you will notice that the room object shows up and is represented with its boundary and two diagonal crossing lines, as shown in Figure 19.9.

FIGURE 19.9
Graphic represen-
tation of a room
object

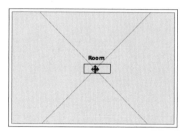

The two diagonal lines might seem strange at first, but they are useful for selecting rooms. Without them, the room element could be selected only at its boundaries—but as those are coincident with many other elements (walls, floors, windows, etc.) the selection is quite tedious. The diagonal lines highlight when the cursor moves over them, so you can select the room (see Figure 19.10). These lines are a subcategory of the room element, and if you wish to see them all the time in the view and not just when hovering over them with the mouse or upon selection, you can turn on the Reference subcategory using the Visibility/Graphic Overrides dialog box. From that point on, all available room elements in your project will be graphically visible. When the Tag on Placement option is checked, your room tag is always placed at the intersection of these two diagonal lines.

FIGURE 19.10
A selected room
element

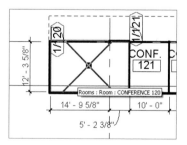

Once a room element is selected, your cursor turns into a move icon and lets you move the entire room somewhere else if needed. When a room is selected and you move it, it automatically takes the extents of the new space. In principle, you are not moving the geometry of the room but you are displacing the room information and assigning it to another space. Moving a room allows you to take all of the data you've entered for the room (wall finishes, ceiling, floors, and so on) and relocate rather than retype it. The same is true for copying a room into a new space.

The graphical room selection can occur in plan and section views. Room selection in 3D views is not possible. The graphical selection of rooms in section view is an improvement added to Revit 2009. You can see, select, change the properties of, and even manipulate the extents of rooms in section views now. When you select a room in section view, two set of editing grips appear that allow you to manipulate the base and top extents of the room by dragging.

SELECTION FROM A SCHEDULE TABLE

To select rooms from a schedule table, simply highlight the room within the schedule while in the schedule view and click the Show button on the Options bar.

Rooms and Room Tags

When you select one of the diagonal or boundary lines of a room, you are selecting the room element and can access its properties. When you select the room tag, you are selecting the tag of that room and can access or change the properties of the tag.

There is a difference between using the Move tool when a room is selected and when a room tag is selected.

When you select a room tag, you are moving the tag around in the room or outside the room: with small spaces, a tag often needs to be taken out of the space the room tag describes because it doesn't fit inside. The most common example is a toilet room. When you attempt to move the tag outside of the room with which it is associated, the tag displays a question mark and you get this warning message:

If you select the tag that is outside the room, a new button appears in the Options bar called Show Related Warnings. It gives anyone who later joins the design team and isn't aware of why the tag shows a question mark the ability to understand the error.

To fix the error and clarify which room the tag is tagging, you can use the Leader option in the Options bar. This connects the room and the tag with a line, and it displays the correct room number and name, which will help you understand the relationship between the tag and the room in the model to which it belongs. Figure 19.11 shows the room tag with the leader line checked.

FIGURE 19.11
(A) A room tag doesn't fit well in a small room. (B) Dragging the tag outside the room it is associated with will turn it into a question mark (?). (C) The tag leader is activated in the Options bar and the room tag connects with the room it is associated with and displays its information.

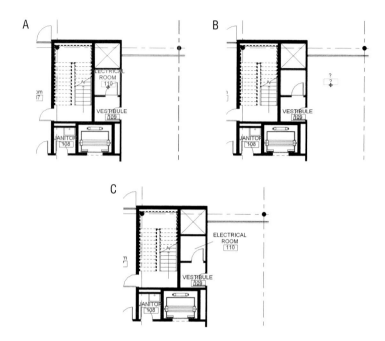

Rooms in Section Views

While you can also tag rooms in a section view, you will not be able to create new room elements in a section view. You can create rooms only in plan views. Revit 2009 brings some important improvements to rooms in section views:

◆ Although it was possible in earlier releases to tag a room in section view, it was not possible to select the room and access any of its properties. That has been changed; now you can select and change room properties within section views. You can also graphically manipulate the base and the top limit of the room, something that wasn't possible in previous versions of Revit.

◆ Color fill of rooms now works in section views, so you are not forced to do it manually using transparent fill patterns anymore. We discussed this in Chapter 15.

VOLUME CALCULATION METHOD DOES NOT AFFECT HOW VOLUMES ARE CALCULATED

Volumes are always calculated up to the wall finish, regardless of the chosen calculation method.

Room Properties

Like all other elements in Revit, rooms have properties. By selecting the room element and clicking the Properties button, you can see the room properties that are available. These properties can be scheduled, displayed in room tags, or used to color-code a floor plan or section with a color fill scheme. The parameters are divided into sections to help organize the information:

Level reports the level on which the room has been placed.

Upper Limit defines the top level of the room. For example, if you have a double-height space (like an open atrium), you might want the upper limit to be more than one floor high so the entire space is treated and scheduled as one element. By default, this is set to be the same as the level on which the room is placed so that you define the actual room height as an offset of Level.

Limit Offset defines the height of the upper limit of the room relative to the Upper Limit setting. This function is critical for volume calculations and gbXML exports. There are some settings that need to be addressed to get accurate results from gbXML exports:

- Limit Offset needs to coincide with the bottom of the ceiling plane above for any given room on floors below the roof line.

- Limit Offset can exceed the top of the roof for rooms that are on the uppermost floor.

- Rooms cannot overlap vertically for accurate gbXML exports. This means the upper limit of a room cannot encroach into the bottom of the room above it.

Base Offset defines the distance at which the lower boundary of the room is calculated, measuring from the base level that itself is defined by the Level parameter. A positive value of the offset sets it above the base level, a negative below. Zero value is set by default and equals the base level.

Area, **Perimeter**, **Unbounded Height**, and **Volume** are noneditable fields that report the metrics of the room element. We will review how these numbers are calculated in the next section.

The **Identity Data** section includes identity information about the room. You can manually add data using these parameters and it will show up in tags. If you're using a color fill scheme, it will also be used to color-code the plan.

Phase is a noneditable field that reports the phase the room was created in.

Area and Volume Calculations

You can set different rules that dictate the automated calculations of area and volume for room elements. The selection of available rules can be found under Settings ➤ Area and Volume Computations. The dialog box, shown in Figure 19.12, gives you the option to select from a number of area calculation schemes by relocating the boundary element of the rooms.

It is important to note the difference between room areas and area plans. *Area plans* follow different rules and treat exterior and interior walls differently. The Area Plans tool places areas automatically in the model, once the Area Plans function is initiated. Room elements have to be manually added in each space within the plan or design, and the rules that are set to define them apply to all the walls.

FIGURE 19.12

Area and Volume
Computations
dialog box

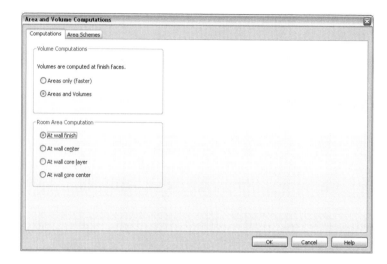

When calculating room area and volumes, you can choose among the following boundary locations, resulting in different calculations:

◆   At wall finish

◆   At wall center

◆   At wall core layer

◆   At wall core center

In addition to calculating room areas, Revit can calculate room volumes. This feature is not enabled by default since volume computation can negatively affect the overall performance of Revit. You can decide at any time to activate the volume computation. This option is available in the Area and Volume Computations dialog box by checking the Areas and Volumes option in the Volume Computation group. We recommend enabling this option only when you need to create or print schedules or other views in which volume computation needs to be visible. How much the volume computation affects the performance depends on the size and complexity of your model and your processor speed, but the general rule is to follow our earlier advice and activate it only when needed.

There are some rules that you should be aware of when activating room calculations:

◆   Every room can have an independent theoretical room height that you define using the Limit Offset room property. This is the height used for calculating room volume if the actual height of the ceiling, floor, or roof above it is higher than the applied height of the room (see Figure 19.13).

◆   If the room height is greater than the height of the existing ceiling, floor, or roof, then the height to the first architectural element the room object hits is used to calculate the volume of the room (see Figure 19.14).

FIGURE 19.13
The Room Offset (bounding box) is set to lower than the ceiling height, and the displayed room volume is 214.72m^3

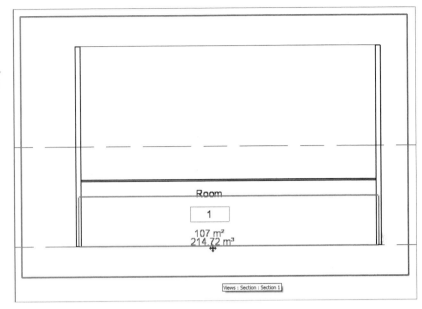

FIGURE 19.14
The bounding box is set to 4100mm (above the ceiling). The tag displays 279.14m^3, which means that the volume was calculated taking a room height only up to the ceiling as a value.

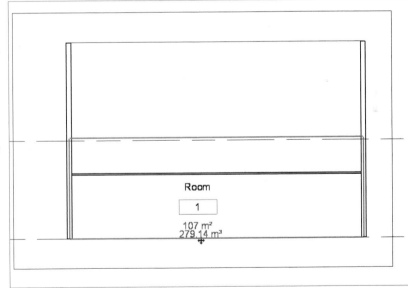

Note that the room height can begin to cause other problems if it extends into the room on a floor above or below (see Figure 19.15).

FIGURE 19.15
A change in the room height doesn't have any effect on the room volume calculation unless it hits the next floor, ceiling, and so on. (A) Computational height is set to the standard 1200mm. Parts of the volume are missing in the calculation. (B) A change of the computational height to floor level allows for correct computation.

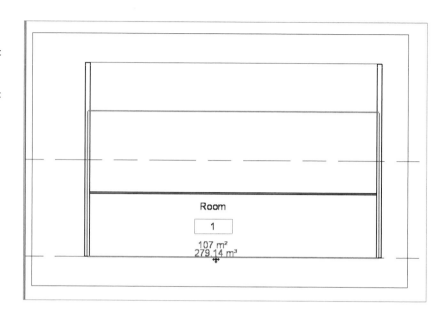

Usually a room height is set to 8′ (3m); so, depending on the default floor-to-ceiling height, it will often not be the real height of the room. You can verify that easily in section, when hovering over and selecting the room element. Adjusting the room height to the actual height of the space is easy in Revit 2009: you can now just graphically pick the room limits in section and adjust the height, as shown in Figure 19.16.

FIGURE 19.16
Arrow grips at the base and top limits of a room element allow you to graph-ically manipulate the height of a room. (A) Default room height; (B) adjusted room height.

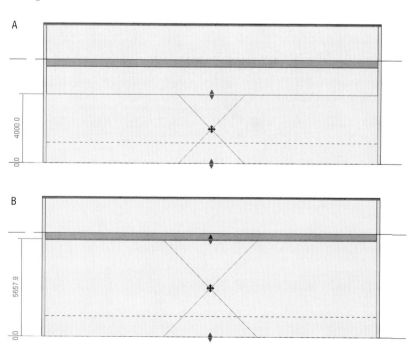

CALCULATING VOLUMES OF ROOMS WITH VARIABLE WIDTHS

Revit Architecture uses the perimeter of the room at the computation height when computing the room area and volume. The computation height is a type property of the Level family and can be changed any time. By default, it is set to 4′-0″ (1200mm).

You can see the computation height graphically when you select a room element in section: it is represented with a dotted line across the lower part of the room (Figure 9.17).

FIGURE 19.17
Computation Height is a type property of the Level family.

To view or change the computation height, select a level line in section or elevation view and access its type properties, as shown in Figure 19.17.

For buildings with vertical walls, the room computation is straightforward, as explained earlier. However, if a building includes sloped walls, you may need to adjust the computation height to achieve more accurate room areas and volumes.

The typical case would be when working with rooms that are bound by nonvertical walls. Having the perimeter calculated at a height of 4′ (1.2m) would result in omitting portions of the floor area. To fix this, you have to adjust the computation height to be close to the floor plane.

Changing the computation height instantly affects the room perimeter, and thus the calculation of the room area and volume shown in Figure 19.18.

FIGURE 19.18
Changing the computational height allows for more accurate computation of rooms with variable width. (A): Computational height is set to the standard 1200mm. Parts of the volume are missing in the calculation; (B): A change of the computational height to floor level allows for correct computation.

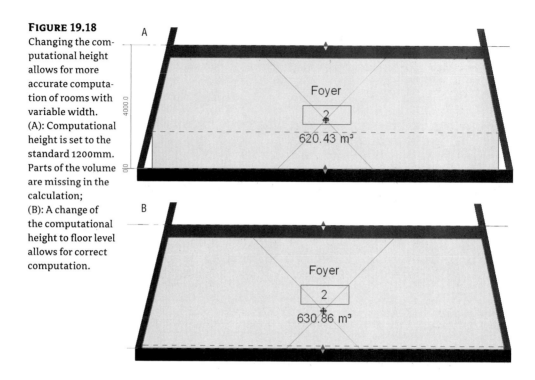

In general, Revit 2009 has brought some improvements in the calculation of volumes: the computations are now more flexible in adjusting to nonorthogonal room sizes and volumes (Figure 19.19).

FIGURE 19.19
Revit 2009 can correctly calculate rooms with nonhorizontal top limits. The room element adjusts its shape to the shape of the space it calculates.

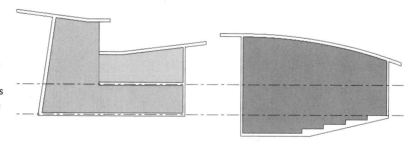

When the volume calculation is off, the room in section appears as if it doesn't recognize the room boundaries (Figure 19.20A); when the room volumes are activated, the room shape adjusts to fit the shape of the space (Figure 19.20B).

FIGURE 19.20
(A) Volume calculation off; (B) Volume calculation on

A

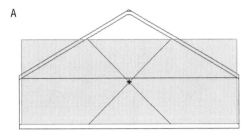

B

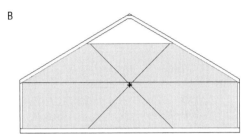

FIGURE 19.21
If room bounding elements narrow as they rise, Revit calculates volume properly.

If, however, bounding elements slope in a way that makes the room widen toward the upper limit, Revit ignores the side spaces when calculating the volume (Figure 19.22).

FIGURE 19.22
If room bounding
elements widen
as they rise, Revit
calculates volume
incorrectly.

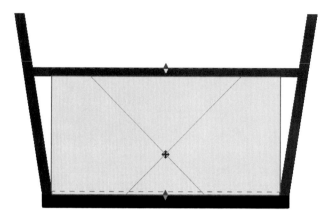

Finally, if a room-bounding element does not reach the upper boundary of the room, the space above the element may not be included in the room volume (Figure 19.23).

FIGURE 19.23
Spaces above
bounding elements
that do not extend
to the limits of
the room will be
ignored by the
room calculation.

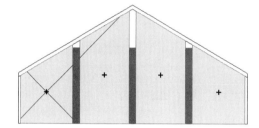

Using Schedule Keys

Once you populate your model with rooms and begin adding information to each room about its department and finishes, you'll most likely discover that information about rooms tends to repeat. Representing this information will be useful when you're generating room and finish schedules. In previous chapters, we discussed ways to report the information in those elements using the schedule functionality. But what if you want to define a common set of parameter values that can be shared across many rooms? For instance, if you are working on a large office project, doing a room finish schedule that lists individual rooms might be unnecessary if many of the rooms share identical finishes. For these situations, a specialized schedule called a *schedule key* can save time. Schedule keys can report any number of values that repeat across similar elements.

Creating a Schedule Key

Since we have already added rooms to the Foundation model, let's make a room finish schedule using a schedule key for the project. To do this, we need to generate two schedules. The first one defines the *room styles* by using what is called a key name. The second schedule links our room styles to the rooms themselves.

Let's begin with the room style schedule. On the View tab in the Design bar, choose Schedule/ Quantities, or from the menu choose View ➤ New ➤ Schedule/Quantities. The same dialog box you use when making any schedule appears. This time, however, you are going to choose some different values.

Choose Rooms from the list on the left, select the Schedule Keys radio button (see Figure 19.24), and click OK.

FIGURE 19.24

Selecting a schedule key

The next dialog box should look familiar (Figure 19.25). It is basically identical to the Schedule Properties dialog box (in fact, it is named the same), but one tab is not included in the dialog box: the Filter tab.

FIGURE 19.25

Making a schedule key

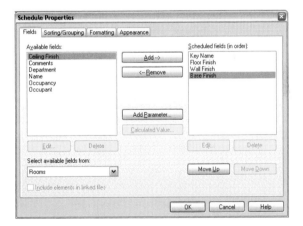

Upon opening the Fields tab, you will notice that one of the values is already on the right side to be included in our schedule: Key Name. Now you want to move the following values from the left to the right (they've already been moved in Figure 19.25):

◆ Floor Finish

◆ Wall Finish

◆ Base Finish

The remaining tabs in this dialog box are identical to the dialog box for other schedule types. For more information on formatting or changing the appearance of a standard schedule, see Chapter 17.

Once you have these values selected, click OK. A blank schedule appears and is available for you to fill in with finish values.

Click the New button in the Options bar to begin to add standard room finishes to the schedule. In this table, the key name is important because it will be the link between the two schedules. Using the New button, add the following room styles to your table: Key Name, Floor Finish, Wall Finish, and Base Finish.

Once the schedule is complete (you can always add to it or modify it later), you need to create the finish schedule to be used in the construction document sheets. Again, select Schedule/ Quantities from the View tab and select Rooms from the list. This time, leave the default value Schedule Building Components selected (Figure 19.26) and click OK.

FIGURE 19.26
Making the finish
schedule

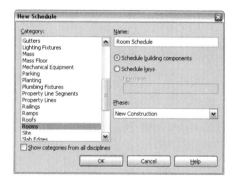

Again, you'll see the standard Schedule Properties dialog box. Add the following fields to the Schedule fields list (the right side) in this order and click OK:

◆ Number

◆ Name

◆ Room Style

◆ Floor Finish

◆ Base Finish

◆ Wall Finish

◆ Area

The schedule that shows up will be a list of the rooms in the project, sorted by room number with (none) set as the value for Room Style. The Floor, Base, and Wall Finish columns will all be blank. Some sample lines are shown in Figure 19.27.

FIGURE 19.27
The finish schedule

From here, adding values and finishes to the rooms by room style is fairly easy. Once you select the (none) value in the Room Style column, you will be given the option to select from the drop-down list of values we defined in the room style table (Figure 19.28).

FIGURE 19.28
Selecting a room style

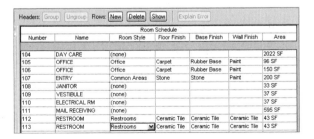

Selecting a value from this list automatically fills in the values for the Floor Finish, Base Finish, and Wall Finish columns to match the values we defined in the previous schedule. As you modify values in the room style schedule, they are dynamically updated in this schedule, adding consistency and predictability to your workflow (Figure 19.29).

FIGURE 19.29
Adding values to the schedule

Number	Name	Room Style	Floor Finish	Base Finish	Wall Finish	Area
104	DAY CARE	(none)				2022 SF
105	OFFICE	Office	Carpet	Rubber Base	Paint	96 SF
106	OFFICE	Office	Carpet	Rubber Base	Paint	150 SF
107	ENTRY	Common Areas	Stone	Stone	Paint	200 SF
108	JANITOR	(none)				33 SF
109	VESTIBULE	(none)				37 SF
110	ELECTRICAL RM	(none)				37 SF
111	MAIL RECEIVING	(none)				595 SF
112	RESTROOM	Restrooms	Ceramic Tile	Ceramic Tile	Ceramic Tile	43 SF
113	RESTROOM	Restrooms	Ceramic Tile	Ceramic Tile	Ceramic Tile	43 SF

Imagine the time it would take if you had to manually enter all these finishes in each schedule in each project! Key schedules are a big time-saver and ensure consistency.

Leveraging Tags

Tags are text labels for elements such as doors, walls, windows, rooms, and a host of other objects that architects typically need to reference in a set of drawings. In Revit, tags are intelligent, bidirectional symbols that report information stored in the properties of an element. A value can be directly edited from the tag; likewise, editing an element's properties affects the tag.

A wall tag, for example (Figure 19.30), can display the wall type that is set in the properties of the wall itself, but it can show much more information, such as the wall's fire rating or area.

FIGURE 19.30

A wall tag

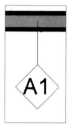

Loading Tags

Revit comes with a variety of tags that can be customized to meet your office's graphic standards or needs. The preloaded tags in the default templates cover many common requirements but are by no means exhaustive.

Every category of a family can be tagged, and you can load multiple types of tags for each category. Tags are loaded like any other family or component in Revit. Navigate to File ➤ Load from Library ➤ Load Family, and browse to the tag you want to add to the project.

Tags you design that you use frequently in your project should be loaded in your office template.

Placing Tags

Tags can be automatically placed during the creation of an element (using the Options bar option Tag on Placement) or can be placed later. You can insert tags from the Tag button on the Drafting tab of the Design bar (see Figure 19.31). Note that only the Room tag is separate from the other tag, and you can find them either in the same Drafting tab, below the other tags, or in the Room and Area tab.

FIGURE 19.31

Tagging options
By Category,
Multi-Category,
or by Material

During tag placement, the Options bar lets you position a tag in several ways.

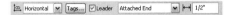

When tagging, should you not find any appropriate tag, the Tag button allows you to load additional tags without having to cancel the command and go back to the Load Families tool. If you click this button but don't have a tag of that category loaded for the element you want to tag, you'll be prompted to load one.

Tags can have a horizontal or vertical orientation and can include or omit a leader line. In the case of a wall tag, you typically have a leader coming from the wall, whereas you probably would not use a leader with a door or window tag.

The Tag button presents three tagging options:

By Category This option allows you to tag elements in the model by category or type. Examples are doors, walls, windows, and other commonly tagged elements. After you choose By Category, the elements you can tag highlight as you hover your mouse over them in your view. Revit also displays a ghost image of the tag you're inserting and the value in that tag.

Multi-Category Use the Multi-Category tag when you want to tag an element across different family types—for instance, when you're using a similar glazing type in your windows and exterior doors and you want to be able to tag the glazing consistently. The Multi-Category tag allows you to have the same tag and tag value for the glazing in both families. (Fire rating is another common application of this tag.)

Material The Material tag lets you tag the materials in a given family. Tagging a wall by material exposes materials used in the wall assembly. This allows you, for example, to tag the gypsum board, sheathing, and studs separately.

Changing a Tag Value

There are two ways to modify text in a tag. Selecting the tag makes the text an active control and turns it blue; just click the blue text and start typing. The second option is to access the properties of the element being tagged. Using a wall example again, if you select the wall, navigate to its properties, and change the Type Mark field, the wall tag updates to reflect this change. See Figure 19.32 for examples of each location.

FIGURE 19.32
Changing a tag value can happen by changing the value directly in the tag (A) or by changing the Type Mark field in the Tag properties (B).

Whichever way you choose, you change the symbol text for every instance of that tag type. Therefore, if you change a wall type from A1 to A2, you change every instance of that wall family that was previously tagged A1.

Some tags only report instance values—values that are unique to the individual element. A room tag or door tag is a common example. The room tag graphics are consistent, but the room name varies from room to room. Doors are often tagged like this, with a unique value for each door. With these types of tags, Revit detects if you enter duplicate values and warns you when that happens.

Tagging Untagged Elements

You can tag many elements at once using the Tag All Not Tagged tool in the Drafting tab of the Design bar. This time-saving feature lets you tag all the elements in a view simultaneously.

During early phases of design, you often are not concerned with tags and annotations but are more focused on the model. Tags can become graphic clutter that obscures the design at times. Later in the process, when the design is more complete, you may want to annotate the drawing quickly. This is where the Tag All Not Tagged tool is helpful. When you select this tool, the dialog box shown in Figure 19.33 appears. You can orient your tag or add a leader to it before tagging all the listed elements in your current view.

FIGURE 19.33

The Tag All Not Tagged dialog box

If you have elements selected, you can choose to tag only the selected elements. Note that this option is grayed out in the sample dialog box in Figure 19.33 because nothing in the model is selected.

TAGGING ELEMENTS IN PLAN: DOORS

Try the following exercise: in the Foundation file we have been using, open the view called Level 1. You'll notice in this file we've moved the documents forward a bit by defining the views we'll be using in our callouts. In this view, using the tools mentioned, let's add tags for the doors and walls. From the Drafting Tab, choose Tag ➤ By Category. Make sure your leaders are turned off in the Options bar before adding any tags to the plans.

Mouse over the door, and click when it highlights. This will insert a tag for the door centered on the door opening. By choosing Horizontal or Vertical for the tag orientation from the Options bar, you can quickly run through the plan placing door tags.

These tags might not be ideally located. As we've mentioned, the tag will come in centered on the door. However, it is a simple process to drag the tag to a more appropriate location if necessary.

Now that you have placed the door tags, you can see how each door is tagged and change the tags if appropriate. As we mentioned earlier, to change the value for any of the tags, simply select the tag, and then click on the blue text. This will allow you to enter a new value in that field. For our drawing set, you are going to number the doors with a door number/room number system, as shown in Figure 19.34. You can also change these values directly in the door schedule.

FIGURE 19.34

Numbering doors in plan

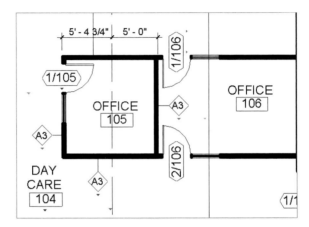

Another way to quickly tag the doors in this plan would be to use the Tag All Not Tagged function shown in Figure 19.33. This feature applies all the tags of a given family type at one time within the model. It's a quick way to populate a view with tags.

Using the Tag ➤ By Category tool in the Design bar again, highlight and select the interior walls. For wall tags, be sure to turn on your leaders, but adjust the leader size in the Options bar to ¼″ rather than ½″. The finished floor plan looks like Figure 19.35.

FIGURE 19.35

Adding wall tags

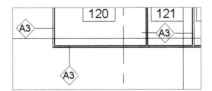

The number of annotations possible in any given view can be rather large, so it's typically a good idea to conserve the available white space on the sheet by not duplicating notes and tags. As Revit is designed to annotate only single items, avoiding duplication in a given view can be a challenge using only the standard tools. In Figure 19.27, you'll notice that in Room 121, the wall tag A3 has a leader going left and right to each wall. The leader on the left is a drafting line (see Figure 19.36). While this eliminates the parametric value for that single wall condition, in many cases adjacent interior walls have the same type. It is recommended that you weigh accuracy against workflow and the space available in your documents for this kind of approach.

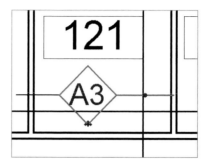

Understanding Project and Shared Parameters

Each Revit element has a set of parameters defined by default, such as material, length, area, or other characteristics that describe the element. Often, however, you need additional parameters to describe an element that you don't find in the standard parameter set. For such purposes, Revit lets you add your own parameters to elements and schedule or tag those parameters. There are a couple of ways to add these custom parameters that offer additional information about the element, depending on how you want to leverage them in the further development of the project and where you want them to be visible:

♦ If all you intend to do with your custom parameter is to schedule it (for example, a parameter called Lockable that describes whether or not a door has a lock), you can take two approaches:

♦ Add that parameter directly in a schedule using the Add Parameter function. This adds that new parameter *only to the element* that you create the schedule for, such as the door element.

♦ Create a new project parameter that you will be able to assign to one or *more element categories*—the difference is that this method allows you to assign the same custom parameter to more than one element (doors and windows, for example).

♦ If you wish to be able to both schedule *and* tag your custom parameter, meaning that you wish to see the value of that parameter being called out by the element tag, you will need to use *shared parameters.* An example for this might be a custom parameter for a room that indicates whether the room is public or private, or heated or not heated, and you want to see that information in the room tag.

As the name indicates, shared parameters in Revit are parameters that can be shared between families and projects. This will allow you to add information to your elements that can be both scheduled and tagged in your project.

In the following sections, we use a detailed example to present the whole process of creating and using a shared parameter, but first we present a basic procedure for creating a custom parameter that doesn't need to be shared.

Creating a Custom Project Parameter

You can create a custom project parameter at any time in the project cycle. You can then assign it to any one or more element categories, and you can generate schedules that will be able to call it out.

In the following example, we want to track whether or not the materials used in the project are recyclable, so we will create a new custom parameter *recyclable* that doesn't yet exist in Revit as a standard parameter and will assign it to the category Materials.

1. To add a new project parameter, choose Settings ➤ Project Parameters and click the Add button (see Figure 19.37).

FIGURE 19.37

Adding a project parameter

2. In the next dialog box, give the new parameter a few definitions (see Figure 19.38):

FIGURE 19.38

Parameter Properties dialog box

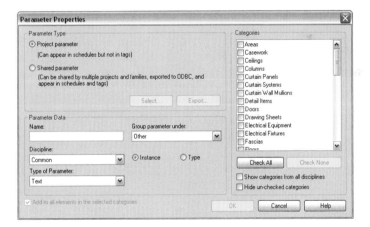

◆ Name, used for describing the parameter.

◆ The group the parameter will belong to. This is specifically for sorting the parameter in the Element Properties dialog box.

◆ The discipline. This is also used as a method to help organize the parameters.

♦ Whether it is an instance or type parameter.

Instance parameters are specific to any instance or insertion. So if you insert three doors, they can each have different instance parameters. An example might be the door number.

Type parameters remain consistent for the family type. So, in the door example, this might be the door width, and you'd create a separate type for each door style (36˝, 34˝, 32˝, etc.) within the project.

♦ What type will it be (text, integer, yes/no).

♦ You will be asked to choose the Revit category to which this new parameter will be applied.

3. Following a scenario in which we are adding a *recyclable* parameter to the materials, name the parameter **recyclable** and assign it to the category Materials. Make it an instance parameter of the Yes/No type (see Figure 19.39).

FIGURE 19.39
Creating a custom
project parameter

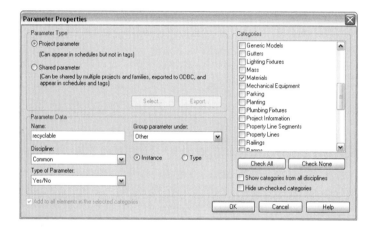

4. Navigate to the Materials dialog box (Settings ➢ Materials) and select the Identity tab. You will find the parameter you just created (see Figure 19.40).

With these steps, you have just assigned the new recyclable parameter to all materials used in the project. What is left to do is to define their state for each material (Yes or No). To do this, you can choose Settings ➢ Materials and, for each used material, set the value of the recyclable parameter on the Identity tab.

Once you do, you can create a material takeoff schedule (View ➢ New ➢ Material Takeoff) and make a schedule that calls out the recyclable parameter. You will then know how much and which of your materials used are indeed recyclable.

Note that you *cannot* tag the parameter you just created—we will not be able to make it appear in the material tag. The reason for that is simple: the existing material tag will not recognize a custom parameter that you create on the fly in a project as it has no label that can call it out attached to it. Tagging a project parameter is only possible using shared parameters. They are used both on the elements and in the tags, and thus the tag understands them and can call them out.

FIGURE 19.40
Locating the new
parameter

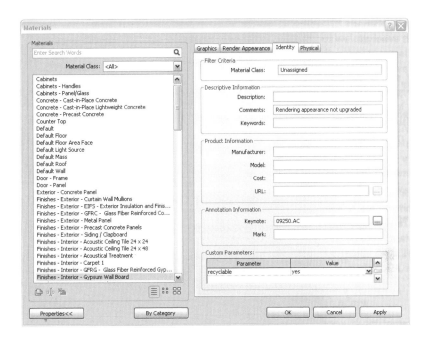

CREATING A CUSTOM PARAMETER WHILE SCHEDULING

When scheduling, you can add a custom parameter to any schedule on the fly. This parameter is assigned only to the category of elements that you are scheduling. To create such a custom parameter,
click Add Parameter in the Schedule Properties dialog box.

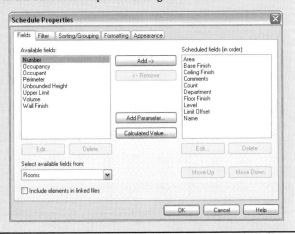

Creating Shared Parameters

When you want to schedule and tag a custom parameter you have created, use shared parameters. For example, you might wish the hardware set information of a door or window to appear in the door or window tag, or the level of radioactivity of medical equipment to appear in the equipment tag, or the door tag to display whether or not a door has a lock. None of these parameters exist by default in any of the families, so you will need to create them and add them to the families if you want to use them. They also don't exist in any of the family tags, so to be able to call out the information of these customer parameters in the family tags, you will need to add the same parameters to the tag families as well. The concept seems complicated, but it's actually straightforward. Imagine this: you have a set of chairs, some that are original Thonet chairs and some that are reproductions. You want to tag the originals with a special parameter called *original*. To do this, you must add that parameter in the tag (by creating a label and calling it out), and you then have to add the parameter to the chairs that are the originals. Now, if you created the original parameter as a project parameter, that parameter would only exist in the project you created. Neither the chair family nor the tag family would be aware of it, as they were created prior to the creation of the parameter and didn't have it among their parameters. That is where shared parameters come in handy—they allow you to reference the same parameter between project and family.

Let's look at the workflow behind creating these, using the example of a hardware set for doors and windows. We will do an exercise that ends up having a door custom parameter called *hardware* that is schedulable and taggable.

1. Create a new shared parameter file. At this stage, it doesn't matter if you are in a Revit project or in the Family Editor. In both environments, you can choose File ➢ Shared Parameters. This opens the Edit Shared Parameters dialog box.

2. Select the Create option and enter a shared parameter file directory path and name. This is where you will store all your custom-created shared parameters. Make sure that the folder you store your shared parameters in is saved somewhere accessible for the rest of your team. Do not store it under the Revit install directory as you might lose them all when you reinstall.

3. Next, create a group by clicking the New button in the Groups cluster of buttons that is now activated. This might be confusing, but in principle every shared parameter belongs to a group as a higher instance in a hierarchy, so you have to create at least one. If you use lot of shared parameters, the groups can come in handy for locating parameters. So, create a group and name it **Hardware**.

4. Once you have created the group, you can create the shared parameter by clicking the New button. Name the new parameter **Hardware Set**. This is the shared parameter that we wish to have visible in our schedules—and more important, that we wish to tag.

The shared parameter you've just created is nothing more than a simple text (.txt) file that you will find in the directory you created at the beginning of the exercise. You can now assign this parameter to any of the following:

◆ The tag family

◆ The project (as a project parameter)

◆ The categories of elements you wish to have that parameter

For this exercise, use the `Foundation.rvt` file located in the Chapter 19 folder on the book's companion web page (`www.sybex.com/go/masteringrevit2009`) to create a shared parameter file.

CREATING THE SHARED PARAMETER FILE

In the following steps, we will first create the shared parameter file:

1. Choose File ➢ Shared Parameters.

2. In the Edit Shared Parameters dialog box, click Create (Figure 19.41).

FIGURE 19.41
The Edit Shared
Parameters
dialog box

3. Specify the directory path and name of the new file; then click Save. The name of the new file that you assign here is not as important as the fact that this file needs to be accessible in Read mode for all team members. Do not give the filename an extension because the `.txt` extension will be appended automatically.

CREATING A GROUP OF PARAMETERS

Revit requires that you create a group before you can create a shared parameter.

1. In the Edit Shared Parameters dialog box, under Groups, click New to create a new parameter group (Figure 19.42).

FIGURE 19.42
Making a new
group

2. Give the new group the name **Doors**. To help you organize your shared parameters, you will want to name the group logically.

CREATING THE SHARED PARAMETER

Now that you've created the backbone for the shared parameters, let's create the parameters themselves.

1. Still in the Edit Shared Parameters dialog box, click the New button in the Parameters section (Figure 19.43).

FIGURE 19.43
Adding a new
parameter

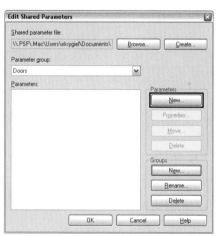

2. In the Parameter Properties dialog box, do the following:

◆ Enter a name for the new shared parameter: **Lockable Door**.

◆ Under Discipline, keep the default, Common.

◆ In the drop-down list under Type of Parameter, select Yes/No.

◆ Confirm by clicking OK.

And that's it! You've just created the shared parameter for door hardware and are ready for the next step: in the Family Editor we will now add it to a door tag and then move into the project environment and assign it to the category Doors. As explained earlier, you can only tag a custom property that you define if you share it across the families and the project.

CREATING A NEW PROJECT PARAMETER USING THE SHARED PARAMETER AND ASSIGNING IT TO A CATEGORY

In the following steps, we'll make our shared parameter a project parameter and assign it to the Door category.

1. Open the file Foundation.rvt.

2. Open the plan view Level 1.

3. Choose Settings ➤ Project Parameters. A list of parameters will appear. The Lockable Door shared parameter that you just created is *not* among them, so you will need to click the Add button (see Figure 19.44).

FIGURE 19.44
Adding the parameter

4. In the Parameter Properties dialog box, in the Parameter Type group you will see a Shared Parameter option. Check it and click Select.

5. The Edit Shared Parameters dialog box opens, and you will see the shared parameter you have just created, automatically selected. Click OK (see Figure 19.45).

FIGURE 19.45
Linking the shared parameter

6. In the Parameter Properties dialog box, set the Group parameter to Identity Data. Make sure you select the Instance radio button.

7. All that is left to do now is select the category to which this shared parameter will apply. In the Categories list, select Doors (see Figure 19.46). Note that you can assign the parameter to as many categories as you wish.

FIGURE 19.46
Assigning
categories

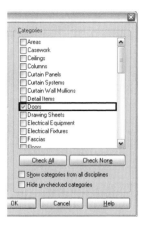

8. Confirm all that you have done by clicking OK.

SETTING THE SHARED PARAMETER IN THE OBJECTS THAT BELONG TO THE SELECTED CATEGORY (DOORS)

Now that you've created a shared parameter, you need to add the tags to show the lockable and nonlockable doors.

1. In plan view, select a door (let's say the door belonging to Room 131—Storage) and open its properties (see Figure 19.47).

FIGURE 19.47
Selecting a door
in plan

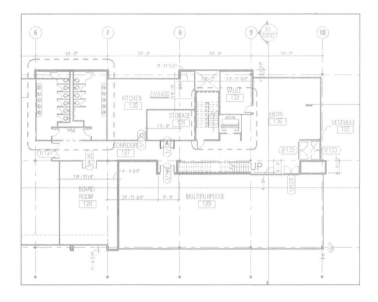

2. Notice that the newly created parameter appears in the group Identity Data, just as we set it to be. Note, however, that the value is gray, meaning that it has not been set.

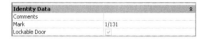

3. To set the parameter to one of the states, lockable or not, click the checkbox. Click again to clear the check box and void the selection.

You don't have to set this parameter one door at a time. You can select multiple doors that will have a lock and check the box using the same method.

ADDING THE SHARED PARAMETER TO A DOOR TAG

If you only wanted to add a new parameter to the door category and schedule it, you could have done so by using a simple project parameter. The point of making a shared parameter is that you will be able to add it to the door tag family as well as tag the door and display the value of the shared parameter in that tag. You will now add this shared parameter to the door tag family so that the tag understands the shared parameter value and displays it. If you just added a new label for the shared parameter and the door is lockable, the door tag for a lockable door would simply display "Yes"; the parameter we made only reports Yes/No values, which is not very helpful. So you'll need to add a static text note next to the label—**Lock** (see Figure 19.48).

FIGURE 19.48
The tag with fixed text

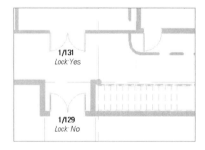

There are two approaches to create a tag that calls out a shared parameter:

◆ You can take an existing door tag, duplicate it, and then add the shared parameter to the duplicate.

◆ You can make a tag from scratch.

For this exercise, we will make a new door tag from scratch.

1. Choose File ➢ New ➢ Family. Choose the Annotation folder.

2. In the New dialog box, select the family template `Door Tag.rft` and click Open.

3. The Family Editor opens in plan view, showing two crossing reference planes. The intersection of the two reference planes represents the insertion point (and center point) of the tag to be created. In the tag, you'd like the following information to be displayed: the door mark and whether it has a lock.

4. Click the Label button in the Design bar. Click with the mouse somewhere close to the crossing point of the two references.

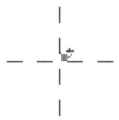

5. In the Select Parameter dialog box, select Mark and click OK (see Figure 19.49).

FIGURE 19.49

Selecting the mark parameter

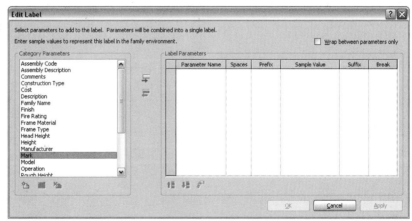

6. The Mark text is set to ⅛″ (3mm) by default, and this might be a bit big if we want to add a mark and a lockable parameter, so we need to make the font size smaller. In the Element Properties dialog box of the mark, click Edit/New. Click Rename in the Type Properties dialog box and enter a new name, indicating the size of the mark, **3/32″** (**1.5mm bold**). Click OK.

7. In the Type Properties dialog box, set the properties of the mark as shown here:

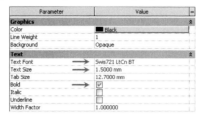

8. Confirm by clicking OK in the remaining dialog boxes when finished. What you see should be similar to what is shown here:

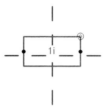

Note that 1i is just a symbolic representation of the label. Once placed in the project environment, it will read and display the mark of the door.

9. Remember, the goal was to display the hardware information about the door within the door tag. For that, we will now add the shared parameter Lockable Door to the door tag. Click again on Label in the Design bar and position this second label below the first, also centered in the tag.

10. In the Edit Label dialog box, click the Add a Parameter button, and then in the Parameter Properties dialog box, click Select. The shared parameter list opens; here you will find the Lockable Door parameter. Select it and click OK in all remaining open dialog boxes.

11. You can also select the Shared Parameter label in the Drawing area, click Modify to access its element properties, and set sample text to Yes.

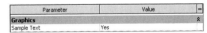

12. You will probably want to change the size of the text here as well to $\frac{3}{32}''$ (1.5mm), so navigate to Edit/New and under Type Properties, select Duplicate. In the Name dialog box, enter **3/32"** (**1.5mm**). Confirm by clicking OK.

13. Clear the Bold parameter and click OK in all remaining dialogs boxes.

14. Adjust the position or the size of the label if needed.

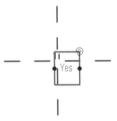

All that remains for you to do is to add the fixed text that will read **Lock:** and position it just in the front of the shared parameter label.

15. Click Text in the property dialog box. In the drawing area, click somewhere in front of the label Yes.

16. Enter the text **Lock:** and in the Options bar, select Properties. Repeat Steps 6 and 7 of this exercise to adjust the size and name of the new text type to match the label we added. Click OK in all remaining open dialog boxes.

The tag is ready. Save it and load it in the project Foundation.rvt. If you have already placed door tags, you can select them all and exchange them with the new tag that contains the shared parameter by simply selecting it in the Type Selector. You will notice that now all your door tags will display the mark on the top and the word *Lock* at the bottom. For doors that you previously defined as lockable, it will also show *Yes*. You will see that many doors have nothing shown in the tag after *Lock:*. Those are the doors that haven't been marked Yes or No, like the one pointed to in Figure 19.50.

FIGURE 19.50
A door without a
Yes or No value
for Lock

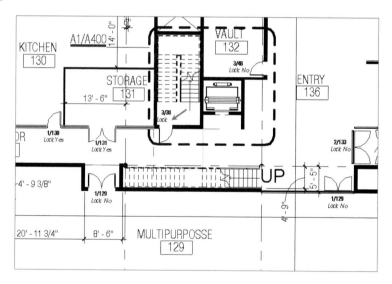

Shared Parameter Notes and Cautions

Keep the following point in mind when you create shared parameters:

♦ Once you have added a shared parameter to your project, you will not be able to change any of the properties of the parameter itself. If you forgot to set the Yes/No parameter, or if you mistakenly selected Type instead of Instance, you will not be able to change this setting. To fix that, you will have to create a new project parameter using the same shared parameter and be more careful the next time.

Adding Text and Keynotes

Notes are a critical part of communicating design and construction intent to contractors, subs, and owners. No drawing set would be complete without written definitions and instructions on how to assemble the building. Revit has two primary ways of adding this information to the sheets. One way is through text. Text in Revit consists of words arranged in paragraphs with or without a leader. Text can be used for specialized annotations, sheet notes, legends, and similar applications. Keynotes—the other way of annotating a drawing—are element-specific and can be scheduled and standardized in the Revit project file. Chapter 4 briefly introduced text and keynotes as elements you can include when customizing your template. In the following sections, we'll explore the use and function of both tools in more detail.

Text

Text is easy to add to any view. However, it's important to understand that text is nothing more than a view-specific annotation. Specific text families maintain a parametric relationship throughout the project, and changing one text family type changes each instance of that type through out the project. However, it is important to recognize that while text is a family within Revit, it is not directly tied to values of other families like keynotes or tags. Text is only text, and it will not dynamically report properties from elements it is pointing to.

T Text

You can access the Text tool from both the Basics and Drafting tabs in the Design bar. Text can be added to any view, including a 3D view. To begin adding text, click the Text button after you've opened the view of your choice, select where in the view you wish to place text, and begin typing. To edit text you've already placed, click the text to highlight it, and then click it again to activate the text box. To move text once you've located it, select it and drag it, or use the Move command.

As with all the elements in Revit, there are ways to change the look and feel of the object being created. Once you've selected the Text tool, the Type Selector and Options bar provide formatting options:

The Type Selector allows you to choose a style for the text you're about to create. Each text style is managed through the Properties dialog box, where you can modify parameters such as font, size, and color. To create a new text style from an existing one, click the Properties button in the Type Selector, choose Edit/New in the Properties dialog box, and then duplicate the type and make adjustments to the properties (see Chapter 4). You can also choose to add a leader to the text note before placing the note.

There are four options for leaders: None, a one-segment leader, a multisegment leader, and an arced leader. Once you've placed the text, selecting the note itself provides additional options. You can add or remove additional leaders and rejustify the placed text. Note that when you are adding or removing leaders, the leaders will be removed in the order they were added to the text.

To edit the text, select the element. The letters will turn from black to blue. You can then click to place your cursor inside the text and begin editing. When you're editing the text, you're given additional formatting in the Options bar for bold, italic, and underline text styles. These apply to whatever text you've selected in the note.

When you use the Move command, you move both the text and the leader. When you move text by dragging the arrow icon, you move only the text box, leaving the leader anchored in its original position. When moving text in this way, Revit will automatically align vertical and horizontal text and leader nodes. This is designed to help you achieve a more consistent graphical appearance. One of the biggest limitations of Revit is the fact that you cannot apply changes in text style to multiple elements (tags, schedules, title blocks, keynotes, or dimensions, for example). If you want to make all text in Revit use a particular font, you will not be able to change a global project setting. You need to edit each element's type individually. A good way to avoid this type of change is to standardize the fonts in your project templates, as covered in Chapter 4.

Keynotes and Textnotes

Keynotes and *textnotes* are written annotations that relate text to specific elements in the model using an external file. You can format font style, size, and justification in the same manner you can format standard text, but keynotes and textnotes behave similarly to a Revit family. This means you can insert different family types of text in Revit, just as you would door or window families. Changing one instance of the family type changes all the instances in the project. Because keynotes and textnotes act as families in Revit, they can also be scheduled. It is important to understand the difference between a keynote and a textnote.

A keynote is a short reference, typically a number followed by a couple of letters. An example would be 03300.AA, which points to a cast-in-place concrete wall. The 03300 portion of the note refers to the specification section the note is generated from, and the AA portion is a sorting mechanism used to differentiate cast-in-place concrete from another note in Division 3 of the specifications.

All of the notes on a given sheet are keyed back to a legend that is typically placed on the right side of a sheet. This reference is an aid to add more detail and understanding to the keynote without having to directly reference the specifications. (See Figure 19.55 later in this section for an example of a keynote and legend.)

Text notes are very similar to keynotes, but they combine a short description of text and the key into one note. This saves you from having to coordinate the legend on the sheet and puts the note right next to the item you are pointing to. (See Figure 19.52, later in this section, for an example of text notes.) No matter which style you prefer, both the keynote and textnote can be created with the same command within Revit. Since the command is called Keynote within Revit, we will refer to the process from here on out as *keynoting* regardless of the style of keynote (or textnote) you choose to use. See Figure 19.51.

FIGURE 19.51

Text notes with keynotes

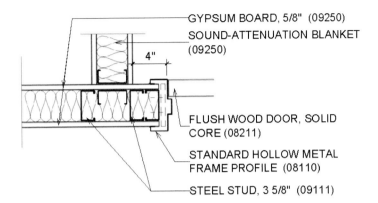

The Keynote command is located on the Drafting tab of the Design bar. When you add keynotes in Revit, you have three options:

Element This option allows you to note an element in the model, such as a wall or a floor. This type of note is typically used if you want to note an entire assembly, such as a wall assembly. You can find this value in the family properties of that element.

Material This option allows you to note a specific material in Revit. You can add a note to concrete, gypsum board, or insulation, even if they are a part of an assembly.

User This option allows you to select any model-based component in Revit and define a custom keynote for it. Notes defined this way differ from those defined as element or material because they're unique to the particular object selected. They can be used in conjunction with element and material notes.

All of these note types can be used in conjunction with one another. Using an element note to add a keynote to a wall doesn't mean you cannot also use a material note to call out the individual materials in the wall assembly.

Keynote Behavior and Editing

A core concept in keynoting is how the notes react in the model. Keynotes are integrated into Revit just like any model element. Keynoting an object in Revit lets you associate a text value with that family's keynote parameter. This value is consistent for every identical element in the model. For example, all doors have a type parameter that lets you set the keynote value. If you keynote a door—anywhere in the model—the keynote will show that value. Likewise, if you ever change the value of the keynote for the door type, all keynotes for that door type will update automatically.

Keynotes are special in that you *cannot edit the text of a keynote directly in Revit*. All the keynotes in Revit are tied to an external text file, which can only be edited in this location. This file can be modified at any point to add or remove values and notes. A sample list looks like this:

03100	Concrete Forms and Accessories	03000
03200	Concrete Reinforcement	03000
03300	Cast-in-Place Concrete	03000
03400	Precast Concrete	03000
03500	Cementitious Decks and Underlayment	03000

This external text file is designed to keep annotations consistent by storing all of them in one repository. Every time you add or change the text of an annotation and reload the text file, it dynamically updates all the keynotes of that type used in the project.

You can edit a keynote text file (.txt) or add one to a project at any time. You can have multiple text files for various projects, but you can have only one text file per project at a time. The text file works just like any other Revit family. Since all the notes are parametric, changing a note in the text file will change all of the notes in the project when the text file is updated.

A powerful way to ensure consistent use of notes throughout your office is to create a master text file for your various project types. These master note lists can be linked to materials or assemblies within your project template so that you can immediately begin inserting common notes into any project. To link keynotes to a material, choose Settings ➢ Materials and select the Identity tab. In the Keynote field, a predefined note can be selected from the master list and added to any material. This same is true for any assembly. Simply choose the assembly's properties (such as a wall or floor) and select the keynote field to enter a note value.

Since the keynote text file is separate from the Revit file, if you send a project file to someone and don't send keynote.txt, that person will be able to see all the keynotes you've added to the views but won't be able to add or edit the notes without the text file.

Keynote Filenaming Conventions

The default Keynote text file in Revit is found in C:\Documents and Settings\All Users\ Application Data\Autodesk\RAC 2009\Imperial Library (or \Metric Library) and is called RevitKeynotesImperial.txt or RevitkeynotesMetric.txt.

To edit this file, open it in Notepad or Excel and follow the format already established in the file. Let's look at that format to get a better understanding of how to customize keynotes.

The first few rows designate the groupings. They consist of a label (in this case, a number) followed by a tab and then a description. An example grouping looks like this:

03000	Division 03 - Concrete

Below the groupings, with no empty lines in the file, are the contents of the groupings. These are shown with a minor heading, a tab, a description, a tab, and the original grouping header. Here's an example:

03200	Concrete Reinforcement	03000

Here, 03200 is the subheading, Concrete Reinforcement is the description, and it all falls under the 03000 grouping from the previous example.

Using this method, you can add or edit notes and groups of notes to the keynote file. It might seem horribly inefficient at the beginning of the process to have to constantly go to the keynote text file to edit or add notes. While this might seem like a burden, it can be a blessing as well. Accessing this file ensures a global consistency within the keynotes on a project that is unattainable in most drafting applications. If you are feeling frustrated with having to access this file to make changes, think about all of the time you are saving *not* having to check your set sheet by sheet to verify that all of the notes pointing to a material are the same.

Keynote Settings

Once you change a keynote text file, you need to reload the file into Revit to update the keynotes. You can open the dialog box to change or update the text file by choosing Settings ➢ Keynoting (Figure 19.52).

FIGURE 19.52
Keynoting Settings dialog box

In the Keynote Table group, you define the path to the text file used for keynoting:

Path Type   Path Type defines how Revit looks for your text file using one of three methods:

Absolute   This option follows the UNC naming conventions and navigates across your network or workstation for a specified location.

Relative   This option locates the text file relative to the Revit project file. If you move the Revit file and the text file and maintain the same folder structure, Revit knows where to look for them.

At Library Locations   This option lets you put the text file in the default library location defined in the File Locations tab of the Options dialog box (Settings ➢ Options).

Numbering Method   Numbering Method defines how the keynotes are numbered:

By Keynote   This option allows you to number keynotes as they come from the associated text file.

By Sheet   With this option enabled, Rivet numbers the keynotes sequentially on a per-sheet basis.

Adding Keynotes to a View

To add keynotes to a Revit model, choose one of the three keynote types from the Drafting tab in the Design bar. In your view, hover your mouse over the various model objects until you find the one you want to note, and click to add the keynote. You'll then be prompted to add a two-joint leader, which will end at a box containing the text of the note you assigned to that material or assembly. Once you've placed the note on the sheet, you'll see a dialog box (Figure 19.53) where you can identify the element you're trying to note if it doesn't already have a note associated with it.

FIGURE 19.53

Selecting a keynote

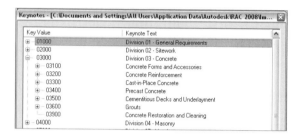

Expand the plus signs until you find your desired keynote and double-click it. Doing so globally associates that particular note with the element or material in the model. As mentioned previously, you need to make this association only once. For example, if you keynote a material called Concrete, then every time you hover the mouse over that material anywhere else in the model with a keynote tag, you'll see the preview graphic of the tag showing "Concrete." This way, you can define the materials and assemblies in the model and begin your documentation process.

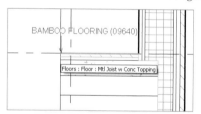

With the exception of detail components (covered later in this chapter), you can't keynote lines or other 2D information.

Keynote Legends

Depending on your workflow and style of annotation, you may want to create a legend on each sheet for your keynotes. You might want only the keynotes that are on a given sheet to appear in the legend. Or you may wish to have one legend for the entire project that will show all keynotes used in the project. The legends allow the builder to reference the note number with the text quickly and easily (see Figure 19.54). These lists usually reside on the side of the drawing near the title block information and can take either of two forms. The first type is all-inclusive and shows every note within the project. This style has the benefit of consistency between sheets in the set. The same note will always be in the same location in the list. The other type of keynote list includes only the notes that are present on a particular sheet. This has the advantage of supplying a list of notes customized for each sheet without extraneous information. As you can imagine, this second list can be very labor intensive and fraught with opportunities for human error. One of the beauties of Revit is its ability to accurately manage this kind of information for you. We will review how to create both types of lists.

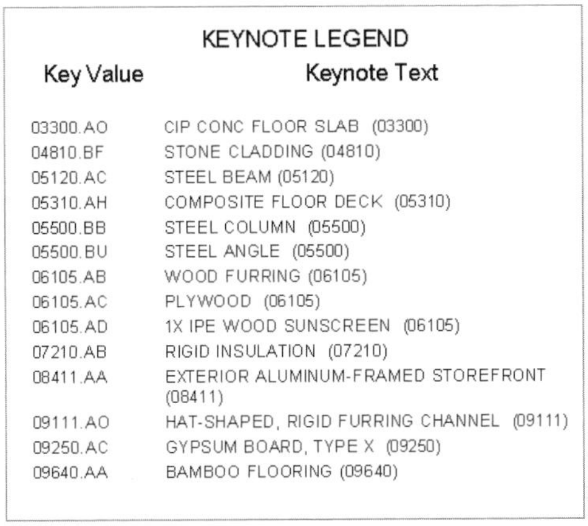

KEYNOTE LEGEND

Key Value	Keynote Text
03300.AO	CIP CONC FLOOR SLAB (03300)
04810.BF	STONE CLADDING (04810)
05120.AC	STEEL BEAM (05120)
05310.AH	COMPOSITE FLOOR DECK (05310)
05500.BB	STEEL COLUMN (05500)
05500.BU	STEEL ANGLE (05500)
06105.AB	WOOD FURRING (06105)
06105.AC	PLYWOOD (06105)
06105.AD	1X IPE WOOD SUNSCREEN (06105)
07210.AB	RIGID INSULATION (07210)
08411.AA	EXTERIOR ALUMINUM-FRAMED STOREFRONT (08411)
09111.AO	HAT-SHAPED, RIGID FURRING CHANNEL (09111)
09250.AC	GYPSUM BOARD, TYPE X (09250)
09640.AA	BAMBOO FLOORING (09640)

FIGURE 19.54
A keynote legend

Creating a keynote legend in Revit is simple: choose View ➤ New ➤ Keynote Legend. The keynote legend, as we've noted previously, is not available from the Design bar; it is only accessible from the pull-down menus. You'll be prompted to name the legend; enter a name and click OK.

There are only two fields available in a keynote legend, and by default, they are both loaded into the scheduled fields side of the Fields tab. Those fields are as follows:

Key Value This field contains the numeric value of the keynote.

Keynote Text This field contains the text value for the keynote.

A keynote legend works very much like any other schedule as far as formatting and appearance. By default, the sorting and grouping are already established because the key value is used to sort. The one special item to note is located on the Filter tab. At the bottom of this tab is a feature unique to this type of schedule: a Filter by Sheet check box (shown in Figure 19.55) is available. Checking this box gives you the ability to filter the list specifically for each sheet set.

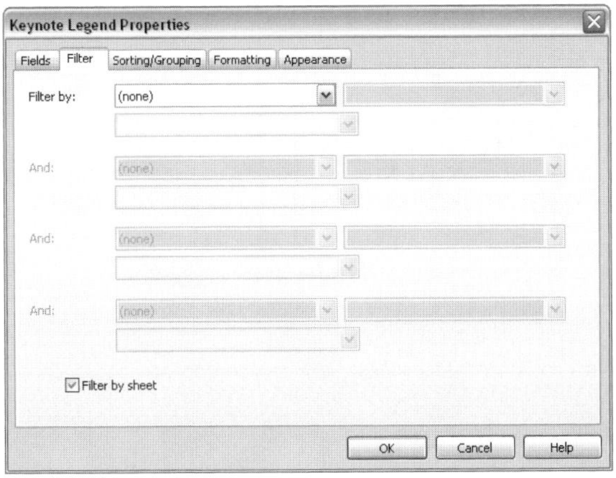

FIGURE 19.55
Filter by Sheet check box located at the bottom of the Filter tab in the Keynote Legend Properties dialog box

Either legend style you make can be placed again and again on every sheet in the project. The filtered legend style dynamically modifies the note list based on each sheet and the contents on each sheet. As views are added or removed from a sheet or notes are added to the project, the keynote legend updates accordingly. If the keynote is not used in the view placed on the sheet, it will not show up in the legend for that sheet.

New to Revit 2009, keynote legends are considered to be another type of legend view: once created, they appear under the Legends branch of the Project Browser.

A SCHEDULE FOR KEYNOTES

Creating a schedule for keynotes is a great way to find rogue notes and typos in a project. If you are working on a project team of any size, there's always a chance that someone could be inserting an incorrect text note into the project. Scheduling the notes is an efficient approach to managing this process and gives you the tools to verify consistency. Scheduling text notes allows you to do two things:

◆ List all of the notes within a project and verify their spelling and accuracy.

◆ Find the odd note; instances of notes that show up only once or twice in the project. Sometimes this can mean the note was accidentally placed in lieu of another note.

The Keynote Family

Revit comes with a keynote family that allows you to produce both keynotes and text notes. If it is not loaded into your project, you can find it under the Annotations folder in the Imperial or Metric library. The family name is `Keynote Tag.rfa`. This family has three family types that let you change note styles within the project. You can see the three note styles in Figure 19.56.

FIGURE 19.56
Note styles available in the default Revit keynote tag

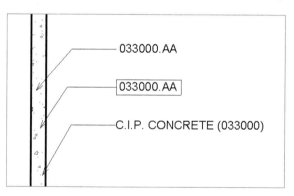

The three default styles are Keynote Number, Keynote Number–Boxed, and Keynote Text. Each of these notes pulls information from the text file we discussed earlier in this chapter. We are simply using the flexibility of family types to report different values within the model from the same note. Like any other family, this family can be edited to change the note length, font style, or other attributes to match your office standards.

ADDING NOTES TO A WALL SECTION BY MATERIAL

As we discussed earlier in this chapter, there are three styles of keynotes: element, material, and user. With all of these styles, there are limits to what you can note within Revit. Understanding this is critical to successfully using the keynote system within Revit so you can optimize the value of your predefined notes.

These three note styles can annotate only objects within Revit. This means you can add notes to elements such as walls, roofs, floors, and families that are a combination of materials or elements; you can add notes to the individual materials themselves or any element that can be given a material; and you can add notes to detail groups and detail components. While this is an extensive list and covers most of what happens in Revit, there are a couple of things you cannot tag with the Keynote tool: detail lines and groups (although you can tag elements within groups).

This becomes a critical issue when you begin embellishing details within a model. As a best practice, it is recommended that you optimize the use of detail components and embed them into the project families. Detail components are families created with 2D linework that can be dropped into any view to represent elements that are not directly modeled. For example, blocking that would appear over a window head is not something you would create as a model element, but it is still necessary to show in a section or detail (see Figure 19.57). We cover the technique of creating and noting detail components in Chapter 21.

FIGURE 19.57
Detail components can be tagged with keynotes.

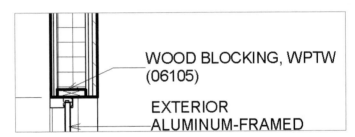

Once you've established your keynote style and made your adjustments to font size and type and linked a keynote TXT file, you can add some notes to the drawing. Adding notes to a drawing from this point is quite simple.

1. On the Drafting tab, click the Keynote button.

2. Select Element, Material, or User from the list. In our example, we've selected Material.

3. When you hover your mouse over the material, Revit will try to identify it. If the material already has a note value defined, Revit will show you a floating note identifying the material.

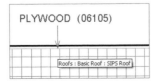

From here, click to place the arrowhead of the note, click again to locate the joint in the leader, then click once more to locate the text. If the material is unknown, Revit shows a question mark to tell you this material has not yet been identified in the project.

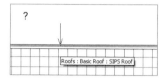

Locate the note using the same method for materials that are already defined (see Figure 19.58), but after you set the text location, Revit prompts you to select a value from the Keynotes table.

FIGURE 19.58
Adding notes to a material

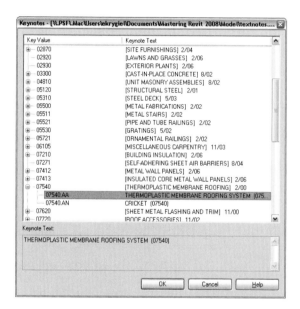

Once you've selected the note for a material, that same note will be applied every time you select that material with a keynote in every other view within the project.

By default, Revit does not include an arrowhead with any of the keynotes. There isn't a way within Revit to preset arrowhead styles for notes unless you preset them within the project template. After you first insert a note into Revit, select it to add an arrowhead. To do this, select the note and navigate to its properties, and then select Edit/New. Here you can globally set an arrowhead style for any of the keynote family types. Most of the common arrowhead styles can be found in this properties box. Selecting one from the list will change the arrowheads for all of the notes of that type within the project.

Once you've added a couple of notes, it's an easy process to continue noting the remaining materials in the wall section. The completed section with keynotes looks like Figure 19.59.

FIGURE 19.59
A wall section annotated by material

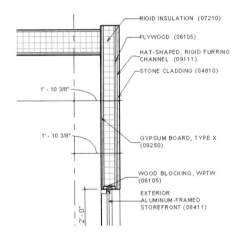

ADDING NOTES TO A WALL SECTION BY ELEMENT

Another way to keynote a drawing is to note by assembly or, within Revit, by element. Keynoting by element means that you are not noting the individual materials as we did in the previous example but the entire assembly at once. So, in lieu of noting plywood and gypsum board, you are noting the entire wall assembly at once. The process to add the notes is very similar.

1. On the Drafting tab, click the Keynote button.

2. Select Element, Material, or User from the list. In our example, we've selected Element.

3. When you hover your mouse over the element or assembly, Revit tries to identify it. If the element already has a note value defined, Revit shows you a floating note identifying the material. From here, click to place the arrowhead of the note, click again to locate the joint in the leader, and finally, click to locate the text. If the material is unknown, Revit shows a question mark to tell you this element has not yet been identified in the project. Locate the note using the same method you used for elements that are already defined, but after you set the text location, Revit prompts you to select a value from the keynotes table.

A wall section noted by element looks like Figure 19.60.

Remember that element, material, and user notes in Revit are different entities and are allowed their own, unique notes. You can note by material, by element, and by user within the same project.

FIGURE 19.60
A wall section
noted by element

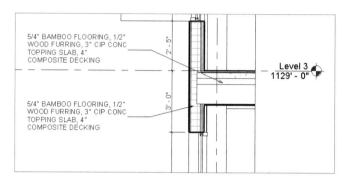

Predefining Keynotes

There are a variety of other ways to add notes to a project without adding them directly in a view. Within the properties of elements and materials is a field to predefine a keynote. By putting a value in this field before noting the drawings, you can avoid selecting notes from the keynote list when you are actually annotating a view. All of the notes would be preselected. Depending on the note type, the location for these settings varies.

Element   This value can be set in the properties of the various families in a Revit project. By selecting a wall, for example, you can select this wall's properties, and then click Edit/New to reach the wall type properties. Under Identity Data, you can then define a keynote (see Figure 19.61). Selecting this field, you will be presented with the same keynote table that you'd receive if you were noting this element in a view. If the note is incorrect for this project or element, you have the option to change the note here as well.

Material   This value can also be set by choosing Settings ➤ Materials. By selecting a material from this list, and then selecting the Identity tab, you can add keynote values directly to your materials (see Figure 19.62). You will again be presented with the familiar keynote dialog box to select your materials.

User   User notes are view-specific and cannot be predefined. While it is still possible to annotate only model elements and detail components with user notes, this tool will allow you to note the same element with different notes in separate views. This can be dangerous to the consistency of your notes in your drawings if used inappropriately. The advantage of this note type, however, is if you need to note something differently in one view based on a unique condition. For example, you might need to note a material or color change in a special location or a special flashing or sealant issue around a unique window condition. This will spare you from having to create a new family type simply to add a different note.

Revit does not support more than one `keynote.txt` file per project, so if you wish to include keynotes from different standards, you can simply add more text entries to the text file that you have for the project and they will all be available immediately within Revit.

FIGURE 19.61

The type properties of the wall showing the pre-defined Keynote field

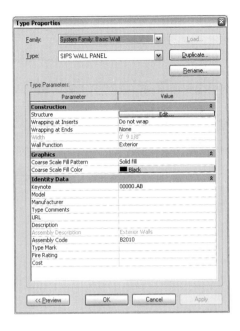

FIGURE 19.62

Defining keynotes for materials

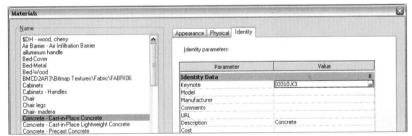

The Bottom Line

Annotating drawings is an essential part of the workflow when preparing construction documents. In most cases, your annotations are "smart" and are tied parametrically to elements in the model. This intelligent behavior will help you quickly and accurately embellish your drawings with critical information.

Annotate views   Room elements are highly useful tools for a number of different applications in a set of documents. Learning how to use them and tag them will help you find areas, create finish schedules, and identify spaces.

Master It   Once the model has been largely built out, you need to start adding information about rooms and finishes. What tools would you use?

Use schedule keys   Adding information to the room element is only part of the documentation and design process. Knowing how to schedule that information allows you to communicate effectively with owners and contractors.

Master It   Tags are used to report information about an element. How do tags work in Revit so that they always report accurate and consistent information about the elements they tag?

Leverage tags   Revit supplies you with three ways to annotate your model and the project. Knowing when to use each and planning for them early in the documentation phase saves time and frustration.

Master It   It is important to understand the relationships between elements and materials in Revit early. How does this help streamline the process of keynoting your project when you reach the documentation phase?

Understand shared parameters   Revit lets its users add as many custom parameters to an element as are needed. When those added parameters need to be visible both in schedules as well as in the elements tags, they need to be created as Shared parameters.

Master It   You added a custom parameter to your door and window elements and wish to schedule and tag it such that each window or door tag displays the information about the hardware set. Schedule works well, but your tags seem not to be able to find the hardware set parameter. What is wrong?

Add text and keynotes   No set of drawings is complete without keynotes or text notes. Understand how to create and modify them for a complete set of documents.

Master It   You will need to add notes in every stage of design to communicate your design intent on a project. How do you create and modify the notes to ensure accuracy throughout all the sheets in the set?

Chapter 20

Developing the Design with Smart Workflows

In this chapter we'll explore scenarios in which elements in a building repeat, and you'll learn how to take advantage of some tools in Revit to help your workflow be more efficient and less prone to error. The tools we'll explore are called *groups* and *links*—tools specifically designed to support design and propagation of repetitive entities, which can range from entire buildings to individual rooms to furniture arrangements.

Both of these tools require an understanding of some basic principles that will help you make decisions about when and where to engage these features in a design. We will introduce the concept behind each tool and present a series of use cases in which groups or links provide a valuable solution to a design problem.

In this chapter, you learn how to do the following:

◆ Work with repetitive elements

◆ Understand the use of groups

◆ Understand the principles of links

◆ Decide whether to use groups, links, or both

Working with Repetitive Elements

Many architectural projects deal with the design and organization of repetitive elements. The concept of a modular unit that is repeatable has been one of the more important principles of modern architecture and continues today in the form of housing, hospitals, schools, and office buildings. A repetitive element can be found at nearly every scale: from repeating buildings to housing units, repeating hotel rooms, classrooms, hospital rooms to bathrooms, closets, and furniture layout. In each case, the basic requirement is to group a collection of elements that is repeatable so that later in the process any change to the module will be propagated to all the other instances (copies) of the module. This propagation results in huge time-savings, as you don't have to manually update the model, element by element. This also guarantees consistency, and fewer red lines to pick up as documents are reviewed. At the same time, there needs to be some flexibility built into the tool to account for edge conditions (where the repetitive unit needs to stray away from base) without breaking its relationship to the essential nature of the module. Revit is remarkably well suited to support a diverse set of design requirements.

Understanding How to Use Groups

Groups significantly improve your workflow when you are working with collections of elements that need to be repeated throughout a project.

When a collection of related elements is made into a *group*, it becomes possible to manage and change *any* single instance of the group and then have the changes propagate throughout the entire model—all in one interaction. It is also possible to execute a change on one group instance only and *not* have that change propagate; as you will see, Revit was designed to be flexible.

You can group elements in a project or even inside a family and use it to quickly lay out entire floor plans. You can also save groups and reuse them in other projects, making them quite versatile.

As we've discussed previously, the Revit categorization schema is intelligent: objects know what category they are and in what views they are visible. This directly impacts how groups are created and organized. For example, model elements (walls, floors, furniture, etc.) are grouped as *model groups*, and 2D, view-specific elements (dimensions, annotations, etc.) are grouped as *detail groups*. There is also a hybrid category called *attached detail groups*, which relates grouped details to a specific model group. If you create a group that contains both types of elements (model and annotations), Revit automatically stores this group as a model group with an attached detail group for the view-specific information. Keeping tags and keynotes associated with a model element in a group is an example of this. That said, there are certain conditions where information *cannot* be attached within a group. For example, if a dimension between two walls is added to a group but only one of the walls is in the group, Revit cannot attach the dimension. The reason is simple: when new instances of the group are placed, where should the dimension go in the absence of the original, ungrouped wall? Remember that dimensions, tags, and keynotes are referencing real model elements and cannot exist without their references (hosts).

Using Groups for Repetitive Rooms

Most architectural firms have projects where repetitive units are used throughout the design. In our first example, we will work on a day-care center for children with cancer project (Figure 20.1). The design calls for many typical bedrooms, most of which will be the same size and have the same accommodations (bed, bathroom, furniture). The ability to design, iterate, and manage all these bedrooms will be a major part of the project, which also has to be easy to maintain, schedule, and update.

We will work with groups to solve this design challenge and then later look at the same issue from the vantage point of using links and examine the differences between the two approaches. As you will see, each method leads to different results.

FIGURE 20.1
Repetitive
elements
sample model

Courtesy of Felipe Manrique Diaz, Universidad de Las Americas

Creating and Managing Groups

As soon as the building design is roughly oriented on the site and you start laying out the modules inside the project, you can immediately take advantage of group functionality by defining the basic room unit that will repeat. Later, you can add more content in one instance of the group, which will then populate into other instances of the group that are placed throughout the project.

Early on, you'll work with walls and rooms to create reliable area schedules in order to see how the design is stacking up against the program requirements. You'll also take full advantage of BIM by keeping all information centralized in one file. Using links (external file references), you would not get these benefits.

Creating and Placing Repetitive Units Using Groups

Let's step through a workflow using groups to lay out bedroom units.

1. Open the Model_groups_01.rvt file from the book's companion web page (www.sybex .com/go/masteringrevit2009). The project should open with the plan view shown in Figure 20.2.

FIGURE 20.2
Floor plan showing just the exterior skin and core (the interior has not yet been designed)

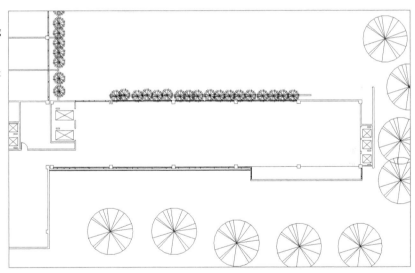

Group

2. Create a room and add a door as shown in Figure 20.3. Select the front wall with the door and one perpendicular wall and create a group by clicking the Group button in the toolbar at the top of the screen.

FIGURE 20.3
Model group
created out of the
elements of the
first room you
created

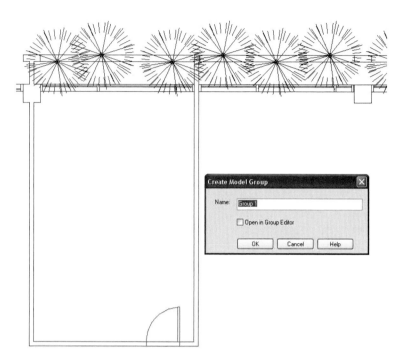

When creating the group, you only chose one of the perpendicular walls (the one on the right side) because you will repeat the module along the length of the space. If you added *both* perpendicular walls to the group, you would end up with *overlapping walls* as the unit is copied along the length of the building. This would result in lots of warning messages to deal with. Not taking these warnings into account would later affect the scheduling of walls, so you need to be smart about how groups are made.

3. Once the Group tool is activated, you'll be asked to name the group. As soon as this task is finished, the new group will appear in the Project Browser under Groups ➢ Model Node. The group is listed as a model group because all elements we selected to become a part of the group were model elements.

4. Before making any changes to the group, take a look at a symbol showing the group origin (Figure 20.4).

FIGURE 20.4
(Left) Group origin
default location.
(Right) Origin
moved to new
location.

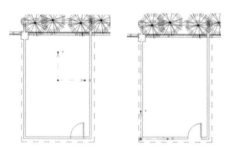

The group origin symbol (insertion point) is placed at the middle of group geometry by default—but you can change it to what you feel will be the most appropriate and practical point of insertion when you pick the group to reuse and place again in the project. Move the group origin symbol to the intersection of two walls, which will help when placing new instances of the group. To do so, place the mouse over the intersection of the X and Y axes and drag it to a new position, or use the Move tool.

There are many possible ways to proceed in the group placement process. You can insert more instances of this group along this wing of the building using the Copy Multiple Instances tool or the Array tool. An alternate approach is to use the Project Browser, and drag and drop the group instances into the view (Figure 20.5).

FIGURE 20.5

The group can be placed from the Project Browser.

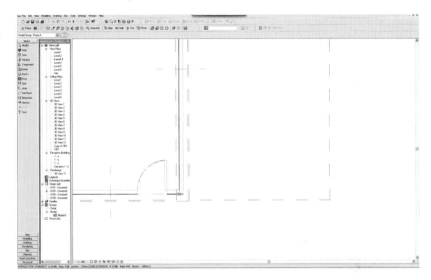

1. For this exercise, let's drag and drop from the Project Browser to place new instances of the group in the floor plan (you can place groups in 3D views as well, but the common use case is in plan). Once you drag the group from the Project Browser into the view, release the mouse button and take your time zooming in to the insertion point in order to get the correct snap without stressing your hand.

   After choosing the insertion point, you'll see that the walls belonging to the group clean up with other walls that do not belong to the group. This is perhaps the most profound difference in behavior between groups and links, (which we'll get into a bit later); but essentially, linked elements cannot interact with elements in the model they are linked to, while walls belonging to a group will clean up with walls from the main model.

2. Continue to place groups, until you arrive at a more developed floor plan (Figure 20.6).

FIGURE 20.6
More groups added
to the floor plan

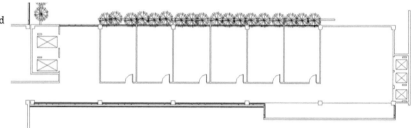

3. With the basic unit established, you can start adding more complexity and really see the power of groups. Because all the groups are instances of the original model group, any changes to this group will affect the others. Select any one of the groups in the floor plan, and take a look at the Options bar.

4. To change a group during the process of design, select the Edit Group option. This takes you to the Group Edit mode, where a new floating toolbar will appear.

The drawing area will turn a pale yellow, indicating that you are now in a special Group Edit mode (Figure 20.7).

FIGURE 20.7
The Group Edit
Mode is indicated
with a pale yellow
coloring of the
drawing area, sig-
nifying the special
mode. The floating
group editing bar
offers group-
specific tools.

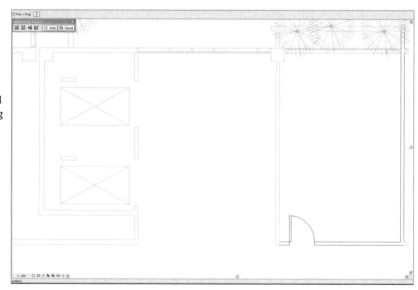

The need to change the design is quite common throughout the lifecycle of a project, where the process is such that designs evolve over time and are not complete with the first iteration. You can make changes and add new elements to a group while in Group Edit mode seamlessly and at any point of your design process. You can now access the modeling commands while editing the group, to add these elements. If you need a new component added to the group, it's just a matter of creating it while in Group Edit mode.

The Group Edit toolbar provides the following features:

Add to Group   This allows you to add any element from the project as the current object in the group.

Remove from Group   This allows you to remove elements from the group.

Attach Detail   This allows you to add view-specific annotations, which will become attached details and will be displayed as a subcategory of the model group in the Project Browser.

Group Properties   This provides access to the Group Properties dialog box, where you can edit the group's name. The level the group is attached to and its offset from that level are presented but not editable.

While in Group Edit mode, move the door to other side of room. When you click Finish, all the other group instances update with the new door location (Figure 20.8).

FIGURE 20.8
Editing one group propagates changes to all other instances of the group.

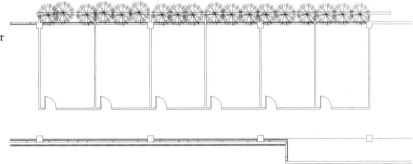

At this stage, you can generate an area report to check the requirements, and the design can continue to evolve. You will now add the bathroom and some furniture. Both of these will expand on the concept of groups by making new groups and nesting them inside of the unit group. You'll also add some details (dimensioning) to create an attached detail group. To conclude, we are going to explore alternatives in the room's layout.

Adding Rooms to a Group

The next step involves adding rooms so that you can schedule the room units by areas or by room type.

1. Select the unit group, and then click Edit Group in the Options bar. Once in Group Edit mode, use the Room tool to place the room. It will automatically be added to the group (see Figure 20.9).

FIGURE 20.9
While in Group Edit mode, place a room.

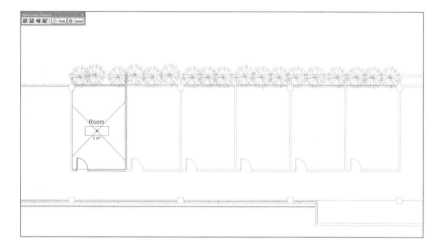

2. Click the Finish button on the Group toolbar to finish the change to this group and populate the change into all other instances of this group.

3. To verify that the rooms now exist, tag them as shown in Figure 20.10.

FIGURE 20.10
Tagging the rooms

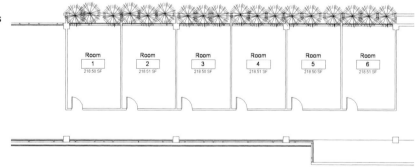

Note that when adding a room tag to a grouped room, the room will get propagated but not the tag. You will still need to tag the rooms.

4. To see how many rooms you have, and their areas, create a room schedule that includes name, number, and area (see Figure 20.11). This can be useful for making decisions about the composition of a floor plan and seeing if you are meeting program requirements as you make changes to the design.

FIGURE 20.11
Room schedule
showing areas

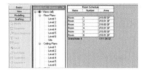

Nesting a Group into Another Group

Often, repetitive units can be a part of other repetitive units. For example, a standardized bathroom unit will repeat throughout many hotel rooms. To support this in an intelligent way, Revit offers a methodology of nesting a group into a group so that the intelligence of the unit is maintained. The bedroom group we just created can be completed with the addition of a nested bathroom group and furniture group.. A nested group appears in the Project Browser as a subnode of its host group.

Following a typical workflow, you can start designing the bathroom by adding walls and plumbing fixtures. Once you've added new walls and fixtures, select and group them, as you did the initial walls (see Figure 20.12). You'll notice that walls in groups clean up with walls outside of the group, making the grouped wall interaction with walls outside of the group seamless.

FIGURE 20.12
Build the bath-
room with walls
and fixtures; then
group them as a
new group.

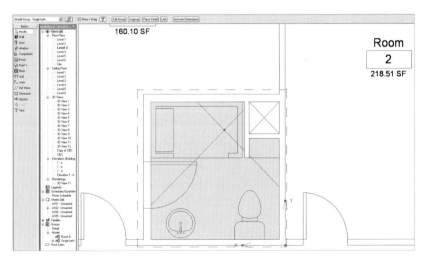

To add the bathroom group that you just created to the bedroom unit group, select the group, click Edit Group, and use the Add to Group button (at the far left of the floating toolbar). By selecting the bathroom group, you add it as a nested group in the Bedroom unit group. You will notice that a new entry appears in the Project Browser under the Bedroom Unit node.

Finish the Group Edit mode by clicking the Finish button on the floating toolbar, and the bathroom will be propagated to all other instances of the group (see Figure 20.13).

FIGURE 20.13
All the instances of the group are updated.

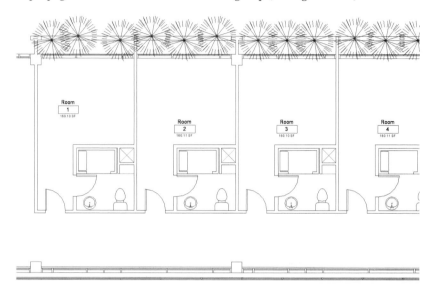

Adding Detail Elements to Groups

Now that the unit is more or less complete, you can start adding some annotations and dimensions to the plan in order to better communicate the design. Begin by dimensioning and adding text or tags in one of the units. To repeat the dimensions in other units, you can again take advantage of group functionality.

With the group unit selected, click Edit Group, and then add your dimensions to the group using the Add to Group button. Because the dimensions are not model elements, you will be prompted to make a new detail group. This will be attached to the unit group as an *attached detail group.*

Once you have a detail group, you can attach it to other instances of the group with relative ease. To do so, select a group and then use the Options bar button called Place Detail to attach the detail group. The details will be added to the group (see Figure 20.14).

FIGURE 20.14
Details can be attached to group instances.

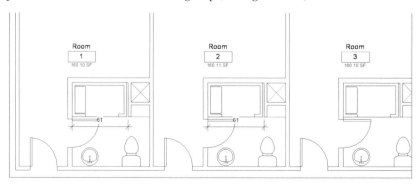

Nesting a Group from a Previous Project

To continue designing the unit, you can add furniture to one of the units. You can place the beds, dressers, and chairs and then group them and nest them just as you did with the bathroom. But suppose you already have a similar grouping of furniture from a previous project that you'd like to use in this project. To use a group from another project, open the other project, right-click on the group in the Project Browser, and choose the Save the Group to File option in the context menu. This creates an RVT file of that group that can be reused in other projects.

To reuse a saved RVT file as a group, select Load from Library ➤ Load File as Group, as shown in Figure 20.15. The dialog box that appears has some special options that let you choose whether to include attached details or levels and grids when loading. With the Attached Details option checked, you will import any details attached to the file, such as dimensions and tags. Levels or grids can also be imported with the group, if necessary, but don't bring in levels and grids if you don't need them.

FIGURE 20.15

The Load File as Group option

Load the file `furniture.rvt` to use it in this project.

The group will appear in the Project Browser and can be dragged into the view like any other group. Drag the group into the view and add it to the unit group. Once you do that, it will propagate to all the other units, as shown in Figure 20.16.

FIGURE 20.16

Furniture group nested into the room group

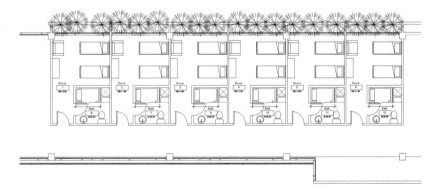

Making Variations to a Group Instance

In just a few steps, you've developed quite a complex structure with extreme flexibility. Not only can Revit manage model and detail groups, it can also work with different levels of nested groups within the main group. For example, if an alternative layout is needed, Revit provides tools that can facilitate a smart workflow. By right-clicking on the group's name in the Project Browser, you'll get a better picture of the possibilities (Figure 20.17).

FIGURE 20.17
The context menu for groups

The options displayed here provide the following functionalities:

Duplicate   Creates a copy of the group with a new name. This allows you to edit a copy of the group without disturbing the original and affecting all other instances of the group. This is helpful when you need a significant geometric variation in design from the first group. You can then at any point swap groups using the Type Selector.

Copy to Clipboard   Provides an easy way to choose a group and copy it to other levels.

Select All Instances   Selects all instances of the group in the entire model. Use this to quickly make selections for the purpose of deletion or swapping.

Create Instance   Provides an alternative means of placing a group—it's as if you were dragging the group from the Project Browser into a view.

Match   Functions the same as the Match Type tool. Enable the tool by selecting it. By first clicking Room Type A and then clicking a room of Type B, you can change room B into a room of Type A. Another way of doing this would be to just select a group in the view and change the type directly using the Type Selector.

Edit   Opens the group for editing in an independent session, not the active project. This allows you to see and edit the group in isolation without the clutter of the project.

Save Group   Allows you to save the group as an RVT file and reuse it later in other projects. This option leads to a dialog box where the new file's name is by default the same as the group's name, and you decide whether or not to include the attached Detail Groups as views.

Reload   Lets you reload a group if you edited the group as a separate file, saved the changes, and then need to reload it to get the most up-to-date version. Reload is not automatic; you'll be prompted to locate the file on disk to do this.

In our example, you can duplicate the unit group, giving it a new name, and then make edits to the newly created group. You can then swap entire groups just as you would any other component in Revit (Figures 20.18 and 20.19). With just a few clicks, you can explore design variations and propagate changes quickly and reliably.

FIGURE 20.18
Groups before
changing types

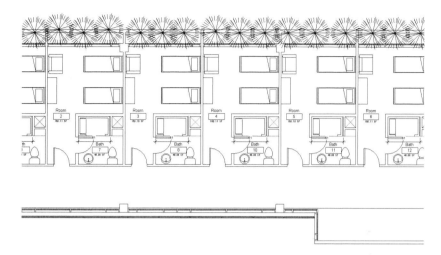

FIGURE 20.19
Groups after
changing type

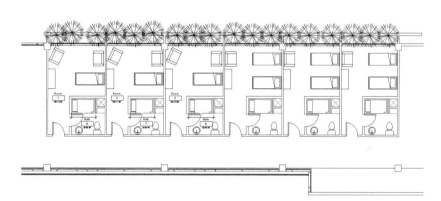

If you create a furniture schedule, you will be able to see easily how the changes to the design affect the quantities (Figure 20.20).

FIGURE 20.20
Schedules update
as groups are
swapped in
and out.

Furniture Schedule	
Family and Type	Count
Chair-Corbu: Chair-Corbu	9
Couch19: Couch19	3
M_Bed-Hospital: 0813 x 2083mm	9
M_Dresser: 1220 x 1830 x 0610mm	6
Seating02: Seating02	1
Grand total: 28	

You should be aware of some other options to understand the full potential of Revit groups. Let's consider a practical example. What would happen if we need just one of the Room A groups to have, say, eight pieces of furniture instead of nine? The intuitive answer would be to duplicate the group and just take away the chair while in the Group Editor. Although this option would work, it is generating an additional new group and thus additional information for the project to handle, thereby adding more complexity, which always makes the project more prone to performance issues.

Revit groups have a feature called *Exclude*, which basically takes away selected objects from selected instances of a group without altering the rest of the group instances. The object is not actually deleted (you have the option to restore excluded objects); it is just *deactivated* in that group and removed from any schedules. This option is more powerful than just overriding the view (by hiding individual elements using the Hide Graphics in View by Element feature) because overriding the view would not update your schedules.

To access this option, Tab-select an element within a group to see the Exclude icon (Figure 20.21).

FIGURE 20.21
The Exclude icon appears when you select an element inside a group.

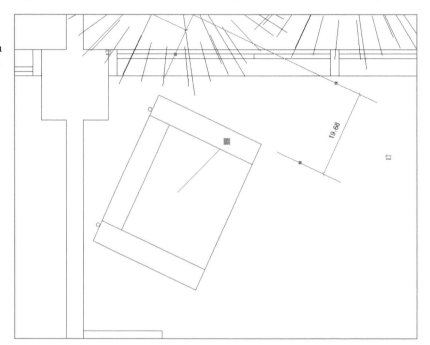

Clicking the icon excludes the element, and it will no longer be counted in schedules (Figure 20.22). You can always add the element back to the group by right-clicking and choosing Restore All Excluded or clicking the icon again.

FIGURE 20.22
The schedule updates to reflect that furniture was excluded.

Furniture Schedule	
Family and Type	Count
Chair-Corbu: Chair-Corbu	8
Couch19: Couch19	3
M_Bed-Hospital: 0813 x 2083mm	9
M_Dresser: 1220 x 1830 x 0610mm	6
Seating02: Seating02	1
Grand total: 27	

Note that the icon will only show up when you are not in Group Edit mode.

Repeating Groups to Other Levels

If parts of the whole floor plan need to be repeated in other levels, you can make a group out of many groups, generating a new high-level group in the Project Browser. For example, you can select the six bedroom-unit groups (also containing nested groups and attached detail groups) and make a new *master* group, which we have called complete level (see Figure 20.23). The result of this action is represented in the Project Browser, shown in Figure 20.24.

FIGURE 20.23

A master group for the entire floor layout

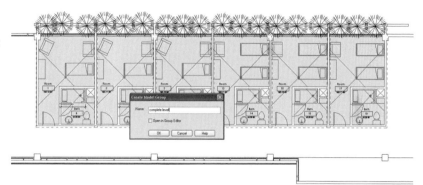

FIGURE 20.24

Complete level group

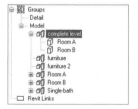

With the entire collection of rooms on the floor now grouped, you can select it and copy it to the clipboard. Choose Edit ➢ Paste Aligned ➢ Select Levels by Name and choose which levels you want the bedrooms copied into. In a few clicks, you can have several floors filled with bedrooms, as shown in Figure 20.25.

To recap, we chose to leave the exterior wall outside of the group to treat it as a single element that spans many levels in the project. We proceeded to make a rough definition of the room unit, which was necessary to fill out the building's wing. If we had instead added a portion of the exterior wall to the group, our exterior wall would have consisted of many separate walls, which would violate typical workflows and expectations. By placing just the initial module, we were able to quickly evaluate the needs of circulation and elevator locations, generate area calculations, and evaluate the design.

Then, by nesting groups, we solved the whole bathroom design and propagated it to the other rooms in one interaction, and likewise the furniture layout. If we had wanted alternatives in the room's layout, a new group made from the previous group could have been created, modified, and swapped out. For more granular changes, such as removing a seat from one single instance of a group, the Exclude option could be used to avoid making unnecessary new group types.

FIGURE 20.25
The bedroom group can be copied and pasted into other levels with a few clicks.

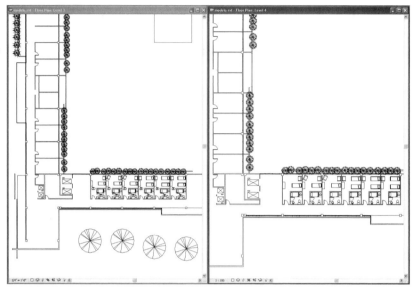

Making the Group a Part of the Project

The ability to make the group a part of the project is a key feature of groups. If there is a slight variation in an instance of a group that requires moving one or more objects, you can select the desired element, and by right-clicking on it, choose Move to Project. This option excludes the object from that specific instance of the group and puts it into the model, where it can be freely edited without editing the group. For AutoCAD users, the closest analogy to this is exploding a block.

 Real World Scenario

MOVING AN ELEMENT IN A GROUP TO A NEW LOCATION

In the bedroom design, the dresser needed to be repositioned in the last unit in the layout without making a brand-new group for such a slight variation. By tabbing into the dresser and selecting it, the designer was able to move it to the project using the context menu.

This action moved the element out of the group, allowing it to be relocated to a new position:

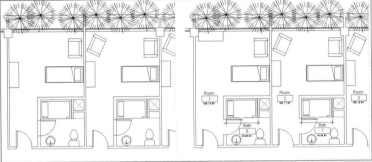

The left image shows the dresser before being moved to the project. The right shows the dresser moved to the project and then repositioned.

In terms of workflow, before deciding whether to move or exclude an element, the main question to ask is whether that change will be reused or not. Exclude and Move to Project are solutions for specific problems in an instance of the group, but that's where their whole power resides. Always remember that when you exclude an object, it also disappears from the schedule, whereas Move to Project does not affect scheduling at all since the object is still around.

Editing a Group in a Separate File

When you are working on a large file, it can be difficult to isolate a group for the sake of editing it. For example, when working in a complex building where you don't want to be burdened with hiding unwanted elements to get a clear view of the group (Figure 20.26), you can use a feature that allows you to edit the group as a separate file. Since this option isolates the group in a single file, you can work from there and then save the file and use the Reload option explained previously. The Edit option that appears when right-clicking a group in the Project Browser opens the group as an independent file outside the project environment, similar to the way you can edit families independently of the project. You can have both the whole project and the single file open at the same time, working with changes that are reflected immediately after saving and reloading.

After editing the group, save it and then go back to the project and reload it from the Project Browser using the right-click context menu. All groups of that type will then be updated.

FIGURE 20.26
Opening a group
for editing in a
separate RVT file

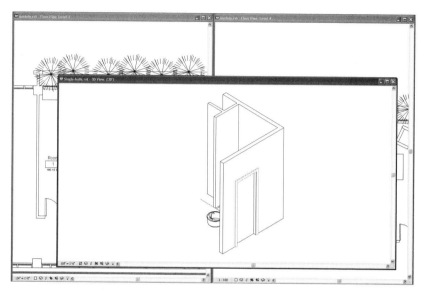

Detail Groups

We have touched on detail groups, but let's look at them a bit closer. You can create annotations to add textual descriptions, add dimensions to measure elements in a group, and then group them in what is called a detail group. The detail group can then be attached to instances of the model group. With a detail group, once it's created, it can be attached to a model group by using the Options bar when a model group is selected. This is a quick way to apply consistent annotations to many groups.

In Figure 20.27, a room is annotated, and then the annotations are grouped.

FIGURE 20.27
Annotations can be
made into a group.

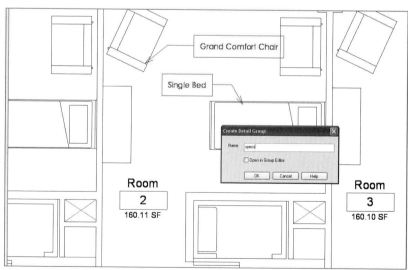

By multiselecting all the unit groups and clicking the Add Detail button, your recently created detail group will be applied to all your groups in one interaction (see Figure 20.28).

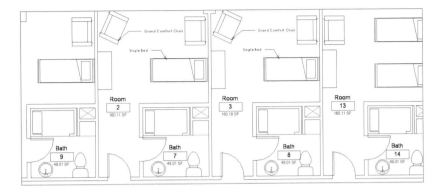

Best Practices for Grouping

Here are some aspects to consider when working with groups:

◆ When using groups on multiple floors (levels), the levels have to have the same floor-to-floor height for groups to work effectively. Currently, there is no way to make walls in a group taller from one floor to the next, so just be aware of that. Always remember that although you are working in a seemingly 2D floor plan, everything is 3D.

◆ Placing multiple instances of a group affects the file size. The group is not a link but an element repeated inside the project, what is called *instantiated*. Once you load a file as a group, it is part of the project and will add to the file size as often as it is used.

◆ If you need to have reduced file sizes, using links instead of groups might be a solution, although it depends on the applicability of the scenario in which you wish to use them, and most important, you should be aware of the consequences of using links.

◆ Try not to mirror groups—create left and right versions instead. While this is more time consuming, it avoids mirrored elements that should not be mirrored (such as plumbing fixtures, equipment, and specialty furniture). As an example, mirroring hospital rooms may easily create inadvertent errors from a utility connection standpoint.

◆ Keep nested elements and their hosts grouped together.

◆ Groups are very processor intensive. You can quickly get to a point of diminishing returns (from a performance standpoint) when groups contain nested groups, or entire floors have been grouped. It works great when you need to disseminate large collections of elements. But editing groups and waiting for them to update can severely affect project workflow.

Understanding the Principles of Links

You've seen that Revit groups can be a powerful tool for streamlining the design workflow, but the performance hit you take from increased file size can be significant. Revit provides another tool that allows you to work with repeating elements and avoid the file size problem: links. Be aware that limitations exist that you might not be comfortable with, so make sure you understand these limitations before deciding to go with the linking method.

To see how links work, we'll continue with our example project. When you select a group, you will notice that the Link button appears in the Options bar.

When you click the Link button, the dialog box shown in Figure 20.29 appears with some options you should understand. Is the information contained in the link going to a new file, or will it be added to an existing file? In this particular case, we are creating a new file, so Revit will automatically create a new file in the folder of the project (by default) and replace the group with a link in the exact same place (see Figure 20.30). The process does not involve any user action at all apart from clicking the Link button. This might look like the ultimate solution for managing file size; in certain cases this may be true, but let's look closely at the implications.

FIGURE 20.29
Converting groups into links

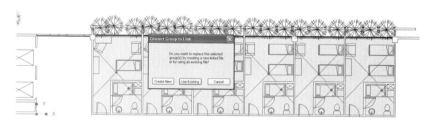

FIGURE 20.30
A group converted into a link on the fly. Note the rooms no longer find boundaries.

The first thing you will notice once you convert the group into a link is that the walls belonging to the link do not clean up with walls belonging to the active host model, because joining between elements in a link and those of the project isn't possible. When we talked about the interactivity of the group with its surrounding context, this was one of the points mentioned as an intelligent behavior specific to the groups. Walls in a linked file will not create clean wall join conditions with the host file, which can make scheduling of rooms particularly difficult.

Real World Scenario

WALL CLEANUPS IN EARLY DESIGN

During the early stages of design, seeing wall joints clean up is necessary for graphical reasons, but it's not needed at this stage for technical accuracy. In conceptual and schematic design, you typically don't want to waste a lot of time dealing with wall join cleanups when you are trying to get the design down. To keep things simple, set the Coarse Fill setting of the wall properties to Solid Fill and set the Color to black. This will give you a great schematic level print of the walls and not show you any of the wall materials. Then, when you are ready to advance the design, change from Coarse to Medium or Fine in your View Level.

If wall cleanups or definition of rooms are not a serious issue in your workflow (an example would be a renovation of an existing building), this could be a good solution to help manage file size. Even so, it is nice to know that as soon as you *bind* the link (convert it back into a group), you'll get wall cleanup and valid rooms again.

Note that binding links will work on any instance of a linked Revit file. This brings the link file completely into the project file and severs the link to the external file. For AutoCAD users, the closest analogy is binding of XREFs.

Common Link Use Cases

Links are well suited for workflows where you don't need a tight connection between elements, such as linking entire buildings or site plans into your project file. Links are commonly used when working with the following kinds of projects:

- Separate buildings on a shared site plan

- A site plan and contextual masses

- Large-scale divisions in building mass and program

- Other disciplines (Structure and MEP)

In the following examples, you'll see various situations when linking files can be useful.

MULTIPLE BUILDINGS ON SHARED SITE PLAN

At Koolhaas's station complex in Lille (see Figure 20.31), there are buildings designed by other architects directly over the station's roof. Interaction between the models is important in order to identify heights and possible restrictions between the buildings. This interaction can easily be created by linking the buildings for coordination, with each model residing in a separate file. What's more, each building could also use nested links or groups. For example, when working on the building over the station, you could link the train station into your model. Within the train station could be links to mechanical system files. All of these elements would be visible in the main host file. This form of nesting keeps file size down and makes working manageable.

FIGURE 20.31
Rem Koolhaas's train station would be a good project candidate for links.

Photograph by Guillermo Melantoni

IDENTICAL BUILDINGS ON SHARED SITE

Another use would be a project where a housing unit is duplicated many times on a site. For example, if you have three identical buildings, you would model it once, link it into a site file, and then make two additional copies. If you then edit the original housing file and update the link, all three instances of the linked file will update in the site file.

COORDINATION WITH OTHER DISCIPLINES

The Linking method is not only applicable to buildings with repeating units but can also be used as methodology for working in a highly coordinated way with other engineers and consultants using Revit Structure or Revit MEP. This workflow is designed as a fully collaborative use of BIM for all the disciplines. Using links, you can integrate structural framing, ductwork, and mechanical systems into your base architectural project for coordination. In a traditional process, this coordination was based on endless revisions, miscommunication, and colliding systems that ended up being resolved on-site during construction at tremendous cost. The Revit BIM platform provides transparent connections between Revit Architecture, Revit Structure, and Revit MEP. In fact, you can open a Revit MEP or Structure file in Revit Architecture because they are all based on the same technology. The only difference will be the available tools; with one of these files you'd be able to select and modify ductwork, but you would not be able to make new ducts.

Linking different disciplines in Revit provides better coordination and even allows for collision detection. This toolset will not be covered now, but you should be aware that it is all possible in Revit using what are called Copy/Monitor and Interference Checking. For further reading on these subjects, consult the Revit help documentation.

Linking Files

To link a RVT file, choose File ➤ Import/Link ➤ Revit. The dialog box involves some decisions in terms of how to position the linked model in a project and which worksets to open, as shown in Figure 20.32.

FIGURE 20.32
The Import/Link RVT dialog box

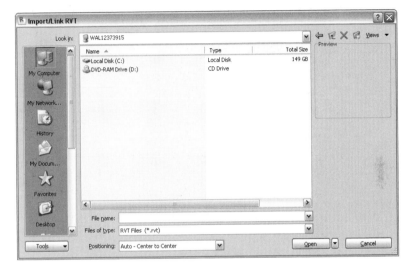

The positioning defines the location of the linked model inside the project and can be manually or automatically done. Automatic positioning of the link provides these options:

Auto - Center to Center   This aligns the 3D center points of both models.

Auto - Origin to Origin   This places the world origin of the linked file at the model's origin point. If the linked model was created far away from the origin point, linking with this option may put the linked file far away from the main model.

Auto - By Shared Coordinates   This places the linked file geometry according to the shared coordinate system created between the two files. If no shared coordinate file has been created, Revit will alert you. These Shared Coordinates settings can be found in the Tools dropdown menu:

> **Acquire Coordinates**   This allows taking coordinates of the linked file into the host model. There is no change to the host model's internal coordinates, but it acquires the true north of the linked model and its origin point.
>
> **Publish Coordinates**   This allows publishing the origin and true north settings into the linked model. Revit understands that there may be other things in the linked file and that you may not want this to be a global change to the linked file. An additional dialog box appears, giving the option to name separate locations for each set of coordinates.
>
> **Specify Coordinates at a Point**   This allows you to manually key in X, Y, and Z coordinates relative to the origin or to define where the (0,0,0) will be.

Report Shared Coordinates This shows the E/W (East/West, X), N/S (North/South, Y), and Elevation (Z) coordinates of any point in the model.

Manual - Origin The imported document's origin is centered on the cursor.

Manual - Base point The imported document's base point is centered on the cursor. Use this option only for AutoCAD 2009 files that have a defined base point.

Manual - Center Sets the cursor at the center of the imported geometry. You can drag the imported geometry to its location.

Special Link Features

As you use links, keep these concepts in mind because they can aid in your workflow and set proper expectations:

Scheduling elements in links You can schedule elements in link files without any trouble by choosing the option Include Elements in Linked Files, located in the Schedule dialog box.

Displaying nested links in the host file This is another big feature because you can have two different states: Attach and Overlay. As with AutoCAD's XREFs, if a file has a nested link set to Attachment, when you link it into another one, you will see both files. If the nested link is set to Overlay, it will not show up in other files. This setting is located in the dialog accessed by choosing File ➢ Manage Links.

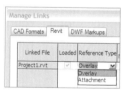

Using nested links in the Project Browser The Project Browser provides the same kind of interaction for links as it does for groups: dragging and dropping will place the link into the view. By right-clicking on the link, you'll get nearly all the options available in the Manage Links dialog box (Reload, Unload, Open, and Reload From).

Making areas and area boundaries in linked files visible and schedulable In Revit Architecture 2009, you can now show areas from linked files, and this includes the ability to create color fill plans that color linked rooms or areas.

Dimensioning to and from elements in a linked file and establishing constraints You can align and dimension to elements in linked files.

Copying and pasting elements from the link into the parent file By Tab-selecting an element embedded in a link file, you can copy it to the clipboard and paste it into the host file.

Controlling and changing the visibility properties of linked file and nested links You can turn categories of linked files on and off, giving you total flexibility in controlling the display of information.

Binding a Revit link within the parent model   This option creates a group inside the parent file, fully integrated to the project. You'll learn more about binding later in the chapter.

UNLOAD AND RELOAD LINKS

If you link a Revit file into the model, you cannot open the link without unloading it from the project. In that case, you will unload the link, make the necessary changes, and then reload the link after saving what you've done, or open a second session of Revit (you can run multiple instances of the Revit application at the same time) and open the link there. This way, you have direct feedback on any changes made in the link by just reloading in the session with the parent file.

Controlling the Visibility of Links

The linked model will display levels, grids, and any annotation they have because the default visibility is defined by the model's visibility. In an elevation, you will see not only the model's levels, but also the linked levels, which may become a problem. To solve this, apply custom visibility settings that override the link in the view. In the Visibility/Graphic Overrides dialog box, choose the Revit Links tab, and override visibility by selecting the Custom radio button.

This allows you to turn off visibility of categories in the link file. To hide levels, choose the Annotations tab and turn them off (Figure 20.33).

FIGURE 20.33
You can turn off visibility for categories in a linked file independently of the host file.

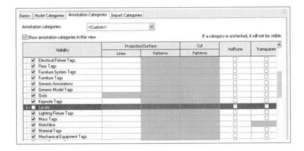

You can control the visibility of all categories in a linked file by using this custom setting, giving you practically unlimited flexibility for what you can display.

Deciding Whether to Use Groups, Links, or Both

So, is it better to use links or groups to handle repetitive content? Or is there a way to capture the advantages of both groups and links without their disadvantages?

The answer depends on the project and definitely on the workflow—the interactivity you need between the elements in the link and the ones in the project. For smaller projects, where file size and performance are not an issue, groups should work fine. If you have a huge project with many instances of repeating elements, linking will reduce file size and make working on the model faster. But if you need control over rooms and cleanups, groups are a better solution.

Had we worked with links for the room units in the previous example, the rooms' file size would not have been a major issue since we are working with instances of a link whose information (and file size) resides outside the project file. If you have a massive repetition of something modular, you might want to consider using links over groups.

If you do go with links but later change your mind, no problem: it is possible to convert the link into a group by *binding the link*, which transforms it into a group and thus adds it to the project. An example would be linking an entire floor plate full of hundreds of rooms.

In our example, we could have linked the furniture since there is not much interaction with anything else in the project. Because models of furniture can increase the file size, this approach could be a smart way of managing size. We can start working with the furniture as simple components in the floor plan and, as soon as we have something, group and afterward link them. As soon as we have the link, we can just copy it around the whole floor plan, resulting in a marginal file size (we don't have 100 beds, but one bed repeated in 100 instances). Keep in mind that there is no way of excluding objects from the link without affecting the rest.

If you need to work with the group as a link to reduce file size during the project, you can link it (thus losing room definitions and wall cleanups) and then later bind it back for final construction documentation. Be careful: when you bind the link, a dialog box opens with some options to be aware of (see Figure 20.34).

FIGURE 20.34
When binding links, you can choose to include details, levels, and grids.

If you bind levels and grids, it will create additional uniquely named levels and grids in the project, duplicating information that could result in problems.

All in all, binding links is a smart workflow that allows working with a sensible file size while restoring the lost relationships within the project as soon as you bind. Depending on the workflow and the size of the project, this seems to be the best of both worlds. You just have to remember that while the file is linked, you lose many key value propositions of using a BIM.

Final Considerations

Now that you've gained an understanding of the basic differences between groups and links, there are still some important things to mention. This is not about using one or the other, but rather about taking full advantage of both tools' potential to solve specific problems. It is again your criteria that should dictate your direction.

The new relationship between groups and links is definitely good news and has greatly improved workflows.

Therefore, if you are looking for a tool for working on a massive repetition of elements with little or no interactivity within the project and you want to keep file size down and still be able to schedule the project's contents, think about using links. You could even have someone else on the team working on that information and eventually bind it all into the model and take advantage of how groups interact with the model.

If you want to keep elements as links but still need rooms, you could use room separator lines as a workaround, and therefore be able to define rooms without binding all the information into the project. This requires some manual work, but it can be a practical solution if you give some intelligence to the separators. Using the Pick Lines tool when drawing room separation lines gives you a chance to lock the line to model elements and thus capture design intent and keep elements connected.

So, when you're looking for a tool that maintains consistency throughout the project and enables the management of repetitive content, when file size is not an issue and interactivity with the rest of the model is crucial, groups are the way to go. And remember, you can at any point swap the group into a link and vice versa.

The Bottom Line

Most architectural projects of any size rely extensively on repeating components, with or without variations. Mastering the tools Revit provides for this kind of repetition—groups and links—greatly simplifies your workflow.

Work with repetitive elements   Many projects have repetitive elements and can benefit by using groups and links efficiently.

> **Master It**   Think of a scenario in your own practice where elements repeat and how you might use Revit groups to solve the problem.

Understand the use of groups   Groups are a powerful design tool. Anyone working with repetitive elements needs to understand how they work.

> **Master It**   Describe a fundamental benefit of using groups.

Understand the principles of links   Links are Revit's second major tool for repetitive elements, avoiding the file size and performance issues associated with groups.

> **Master It**   Using a link paradigm means that the BIM model now depends on links to external files. Even so, the links can be scheduled, dimensioned to, and graphically altered. Despite that, there are still some limitations. What are they?

Decide whether to use groups, links, or both   Knowing when to link a file can improve file performance and provides an easy way to operate on large clusters of building data. You can hide links, remove them, and work on them independently. Knowing when to use groups can help replicate repeated elements quickly. Knowing how and when to use both helps speed the documentation process.

> **Master It**   Know that links can reduce the overall file size and thus improve performance when working in Revit; imagine a scenario in which you would most certainly want to employ links over groups.

Chapter 21

Moving from Design to Detailed Documentation

In this chapter we discuss how to expand the model and create details for documentation. Typically, details are created by taking the model data in section or plan and embellishing it with 2D elements. Understanding the 2D detail families within Revit allows you to quickly and easily complete a set of documents for a client or contractor without the burden of having to model every component and detail within the project.

In this chapter, you learn how to do the following:

◆ Create drafting views

◆ Import and link CAD details

◆ Create 2D detail components

Advancing the Design

In the lifecycle of a project, eventually it becomes necessary to add details to the model that are then used to actually build the building. Historically, the conceptual design, schematic design, and design development project phases progressed through a series of refinements to develop the final set of construction documents. With a BIM process, these discrete phases are being redefined, but the workflow remains essentially the same. At the stage prior to adding details, the "big idea" is refined and most plans and building sections are in place. Materiality is added to the design, and the assemblies that make up walls, floors, and ceilings are added. Creating wall sections, schedules, and enlarged plans helps to describe the project further. Eventually, the systems solidify and details are created that truly begin to define how many of these elements are put together in the field. In this chapter, we are going to explore a few scenarios for detailing the model and creating some of the smaller-scale drawings that go into construction documents. We will look at some of the more common methods:

◆ Creating details from scratch

◆ Importing details that have already been drawn

◆ Creating the detail from the model and embellishing it using 2D detailing tools

Creating Drafting Views

It isn't feasible to model every single construction detail in 3D within Revit. A 2D detail often provides enough information for construction in the field. To this end, Revit provides a means of drafting in views strictly used for 2D information that can be placed on sheets like any other view. These views are called *drafting views* and document typical or special details of the project. They can be created by either drawing the details directly within the view or by importing details. They can also have legends, maps, text, or any of a variety of things necessary for a construction document set. When placed on a sheet, drafting views have the same intelligent referencing as all the other views within Revit. Even though drafting views present only 2D information, they are still tied parametrically to sheets, so all the references are dynamic and coordinated.

To create a new drafting view, follow these steps:

1. From the View tab in the Design bar, choose the Drafting View tool.

2. In the dialog box that appears, enter a name in the Name field (Figure 21.1) to name the view. This is the default name that will appear when the drafting view is placed on a sheet in the drawing set.

FIGURE 21.1
Making a new
drafting view

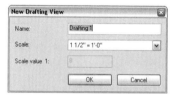

3. Using the Scale drop-down list, choose a scale.

4. Click OK. A new node, Drafting Views, is added to the Project Browser. This new drafting view is primed for either drafting a new detail or importing existing CAD details. This essentially creates a blank sheet within Revit for you to begin drafting (or importing) 2D details.

Importing and Linking CAD Details

It is common to have details from manufacturers you'd like to include in your drawing set, or you may have standard details from an office detail library that need to be included in your documents. What if all these files were created in a 2D CAD application? As we discussed earlier, you can easily import these 2D details into Revit to be used and reused across many BIM projects.

FIGURE 21.2
The Import/Link
dialog box

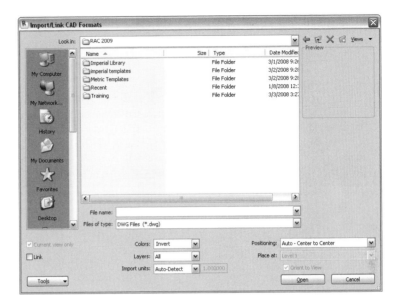

To see the types of files you can import into Revit, choose File ➢ Import/Link to open the dialog box shown in Figure 21.2. The Files of Type pull down menu contains all the file types you can import into Revit:

Category of File	Typical Extensions
CAD formats	.dwg, .dxf, .dgn, .sat,.skp
Images	.jpg, .bmp, .pgn, .tif, .jpeg
Revit	.rvt
Link DWF Markup Set	.dwf
IFC	.ifc

Later in this chapter, we'll see how each of these file types is used, but first we want to make sure you understand the distinction between importing and linking.

Linking vs. Importing

Use linking when you have files that will update throughout the design process. Imagine having a person in your office who does nothing but develop 2D details and who is working in parallel with you. The details will update constantly, and you'd want to link them so that you get the latest states of those details. By linking the file into Revit, you ensure that the information will update as the source file changes. Linking creates a *live* connection to a file. This allows you to work on the linked file and then have the Revit model update to reflect the changes in the link. This behavior is similar to an XREF in AutoCAD.

Use importing when you are looking to embed the CAD file within the project file itself. This might be of value if you need to slightly modify imported details, because unlike linked files, imported files can be exploded and thereby modified.

LINKING CAD FORMATS

The ability to link one file into another can be helpful in a collaborative environment. Perhaps someone on your team—a person working on details within your office or an external consultant—is working in a CAD environment while you build up the project in Revit. Linking lets you have their latest work updated in your Revit model. If you import without linking, you get a static file that will not update if changes are made to the original file. When you link, however, it's possible to always get the latest state of the DWG by updating the link within Revit. From the Manage Links dialog box shown in Figure 21.3 (choose File ➤ Manage Links), you can reload, unload, import, or remove a CAD link—or see what is already loaded.

FIGURE 21.3

The Manage Links dialog box

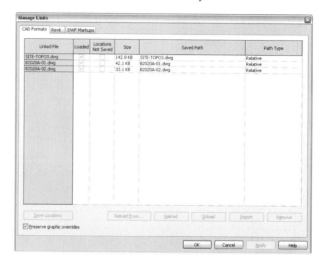

IMPORTING OR LINKING CAD FORMATS

Site plans, consultant files, and details or drawings done with CAD technologies on prior projects are all examples of information you may want to link or import into Revit. This isn't limited to 2D data; you can link 3D files as well. The data you import or link into your model can be view specific (imported in *one* view only—using the Current View Only import option—as opposed to all views). Start by opening the view into which you want to bring data. Choose File ➤ Import/Link ➤ CAD Formats. The CAD Formats tab in the Manage Links dialog box includes additional options. You can link or import five types of CAD files in 2D or 3D in Revit:

Extension	Types of Files
.dwg	Files made from AutoCAD or other applications that can export to this industry standard format.
.dxf	Drawing Exchange Format files. Most software packages can write to DXF in addition to their native format.
.dgn	MicroStation native files.
.sat	Standard ACIS text files; many modeling and fabrication applications can write to this file type.
.skp	SketchUp native files.

The Link option in the Import/Link dialog box gives you the option to import your file or link it. There are some pros and cons to each option:

Linking   If you link a file, any changes made in that *original file* will be apparent in the Revit file in which it was linked. If your office or team workflow has personnel who are dedicated to working solely on details in a 2D environment, they can continue creating and changing the details in CAD and you can update the link to reflect the changes automatically. You can also manipulate the linked file through the Manage Links dialog box (select File ➤ Manage Links). *You cannot modify a linked import since modifying any information requires explosion of the import, which the linking method does not allow.* However, you do have the ability to manage the layers in the linked file and turn them on or off as needed, without the ability to explode the file. This can all be done through the Visibility/Graphic Overrides dialog box.

Importing   An import is not tied to an external file, which means you can modify the CAD drawing directly in Revit by first exploding it. Once an import has been exploded, the import ceases to exist and everything becomes part of the Revit file. The import is translated to a bunch of lines and they are just that: lines, with no inherent intelligence. In addition, any line names or styles from the CAD layers that have been imported will become Revit line styles.

OPTIONS DURING IMPORT/LINK

There are a series of options that you will need to understand and set during the Import/Link function depending on the result you would like to achieve with the file that will be imported or linked:

Current View Only   Selecting the Current View Only check box brings the linked or imported file into *only* the view that is currently active. It's not always desirable to see your CAD files in all the views in your model. A site plan, as an example, doesn't have to be seen in all floors of a building—just the site view and maybe the Level 1 (ground floor) view. More often than not, you'll want to select this check box, because you will likely want to limit the number of views in which your linked files appear. If you import with this option unchecked, the file will be visible in *all* of your views (and any new views you create), plus you'll need to manage the visibility via the Visibility/Graphic Overrides dialog box or view templates. If you import your CAD file into one view and would like to have it in others, you can easily copy and paste it from one view to the next.

Layers   The Layers drop-down menu gives you the option to import or link in all the layers, only the layers that were visible at the time the CAD file was last saved, or a selected group of layers from a secondary dialog box. (Layers are a DWG-based naming convention. Revit allows the same functionality with levels from DGN drawings.)

Layer/Level Colors   The default view background in AutoCAD is usually black, so the colors used in AutoCAD are easily visible on a black background. When you import a DWG file into Revit, which has a white background, many of the colors usually used in AutoCAD (yellow, light green, magenta, cyan) are often difficult to read. Revit recognizes this issue, and in the Layer/Level Colors section of the Import/Link dialog box you have the option to invert these colors. You also have the option to not change the colors or to convert them to black.

Scaling   The Scaling section of the Import/Link dialog box allows you to let Revit autodetect the scale at which the imported or linked drawing was created and convert accordingly. Or you can do the detection manually and apply a scale factor.

 **Real World Scenario**

TIPS ON IMPORTING CAD DETAILS

It is not possible, or always desirable, to communicate the entire project in 3D. At times your work-flow will demand using 2D graphics from a past project, manufacturer's library, or other resource. In order to optimize the performance of imported CAD files in your model, it is strongly recommended that you delete all the superfluous data in the CAD file *before* importing it into Revit. Here are some general tips to help your workflow:

♦ If your import contains hatches or annotations that you don't intend to use in Revit, delete them before importing.

♦ Import only one detail at a time so you can take better advantage of Revit's ability to manage sheet referencing. If you have a series of details organized in a single CAD file that you'd like to import into Revit, isolate each detail, save it as a separate file, and then import.

♦ Consider annotating in Revit and removing the annotations from CAD. This can help keep consistency in your documents. If you use arrowheads or leaders in your CAD file, they will import into Revit (when exploded) as polylines. Consider drawing the arrows within Revit.

♦ Make sure you import the CAD details using the proper line weights, colors, and styles. Check your CAD file before importing into Revit to make sure it is consistent with your office's standards.

♦ Every time you explode a CAD file in Revit, you add objects to the database. An inserted CAD file is one object. An exploded CAD file in Revit consists of many objects—maybe thousands of objects. For best performance, it is recommended to explode CAD files as seldom as possible. If you must explode the CAD file, make sure to remove any unwanted or unneeded linework from the file in CAD before inserting it and exploding it in Revit.

IMPORTING CAD DETAILS

The ability to communicate and share design intent with others is critical to any design and documentation process. With that inevitably comes the need to translate or transfer ideas, drawings, and information from one format to another to create a versatile workflow. Revit recognizes this need to share information and allows you to import and export CAD-based drawings to aid in communication.

If you're working with someone who produces details using only CAD, you can incorporate their work into your Revit model without disrupting the workflow.

IMPORTING A CAD DETAIL

It is common to have a library of existing details that can be used for many projects. This example demonstrates the process of getting these details into a Revit project using a DWG file you can download from the book's companion web page (www.sybex.com/go/masteringrevit2009):

1. Create a new drafting view. Under the View tab, choose Drafting View and give it a custom scale of 1:1.

2. Import/link your CAD detail. In this example, we have a typical doorjamb detail that is already noted and dimensioned. Choose File ➢ Import/Link ➢ CAD Formats and select the following options:

- ◆ Link (instead of Import)
- ◆ Colors: Black and White
- ◆ Positioning: Automatically Place Center to Center (the default)

3. Choose detail B2020A-01.dwg (located on this book's companion web page), and click OK.

This will import your CAD file into a new drafting view. Now you can change your view scale to match the scale in which you'd like your detail to be displayed. For our detail, we will change the scale to read 1½″ = 1′-0″.

It seems that in our detail the wall tags are unnecessary. Unfortunately, we did not delete them in CAD as recommended before we linked the file.

So, we have two options. One is to address the issue in CAD—delete them there and re-import/link the file. For this exercise we'll assume that's not feasible. Our second option is to manage the layers of the import/link within Revit and simply turn off the layer on which the tag has been placed. As mentioned earlier, you can do this using the Visibility/Graphic Overrides dialog box. You can also do it through Revit's graphical interface. Selecting the detail will expose some tools in the Options bar. We have already discussed the Explode options. Now let's focus on the Query tool.

Clicking the Query button allows you to select elements in the import and discover what layer they belong to. With Query enabled, you can select any of the lines or hatches within the CAD file. Choose the border of the wall tag. This gives you the dialog box shown here, which tells you the entity, its layer, block name, and style:

The Import Instance Query dialog box also allows you to delete the entity (which we do not want to do here) or hide the layer. Choosing Hide in View turns that layer off in this view. It can be turned on again with the Visibility/Graphic Overrides dialog box.

Now, the detail is complete, and we can drag and drop the drafting view from the Project Browser onto the sheet A350 Details. If we need more details from CAD files for our project, we will simply create more drafting views.

The finished detail is shown here. The imported detail on the printed sheet should be indistinguishable from the details created in Revit.

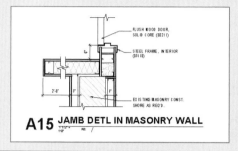

Creating 2D Detail Components

Creating two-dimensional detail components is a powerful way to utilize Revit's parametric capabilities to produce the necessary details that will help tell the contractor how to create the building. Learning how to leverage these detail types can make the detailing process much more efficient.

Detail Groups

Detail groups are similar to blocks in AutoCAD. They're collections of 2D graphics (drafting lines, other detail groups, 2D content) and represent details that you'll probably want to use again and again in the same or different views. A classic example is wood studs or blocking. You can easily and quickly set up a Revit group and use that group over and over in the model. Doing so helps control consistency throughout the drawing.

To make a detail group, create the detail elements you'd like to group and then group them using Edit ➤ Group ➤ Create Group. When you're prompted for a group name, name the group something clear rather than accepting the default name Revit wants to give it (Group 1, Group 2, and so on).

To place a detail group, use the Detail Group button in the Drafting tab. Then use the Type Selector to choose which group you want to place.

Detail Components

Detail components are 2D families that can be parametric or static. They're similar to detail groups but are created in the Family Editor and can be designed with dimensional variation built right into the family. In other words, a full range of shapes can be available in a single detail component. Because they are families, they can also be stored in your office library and shared across projects easily.

To add a detail component to your drawing, select the Detail Component button in the Drafting tab and select one from the Type Selector. If you already have preloaded detail components in your project, you can search in your Project Browser, under Families/Detail Items.

If you need to load a new component, click the Load button in the Options bar and browse to the Detail Components folder. Revit has a wide range of common detail components in the default library.

To make a new detail component, use the Family Editor and choose File ➤ New Family ➤ Detail Component.rft. From there you begin drawing lines, as you did in the project, adding parametric values, and then save the file as an independent family that can be loaded into any project.

Masking Regions

A masking region is designed to hide portions of the model that you don't want to see in a certain view. This tool is known to many users of AutoCAD as the "wipeout" tool and serves to make white masks over graphics or text. The masking region places a 2D shape on top of the model that masks elements behind it.

☐ Masking Region

To add a masking region to your view, click the Masking Region button on the Drafting tab of the Design bar.

This takes you to a Sketch mode where you draw a closed loop of lines over the area you wish to mask. When you draw a masking region, you can assign the boundary lines different line styles—check the Type Selector to make sure you're using the line style you want. One of the line styles that is particularly useful for the Masking Region tool is the Invisible line style. It allows you to create a borderless region, which is ideal if you want to mask an element in the model. A masking region is shown in Figure 21.4. Note that masking regions do not mask text, annotations, or leaders.

FIGURE 21.4
(A) The detail without a masking region; (B) portion of the detail covered with masking region; (C) masking region with invisible line style outline

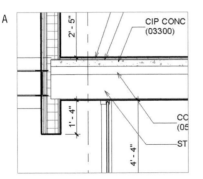
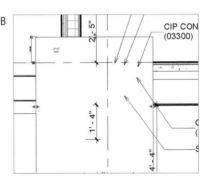
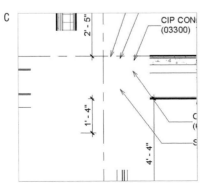

Creating a Repeating Detail Element

Repeating details are a common occurrence in architectural projects. Masonry walls, metal decking, and roof tiles all comprise a series of repeating shapes that can create a repeating detail. Most of these elements aren't modeled as 3D components in Revit but are repetitions of symbolic detail components.

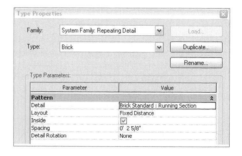

You create repeating details in Revit by clicking the Repeating Detail button on the Drafting tab of the Design bar.

This tool takes a single detail component and arrays it along a straight line at regular intervals. Open the Element Properties dialog box of any available repeating detail (click the Repeating Detail command and look in the Type Selector) to get a feel for how it's laid out. Figure 21.5 shows the Type Properties dialog box for a repeating brick detail. When you select a repeating detail, the Type Selector is activated so that you can select any repeating detail you've already loaded in the project. Repeating details are similar to families: they have types and properties. If you don't have the repeating detail that you want loaded, it's easy enough to create one on the fly. All you need is a detail component that you wish to repeat.

FIGURE 21.5
Repeating detail
type properties

Placing a repeating detail is similar to drawing a line: it requires one click as a start point and a second click as an end point; repeating 2D geometry will fill in between the clicks. Take these steps to create a repeating detail:

1. Click the Repeating Detail tool on the Drafting bar.

2. Click the Properties button next to the Type Selector.

3. Click Edit/New.

4. Click Duplicate.

5. Give your new repeating detail a name.

6. Select a detail component to repeat.

The default repeating detail in Revit is a running brick pattern. If you look at it in detail, it consists of a brick detail component and a mortar joint (Figure 21.6).

FIGURE 21.6
Single brick detail
component

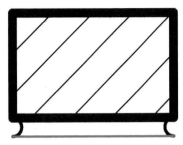

When you create a repeating detail layout, measure the distance between the beginning of the brick and the end of the mortar joint to understand the module on which the detail will repeat. When the detail component is inserted, it acts like a Line tool and allows you to pull a line of brick, as shown in Figure 21.7. This line can be lengthened, shortened, or rotated like any other line. The line will automatically expand in length based on the module of the repeating detail.

FIGURE 21.7
A repeating brick
detail

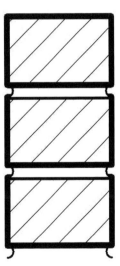

Detail Component Properties

If you're making a repeating detail from a component that isn't loaded in your project, you won't find it listed next to the Detail parameter in the Type Properties dialog box. You first need to load that detail component in your project and then make a repeating detail component with it. The Properties window will then look like Figure 21.8.

FIGURE 21.8
Repeating detail
type properties

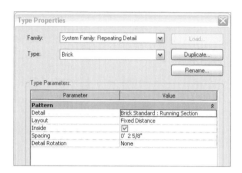

Detail   This allows you to select the detail component to be repeated.

Layout   This offers four different modes:

> **Fixed Distance**   The path drawn between the start and end point when the repeating detail is the length at which your component repeats at a distance of the value set for spacing.
>
> **Fixed Number**   This mode sets the number of times a component repeats itself in the space between the start and end point (the length of the path).
>
> **Fill Available Space**   Regardless of the value you choose for Spacing, the detail component is repeated on the path using its actual width as the Spacing value.
>
> **Maximum Spacing**   The detail component is repeated using the set spacing, and the number of repeated components is set so that only complete components are drawn. Revit creates as many copies of the component as will fit on the path.

Inside   This option adjusts the start point and end point of the detail components that make up the repeating detail.

Spacing   This option is active only when Fixed Distance or Maximum Spacing is selected as the method of repetition. It represents the distance at which you want the repeating detail component to repeat. It doesn't have to be the actual width of the detail component.

Detail Rotation   This allows you to rotate the detail component in the repeating detail.

Creating Custom Line Types Using Repeating Details

You can use the Detail Component tool to create custom line types (lines with letters or numbers for various services such as fireproofing, rated walls, fencing, and so on). Note that when you create a detail component, you can't use text for the letters; you need to draw the letters or text using lines. Figure 21.9 shows the creation of a detail component in the Family Editor and the final result used as a repeating detail in the project environment.

FIGURE 21.9
Repeating detail:
(A) in Family Editor;
(B) used in project

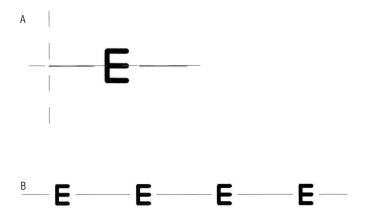

Miscellaneous Line Tools

The Insulation tool, Filled Region tool, and Show/Remove Hidden Lines tool serve important specific purposes in your drawings.

INSULATION

Designed as a symbolic representation for batt insulation, the Insulation tool works just like any other line type. When it's selected, two blue grips appear at the ends and let you change the length. The element properties of the insulation include two editable parameters:

Width This parameter is used to control the thickness (referred to as *Width* in Revit) of the insulation that is used. The Width parameter is also available in the Options bar when Insulation is selected (see Figure 21.10).

FIGURE 21.10
Insulation can be
created simply
in Revit in two
clicks defining
the length. The
Width is set in the
Options bar.

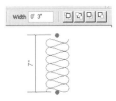

Insulation Bulge to Width Ratio This parameter is used to control the density of the circles used in the insulation line and can be set in the Options bar when the tool is selected. In most cases, you'll have two lines representing the space in the wall where the insulation needs to fit. Revit allows you to place the insulation using the centerline of the insulation as a location line.

FILLED REGION

☐ Filled Region

The Filled Region tool is a drafting tool for making 2D hatch shapes and solid fill shapes. It can help you color surfaces or areas for graphic representations during the conceptual or design-development phase. It is also a useful tool for showing materials at finer levels of detail.

A filled region consists of a boundary—which can be created using any line style—and a fill pattern, which fills the area defined in the boundary. Figure 21.11 shows a filled region with a tile hatch pattern used to show tile in an interior elevation. In lieu of a complex stacked wall condition for bathroom walls, a filled region with a 4″ square model pattern is used to represent tile on the restroom wall. While this will not be reflected in any material take-offs, it is a quick way to create interior elevations.

FIGURE 21.11
Filled regions used
for quick graphic
representation of
tile wall finish

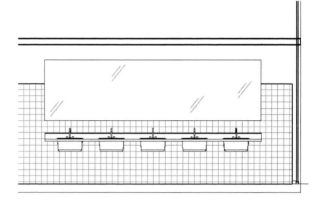

Filled regions can be either transparent or opaque to show or hide what is behind them. Figure 21.12 shows two filled regions—the left one is opaque and the right one is transparent—and how they interact differently with a model component.

Filled Region Type Properties

Filled region type properties define how a fill appears, including pattern, pattern color, and transparency (Figure 21.13). Notice that the boundary lines of the region are not part of the type properties and are defined independently when the sketch is edited. To change the line thickness of the boundary, select the pattern, click Edit in the Options bar, and change the line pattern in the Element Properties dialog box or from the Type Selector.

For each filled region that has a different pattern, transparency, or other variation in appearance, you need to make a new type. Remember that type properties propagate to all instances of the type, so making a change to one type may affect many instances in many different views. If you want to make a filled region that uses a new pattern, be sure to duplicate an existing type before you start changing type parameters.

FIGURE 21.12
Opaque and
transparent filled
regions

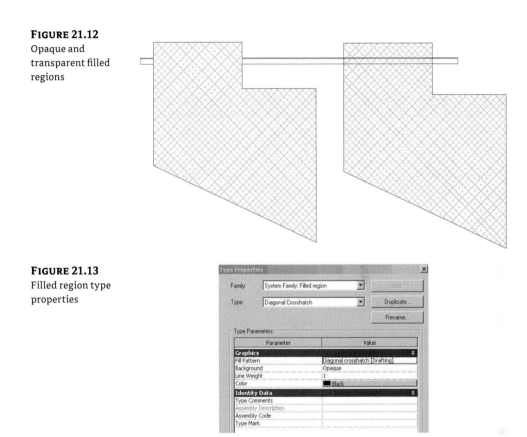

FIGURE 21.13
Filled region type
properties

Filled regions can use both drafting and model patterns, making them a flexible and handy tool for 2D workflows. As previously noted, drafting patterns are patterns that will maintain their separation distance relative to the printed sheet. Model patterns will maintain their separation distance relative to the model element. To describe this further, let's use two examples. If you were looking to use a cross-hatched pattern of lines, as in the example earlier for 4″ restroom wall tile, you would want to use a model pattern. The pattern would be set to 4″ and it would maintain a 4″ pattern regardless of what scale the drawing was set to. So, the pattern in a ⅛″ scale drawing will appear twice as tight as in a ¼″ scale drawing. In the example of a drafting pattern, you would want to use this in places where graphical consistency is more important than actual dimension. So, when creating a filled region that represents rigid insulation, the pattern might be set to a ⅛″ grid. It will always print as a ⅛″ grid regardless of what scale the view is set to. Just keep in mind that all of these are truly just 2D shapes with no 3D BIM characteristics.

SHOWING HIDDEN ELEMENTS WITH DASHED LINES

In visual communications between architects and engineers, when one element obscures another, the hidden element is usually graphically represented with dashed lines. Often, just a portion of an element is hidden. In the 2D CAD application, it can take a lot of manual work to make this possible: you will need to explode the block representing the element that has to be half-hidden, and split lines so that one portion remains solid and another converts to dashed.

Revit has a special tool, Show Hidden Lines, for recognizing obscured elements and representing the portion that is hidden with dashed lines while still maintaining the complete object.

1. Select the Show Hidden Lines tool in the toolbar.

2. Click the element that obscures the object.

3. Click the element that is obscured. The hidden portion of the element becomes dashed. If an element is obscured with more than one element, keep repeating this operation until you get the desired look.

When you relocate or delete the obscuring element, the hidden element responds intelligently to those changes. Figure 21.14 shows an I-beam hidden by another beam. Figure 21.15 shows the results after using the Show Hidden Lines tool when the second beam is selected as an obscuring element and the I-beam is selected as an obscured element.

FIGURE 21.14
An I-beam hidden
by another element

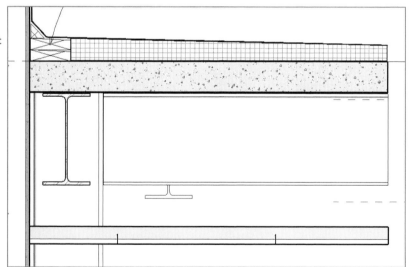

FIGURE 21.15
The I-beam after using the Show Hidden Lines tool

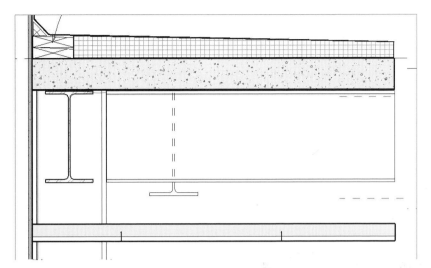

The Show Hidden Lines tool applies to 2D and 3D elements in all possible combinations: detail over detail, detail over model, model over detail, model over model. Right next to the Show Hidden Lines tool is the Remove Hidden Lines tool, which resets the graphical display of the elements so they look as they did before you applied the hidden line behavior.

Linework

While Revit does a lot to help you manage your views and line weights automatically, it does not cover all requirements all the time. Sometimes you wish some lines to punch out and be stronger while keeping others thinner. This is where the Linework tool comes into play; it allows you to choose any existing line style and apply it to individual edges of elements with a few clicks of the mouse.

To use this tool, click the Linework button in the toolbar, choose a line style from the Type Selector, and begin picking lines in any view. Once a line style is selected, you can continue selecting lines to override. To change the length of the new Linework that has been applied over the existing model element, use the blue grip controls. Figure 21.16 shows an unaltered elevation of a window and the finished view.

FIGURE 21.16
The outer boundary of the window with linework applied

Before...

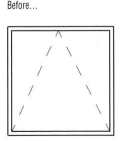

After...

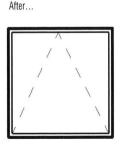

Using Callouts

Callouts are just one other view type in Revit. They are used extensively in plans and sections to indicate a more detailed view of various conditions in any type of construction document package. Figure 21.17 shows two callouts in a wall section.

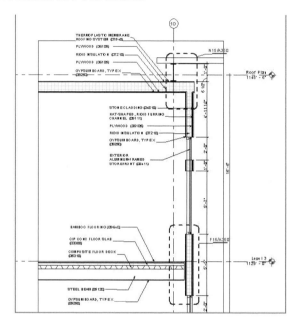

In Revit, there are two types of callouts you can choose when creating new details: one for floor plans and one for details.

Depending on the type of callout you select, it will appear under different folders in the Project Browser. Choosing a floor plan callout will add a new view under Floor Plans in the Project Browser called Callout of *view name*.

Choosing Detail Callout will add a new view under the Detail Views (Detail) heading. The subsequent view will be by default named Detail 0, Detail 1, Detail 2, and so on (Figure 21.18). For the ease of finding and organizing your views, be sure to choose the correct view type when creating a new view.

FIGURE 21.18

The new detail views in the Project Browser

Adding Information to Your Details

Now that we have discussed many of the tools used for detailing within Revit, let's step through a detail and see how these tools can be put to practical use. For this exercise, a detailed wall section will be used to illustrate a workflow. In the Foundation file found in the Chapter 21 on this book's companion web page, Detail A14 on Sheet A301 (Figure 21.19) is a wall section at the east entry. Since we already discussed dimensioning and keynoting previously (Chapter 19), those items have already been added to the view.

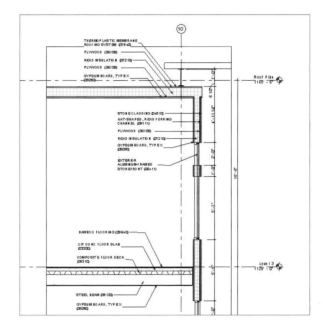

In this view, the only things that have been added are text notes and dimensions. The rest of the model graphics were automatically generated the moment the section was placed in plan view. To add more detail, start by adding callout detail bubbles at each major construction joint, as shown in Figure 21.20. In this wall section we need four 1″ = 1′-0″ callouts:

- The roof/wall condition (*Roof Detl, Typ*)

- The wall/floor condition capturing window heads and sills (*Floor Detl, Typ*)

- The exterior storefront (*Head @ Storefront, typ*)

- The interior storefront (*Storefront Head Detl*)

Using the Callout tool in the Detail tab of the Design bar, create callouts in those locations. You can make the first three callouts by choosing the Callout tool and drawing a rectangle around the detail condition. New views are automatically generated and can be renamed as shown in Figure 21.20. For the interior storefront, a different method will be used that takes advantage of an existing CAD drawing by referencing it rather than making a new view of the model.

FIGURE 21.20
Detail A14/A301

To do this, follow these steps:

1. Create a new drafting view. Under the View tab in the Design bar, choose Drafting View and give it a custom scale of 1:1.

2. Import your CAD detail in the drafting view. In our example, we have a typical doorjamb detail that is already noted and dimensioned. Choose File ➤ Import /Link ➤ CAD Formats. Choose the detail B2020A-02.dwg found in the project directory and select the following options in the dialog box:

   ◆ Link

   ◆ Colors: Black and White

   ◆ Positioning: Automatically Place Center to Center (the default)

   Click OK to link the file into the view.

3. Change the view scale to match the scale in which you'd like your detail to be displayed. For this detail, set the scale to 1″ = 1′-0″.

4. Right-click the view in the Project Browser (in the Drafting Views node) and rename it **Storefront Head Detl**.

5. With the drafting view for our detail created, you can now reference that detail when making new callouts. Choose the Callout tool from the View tab, but do not draw a rectangle in the view yet. First go to the Options bar and check the Reference Other View box. This activates a drop-down menu from which you can choose the detail named *Storefront Head Detl* (Figure 21.21).

FIGURE 21.21
Choosing the
*Storefront Head
Detl* detail from the
drop-down menu

6. Once the reference view is selected, draw the callout at the interior storefront head condition.

7. Keep the views related by dropping them onto sheet A350.

Embellishing the Wall Section: The SIM (Similar) Condition

With the four details identified, we can begin to add embellishment to the wall section. Beginning with the most recent detail you cut—the Storefront Head Detail condition—you need to do a little work in the section to match the CAD detail we plan to use for this condition. Because this is a unique condition we will see in only this one detail, we have decided not to model the assembly but to create it using the drafting tools. In Figure 21.22, you can see the current condition of the modeled wall section (A) and what we have imported as a similar condition (B) for our CAD detail.

FIGURE 21.22

The callout (A) and its reference 2D detail (B)

A

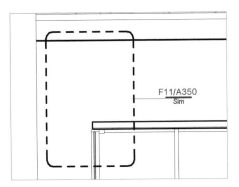

B

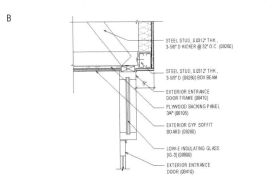

F11 **Storefront Head Detail**
1" = 1'-0"   REA14/A301

You need to show the soffit and head condition at a lower level of detail within the wall section to make the detail work. As you can see in the detail and wall section shown in Figure 21.22, the ceiling's condition above the window head does not coincide. The wall section needs to be edited to match the detail by extending the ceiling so that it overhangs 5" (13cm).

1. In the section view, select the ceiling and choose Edit from the Options bar. Revit will alert you to the fact that the ceiling cannot be edited in the section view and will let you switch views (Figure 21.23). Choose Reflected Ceiling Plan: Level 1.

2. The Reflected Ceiling Plan (RCP) view will open, and you'll be placed in Sketch mode to modify the ceiling over the entry. According to the detail, we need a 5″ (13cm) projection past the head of the door for the design (Figure 21.24).

3. Finish the sketch and return to the section view to see the effect (Figure 21.25).

FIGURE 21.23
Choosing a new view to edit the ceiling

FIGURE 21.24
Editing the ceiling in plan view

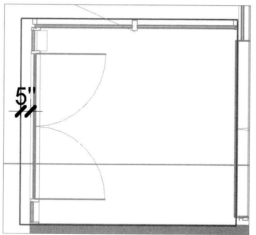

FIGURE 21.25

The edited ceiling in section

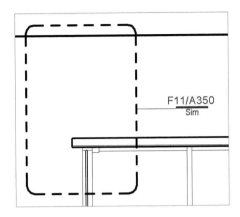

Adding Detail Components

Looking at the detail, we need to add some blocking and 3½″ (8cm) studs. This type of element is likely to be used throughout the model, so it makes sense to use a detail component rather than draw them as individual 2D lines. There will be some strictly 2D drafting lines to add later to this wall section for sealant and flashing, but first we add architectural elements like blocking.

To represent the blocking we need above the window head, we'll use a premade detail component from the Revit library and load it in the project.

1. Navigate to File ➤ Load from Library ➤ Load Family, browse to Detail Components ➤ Div 06-Wood and Plastic ➤ 061100-Wood Framing, and choose Nominal Cut Lumber-Section.rfa.

2. A list of predefined types will show up at the bottom of the dialog box. Since we are not sure which type we want right now, select a few of them by holding down the Ctrl key and selecting 2 × 4, 2 × 6, and 2 × 8 from the menu (Figure 21.26).

FIGURE 21.26

Choosing detail components

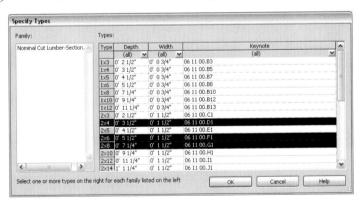

3. This loads the family and the types into the project. Click the Detail Component button and choose 2 × 4 from the Type Selector. Insert it in the general location shown in Figure 21.27. We can then rotate it and move it into place.

FIGURE 21.27
The finished detail
component

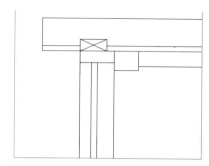

DETAIL COMPONENTS AND PROJECT TEMPLATES

If you find you are inserting the same detail components over and over again, load them into your
project templates and make them readily available when you begin any new project.

EDITING A DETAIL COMPONENT

For printing purposes, the line weight for the default 2×4 detail component is too thick and needs
to be adjusted. Because elements are so simple to modify, you will find yourself changing stock
components to better meet the needs of your office.

1. For the 2×4 we just inserted, the line weight of the border can be changed by selecting the
   component and clicking the Edit Family button in the Options bar. You'll get a confirmation
   dialog box before going directly to the Family Editor to change the component. Click Yes.

2. To change the thickness of the border, first hover the cursor over the element to see what
   it is. You'll see that this component is made of a masking region and some detail lines.
   Select the masking region (Figure 21.28) and click Edit in the Options bar.

FIGURE 21.28
The masking
region

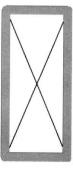

3. This opens the Sketch mode of the masking region. Select the boundary lines and use the Type Selector to change them from heavy lines to medium lines. These line styles are actually subcategories of the Detail Items category, which you can access from the Object Styles dialog box shown in Figure 21.29 (select Settings ➤ Object Styles). That is where you can change the line color, thickness, or pattern of the object style.

FIGURE 21.29
Viewing the line object styles

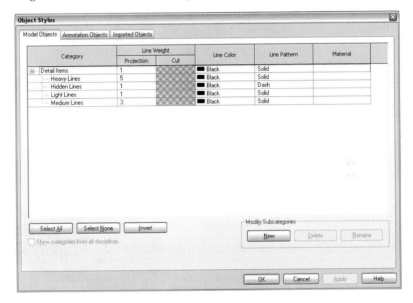

4. Clicking Finish Sketch completes the masking region. Clicking the Load into Projects button loads the changes back into the model. You will be prompted to override parameter values of existing types. Click Yes, as we have not modified any of the values for this type.

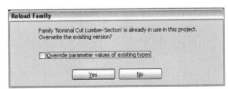

The blocking displays much better, as you can see in Figure 21.30.

FIGURE 21.30
(A) Before changing the detail component line weight.
(B) After changing the detail component line weight.

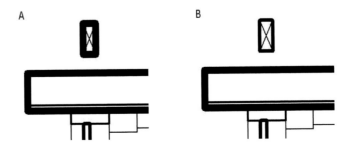

5. Moving the component into place, we use the fact that it was created as a masking region to cover some unwanted gypsum board above the door head.

Don't forget that you have the ability to see multiple views at once. By closing all views but this detail and the wall section, you can choose Window ➤ Tile View and see both views side by side (Figure 21.31).

FIGURE 21.31
Callout view (left);
Drafting view
(right)

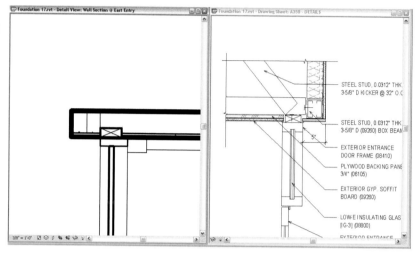

6. The same procedure can be followed to place metal studs in this detail by loading them from Detail Components ➤ Div 09-Finishes ➤ 09100-Metal Support Assemblies ➤ 09110-Non-Load Bearing Wall Framing ➤ Interior Metal Studs-Section.rfa. Place them in a similar location to what is shown in the drafting detail view.

There is one more element to add before we begin drafting lines to finish the detail. There is a ¾″ piece of plywood backing over the entryway in our detail that does not appear in our wall section. We can represent that with a filled region.

1. Select the Filled Region tool from the Drafting tab.

2. Set the boundary lines to thin lines using the Type Selector and draw a box ¾″ tall on top of the gypsum board that will represent our plywood.

3. Choose Region Properties in the Sketch tab in the Design bar; select Edit/New and then Duplicate. Name it **Plywood**.

4. Change the background to opaque.

5. Set the fill pattern to Wood_Glu-LamBeam pattern (Figure 21.32).

6. Click OK to complete the new type; then finish the sketch of the filled region.

FIGURE 21.32

Select a plywood-style fill pattern

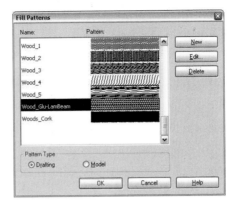

FINISHING THE DETAIL

To complete the detail, use detail lines from the Drafting tab. These lines are similar in nature to most drafting applications. Choose the Detail Lines tool, select the desired line type from the Type Selector, and start drafting. By using some thin, medium, and hidden lines, you'll be able to quickly complete this detail (Figure 21.33).

FIGURE 21.33

The finished ceiling detail

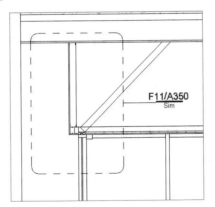

Embellishing the Wall Section: The Model Details

Now that you have explored the use of some of the drafting tools on an atypical detail, let's look at some of the more common detail types when there is no SIM (Similar) condition and only the model data. You will begin this exercise by working on the detail in the same wall section at the floor of Level 3. This will allow you to work on the head and sill conditions of the windows at the same time. The detail right out of the model looks like Figure 21.34 (again, using the tiled views to see both conditions at same time). Since Revit is parametric, you can actually work in either the detail or wall section as the model changes will occur everywhere. For this exercise, you will be working directly in the detail with the understanding that the wall section will also be updated. The finished detail we are going to create is shown on Figure 21.35.

REUSING DRAFTING LINES

Design is cyclical in nature. Just because you think that in one phase you won't need more than one detail of a condition doesn't mean it will remain like that throughout the rest of the project. We have found using Copy and Paste and filtered selections together useful.

For instance, if we needed to make another detail similar to the drafting lines we just drew in this exercise, we can make a selection box over a large portion of the detail and then use the Filter button in the Options bar to filter out all but the drafting lines and detail components, basically taking the detail with us when we click OK and add a simple Ctrl+C to copy.

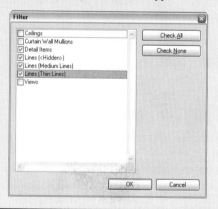

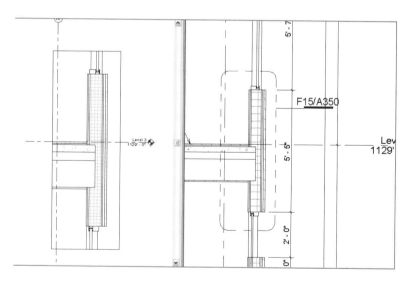

FIGURE 21.34
The detail and the related wall section

FIGURE 21.35
The finished detail

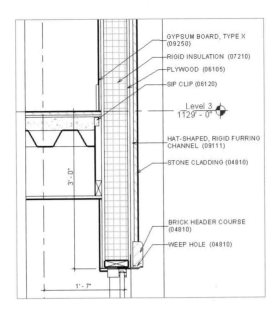

The first thing you need to modify for this detail is the floor condition. Since we are using a structurally insulated panel (SIP) for the skin, we cannot have the floor slab bearing on the insulation inside the panel. In reality, the panel will be clipped and hung from the side of the floor system. We need to pull the edge of the floor back to 1½″ from the inside face of the wall. You can do this the same way you fixed the ceiling in the detail earlier.

1. Select the floor and choose Edit from the Options bar.

2. When prompted for a view to edit the floor in, choose Floor Plan: Level 3.

3. Move the slab edge on that wall 1½″ from the inside face of the wall and click Finish Sketch.

The revised detail should look like Figure 21.36.

FIGURE 21.36
The modified floor

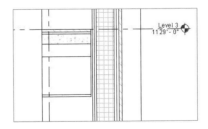

Obviously, we can't run gypsum board back behind the slab and we still don't have a clip to hold up our SIP panel. However, based on all the wall sections and details we have, it doesn't make sense to create this out of detail lines, and there is no default Revit detail component for this condition. So we will make our own detail component to reuse when we encounter this condition.

1. Navigate to File ➤ New ➤ Family ➤ Detail Component.rfa. Here in the Family Editor, you will make a quick and simple detail component.

   Detail components are like any other family in Revit. Once added to the drawing, you can always reedit and update them with new information.

2. Let's start with a masking region to hide the gypsum board on the SIP wall system. Select the Masking Region tool from the Family design bar.

We need to create a masking region ⅞″ wide × 1′-8″ long to hide that run of gypsum board. We also want to make three sides (top, bottom, and right) medium lines because they will represent cut material and the left line an <Invisible Lines> type to keep it hidden. Invisible lines will show as gray when drawn in Sketch mode but will not appear at all and hide other lines (if on top) in model views. Since we have overextended the masking region, we need to cut the top and bottom lines. Notice in Figure 21.37 that the left line of the rectangle appears as gray because it is an invisible line.

FIGURE 21.37
Creating the masking region

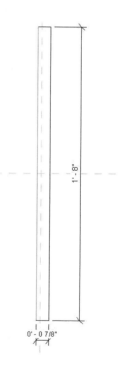

Masking regions are very precisely shaped elements. The reason this masking region is ⅞″ wide is to cover the ⅝″ gypsum board, taking into account that the line weight of the gypsum adds thickness to the line; this needs to be covered by the masking region.

1. Now you need to draw the clip. For the moment, the clip can be represented by a simple filled region box 2″ high and 1″ wide, located 1½″ down from the top of the finished floor

on the right side of the masking region. Using medium lines, create the box as shown in Figure 21.38.

2. Before finishing the sketch, choose Region Properties and select the Aluminum pattern. Click OK and then choose Finish Sketch. The finished component should look like Figure 21.39.

FIGURE 21.38
Creating the filled region

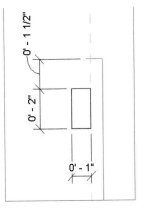

FIGURE 21.39
The finished component

3. If you choose Load into Projects right now, it will load with a default name of Family1, which is not highly descriptive and not easy to relocate when you want to use it again. Take a moment and save the detail component to your project directory or library as SIP Clip.rfa. Now load it into your project, as shown in Figure 21.40.

4. Because you have chosen a detail component, you have the added benefit of being able to keynote it, which you will need for the detail. Because this is a 2D, view-specific element, you'll use the User keynote.

A NOTE ON ANNOTATION CROP REGIONS

The annotation crop region is designed to allow you to crop annotations separately from model elements. Be aware that if your annotations extend past the annotation crop region in any way, they will not appear in the view. The annotation crop region needs to be outside the entire keynote or other annotation for it to appear in the view.

FIGURE 21.40
The component
placed in the view

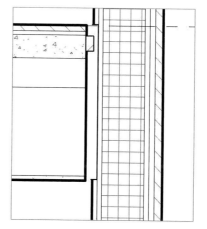

To finish cleaning up this floor condition, a few more items can be added by placing base molding around the floor/wall condition and then bringing the ceiling finish of the second floor to meet the wall and the floor finish to meet the wall.

ADDING THE BASE MOLDING

For this detail, it is easiest to make a simple detail component. This will make it reusable and taggable—something you wouldn't get with mere lines.

1. Choose File ➢ New ➢ Family ➢ Detail Component.rft.

2. Draw a simple 6″ × ½″ rectangle using a masking region and thin lines.

3. This time, add a parameter to the base in case we want to change the height later in the design. Add a dimension to the base from top to bottom (Figure 21.41). Selecting the dimension, choose the Label drop-down from the Options bar and choose <Add Parameter...>.

4. In the Parameter Properties dialog box, name it **Height** and choose Dimensions from the categories (Figure 21.42).

FIGURE 21.41
Adding a
dimension to
the baseboard

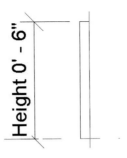

FIGURE 21.42
Setting the height
as a parameter

If you choose to change the height of the base later in the project, you don't have to reedit the family. It is simply a matter of changing the parameter:

1. Save the file to your project director or library as 6in base.rfa and load it into the project.

2. Place it in the model (Figure 21.43).

FIGURE 21.43
Creating a param-
eter to control the
baseboard height

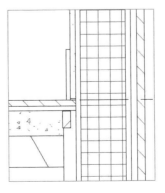

MODIFYING THE FLOOR AND CEILING CONNECTIONS AND DETAILS

In Revit there are a number of ways to create a detail. There is not one best solution, just as there is not one way to build something on site. We chose to cut the floor back from the wall and use filled regions to re-extend the floor to meet the wall condition. We could have left the floor connected to the wall and simply used masking regions and filled regions to give the appearance of the floor structure being pushed back instead of the floor finish being pulled forward. We chose our particular method because our contractor had requested the use of the Revit model to do some concrete take-offs, so we needed to make sure the volume of concrete was as accurate as possible. Overextending or underextending that condition, even by a few inches, would have changed the volume of concrete reported in the schedule. Before choosing a direction for a workflow, it's a good idea to understand all the uses for your model (beyond documentation) and keep those in mind when making these kinds of decisions. In the following steps, we'll walk through the techniques we used.

We cut the floor line back to make room for our clips, but now we need to finish out the subfloor and finish floor to meet the wall. To do this, we are going to create some simple filled regions.

1. Using the Filled Region tool on the Drafting tab, draw a rectangle at the ceiling of the second floor to close the gap for the gypsum board under our blocking (Figure 21.44).

FIGURE 21.44
Using a filled region to graphically clean up a detail

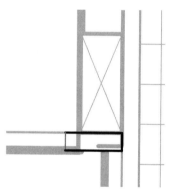

2. When drawing the filled region rectangle, be sure to define the left line as invisible so it appears continuous with the gypsum ceiling. Make the top a thin line, the right medium, and the bottom wide. Be sure to overextend the invisible line a bit to compensate for the line thicknesses.

3. Open the Region Properties dialog box, set Type to Gyp, and click OK. Verify that the filled region is opaque so we don't see the model geometry through the filled region.

Once you click OK, the filled region looks like Figure 21.45. Somehow, it is not quite right. This is because the filled region and the detail components layer can rest on top of the others. You need to resolve their order by pushing the gyp filled region to the top.

By selecting the filled region, you will be given some layering options in the Options bar. In order from left to right, these are Bring to Front, Send to Back, Bring Forward, and Send Backward. Select the first button, Bring to Front, and the gyp hatch will appear correctly on top of the detail component (Figure 21.46).

FIGURE 21.45
The filled region
does not look
correct yet.

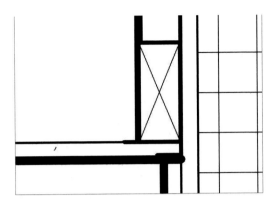

FIGURE 21.46
The graphically
modified condition

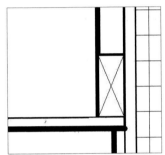

Using this same example, you can build simple filled regions for the floor extension under our base. The floor condition looks like Figure 21.47.

FIGURE 21.47
Floor detail
condition

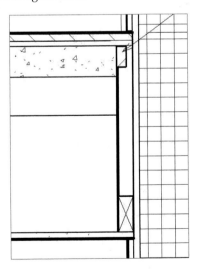

ADDING REPEATING DETAILS

To finish this portion of the detail, you need to add material definition to the floor. The concrete has been poured on top of a corrugated metal deck, but it is not possible to add a corrugated metal material pattern as part of our floor materials, so we want to make a repeating detail in the form of our 3¾″ corrugated deck. While the structural engineer will show this in detail, we still want to show the material architecturally in our sections and details. First, we need to make the profile of the deck.

1. Create a new detail component using the steps described earlier. You need to make a corrugated metal deck 3¾″ tall to mimic the height in the model (Figure 21.48). There are a couple of ways to make the decking in the Family Editor. One option is to simply use lines. Another option would be to create it as a masking or filled region. It's a matter of personal preference, and one might be better for your project workflow than the other. We only need to draw a section that can be repeated. When you're finished, save the detail component as Mtl Deck.rfa to the project folder or library.

FIGURE 21.48
Metal deck detail
component family

2. Once the detail component is loaded into the project, click the Repeating Detail button on the Drafting tab of the Design bar. You will need to make a new type, so click the Properties button next to the Type Selector, choose Edit/New, and choose Duplicate. Name the new type **Metal Deck**.

3. In the Detail field, choose Mtl Deck from the drop-down menu.

4. Change the Detail Rotation field to 90 Degrees Clockwise.

5. Start drawing the element as you would a line.

Since this is a 2D element, you will also want to go back to the wall section and add the corrugated deck to all of the appropriate locations. The finished deck in detail and section looks like Figure 21.49.

NESTING DETAIL COMPONENTS

You have a couple more conditions to address to finish this detail. The head and sill conditions for the storefront system will probably not be affixed directly to the rigid insulation as the detail currently shows. You'll need to add some blocking and flashing to those locations. Again, since you will want to reuse this condition in other views, you can make it with a detail component. This time, however, you are going to add a more significant level of detail to the detail component before inserting it into the model. You'll do this by nesting detail components within each other. Let's start with the storefront head condition.

1. Start a new detail component family using the process described earlier.

2. Notice that in the Family Editor, there is a Detail Component button, similar to the one in the project environment. Click it and load a 2 × 6 from the same path we used earlier (Detail Components ➤ Div 06-Wood and Plastic ➤ 06100-Rough Carpentry ➤ 06110-Wood Framing ➤ Nominal Cut Lumber-Section.rft).

3. Use the horizontal reference plane to simulate the top of the storefront. We want to place our blocking ¼″ back from this line, centered on the vertical reference plane.

4. Using a masking region, draw a shim under the 2 × 6.

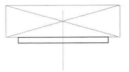

5. Once you click Finish Sketch, because this is a shim, you'll want to show it with a single diagonal line through it. Using the Lines button, you can add a detail line to make this condition.

FIGURE 21.49
The metal deck in section and detail

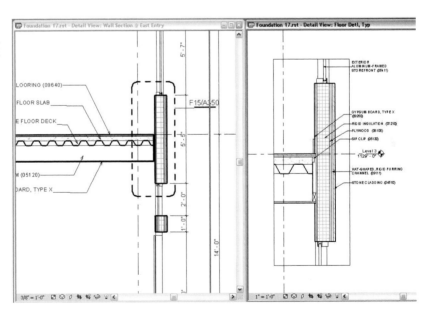

To help finish the window on the exterior, place a stone header over the window opening. This can be created with a filled region and a new region type for stone. The stone head is 6″ high by

2¼″ wide and placed 1⅜″ from the edge of our 2 × 6. (This measurement isn't arbitrary: it is taken directly from the wall condition in the model.) Figure 21.50 shows your current progress.

FIGURE 21.50
Nested detail
component

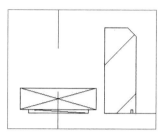

1. We need to add a steel lintel for the stone header. Revit does not provide these as default detail components, so we can create one with a filled region.

2. Save this condition as SIP Storefront Head.rfa and load it into the project.

Our detail component inserted into the model looks like Figure 21.51.

FIGURE 21.51
Inserting the
nested detail
component

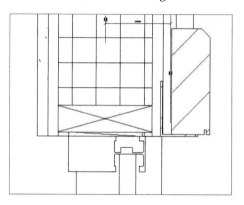

Using simple detail lines and filled regions, you can add any necessary flashing and gypsum returns to the window. The completed head condition should look like Figure 21.52.

FIGURE 21.52
Final detail at head
condition

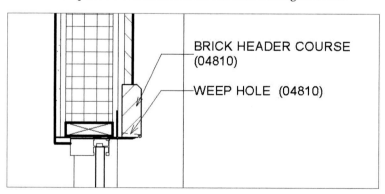

FINISHING THE DETAIL

By combining the simple tools used in the previous sections, you can easily complete this detail. As we have mentioned throughout this chapter, many of the elements that were imported or created need to be made only once. All of the families and detail components you built in the course of this detail are now available in the project for use in other views. The finished detail looks like Figure 21.53.

FIGURE 21.53
The completed detail with the nested component

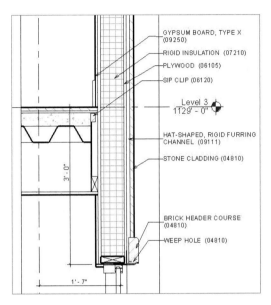

GYPSUM BOARD, TYPE X (09250)

RIGID INSULATION (07210)

PLYWOOD (06105)

SIP CLIP (06120)

Level 3
1129' - 0"

HAT-SHAPED, RIGID FURRING CHANNEL (09111)

STONE CLADDING (04810)

BRICK HEADER COURSE (04810)

WEEP HOLE (04810)

3' - 0"

1' - 7"

You can easily mimic this process to complete details for the other conditions.

GENERAL TIPS FOR DETAILING

When detailing, keep these ideas in mind:

◆ If your model is detailed to begin with, the detailing will go much faster because you will need to add fewer components. However, you must strike a balance and not make an overly detailed model, because that will negatively impact performance. When wondering what to model or what to make into a detail component, ask yourself the following questions:

   ◆ Will I see or use this in other views in the project?

   ◆ Will it affect other aspects of the project (like material take-offs)?

   ◆ How large is it? (Our office tends to use 2D detailing for details 1½˝ and smaller.)

- ◆ If you insert User keynotes and in the Options bar choose the option for Free End for the Leader, you can drag the notes around anywhere on the view and add as many as you'd like. The benefit of this method is that it allows you the consistency of *always* pulling your notes from the keynote text file. And if the note is updated in the text file, it will be updated in the project.

- ◆ Remember to import only CAD files that you have cleaned up first. Only bring in what you need, to reduce your overhead and keep file performance optimal.

- ◆ There is no limit to how much information you can place in a detail component. If you will be seeing similar conditions throughout the model, put in as much as you can.

- ◆ You can use detail components at every scale within the model, so it is a great way to draw the information only once.

- ◆ If the lines describing geometry merge when printed into a single graphic element, there's little point in showing that geometry at that scale. You might consider making the model simpler.

The Bottom Line

Revit provides a full set of detailing tools to help you create finished construction documents.

Create drafting views   Not every drawing or view in Revit is created with model elements. Some of the views on sheets will be made solely with 2D drafting views. Knowing how to create and use these views is critical to any documentation package.

> **Master It**   Keeping views hyperlinked together is a key benefit to using Revit. How do you draw simple, 2D details in Revit but still keep them parametrically linked to sheets?

Import and link CAD details   Even if you've been using Revit for years, you will need to import 2D geometry from an old library of standards or manufacturer drawings. Understanding how to do this effectively will keep you from having performance issues with your model.

> **Master It**   Your office has a huge repository of standard details. How do you reuse details drawn in CAD in a Revit project?

Create 2D detail components   Detail components can be used again and again within a model to graphically show in 2D different typical building components. Mastering these will result in enhanced productivity when you work on a project.

> **Master It**   Detailing is a process of adding more granular layers of information and graphics to the model and view. What tools would you use to add 2D detail?

Chapter 22

Advanced Detailing Techniques

Chapter 21 covered the transition from design to construction documentation. Now you will continue building your skills and learn some additional techniques for more detailed construction documentation. As your project experience grows, your library and detailing capacity within Revit will grow with it. This chapter is dedicated to tools and functionality that you can employ after you become comfortable with creating details in Revit. By building your library and knowledge of detailing workflows, you can cut down the time you spend detailing, leaving more time for design.

In this chapter, you learn how to do the following:

◆ Create 3D details

◆ Add detail components to families

◆ Reuse details from other Revit projects

Creating 3D Details

As building designs become increasingly complex and the construction industry continues to specialize its assembly methods, it has become imperative that information be communicated effectively between designer and contractor. A technique for showing construction assemblies that goes way back in the history of architectural representation is the use of 3D detail drawings (Figure 22.1) that show a sectional cut through the building in a 3D format (axonometry or perspective). This type of drawing has been used to convey detail and constructability information rather than create a multitude of abstract sections and elevations. In recent years, this documentation technique has fallen into disuse because it has been difficult or time consuming to re-create such axonometric details in a 2D CAD-based environment.

With Revit's 3D modeling capabilities, it is easy to create such 3D details. By using 3D views and the *orient to other views* command, you can quickly generate 3D views that focus on a construction condition. These can be for constructability or to demonstrate critical building concepts. Figure 22.2 shows a detail of a sustainable solution employed on the Foundation project. In this sectional axonometry, we are able to demonstrate many of the green building concepts simultaneously while also showing dimensional depths of the sunshading and daylighting systems.

FIGURE 22.1
Hand-drawn
perspective detail

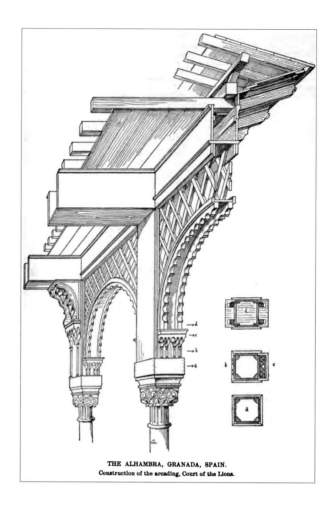

THE ALHAMBRA, GRANADA, SPAIN.
Construction of the arcading, Court of the Lions.

FIGURE 22.2
Sectional axonom-
etry showing de-
tails of sunshading
solution

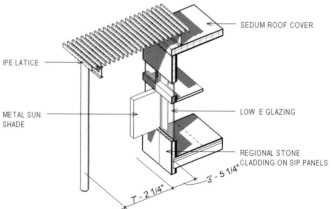

IPE LATICE

METAL SUN
SHADE

SEDUM ROOF COVER

LOW E GLAZING

REGIONAL STONE
CLADDING ON SIP PANELS

7' - 2 1/4"

3' - 5 1/4"

Creating these kinds of 3D details in Revit is quick and easy to learn and do. There are two methods you can apply:

◆ Turning on the Section Box tool, and then adjusting the section box to focus on your detail.

◆ Orienting a 3D view to an existing view. This method adjusts a 3D view to resemble a chosen 2D view. You can then rotate the cropped 3D view to any new orientation. This method is much more practical because it is much faster to generate details and because the size of the detail condition is focused on an existing, pre-established scope.

3D Details: Enabling a Section Box in 3D View

Take the following steps to enable the Section Box tool in a 3D view:

1. Start by creating or opening a 3D axonometry of the building. To create one, click the Default 3D View button in the toolbar at the top of the screen. Be sure to rename your view something unique.

2. Open View Properties and enable the Section Box parameter. A large section box that surrounds the entire model will appear in the view. This is a 3D clipping box that allows you to cut the model from six directions.

3. By clicking and dragging the blue arrows, you reduce the size of the box to a clip that represents the detail area you wish to indicate (Figure 22.3). Manipulating a section box can take a bit of trial and error, regardless of your experience with Revit. Later in this chapter, we'll discuss some ways to make this quicker and more accurate.

FIGURE 22.3
Drag the blue arrows to resize the section box.

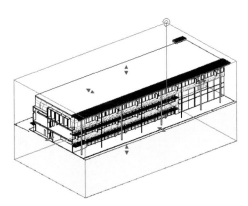

3D Details: Orienting to View

An alternative for creating a 3D detail is to use the technique of *orienting* the 3D view to an existing view. Do this by first creating a detail callout where needed, let's say in a wall section, as shown in Figure 22.4. Then, give the callout detail view a recognizable name by selecting the callout and editing its element properties. Call it **Sunshade Detail**. Having a recognizable name will be useful for finding the detail later, as the number of details in a project can become quite large.

FIGURE 22.4
Creating a callout
detail in section

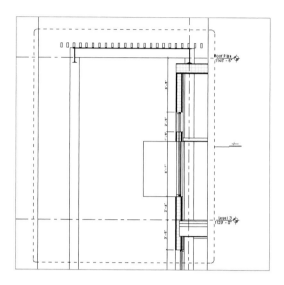

1. After creating the callout, open the default (3D) view by selecting the 3D view icon from the toolbars and choose View ➤ Orient ➤ To Other View, and select our Sunshade Detail from the list (Figure 22.5).

FIGURE 22.5
Selecting a view
from View ➤
Orient ➤ To
Other View

2. Once you click OK, the 3D view reorients and appears in the form of a section—just like the detail callout. However, this is a 3D view. By orbiting this view (using either the ViewCube or combining Shift and the middle mouse button), you'll be able to visualize the sectional detail in 3D (Figure 22.6).

FIGURE 22.6
Top: Oriented to
other view, detail
looks like a flat sec-
tion. Bottom: The
rotated (orbited)
view reveals a
3D detail.

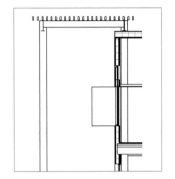

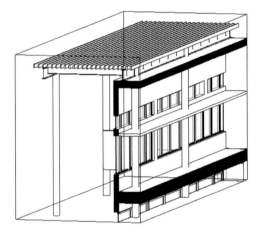

The crop boundaries of the 3D detail correlate to the boundaries of the callout, so there is no
need to alter the section box as was the case with the first method of creating 3D details. The
depth of the section box in this view is defined by the depth of the view you have used for orientation. You can edit the section box using the grip controls as you would any other section box.
To hide the section box lines but keep it cutting the model, select it, right-click it, and choose
Hide in View ➤ Elements from the context menu.

CREATE A 3D VIEW OF ONE SINGLE FLOOR

Reorienting to view is also practical when you want to isolate an entire floor and show a 3D view on
one floor only.

Adding Annotations to the 3D Detail

Even if 3D details are much richer and clearer in information than 2D details, they still need annotations (dimensions, text notes) that add to the graphical explanation. To add dimensions to a 3D view, you first need to define a work plane where the dimensions will appear, as they cannot float free in the 3D space; they need a surface (work plane) to be drawn against. (See Chapter 6 for more on work planes.) We are showing our dimensions at Level 3 in the view. Click the Work Plane button on the toolbar and select Level 3 from the drop-down menu. Using the Work Plane Visibility toggle, you'll be able to see what plane the dimensions will be created on, as shown in Figure 22.7. Dimensioning along this plane is similar to dimensioning in any plan view. By selecting parallel elements, you can apply the necessary dimensions.

FIGURE 22.7
Setting and visualizing the work plane in a 3D view

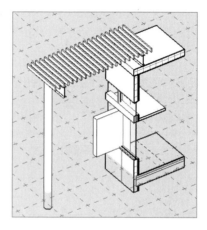

You can then begin to add text notes to this view. Note that in a 3D view, you can add text and dimensions but not keynotes or tags. Also, be careful *not to rotate the 3D view* after you apply your notes. Text is placed perpendicular to the view you have created and will maintain that relationship. Rotation of the 3D detail after you've added text will result in leaders or text not pointing to the desired building elements.

By turning on the shadows in the view, you'll be able to give the view a better sense of depth, as shown in Figure 22.2 earlier.

Be sure the ground plane is enabled in the Sun and Shadows Settings dialog box for the view. A good choice is either Sun from Top Right or Sun from Top Left. See Chapter 15 more detail on presentation techniques.

Adding Detail Components to Families

In the previous chapter, we investigated how to add levels of detail to a detail component by creating one detail out of a number of separate components, making it easier to replicate a detail condition across various project views. Again, this idea of drawing it once and repeating that detail easily is a core theory in Revit. Combining these principles, we can extend this theory to family creation, where you can turn details on or off within a family depending on the Level of Detail view setting.

When we explored the notion of the view detail earlier, we mentioned the ability to show different levels of detail at coarse, medium, and fine settings. Combining this with detail components, you can embed details for typical conditions directly within the families themselves, so that you do not need to add more drafting elements to your views. Figure 22.8 shows the same window family in coarse, medium, and fine views. All of the detail has been added to the family itself, and the detail is activated by switching between the levels of detail. Note that the fine detail level in this series shows the actual CAD detail from the manufacturer's website and is not modeled in detail in 3D. Modeling this level of detail within the Revit model would be a huge performance killer. Because the detail was created as part of the window family, this highly detailed information will be displayed each time any section or plan view is made that cuts through the window. This method enables you to have the level of detail always present in the drawings without having to give up performance or over-model the building.

FIGURE 22.8
The same awning window shown in
(A) coarse,
(B) medium, and
(C) fine view

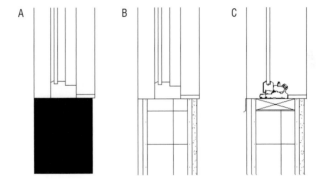

Building this type of window family is not complicated, but it does require a bit of knowledge about how a family is created and assembled. For our purposes, we are going to assume that the window family has been created correctly and we are simply trying to apply more detail to the window itself so that it displays much more detailed information in fine view. Since we have already created the sill condition, let's now focus on creating the head detail.

Adding Details to a Window Family

Start by locating the family within the project using the Project Browser. Select it and choose Edit Family from the right-click context menu. The interface changes to the Family Editor environment. Open a section view (or if there is no section view, create a new one using the Section tool). The sectional view of the window family head looks like Figure 22.9.

FIGURE 22.9
Sectional view of the window family head

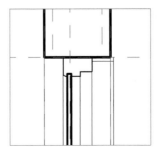

In Chapter 21, we discussed how to insert default Revit detail components. For the blocking above the window head, we can load a detail component from the Revit default library.

1. Navigate to File ➤ Load from Library ➤ Load Family. Then, once the browsing window opens, you will need to follow the path Detail Components | Div 06-Wood and Plastic | 06100-Rough Carpentry | 06110-Wood Framing and choose Nominal Cut Lumber-Section.rfa.

2. Insert this component 1¼″ (3cm) from the exterior face of the wall. This ensures that it ends up in the right location relative to the wall it will be inserted into. If this window was going to be inserted into a variety of wall types, you could make the 1¼″ (3cm) dimension a parametric family parameter.

3. Once the component 1¼″ (3cm) is inserted, lock it to the reference plane that is at the window head. This ensures that as window sizes are changed, the blocking moves as well.

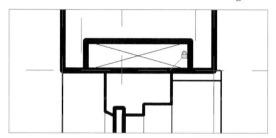

4. Based on the window type, the blocking needs to always be set 1¼″ (3cm) from the front face of the wall, so you can add a constraint there as well. Add a dimension to the left edge of the blocking and the left edge of the wall, and lock it into place (Figure 22.10).

FIGURE 22.10
Adding a dimension and locking it into place

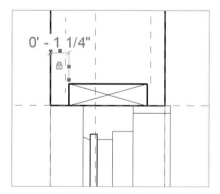

5. We want to create a new detail for the window head showing an added level of detail at the head condition. For this, we've downloaded the manufacturer's standard CAD detail and we want to incorporate it into our window. To begin, you need to create a new detail component using this CAD detail. Choose File ➤ New ➤ Family and choose Detail Component to open the Family Editor.

6. To import our CAD detail, follow the steps we discussed in the previous chapter. Choosing File ➤ Import/Link ➤ CAD Formats will bring up the dialog box to insert the CAD detail. This time, you'll want to choose slightly different options than we did last time. Accept the defaults for all but the following:

◆ Select the Black and White option in the Layer/Level Colors area.

◆ In the Import or Link area, change the Layers setting to Select (we want to pick the layers to import).

The dialog box will look like Figure 22.11. Click Open.

FIGURE 22.11
Importing CAD detail into a detail component

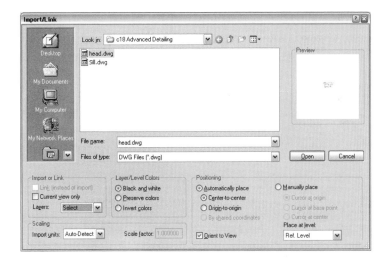

7. A dialog box similar to Figure 22.12 opens, asking you to choose the correct layers to import. Hatch is something we do not need, and typically, manufacturers are fairly good about keeping their layer management for CAD details simple and easy to understand. We want to deselect any layers that reference hatch or any layers we know we will not need as part of our detail. Deselect the box and click OK.

FIGURE 22.12
Selecting layers to import

8. With the detail inserted, position it using the reference planes in the detail component. While you can reposition things within the Revit families fairly easily, these reference planes provide invisible snap references when loaded into a project—making placement and dimensioning easier and more specific. Because the top of the head and the face of the glass are key to this detail, use those to place the imported file, as shown in Figure 22.13.

FIGURE 22.13
Aligning the reference planes

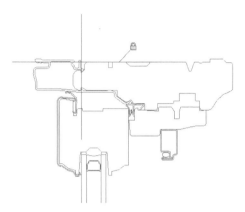

9. You are nearly done with this family. Because this detail has such a simple construction (very few lines) and we have removed the hatch, we are going to explode the detail. Select the detail and click the Full Explode button on the Options bar. This converts the detail into Revit detail lines and allow you to modify some of the line weights and the detail geometry to better fit the family. A detail with too many lines or lines that are very, very small (< 0.3mm) will be deleted when the detail is exploded.

10. With the detail exploded, you can now remove the glazing, which is only partially drawn. We have modeled glazing in the family itself, so including it in the detail as well is a bit redundant. Select the lines shown in Figure 22.14 and delete them. Instead of exploding the detail, another way to do these same steps is to go into the original CAD file and remove the lines and layers you don't need before inserting the detail into a Revit detail component.

11. The last thing you need to do before saving the model is change the line weights. Select all of the lines in the detail by creating a selection box around them, and while they are selected, choose Detail Items from the Type Selector. You could keep all of the lines the way they had been imported from CAD and change them to the appropriate line weight using Settings ➢ Object Styles. However, this is a little cleaner for future tweaks.

FIGURE 22.14
Select the lines for
the glazing and
delete them.

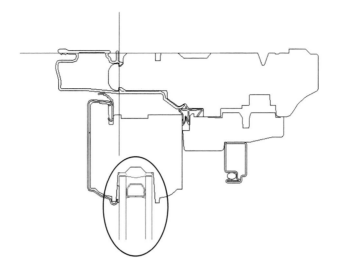

12. Save the detail as Head.rfa in your project folder or library and import it into the window family using the Load into Projects button.

13. Back in the window family, place the detail component over the existing extruded window frame and lock it to the reference plane that defines the head opening (Figure 22.15).

FIGURE 22.15
Detail component
in window head
detail

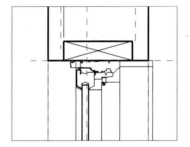

Visibility Settings

With the detail components in place, you can now establish rules for when each of them will be visible when loaded into the model. You might not want to have your details shown in coarse or medium scales of 1:200 or 1:100, but you might wish to show them in 1:50 or 1:20 scale. In the next steps, visibility settings will be applied to some of the model elements and detail components that will link these items to the detail level setting. For this family, we need the detail component to be visible only in fine levels of detail and the 3D solid form window frame sweep to be hidden in fine levels of detail.

1. Still in the Family Editor environment, select the detail component. In the Options bar, click the Visibility button. Clicking this button opens the Family Element Visibility Settings dialog box shown in Figure 22.16.

FIGURE 22.16

The Family Element Visibility Settings dialog box

2. This dialog box is as simple as it looks, but it's quite powerful at the same time. By deselecting any of the options here, you limit the visibility of components to specific detail levels. For this example, clear the Coarse and Medium check boxes and click OK.

Now you will notice that a funny thing happens—or actually, doesn't happen. If you change the visibility of detail levels, the detail component still appears, although now drawn in a gray tone, as if it ignores the visibility settings you just made. You can quickly confirm that you deselected those view levels by checking the visibility settings again. Don't worry. You have done nothing wrong. In the Family Editor, for editing purposes, you will always see everything in each view detail level regardless of its setting. Only when you load the family in the project environment will you really understand if you have modified the visibility correctly.

The goal was to see the highly detailed representation of the window when switching to fine detail view. At the same time, you don't need to see the original 3D window frame because the linework of the frame will overlap with the linework of the newly inserted 2D detailing components. You need to turn off the visibility of the window frame from within the family when in fine detail view:

1. Select the 3D sweep created to represent the window frame and click the Visibility button in the Options bar. The dialog box that appears is the same as you saw previously when you selected the 2D detail component, but since this 3D element appears in more views, you now have more visibility options (Figure 22.17).

FIGURE 22.17

Visibility settings for a 3D element

2. You still want to see the window frame in plan, reflected ceiling plan, and elevation, so leave those boxes checked for now and just uncheck the When Cut in Plan/RCP and Fine boxes, mirroring the settings for the detail component above.

CONTROLLING VISIBILITY IN PLAN VIEWS

The same rules can be applied to plan views using this technique, so that the sweep does not show up in fine levels of detail. By clearing the Plan/RCP check box, you turn off the visibility of the window frame in plan view as well.

We will now add a trim. Use a masking region to cover the trim piece above the window frame on the exterior side of the glass. Because the masking region has a boundary, you don't need to have the shape previously drawn to show the lines. Create it on the fly (Figure 22.18). While visually scanning through the manufacturer's product information, we selected a trim piece, but we don't have any Revit or CAD details for it. So, you have two options: make a new detail family and import it or build it on the spot.

FIGURE 22.18
Draw a masking region for trim

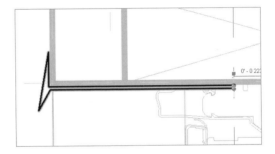

Adding More Information Using Symbolic Lines

At this stage of the detailing process, you need to add sealant, flashing, and trim at the window head. For that you can use symbolic lines. Symbolic lines are 2D lines that are visible *only in the view in which they were added*. An example of the use of symbolic lines would be to represent a door swing in elevation. The dashed lines that represent the hinge points are symbolic lines.

1. Using symbolic lines, add sealant to the detail, as shown in Figure 22.19.

FIGURE 22.19
Adding symbolic lines for the sealant

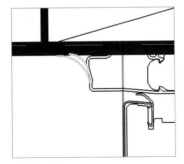

2. Before loading the detail into the project, you need to make sure the visibility of the symbolic lines and the masking region are correct. You cannot change the visibility of those elements simultaneously, so you'll need to select each one independently (choosing the masking region, then the symbolic lines) and set the visibility to show them only in fine detail views.

 **Real World Scenario**

DOORS AND SYMBOLIC LINES

Doors are typically modeled in a closed position but shown as open and with a door swing direction in plan view. To get this dual representation, in the Family Editor turn off the visibility of the door panel (extruded solid form) in the plan view and draw the 90-degree open door panel and its swing using symbolic lines. Symbolic lines can be controlled using the same visibility settings available for detail components and the solid model elements in the family. You can use the same logic and draw the dashed lines that represent the door opening direction in elevations.

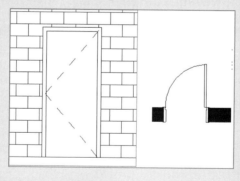

Save the family with a unique name before loading it. Once it is loaded, you can quickly cycle through the various view detail options and see the power of using visibility settings in the family, as in Figure 22.20.

FIGURE 22.20
Cycling through
to different levels
of detail of the
window

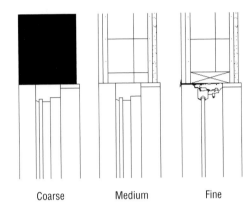

Coarse   Medium   Fine

Imagine that the door has already been modeled and you are adding the lines representing the swing. For that you add the symbolic lines in both plan and elevation to complete the element. When drawing new symbolic lines, use the Type Selector to define the subcategory of the lines.

Reusing Details from Other Revit Projects

There are many times in a project workflow when you want to leverage details already created in other projects and reuse them. So far we have covered how to do this using CAD files from other projects or from manufacturers' websites. This workflow is also possible using details created from other Revit projects. We will explain how to take an active project file and export key details to the library. We'll also discuss how to pull details out of a Revit file and put it into your active project.

Exporting Details from Revit Projects

As you create more and more details in Revit, you will inevitably want to save some of them to your office's standard library so you can reuse them in other projects and save the work you've invested. Saving a view out of a project creates a separate RVT file that contains only that view. There are a couple of ways to do this, either of which will result with the same outcome. First, if you have a 3D model detail that you've embellished with 2D components and would like to save it for future projects, you can save it as a Revit file.

Right-click any view (or schedule) in the Project Browser and choose Save to New File. It might take Revit a minute to compile the view content, but you will be presented with a dialog box asking you for a file location to save the view (Figure 22.21). The default filename will be the same as the view name in the project.

FIGURE 22.21
Exporting a drafting view from Revit

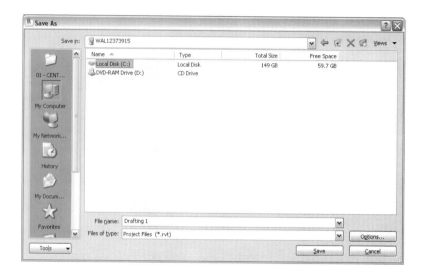

Once the view is exported, it functions like any other RVT file. Opening the view directly will allow you to edit and manipulate any of the elements you exported in the view. You will also see a streamlined version of the Project Browser (Figure 22.22) with only the related views present. These Revit files can be kept in a project library for later use.

FIGURE 22.22
Project Browser only has views appropriate to the ones for the exported view.

The second way to export a view from Revit is to navigate to File ➢ Save to Library ➢ Save Views. This opens a dialog box of all the exportable views from the project file. Here, you can select any number of views to be simultaneously exported into separate library files (Figure 22.23). This is a great way at the end of a project to export all of the detail views you would like to keep in a project library. Select the desired views by checking the appropriate boxes and click OK.

Importing Views into Revit Projects

To import any of these files into a new project, choose File ➢ Insert from File ➢ Views with the project open. This lets you navigate to your library containing your exported details. When you choose the exported detail file, a dialog box opens allowing you to select the view (Figure 22.24).

FIGURE 22.23
Multiple views can be saved as separate Revit files.

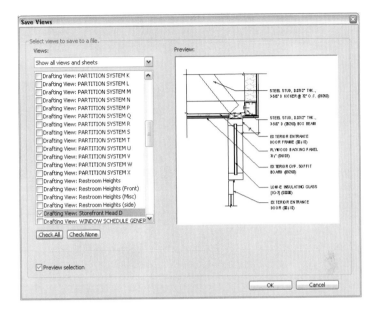

FIGURE 22.24
Selecting a file to import into the current project

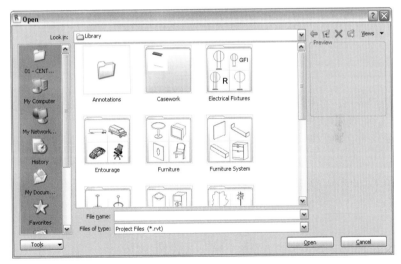

Notice that the view is described by both its location within the Project Browser (Drafting View) and its view name (Storefront Head Detail). Selecting this view and clicking OK merges the view into your current project. The view will appear in the location called out by the view name. In this case, you can find this view in the Project Browser under Drafting Views.

Another way to insert content into Revit is to use the 2D views from exported files. For example, elements of a detail you have in your library may need to be inserted into a view you are working on to augment that view. An excellent use case for this would be if you are creating a new detail and want to reference or use parts of one from another project that is similar but not exactly the same. An example of this might be a new detail of a window head in a concrete opening and you are reusing parts of a detail from a masonry opening. You may only want to use a selected portion of the new view in the current detail you are working on. To import the 2D content into your view, follow these steps:

1. Open the view you want to import into and navigate to File ➢ Insert from File ➢ 2D Elements. This dialog box looks similar to the one for importing the full view but with some slight differences (Figure 22.25).

FIGURE 22.25
Importing
2D content

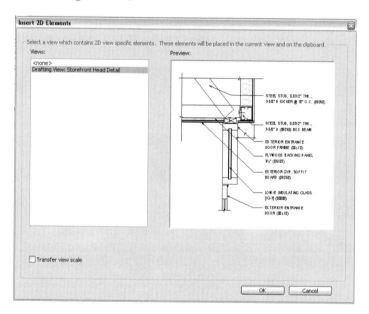

Unlike Insert Views, the Insert 2D Elements dialog box allows you to choose only one view at a time to insert. There is also an option to transfer the view scale with the view elements. Checking this box reconfigures the view you are inserting into to match the view that you have inserted.

2. Select the drafting view and click OK. This brings all of the 2D elements in the selected view into your active view. You can repeat this command multiple times in the same view window if you need to repeat the content.

🌐 Real World Scenario

USING DETAILING TO CREATE A SHAFT OPENING

Within Revit, there are a couple of ways to create an elevator shaft. One commonly used way that we've seen discussed on the community forums is to create a door family that also contains all the elevator information (essentially, a combined door and elevator family in 3D). As a door family, it cuts a hole into a wall and gives proper representation of both the door and the elevator. This will give you your elevator, but then you need to perform a secondary task of editing the floor slab profiles to accommodate the shafts. Although this method will work, it can cause a problem with making sure the floor openings stay aligned between the floors. In our practice, we use a different method, which was used in creating the Foundation model. By using the Opening tool on the Modeling tab, we can create a shaft opening.

This tool allows you to create one vertical shaft through multiple floors. This has a few benefits over the other method:

◆ The openings in the floors will always be aligned.

◆ We can extend this shaft through as many or as few floors as desired.

◆ The constraints of the shaft can be locked to reflect the manufacturer's required size.

◆ Symbolic lines can be embedded in the opening to represent the elevator cab and can be drawn (or imported) to reflect the manufacturer's cab sizes and proportions.

This last point is very valuable within our office. After creating the shaft, we can add the elevator cab plan directly from the manufacturer's CAD detail as symbolic lines.

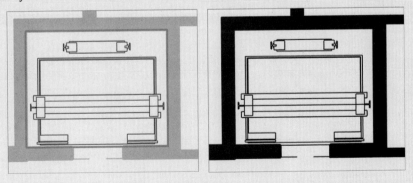

Now, any time we cut the shaft in plan, it will display the elevator cab using these symbolic lines. If our building is complex in form and we need to move our view range up or down, we will always maintain the elevator cab in the plans.

The Bottom Line

Revit's tools for detailing can go a long way toward helping you make construction documents read clearly and concisely. Understanding how to detail within Revit is critical to producing any set of documents.

Create 3D details   3D axonometric details are a great way to demonstrate more complex assemblies and conditions in any document set. Knowing how to create them in Revit will expand the ways in which you can detail.

Master It   Use a 3D axonometric detail to demonstrate constructability in a unique assembly condition.

Add detail components to 3D families   Adding detail components to 3D families can save time by embedding the linework of a detail within the family itself and making it instantly available throughout all the locations that family is placed.

Master It   Create a detail by embedding it into a family so it can be expressed by simply modifying the detail level of a view.

Reuse details from other Revit projects   There are times when details are common between projects. Knowing how to use details from other Revit projects will cut down on your documentation time.

Master It   Use details you created in your other Revit projects.

Chapter 23

Tracking Changes in Your Model

Once a project is under way in the construction document phase, changes to the design need to be tracked. This is typically done on a per-sheet basis by adding revision clouds around elements that are changing in the drawings and documenting those changes in the title block of the sheet. The revision history of each sheet is then tracked in the title block with a number, description, and issue date. In this chapter we will look at adding new revisions, adding revision clouds to sheets, and assigning a cloud to a revision, as well as explore some best practice tips and tricks for performing revisions in Revit. We will also investigate using Autodesk Design Review to pass comments and markups back and forth between team members.

In this chapter, you learn how to do the following:

◆ Add revisions to your project

◆ Understand BIM and supplemental drawings

◆ Use Autodesk Design Review

Adding Revisions to Your Project

Revisions allow designers and builders to track changes made to a set of construction documents. Typically, these changes are recorded after a set of documents has been issued and permitted. Since the construction documents usually consist of numerous sheets, this methodology allows everyone on the team to track and identify which changes were made by whom and when during the construction process those changes were made. The purpose is not only to ensure correct construction but also to create *as-built* documentation at the end of the construction process that can be delivered to owners for their continued use of the building.

In a typical workflow, the revisions will look something like Figure 23.1 when they are created in Revit and issued as part of the drawing set.

To create a revision, choose Settings ➢ Revisions. This opens the Sheet Issues/Revisions dialog box (Figure 23.2). Here you can add, delete, merge, issue, and define the behavior of revisions. Let's go through the major elements of this important dialog box.

FIGURE 23.1

A revision cloud
and triangle-shaped
revision tag

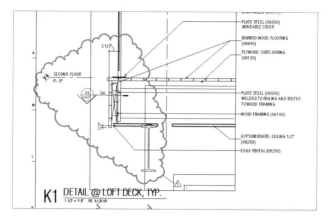

FIGURE 23.2

The Sheet Issues/
Revisions
dialog box

The numbering method You can choose to number revisions *By Sheet* or *By Project*, which is a global project setting. Which method you choose mainly depends on how your firm tracks revisions. By Sheet allows you to have as many revisions as you want within the drawing set, but on each sheet, the revision numbers always start with 1. In the example shown in Figure 23.2, the tags and revision schedule are unique for each sheet, depending on what revisions are on each sheet. The revisions on each sheet are presented sequentially by sheet. This means, you are chronologically numbering/tracking the changes that happened on one particular Sheet, not all the changes that happened in the entire project.

Using By Project will tag your revision clouds based on the global sequence established within the project as a whole. In this example, all revisions with the same issue date within the model would have the same revision number. So you might skip a revision number on any given sheet. You can also set up this numbering method in your default office templates.

The revision table The Sheet Issues/Revision Setting dialog box starts with one default revision already in place, even though you may have not made a revision yourself. This is only so that you have a place to start—no revision will appear in your title blocks until you add revision clouds to your sheet. Each revision has a fixed number of parameters that you can fill out. As you can see in the dialog box, they are fairly self-explanatory and include Numbering, Date, Description, and an Issued check box, in addition to Issued To and Issued By columns and options for showing clouds and tags.

The Add button   To create a new revision, click the Add button. The new revision will automatically be placed in sequential order. Only the sequence number will be automatically updated. You'll need to add your own description and date.

Revision numbering   The Numbering option allows you to number each revision numerically, alphabetically, or not at all. If you choose alphabetic sequence, the sequence is defined in the Alphabetic Sequence Options, in the lower right of the dialog box. Click the Options button to set your sequence and remove letters you don't want (Figure 23.3). By default, an entire alphabet will appear here. The None option will allow you to add milestones—non-numbered entries that appear in revision tables—to sheets without having to add revision clouds.

FIGURE 23.3

Sequence options allow you to use any order of letters you want.

Revisions   To issue a revision, click the check box in the Issued column. This will lock the revision clouds placed on sheets or in views associated with that revision, preventing them from being moved, deleted, or otherwise edited. The parameter values will gray out and become noneditable. This is to guarantee that the clouds and data do not change downstream once you issue a set of drawings.

REVISIONS IN A LIVE MODEL

Keep this in mind: while the clouds can become fixed in the project, the model will not be. So, if you need to maintain an archive of all project phases and of each revision, be sure to export the sheets either as DWF or PDF files as a snapshot of the sheets at time of issuance.

Revision clouds and tags   The visibility of revision clouds and tags related to issued revisions is controlled from this dialog box. As issues occur, you may want to hide clouds or tags of previous revisions. This is where the Show parameter comes in handy. For example, if you've issued a revision and then have additional revisions later and want to declutter your drawing, you can choose to show the issued revision as the tag only (typically a small triangle with the revision number inside it, as in Figure 23.4) or not show anything at all by using the None option (Figure 23.5).

FIGURE 23.4

A revision tag

FIGURE 23.5

Use the Show parameter to hide clouds and tags of issued revisions on your sheets.

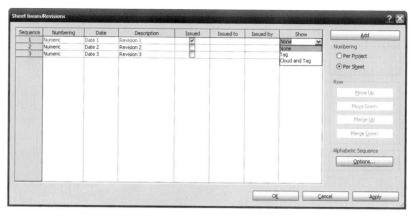

Merge Up or Merge Down If you need to combine two revisions into one, use the Merge Up or Merge Down button. All associated revisions on sheets and tags will update automatically.

TRACKING REVISIONS IN THE TITLE BLOCK

The revision is typically a part of the architectural sheet and is located in a prominent position in the title block to alert readers to changes made in the documents. These revisions can be incorporated into your title block design so they are parametrically read from the sheet into a revision table. To add a revision schedule to a Title block, you will need to go in the Family Editor and make changes in the Title block. Please refer to Chapter 4 to understand how that can be done.

Placing Revision Clouds

To place a revision, open a view in which changes to the model have occurred and use the Revision Cloud tool found in the Drafting tab in the Design bar to mark the location of the change. Once you activate the tool, you will be dropped directly into Sketch mode. Start drawing lines around the area you are calling out as a revision in a clockwise direction. Revit automatically creates a line that makes a *cloud* (or arc), as shown in Figure 23.6. When you're finished creating the cloud, click Finish Sketch in the Design bar.

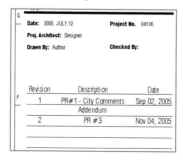

FIGURE 23.6
Clouds are drawn for you as you sketch.

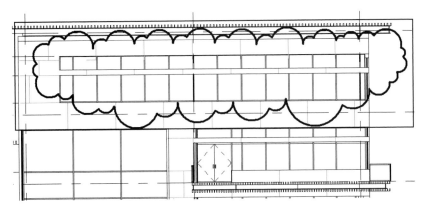

The graphics for revision clouds are controlled in the Object Styles dialog box on the Annotation Objects tab, shown in Figure 23.7.

FIGURE 23.7
You can change the graphic appearance of revision clouds globally using the Object Styles dialog box.

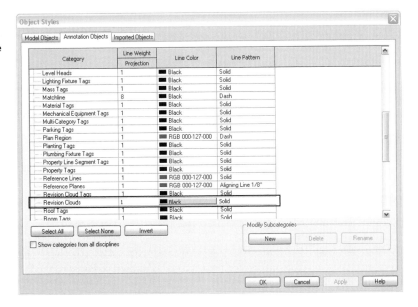

Use this dialog box to make revision clouds have thicker line weights or to change patterns or colors. As we mentioned in Chapter 4, the graphical appearances of your elements should be set up in your office templates in advance to guarantee consistency between projects.

By default, each new revision cloud will be assigned to the last revision in the Sheet Issues/Revisions dialog box found in the Settings menu under Revisions. If you need to change the revision a cloud belongs to, select the cloud and use the drop-down list in the Options bar to change it. This information is also stored in the Element Properties dialog box of the cloud, as shown in Figure 23.8.

FIGURE 23.8

The revision
cloud's Element
Properties
dialog box

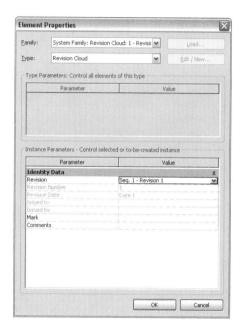

As soon as you have placed a revision cloud onto a sheet, the revision schedule in your title block will update to include the revision number, description, and the date you assigned in the Sheet Issues/Revisions dialog box earlier.

Rev. #	Description	Date Issued
1	Windows Changed	6/15/07

UPDATES IN CUSTOM TITLE BLOCKS

If you are using the default Revit title blocks, updates will happen automatically. If you are using custom title blocks, be sure you've added a revision schedule to them in the appropriate location so you can take full advantage of using a parametric model. (See Chapter 4 to learn how to add revision schedules to your title block families.)

Tagging a Revision Cloud

Revision clouds can be tagged like many other elements in Revit. The tags are intelligent and designed to report the revision number or letter that has been assigned to the cloud. Place a revision tag using the Tag ➤ By Category option on the Drafting tab.

If a tag for revisions is not in your template, you will be warned that no such tag exists in your project. To continue, simply load a revision tag. The default Revit tag loaded by default in Revit is named `Revision Tag.rfa` and is located in the default Annotations folder created with a standard installation (see Figure 23.9).

FIGURE 23.9

Load a revision tag if it's not already part of your template.

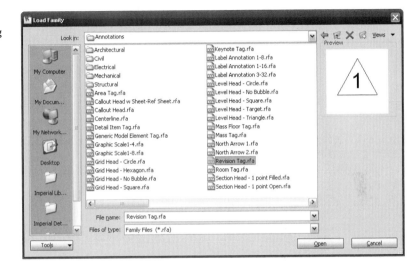

Once you have a tag loaded, you are ready to go. Hover the cursor over a revision cloud and click to place the tag. You will see a preview of the tag prior to placing. Once the tag is placed, you can drag it around the cloud to reposition it, and it will stay associated with the cloud.

CUSTOMIZING THE TAG

Just like the majority of annotations in Revit, you can design your custom revision tag as you need it. You can follow the steps presented in Chapter 4 to make a custom annotation tag from scratch or you can customize the default revision tag provided with the software. To customize the appearance of the default revision tag, select a tag already placed in the project and click the Edit Family button in the Options bar. Editing the tag within the project will take you to the Family Editor, where you can tweak its size, font, and appearance. Once you've made your customizations, save the tag to your local library, then load it into your project and swap it with the default tag using the Type Selector.

DISABLING THE LEADER

You can choose to use a leader line between the tag and the cloud depending on your preference or your office standards. In many cases, the tag just needs to be near the cloud and a leader is not necessary. Disable the leader by selecting the tag and clearing the Leader option in the Options bar (shown in Figure 23.10).

FIGURE 23.10

A revision tag can be made to have no leader by using the Options bar.

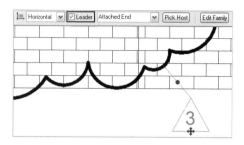

BIM and Supplemental Drawings

The process of making supplemental drawings (SDs) entails making a change to an existing drawing and then issuing that change as a separate package. Sometimes this can be a single 8½″ × 11″ sheet where the new detail is then pasted over the old one in the construction set in the job trailer. From a workflow perspective, this can be a little disruptive in Revit for a couple of reasons:

- ◆ Placing the new detail into an 8½″ × 11″ or smaller sheet to issue the individual drawing can lead to other problems. You will need to either remove the view from the sheet it was issued on temporarily (and remember to put it back) or duplicate the view and hope that you do not need to make last-minute additional changes.

- ◆ An SD, once issued, is like a snapshot in time. It becomes a numbered change made to the drawing set at a given date. Since the model and all the views in the model always reflect the most current state of the project, making separate SD sheets and views within Revit will show any additional changes made to that view.

As a best practice, some architects leave all of the revisions directly on the sheets where they were originally issued. The sheets are printed to PDFs and the PDFs (with the revision clouds) are imported into Adobe Illustrator or a similar application where they can be properly scaled and cropped to the view or detail in question and then placed on an 8½″ × 11″ template to be issued for the revision. This process not only creates a historic record of the revision, but also allows you to avoid issuing the full sheet.

 **Real World Scenario**

TRACKING CHANGES IN THE FOUNDATION PROJECT

To see the change-tracking process in practice, you can try an example using the Foundation project. Assume that you have already submitted a CD documentation set, and after some review with the client have decided on some additional changes. Imagine that you need to change some windows from sliders to casements.

Another team member implements this change, and now you need it to be tracked on your sheet as a revision to the original document set.

When you open the sample file, `Foundation.rvt`, from the Chapter 23 folder on the companion web page (www.sybex.com/go/masteringrevit2009), you'll see some markup notes on the sheet indicating the desired changes, along with the revised window design itself.

You first open the Sheet Issues/Revisions dialog box, click Add to add a new revision, and give the revision a description: **Window Modifications**. Click OK and move to the Drafting tab, where you select the Revision Cloud tool, sketch a cloud around the windows, and click Finish Sketch. Then, to place a tag, choose Tag ➤ By Category, clear the Leader check box in the Options bar, and tag the revision cloud. Your workspace should look like this:

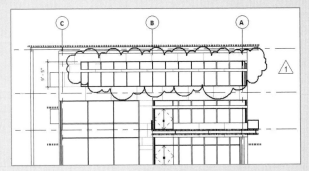

Notice the Revit revision cloud and tag. In the title block, note that a new entry appears in the revision schedule. Your revision tag, the cloud, and the revision number are parametrically associated.

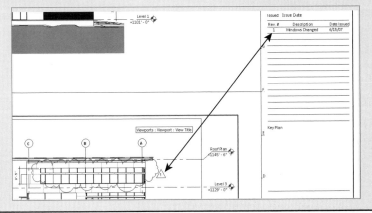

Using Autodesk Design Review

Autodesk Design Review offers a fast, efficient way to view and mark up 2D and 3D designs for review. This workflow is different from what we just covered and is geared more toward informal design review rather than management of sheet issues. For example, if your drawings must be reviewed for quality checking and overall design comments by a senior designer who neither owns Revit nor knows how to use it, this tool can streamline the process and offer a middle way to achieve that. The senior designer, consultant, or any other third party can make comments and review changes and send it back to the Revit user who needs to follow up on those reviews.

Note that in Revit 2009, a new file format for DWF was introduced: DWFx. This is the next generation of the DWF format—one that is more closely aligned with emerging technology standards supported by Microsoft. Once a DWFx is published from Revit, it can be opened in Design Review, marked up, and then linked back into the Revit file, where changes can be picked up and tracked. If you export the drawing sheets from Revit to DWFx, when the DWFx is linked back into Revit, Revit will automatically place the DWFx under the corresponding sheet so there is no need on your part for any sort of alignment or placement of the revisions.

The DWFx format allows you to share drawings and models with stakeholders with a lightweight and easy-to-use application. The navigation and ability to hyperlink between views works well with Revit and is easy to learn.

Design Review is a free tool that you can download from the Autodesk website: `www.autodesk .com/designreview`.

Once it's installed, you can open any DWFx or DWF file produced by any Autodesk or non-Autodesk software packages.

The Design Review User Interface

The interface for Design Review is straightforward, as shown in Figure 23.11. It contains a main view window, toolbar, and navigation pane.

FIGURE 23.11

The Autodesk Design Review interface

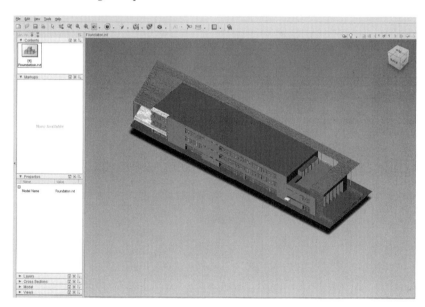

The view window   The main window shows the active view. Using the middle mouse button, you can zoom and pan. If you are looking at a 3D DWF, you'll also see the ViewCube in the upper-right corner of the view. Use this cube to rotate the model by clicking it, or you can hold the mouse down and rotate the cube. Before you start rotating the model, make sure the orbit method is set to Turntable in the toolbar.

This will keep your model rotating with the Z axis always pointing up. If you use the Orbit option, your model will tumble around freely in space on all axes.

The toolbar   Located at the top of the application, the toolbar contains tools for spinning, zooming, panning, cutting cross sections, moving and rotating elements, and adding markup. Feel free to experiment with all these features.

The navigation pane   Located on the left side of the application, this feature is a lot like the Project Browser in Revit: it contains lists of all the views, components, element properties, markups, and layers. Use this to move between views, check properties of objects, and show or hide elements in the view.

SELECTING ELEMENTS IN DESIGN REVIEW

Selection is very much the same in Design Review as in Revit for certain types of elements. For example, when you select a wall, level, grid, or section marker, that element will highlight in other views as well—not just where your cursor is. It behaves this way because the DWFx originated from Revit, where every element is a unique, model-based element and not just a set of abstract lines. When an element is selected, check out the context menu; it contains many options that allow you to zoom, hide elements, make them transparent, and even move them (Figure 23.12).

FIGURE 23.12
The Autodesk
Design Review
context menu

Publishing to Design Review

The DWFx format allows others to examine your design without needing to own or know how to use Revit. The files are also small, which makes them easy to email, something you cannot do with a large Revit file. There are two ways to share your model using Design Review: as 2D information or as 3D information. If you publish to 3D, you create a single 3D representation of your model. Publishing to 2D can create either a view or a whole collection of interconnected views and sheets all packaged as one file.

ARCHIVING WITH DWFS

A 2D DWF of all the sheets of the drawing set is a great way to keep an archive of your project. This allows you to take a snapshot in time of the state of your drawings in a single, small file that is easy to print and easy to reference back into the model should you ever need to return to a previous state in the design. Again, make sure you export sheets, not views.

3D DWF

From a 3D view, choose File ➤ Publish DWF ➤ 3D DWF. Give your file a unique name and save. Then open the file with Design Review to see the result. When in Design Review, experiment with some of the viewing options in the toolbar (Figure 23.13). The Perspective toggle is a nice feature that lets you toggle the 3D view between isometric and perspective with a single click.

FIGURE 23.13
Options for viewing the model—note the Perspective toggle.

2D DWF

From any view, choose File ➤ Publish DWF ➤ 2D DWF. You will be given options similar to the Print dialog box, allowing you to publish the active view or sheet or a selection of views and sheets. At the bottom of this dialog box, the Range group is where you choose to publish the current view or a selection of views and sheets. Click the Select button to choose from a list of views and sheets in your project. By default, all your views and sheets will be combined into a single DWF file. If you want a separate file for each view and sheet, clear the option Combine Selected Views and Sheets into Single dwf File. Let's walk through this:

1. Open the Foundation.rvt model in the Chapter 23 folder on the companion web page.

2. Choose File ➢ Publish DWF ➢ 2D DWF to open the dialog box shown in Figure 23.14.

FIGURE 23.14

The Publish DWF
2D dialog box

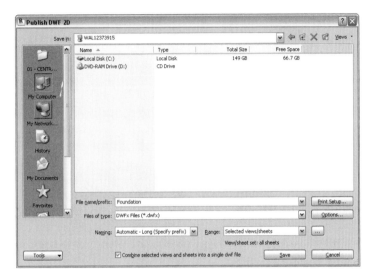

3. Make sure you are combining all sheets into a single DWF file.

4. For Range, choose Selected Views/Sheets. Click the button next to the option to open the View/Sheet Set dialog box.

5. Click the Check All button on the right side of the dialog box. The dialog box should look like Figure 23.15.

FIGURE 23.15

You can publish
sets of sheets into a
single DWF file.

6. You'll be asked if you want to save this selection set for later use. Click Yes and name the set **all sheets**.

7. Click the Print Setup button. In the resulting dialog box (see Figure 23.16), for Paper Size choose <Use Sheet Size>. Rivet will automatically detect the size of sheet being used and publish to that size. The remaining settings should be fine.

FIGURE 23.16
Set the <Use Sheet Size> option and Revit will auto-detect the size of your sheets when publishing to DWF.

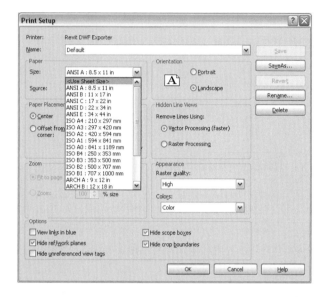

8. Save the file as foundation_all_sheets.dwfx to a location on your hard drive.

9. This process will take some time because it is publishing all the views on all these sheets. When the process completes, open the file with Design Review. You'll see all the sheets displayed with previews in the navigation pane in the Contents tab (Figure 23.17).

Marking Up the Model Using Design Review

Once you have published a DWF, you can open it in Design Review and add textual markups that can then be shared with your team, or even linked back into Revit. To mark up a view in Design Review, click the down arrow next to the Create Markup button and select from the array of graphic styles (Figure 23.18).

Draw the shape using the tool, and then add your text. Figure 23.19 shows a clouded area and associated text note.

FIGURE 23.17
Sheets are displayed in Design Review as previews in the navigation pane

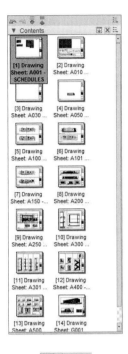

FIGURE 23.18
Design Review has a variety of markup graphic styles.

FIGURE 23.19
Type in comments and use the grips to position your markups as desired.

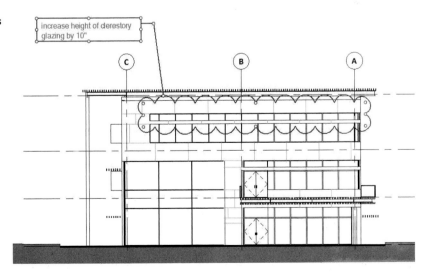

Importing a Design Review Markup

Once you've added markups in Design Review, save the file. You can then link these back into the Revit project. Choose File ➤ Import/Link ➤ Link DWF Markup Set.

When a DWF file is selected, Revit will link and show only the markups, not the entire DWF file. So if there are no markups in the DWF file, nothing will come into Revit. Markups are any text note, markup, or stamp added in Design Review. Figure 23.20 indicates that three sheets have markups.

FIGURE 23.20
For each markup, there is an associated Revit view.

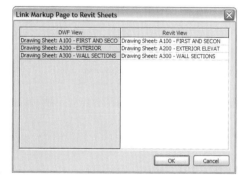

Note that markups can only be linked to sheets. If you export a view and mark it up, it will not show up in Revit. Always work from sheets when using Design Review for markup transfer.

You cannot move or delete linked DWF markups—they appear with a pin when selected. You can do a number of things to graphically indicate that you've dealt with a markup:

Change its graphic appearance Let's say you have 20 redline markups on your sheet. You need to keep track of which ones you've dealt with. One way to do this is to graphically override each one as you finish. Select the markup, then use the context menu option Override Graphics in View ➤ By Element. Choose a color to indicate "done." Yellow works well because it suggests a highlight marker.

Hide it This approach is similar to the graphic override, but you hide the markup altogether. Select the markup, and use the context menu option Hide in View ➤ Element.

Remove it You can remove markups by choosing File ➤ Manage Links. In the Manage Links dialog box, select the markup and click the Remove button. This removes all markups associated with the link.

The Bottom Line

Any changes in a construction documentation set, once issued, need to be recorded with revisions so that changes can be tracked. Revit's revision tools provide intelligent support for this in order to facilitate correct documentation of changes in the model.

Add revisions to your project   You need the ability to track changes in your design after sheets have been issued. Adding revisions to a drawing is an inevitable part of your workflow.

Master It   Add revisions to your project that automatically get tracked on your sheet.

Understand BIM and supplemental drawings   Making an actual revision to a construction document involves adding graphics and coordinating the clouds with revisions.

Master It   You need to cloud a design change. How would you do this using Revit?

Use Autodesk Design Review   You'll often need to share your design with people who do not have Revit, so that your design can be examined and marked up.

Master It   How can you export your designs in a lightweight file format?

Chapter 24

Worksharing

Most projects involve more than one person working on a project at any given time. It's common for many people to work together to meet deadlines and crank out a set of construction documents. Keeping with the theme of an integrated single-file building model, Revit allows for this work-flow without breaking apart the model. A complex model can be edited by many people at once using a feature called *worksharing*. In this chapter, we'll focus on enabling the worksharing feature of Revit.

In this chapter, you learn how to do the following:

◆ Set up a project with worksets

◆ Understand worksharing basics

◆ Manage workflow with worksets

◆ Understand element ownership in worksets

Setting Up a Project with Worksets

Worksharing in Revit refers to the use of *worksets* to divide up the model for the purpose of sharing data between many people. A workset is a collection of building elements and components (floors, roofs, walls, windows, and so on) that can be used to manage project workflow and responsibilities by separating various building components into subsets that allow control over visibility and element ownership. By default, worksharing is not enabled when you start a project in Revit, because the software assumes you are working in a single-user environment until you tell it otherwise.

WORKSHARING WARNING

Once you enable worksharing in a model, you can't undo it. We suggest that you make a copy of your project file before you enable worksharing so you keep an unshared version as a backup.

You share your work by saving a *central file* to a shared network location. This central file becomes the repository where all the individual work on the project is collected and permissions are managed.

Once the central file has been established, each team member then makes a local copy of it and works on that local copy. All work is done directly in these copied—but still associated—

local files. This enables all users to open their local files simultaneously and work in them (see Figure 24.1).

FIGURE 24.1
The worksharing concept

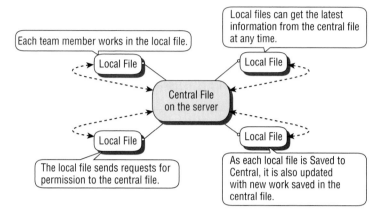

The elements in each separate file are tied to an ownership rule linked to the central file, making it impossible to edit an element in your local file if that same element is owned by someone else in another local file. Remember, Revit is a database. In effect, you're getting permission to edit one or more elements from the central database. Once you have permission to modify an element, no one else can make changes to that element until it is reconciled with the central file. This occurs when you use the Save to Central command (hereafter referred to as STC) copy your work back to the network. If one user has ownership of an element, no other user can edit that element until its permissions, and any changes to it, are reconciled with the central file.

Worksets allow you to group many elements into virtual collections of objects for the purpose of managing visibility and file performance. To that end, there are a number of benefits to enabling worksets beyond allowing multiple team members to work within the same file:

◆ Using worksets, you can turn the visibility off and on for elements that aren't being worked on or that are not needed for the current tasks.

◆ Closing worksets is different than turning them on or off in only one view, as it allows you to close a particular workset globally across all views and also remove it from active memory, thus improving performance.

◆ You can quickly request and obtain permission to work on groups of elements belonging to someone else.

When you enable worksharing, a new tab appears in the Visibility/Graphic Overrides dialog box for the worksets (see Figure 24.2). You can turn any workset on or off in any view using this tab. Additionally, you can make those settings part of any of your view templates.

FIGURE 24.2
Workset visibility

Understanding Worksharing Basics

Revit's worksharing features are designed to accommodate any division of labor you see fit. There are no inherent restrictions in how you use worksharing to divide up a model. For example, you can break up a model and have one group work on the shell and another work on the interior core of a building. You can turn worksharing on at any stage of the project, and you can create or remove individual worksets during the project cycle.

By default, the Worksets toolbar isn't visible in the Revit UI. To turn on the toolbar, right-click in a blank area of the toolbars at the top of the screen and select Worksets from the context menu.

You can then start worksharing in one of two ways:

◆ Choose File ➢ Worksets from the main menu.

◆ Click the Worksets button on the Worksets toolbar. It will be the only active button on the toolbar.

Either of these actions opens a dialog box telling you that you're about to enable worksharing for your project and that once it's enabled it can't be undone (Figure 24.3). After confirming that you do want to proceed, Revit will automatically create two worksets: Shared Levels and Grids that contains all the levels and gridlines from the project, and Workset1 that will contain everything else in the model.

FIGURE 24.3
Activating worksets within a project

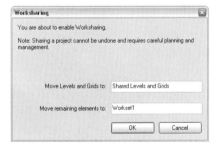

In addition to the two worksets created automatically when you initialize worksharing, Revit maintains three other types of worksets in a project:

View worksets   Each view in a project has a dedicated view workset. It contains the view properties and any view-specific elements (text, dimensions, tags, and so on). View-specific elements cannot be moved to another workset. You can take ownership of any view in Revit by simply right-clicking it in the Project Browser and choosing Make Workset Editable (see Figure 24.4). This will give you ownership of the view workset and all of the view-specific annotations, allowing you to easily and quickly make modifications to any of the 2D content within the view. This is a handy feature during the construction document phase when much of the work is segregated to view worksets for dimensioning and annotations.

FIGURE 24.4
Making a view
workset editable
is a property of
any view in a
workset file.

Family worksets   For each family loaded in the project, a workset is automatically created. When editing properties of a family, you will take ownership of that family unless someone else already owns it. You can add families to each of the views without having ownership over view worksets, but you cannot make changes to the families or their properties without having permission.

Project standards worksets   This workset is dedicated to all the project settings like materials, line styles, tags, dimensions, and so on. Any time you need to edit a project-wide setting, you will be taking ownership of a workset for that setting. Something to keep in mind: you can always add new information, materials, or line styles to a project without having to own the workset. You only need to take ownership of a workset to edit existing settings.

Once you've activated the worksets, you'll see the dialog box shown in Figure 24.5. Also note at the bottom of this dialog box that you have the option to turn on visibility for the automatically created worksets we discussed earlier. By default, they are not activated.

FIGURE 24.5
Worksets
dialog box

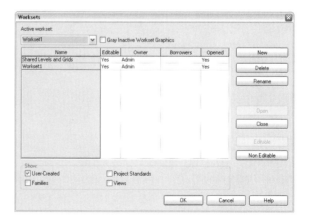

The Worksets dialog box lets you add and remove worksets from the project. A new workset does not contain any model elements or components initially; it is a blank container that you can then begin to fill.

When you activate a workset, you become the owner of that workset and all the elements in it. This ownership is what the Yes value in the Editable column refers to; if you are the owner of a workset, the value in the Editable column will be Yes, but if you are not the owner, the value will be No.

WHO CONTROLS WORKSETS?

Worksets are usually activated by the team's project manager, who initially enables worksharing, creates user worksets, and assigns people and tasks for the project. However, worksets are managed by the team itself. It is up to the team members to make sure they are working on the correct workset. It is also not currently possible to lock a workset from use.

Workset Organization

It's important that you think of your project as a holistic building when dividing it into worksets. Technically speaking, you don't need any more than the initial default worksets because Revit manages ownership of elements on a per-element basis and relinquishes elements automatically when you save your changes to the central file. However, you might want to divide up the model into worksets for some of the reasons we described earlier. Some good examples of typical worksets are Shell and Core, Exterior Skin, and First Floor Interior Partitions.

THINKING WORKSETS

One of the biggest challenges facing teams new to Revit is losing the legacy of layers. Many teams that have been drafting in 2D CAD immediately want to begin managing worksets as they would manage a CAD drawing. They make a workset for doors and one for walls and one for windows. Remember that all of your objects are in one file and you can control visibility of those objects through the Visibility/Graphic Overrides dialog box. Not only is there no need to put your doors into a separate workset, but doing so will actually make your model more difficult to manage. What happens when you have ownership of the doors, your teammate has ownership of the walls, and you want to move or add a door? You can't do so because you don't own the entire assembly. You have to own the door *and* the wall it goes into to make those changes.

Divide your project into worksets that relate to the roles and responsibilities of people working on the project. By default, you don't need more than two to three worksets per person on the job. When making new worksets, remember the Ludwig Mies van der Rohe dictum, "Less is more."

For our Foundations project, we have divided the model into four worksets (see Figure 24.6):

FIGURE 24.6
Workset
organization

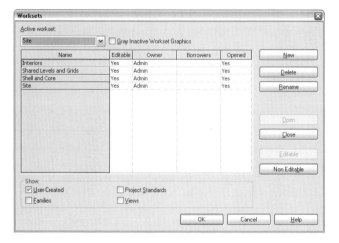

Interiors   All of the interior walls, furniture, and other items are managed with this workset.

Shared Levels and Grids   The workset Shared Levels and Grids contains the level and grid information from the model, as was originally established when worksharing was enabled.

Shell and Core   All the exterior skin of the building as well as the elevator, stair, and toilet cores that are grouped in any typical office building are in this workset.

Site   The topography (toposurface) and any site-specific elements in the project are put into this workset.

KEEPING IT SIMPLE

For our project, creating the Site workset meant renaming Workset1. Because the Shell and Core workset will have the most elements in it, renaming allowed us to forgo the additional work of moving all those objects to a blank workset.

Notice that Workset1 has been renamed. The title is not descriptive enough to be of use, so it can be modified once all the model elements have been moved to relevant worksets. The worksets we've set up demonstrate how a typical breakdown might occur in a project of this size, but it's by no means limited to this scheme. Depending on how you structure work in your office, the worksets might be quite different.

Once in a workset environment, you can see or change an object's workset by accessing its element properties. At the bottom of the Element Properties dialog box, you can see which workset an object or group of objects belongs to, and you can change what workset the element belongs to (see Figure 24.7). Note that you can move elements to other worksets only if you own the elements. You do not need to own the entire workset to do this—just the individual elements.

FIGURE 24.7

Change the work-
set to which an
element belongs
by selecting a
different workset
using Element
Properties.

Element Properties			
Family:	System Family: Surface	▼	Load...
Type:	Default	▼	Edit / New...

Type Parameters: Control all elements of this type

Parameter	Value

Instance Parameters - Control selected or to-be-created instance

Parameter	Value	
Materials and Finishes		⌃
Material	Site - Earth	...
Dimensions		⌃
Projected Area	770947.01 SF	
Surface Area	772290.10 SF	
Identity Data		⌃
Comments		
Name		
Mark		
Workset	Shell and Core	
Edited by	Admin	
Phasing		⌃
Phase Created	New Construction	
Phase Demolished	None	

OK   Cancel

Additionally, you can tell what workset an object belongs to by hovering your cursor over the object and waiting for the tooltip to appear. This tooltip will give you a host of information about the object in question. In the following example, the workset is Shell and Core, the element is also part of the Walls category, the name of the family is Basic Wall, and the family type is A3 - 4 ¾":

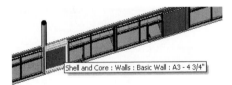

Shell and Core : Walls : Basic Wall : A3 - 4 3/4"

PRACTICE GOOD WORKFLOW

As a best practice, do not work directly in the central file once the worksets have been established. Every user should be working in their user, local file. Working directly in the central file will change the file attributes and nullify anyone's ability to use the STC command. *Once someone has worked directly in the central file, any work by anyone else will be lost and everyone will be required to make new local copies.* Working in the central file should *only* occur with full knowledge of all the team members and only if there is a file upgrade or some other historically significant event occurring.

Moving Elements between Worksets

Once the worksets are created, there are some simple steps for moving elements quickly and easily to other worksets. As mentioned, the easiest way to move the bulk of the objects is to not move them at all but simply rename Workset1. After that, it is easiest to move elements in a subtractive method from a 3D view. The following exercise will walk you through moving elements to their new worksets using a subtractive method to locate model geometry. Note that this should be done while one person is still the solitary owner of all the worksets.

1. Open the default 3D view ({3D}) so that you can see all of your model elements within the project.

2. Open Visibility/Graphic Overrides dialog box, turn off the Site workset, and click OK. Since nothing is in the Site workset, the view should look the same when you are done.

3. Now, in the 3D view select a comfortable number of the site elements and click the Properties button—*comfortable* meaning you don't have to try to select them all at once. In the first image in Figure 24.8, the toposurface and some trees have been selected and are highlighted.

FIGURE 24.8
Moving objects between worksets

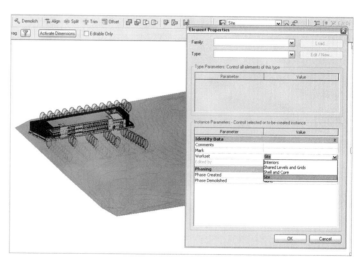

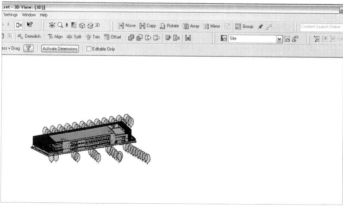

4. In the Element Properties dialog box, select Site for the Workset value and click OK. All of the elements you selected will disappear (the second image in Figure 24.8). Not to worry: remember, you turned the Site workset off using the Visibility/Graphic Overrides.

5. Using the same technique, you can move the remainder of the site elements to the Site workset. The same procedure is repeated in order to move the interior walls to the Interior workset.

At any point in this process, you can check your work by opening the Workset tab in the Visibility/Graphic Overrides dialog box and clearing all of the boxes but one to see what is in each workset. Figure 24.9 shows the Interiors workset with all of the interior elements. As you can see, this is a great way to manage visibility without using the object categories.

FIGURE 24.9
The Interior
workset

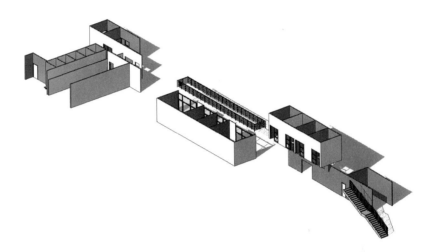

MOVING EVERY INSTANCE OF AN ELEMENT

A quick way to move every instance of a single element to a new workset is to use the Select All Instances option from the context menu. For example, select a tree in the model, right-click on the tree, choose the Select All Instances command from the context menu, and open Element Properties. You can then change the workset for all those elements in one action.

Managing Workflow with Worksets

With worksharing there is always one central file that spawns local files and manages element ownerships. This is the file that collects all the work being done by your team members, and allows the team to get regular updates of new work saved to the central file. Once the worksets are initialized and the model is divided into various worksets, you will need to complete a few more steps before the team can jump into the model and begin working in a multiuser environment.

To use Revit in a workset environment, you do everything any IT manager ever yelled at you for doing: you make a local copy of the central file and work directly off your C: drive. Although this approach is a bad idea for most work in an office environment, for the Revit database there are several good things about it:

◆ It allows more than one user to make changes to the central file by editing local files and synchronizing those changes with the central file.

◆ Your local copy will be more responsive than a networked file because your access speed to your hard drive is much faster than it is across most networks.

◆ Should anything bad happen to your network or your central file, you will have an up-to-date backup to which you can easily apply the Save As command to make a new central file.

Creating a Central File

Now that you've turned on worksharing, you need to set up the central file to be used by more than one person. To do this, you first create a central file located on your network; then you create the local files to begin working on the project. To create the central file, choose File ➢ Save As and give the model a new name. Before you save, click the Options button at the bottom of the dialog box and verify that the box Make This a Central File After Save is checked (see Figure 24.10).

FIGURE 24.10
Creating a central file

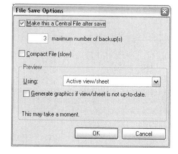

The reason for the new name is twofold. First, it gives you a backup of your old file before you made the worksets. Backups never hurt. Second, Revit sometimes does not like to have a new file saved over an active file or a file of the same name. It can cause file corruption.

Creating the Local File

Now that the central file has been created, you need to create the local files to work from:

1. Make a new, local copy of the central file by dragging the file you just created to your desktop or another location on your hard drive. Be careful not to *move* the file; you just want to make a copy of it.

2. Now, open this new, local file. The first time any local file is initialized, you will receive the warning message shown in Figure 24.11. All this means is that you've made a local file

and you will be the owner of the local copy. If you don't see this message, check to make sure you're opening the correct file.

FIGURE 24.11
Opening the
local file for the
first time

Once you click OK, you are set and ready to begin working in a worksharing environment. Now that you're in a worksharing environment, every element added to the file belongs to a workset. Try to keep model elements in a workset other than Shared Levels and Grids because these worksets may be locked down at some point to avoid accidental movement of key datums. To make sure you're placing elements in the proper workset, check the Worksets toolbar to see what the active workset is. All newly created elements will be assigned to the workset shown in this box. Remember, you don't have to be the owner of this workset, nor does the workset need to be editable in order for you to add new elements to it.

A helpful toggle in the Worksets toolbar is the Gray Inactive Workset button. It grays out all elements that aren't in the active workset, helping you identify which elements in the workset are active. This is a temporary view state and will not affect any print output.

Saving Shared Work

Once you begin working in a worksharing environment, it becomes necessary to not only save your work but also to share it with others. There are three ways to save your work when you're using a workshared file:

Save   The Save tool saves the work you've done to your local copy only; the work isn't shared or saved back to the central file. This is useful when you're in the design phase and trying out different designs, or if you're not ready to share your work with others but you definitely want to save the work you're done.

Save to Central   Next to the Save tool is the Save to Central button. Use this to publish your work into the central file. When you do so, your work appears in the central file and becomes available to the entire team. Using Save to Central also acquires the changes that others have made (and likewise saved to the central file) and loads them into your local model. By default, saving to the central file will relinquish any permissions you have over objects and worksets within the model.

File ➢ Save to Central   Using the menu option for STC is a good way to save yet maintain permission over the elements you are creating. Choosing this option will open the dialog shown in Figure 24.12, which allows you to customize how you save to the central file. You can choose to relinquish some permissions or none of them, and you can choose to save a local copy at this time (or not). You can also add comments about this particular version you are saving. The comments are available in the History dialog box (covered later in this book).

FIGURE 24.12
Save to Central
dialog

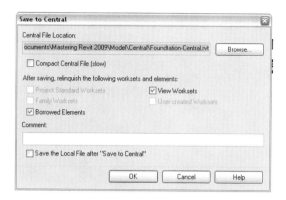

In addition, Revit will remind you regularly to save your work. In a worksharing environment, you will see a reminder to save to the central file and a separate reminder to save locally; however, there is no autosave feature in Revit. You can dismiss this dialog box from time to time, but remember it's always a good time to save (and not lose work).

The reminder time shown in the dialog box can be modified across the application in the Settings ➤ Options dialog box under the General tab.

Loading Work from Other Team Members

It's possible to update your model from the central file without committing your changes to the central file. Think of this process as getting an update of the model. To do so, choose File ➤ Reload Latest. Revit finds the latest changes saved to the central file and brings them into your local file without publishing any of the changes you've made.

RELOAD LATEST

Mapping Reload Latest to a keyboard shortcut can help you see others' edits quickly. Also, much of the time in a Save to Central process is consumed by reloading the latest changes. More frequent use of Reload Latest will shorten the time to save when you use Save to Central.

Understanding Element Ownership in Worksets

While you are working in a worksharing environment, it might become necessary to see if you have ownership of an element. To do so, select the element. If you own it, it will be highlighted in red and can be readily moved or modified. If you do not own it, it will still be highlighted red, but you will also see an icon resembling a puzzle piece in blue. This indicates that you do not currently have ownership of that element.

You can obtain ownership of the element in a few ways:

◆ If you edit or move an element, Revit will automatically grant you permission to own it provided no one else currently owns it.

◆ If you can click the puzzle piece icon, and if the element is available, Revit will grant you permission to edit or change it.

◆ You can right-click the element and choose Make Elements Editable from the context menu (see Figure 24.13).

FIGURE 24.13
Making an element
editable

Note that in this context menu, you also have the option to make worksets editable and take permission of the *entire* workset the object is assigned to.

Real World Scenario

RECOVERING FROM MISTAKES

Inevitably, with any team of people, someone is bound to make a mistake somewhere in the process. It happens; it's just human nature. The important thing is knowing how to recover when those accidents happen. On one project, someone new to our team kept accidentally deleting the west wall of the project while deep into Construction Documentation. Since Revit is a database and everything is linked to everything else, every time this happened, not only the plans were messed up, but we'd lose the west elevation, wall sections, the door and window details in those sections, and so on. You get the idea. The west wall would be deleted and the user would issue the Save to Central command, thereby changing the central file. Fortunately, we caught the mistake in time and thus did not have to resort to a backup from the previous night and lose a day's worth of work. Each local copy is a fully functional copy of the model. All we had to to do is find the latest local version with the wall in it, and perform a simple File ➢ Save As. Click the Options button and then select Make This a Central File after Save. Once everyone on the team made a new local copy, we were back in business.

Borrowing Elements

By borrowing elements, team members can take ownership of some of the elements within a particular workset that belongs to someone else. This can typically be used if you need to modify only one or a few elements in a given workset and do not want to take ownership of the entire workset. This is also valuable if you need to edit elements in a workset and someone else already owns it.

The key idea here is that you can borrow elements individually rather than by workset. If you need to work on an element that belongs to someone else, you'll be informed of that and given the option to send a notification asking to borrow it. The owner of the element can then grant permission for you to take ownership. This is referred to as *relinquishing* permission.

Borrowing is a critical technological concept in Revit; it allows users to fluidly transfer permission of objects without having to constantly save all their work to the central file and relinquish all worksets. Let's look at this workflow in more detail.

Requesting Permission

Say you are happily working away on your model and realize that someone else is the owner of an element you need to modify. Should that occur, you will be presented with a dialog box shown in Figure 24.14. This will occur every time you are working in a model in which worksharing is enabled and you are attempting to edit an element that is already owned by someone else on the project.

FIGURE 24.14

Placing a request
for permission

You have the option to click Cancel, which will undo any edits you have made to that element, or you can click Place Request to ask the other user to relinquish permission over the element in question. If you opt to place a request, you will see the following dialog box:

It is important to note that the other user does not receive an explicit notification that you have placed the request. To make sure your colleague knows of your request, you'll need to call or instant message (IM) that person, and get them to grant the permissions. If owning this element is critical to your task at hand, keep in mind that you will not be able to perform any more work in relation to that element until that other user grants you permission to borrow it. Once you've made your phone call, or gotten the other user to relinquish ownership, click the Check Now button to see if you do in fact own the element. Or if you want to just keep working, click the Continue button. This will undo your last command and return you to the view to continue your work.

GET THEIR ATTENTION!

Asking another user to grant permission to an element is a great reason to use an intraoffice IM or chat service. It is invasive enough to alert another user to the fact you are requesting permission for an element. However, the phone works well, too. Formatting a Revit username as *Your Name + Phone Extension* can be a good idea as well.

Once you've received notice from the other user that your request has been granted, click Check Now and you will receive the message shown here.

Clicking OK will apply your edits and you will then be the borrower of that element.

You can check to see who owns which worksets and who is borrowing from a workset at any time in the Worksets dialog box, as shown in Figure 24.15.

FIGURE 24.15
Owning and borrowing worksets

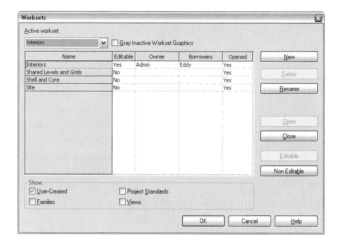

Granting Permission

Now suppose that you have been happily modeling along and you receive a phone call, IM, or tap on the shoulder from someone looking to get permission for an element you own in the model. How do you grant permission for someone else to use this element? On the Worksharing toolbar is a button called Editing Requests, which allows you to see outstanding requests that have been sent your way. Clicking this button gives you the dialog box shown in Figure 24.16.

FIGURE 24.16
Editing Requests
dialog box

From here, you have a few options:

Grant   Gives permission for the requested element to your teammate

Deny/Retract   Denies permission to your teammate

Show   Shows you exactly which element or elements have been requested to help you make an informed decision

Once you are ready to grant permission, one of two things will happen. If you haven't made any changes yourself that need to be saved, you can simply grant the permission and notify your teammate that you have done so, and then both of you can continue to work. If you have been editing the requested element, you'll need to save your changes to the central file before anything else can happen. Changes of this nature are specially flagged in the Editing Requests dialog box with an asterisk before the request indicating that the element has been modified and a Save to Central command must be issued before permission can be granted (see Figure 24.17).

FIGURE 24.17
Editing requests for changed elements

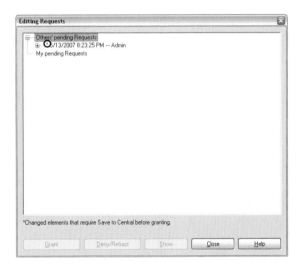

Trying to grant permission at this point will give you the dialog shown here:

In order to remedy this issue, close the dialog and perform a Save to Central using one of the methods we discussed earlier. Keep in mind that if you choose File ➢ Save to Central and uncheck the boxes for relinquishing permission, you will need to come back to the Editing Requests dialog box to grant permission for this element. Once you have saved to the central file and notified the other user, he or she can then click the Check Now button to continue to work.

The user who is requesting permission of the element will see this dialog box after clicking Check Now:

This means that the object the other user was trying to use has been edited and he or she will have to choose File ➤ Reload Latest or Save to Central to reload the most current copy of that object before it can be edited. Unfortunately, any modifications to this element will be lost as the element is changed in the central file.

The Bottom Line

Understanding worksharing is important to any team environment or any project in which you plan to have more than one person working on the file at a time. The idea that everyone is essentially editing one shared model is a novel concept but one that works surprisingly well. Understanding worksharing can help support good project communication and efficient workflow across the project lifecycle.

Set up a project with worksets   Knowing how to activate worksharing and set up the project file for more than one person at a time is critical in any office environment.

> **Master It**   How do you work in a single Revit file on a project team with more than one member in the file at a time?

Understand worksharing basics   Once you've enabled worksharing, you'll need to understand the dynamics of central and local files to fully leverage working in a worksharing environment.

> **Master It**   Once you have enabled worksets to allow for multiple users, what's the best way to implement and use the file?

Manage workflow with worksets   Saving to and loading from the central file allow you to view other team members' work and allows them to see what changes to the project you have added.

> **Master It**   How can you translate the changes you've made in your local file to the central file on the network? How do you download changes from other team members to your local file?

Understand element ownership in worksets   Editing elements in a central file means you have sole ownership over further changes to those elements. Understanding the permissions will be critical to working in a team.

> **Master It**   How do you edit an element in the model if someone has already taken permission of it in a worksharing environment?

Appendices

In this section you will find:

Appendix A

The Bottom Line

Each of The Bottom Line sections in the chapters suggest exercises to deepen skills and understanding. Sometimes there is only one possible solution, but often you are encouraged to use your skills and creativity to create something that builds on what you know and lets you explore one of many possible solutions.

Chapter 1: Understanding BIM: From the Basics to Advanced Realities

Building information modeling is a departure from the conventional approach of representing buildings with lines on paper; instead, BIM stores a description of the building as data that can be used to generate all of your drawings.

Identify the advantages of building information modeling   The traditional architectural design tools you've mastered are probably serving you well. New software and a new conceptual model of the building process will inevitably involve some adjustments, so they need to provide significant benefits.

Master It   What are some of the advantages of using BIM over traditional CAD tools?

Solution   BIM is a model-based tool that keeps your documents coordinated in a single file. As a modeling tool, representational drawings such as plan and section are by-products of modeling, not separately managed drawing files. BIM is also well suited for making early design decision and iterating in the design, because you can run analysis early and frequently.

Know what to expect from BIM   A BIM project is based on a single, centralized database of information. You need to anticipate how that change can affect workflows based on more independent functions.

Master It   How can your work process be affected by the adoption of BIM?

Solution   BIM changes the way projects are managed and worked on. You'll find that teams must communicate on a regular basis when working on a shared BIM model. This encourages members of the team to take active responsibility for their parts of the model and understand the impact that design changes have on other parts of the model. Using BIM also means you have to shed some old habits and expectations and be willing to change the way you think about producing construction documents. Moving from a drafting-centric workflow to a model-based workflow can be jolting at first, but once you take the plunge, you're unlikely to look back.

Chapter 2: Revit Fundamentals

The Revit user interface is fairly straightforward. Once you know how to access settings, add elements to a view, and navigate views, you'll be off and running. Get used to the idea of editing properties of elements to change their appearance and behavior. This applies to model elements, annotations, and views.

Understand Revit parametric elements   Although you can find references to objects, families, instances, and components, in the end everything is an element.

Master It   What are Revit elements, and how are they managed graphically?

Solution   Anything you can select in the view is a Revit element. By using a fixed category structure, Revit lets you quickly identify elements, control their visibility and graphics, and generate reports based on this information. The data is highly structured, but you have tremendous liberty when it comes to the representation of that data.

Work with the Revit user interface   As in any software application, you need to know where all the major components are and what tasks they support.

Master It   How do you change the graphics of a category for all views? What if you need to change the graphics for only one view?

Solution   Use the Object Styles dialog box to set up and edit the graphics for all elements in the model. This establishes a default behavior for all views. To change the graphics on a per-view basis, use the Visibility/Graphic Overrides dialog box, which you can access from the context menu when elements are selected or by pressing the VG keyboard short-cut. The sooner you embrace this concept and start exploring the opportunities it presents, the better. If you can't get your drawing to look just right, chances are you haven't dug deep enough.

Use the Project Browser   This UI component provides access to all elements in your model. Become accustomed to using it to locate views, families, groups, and links.

Master it   Knowing how to navigate views in Revit is essential to completing work. What are some of the ways to open views in Revit?

Solution   You can open views from the Project Browser by double-clicking any view. In addition, you can double-click view tag symbols directly (level heads, section heads, elevation tags, and callout bubbles) to open the view.

Navigate views and view properties   Views are also elements. Just like the walls, floors, and roofs you add to the model, you'll also add views. They have properties you should become familiar with.

Master it   You need to change the scale of a plan view from ⅛″ to ¼″. How do you do this with Revit?

Solution   Using either the View Properties option on the view's context menu or the view controls at bottom of the view, change the scale. The annotations and hatch patterns will update automatically. You can change the scale of any view at any time.

Chapter 3: Know Your Editing Tools

Get to know the basic commands with Revit. The faster you become, the more productive you'll be. The more you use Revit, the more you'll find that certain commands are better suited for certain tasks.

Select, change, and replace elements   Learning the basic mechanics of the interface is crucial to just about everything you'll do in Revit.

> **Master It**   Selecting elements in the model happens all the time. What are some of the capabilities that the Revit user interface provides when you select elements?
>
> **Solution**   Any time an element is selected, you'll notice that a few things change in the user interface. First, the element changes color, indicating that it's selected. Second, if you select a model element, you get temporary dimensions to help you position the element. Third, icons appear for graphic controls such as drag grips, check boxes, and flip arrows. And finally, the Options bar updates with element-specific tools. All these features help keep the user interface out of your way until you need it.

Edit elements interactively   The architectural process inevitably involves revision, so be sure you know how to make changes on the fly.

> **Master It**   You need to make some major changes to a floor plan, moving the bathroom 20′ down a corridor. How might you do this with Revit?
>
> **Solution**   Box-select all the walls, fixtures, and doors that are part of the bathroom. Use the Filter tool to make sure you have the right categories selected. Then, select the Move tool in the toolbar. Click anywhere in the model, and move the mouse in the direction you need to move the bathroom. Type 20′. The whole set of elements then moves 20′.

Use other handy editing tools   Revit provides a wide range of tools for making changes in a project.

> **Master It**   In a section view, you notice that the walls and floors aren't cleaning up neatly—you're seeing lines overlap. What tool could you use to try to clean that up?
>
> **Solution**   For quick join cleanups, use the Join Geometry tool. Activate the tool, and then select the elements you want to join. With each click of the mouse, you see the overlapping lines disappear, and your drawings start to clean up immediately.

Chapter 4: Setting Up Your Templates and Office Standards

If you set up your templates from the beginning, you'll save yourself headaches downstream. Experiment with object styles, annotations, and tags to get the right look and feel for your practice.

Start a project with a custom template   Creating a template that incorporates your firm's styles and preferences is an essential first step in putting Revit to work.

> **Master It**   Your firm has some deeply established graphic conventions that were defined in AutoCAD. How would you go about matching these graphics and setting up a Revit template?
>
> **Solution**   Using object styles to customize how elements appear in both projection and cut, you can get model and annotation categories to match the line weight, color, and pattern of those used in AutoCAD.

Create custom annotation tags   Styles for annotations, dimensions, and text are all governed by office standards, and the Family Editor is your tool for setting up those standards in Revit.

Master It   You need to create dimensions, text, and annotations that match your office standards. How do you do this with Revit?

Solution   Make new types of system families for text and dimensions. With these families, you can control font, color, and size. For tags, open an existing tag and customize its graphics to suit your needs. Be sure to add parametric labels to make your tags smart and associative. This will save you huge amounts of time later.

Create custom titleblocks   Titleblocks are another important element of office standards that you can configure in the Family Editor.

Master It   Most offices have several titleblocks with lots of information embedded in them. How would you add multiple titleblocks to your project template file?

Solution   Make your own titleblocks as parametric families, and then load them into the template using the Load from Library option. With smart labels, you need to define these only once in the Family Editor; they will adapt to whatever project you load the titleblock into.

Chapter 5: Customizing System Families and Project Settings in Your Template

Project templates save you time by capturing settings and modeling standards in a preset file that will help your office maintain a consistent look and feel across different projects. Templates allow you to load a set of commonly used families in advance, so that you won't have to search and load those elements with each new project you start. Having complete and well designed templates will help create a more efficient and productive working environment.

Create new types of system families   Incorporating common building components in your project template is fundamental to using Revit effectively.

Master It   How do you add/remove wall, floor, and roof types to your template?

Solution   Start with an existing template, and draw all the walls, floors, and roofs you're likely to need in your own projects. Then, purge unused wall, floor, and roof types from the file using the File/Purge tool. That way, all unused types will be removed from the template. If you need to add types, duplicate a type, name it, and make changes to properties as needed. When you're done, save your file as a new Revit template (RTE file).

Use type catalogs   Revit's type catalogs are an important tool for keeping the types you create accessible in a project.

Master It   What are type catalogs used for?

Solution   A type catalog is a tool that lets you easily and quickly create many types of a family that have different dimensions and sizes. The type catalog is a text file connected with a Revit family. This text file can store many definitions of family types. It is imperative that the type catalog have the same name and be located in the same folder as the family for which it defines additional types; otherwise there will be no association between them and the type catalog will fail. When you load a family with an associated type catalog, you can selectively load types from the catalog.

Customize project settings in your template   View templates allow you to tailor views according to the requirements of a project.

Master It   How would you set up a new view template for plan views where the surface pattern of floors is turned off?

Solution   You can turn off categories and patterns and override the graphics for any view, and store these settings in a view template so they can be applied to many views. First, choose Settings ➤ View Templates. Duplicate an existing plan-view template type, and give it unique name. Next, click the Visibility/Graphic Overrides button, which takes you to the Visibility/Graphic Overrides dialog box. Scroll down to the Floors category, and click the Surface Pattern Override button. Deselect the Visible option, and click OK twice to get back to the View Templates dialog box. You can now apply this view template to your plan views by right-clicking the view name in the Project Browser and using the Apply View Template feature.

Chapter 6: Modeling Principles in Revit I

Creating elements in Revit requires modeling in 3D, which can be quite a change from traditional 2D workflows. Learning how to model your building project in Revit is the first step to leveraging the functionalities of BIM.

Understand the basics of modeling with Revit   Modeling with software is an extension of the traditional art of modeling with the hands. Free-form 3D modeling tools are not designed with BIM workflows in mind, however, it is still possible to import shapes into Revit for downstream use. At the same time, Revit provides some basic tools for 3D design, and you should familiarize yourself with these.

Master it   Tools such as Rhinoceros, 3ds Max, Maya, and SketchUp allow you to create free-form shapes with relative ease. How does Revit let you take advantage of such shapes?

Solution   In Revit you can import shapes into the project and family environments and reuse them intelligently in a parametric setting. You can also create shapes from scratch in Revit.

Understand sketch-based design   Sketch-based design allows you to define some basic parameters and shapes in Sketch mode within Revit.

Master it   Revit uses a 2D sketch-based approach to modeling. What modeling elements in Revit use this 2D sketch principle to generate their form?

Solution   Every model element in Revit has at least one 2D sketch in it. Even walls, while not made initially using a Sketch mode, have a sketch that can be edited. All 3D content is composed of combinations of forms that all derive from 2D sketches.

Understand work planes, levels, grids, reference planes, and reference lines   Using these tools gives you the ability to better control your model and your design by applying and controlling parameters.

Master it   In order to sketch a form, the form must reside on a work plane. How do you define and visualize the work plane in Revit?

Solution   To see the active work plane in a view, click the Work Plane Visibility toggle in the Options bar. Right next to that button is the Work Plane tool, which allows you to change the work plane by choosing an existing level, or by clicking on an existing model face.

Chapter 7: Modeling Principles in Revit ll

Revit provides a set of modeling tools and techniques that enable you to build your model and all the elements that go into the model. Mastering them is what will make the transition to working in 3D BIM easy.

Understand the principles of modeling in Revit   Understanding how to use Revit's modeling tools is an important part of project documentation. Knowing which modeling tools to use when will aid not only in project visualization but also in documentation, scheduling, and rendering.

Master it   There are many unique design elements in any project. Know when to use the appropriate modeling tools at the right times. What tool in Revit might you use to model the following elements?

◆ Reception counter

◆ Entry canopy

◆ Massing study

◆ Custom furnishings

Solution   While there is no *right* tool within Revit for a given task, there are some that tend to work better than others:

◆ Reception counter: Use the Create tool on the Modeling Tab.

◆ Entry canopy: If there is only one, you might use the Create tool or the Family Editor.

◆ Massing study: Use the Massing tab and the mass and void tools there.

◆ Custom furnishings: Use the Family Editor.

Model with five basic forms   These tools are at the root of practically all form modeling.

Master it   Having learned the basics of Revit's form-making tools, imagine how you would build this faucet designed by Philippe Starck.

Solution   Start a new generic model family. In the family, use revolves, sweeps, and blends to create the faucet. In this example you would model the base as a revolve, the spout a sweep, and the toggle switch as a blend.

Master it   In some cases, a form uses multiple sketch lines to generate its form. What form-making tools in Revit use more than one set of 2D sketches to generate the form?

Solution   Sweeps have a profile sketch and a path sketch.

Revolves have a profile sketch and an axis line.

Blends have two sketches: one for the base and one for the top.

Combine solids and voids to create complex and intriguing forms   Revit's five basic forms can be expressed as either positive space (solids) or negative space (voids).

Master it   To make more complex forms, both solids and voids can be used. Think of a case where the using voids as a subtractive element makes sense.

Solution   If you create an extrusion in plan form, and then need to edit it in elevation, a void is a perfect match. With the void, you can carve the top of the extrusion to give it a unique shape.

Chapter 8: Concept Massing Studies

Projects begin with broad, gestural strokes that are eventually refined with more detail. The ability to quickly generate conceptual 3D massing form aids in the development of a project. With Revit, you can make parametric abstract mass forms and use those forms downstream in your process as the design progresses.

Understand massing workflows   Using generic forms, you can create early conceptual models and then use the mass to create the walls, floors, and roofs.

Master It   You need to explore a design idea early on, in 3D, using abstract forms. How would you do this with Revit?

Solution   One way to start work on a project is with an early conceptual sketch and massing study. Revit tools allow you to create massing studies and work through iterations to arrive at the design solution you need. You can import a hand sketch or a DWG and model from it or start from zero using the modeling tools. Once you've created some forms, you can make views, do shadow studies, and calculate area and volumes.

Start a conceptual massing study   In the project environment, you can make massing forms at any time. For generic forms that might appear in multiple projects, consider using the Family Editor and create mass families.

Master It   You've imported a 2D site plan, and now you need to start building a massing study model in the project. How would you approach this with Revit?

Solution   Start the Massing tool on the Massing tab of the Design bar, select Create Mass, and use the extrusion tool while selecting the existing 2D shapes of the imported site plan as a base reference. Create a new massing form to begin experimenting with your design, and see how it impacts the surrounding context.

Understand how massing can be used downstream as the design progresses   Creating a mass is one thing, but leveraging that mass for conceptual analysis and quantity take-offs can further aid and inform the design process.

Master It   Once you've settled on a basic massing study, what information can you derive from it? How can this be represented?

Solution   Using levels, the mass can be sliced into floors to perform area calculations. These can then be used to track progress of the design against the design requirements. You can also attach walls, floors, and a roof to the mass, which can in turn be scheduled early in the process.

Chapter 9: From Conceptual Mass to a Real Building

One typical way to start a design process is a creation of conceptual masses. Revit can create or read concept masses created in other tools and apply conceptual analysis and convert those masses in real building elements using a set of smart tools called the Building Maker.

Make conceptual designs and early studies in Revit   You can use massing studies to validate a design against the program requirements.

Master It   Conceptual modeling is used early in the design process to explore building shape and program. How do you approach schematic design using Revit and perform feasibility studies?

Solution   Revit lets you import a site DWG file and begin building a 3D massing study of the surroundings using the lines from the CAD import. Then, using the massing tools, you can model your conceptual composition. Using design options, you can make a few different proposals. With mass and floor schedules, you can measure what you've done and test against the local regulations as well as program requirements.

Build a real building out of a 3D concept mass   Moving from massing to actual building components is easily done with Revit.

Master It   You've got the basic massing nailed down, and now you need to study more details such as wall and window fenestrations. How do you approach this with Revit?

Solution   Once a final design is selected, you can use the Building Maker concept to quickly turn the mass model into a BIM model that contains walls, floors, roofs, and other architectural elements. In the early stage of this conversion, you can keep the dependency with the mass model so that if you decide to make changes you can use the Remake functionality to update the converted building accordingly. The idea is simple—you move from mass to a final building seamlessly, without data loss.

Use imported geometry from other applications for massing   You can make your own conceptual massing forms using standard Revit form-making tools or by importing geometry from other applications.

Master It   How can you reuse conceptual models created in other modeling applications and turn them into a measurable and documentable building in Revit?

Solution   The concept of Building Maker allows you to import models from SketchUp, Rhino, Maya, 3ds Max, and Inventor. You import early concept studies into a mass element and then apply real components (walls, roofs, floors, and so on) to its faces:

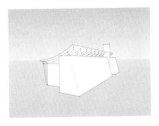

Use smart relationships between building mass and the underlying mass   It's not always possible to start a project directly within Revit. Knowing how to import model geometry from other applications is critical to a good workflow. You can also avoid replicating model geometry just because you're moving from one software package to another.

> **Master It**   Import model geometry from other applications (such as Rhino or SketchUp) into Revit in a way that allows you to cut them in plan and section.

> **Solution**   By creating a mass, then importing the geometry into the mass while in Edit mode, you can cut the new geometry once the mass is finished.

Chapter 10: Working with Design Options

If you need to explore alternate design ideas in your model, try using design options. Doing so will save you from having to try to merge information downstream if you tend to make separate files for each design. Rather than going through a laborious copy–paste workflow and maintaining two or three models in separate files, you can use design options in one model of your building and thus streamline your workflow. Just keep in mind that you're working with a 3D parametric model that creates lots of relationships between elements. Often, editing a floor or roof also involves editing walls that are attached to that roof, even if you aren't burdened with having to make the edits manually.

Use Revit design options   Design options provide a means to maintain two or more alternative designs for the same project or component.

> **Master It**   What are design options in Revit?

> **Solution**   Design options allow you to explore alternatives to your current design direction. By creating option sets from the Design Options dialog box, you can make an unlimited number of variations to your design theme. These can be controlled with Visibility/Graphic Overrides, which lets you see the options in any number of view types: plans, elevations, sections, perspectives, schedules, and so on.

Decide on a design solution   The end result of exploring multiple options is to choose one alternative and implement that choice.

> **Master It**   You've explored a number of design options for an entry scheme. Your client has selected one, and you need to incorporate it into the rest of the model and remove the unwanted alternates.

> **Solution**   In the Design Options dialog box, select the desired option, and click the Make Primary button. Doing so pushes that option into all your views in the project as the default option. Now, select the option set and click the Accept Primary button. Each of your other unwanted options is eliminated, and your primary option is incorporated into the design.

Use design options with parametric design   Making quantitative differences visible is an essential part of presenting multiple alternatives.

Master It   You need to look at some seating layout options for an auditorium space based on different-sized seating and show the seating counts.

Solution   Using design options and a Revit auditorium seat family, you can create two design options for the layout: one for seating 20″ wide and one for seating 24″ wide. Once these are laid out in their respective design options, you can create a schedule to count the seating based on size. By creating a seating schedule and then duplicating it, you can change the Visibility/Graphics Overrides parameter of the second schedule to count the second design option. In the following views, the two schemes have 276 and 234 seats, respectively.

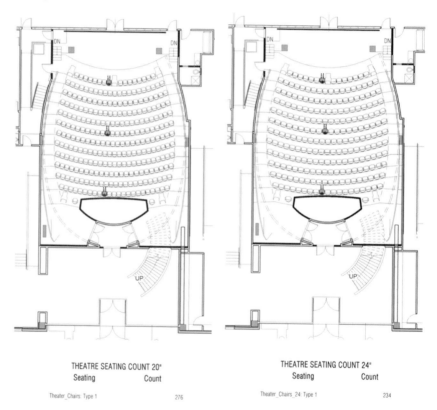

THEATRE SEATING COUNT 20″		THEATRE SEATING COUNT 24″	
Seating	Count	Seating	Count
Theater_Chairs: Type 1	276	Theater_Chairs_24: Type 1	234

Chapter 11: Creating Custom 3D Content

Models are full of content, and while the majority of the time you can find the needed content in the Revit library or on the Web, at some point you'll need to make your own designed content. Don't be afraid to dive into the Family Editor and start creating your own custom content. Begin with simple families, and elaborate as you go. When approaching an element you wish to model, think first of how it's constructed and what aspects of it you need to control parametrically—not all components need to be full-blown parametric objects. Also think about how you might break a component into subcomponents. Consider the eventual application of the family—will it be hosted in walls, ceiling, or roofs? Or is it a stand-alone object? As you become more familiar with how parameters work, start considering formulas and parameter linking to save time and embed intelligent behavior.

Model parametric 3D families   When you're making a new family, consider how it will be used in the model, and choose an appropriate template.

Master It   You found a ceiling-mounted lighting fixture that you want to use in your existing project, but you can't find a Revit family for it in any libraries or online communities. How would you start?

Solution   Knowing that you need to build a lighting fixture from scratch, begin by opening the `Lighting Fixture ceiling based.rft` template file. This will ensure that the family is hosted by ceilings and will thus move and stay connected with the ceiling in which the light is placed.

Look carefully at how the fixture is built, and consider what Revit form-making tools are best suited for building it. Proceed to build the family, and assign it materials and any dimensional parameters using reference planes and labeled dimensions. When you think you're done, save the file with a unique name, load it into your project, and place it. Remember, if you need to make edits, the process is simple: select the family, and then click the Edit Family button on the Options bar. You'll be taken directly into the Family Editor, where you can tweak the design. Clicking the Load into Project button reloads the family into your project and updates all instances of the type with your changes.

Nest one family into another   The ability to nest families in other families lets you create content that's easier to manage and improves your workflow.

Master It   Building components are often composed of a series of subcomponents that form an overall assembly. Think of some common examples and what strategies you could use to build such content in Revit.

Solution   Consider an office workstation. Typically, a workstation is made of modular components: the desk surface, vertical partitions, file cabinets, bookshelves, and a chair. You could load these elements into a project and manually manage all the parts, maybe even using groups to do so. A more efficient and easier-to-manage method is to nest various parts into one family. Starting with a blank Furniture Systems family template, you could load the desk, partitions, cabinets, and chair into one family. By making each nested family a shared family, you can tag and schedule all the elements.

Build relationships between parameters with formulas   Create smart connections between geometry and dimensions to create efficient and parametric content.

Master It   You can use dimensional relationships to tie the size of one object to the size of another. How do you do this in the context of a family?

Solution   Using the Family Types dialog box, you can add new parameters and then create formulas that tie the value of one or more parameters to any other parameter. Using a conventional mathematical formula, you can create families that are extremely flexible and dynamic.

Chapter 12: Extended Modeling Techniques—Walls

Revit provides you with the tools to create everything from standard walls to more complex assemblies. In all cases, the walls will behave intelligently and relate to other elements in the model. Digging deeper into the wall properties, you'll discover some great ways to improve workflow, and get more detailed designs out of the model.

Use advanced modeling techniques for standard walls   Many design situations require more than just the basic wall features; learn to use the more advanced Revit tools.

Master It   A design calls for a horizontal soldier course in a brick wall every 12´ on the façade. Using Revit, how would you build this into a wall element?

Solution   Create a new wall type and add integrated wall sweeps into the wall definition. Each wall sweep can have a material assigned to it, so you just need to define the correct size and materials to the sweep to get it to look correct. Place several instances at 12´ intervals. You can change the preview sample size of the wall to be any height in order to add additional sweeps above the default 20´.

Use advanced modeling techniques to create stacked walls   Walls along a building façade usually have different construction layers from foundations to the top of the building. Stacked walls allow for a single wall to be constructed with varying wall types along its height.

Master It   You have a building project where you are still experimenting with a number of floors but have already defined the wall types for the foundation, typical floor, and the attic and have combined them in a stacked wall type. How do you define the stacked wall so that it will accommodate middle floors with varying heights?

Solution   Stacked wall types allow for one of the walls in the stacked wall to have a variable height. In this case, set the middle wall type as a variable height layer. Thus you will assure that the stacked wall updates correctly when floor to floor heights change.

Use advanced modeling techniques for curtain walls   Curtain walls find their way into many architectural projects and designs. Knowing how to manipulate curtain walls in Revit is a key piece of the software for many design solutions.

Master It   You've got to add a doorway to a storefront façade you've made. How would you go about doing this?

Solution   Load a curtain wall door panel and then swap out a glazed panel with the door. Remember—you cannot use standard door families with curtain walls.

Chapter 13: Extended Modeling Techniques— Roofs and Slabs

Revit provides extensive tools for modeling roofs, allowing for tremendous flexibility.

Understand the various roof creation methods   There are multiple methods for creating roof forms in Revit, and you should become familiar with each.

Master it   When would you use a Roof by Extrusion method?

Solution   The roof by Extrusion method for creating roofs is great for barrel vaults, sawtooths, or any roof with an arc profile.

Create all kinds of roofs   Roofs are an integral part of any building. Knowing how to create them in a variety of shapes and sizes is critical to the success of a project.

> **Master It**   In the early design phases of a project, you are exploring a variety of roof forms for your building. Create the base building form and explore different roof options and shapes.

> **Solution**   Create a roof using the Roof by Footprint tool. Then by editing the roof, modify the slope on the various roof edges (at times setting some of them to 0) to explore different roof shapes.

Work with advanced roof and slab shape editing   Roofs are another seemingly simple element that present architectural challenges, and Revit has tools for them.

> **Master It**   You are working on a flat roof retail project, but the roof is not really flat and will need to drain. Using Revit roof tools, how would you go about modeling this?

> **Solution**   Create your roof flat initially, and then select it. Use the shape modification tools to add ridges and low points to the roof. By selecting points, you will get temporary dimension controls to accurately set the height and get correct slopes for drainage.

Chapter 14: Extended Modeling Techniques— Railings and Fences

Revit provides extensive tools for modeling basic elements such as walls, roofs, and railings, allowing for tremendous flexibility.

Work with railings and fences   Railings are a bread-and-butter architectural element whose design can be streamlined with Revit.

> **Master It**   You've found some nice-looking railing panels and balusters while scouring the Web for interesting rail designs. How do you go about building the railing in Revit?

> **Solution**   Start by figuring out what is baluster and what is rail. For the rails, you'll need to make custom profile families and use those when you define the rails in the system. For the balusters, use the baluster family templates as a starting point and break the system down into Revit-centric constructs: extrusions, blends, revolves, and sweeps. Once you have the baluster made, load it into your project, create a new railing type, set up the baluster spacing, and establish the rail pattern.

Use balusters and rails to construct railings   A Railing is a complex set of sub-elements that Revit lets you organize and control with a series of rules and settings.

> **Master It**   You want to make a railing where the balusters are glass panels with fixed width. You wish to create a railing that contains the maximum number of those panels and you wish them to be spread symmetrically. How do you do that?

> **Solution**   In the Edit Baluster placement dialog box, under Main Pattern, set Justify to Center and Excess Length Fill to None. Justify Center will assure spreading a full number of patterns from the center toward the two ends of the railing, and the Excess Length set to None will assure that no pattern is truncated and only a full number of patterns find their place in the length of the railing.

Adjust additional settings   Stair railing details are particularly difficult to design and plan at landings. Revit helps you fine tune the details using additional settings.

Master It   After designing the stair railing, you notice that there is a gap between the Rails following the Stair flight and the horizontal Rail on the landing. What options do you have to resolve this situation?

Solution   Using the options under the Angled joints in the Type Properties dialog box of the railing, you can choose to add horizontal/vertical connectors that fill the gap or leave the gap as is by choosing No connector.

Chapter 15: Presentation Techniques for Plans, Sections, and Elevations

Revit is a complete solution that allows you to conceptualize a design and generate construction documentation while also providing powerful presentation tools. Using some automated routines to render shadows, depth, color, lighting, and materiality, you can create compelling plans, sections, and elevations directly in Revit and at any stage of your design. The value of doing this is that as the model changes, your presentation views automatically change as well. You won't have to redo your presentations as is usually the case when you exit modeling software and go to image-editing tools such as Photoshop. Your nice-looking views you've set up are maintained and updated automatically.

Use shadows for presentation purposes   Presenting your design to stakeholders is a critical part of your workflow and allows you to sell your ideas. Having tools that make this process easier without compromising your creativity is essential to being successful.

Master It   You've been asked to show the effect of your building's shadow on its surrounding site during the winter solstice. How would you do this with Revit?

Solution   Use a site-plan view, and enable shadows from the View Control bar. Set the Sun and Shadows Settings to the correct date, time, and place. Remember to set the correct place, because this affects how shadows are calculated.

Create presentation-quality plans and sections   Creating clean, easy-to-read plan and section views using Revit is a huge time-saver.

Master It   Your latest design is all the rage, and you've been asked to publish the plans and sections in a magazine. How do you make these?

Solution   Turn off all the clutter in the view by selecting unwanted categories and elements and hiding them in the view. Then, give the walls, columns, roof, and floors a bold solid fill hatch override when cut. This will make the drawings punch on the printed page.

Create elevation drawings that convey depth   Two-dimensional drawings can be hard for clients to read, which makes shadows a useful mechanism for illustrating recesses and projections.

Master It   You need to give your elevation view more variation in line weight to convey depth beyond the default line styles established in the Object Styles dialog box. How do you do this?

Solution   Use the Linework tool to apply heavier lines to element edges in the foreground. Use element overrides to apply halftone or thin line weights to elements in the background.

Chapter 16: Presenting Perspective Views

Revit is a complete solution that allows you to generate construction documentation while also providing powerful presentation tools. Using the new rendering functionality, you'll be able to generate photorealistic results with minimal effort. That said, setting up cameras and assigning good materials is still an integral part of creating a solid presentation, and they deserve attention.

Create perspective views   Design visualization is a key benefit to using Revit as a documentation solution. Being able to snap quick perspectives of your spaces and building forms can be critical to making good design decisions.

Master It   Create a new perspective view showcasing a critical design feature. Using the Rendering tab, apply lighting and materials and complete the rendering.

Solution   Using the Camera tool on the View tab, you can quickly create a perspective from a view that is important to describe the design intent of the project. Using the tools described in this chapter, create a quick rendering to further analyze the design.

Create photorealistic renderings   You know those signs that are put up at the site before and during construction—the ones with the nice rendering showing the final product? Well, you can generate those directly in Revit!

Master It   You've been asked to produce an exterior rendering of the building. Can you do this in Revit? Can you tweak the results in Photoshop?

Solution   Set up some dramatic exterior camera shots, and assign photorealistic materials supplied in the new Render Appearance Library. Add RPC entourage such as trees, cars, and people. Render the view, and then export the image so it can be touched up in Photoshop. Send the image to the print shop, and get the rendering up on the billboard!

Create animated walkthroughs   Creating animated walkthroughs is an excellent way to visualize the spaces within the project in a more dynamic fashion than still renderings.

Master It   You want to create a compelling animation showing an entry approach to the building. How would you do that with Revit?

Solution   Start with a plan view and choose the Walkthrough tool from the View tab of the Design bar. Draw your path, and then adjust the camera at each keyframe to get the desired look and feel.

Export the 3D model for use in other applications   Revit is an excellent application, but there are a variety of other tools out there that you might want to use for rendering, modeling, or other BIM features such as 3D printing.

Master It   You've modeled your project in Revit and assigned materials, and now want to make an animation sequence with 3Ds Max 2009. What should you do?

Solution   Use the new option to export the model to FBX. This will create a file that can be opened directly with 3Ds Max 2009, where you can take advantage of animation tools. To do so, choose File ➢ Export ➢ CAD Formats ➢ 3ds Max (FBX).

Chapter 17: Fine-Tuning Your Preliminary Design

Remember that area plans and schedules are nothing more than different ways to view your model and the parametric data inside it. Learning how to leverage these view types can be a huge time-saver for your project. In this chapter you created some area plans and schedules, but remember that this data will be constantly updating itself to reflect the most current status of your project. Set it up once and you have a tool you can regularly refer back to for project metrics.

Quantify your preliminary designs   Once your plans are established, create your own area plans to dynamically track changes in the project.

> **Master It**   Establish your preliminary design, and then create area plans so you can keep up to date with space sizes, allocations, and your project program.

> **Solution**   Use the tools for figuring gross area and rentable area to establish these baseline plans.

Create schedules   One of the benefits of Revit is the ability to manage not only your drawings, but also other information about the project. Create schedules for your project templates to manage the materials within the project.

> **Master It**   Schedules have a multitude of uses and value at all levels of the project. Explore a variety of schedules to optimize your workflow and maximize what you can get from the model.

> **Solution**   Here is a list of schedules you might try:

> ◆   Wall schedules showing length and area by wall type

> ◆   Multicategory schedules showing a full list of all the families in a project

> ◆   Material schedules—for example, a schedule for reporting the cubic volume of concrete in the project

> ◆   Auditorium seating schedules

> ◆   Door schedules

> ◆   Parking stall schedules for parking counts by type (stalls, accessible stalls, and so on)

Use schedules for preliminary cost estimates   Create a schedule that tracks project costs based on an estimated cost per square foot.

> **Master It**   Many developers and facilities managers use BOMA calculations for figuring rentable area, gross area, and R/U (rentable/usable) ratios. Establishing area plans and schedules can help you find these numbers much quicker than a legacy CAD system would have allowed.

> **Solution**   Establish the schedules as part of your default templates, and as you create your area plans, the schedules will dynamically fill. Also, become familiar with the typical methods of calculating space. These are some of the formulas you can also incorporate in your default templates:

> building rentable area + pro rata building common area = rentable area

> gross rentable area / usable area = R/U ratio (load factor)

> usable area   (1 + load) = rentable area

Chapter 18: Evaluating Your Preliminary Design: Sustainability

Sustainability is an increasingly important goal for your clients. Revit, thanks to its BIM database of project information, provides tools that greatly simplify sustainability analysis.

Incorporate a sustainable approach from the very beginning of the project development Sustainability is quickly becoming a core approach to any design. Learn to leverage the Revit model for a more holistic approach to sustainability.

Master It BIM is also a computational database that can report information about the virtual building. The important thing about a sustainable approach is to know which questions to ask and to ask them at the right time. What is a strategy for doing this?

Solution Come up with your sustainable goals early on in the project process and revisit them regularly to make sure you stay on track.

Use Revit to create sun studies Understanding the sun's effect on a building is paramount to sustainable design.

Master It How can you use the tools within Revit to produce still and animated solar studies from interior and exterior views in order to understand shading and the sun's effect on the building and space?

Solution Use the Advanced Model Graphics dialog box to set the global location of the project. Next, establish a time of day to view the effects of the sun. Create key interior and exterior views of the project and apply these sun settings to the new views. To see the effects of the sun at that time throughout the year, animate the solar study for each week throughout the year.

Track recycled materials and other sustainability strategies using schedules Keeping track of project goals is an important part of any project process. By using the schedules and other tools in Revit, you can also track key sustainability goals.

Master It Tracking recycled material usage is key to LEED credits and sustainability. Create a material schedule that tracks recycled content volume for concrete.

Solution Create a schedule for the concrete in the building. Using a custom calculated field, apply your percentage of recycled content by building a formula to multiply the percentage of recycled content by the volume of concrete in the model. As you build and refine the design and the model, this value will dynamically update.

Chapter 19: Annotating Your Model

Annotating drawings is an essential part of the workflow when preparing construction documents. In most cases, your annotations are "smart" and are tied parametrically to elements in the model. This intelligent behavior will help you quickly and accurately embellish your drawings with critical information.

Annotate views Room elements are highly useful tools for a number of different applications in a set of documents. Learning how to use them and tag them will help you find areas, create finish schedules, and identify spaces.

Master It   Once the model has been largely built out, you need to start adding information about rooms and finishes. What tools would you use?

Solution   Once the rooms in the project are roughly defined by walls, you can use the Room tool to add room elements to your project. After these are defined, use the schedule key in combination with a room finish schedule to quickly create finish values for each room that are easy to control and define.

Use schedule keys   Adding information to the room element is only part of the documentation and design process. Knowing how to schedule that information allows you to communicate effectively with owners and contractors.

Master It   Tags are used to report information about an element. How do tags work in Revit so that they always report accurate and consistent information about the elements they tag?

Solution   Elements defined in Revit such as walls, doors, and rooms all have parameters. These parameters can be used to drive information into tags by adding labels to the tag families. If you change the parameter value, the tag will update automatically. Likewise, by editing the value in the tag, you are affecting the element.

Leverage tags   Revit supplies you with three ways to annotate your model and the project. Knowing when to use each and planning for them early in the documentation phase saves time and frustration.

Master It   It is important to understand the relationships between elements and materials in Revit early. How does this help streamline the process of keynoting your project when you reach the documentation phase?

Solution   If this is your first project in Revit, discuss the keynoting strategy used within your office and see how easily that transitions into Revit. Set up your keynotes and schedules for those notes long before you need to document the project. This will ensure that when the time comes to begin laying out your sheets, you can do it with a minimum amount of disruption to your workflow.

If this is not your first project in Revit, begin embedding notes into your project template, building from the experiences of past projects.

Understand shared parameters   Revit lets its users add as many custom parameters to an element as are needed. When those added parameters need to be visible both in schedules as well as in the elements tags, they need to be created as Shared parameters.

Master It   You added a custom parameter to your door and window elements and wish to schedule and tag it such that each window or door tag displays the information about the hardware set. Schedule works well, but your tags seem not to be able to find the hardware set parameter. What is wrong?

Solution   In order to be able to display a custom parameter in a tag, that parameter needs to be created as a shared parameter. Create a shared parameter as a `.txt` file, assign it to the tag family and also in the project environment, to the Door and Window category, to achieve the desired result.

Add text and keynotes   No set of drawings is complete without keynotes or text notes. Understand how to create and modify them for a complete set of documents.

Master It   You will need to add notes in every stage of design to communicate your design intent on a project. How do you create and modify the notes to ensure accuracy throughout all the sheets in the set?

Solution   Use the Keynote tool on the Drafting tab to insert element, material, and user notes. As these notes are all tied to a single file and are not modifiable within the project, they will always be identical. To modify the notes, simply modify the linked text file found under Settings ➤ Keynotes.

Chapter 20: Developing the Design with Smart Workflows

Most architectural projects of any size rely extensively on repeating components, with or without variations. Mastering the tools Revit provides for this kind of repetition—groups and links—greatly simplifies your workflow.

Work with repetitive elements   Many projects have repetitive elements and can benefit by using groups and links efficiently.

Master It   Think of a scenario in your own practice where elements repeat and how you might use Revit groups to solve the problem.

Solution   A hotel room in a multistory tower is a good example of where groups could come in handy. You can draw the walls, add the bathroom and all the fixtures for one unit, and then group them in what will be a typical hotel room. Once they're grouped, you can place instances of the group throughout the model to fill out the design. From there on out, any change to any group will propagate to the other group instances.

Understand the use of groups   Groups are a powerful design tool. Anyone working with repetitive elements needs to understand how they work.

Master It   Describe a fundamental benefit of using groups.

Solution   When you make a group of elements and then duplicate it many times, it is important to maintain consistent and predictable results. Using groups, you are guaranteed that a change to one instance will propagate to all other instances in the model. At the same time, Revit recognizes that some group instances might have to be slightly different from the rest and that it must be flexible enough to support slight differences without the necessity of creating a separate new group.

Understand the principles of links   Links are Revit's second major tool for repetitive elements, avoiding the file size and performance issues associated with groups.

Master It   Using a link paradigm means that the BIM model now depends on links to external files. Even so, the links can be scheduled, dimensioned to, and graphically altered. Despite that, there are still some limitations. What are they?

Solution   One of the major limitations is how walls in a linked file interact with walls in the host file. For example, when a Revit link is used, none of the walls in the link will clean up with the host walls and rooms will not be calculated.

Decide whether to use groups, links, or both   Knowing when to link a file can improve file performance and provides an easy way to operate on large clusters of building data. You can hide links, remove them, and work on them independently. Knowing when to use groups can help replicate repeated elements quickly. Knowing how and when to use both helps speed the documentation process.

Master It   Know that links can reduce the overall file size and thus improve performance when working in Revit; imagine a scenario in which you would most certainly want to employ links over groups.

Solution   A campus layout master plan would be a great candidate for using links. By building a master site file and building each campus building as a separate file, you could then link them all together in the master file and have good performance in each of the separate files. This also keeps levels and grids from neighboring buildings from interfering with your workflow.

Chapter 21: Moving from Design to Detailed Documentation

Revit provides a full set of detailing tools to help you create finished construction documents.

Create drafting views   Not every drawing or view in Revit is created with model elements. Some of the views on sheets will be made solely with 2D drafting views. Knowing how to create and use these views is critical to any documentation package.

Master It   Keeping views hyperlinked together is a key benefit to using Revit. How do you draw simple, 2D details in Revit but still keep them parametrically linked to sheets?

Solution   By creating drafting views, you can use detail lines (found on the Drafting tab) to draft 2D details in from within Revit. These drafting views can then be placed on sheets, keeping all the same parametric values maintained by any other view created in Revit. You can also reference these drafting views with the Callout tool.

Import and link CAD details   Even if you've been using Revit for years, you will need to import 2D geometry from an old library of standards or manufacturer drawings. Understanding how to do this effectively will keep you from having performance issues with your model.

Master It   Your office has a huge repository of standard details. How do you reuse details drawn in CAD in a Revit project?

Solution   Make sure the CAD detail is free of extraneous information and then import it into a drafting view at a 1:1 scale. Reset the scale to the proper scale of the view and place the new drafting view in the appropriate sheet. When forming a new detail callout from a plan or section, check the box Reference Other View on the Options bar and select the CAD detail from the list. This will give the new detail a SIM (similar) annotation.

Create 2D detail components   Detail components can be used again and again within a model to graphically show in 2D different typical building components. Mastering these will result in enhanced productivity when you work on a project.

Master It   Detailing is a process of adding more granular layers of information and graphics to the model and view. What tools would you use to add 2D detail?

Solution   Create detail components for content that can be reused in other views. Add as much detail to the component as is applicable, including nesting components within one another. Use masking regions (also referred to as whiteout) to cover unneeded model geometry, taking care to balance proper modeling techniques with efficiency and productivity. Use filled regions to add additional levels of detail and materiality to the view. Use repeating details in lieu of copying or arraying simple 2D elements. Finish the detail by drafting necessary areas with detail lines.

Chapter 22: Advanced Detailing Techniques

Revit's tools for detailing can go a long way toward helping you make construction documents read clearly and concisely. Understanding how to detail within Revit is critical to producing any set of documents.

Create 3D details   3D axonometric details are a great way to demonstrate more complex assemblies and conditions in any document set. Knowing how to create them in Revit will expand the ways in which you can detail.

Master It   Use a 3D axonometric detail to demonstrate constructability in a unique assembly condition.

Solution   Locate the new detail in a wall section or enlarged plan. Navigate to the default 3D view, and using the Orient to View tool, orient the 3D view to match the desired detail. By orbiting the orientated view, you can begin adding annotations and dimensions to describe the construction of the assembly.

Add detail components to 3D families   Adding detail components to 3D families can save time by embedding the linework of a detail within the family itself and making it instantly available throughout all the locations that family is placed.

Master It   Create a detail by embedding it into a family so it can be expressed by simply modifying the detail level of a view.

Solution   Open the family in the Family Editor. By adding detail components to the family, you can begin building the corresponding detail (flashing, blocking, sealant, trim, etc.). Next, select these elements and modify their visibility to make them viewable only in specific conditions (in this case, fine level of detail). Reinserting the family into the project allows you to control what is displayed in any view by modifying the view detail in each view.

Reuse details from other Revit projects   There are times when details are common between projects. Knowing how to use details from other Revit projects will cut down on your documentation time.

Master It   Use details you created in your other Revit projects.

Solution   After finishing the detail or project, choose File ➢ Save to Library ➢ Save Views to select a variety of views and export them to your project or office standards library.

Chapter 23: Tracking Changes in Your Model

Any changes in a construction documentation set, once issued, need to be recorded with revisions so that changes can be tracked. Revit's revision tools provide intelligent support for this in order to facilitate correct documentation of changes in the model.

Add revisions to your project   You need the ability to track changes in your design after sheets have been issued. Adding revisions to a drawing is an inevitable part of your workflow.

Master It   Add revisions to your project that automatically get tracked on your sheet.

Solution   Choose Settings ➤ Revisions and use the resulting dialog box to add, edit, and manage revisions. Be sure to set the numbering scheme to By Sheet.

Understand BIM and supplemental drawings   Making an actual revision to a construction document involves adding graphics and coordinating the clouds with revisions.

Master It   You need to cloud a design change. How would you do this using Revit?

Solution   Draw clouds with the Revision Cloud tool. Next, tag your revision clouds with parametric tags. In turn, your title block will also be parametrically tied to each revision placed on the sheet.

Use Autodesk Design Review   You'll often need to share your design with people who do not have Revit, so that your design can be examined and marked up.

Master It   How can you export your designs in a lightweight file format?

Solution   Publish your sheets to Autodesk Design Review by choosing File ➤ Publish to DWF. You can publish either 2D or 3D data.

Chapter 24: Worksharing

Understanding worksharing is important to any team environment or any project in which you plan to have more than one person working on the file at a time. The idea that everyone is essentially editing one shared model is a novel concept but one that works surprisingly well. Understanding worksharing can help support good project communication and efficient workflow across the project lifecycle.

Set up a project with worksets   Knowing how to activate worksharing and set up the project file for more than one person at a time is critical in any office environment.

Master It   How do you work in a single Revit file on a project team with more than one member in the file at a time?

Solution   Worksharing allows for multiple users in a Revit environment. Understanding and using worksharing is a vital part of any large-scale project where you will have more than one person doing the drawing. Worksharing will be the most successful when implemented in an organized, well-thought-out division of model assemblies. To set up worksets, first enable worksharing (File ➤ Worksets). Then save the file as a central file and inform team members to make their own local files.

Understand worksharing basics   Once you've enabled worksharing, you'll need to understand the dynamics of central and local files to fully leverage working in a worksharing environment.

> **Master It**   Once you have enabled worksets to allow for multiple users, what's the best way to implement and use the file?
>
> **Solution**   Set up a central file on your network. Each of your users makes new, local files from the central file on their local drives and works directly in these copies. These files are smart enough to be able to manage changes between all the members of the project team while updating the central file.

Manage workflow with worksets   Saving to and loading from the central file allow you to view other team members' work and allow them to see what changes to the project you have added.

> **Master It**   How can you translate the changes you've made in your local file to the central file on the network? How do you download changes from other team members to your local file?
>
> **Solution**   Use the Save to Central command on the File menu. This will copy all of your changes up to the networked central file *and* download their changes to your local file. If you are simply looking for changes others have made to update your local copy (without posting your own changes), you can use the File ➤ Reload Latest command.

Understand element ownership in worksets   Editing elements in a central file means you have sole ownership over further changes to those elements. Understanding the permissions will be critical to working in a team.

> **Master It**   How do you edit an element in the model if someone has already taken permission of it in a worksharing environment?
>
> **Solution**   By simply trying to edit the element, you can request permission for the object from another user on the team if permission is not readily available. They can similarly grant or deny you permission for any element they own by using the Editing Requests button on the Worksharing toolbar.

Appendix B

Tips and Troubleshooting

This appendix provides tips and tricks about how to keep your project file running quickly and smoothly. Listed here are some pointers to keep you from getting into trouble, along with some solutions in case you do. Topics we'll cover include:

- Optimizing performance
- Using best practices
- Dealing with file corruption
- Getting a project started
- Finding additional resources

Optimizing Performance

It should make sense that a small file on a good network runs the quickest. Depending on your hardware configuration, typical file sizes can run a large gamut. We've seen them range from 30MB to 200MB. Much of that variation depends on the level of detail you've put into your model, the presence of imported files (like other 3D files or CAD files), and the overall complexity of your model. However, there are a number of things you can do to be proactive about keeping your model performance optimized. Here are a few we recommend:

Use the 3 GB switch. Revit now supports Microsoft XP's 3GB switch. Windows XP allows any given application access to only 2GB of RAM at a given time; if the application needs more, it gets the rest from virtual memory. Microsoft's switch (which is available in XP Service Pack 2) allows you to change that 2GB limit to 3GB. To find out how to do this, visit www.autodesk.com/support, choose Revit Building from the menu, and read the support article on enabling the 3GB switch. Of course, you need more than 2GB of RAM in your workstation for this switch to do you any good.

More information on RAM and virtual memory can be found at the Autodesk knowledge website. Visit this site for details: http://usa.autodesk.com/adsk/servlet/ps/item?siteID= 123112&id=8018971&linkID=9243099.

Don't explode imported CAD files. A CAD file imported into Revit is a collection of objects that is managed as single entity. If you explode a CAD file, the single object immediately becomes many—and becomes that much more data for Revit to track. If you're unfortunate enough to explode a hatch pattern, one object becomes many thousands. If you're importing DWG files, leave them unexploded as much as possible. If you need to hide lines, use the Visibility/Graphic Overrides dialog box to turn layers on and off. Explode *only* when you need to change the imported geometry, and start with a partial explode. Figure B.1 shows the tools available in the Options bar when you select an imported or linked DWG file.

FIGURE B.1

Import explode
options

Another option is to change the DWG file directly in CAD—delete lines and layers you don't need, then reimport.

Delete or unload unused DWGs. Often, you import a DWG as a reference, but then you don't need it later in the process. It's easy to forget, but if you no longer need an import, go ahead and delete it by selecting it in the view and deleting it. This will delete the import in all views.

Close unused views. Keeping the number of open views to a minimum helps the model's performance. Choose Window ➤ Close Hidden Windows often (Figure B.2), because it's easy to have many views open at once, even if you're concentrating on only a few views. Once you reduce your open views to just two or three, you can take advantage of the view switch toggle: press Ctrl+Tab, and you'll cycle through your open views. Press Ctrl+Shift+Tab to reverse the view cycle.

FIGURE B.2

Close hidden
windows that
you're not using.

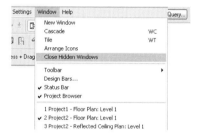

Turn on volume calculation only when necessary. You can turn on room volume calculation by choosing Settings ➤ Area and Volume Computations. Check Areas and Volumes under Volume Computations (shown in Figure B.3) only if you need room tags or a schedule to display volumetric information. Don't forget to switch off this option after you print or view the information. Otherwise, the volumes will recalculate each time you edit something in the model, and this can affect the overall performance of your file dramatically.

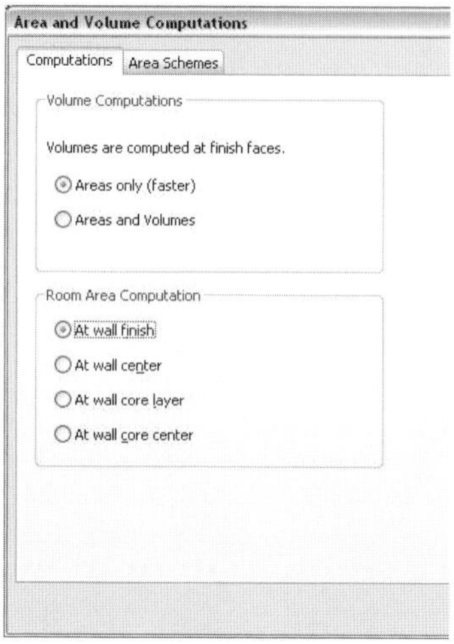

FIGURE B.3

Do not compute
room volumes
unless necessary.

Best Practices

The following best practices will not only help you keep your project files running smoothly but will also keep frustration levels with poorly performing files low.

Workshared files: Make a new local copy once a week. Sometimes in a workshared environment, your local copy can begin to perform poorly but others on your team don't have the same problems. If this is the case, we recommend that you make a new local file. Local files can become problematic because of any of the things that commonly cause issues with large files in a networked environment. As a general practice, it's a good idea to make a new local copy once a week.

Use graphics card options to improve drawing performance. In the Settings ➤ Options ➤ Graphics tab, make sure you have both Use OpenGL Hardware Acceleration and Use Overlay Planes to Improve Display Performance checked (Figure B.4). Deselecting the overlay planes check box can cause significant degradation in performance—we recommended you never deselect this option.

FIGURE B.4

Enable video card options for better performance.

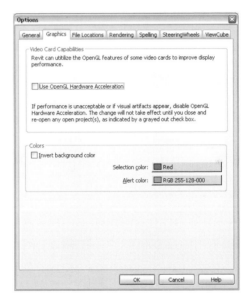

Import or link DWGs in one view only. Importing in all views can seriously affect performance. Figure B.5 shows the Link (Instead of Import) check box in the Import or Link dialog box. Linking is better than importing if you don't need to edit the geometry. (The exception to this rule is when you need to generate topography out of an imported DWG file of a site. In that case, you have to import it in all views; otherwise you will not be able to generate the topography.)

FIGURE B.5

Import into one view.

Watch out for imported geometry. Although Revit has the ability to import files from a number of other sources, you should exercise caution when doing so. If you're importing a 60MB NURBS-based Rhino file into your model, expect your Revit model to grow in size and react a bit slower than it did before. Delete unneeded imports to reduce file size and improve overall performance.

Purge unused elements. Revit has a built-in tool that allows you to purge unused families and content. This is a good way to reduce file size, improve performance, and minimize the list of things you need to search through when adding content in the project. Loaded but unused families can make your file grow quickly. To purge, choose File ➢ Purge Unused. If your file is very large, it may take a few minutes to run this command before you see the dialog box shown in Figure B.6. Here, you can opt to keep or purge families individually.

FIGURE B.6
Use the Purge Unused dialog box to reduce file size.

USE PURGE TO REDUCE FILE SIZE

Some Revit families can only be removed from the project with the Purge command. You will notice with elements such as dimensions and text notes, there is no way to delete a family type from the Properties dialog box. To get rid of unused types, use Purge. Everything included in the Other Styles group falls into this category.

This is typically *not* a good idea at the beginning of a project, because your template may contain families that you intend to use but haven't yet inserted (such as wall types).

Manage the amount of information shown in views.   Learn to manage the amount of information needed in your views. Don't show more than you need to show in a view either in depth or in your level of detail. Here are a few easy ways to keep your views opening and printing smoothly:

Minimize the level of detail.   Set your detail level (in the View Control bar) relative to the scale you're viewing. For example, if you're working on a $\frac{1}{32}''$ (1:50) plan, you probably don't need Detail Level set to Fine—it will cause your view performance to suffer needlessly.

USE LEVEL OF DETAIL TO SPEED UP VIEW PERFORMANCE

One project was taking upward of 20 minutes to open plan views. As you can imagine, this was very frustrating for the users, especially when you opened those views accidentally. As it turned out, the views were set to a $\frac{1}{16}''$ scale and a fine level of detail. For the elements in the plan, none of them showed any significant information at this level of detail. By setting the View Detail to Coarse, they were able to reduce the time to open those views to under two minutes. We further optimized view performance by modifying complex families in the view to show less detail at a coarse level.

Minimize view detail.   This goes along with the level of detail, but this tip is more user based than tool based. If you're printing a $\frac{1}{32}''$ (1:50) drawing, make sure you're showing the proper level of detail in the view. Even if Detail Level is set to Coarse, do you really need to show balusters in an elevation on your railing at that scale? They will print as a thick, black line. Turning them off in this view will help improve not only your printing speed but also the quality of the resulting printed sheet.

Minimize view depth.   View depth is a great tool to enhance performance. It's especially valuable in section views. A typical building section is shown in Figure B.7. The default behavior causes Revit to regenerate all of the model geometry the full depth of that view every time you open the view. To reduce the amount of geometry that needs to be redrawn, drag the section's far clip plane (the green dashed line when you highlight the section) in close to the cutting plane.

Turn off shadows.   Shadows can help you make beautiful presentations, give a sense of depth in façades, and show the effect of the sun in a site-plan view; however, shadows are performance intensive and can significantly slow a view's time to open, print, or regenerate as you pan and move around in it. Make sure you turn shadows off whenever you don't need them.

Open only what you need.   One of the benefits of having worksets is that you don't have to turn them all on at once. When you open the project, go to the Workset dialog box. There, you can highlight a workset and click the Close button (see Figure B.8). Doing so drops that workset from active memory and gives you better performance. Remember, if worksets are closed, you can't do anything with them. If a workset isn't visible, it won't print. To print a current copy of the whole model, you'll need to turn the worksets back on.

FIGURE B.7
Minimize the
section's Far Clip
Offset.

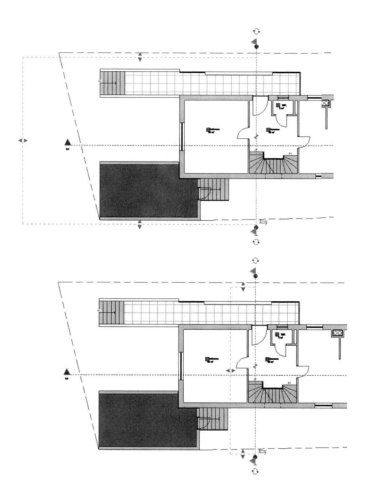

FIGURE B.8
Worksets can be
closed to reduce
the amount of
memory used to
open a file.

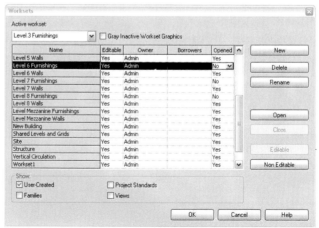

Break up your model.   For larger projects, or campus-style projects, you can break up your model into smaller submodels that are referenced together. You can also do this on a single building. If you decide to divide your project, make your cuts along lines that make sense from a holistic-building standpoint. Don't think of the cuts as you would in CAD, but think about how the actual assemblies will interact in the building. As an example, don't cut between floors 2 and 3 on a multistory building unless you have a significant change in building form or program. Here's a list of some good places to split a model. See Figure B.9 for an example:

- ◆ At a significant change in building form or massing

- ◆ At a significant change in building program

- ◆ Between separate buildings on the site

- ◆ At the building site

FIGURE B.9
Splitting up a model can improve performance.

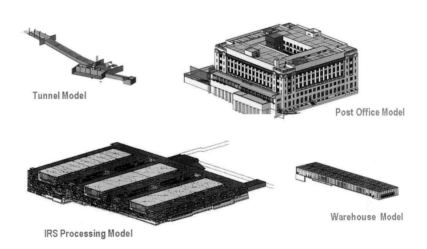

Tunnel Model

Post Office Model

IRS Processing Model

Warehouse Model

Consider printing paper, DWFs, or PDFs.   Printing big Revit files can sometimes take a long time. Enabling raster printing speeds up printing, although there is a trade-off compared to the quality that vector printing offers. Depending on the printer, you may get better line quality by going to a DWF or PDF first, then printing your physical sheets. Experiment on a few sheets to see what your printer responds to best before sending your entire set. Printing a digital set first will also give you a record copy of what you have just printed as well as a quick way to make additional copies later if needed.

Model just what you need.   Don't fall into the trap of overmodeling. Just because you *can* doesn't mean you *should*. Be smart about the level of detail you choose to model based on the complexity and size of your project. Some data is just easier and better to show in a 2D detail rather than as 3D model data. The amount of information you model or do not model should be based on your project size and complexity, your timeframe, and your comfort level with the software.

Don't overconstrain. User-defined relationships and constraints are important to embed in the design to help keep important dimensions constant. However, if you don't need to lock a relationship, don't. Even though the option to lock all alignments is available, it's often not necessary to do so. Overconstraining the model can cause problems later in the project process when you want to move or modify an element and you need to figure out (or remember) what you locked and where to allow the particular element to be moved or modified.

Assign proper view detail. It is possible to create families in Revit with a seemingly infinite amount of detail. Use the Visibility tool found in the Family Editor. Make sure when creating families that you are setting the elements within the family to the right level of detail. Setting elements to Coarse, Medium, or Fine can keep your families from looking like blobs in Coarse view and quicken your screen-refresh times.

Fix an overconstrained object. If you keep encountering a dialog box telling you the model is overconstrained and this is impeding your workflow, you can delete the constraint. If it is a simple element (such as a wall with no openings or sections), it might be easier to simply delete and redo the troubled object.

Close Revit with an empty view. To avoid long opening times for really large files, establish an office standard that you always close your last view as a drafting view or legend that is empty, or maybe contains only some text with the project name. This way, when Revit first opens the project it will need much less processing time. By default, Revit always opens with the view from when the project was last saved. We've seen some nice-looking "project pages" made with a drafting view using text and some simple instructions.

File Corruption

If your file becomes corrupted and begins to crash frequently, there are a few things you can do to help fix the problem before you call Revit Support in a panic. To proactively avoid this issue, focus on the previous tips before you begin having problems. Otherwise, here are some suggestions on what to do when you get into trouble:

Audit the file. Auditing the file will review the data structures and correct problems that are found within the model. An audited file won't look any different when the audit is completed; however, it should (ideally) not crash. This is not a cure-all, by any means, but it can help you get out of a tight spot when necessary.

Get everyone out of any worksets and local files, and have them relinquish their permissions. Open the file using File ➢ Open. The resulting Open dialog box lets you browse to a project location. Select your project and before clicking the Open button to open the file, select the Audit check box in the lower-right corner (shown in Figure B.10). Revit gives you a warning before performing an audit on your file. The audit itself can take several minutes to complete. When this process is finished, save the project with a new name or in a new file location; don't save this file over the old Revit file. Saving over an existing Revit file can sometimes lead to instability. When you're finished, have everyone make a new local file, and you can get back to work.

FIGURE B.10
The Audit option is located in the Open dialog box.

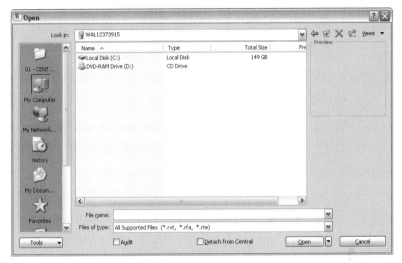

Review warnings. Each time you create something that Revit considers a problem, a warning is issued. If you ignore warnings, they will accumulate if left unresolved. Think of all these errors as unresolved calculations. The more there are, the more your computer will have to struggle with trying to resolve them. Revit provides an interface where you can review all the warnings in the project and fix problems.

Try to read and react to the warning that Revit sends. You don't have to do it when you're under a tight deadline or when doing so will interrupt your work. But once a week, you should spend 30 minutes reviewing the warnings, as this can improve your model's overall performance. You can find the list of warnings in your file under Tools ➢ Review Warnings (Figure B.11).

Purge unused elements. We referred to this earlier in the "Best Practices" section. Purge can also be used to get rid of poorly built families that might be wreaking havoc in your file.

FIGURE B.11
Review the warnings in this dialog box.

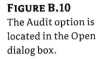

Tips for Getting Started in Revit

Knowing how and where to begin your journey can be a challenge, and we want to give you a few pointers to help you get started. Although this list isn't complete by any means, it should help steer you in the right direction:

Begin with the end in your mind.   When you begin any project, planning is always a good way to start. You can set yourself up for a successful implementation from the beginning by using a bit of forethought about your process, workflow, and desired outcome.

Get your project and office standards in place early.   As design professionals, we have a tendency to develop unique graphic conventions and styles for our documents. This is a specific area where good planning leads to a good project. If possible, get your standards in place before you begin a project. Revit does an excellent job of getting you started with a good template of graphic standards to work with. However, if you're like most architects, an application right out of the box is never quite nice enough. Revit provides a good starting point for customization, and with some up-front time, you soon can have your project and office standards up and running. Once you nail down your standards, they can be easily applied to your project using Transfer Project Standards.

Remember that the first project you do in Revit is a change in methodology.   You're leveraging technology to help you change the way you approach design and documentation. Don't expect the process to have the same workflow as it did in a CAD-based system. Try to stay flexible in your expectations and schedule and allow yourself time to adapt to the change.

Don't try to conquer the world on the first project.   There are many advantages to using BIM as a design and documentation methodology. As this process becomes more mainstream within the industry, those benefits will only increase. All of these things and more are possible with the use of Revit, but it will take a couple of projects to get there. Tailor the use of BIM to the project, and use the features that will maximize the benefits of using BIM. Choose your goals realistically based on the expertise of your project team, and plan ahead so those goals can be met successfully. Consider a project that is less complex for your initial pilot.

LEARNING A MODELING WORKFLOW

One of the most important rules to follow as you begin your project is to model the building as it will be built, but keep in mind that you do not need to model every condition three-dimensionally. Use Revit to get the essential dimensions and building form coordinated. You can then embellish the model with 2D details to convey the fine grain.

Model correctly from the beginning.   We can't stress this enough. As you refine your design, it's critical to model correctly right from the beginning so you don't have to fix things later. What does this mean? As an example, think of a wall. Does it sit on the floor, or does the floor attach to the wall? If you can begin to think about how your project will be assembled, it will save you a lot of time at the end. It's good practice to plan ahead, but remember that Revit will allow you to make major changes at any stage in the process and still maintain coordination. If you are still in early phase of design and do not know the exact wall type, use generic walls to capture your design intent; changing these later will be simple.

Get information into the project as soon as it is known. A key advantage of using Revit is the ability to change your project schedule. In a traditional design process, most of the effort on a project is realized during the construction-document phase. At that time, a typical project has the most staff working on the project, and it can be fairly difficult to implement major changes to the project design. This is due to the complexity of the documents by this time and the amount of effort for the team to redraw all the changed information. You'll find that with Revit, design change is largely managed by the software itself. This gives you a great deal of flexibility in both your design and documentation. Take advantage of this shift in the process, and add information to your model early. It can be in the form of more detailed content or showing the material construction of your wall system. Remember that you can change all this information much more quickly and easily than you ever could in CAD, so don't assume you're locked into the information you displayed early in the design process.

Plan for better communication among team members early in the process. Communication within a team is critical for understanding a project and documenting it successfully. One of the downfalls inherent in a CAD-based system is that there is no connection among the different files that make up the drawing set. This phenomenon carries through to the project team and is a function of project workflow and project management. In CAD, it's possible for team members to work in some degree of isolation. They aren't forced to immediately reconcile their changes with changes made by their teammates. Revit's single-file environment forces a much higher degree of team communication between not only the architects but also your structural and mechanical engineers.

Don't try to model everything. Most of us have drafted in a 2D environment until now. Moving to a 3D world is a significant change. Do you have to model every single screw? Every mullion? Every stud? That's a good question. The simple answer is no, you don't have to, and in fact you should not attempt to do so. Like any BIM system, Revit isn't 100 percent 3D information. Typical workstations aren't capable of handling all the data of a building in model form. Additionally, few projects have the time in their schedule to model the screws in a sheet of gypsum board or the sealant around all the windows; some of that information is best presented in 2D or in the specifications. This still leaves you with a wide range of options for modeling. In the beginning, err on the side of simplicity. It's far easier to add complexity to your model later on as you gain experience and confidence than it is to troubleshoot overconstrained parameters early in the process. Start with the big ideas: walls, openings, roofs, and so forth. Work your way down to a comfortable level of detail for both you and your computer.

Organize your team. A BIM project team includes three basic technical roles. These roles are interchangeable, especially on smaller projects with fewer team members. However small the team, it's useful to make sure all these roles are filled:

Building designer This is the person or team whose primary responsibility is to figure out what the project will look like and how it will be made. They create walls, floors, and roofs and locate windows, doors, and other building elements.

Content/family creator The family creator's primary role is to create the parametric content in the Revit model. This is typically someone with 3D experience who also has a firm understanding of Revit and Revit families. The families, as you'll see later, have parameters that can control visibility, size, color, proportion, and a number of other things.

Documenter   This role supplies the bulk of the documentation. It consists of drafting some of the 2D line work over portions of the 3D model to show detail, adding annotations and keynotes, and creating details.

Ask for help.   If you get stuck along the way, don't assume you're alone. There are myriad resources in the help file, in books, or on the Web to help you find a specific solution to your problem. Chances are, someone has tried the same thing before. In our digital age, a wealth of information is available online; powerful communities of passionate users are out there willing to help. So before you spend hours trying to work through a particular problem on your own, try tapping some of the existing resources:

Revit Help menu   Your first stop, if or when you get stuck, should be the Revit Help menu. It's one of the easier and more robust help menus out there, and it can give you a lot of useful information very quickly. It's also the most accessible help source. As with most applications, it's at the far right of the menu bar.

Subscription Support   If you have bought Revit on subscription, Revit Subscription Support offers an exemplary web-based support system. Their responses are speedy, and their advice is top-notch. If you need information more quickly, Revit also has an online knowledge base of FAQs that is available without a subscription. Both of these resources can be accessed at www.autodesk.com/revit.

AUGI   Autodesk User Group International (AUGI) is also an excellent source for tips and tricks. It's an online user community free to participate in, ask questions, get answers, and share families and examples. To get the benefit of this fantastic online resource, go to www.augi.com and look for Revit Architecture as a product. If you never logged in, you will have to register once; from then on it's easy!

Revit City   Looking for content and families? Revit City, another free online service, has a growing database of free families posted by other users. Its address is www.revitcity.com.

Autodesk Discussion Groups   These pages offer insightful discussions and some great Q&A threads: http://discussion.autodesk.com/.

AECbytes   A website dedicated to following and reporting on the trends in the AEC industry, with a strong focus on BIM, technology, and the direction of the industry—put together by Lachmi Khemlani: www.aecbytes.com.

Blogs   Revit OpEd is a blog with some great information, useful links, and helpful tips and tricks. Put together by a longtime Revit guru, and friend Steve Stafford: http://revitoped.blogspot.com/. And there are numerous blogs from passionate, experienced Revit aficionados such as these:

- www.allthingsbim.blogspot.com (James Vandezande)

- www.dorevit.blogspot.com (Robert)

- www.greenrevit.blogspot.com (Beau Turner, Bradley Hardnagle)

- www.revitbeginners.blogspot.com (David Duarte)

- www.revitcoaster.blogspot.com (Troy Gates)

- www.revitfamilies.blogspot.com (Shaun Van Rooyen)

- www.revit-alize.blogspot.com (Bruce Gow)

- http://revit4you.blogspot.com (Philippe Drouant) (French)

- http://revitez.blogspot.com (Yves Gravelin) (French)

- www.revitrants.blogspot.com (Chris Price)

- www.revitlution.blogspot.com (Christopher Zoog)

- www.revit-up.blogspot.com (The PPI Group's Revit evangelist)

- www.revitup.co.za (Justin Taylor)

- www.autodesk-revit.blogspot.com (David Light)

- www.auservice-bim.blogspot.com (Simone Cappochin) (Italian)

- www.cmotion.net/products/revit-tools.html (Siggi Pfundt and Gotthard Lanz) (German and Italian)

Index

Index